Protecting Study Volunteers in Research

A Manual for Investigative Sites

Fourth Edition

Cynthia McGuire Dunn, M.D.

Gary L. Chadwick, Pharm.D., MPH, CIP
Associate Provost at the University of Rochester
and Professor of Clinical Community and
Preventive Medicine and Medical Humanities in
the School of Medicine and Dentistry; Director
of the Office for Human Subject Protection

Protecting Study Volunteers in Research, Fourth Edition

by Cynthia McGuire Dunn, M.D. & Gary L. Chadwick, Pharm.D., MPH, CIP

Managing Editor   Cheryl Rosenfeld
Cover and Interior Design   Holly Rose

 CenterWatch

10 Winthrop Square, Fifth Floor
Boston, MA 02110
www.centerwatch.com   ISBN 978-1-930624-64-1

Welcome to the fourth edition of *Protecting Study Volunteers in Research*. When this training manual was first developed, the need for education in the ethics of research involving human subjects was a novel idea. Over the past 15 years, most research institutions have adopted some form of required educational program in the basic ethical theories and regulatory framework that underpin sound research. Institutions can take comfort that their investigators have a core familiarity with research topics and an increasing sensitivity to the special concerns when research involves human volunteers. For me, the exciting development is that investigators and research staff are increasingly asking for educational programs and contributing to the development of the literature of human subject research. Ethics education is not an imposition, but a chance to puzzle through past difficulties and prepare for future challenges.

As with prior editions, updates have been made to the chapters to keep up with current events, thinking and the ever expanding frontiers of science. Federal regulators have been engaged in updating their guidances and the FDA and HHS/OHRP have undertaken an effort to harmonize their advice to lessen confusion and to focus on procedures that truly protect human subjects without excessively burdening investigators, sponsors and institutions. Likewise, European regulatory authorities are looking at "right-sizing" regulations and moving the research enterprise forward. Countries seeing an increase in clinical trial activity are looking to the U.S. for regulatory models and educational materials. It is gratifying to see how well received this manual has become internationally.

In many ways, this manual is a self-help book. Study coordinators/administrators led the way into individual certification many years ago. Certification programs for IRB professionals and investigators have since been developed and readily accepted by the research community. More recently, formal organization of institution-wide programs—human research protection programs—has become expected, and the accreditation of these programs has become a growing standard of excellence. Research sites, sponsors, contract research organizations, regulators and individuals are all working together as a system. This effort is to ensure acceleration in the discovery and application of new knowledge while providing a research environment that is respectful of patients and subjects, protects their rights and well-being and honors the principles of beneficence and justice. This manual continues to be dedicated to all people in the human subject protection system who are doing right because it is right.

—*GLC*

ACKNOWLEDGEMENTS

Manual Development Coordination

William Kelvie, CCRC
Director, Research Education
Office for Human Subject Protection
University of Rochester

Advisory Review Committee

David Forster, J.D., M.A., CIP
Chief Compliance Officer
Office of Compliance
Western Institutional Review Board

Peggy Galluzzi, B.S.N., M.S.
Vice President, Clinical Operations
MannKind Corp.

Paul W. Goebel, CIP
President
Paul W. Goebel Consulting, Inc.

Jeanne Grace, R.N., Ph.D.
Professor emeritus
University of Rochester

Louis Lasagna, M.S.
Tufts University

Robert Levine, M.D.
Yale University School of Medicine

Dale W. McAdam, Ph.D.
University of Rochester

P. Pearl O'Rourke, M.D.
Partners Healthcare System

J. Thomas Puglisi, Ph.D
Chief Officer, Office of Research
Oversight
Dept. of Veterans Affairs

Harold Vanderpool, Ph.D., Th.M.
University of Texas Medical Branch

Karen Woodin, Ph.D.
Independent consultant

Gary Yipling, J.D.
K&L Gates LLP

Contributing Authors

Mary Adams, M.T.S., CIP
Director, Research Subjects Review
Board Office
University of Rochester

Christine Burke, J.D.
Associate Vice President and
General Counsel
University of Rochester Medical
Center

Nora Cavazos
Director, Clinical Development
Relypsa

Nancy Chin
Associate Professor
Community and Preventative
Medicine
University of Rochester Medical
Center

Ann M. Dozier, R.N., Ph.D.
Associate Professor
Community & Preventative
Medicine
University of Rochester Medical
Center

Cindy Dunn, M.D.
Maximus Corporation,
Federal Services

Judith Farrar, Ph.D.
Editor-in-Chief
LifeSciences Press

Chin-to Fong, M.D.
Associate Professor
Pediatrics-Genetics
University of Rochester

David Forster, J.D., M.A., CIP
Chief Compliance Officer
Office of Compliance
Western Institutional Review Board

Tim Hackett
Director, Regulatory and Technical
Affairs

Center for Human Experimental
Therapeutics (CHET)
University of Rochester

Cornelia Kamp, M.B.A., CCRC
Senior Associate, Executive Director
Strategic Initiatives
Clinical Materials Services Unit
Center for Human Experimental
Therapeutics
University of Rochester

William Kelvie, CCRC
Director, Research Education
Office for Human Subject
Protection
University of Rochester

Scott Kim, M.D., Ph.D.
Associate Professor, Psychiatry
University of Michigan Health
System

Joanne Larson
Michael W. Scandling Professor of
Education
Chair of Teaching and Curriculum
Margaret Warner Graduate School
of Education and Human
Development

Gunta Liders
Associate Vice President for
Research Administration
Provost Office
University of Rochester

Terri O'Reilly, M.D.
Novar Research

Roy M. Poses, M.D.
Associate Professor of Medicine
Brown University School of
Medicine

Carol Pratt, Ph.D.
Partner, K&L Gates LLP

Aileen Shinaman, J.D.
Senior Counsel, Office of Counsel
University of Rochester Medical
Center and Strong Health

Jeanine Smith, M.S.
Pfizer, Inc.

Rebecca Thom, Ph.D.
Clinical Research Specialist
3M Drug Delivery Systems Division

Editorial Reviewers

Heather Cline, MPA, CIP
IRB Liaison
Independent IRB, A Schulman Company

Carrie Fisher, Ph.D.
Director, Enterprise Programs Development
Western Institutional Review Board

David G. Forster, JD, MA, CIP
Chief Compliance Officer, Office of Compliance
Western Institutional Review Board

Cynthia M. Gates, RN, JD, CIP
Vice President, Education and Consulting Services
Western Institutional Review Board

Kenneth A. Getz, MBA
Director of Sponsored Research Programs
Tufts Center for the Study of Drug Development,
Tufts University
Founder and Board Chair, CISCRP

R. Bert Wilkins, JD, MHA, CIP
Director, Regulatory Affairs
Western Institutional Review Board

Instructions for Obtaining Credit

Needs assessment

This training manual was designed for biomedical and behavioral investigators to ensure they are aware of the fundamental requirements, responsibilities and ethical and regulatory issues related to the conduct of human subject research. The initial *Protecting Study Volunteers in Research* training manual was published in 1999 and responded to a need to provide a resource for investigators and their research staffs who work with human volunteers. The purpose of the fourth edition is to update the information and to expand on previous topics contained in the first three editions. The national trend for requiring completion of programs on human subject protection for researcher continues and is now almost a universal requirement. This fourth edition is intended to add to these training programs.

In an effort to make this manual as relevant to your work as possible, we have focused on topics, regulations and guidelines most pertinent to academic research. This manual does not include specific code references to the regulations, nor does it provide sample documents. While some of the regulations are included in the appendix, the regulations, codes and guidance documents are subject to change. Specific resources that can provide additional information are listed in the References, Resources and Suggested Reading section of the appendix. Also, remember to contact your Institutional Review Board (IRB) with any questions and for updates on relevant regulations and documents.

Certification

For physicians

The University of Rochester School of Medicine and Dentistry is accredited by the Accreditation Council for Continuing Medical Education to provide continuing medical education for physicians.

The University of Rochester School of Medicine and Dentistry designates this educational activity for a maximum of 7.5 AMA PRA Category 1 Credits™. Physicians should claim only credit commensurate with the extent of their participation in the activity.

Author declarations

The Accreditation Council for Continuing Medical Education (ACCME) Standards of Commercial Support requires that presentations are free of commercial bias and that any information regarding commercial products/ services be based on scientific methods generally accepted by the medical community.

The following authors have disclosed financial interest/arrangements or affiliations with organizations that could be perceived as a real or apparent conflict of interest in the context of the subject of their contribution(s). Only current arrangements/interests are included.

Authors

None of the authors has financial interests or arrangements to be declared.

ACCME Standards of Commercial Support of CME requires that presentations be free of commercial bias and that any information regarding commercial products/services be based on scientific methods generally accepted by the medical community. When discussing therapeutic options, authors are requested to use the generic names. If they use a trade name, then those of several companies should be used. If any information is provided on unlabeled or investigational use of a commercial product, the authors are required to disclose this to the readers.

Category 1 credit valid through May 31, 2015.

To obtain credit

1. Read the manual.

2. Answer the exam questions on the answer sheet provided. Questions and answers are based on information in the manual. Participants who answer 85% of the questions correctly will receive up to 7.5 AMA PRA Category 1 Credits™.

3. Complete the evaluation questions on the *Protecting Study Volunteers in Research* evaluation form. Note: Credit cannot be issued if the evaluation form is not received with the answer sheet.

4. Complete the mailing information portion of the answer sheet.

5. Detach and mail the answer sheet and evaluation form by May 31, 2015.

University of Rochester
Center for Experiential Learning
601 Elmwood Avenue, Box 677
Rochester, NY 14642-8677

6. You will receive a certificate in the mail within two to four weeks.

7. Call (585) 275-4392 with questions or for further information.

> This material is presented as an interpretation of the research process based on the expertise and experiences of the authors. Although designed to be of general application, not all material will be relevant in every situation. Each situation must be individually assessed and appropriate actions chosen based on individual knowledge and institutional and sponsor requirements.

Sponsored by:

Office of Continuing Professional Education

CHAPTER ONE

Historical Perspectives on Human Patient Research

At the conclusion of this chapter, readers will be able to:

- Describe three events that had significant impact on the federal regulations for the protection of human research volunteers.

- Have a better understanding of why we need federal regulations and how compliance helps protect the rights and welfare of human research volunteers.

Introduction

History is not static. Yesterday's events are today's history. The public's perception of research, its benefits and its risks are shaped by the way research is conducted. Many events have renewed concerns about research ethics. Included are issues regarding informed consent for incapacitated patients (TD v. New York State) and responsibilities of researchers for patient welfare (after the deaths of volunteers in research studies at Johns Hopkins, Penn and Rochester and the suicide of a schizophrenic patient during a study "washout period" at UCLA). In June 2001, Ellen Roche, a healthy volunteer, died in an experiment at Johns Hopkins University.

Partially in response to this death, the death of Jesse Gelsinger and other similar events, the Maryland Legislature passed a law in 2002 that extends the federal protection requirements to all research involving human volunteers conducted in the state, regardless of funding source or FDA jurisdiction. In the United States, concerns such as these often result in government action affecting the conduct and monitoring of research.[1]

> **The public's perception of research, its benefits and its risks is shaped by the way research is conducted.**

There are three events that have had significant impact on federal regulations for the protection of human research volunteers. In chronological order, they are the 1946 Nuremberg Doctors Trial, the 1960s Thalidomide

Tragedy and the 1972 Tuskegee Syphilis Study Exposé. While other events such as the Willowbrook Studies, the Wichita Jury Study, the Jewish Chronic Disease Hospital Study and the San Antonio Contraceptive Study also played a role, the cases discussed below had the most direct impact on shaping federal regulations.

One additional case, the Milgram Study, will be reviewed. While it did not have the same scope or impact on federal regulations, this study is included because it often is cited in ethics literature as illustrative of potential problems in behavioral research. Also presented is the 1995 report on Human Radiation Experiments that measured how well the regulations are working. Finally, the unfortunate incident at the University of Pennsylvania and the effect it is having on human patient protections, particularly conflict-of-interest standards, is noted.

The Nuremberg Doctors Trial of 1946

Background

At the beginning of World War II, Germany was the most scientifically and technologically advanced country in the world, and it even had a notable code of research ethics. In the field of medicine, the Nazi government supported midwifery, homeopathy and nutrition programs, as well as research into ecology, public health, human genetics, cancer, radiation and environmental risk factors such as asbestos. It was the first to ban smoking in public buildings. Women were denied tobacco ration coupons because of concern about the effect of nicotine on a fetus. German physicians stressed the importance of preventive medicine as well as curative medicine. The Nazis, however, exploited people's trust in physicians to disguise discrimination and murder as public health and medical research.

Medical Experiments

Legitimate concerns of the Luftwaffe (the German air force) were the survival of pilots at extremely high altitudes and the determination of the maximum safe altitude for bailing out of damaged aircraft. In one series of experiments, researchers placed victims in vacuum chambers that could duplicate the low air pressure and lack of oxygen at altitudes as high as 65,000 feet (about two to three times the maximum altitude aircraft were flying). Approximately 200 internees at Dachau prison camp were used in these experiments and about 40% died as a result. Some deaths were caused by extended anoxia; others were attributable to lungs rupturing from the low pressures created in the chamber.

Another Nazi concern was survival time after parachuting into the cold water of the North Atlantic. Some victims of this research were immersed for hours in tubs of ice water; others were fed nothing but salt water for days. Still others were penned outside, unclothed and unsheltered in sub-freezing temperatures for 12 to 14 hours. Some of these "freezing victims" were sprayed with cold water. No attempts were made to relieve the tremendous pain and suffering caused by these experiments. Three hundred Dachau prisoner-subjects suffered a mortality rate of about 30%.

Experiments involving battlefield medicine included treatment of gunshot wounds, burns, traumatic amputations and chemical and biological agent exposures. While these were valid concerns for a country at war, the techniques that were used were inhuman. In these experiments, wounds were first inflicted upon victims (by gunshot, stabbing, amputation or other traumatic method) and then treated by various techniques. For example, in a study of sulfanilamide at the Ravensbrueck camp, Polish women were shot and slashed on the legs. The resulting wounds were stuffed with glass, dirt and various bacteria cultures and sewn shut. The infected wounds were then treated with experimental anti-infective agents. In another experiment, a mixture of phosphorus and rubber was applied to the skin of victims and ignited. After burning for up to two minutes, the fire was extinguished and the resultant burn treated with various chemicals and ointments. Another series of experiments involved amputation of upper and lower limbs and attempted treatment with transplanted bones, muscle and nerves. About half of the amputation victims died; the rest were maimed for life.

In the experiments on treating exposure to chemical-warfare agents, prisoners were forced to drink poisoned water and breathe noxious gases. Some were shot with cyanide-tipped bullets or given cyanide capsules. A mortality rate of at least 25% was typical.

The Nuremberg Trial

On Aug. 8, 1945, representatives of the British, French, Soviet and United States governments established the International Military Tribunal in Nuremberg, Germany. After the initial Nuremberg Trial of the Nazi leadership, a series of supplemental trials was held. The trial, officially known as 16 Historical Perspectives on Human Subject Research United States v. Karl Brandt et al., and popularly referred to as "The Nazi Doctors Trial," was held from Dec. 9, 1946, to Aug. 20, 1947. As the title indicates, for this trial the judges and prosecutors were all from the United States. The 23 defendants (including 20 physicians) were charged with murder, torture and other atrocities committed in the name of medical science.

Upon completion of the Nazi Doctors Trial, 15 of the 23 defendants were found guilty. Seven were sentenced to death. Although, at the time, the trial was called "The Trial of the Century," it probably would have been forgotten, except for the fact that the judgment included a set of standards known as the Nuremberg Code. The Code was the "ethical yardstick" by which the defendants had been measured and guilt determined. The "Modern" era of human patient protection is routinely dated from the promulgation of the

Nuremberg Code. It set standards that have been accepted and expanded upon by the international research community.

The Code stated that:

- Informed consent of volunteers must be obtained without coercion in any form.

- Human experiments should be based upon prior animal experimentation.

- Anticipated scientific results should justify the experiment.

- Only qualified scientists should conduct medical research.

- Physical and mental suffering and injury should be avoided.

- There should be no expectation of death or disabling injury from the experiment.

> **The "Modern" era of human patient protection is routinely dated from the promulgation of the Nuremberg Code in 1947.**

Post-War Years

In 1953, the World Medical Association (WMA) began drafting a document that would apply the Nuremberg Code principles to the practice of medical research. The WMA code became known as the Declaration of Helsinki. This statement of ethical principles, first issued in 1964, defined rules for "therapeutic" and "non-therapeutic" research. It repeated the Nuremberg Code requirement for consent for non-therapeutic research, but it did allow for enrolling certain patients in therapeutic research without consent. The Declaration of Helsinki also allowed legal guardians to grant permission to enroll patients in research, both therapeutic and non-therapeutic. Several revisions have been made to the Declaration of Helsinki to keep it aligned with modern ethical theory and current clinical and research practices.

In 1966, following the publication of the Declaration of Helsinki, Dr. Henry K. Beecher reported in the *New England Journal of Medicine* (NEJM) on 22 studies that had serious ethical problems. Beecher cited various problems related to study design and informed consent. Probably even more than the Nuremberg Trial/Code or the promulgation of the Declaration of Helsinki, this article helped spur the debate on research ethics in the United States.

In addition to the expanding number of ethical statements and codes, in 1982, the Council for the International Organization of Medical Sciences (CIOMS) published the International Ethics Guidelines for Biomedical Research Involving Human Subjects (CIOMS Guidelines). These were designed to guide researchers from the more technologically advanced countries when conducting research in developing countries. The guidelines sought to correct perceived omissions in the Nuremburg Code and Declaration of Helsinki, especially as applied to cross-cultural research. The CIOMS Guidelines allow for cultural differences in ethical standards. Like the Declaration of Helsinki, the CIOMS Guidelines have been revised to account for current thinking and practices.

The Milgram Study

Background

Stanley Milgram was a researcher in social psychology who, after reading accounts of the Nazi Holocaust, became interested in obedience and humans' response to authority. The defense proposed at Nuremberg of "I was only following orders" and the German citizenry's seeming acceptance of and complacency with the atrocities presented an interesting question. In 1963, Milgram published the results of his study on obedience, which raised criticism with implications even today. His 1972 book, *Obedience to Authority*, describes the series of studies and addresses some of the concerns they engendered.

While the Milgram studies come nowhere close to the ethical violations of the Nazi experiments or the other studies often cited, it is a well-known behavioral study that is instructive even today. Importantly, these studies served to remind the drafters of the first federal regulations that even studies that do no physical damage or permanent harm have important ethical considerations that must be addressed.

The Experiment

Adult patients were recruited by means of newspaper advertisements asking for volunteers for a study of "memory and learning." Participants were paid a modest amount for the one-hour experiment. Study participants were part of a triad that consisted of themselves, the investigator and a third person. The investigator explained that the experiment was to study learning and memory, specifically what role punishment played. The volunteer was to play the role of "teacher," while the third person was to be the "learner." The investigator would monitor the process and record the data.

The learner was placed in a chair with wire leads that ran from a control panel to the chair and were attached to the learner's body. The control panel had switches labeled from 15 volts to 450 volts.

For the experiment, the investigator instructed the volunteer-teacher to ask the learner a question (word-pair matching) and when the wrong answer was given, to administer "punishment" to the learner in the form of electric shocks in an escalating amount. The learner would display visible evidence of pain from the shocks. After one-third of the shock levels had been given, the learner demanded to stop. At this point, the volunteer-teacher usually would ask the investigator to stop, but the investigator would state that the procedure should continue. After two-thirds of the shocks had been administered, the learner fell silent and non-responsive. Under the study design, a non-response was treated as a wrong answer and punished. When they continued to seek permission to stop, the highly conflicted volunteer-teachers were told that the experiment was important to complete for the advancement of science. Fully 60% of volunteer-teachers were persuaded to administer shocks up to and including the highest level.

The volunteers were deceived about a number of things. The third person who played the role of learner was in fact a confederate of the investigator. No shocks were administered. The learner (who deliberately gave wrong answers) only pretended to receive shocks and be hurt. The real intent of the experiment was to see how far the volunteer would go under the guise of complying with authority. At the completion of the experiment (either after the maximum shock was ostensibly given or upon firm refusal by the volunteer to continue), the confederate came out of his room and demonstrated to the volunteer that he was uninjured. A debriefing with the volunteer was held that explained the deception and the real purpose of the study. During the debriefing interviews, volunteers often justified their actions by saying they were only trying to follow instructions.

"I observed a mature and initially poised businessman enter the laboratory smiling and confident. Within twenty minutes he was reduced to a twitching, stuttering wreck, who was rapidly approaching a point of nervous collapse."

—*Stanley Milgram, Obedience to Authority*

Impact

Criticism of the Milgram study centered upon the psychological stress experienced by some volunteers and on the fact that due to the deception involved, true informed consent had not been obtained. The role of deception in human patient research continues to be debated even today. Common sense and experience tell us that people act differently when they know they are being studied. Ethical codes such as the Nuremberg Code, the Declaration of Helsinki and the Belmont Report point to the importance of obtaining consent that is informed, understood and voluntary. The federal regulations specifically allow for deception in research, but only in limited conditions and only with institutional review board (IRB) approval.

As a result of this study and other problematic behavior, the federal guidelines specifically instruct investigators and IRBs to consider not just physical harm that may be attached to research, but also psychological, social, legal and economic harm.

An additional implication can be drawn from this study that has relevance to today's informed consent process. Milgram demonstrated that the phenomenon of obedience to authority is real. In many research studies, the in-

When deception is involved, true informed consent cannot be obtained.

vestigator (or other person obtaining consent) is in a position of authority or power over the potential patient. This response to authority, especially when combined with a general feeling of trust, has led many to question whether consent is truly a voluntarily considered decision. This is of special concern in the medical care setting, as well as in student-teacher and employer-employee situations.

Thalidomide Tragedy

Background

Thalidomide was approved as a sedative in Europe in the late 1950s. Although the U.S. Food and Drug Administration (FDA) had not approved the drug, the manufacturer supplied "samples" to U.S. physicians who were paid to study its safety and efficacy in what was loosely termed "research" by giving the experimental drug to patients. This was a common practice at the time. By 1961, experience in Europe, Canada and, to a lesser extent, the United States showed that while thalidomide was not harmful to the mother, it was extremely damaging to the fetus if taken in the first trimester of pregnancy. It interfered with the normal development of blood vessels and particularly affected development of arms and legs. Based upon its teratogenicity, use of the drug as a sedative was banned worldwide. [Note: Thalidomide was approved in 2006 for treatment of multiple myeloma, but because of its teratogenicity, the FDA is controlling its marketing in the U.S. through a mandatory registry.]

Thalidomide Hearings and Their Impact

A U.S. Senate Antitrust and Monopoly subcommittee, chaired by Tennessee Senator Estes Kefauver, had been holding hearings (1959–1962) into the business practices of pharmaceutical companies. At his request, two other congressional subcommittees, one chaired by Representative Emanuel Celler and the other chaired by Senator Hubert Humphrey, heard testimony about the thalidomide disaster. In the Celler hearings, Dr. Helen B. Taussig of Johns Hopkins University showed slides of the birth defects caused by thalidomide. The pictures of deformed and limbless babies raised questions about the procedures used to test experimental drugs. Dr. Frances O. Kelsey of the FDA testified in the Humphrey hearings about holding up approval for thalidomide because of safety concerns and questions about the drug's testing. In the hearings, it was learned that many people who were taking unapproved drugs were neither informed that they were being given an experimental substance, nor had they been asked to give their consent.

The public concern over research practices addressed in these three committees led to the passage of the Drug Amendments of 1962 to the Food, Drug and Cosmetic Act (sometimes referred to as the Kefauver-Harris Amendments). New York Senator Jacob Javits added language to the bill requiring informed consent of patients receiving experimental drugs. This was the first U.S. statute that required researchers to inform patients of a drug's experimental nature and receive their consent before starting the research. In 1964, Representative Richard Harris wrote a book on the Amendment's passage process. In homage to Kefauver's tenacity, courage and public spirit, *The Real Voice* referred to the voice of the people being heard in national legislation.

In February 1963, the FDA issued regulations with consent requirements, but it allowed widespread exemptions. Responding to concerns that consent still was not being appropriately obtained, the regulations were rewritten in 1966 to clarify that consent was required except in cases of emergency or experimental therapeutic treatments with children and similar situations. The 1966 rewrite also contained the requirement for documenting consent in writing and informing patients that they might receive a placebo.

The Study of Untreated Syphilis in the Negro Male

Background

The treatment for syphilis at the turn of the twentieth century was, at best, crude and involved the use of "heavy metal" (mercury and arsenic) compounds. These were poisons, highly toxic to humans, and had to be administered for a year or more. Severe reactions, even death, were not uncommon from the treatment and some evidence suggested that treated patients lived shorter lives than those untreated.

An agency of the U.S. Public Health Service (PHS), which was to become the Centers for Disease Control and Prevention (CDC), designed a study to demonstrate the need to establish syphilis treatment programs by investigating the effects of untreated disease. This evolved from a genuine concern about minority health problems. The PHS was a key force in promoting rural medical care. Macon County, Alabama was selected as the site for the project because previous epidemiological studies had shown an extremely high rate of disease. Thus began the Tuskegee Study of Untreated Syphilis in the Negro Male.[2] To secure the cooperation of the black patients, the participation of black physicians was seen as essential. The Tuskegee Institute and its John A. Andrew Hospital were used because of their position of trust in the local community. A local nurse who had trained at the Tuskegee Institute was hired to be the on-site representative. The project was scheduled to end after assessing what health effects had occurred.

In the beginning, there was no intent to deny anyone treatment on a long-term basis. The study called for 200 to 300 syphilitic black males, aged 25 and older, to be enrolled. They were to be given complete physical examinations, a thorough medical history and then followed for six to eight months. During that time, they would not be treated. This study demonstrates how competent and well-intentioned researchers may run into problems if they do not identify and examine the ethical assumptions and consequences of their actions.

The Experiment

In October 1932, volunteers were sought and encouraged to participate in the study with offers of free examinations and medical care. The men were not informed about their disease or the fact that the research would not benefit them. Non-therapeutic spinal taps, which were conducted in May 1933, were supposed to end the experiment; but a second phase, or follow-on study, began in late 1933. This phase introduced new procedures to strengthen scientific validity and gain more information. A control group of 200 black men and autopsies of deceased patients were added to the study. Like the original volunteers and according to the conventions of the day, the members of the control group were not informed about the purpose of the study but were told that "government doctors" were examining people for "bad blood."

Each year, new physicians were sent on special assignment to Alabama to conduct the "roundups" and medical examinations. The study procedures became so routine that the study continued without any exploration or understanding of the potential ramifications of the project. Many of the itinerant physicians later filled positions of authority in the PHS and/or the CDC.

In 1943, penicillin was accepted as the curative treatment for syphilis. However, during World War II, to keep the syphilis study patients from receiving treatment, it was arranged with the local draft board to exempt them from the military. By 1951, penicillin was widely available as the treatment for syphilis, but it continued to be withheld from the study patients.

Actually, the availability of penicillin was used by the study investigators as justification for continuing the study, because it made the protocol a "never-again" scientific opportunity. Neither the ethical issues nor the fact that the supposedly untreated patients had received some minimal treatment was addressed. Announcement of the Nuremberg Code and its requirement for informed consent and avoidance of harm had no impact on the study. Publication of the Declaration of Helsinki in 1964, with its extensive set of ethical requirements, had no effect on the study.

Exposé

After obtaining copies of letters and other study-related documents in 1972, the Associated Press assigned an investigative reporter, Jean Heller, to uncover the story. Her best source of information was the CDC itself. The study had never been hidden. Several articles had been published and CDC officials discussed it candidly. Her story was published in *The New York Times* and the *Washington Star* on July 25, 1972.

The public reaction to the Syphilis Study was strong. James B. Allen, a U.S. Senator from Alabama, denounced the study as appalling, "a disgrace to the American concept of justice and humanity." The fact that the PHS had conducted the study was particularly distressing, because instead of protecting citizens it had used them for research. Some people thought the study was racist. Others believed social class was the critical issue, i.e., that poor people, regardless of race, were the ones at risk because, at that time, they made up a disproportionate share of patients in most medical experiments.

An article that appeared in the *Atlanta Constitution* on July 27, 1972, stated, "Sometimes, with the best of intentions, scientists and public officials and others involved in working for the benefit of us all, forget that people are people. They concentrate so totally on plans and programs, experiments, statistics—on abstractions—that people become objects, symbols on paper, figures in a mathematical formula or impersonal 'subjects' in a scientific study." Many saw a need to protect people from experiments and scientists who ignored human values.

In reaction to the revelations about the Syphilis Study and other research "scandals," several bills to regulate research were introduced in Congress. During February and March 1973, Senator Edward Kennedy held hearings on experimentation with human subjects. In March 1973, the Syphilis Study was stopped and treatment was given as needed. In April 1973, the CDC informed the survivors that the government would pay all of their medical expenses for the rest of their lives. In 1975, the government extended treatment to the wives who had contracted syphilis and to their children who had been born with congenital syphilis. This money continues to be paid to these citizens today. In a formal White House ceremony in 1997, President Bill Clinton apologized to study patients and their families and called for renewed emphasis on research ethics.

In 1974, Congress passed the National Research Act. The Act required regulations for the protection of human patients that included requirements for informed consent and review of research by institutional review boards (IRBs). It also created the National Commission for the Protection of Human Subjects of Biomedical and Behavioral Research. In 1979, the National Commission published the "Belmont Report," which is the cornerstone statement of ethical principles upon which the federal regulations for the protection of subjects are based.

In 1981, the DHHS and the FDA published convergent regulations based on the Belmont Principles. These mandated a role on the IRB for persons with broad backgrounds and members who could represent community attitudes. Informed consent was required for participants, and specific elements of information were required. After years of negotiation and coordination, 17 federal departments and agencies agreed to adopt the basic human subject protections. These were published in 1991 and are referred to as the "Common Rule." Thus, essentially all federally sponsored research is now covered by a common set of regulations that has its origins in the National Research Act and the Syphilis Study. 45 CFR 46 subpart A is the Common Rule. All 15 government entities, including HHS, NSF (National Science Foundation) and DOD (Department of Defense) that now subscribe to the Common Rule have this wording in their own regulations.

Human Radiation Experiments

Background

In November 1993, the *Albuquerque Tribune* published a series of articles by Eileen Welsome that revealed that, under government sponsorship, researchers at several major universities had injected plutonium into unknowing patients to study the effects of the atomic bomb. That same month, a congressional report described 13 cases in which nuclear facilities had intentionally released radiation into the environment for government experiments.

These revelations raised concern about the adequacy of protection provided by federal laws and regulations. In January 1994, President Clinton created the Advisory Committee on Human Radiation Experiments (ACHRE) to explore human radiation experiments and determine the ethical and scientific standards for evaluating these events. When he accepted the committee's final report in 1995, President Clinton ordered the creation of the National Bioethics Advisory Commission (NBAC), which reviewed human experimentation and made recommendations on a variety of research topics and regulations.

Experiments

The Advisory Committee discovered that several thousand government-sponsored human radiation experiments and hundreds of intentional releases of radiation from nuclear facilities were conducted from 1944 to 1974. Many well-known and well-respected researchers and research institutions conducted these experiments either without thinking of the ethical implications or subordinating the interests of their human patients to scientific pursuit or national interest. Other experiments were not so benign.

The "Manhattan Project" plutonium injection experiments were conducted for national security and to gather safety data to protect the health and safety of nuclear weapons workers. The results are still used in the nuclear industry today. In one series of experiments, over 100 prisoners submitted to non-therapeutic testicular irradiation. Up to 3,000 military personnel served as subjects of research, sometimes unknowingly, in connection with atomic bomb tests. About 2,000 cancer patients were subjected to total body irradiation strictly to find answers to problems in the development and use of atomic weapons. A review conducted by the Atomic Energy Commission

(AEC) in 1974 found that while 18 subjects were given plutonium injections between 1945 and 1947, the records documented only one subject's consent.

Eighty-one examples of pediatric radiation research projects were identified by the ACHRE. Fortunately, although children are more susceptible than adults to harm from low levels of radiation, the exposures to radiation were very low and probably did not pose a risk of physical harm to these children.

Response

In addition to exploring the case studies summarized above, the ACHRE Report discussed the historical development of research ethics and examined issues related to implementing and interpreting current federal regulations. Clearly, the Nuremberg Code and later the Declaration of Helsinki seemed to be disregarded in the Cold War radiation experiments. Some contemporary consent documents were found to be difficult to read, uninformative and even misleading. Informed consent was particularly troubling to the Advisory Committee members in research involving patient-subjects with poor prognoses because these patients were so vulnerable and were often confused about the relationship of research to treatment; this situation is often called "therapeutic misconception." There was also concern about the inappropriate use of the word "treatment" in consent forms, especially in phase I trials of new drugs, designed to find toxicities and maximal doses rather than to treat an existing condition.

The ACHRE found that, when compared to the information in the grant proposal and/or protocol, consent forms often overstated the benefits and therapeutic potential of the research. Such overstatements may inappropriately induce enrollment by playing on the hopes of patients or on the altruism of volunteers. The review also showed that consent forms did not always discuss the risks that volunteers faced when removed from standard treatment in order to be placed on experimental interventions. They found that frequently there was little mention of how participation would affect the volunteer's daily life or quality of life. Psychosocial risks were often inadequately addressed in proposal documents, as were potential financial costs that could be incurred by volunteers.

The final portion of the report included recommendations to better ensure that those who conduct research involving human subjects act in a manner consistent with the interests and rights of patients, and with the highest standards of medical and scientific ethics. The recommendations stated it is essential that the research community come to value the ethics of research as central to the scientific process. Because the future of science depends to a great extent upon public support and public trust, scientists must have a clear understanding of their duties to human volunteers, and scientific leaders must value good ethics as much as they do good science. The ACHRE's call for making ethics the centerpiece of the research enterprise and recommending increased training in research ethics represents an important step in the continuing evolution of human subject protections.

> **"It is essential that the research community come to value the ethics of research as central to the scientific process."**
>
> —National Bioethics Advisory Commission

When the NBAC charter expired in 2001, President George W. Bush appointed the President's Commission on Bioethics (PCB), followed by President Barack Obama's Presidential Commission for the Study of Bioethical Issues, appointed in 2009. These groups, like their predecessors, serve to focus national debate and advance ethical thinking in the area of human experimentation.

The University of Pennsylvania Gene Transfer Experiment

In 1999, an 18-year-old volunteer in a gene transfer experiment died. The experiment was conducted at the Institute for Human Gene Therapy at the University of Pennsylvania (Penn). The principal investigator and the university owned shares in the private startup company that owned the technology used in the experiment. The young volunteer's name was Jesse Gelsinger.

At first, Jesse's father, Paul Gelsinger, defended Penn and the investigator. But as more information about the study surfaced, Paul Gelsinger's initial defense turned into anger at trust abused. The study raises issues and contains lessons to be learned about informed consent, study design and safeguards for the welfare of patients, protocol adherence and the motivations and influences acting upon institutions and investigators. This last issue—conflict of interest—has been the major focus of response in the research community.

In reaction to the negative publicity surrounding this event and *The Seattle Times'* exposé of oncology studies at the Fred Hutchinson Cancer Center (in which the Center and the investigators had financial interests), several groups have published guidelines and statements on conflict of interest. The American Association of Medical Colleges (AAMC) and the Association of American Universities (AAU) both formed national task forces and published guidance documents addressing steps that should be taken by institutions to avoid or mitigate the effects of conflict of interest on investigators. The concern is that even the perception that investigators may be influenced by interests, such as fame and money, to ignore the welfare of human volunteers will weaken the public's trust in researchers and in research institutions.

The Department of Health and Human Services (HHS) issued a final guidance on Financial Relationships and Interests in Research Involving Human Subjects in 2004. This guidance is designed to promote objectivity in research by helping institutions manage, reduce or eliminate conflicts of interest in their research projects. As institutions, IRBs and researchers consider potential financial conflicts of interest, they can refer to the guidance for possible mechanisms to manage such conflicts. These mechanisms include:

- Separating institutional responsibility for research activities from management of the institution's financial interests

- Establishing conflict of interest committees (COICs) or identifying other bodies or persons and procedures to address financial interests in research

- Using independent organizations to hold or administer the institution's financial interest

- Determining whether current methods for managing conflicts of interest are adequate for protecting the rights and welfare of human volunteers and whether other actions are needed to minimize risks to volunteers

- Determining the kind, amount and level of detail of information to be provided to research volunteers regarding funding and financial interests

- Using special measures to modify the informed consent process when a potential or actual financial conflict exists.

Recognizing that these guidances and voluntary corrections may not be sufficient, Senator Edward Kennedy, who chaired the 1973 Syphilis Study Hearings, which led to the 1974 National Research Act, and Senator Bill Frist (a physician) held hearings in the spring of 2002 re-examining human subject protection issues. Coupled with a detailed report by the NBAC on ways to strengthen and change volunteer research protection, this interest and parallel legislation proposed in the House by Congresswoman Diana Degette has led to new and/or revised federal human subject protection laws and regulations. For example, IRBs that review research regulated by the FDA must register at a site maintained by the Department of Health and Human Services (HHS), and there have been changes in the required reporting of adverse reactions. The FDA also has issued numerous guidance documents that define its current thinking on several aspects of research involving human volunteers. Many of these are discussed in more detail throughout this book.

Even today, with increased regulation and increased awareness of human patient protection, problems still occur in clinical trials. The TeGenero trial is a case in point.

The TeGenero Phase I Trial

In England in 2006, the first phase I clinical trial of TGN1412 was conducted by PAREXEL, a large contract research organization (CRO), for the sponsor company that had developed the compound, TeGenero Immuno Therapeutics. The compound was an immunomodulatory drug originally intended for the treatment of B cell chronic lymphocytic leukemia and rheumatoid arthritis. Healthy volunteers were recruited to the study, and were paid a fee for participating. The trial was a double-blind, randomized, placebo-controlled study. Eight patients were given the first dose, six receiving a low dose of the study drug and two receiving placebo. All six of the trial patients who received the drug were male, aged 19 to 34; none had a notable medical history, and all were well during the two weeks before the trial. Soon after the last patient had been dosed, the first patient started to develop serious problems. Shortly after, the remaining participants who received the actual drug also became ill, vomiting and complaining of severe pain. All six were hospitalized for immediate and severe problems, including multiple organ dysfunction in four of the six. Eventually all six were released from the hospital.

The Medicines and Healthcare Products Regulatory Agency (MHRA) in England investigated the situation. They found no deficiencies in TeGenero's pre-clinical work, including the animal studies, and PAREXEL's records and processes appeared in order (including dose measurement and administration); the MHRA felt that their actions did not contribute to the serious adverse events. The only issue raised about the procedures used was the timing of the dosing. Although they were to wait at least 10 minutes before dosing each new patient, it appeared that the time was actually considerably less than that, and it would probably have been better if they had waited a longer time between dosing the six patients. That would have allowed them to see the adverse reaction in the first patient before dosing the others.

So what went wrong? The MHRA concluded that the most likely cause of the reaction in trial patients was an unpredicted biological action of the drug in humans. When new compounds are being tested in humans for the first time, it is never known whether or not unexpected problems will be found. Tight control and close monitoring are critical; in this case, had they waited at least a few hours between the dosing of the first patients, the latter patients probably would not have received the drug at all.

The development of this drug was stopped, and the sponsor went out of business.

Conclusion

Investigators bear the ultimate ethical responsibility for their work with human volunteers. Society entrusts them with the privilege of using other humans to advance scientific knowledge. In return, society expects that investigators will show respect for research volunteers. Unfortunately, as events have shown, some scientists continue to value the quest for knowledge and the potential for personal fame and financial gain more highly than respect for basic human rights. The research community as a whole suffers when even a few investigators ignore the basic principles of ethics. Compliance with human patient protection regulations should not be seen as something that must be done just because it is required by the regulations. Compliance should be seen as the "right thing to do" because it helps protect the rights and welfare of the patients of human research and maintains public trust in research.

References

1. Examples are the congressional *General Accounting Office (GAO) Report on Human Subject Research (1994); the Department of Health and Human Services (DHHS) Report on Institutional Review Boards (1998); Research Involving Subjects with Disorders that May Affect Decision-making Capacity: a draft report of the President's National Bioethics Advisory Commission (NBAC); Third Report of the [Maryland] Attorney General's Research Working Group;* and the *1998 New York State Department of Health (NYS-DH) report on human subjects in research.*

2. The Tuskegee Study of Untreated Syphilis in the Negro Male has been most commonly called the Tuskegee Study. Due to concern for the negative connotations for the Tuskegee Institute, some are calling for a change in the shorthand name. Therefore, this manual will use the term "The Syphilis Study."

CHAPTER TWO

Ethics and Federal Regulations

At the conclusion of this chapter, readers will be able to:

- Describe the relevance of the Belmont Report on federal human subject protection regulations.

- Identify what populations are considered vulnerable and develop an awareness of circumstances requiring sensitivity.

- Define informed consent and describe the three components of valid informed consent.

- Describe the purpose and function of the Institutional Review Board (IRB).

- Define scientific misconduct and describe how it is reported.

Introduction

The ethics of human subject research and federal regulations have evolved over the past 50-plus years. Professional associations and international organizations have developed codes of ethics that cover research with human volunteers. This chapter emphasizes federal regulations because they are seen as a standard for the conduct of research. Compliance with the requirements of federal regulations, even for non-federally sponsored/regulated research, protects the rights and welfare of research participants. Most research institutions require compliance with federal regulations for all studies regardless of the source of support.

The Belmont Report

In 1974, Congress passed the National Research Act. The Act created the National Commission for the Protection of Human Subjects of Biomedical and Behavioral Research. The National Commission wrote the Ethical Principles and Guidelines for the Protection of Human Subjects of Research (commonly called the Belmont Report), published in the *Federal Register* in 1979. This document is the cornerstone statement of ethical principles upon which the federal regulations for the protection of subjects are based. A copy of the Belmont Report is included in Appendix B and should be considered mandatory reading for anyone involved in the research enterprise.

> **The Belmont Report contains the ethical principles upon which the federal regulations for protection of human subjects are based.**

The Belmont Report begins by stating, "Scientific research has produced substantial social benefits. It has also posed some troubling ethical questions. Public attention was drawn to these questions by reported abuses of human subjects in biomedical experiments..." As a result, national and state laws and regulations, as well as international and professional codes, have been developed to guide investigators. Such rules are based on broader ethical principles that provide an analytical framework to evaluate human actions. The Belmont Report describes three basic principles relevant to the ethics of human subject research: respect for persons, beneficence and justice.

Basic Principles of the Belmont Report

> **Basic principles of the Belmont Report**
> 1. Respect for persons
> 2. Beneficence
> 3. Justice

1. Respect for Persons

The Belmont Report says, "Respect for persons incorporates at least two ethical convictions: first, that individuals should be treated as autonomous agents; and second, that persons with diminished autonomy are entitled to protection. The principle of respect for persons thus divides into two separate moral requirements: the requirement to acknowledge autonomy and the requirement to protect those with diminished autonomy."

> **The principle of respect for persons is applied in the consent process.**

Vulnerable Populations

By definition, "vulnerable populations" are those groups that may contain some individuals who have limited autonomy (i.e., they cannot fully appreciate or participate freely in the consent process). Such groups include children, some mentally incapacitated individuals with dementia and other cognitive disorders and prisoners. Special considerations apply when conducting research with these populations. Pregnant women are also recognized by the regulations as a vulnerable population because of the additional health concerns during pregnancy and because of the need to avoid unnecessary risk to the fetus. Many institutions have also included the elderly, terminally ill and hospitalized patients, students and employees in the definition of vulnerable populations deserving special consideration by investigators and IRBs.

> **Vulnerable populations include some individuals who have limited autonomy such that they cannot fully participate in the consent process.**

Prisoners—The regulations for human subject protection make special provisions pertaining to research with prison populations. The incarcerated may be at greater risk for true coercion (threat of force) as well as undue influence. Special considerations for prison studies include ensuring that:

- Any potential advantages to the prisoner for participating do not interfere with the ability to make a voluntary choice by outweighing the risks (e.g., parole decisions will not be affected by study participation)

- The risks of participating would be acceptable to non-prisoner volunteers

- Selection of subjects within the prison system is fair

- Adequate follow-up care is provided, if necessary.

Children—Legally, children have not attained the age at which they can grant consent for research or treatment. Additional regulatory protections are established for research with children. Under these regulations, some of the exempt categories are deemed not to apply to research with children. Research that qualifies for exemption with adult subjects, but not for children, includes the use of survey, questionnaire or interview procedures and participatory observation. This is because a child's responses are less guarded than an adult's and, therefore, information may be divulged inappropriately.

Consent cannot be given by another person. Only an individual can provide consent for oneself. Parents or guardians, however, may provide "permission" for their child to participate in a research study. Furthermore, to the extent that they are able, children should be asked about their willingness or "assent" to participate. Information about the research study must be presented to children at their developmental level, so they can understand what is being requested of them. The combination of "assent" (agreement) of the minor subject and "permission" of the parent or legal guardian is recognized by the federal regulations as an adequate substitute for consent.

Adequate provision must be made for soliciting the assent of those children capable of providing a meaningful agreement. The process must be appropriate to the study as well as to the age, maturity and psychological state of the child. An exception to the assent requirement is made for children with life-threatening illnesses who are entered into "open-label treatment protocols" with the expectation of direct benefit. In these cases, the permission of the parent is sufficient, but the understanding by the minor subject is still desirable.

Documentation of the minor's assent and the parents' permission also depends on the nature of the research and the maturity of the child. For research with very young children (preschool and younger), only the parents' permission typically is needed. For teenagers, a single form that both the minor and the parent(s) sign may be adequate. For children in between (i.e., ages seven to 12), two forms are generally advisable. One is written at a basic level for the child (as a "script" for oral presentation or for reading), and a more detailed form is for the parents' understanding and signatures.

Research in schools—In addition to the federal children's regulations, investigators who conduct research in schools should be aware of laws governing these studies and disclosure of information. Two laws, the Family Educational Rights and Privacy Act (FERPA) and the Protection of Pupil Rights Amendment (PPRA) apply to research in schools.

FERPA defines the rights of students and parents concerning reviewing, amending and disclosing education records. Except under certain circumstances involving treatment, subpoena, educational or financial aid, FERPA requires that written permission must be obtained to disclose personally identifiable information from a student's educational records. Researchers who wish to inspect student records must obtain parental permission if identifiers are linked to the data.

Survey research in schools is regulated under PPRA. This law states that surveys, questionnaires and instructional materials can be inspected by parents or guardians, and parental permission must be obtained to allow minors to participate in a survey revealing information concerning the following:

- Political affiliations

- Mental and psychological problems

- Income

- Sexual behavior and attitudes

- Illegal, anti-social, self-incriminating and demeaning behavior

- Critical appraisals of other individuals with close family relationships

- Legally recognized privileged relationships (e.g., lawyers, physicians, ministers).

Subordinate individuals—College students, employees and other persons in subordinate positions or positions of lesser power/status provide an easily accessible group with the potential for undue influence to impede free choice in the consent process. IRBs and investigators should carefully consider how to protect the autonomy and confidentiality of employees and students. Employees must not be pressured to participate in research due to fear of job loss, delayed promotion or other influence of a superior. For student subjects, investigators need to consider the following:

- If course credit is given for participation, alternatives should be available for receiving equal credit that are no more burdensome than the participation in research.

- Policies regarding course-related research participation must be understood clearly.

- Incentives for participation should not present undue influence.

- Student subjects must have the ability to decline participation.

- Confidentiality must be maintained for self-disclosures of a personal nature.

Decisionally impaired—The regulations for human subject protection do not yet make special provisions for persons whose mental status is impaired. This vulnerable population may include persons with psychiatric illness, neurological conditions, substance use and various metabolic disorders. Even persons suffering from acute emotional or physical stress may have impaired decisional capacity. The level of impairment may range from poor judgment to frank coma. The National Bioethics Advisory Commission (NBAC) and several states have examined the issue and have published recommendations and suggested rules.

Until there are federal regulations, most investigators and IRBs use a combination of special protections gathered from the DHHS regulations for children and prisoners. As with children, some individuals in this group may not be able to give informed consent. A combination of "permission" from legally authorized representatives and the "assent" of subjects to participate are substituted for consent. Witnesses to the consent process, periodic re-consent and formal checks of comprehension may be included as additional protections. Special considerations for studies in this population include ensuring that:

- The risks of participating would be acceptable to volunteers in the general public.

- Selection of subjects is fair.

- The consent information is understandable given the expected level of function.

- Adequate follow-up is provided.

Informed Consent

The Belmont Report tells us that, "Respect for persons requires that subjects, to the degree that they are capable, be given the opportunity to choose what shall or shall not happen to them." Informed consent is not just a form or a signature, but a process of information exchange that includes subject recruitment materials, verbal instructions, written materials, question/answer sessions and agreement documented by signature. The Belmont Report states that "the consent process can be analyzed as containing three components: information, comprehension and voluntariness." The Report regards these components as ethically required.

> **Informed consent process:**
>
> - Information
> - Comprehension
> - Voluntariness

> **Informed consent is a process of information exchange that takes place between the prospective subject and the investigator, before, during and sometimes after the study.**

Information

Most research codes and regulations establish specific items for disclosure intended to ensure that subjects are given sufficient information. These items generally include: the research procedure; its purpose, risks and anticipated benefits; alternative procedures (where therapy is involved) and a statement offering the opportunity to ask questions and to withdraw at any time from the research. Investigators should consider these items necessary, but often not sufficient, for fully informed consent.

> **Freely given informed consent should be obtained from each volunteer before research procedures are begun.**

For judging how much and what sort of information should be provided, a standard of "the reasonable subject" should be used. This implies that the extent and nature of information provided should be such that a reasonable person has enough information to decide whether or not to participate in the research. "Even when some direct benefit to them is anticipated, the subjects should understand clearly the range of risk and the voluntary nature of their participation," declares the Belmont Report.

Regarding deception or incomplete disclosure, the Report states, "In all cases of research involving incomplete disclosure, such research is justified only if it is clear that (1) incomplete disclosure is truly necessary to accomplish the goals of the research, (2) there are no undisclosed risks to subjects that are more than minimal, and (3) there is an adequate plan for debriefing subjects, when appropriate, and for dissemination of research results to them. Information about risks should never be withheld for the purpose of eliciting the cooperation of subjects, and truthful answers should always be given to direct questions about the research. Care should be taken to distinguish cases in which disclosure would destroy or invalidate the research from cases in which disclosure would simply inconvenience the investigator."

Comprehension

"The manner and context in which information is conveyed are as important as the information itself. For example, presenting information in a disorganized and rapid fashion, allowing too little time for consideration or curtailing opportunities for questioning all may adversely affect a study subject's ability to make an informed choice," explains the Belmont Report.

"Because the subject's ability to understand is a function of intelligence, rationality, maturity and language, it is necessary to adapt the presentation of the information to the subject's capabilities. Investigators are responsible for ascertaining that the subject has comprehended the information." The investigator should encourage the person to ask questions. Investigators should make every attempt to ensure that the person understands the information, which may involve probing for unresolved questions and not just accepting immediate agreement. Investigators must give an opportunity for subjects to resolve any concerns before agreeing to participate in the study. Subjects should feel free to ask questions at any time before, during and even after the study.

The Report says, "Special provision may need to be made when comprehension is severely limited—for example, by conditions of immaturity or mental disability. Even for these persons, however, respect requires giving them the opportunity to choose, to the extent they are able, whether or not to participate in research." In addition to this "assent" process, "respect for persons also requires seeking the permission of other parties in order to protect the subjects from harm."

Voluntariness

An agreement to participate in research constitutes valid consent only if voluntarily given. This component of informed consent requires conditions free of coercion and undue influence. Coercion occurs when an overt threat of harm is intentionally presented by one person to another in order to obtain compliance. Undue influence, by contrast, occurs through an offer of an excessive, unwarranted, inappropriate or improper reward (benefit) or other overture to obtain compliance. Investigators should assure that the circumstances (context) in which consent is obtained are free from undue influence.

Subjects must understand that they are free to decline participation and to withdraw from the study at any time after it has begun.

2. Beneficence

According to the Belmont Report, "Persons are treated in an ethical manner not only by respecting their decisions and protecting them from harm, but also by making efforts to secure their well-being...Two general rules have been formulated as complementary expressions of beneficent actions: (1) do not harm and (2) maximize possible benefits and minimize possible harms."

"The obligations of beneficence affect both individual investigators and society... Effective ways of treating childhood diseases and fostering healthy development are benefits that serve to justify research involving children—even when individual research subjects are not direct beneficiaries." The principle of beneficence is reflected in regulations as a requirement to perform risk/benefit assessments.

Assessment of Risks and Benefits

"The assessment of risks and benefits... presents both an opportunity and a responsibility to gather systematic and comprehensive information about proposed research. For the investigator, it is a means to examine whether the proposed research is properly designed. For a review committee, it is a method for determining whether the risks that will be presented to subjects are justified. For prospective subjects, the assessment will assist their determination whether or not to participate," instructs the Belmont Report.

The Report further says, "The term 'risk' refers to a possibility that harm may occur... both in the chance (probability) of experiencing a harm and the severity (magnitude) of the envisioned harm. The term 'benefit' is used in the research context to refer to something of positive value related to health or welfare... Accordingly, so-called risk/benefit assessments are concerned with the probabilities and magnitudes of possible harm and anticipated benefits... While the most likely harms to research subjects are those of psychological or physical pain or injury, other possible harms should not be overlooked." Except for a narrow segment of research, the potential benefits accrue to society and there are no benefits to individual study participants. Often, determining the balance between personal risk borne by the study participant and potential societal benefit constitutes a key ethical dilemma in research.

According to the Report, "Risks and benefits of research may affect the individual subjects, the families of the individual subjects and society at large (or special groups within society)...Beneficence... requires that we protect against risk of harm to subjects and also that we be concerned about the loss of the substantial benefits that might be gained from research."

The principle of beneficence is applied in risk/benefit assessments.

3. Justice

The principle of justice requires fairness in distribution. The Belmont Report says, "An injustice occurs when some benefit to which a person is entitled is denied without good reason or when some burden is imposed unduly... For example, the selection of research subjects needs to be scrutinized in order to determine whether some classes of subjects (e.g., welfare patients, particular racial and ethnic minorities or persons confined to institutions) are being systematically selected simply because of their easy availability or their compromised position..." Belmont also says that, "justice demands... That such research should not unduly involve persons from groups unlikely to be among the beneficiaries of subsequent applications of the research." This principle also requires inclusion of diverse populations/groups so they may benefit from the findings of research. In the regulations, the principle of justice requires review of procedures for the selection of participants and the outcome of those procedures.

Selection of Participants

Justice is relevant to the selection of research participants at two levels: the social and the individual. Individual justice in the selection of participants would require that researchers exhibit fairness. Justice requires fairness in the exclusion and inclusion criteria. Investigators and IRBs must consider subject selection issues including the encouragement by federal agencies for increasing enrollment of women, children and minorities. "Social justice requires that distinction be drawn between classes of subjects that ought and ought not to participate in any particular kind of research, based on the ability... to bear burdens and on the appropriateness of placing further burdens on already burdened persons...Certain groups, such as racial minorities, the economically disadvantaged, the very sick and the institutionalized... given their dependent status and their frequently compromised capacity for free consent... should be protected against the danger of being involved in research solely for administrative convenience or because they are easy to manipulate as a result of their illness and/or socioeconomic condition." Research should not use underprivileged persons to benefit the privileged. The principle of justice is applied in the selection of research participants.

Federal Regulations

Human Subject Protection Regulations

The federal regulations were directly derived from the ethical principles discussed above. In 1991, 17 federal departments and agencies adopted a common set of regulations, called "the Common Rule," governing human subject research sponsored by the federal government. The Common Rule was derived from the first of four subparts of the Department of Health and Human

Services (DHHS) regulations for the protection of human subjects. These regulations date from 1981, when they were published together with FDA human subject protection regulations as a response to the National Research Act of 1974 and the 1979 Belmont Report on research ethics. The Common Rule governs research conducted or supported by these federal agencies. The equivalent FDA human subject protection regulations govern research with drugs, biologics and devices regardless of study sponsorship. The Common Rule has established three main protective mechanisms: review of research by an institutional review board (IRB), required informed consent of participants and institutional assurances of compliance.

Protective mechanisms established by the Common Rule:

1. Review of research by an IRB.

2. Informed consent of subjects.

3. Institutional assurances of compliance.

---

1. Review of Research by an Institutional Review Board (IRB)

Peer scientific review and independent ethical review are key components of the research monitoring system. Scientific merit and methods are reviewed under a system of peer review at major research institutions. The purpose of the IRB is to review research and determine if the rights and welfare of participants in research are adequately protected. Institutions establish policies that ensure peer review and IRB review are properly conducted. By institutional policy, even studies that otherwise may be exempt from federal regulations may require review and/or verification of exempt status. Documents provided to peer review committees and IRBs by investigators must contain enough information to allow valid judgments about the science and ethics of the research.

The IRB has the authority to approve, require modification of (to approve) or disapprove all research activities, including proposed changes in previously approved human subject research. Based on factors including risk to participants, IRBs determine which activities require continuing review more frequently than once a year and which need verification that no changes have occurred since the previous review and approval.

- Before human volunteers are involved in research, the IRB must consider:

  - The risks to participants

  - The anticipated benefits to participants and others

  - The importance of the knowledge that may reasonably result

  - The informed consent process to be employed.

- The IRB must report promptly to the appropriate institutional officials, OHRP, the FDA and any sponsoring agency of the federal government:

- Injuries to human volunteers or other unanticipated problems involving risks to volunteers or others

- Serious or continuing noncompliance with regulations or requirements of the IRB

- Suspension or termination of IRB approval for research.

• Initial and continuing review and approvals must be in compliance with federal regulations. Continuing reviews must be preceded by IRB receipt of appropriate progress reports from the investigator, including available study-wide findings.

• Investigators must request proposed changes in previously approved human subject research activities to the IRB. Proposed changes to the protocol may not be initiated without IRB review and approval, except where necessary to eliminate apparent immediate hazards to the participants.

2. Informed Consent of Volunteers

As described in the Belmont Report, consent must be informed, understood and voluntary. These are the essential ethical and conceptual hallmarks of consent and provide respect for persons by honoring their autonomy. The requirements to ensure "legally effective" consent are intended to maximize the likelihood that consent is an informed autonomous decision.

Consent forms should reflect, in language that is understandable to volunteers, relevant information about the study. Consent, whether written or oral, may not include waivers or the appearance of waivers of any of the volunteer's legal rights. The same is true for releases (or appearance of releases) from liability for negligence of responsible parties. Technical language should be eliminated or explained in lay terms. Overly optimistic language should be avoided (e.g., "this product has been extensively and safely used elsewhere"). The form serves as a baseline of information for initial presentation and a reference source during the study, as well as documentation of voluntary participation. Especially for long and/or complicated studies, investigators should stress to subjects the importance of keeping their copy of the consent form for reference. The original consent form, which is kept in the investigator's records, needs to be signed and dated by the participant.

3. Institutional Assurances of Compliance

Before a federal grant or contract can be awarded, the institution must file an "Assurance of Compliance" with the government. This assurance is called a Federalwide Assurance (FWA). In the Assurance, the institution agrees to apply the federal regulations and be guided by the ethical principles of the Belmont Report.

The Office for Human Research Protection (OHRP) is the office within the federal government that negotiates Assurances for DHHS and oversees institutions' compliance with their Assurances. Research institutions must periodically reapply for and negotiate the terms of their Assurances as one mechanism by which the OHRP can address any concerns that may have come to its attention regarding the conduct of human subject research at a particular institution.

> **An Assurance imposes requirements on the institution and its researchers with respect to the conduct of human subject research.**

A Federalwide Assurance (FWA) is required only for federally sponsored research; however, most institutions voluntarily choose to extend the procedures and protections to all research conducted at the institution. Institutions must maintain certain conditions and requirements in connection with the conduct and review of research projects. One fundamental condition of an Assurance is that the institution must name an institutional review board (IRB) to oversee the conduct of research.

> **The IRB review system is a requirement set forth in the Assurance.**

Assurance violations: In the past several years, OHRP has enforced sanctions at some major research institutions. These sanctions ranged from the withdrawal of the institution's Assurance to the placement of limitations on the institutional Assurance and temporary suspension of federal research at institutions. In some cases, the suspension lasted a few days, but in others all human subject research across the entire institution was stopped for months.

Given the potential ramifications of violating an Assurance, it is important for researchers to be compliant with the procedures established by the institution's Assurance for the review and approval of research and to be compliant with applicable laws governing the conduct of human subject research.

If OHRP determines that the obligations set forth in an Assurance have been violated, it has the authority to terminate or suspend it. This means no federally funded research can be conducted until the Assurance is reinstated. Typically the termination or suspension of an institution's Assurance arises in situations in which there have been repeated and systematic violations of human subject research requirements by an institutional review board or by researchers and, as a result, the safety and welfare of research participants is believed to be at risk.

Another significant sanction available to OHRP is to temporarily suspend new enrollments in existing research protocols. OHRP also may place certain restrictions on the institution's ability to conduct human subject research and/ or require that the institution take corrective actions. OHRP monitors the implementation of these corrective actions by requiring the submission of periodic progress reports and conducting site visits. If the institution fails to adequately apply the corrective actions, more severe sanctions are imposed.

OHRP also has the authority to impose sanctions on individual researchers. Sanctions that may be imposed on an individual researcher include:

- Recommending to the DHHS that the researcher be barred from receiving federal funds for conducting research

- Requiring OHRP approval for each study conducted by the researcher

- Requiring the researcher to undergo remedial training or education

- Placing certain restrictions on the researcher's ability to conduct research (e.g., requiring supervision of the researcher).

Concerns regarding a particular researcher can come to the attention of OHRP through a number of mechanisms, including complaints by subjects. One mechanism is through a mandated IRB report to OHRP. Federal regulations require the IRB to report to the OHRP (and FDA as appropriate):

- Any serious or continuing noncompliance with regulations or requirements of the IRB

- Any injuries or unanticipated problems involving risk to research participants

- Any suspension or termination of IRB approval for research.

Violation of the obligations of Assurance can result in:

- Termination or suspension of the institution's Assurance.
- Suspension or restrictions to ongoing studies.
- Departmental restrictions.
- Individual restrictions

Additional FDA regulations and sanctions: As stated previously, the FDA has regulations for the protection of human research subjects that are also based on the Belmont Report ethical principles (21 CFR Parts 50 and 56). In addition, the FDA has specific regulations governing the way FDA-regulated products (primarily drugs, biologic products and medical devices) may be used in clinical research settings. These regulations also are intended to protect volunteers as well as ensure sound data on which to base product approvals. Therefore, it is important that investigators who use FDA-regulated products be familiar with these regulations so that research is conducted in compliance. Like other FDA regulations, these rules are contained in the Code of Federal Regulations (CFR) and are available in IRB and legal offices as well as on the internet. The

Figure 1: Most common deficiencies found in FDA inspections

Investigative sites	• Failure to follow the investigational plan (protocol)
	• Protocol deviations
	• Inadequate record keeping
	• Inadequate accountability for the investigational product
	• Inadequate participant protections, including informed consent issues
IRBs	• Inadequate initial or continuing review
	• Inadequate standard operating procedures (SOPs)
	• Inadequate membership rosters
	• For devices, lack of or incorrect SR/NSR determination
Sponsors	• Inadequate monitoring
	• Failure to bring investigators into compliance
	• Inadequate accountability for the investigational product

Source: www.fda.gov

specific references for drugs and devices are 21 CFR Parts 54, 312, 314, 600, 812 and 814, some of which are included Appendix C.

The FDA has an inspection program, the Bioresearch Monitoring Program (BIMO), that conducts routine and "for cause" audits of FDA-regulated research. Investigators, research sites, sponsors and IRBs are inspected under this program. In 2010, the FDA conducted 1037 inspections, including 680 at investigative sites, 203 at IRBs and 154 at sponsors, according to www.fda.gov. The most common deficiencies for each group are shown in Figure 1.

The FDA works with individuals, companies and institutions to help promote compliance with the laws and regulations that govern clinical research. Most cases of noncompliance are due to misunderstanding the regulations or the responsibilities of individuals conducting clinical research. Institutions and individuals who work to resolve areas of noncompliance are generally met with the cooperation of the FDA. Disregard for the regulations and/ or their intent, especially after initial goodwill efforts by the FDA, may lead to various levels of sanctions. Often correlated with the level to which research participants are placed at risk, these include:

- Longer review of applications. Once a level of trust is broken with the FDA, additional safeguards, including more detailed review cycles, often are required.

- Warning letters for specific documented concerns. These letters require immediate action, usually to cease all noncompliant activity until compliance is assured. Warning letters are made public and posted on the FDA's web site and can be searched by individual, institution,

Figure 2: FDA warning letter excerpt

1. You failed to assure that an Institutional Review Board (IRB) that complies with the requirements set forth in 21 CFR Part 56 was responsible for the continuing review and approval of the clinical investigation [21 CFR 312.66].
   a. IRB approval of your research study, [   ], expired on March 17, 2004. Our investigation found that the IRB requested information from you on this study on February 18, 2004, before approving the study under continuing review. The requested changes were not submitted by you to the IRB until May 12, 2004, approximately two months after IRB approval had expired. IRB approval was not granted until May 19, 2004.
2. You failed to adequately document informed consent [21 CFR 50.27]. Specifically,
   a. Our investigation failed to find documentation of informed consent for Subjects [ ]/013 and [ ]/016 who participated in study [   ].
   b. Our investigation failed to find documentation of informed consent for Subject [ ]/007 who participated in study [   ].

Source: www.fda.gov

company, date or compliance type. Frequently, although the warning letter may be specific to an individual investigator, it is directed to the institution and may result in action against the institution.

- Disqualification/debarment of individuals from conducting clinical research (this can be temporary or permanent). Both the list of disqualified investigators and the list of debarred persons are posted on the FDA's web site. Once a name is placed on the list, it stays on the list even if the sanction is removed. It should be noted that this list is reviewed by companies as they choose investigators and sites for their clinical studies. It also is available to future employers, fellow investigators and researchers.

- Disqualification of institutions and/or IRBs from conducting or approving clinical research. Again, once an institution becomes known for noncompliance, it will take time and effort to re-establish trust with the agency.

- Other sanctions including seizures, injunctions, criminal charges and monetary penalties. These types of penalties are applied when there is evidence of willful serious disregard for the regulations and participant safety. For individual researchers, these often are last-resort efforts to halt criminal activity.

Scientific misconduct: In addition to enacting regulations that implement the principles of the Belmont Report, the federal government also has enacted regulations governing misconduct in scientific research.

As a condition of accepting federal funding for research, institutions are required to adhere to the Public Health Service (PHS) regulations that apply to scientific misconduct. The regulations require that research institutions have written policies and procedures for investigating scientific misconduct. The current PHS definition of scientific misconduct is as follows:

Misconduct in science means fabrication, falsification, plagiarism or other practices that seriously deviate from those that are commonly accepted within the scientific community for proposing, conducting and reporting research. It does not include honest error or honest differences in interpretations or judgments of data. (42 CFR 50.102)

The Public Health Service defines falsification to mean changing or falsifying existing data. It defines fabrication as the creation of data out of "thin air." It is important to note that honest errors or differences in interpretation are not considered misconduct. Although they are serious charges, incompetence and negligence also are not considered misconduct. Within the definition of scientific misconduct, however, there is a significant gray area, particularly with respect to "other practices that seriously deviate from those that are commonly accepted." In light of this, if there is a concern an individual may have engaged in practices that seriously deviate from acceptable research standards, the matter should be brought to the attention of the individual's immediate supervisor, who can then confer with institutional officials regarding the appropriate action to be taken. If an individual has a concern with respect to his/her immediate supervisor, most institutions' policies designate other institutional officials who can be contacted.

> **The definition of scientific misconduct does not include "honest errors" or "differences in interpretation of the data."**

Misconduct allegations: When an allegation regarding scientific misconduct is made, regulations require that the institution investigate the allegation in two phases: the inquiry phase and the investigative phase. During the inquiry phase, the accused researcher, the complainant and anyone with knowledge relevant to the inquiry must be interviewed. The purpose of this phase is not to determine conclusively whether or not there was misconduct. Instead, the purpose of the inquiry phase is to determine whether or not there may be reason to believe that misconduct could have occurred. PHS regulations require that the inquiry phase generally be completed within 60 days of receipt of the allegation. At the conclusion of the inquiry phase, the institution is required to write a report summarizing the results of the inquiry.

If, after the inquiry, institutional officials believe misconduct may have occurred, the institution is required to conduct a more in-depth investigation. The institution is required to report its intention to conduct an investigation

A recent case of scientific misconduct

In 2006, Dr. Anil Potti, a cancer researcher at Duke University Medical Center, Joseph R. Nevins, a senior scientist at Duke, and their colleagues published a paper in *Nature Medicine*. They wrote about genomic tests they had developed that looked at genetic traits of a cancerous tumor and determined which kind of chemotherapy might work best to cure the tumor. This was a major breakthrough in cancer treatment, and other cancer researchers were looking forward to using this huge discovery with their own patients.

Two statisticians at M.D. Anderson Cancer Center in Texas, Dr. Keith Baggerly and Dr. Kevin Coombes, were asked to check the work for possible application. Dr. Baggerly and Dr. Coombes found errors almost immediately. Some seemed careless—moving a row or a column over by one in a giant spreadsheet—while others were significant, and not so easily explained. When they questioned the Duke researchers about these findings, they were dismissed as "clerical errors" and the researchers continued to publish papers on their genomic signatures in prestigious journals. Meanwhile, the Duke group started additional trials using the work to decide which drugs to give patients.

At this time the Duke researchers even had set up a company that was planning to sell their test to determine optimal cancer treatments. It appeared this was poised to be a gold mine for the Duke researchers and for the university. The promise of the company's future was widely reported in the national media.

Dr. Baggerly and Dr. Coombes tried to alert people to the problems they were seeing and finally got the attention of the National Cancer Institute, whose own investigators wanted to use the Duke system in a clinical trial but were concerned about the criticisms. Eventually, Baggerly and Coombes published their analysis in *The Annals of Applied Statistics*, a journal read primarily by statisticians.

Because of the National Cancer Institute's concerns, a major external review of the Duke research was conducted. This review found no errors in the conclusions. However, it was based on data supplied to them by Duke, which now is known to have been falsified.

Then in 2010, The Cancer Letter reported that the lead researcher, Dr. Potti, had falsified parts of his résumé, falsely claiming, among other things, that he had been a Rhodes Scholar. "It took that to make people sit up and take notice," said Dr. Steven Goodman, professor of oncology, pediatrics, epidemiology and biostatistics at Johns Hopkins University.[1]

This "seemingly minor" resume padding triggered further investigations. These finally uncovered false statements in grant applications, that some of the actual data from the research had been significantly falsified and that the claimed and published conclusions were false.

The impact on Duke was massive. Duke shut down its three new trials based on the results of a re-evaluation the earlier work, and several lawsuits were filed on behalf of study participants and their families. Duke may be asked to return some of the grant funding related to this research and these trials. Four significant related

A recent case of scientific misconduct (cont'd)

scientific papers from major journals were retracted, which is extremely rare. Dr. Potti resigned from Duke and his collaborator and mentor, Dr. Nevins, no longer directs one of Duke's genomics centers. Duke University Medical Center was embarrassed and its reputation tarnished.

Researchers everywhere are realizing huge data sets, complicated analyses and the resulting scientific publications can't always be relied on. Worst of all, the cancer research community and cancer patients had their hopes of a promising new therapy crushed.

Sources: Gina Kolata. "How Bright Promise in Cancer Testing Fell Apart." New York Times. July 7, 2011.

www.nytimes.com/2011/07/08/health/research/08genes.html

www.economist.com/node/21528593

Institutions are required to report to the Office of Research Integrity when the institution decides to commence an in-depth investigation into an allegation of scientific misconduct.

---

to the Office of Research Integrity (ORI). ORI is a division of the PHS that oversees investigations of allegations of scientific misconduct.

When a further investigation is conducted into the allegation of misconduct (the investigative phase), the institution is required to interview the accused researcher, the complainant and others with knowledge relevant to the investigation. Relevant documents are also reviewed. At the conclusion of its investigation, the institution is required to write a report of its findings and its determination as to whether or not the accused individual committed scientific misconduct. The report is submitted to institutional officials, who determine the final action to be taken. The report is also submitted to ORI, which has the authority to either accept or reject the findings. In general, the investigative phase takes no more than 120 days. The PHS regulations require inquiries and investigations into allegations of misconduct be conducted as confidentially as possible without compromising the ability to conduct an effective investigation.

Individuals who have, in good faith, made an allegation of misconduct ("whistle-blowers") should not be the object of retaliation. Indeed, retaliation against a whistle-blower who made an allegation of misconduct in good faith may itself be construed as an act of misconduct.

Retaliation against a "whistle-blower" may be construed as an act of misconduct.

If an individual is found guilty of scientific misconduct, the institution and ORI may utilize a range of penalties. For the institution, penalties may range from requiring further training or supervision for the individual to terminating his or her appointment. The ORI may impose penalties that range from researcher supervision to the maximum penalty of researcher debarment from conducting federally funded research. Additionally, in some cases, the institution or ORI may require any publication related to the research in question be retracted or corrected.

The Ketek case, excerpted in part from an FDA warning letter, Ref. 07-HFD-45-0501, is an example of misconduct. A whistle-blower also was involved in this situation.

The Ketek case

In 2004, after three reviews, the FDA approved a drug called Ketek (telithromycin) for the treatment of community-acquired respiratory tract infections such as sinusitis, bronchitis and pneumonia. During the first review, FDA reviewers identified some substantial safety concerns, so they asked the manufacturer to obtain additional safety data by conducting a study involving patients who might be prescribed Ketek if the drug were approved.

The company recruited more than 1,800 physicians to conduct this unblinded, randomized, controlled trial in which the incidence rates of hepatic, cardiac and visual adverse events in patients receiving Ketek were compared to those receiving another antibiotic. The study enrolled over 24,000 subjects and was completed in five months. The results professed to show Ketek was as safe as the other treatment. In its second review, the FDA reviewed this study.

Before the second review, the FDA completed its routine inspections of some of the sites involved in this large study. They found the clinical investigator who had enrolled the highest number of subjects, over 400, had fabricated data and subjects. (She subsequently served several years in a federal prison for her actions.) The FDA also inspected nine other sites and found other serious violations of trial conduct at three of these sites; overall, four of the 10 inspected sites were referred to the FDA's criminal investigation unit for additional inspection. These issues with data integrity were not shared with the review committee. Also, the manufacturer knew about the data issues before submitting its study for review but did not tell the FDA about the problems.

When these problems came to light, the FDA held a third review of Ketek. Because of the potential unreliability of the data, FDA managers proposed using foreign post-marketing safety reports as evidence of the drug's safety. The post-marketing data submitted by the company were reviewed by the FDA without any verification of their accuracy or completeness, which was not the usual FDA policy.

At the same time, the efficacy of Ketek came into question because the only trials conducted had been noninferiority trials, which do not directly compare the new drug (Ketek) against a standard control or placebo. Although noninferiority trials had been standard procedure for antimicrobial drugs in the 1990s, by 2004 they

The Ketek case (cont'd)

had fallen out of favor. Despite this, the FDA accepted the trials as completed, and approved the drug for marketing.[1]

In February 2005, seven months after the drug was introduced in the U.S. market, the first death from Ketek-associated liver failure was reported to the FDA; it occurred in a patient treated for a mild respiratory tract infection. During the next few months, there were several reports of liver, cardiac and visual adverse reactions associated with the use of Ketek, including cases of severe liver damage and some deaths.

In 2007, the FDA revised the labeling for Ketek and banned its use for two of the three previously approved indications, although the drug is still approved to treat pneumonia. The new labeling warns that cases of acute hepatic failure, including fatal liver injury, have been reported, with some requiring liver transplants and some occurring after only a few doses. The new labeling also includes a black box warning that the drug is contraindicated in some patients and updates the occurrence of other potentially serious disorders.[2]

References

1. www.nejm.org/doi/full/10.1056/NEJMp078032

2. www.lawyersandsettlements.com/articles/drugs-medical/ketek-scandal-00680.html

CHAPTER THREE

Roles and Responsibilities of Institutions in Human Subject Research

At the conclusion of this chapter, readers will be able to:

- Describe the responsibilities of research institutions and federal regulatory agencies in conducting clinical research.
- Discuss the legal basis and the intent of the regulations governing clinical research.
- Describe the term "Good Clinical Practice" and how it applies to clinical research.

Introduction

The roles and responsibilities of federal agencies, institutions, IRBs and investigators in conducting human subject research are defined in federal and state laws and regulations. This chapter provides a general review of these roles and responsibilities.

Research Institution

The research institution bears responsibility for compliance with the Department of Health and Human Services (DHHS) and the Food and Drug Administration (FDA) regulations for the performance of all research activities that involve human subjects. Institutions are required to use additional safeguards for research in vulnerable populations. This is true for research conducted at sites under the direction of any employee or agent of the institution. The institution has responsibility for educating researchers on issues of research ethics and scientific integrity. It also has a mandated responsibility to investigate alleged cases of scientific misconduct. In addition, the institution has a responsibility to have and enforce a policy on conflict of interest.

Issues that require institutional review

- Ethical (i.e., IRB) review (of the protocol and informed consent).
- Administrative review of proposals, contracts and grants.
- Scientific peer review.

1. Ethical Review

Institutions protect the rights, safety and welfare of their research participants by assuring an Institutional Review Board (IRB) operating in compliance with federal regulations is in place. By regulation, when approving research the IRB must determine the following requirements are satisfied:

- Risks to volunteers are minimized:

  - by using procedures consistent with sound research design and that do not unnecessarily expose volunteers to risk, and

  - by using procedures already being performed on the volunteers for diagnostic or treatment purposes, when appropriate.

- Risks are reasonable in relation to anticipated benefits to volunteers, if any, and to the importance of the expected knowledge. In evaluating risks and benefits, the IRB considers only those risks and benefits that may result directly from the research (as distinguished from risks and benefits to people even if they were not participating in the research).

- Selection of participants is equitable. In making this assessment, the IRB takes into account the purpose(s) of the research and the setting in which the research will be conducted.

- Informed consent will be sought from each prospective volunteer, or the volunteer's legally authorized representative, unless waived in accordance with regulations.

- Informed consent will be appropriately documented, usually with a signed written consent form.

- The research plan makes provisions for monitoring the data collected to ensure the safety of participants.

- There are provisions to protect the privacy of participants and to maintain the confidentiality of data.

- Additional safeguards are included in the study to protect the rights and welfare of participants when some or all of them are likely to be vulnerable to coercion or undue influence (children, prisoners, pregnant women, handicapped or mentally disabled persons or economically or educationally disadvantaged persons).

The IRB reviews the study design/protocol and the information from the IRB review application to make the above determinations. IRB approval is based on the information provided, and the board expects the researcher to abide by the protocol as written. Most changes in the study must receive prior approval by the IRB before being instituted. Sponsors require any changes made by the IRB be relayed to them for concurrence.

Some funding/sponsoring organizations require IRB review of projects before they can be considered for funding/sponsoring. Often, the funding/sponsoring organization's review results in changes to the study design. It is essential that the investigator know that, if the study is to be funded and conducted, all changes must be reviewed and approved by the IRB before the study may begin.

> **To ensure an effective review by the IRB, the board must be provided with certain critical information, including: the protocol/study design, consent form(s) and subject recruitment materials.**

This also is true for changes required by a regulatory agency. For example, in the Investigational New Drug Application (IND) or the Investigational Device Exemption (IDE) review process, if the FDA requires changes to the study protocol, these changes must be submitted to the IRB for approval.

After the initial approval, studies must undergo continuing review by the IRB to ensure that the risk/benefit relationship of the research remains acceptable, the informed consent process and documents are still appropriate and the enrollment of subjects has been equitable. By federal regulation, the maximum period between these IRB reviews is one year. As part of the continuing review, the IRB will assess appropriate information such as enrollment figures and demographics, adverse events and unanticipated problems, subject withdrawals, preliminary study results and publications and the consent process. The investigator is responsible for applying for continuing review in a timely manner to ensure IRB approval is continuous. If a study is not re-approved before its expiration date, it is automatically suspended until formal notice of re-approval from the IRB is received. Sponsors require copies of IRB approvals (initial and continuing) and will not ship study materials until the initial approval is received.

Note that not all IRBs are associated with institutions. There are also independent, or "central," IRBs that can be used by any investigator not affiliated with an institution, who will not be conducting clinical trials at an institution or whose institution does not have an IRB. Independent IRBs are frequently used for multi-center studies in non-hospitalized patients.

In 2009, the FDA began requiring registration of IRBs that review FDA-regulated studies. Registration gives the FDA more complete information about the IRBs that review these studies and:

- Facilitates sharing educational and other information with the IRBs

- Assists the FDA in scheduling and conducting IRB inspections

- Helps the FDA prioritize IRB inspections.

Once registered, IRBs are required to review and submit current information every three years, although some information, such as a change in the IRB chairperson, are required to be submitted within a certain amount of time after the change occurs.

IRB registration is not accreditation or certification by the FDA, nor does it address issues of the IRB's competence, expertise or ability to conduct review.

An Interesting "Sting" Operation

In 2009, the Government Accountability Office (GAO) conducted an undercover operation to investigate three key aspects of IRB operation: establishing an IRB, obtaining an HHS-approved assurance and obtaining IRB approval. For this "sting" operation, GAO created a fictitious IRB, medical device company, a device it supposedly was developing and investigators. GAO developed a protocol based on the fictitious device and, using its medical device company cover, submitted applications to three independent IRBs for approval of the protocol and investigators to test this medical device on humans.

The device was a gel called Adhesiabloc, which was to promote post surgical healing and would be classified by the FDA as a significant-risk device. One IRB, Coast IRB, approved the protocol for human testing. The other two IRBs did not approve the protocol, calling it "junk" and "the riskiest thing I've ever seen on this board."

Considerable publicity resulted from this investigation, and Coast IRB since has ceased operations. In the aftermath of the media attention, IRBs across the country have asked themselves what they can learn from this investigation and assessed their vulnerability to unethical manipulation.

The GAO has stated that failure to check the credentials of investigators to ensure they were qualified to conduct clinical trials was a key finding. None of the three IRBs that reviewed the protocol discovered that the company, investigators and device were all fraudulent.

The GAO investigation has encouraged most IRBs to examine their practices and increase their vigilance when assessing investigators and protocols.

GAO's report on the operation stated, "the process for obtaining HHS approval for an assurance lacks effective controls."[1] When HHS was briefed on the findings of the investigation, it agreed the assurance process does not offer protection against unethical manipulation. HHS also indicated it does not review applications to assess whether the submitted information is factual. This has left many people wondering how meaningful an assurance is, beyond being a regulatory requirement.

2. Administrative Review of Proposals, Contracts and Grants

Most research institutions establish an office that reviews and authorizes proposals to external sponsors, accepts grants and reviews or approves contracts for all associated researchers.

This review office generally ensures that proposals and associated budgets are in compliance with institution and sponsor policies (including IRB review where appropriate) and that investigator assurances are current. These assurances include determination that a financial interest does not have a significant effect upon the design, conduct or reporting of the proposed study. Generally, if the investigator has a financial interest in the sponsor funding the clinical study, the institution will need to determine if the conflict can be managed. Some institutions will not accept funding if this situation exists.

By authorizing a proposal to an external sponsor, the institution is:

- Stating that in the institution's best estimation, the statement of work or protocol can be performed at the proposed funding level

- Any unique policies of the institution have been considered

- The proposal meets the requirements of the potential sponsor

- The institution will comply with all federal and state laws and regulations, as well as institutional policies.

The review office addresses contractual issues inherent in clinical research contracts, such as ownership of data, appropriate sharing of liability, responsibility for participant injury and protection of publication rights for researchers. They are also responsible for negotiating terms on which sponsor confidential information will be accepted.

Institutions that receive Public Health Service (PHS) funds are mandated to have a conflict-of-interest (COI) policy and a mechanism for reviewing potential conflicts. Usually, institutions have followed the model PHS policy and have established a COI committee that sets institutional policy, reviews reports of potential conflicts and recommends procedures to eliminate, manage and/or minimize conflict. These policies have focused on individual financial COI. However, with greater involvement with industry partners and the fostering of technological transfer through institutionally sponsored start-up companies, institutional COI is becoming an issue that must be dealt with. Chapter 8 discusses conflict of interest in more detail.

3. Scientific Peer Review

Peer review ensures that sound research design and methods are employed. An institutional peer review committee focuses on the scientific concerns of studies. This committee generally will examine the composition and qualifications of the research team and they may also consider resource issues.

Scientific review for both biomedical and behavioral/social science research considers the soundness and worth of the hypothesis, the procedures used to test the hypothesis and the adequacy of the analysis to be employed.

For clinical trials, sample size justifications are based upon statistical significance and predicted results. For both behavioral and biomedical research, it is important that scientific rigor be maintained because, as the Belmont Report indicates, exposing volunteers to any risk is unethical if valid scientific results are not possible.

Institutions have set up various methods to perform scientific review. At most universities and larger research institutions, peer review is conducted by a committee of scientists within the investigator's department. Smaller facilities have assigned this to department heads, or even to the IRB. When the IRB is responsible for scientific review, in addition to its mandated role as reviewer of participant rights and welfare, additional information must be reviewed and, usually, scientifically qualified people must be added to the IRB. Some IRBs in this dual role have established a subcommittee to accomplish the scientific review. The major concern is that it may detract from the IRB's ability to comply with the federal human subject protection regulations and institutional responsibilities. It is important for continued public trust and support that research institutions be seen as dedicated to the development of unbiased scientific knowledge for the betterment of humankind.

Federal Agencies

While several federal agencies, such as the Department of Education, the Department of Defense and the National Science Foundation, fund and regulate research, they generally follow the lead of the Department of Health and Human Services (DHHS).

Department of Health and Human Services (DHHS)

In addition to the FDA, the DHHS houses several other agencies that regulate or fund research. The National Institutes of Health's (NIH) mission is to uncover new knowledge that leads to better public health. The NIH's role in research primarily is to conduct studies with its own investigators and provide funding for research projects at other institutions, especially multi-site national studies. To a lesser extent, other DHHS agencies also function in the role of research conductor/sponsor, including the Centers for Disease Control and Prevention (CDC) and the Agency for Healthcare Research and Quality (AHRQ).

Agencies within the DHHS promulgate regulations applicable to Public Health Service (PHS)-funded research. An example is the conflict-of-interest rule that establishes standards and procedures to be followed by institutions to ensure the design, conduct or reporting of research funded under PHS grants, cooperative agreements or contracts will not be biased by any conflicting financial interest of its investigators.

The Office for Human Research Protection (OHRP) regulates, in a manner similar to the FDA, research involving human subjects for studies conducted with DHHS funds to protect the rights and safety of participants. This includes regulations for IRB review of studies and informed consent documents.

The Office of Research Integrity (ORI) conducts investigations into misconduct in research. As a condition of accepting federal funding for research, institutions are required to adhere to the PHS regulations that apply to scientific misconduct. If an individual is found to have committed scientific misconduct, the institution and the ORI may impose a range of penalties.

Food and Drug Administration (FDA)

The FDA is the federal consumer protection agency within the DHHS that enforces the Food, Drug and Cosmetic Act (the FD&C Act) and related federal public health laws. According to these laws, only drugs, biologics and medical devices that have been proven safe and effective can be marketed.

To allow for research with human subjects to determine the safety and effectiveness of new (i.e., investigational) drugs, biologics or device products, the FDA has established regulations that govern study sponsors, investigators and IRBs.

Prior to the initiation of a human research study with an investigational product, an application to the FDA is usually required.

> **Although FDA oversight may not be necessary, the protocol and informed consent still needs to undergo review by the IRB.**

The FDA monitors research through review of required reports from sponsors, as well as through a program of on-site inspections and audits. The biomedical monitoring program (BIMO) inspects all players in the research enterprise, including sponsors, investigators and IRBs. It conducts both routine inspections, primarily looking at studies that support a marketing application, and for-cause inspections, for which there is suspected non-compliance.

Good Clinical Practice

GCP is an ethical and scientific quality standard for designing, conducting, monitoring, recording, auditing, analyzing and reporting drug trials that involve participation of human subjects. GCPs are consistent with ethical principles put forth in the Declaration of Helsinki. The main purposes of GCP are:

1.   To protect human subjects during clinical studies.

2. To ensure that the integrity of the data collected in clinical studies is maintained.

> **GCPs offer protection for human subjects in clinical trials.**

There is no one source of guidance for GCPs. They are embodied within laws, regulations and guidelines such as:

- Ethical codes
- IRB and consent regulations
- Guidelines on the obligations of investigators, sponsors and monitors
- Code of Federal Regulations pertaining to drugs and devices
- ICH Guidelines
- Official guidance documents.

> **Following GCPs ensures the accuracy and reliability of the data generated in the course of a clinical trial.**

Compliance with GCPs during clinical trials will ensure that:

- The rights and safety of human subjects are not compromised
- Appropriately and adequately trained staff manage the study
- The study is carefully documented
- Protocol is strictly adhered to.

GCPs, therefore, encompass all aspects of a clinical trial including (but not limited to):

- Obtaining informed consent
- Documenting accurate case histories
- Maintaining complete "paper trails" for all study documents
- Reporting adverse events
- Proper record retention.

The International Conference on Harmonization (ICH) is composed of expert working groups from industry and regulatory bodies in the European Union, Japan and the U.S. ICH has published guidelines for GCP. This worldwide GCP document offers standardization for clinical trials.

In the U.S., FDA regulations are the basis for the practices that govern clinical research. Compliance with these standards provides public assurance that the rights, safety and well-being of trial participants are protected and that the clinical trial data are valid and accurate. Most ICH standards also have been accepted by the FDA, and most trials conducted in the U.S. adhere to both FDA and ICH guidelines. Since many clinical trials are used for registration in both the U.S. and other countries, adherence to both FDA and ICH standards helps to ensure acceptability by regulatory agencies around the world.

References

1. *Undercover tests show the institutional review board system is vulnerable to unethical manipulation.* GAO. March 26, 2009.

CHAPTER FOUR

Roles and Responsibilities of the Investigator and the Study Process

At the conclusion of this chapter, readers will be able to:

- Describe the roles and responsibilities of the investigator and research team.
- List the items that should be included in a protocol (study design).
- List the required elements of a consent form.
- Describe the issues to consider in patient recruitment for a study.

Introduction

The complex responsibilities of conducting research can make the investigator's role difficult and challenging. On the other hand, once the investigator understands the responsibilities involved, research can be rewarding for both the investigator and for the patients who participate. The study process begins before the first patient is entered and continues after the last patient has completed his or her study involvement. This chapter provides an overview of the responsibilities of investigators, the roles of the research team members and the steps involved in the process of conducting a successful research study.

Investigator's Roles and Responsibilities

Investigators share with research institutions and sponsors the responsibility for ensuring that study volunteers are adequately protected. They are required to assure that the Institutional Review Board (IRB) reviewing the study is in compliance with federal regulations. Studies must be properly designed so that they are scientifically sound and likely to yield valid results. Investigators must be appropriately qualified to conduct the research. The investigator is responsible for ensuring that the research is conducted according to the research design as approved by the IRB. Respect for study volunteers' rights and dignity requires that informed consent be obtained before a person participates in a study.

> **The safety and welfare of research volunteers ultimately rests with the investigator.**

Professional Judgment

The ultimate responsibility for the acceptable conduct of research with human volunteers rests with the investigator. Only sound professional judgment can ensure the protection of study volunteers. It is up to the investigator to see that:

- The personal dignity and autonomy of the research volunteer are respected.

- Volunteers are protected from harm by maximizing anticipated benefits and minimizing possible risks.

- The benefits and burdens of research are shared fairly.

The challenge arises in deciding how to protect the study volunteers while also achieving progress in science. Although the two objectives are not mutually exclusive, they also are not without conflict. Understanding the distinction between research and regular practice is fundamental to resolving any conflict that may arise. It is also essential to recognize the potential for confusion on the part of the volunteer (e.g., patient, client, student) about his/her relationship to the investigator, who may also be his/her physician, social worker, mentor or teacher.

The purpose of medical or behavioral practice is to provide diagnosis, preventative treatment or therapy. "Practice" involves interventions designed solely to enhance the well-being of the patient or client. These interventions are undertaken because there is a reasonable expectation of a successful outcome. "Research" constitutes activities designed to contribute to generalizable knowledge. Typically, in research, a set of activities is consistently applied to groups of individuals in order to test a hypothesis and draw conclusions. The activities do not necessarily provide direct benefit.

The line between practice and research is often blurred. Novel procedures do not necessarily constitute research and often, research and practice occur simultaneously. The investigator's professional judgment is essential to maintain the integrity of the research process and to keep the study volunteer informed of his/her role in the process and relationship with the investigator(s). People who are used as research subjects without their consent may be wronged, even if they are not harmed.

Good judgment is required throughout the research process to provide the necessary checks and balances. No balance of research/therapy is acceptable if it is likely to result in less than adequate care for the patient. It can be tempting to value knowledge more highly than basic human rights when excited by the prospect of a new scientific method or new understanding of behavioral processes. To avoid this, consider the following questions before undertaking a new study.

- What types of people will be enrolled? Address this from an ethical perspective as well as on the basis of entry criteria.
  - What alternatives are available?
  - Would some potential patients incur more risks than others? Accrue more benefits?
  - Are all patients capable of understanding the consent process?
- What is your relationship to the patient?
  - Are you also his or her caregiver, teacher, employer or in any other position of authority?
  - Does the patient delegate his or her decisions for participating in research to you?
  - Is the patient comfortable asking you questions? Are you comfortable asking probing questions to ensure he or she understands the study?
- How do you treat someone with an intervention that has not been proven to be safe or effective?
- Are you so involved with the "science," publishing, presenting or grant review that there is significant potential for conflict?

> **Good judgment is required throughout the research process to provide the necessary checks and balances.**

These are among the many questions that investigators must ask themselves regularly.

There is no standard operating procedure to address the potential issues that can arise when human patients are involved in research. Because the future of science depends on the goodwill and trust of the public, investigators must understand and meet their duty to human volunteers.

Study Conduct

The investigator is personally responsible for the conduct of the research project and for the actions of personnel under his/her supervision. Many studies are conducted by one investigator, commonly referred to as the principal investigator (PI) or, to use the FDA term, clinical investigator (CI). The investigator of a study is required to conduct the study according to the:

- Investigational plan (including the protocol and IRB stipulations)
- Institutional policies

- All applicable regulations.

Additional responsibilities for FDA-regulated studies are to:

- Comply with the signed investigators' statement (Form FDA 1572)
- Supervise use of the test article(s)
- Maintain accurate study records
- Maintain control of all test articles, ensuring that no people other than those identified to the FDA are given access to the test articles.

The investigator is responsible for the study conduct.

The term "co-principal investigator" (co-PI) is used when a study is conducted by more than one investigator, each of whom assumes equal responsibility for the conduct of the study and adherence to the regulations. The reasons for a study to be conducted by co-principal investigators are varied. For example, co-PIs might be used in drug studies when an investigator has multiple sites at which a different investigator is responsible at each location. Note that in FDA-regulated studies, each co-investigator is fully responsible for fulfilling the obligations of an investigator, and each must sign a Statement of Investigator (Form FDA 1572) form.

Principal investigators must be qualified by education, training and experience to assume responsibility for the proper conduct of the research project. They should meet all of the qualifications specified by the applicable regulatory requirements and provide evidence of such qualifications through an up-to-date curriculum vitae and relevant documentation as requested by the sponsor, the IRB and/or regulatory authorities.

Administration of the Study

Because investigators are required to conduct the study in accordance with institutional policies and all applicable regulations, their responsibilities go beyond the scientific conduct of the study itself.

Other responsibilities of investigators include:

- Compliance with federal/state laws and regulations, including a conflict-of-interest disclosure
- Assuming fiscal management
- Supervising and training of students, post-docs, residents, and other staff who will be involved in the study
- Complying with the terms and conditions of the sponsor's award/grant, for example, non-disclosure of sponsor confidential information

- Submission of all technical, progress, invention and financial reports on a timely basis.

By accepting the study, the investigator must remain cognizant of these responsibilities. Violations or delinquencies may result in loss of funding or even debarment in certain instances.

Research Team Roles and Responsibilities

The composition of the research team may vary according to the scope and complexity of the research project and the number of investigational sites involved. In some instances the study may be conducted by one individual. Most biomedical studies involve a team of individuals. Investigators who conduct clinical trials of drugs are required to personally conduct or supervise the trial and the individuals on the study team. When study activities are delegated to other individuals, the investigator must ensure these people are qualified by education, training and experience (and state licensure where relevant) to perform those activities. In all cases, a qualified physician (or dentist) should be responsible for all trial-related medical (or dental) decisions and care.

When the investigator delegates responsibility to various members of the research team (e.g., survey instruments, follow-up tests, exams or laboratory procedures), the investigator is responsible for providing adequate supervision of all team members to ensure they perform these procedures as the protocol requires. In assessing the adequacy of the investigator's supervision, the FDA focuses on four major areas:

1. Were the individuals who were delegated tasks qualified to perform these tasks?

2. Did the study staff receive adequate training on how to conduct their tasks and were they provided with an adequate understanding of the study?

3. Was there adequate supervision and involvement during the study?

4. Was there adequate supervision or oversight of any third parties involved in the conduct of the study?

The investigator is accountable for any regulatory violations resulting from failure to adequately supervise the conduct of the clinical study.

Normally, the research team meets periodically to discuss study progress and problems as they arise. It is usually helpful to keep notes or minutes, thereby documenting that the investigator is effectively managing the study.

Subinvestigator

A subinvestigator is any team member (e.g., study coordinator, junior faculty, graduate student, resident, lab staff) other than an investigator who may help in the design and conduct of the investigation, but does not actually direct its conduct. A subinvestigator can be any member of a research team designated and supervised by the investigator to perform study-related procedures and/ or make important study-related decisions. The investigator often delegates responsibility to others within their sphere of expertise.

Subinvestigators designated and supervised by the investigator should be qualified by education, professional qualifications and experience to perform the procedures delegated by the principal investigator. The competency of a subinvestigator is usually documented with a curriculum vitae.

> **The subinvestigator may help conduct the study, but does not direct it.**

Clinical Research Coordinator (CRC) or Study Coordinator

The Clinical Research Coordinator (CRC) is a specialized research professional working for and under the direction of a clinical investigator. The CRC is responsible for screening and recruiting patients, collecting and recording clinical data, maintaining clinical supplies where applicable and many of the operational aspects of a clinical trial.

Other Team Members

The principal investigator can delegate study-specific tasks, but the level of responsibility must coincide with the experience and/or capabilities of the team member. Other team members may include a variety of professionals, trainees, statisticians, laboratory technicians and administrative staff.

The investigator always should document in writing the responsibilities delegated to all members of the research team and the time period during which each team member participated. This is especially important in the event team members change during the course of the study. This "Delegation of Authority" log should be maintained and updated throughout the study and should be kept in the study documents file.

Study Process

The internal (within an institution) study process usually includes protocol development, departmental scientific review, funding applications, administrative review of contracts/grants and the application to the IRB. When an investigator is developing a study design, it may be useful to consult with the IRB regarding human patient protections. Other institution officials and administrators should be advised and consulted as necessary. When an award is made, most institutional and sponsor policies require that the protocol and associated contract be formally accepted by the investigator and an official of the institution.

When an investigator conducts a study for an outside sponsor, such as a pharmaceutical company, the protocol and other study-related materials are provided by the sponsor, and the investigator must follow the study procedures required by the sponsor. Institutional policy still may dictate internal scientific review and involvement of the grants and contracts administration.

Protocol (Study Design) Development

The protocol is a formal document that establishes the conditions under which the research is to be conducted. A protocol should contain all applicable sections—example items are listed below:

- The specific scientific objectives (aims of the research)
- Budget, personnel and facility considerations
- The research method(s) and all procedures
- The statistical/analytical methods to be used, including justification for the number of patients expected to participate
- If a data monitoring committee is used, describe its operation (e.g., membership, stopping rules and frequency of review and reports)
- Security measures to protect the research data
- Human volunteer issues such as:
  - The inclusion criteria
  - The exclusion criteria
  - Justification for inclusion of vulnerable patients (e.g., those with limited autonomy or those in subordinate positions)
  - The intended sex distribution of the volunteers
  - The age range of the volunteers [Note: Special considerations apply to NIH-funded research, which must address the inclusion of children.]
  - The intended racial and ethnic distribution of the volunteers
  - The potential risks associated with the study
  - Any potential benefit(s)
  - Alternatives that are available should the patient select not to participate in the study
  - The recruitment methods
  - Who will obtain consent and how the process of informed consent will be structured
  - Additional protections if all patients will not be capable of giving consent
  - Assessment of understanding of the information presented

- Justification of any non-disclosure and description of post-study debriefing

- Justification of any costs the patients will incur

- Description of any reimbursements or incentives such as cash payments.

When the investigator performs a study for a sponsor, especially if the study will be done under FDA regulations (drugs and devices), there are other protocol requirements, which can be found in 21 CFR 312. For example, phase II and phase III protocols are required to contain:

- A statement of the objectives and purpose of the study

- The criteria for patient selection

- A description of the study design, including the control group, and the methods for minimizing bias

- Dosing information, including maximum dosage and duration of exposure to the drug

- The observations and measurements to be made

- A description of clinical procedures, laboratory tests and other measures to monitor the effect of the drug and to minimize risk.

The investigator will want to carefully review the protocol to be sure all of the required elements are included.

Informed Consent Requirements

The regulations, codes and institutional policies state items that must be disclosed to satisfy the informed consent requirements. Although each research study involving human patients is unique, federal regulations require that all consent forms contain the following information:

- A statement that the study involves research

- Purpose of study

- Description of study procedures (identifying any that are experimental)

- Duration of patient involvement

- Potential risks or discomforts of participation

- Potential benefits of participation

- Alternatives (medical treatments or other courses of action, if any)

- Confidentiality of records description

- Compensation for injury statement (for greater than minimal risk studies)

- Contact persons

- Statement of voluntary participation

It is important to include several other elements of information if they apply to the study and are important for volunteers to know. These include:

- Unforeseen risks statement (if applicable)

- Reasons for involuntary termination of participation (if applicable)

- Additional costs to participate (if any)

- Consequences for withdrawal (e.g., adverse health/welfare effects if any)

- New findings statement (to be provided if relevant)

- Number of patients (if it may have an impact on the decision to participate)

- Payments (incentives and/or expense reimbursements if any).

Informed consent is not just a form or a signature, but a process of information exchange that includes:

- Patient recruitment materials.

- Verbal instructions.

- Written materials.

- Question/answer sessions.

- Agreement documented by signature.

Further information on the informed consent can be found in Chapter 9.

Recruitment Issues

Recruiting patients is one of the most important, and often difficult and time-consuming, aspects of conducting research. Recruiting is an aspect of a study that must be considered before the study and must continue throughout the duration of the trial. The biggest stumbling block to the timely completion of studies is recruiting an adequate number of patients within the designated enrollment time period. Recruitment is discussed in more detail in Chapter 13.

A variety of recruitment methods and materials are used by researchers, including:

- Formal referrals or informal word-of-mouth

- Health workshops, screenings and health fairs

- Internet and social media

- Direct advertising

- Community meeting places (barber shops, recreation spots, etc.)

- Computerized database

- Chart/record review.

It is unacceptable to use confidential/private data to which the investigator would not ordinarily have access to approach patients for a research study (i.e., cold contacting). The initial contact with potential patients should be made by those having legitimate access to the information; these people can convey referral or contact information.

Payment to Volunteers for Participation

Payment for participation requires conscientious judgment calls on the part of the researchers and the IRB. It is not uncommon for people to be paid for their participation in research, especially for research with no direct benefit to the subjects, for example, survey research or the early phases of investigational drug, biologic or device development. The amount of payment must not be an undue inducement to participate in the research.

> **The payment to volunteers for participation is not considered a benefit, but a recruitment incentive.**

Protocol Adherence

The investigator must follow the IRB-approved protocol. This is a specific requirement for the investigator's compliance with the regulations. The time to evaluate study procedures and the inclusion/exclusion criteria is while the protocol is in its draft form, or before agreeing to do the study. Once the protocol is final and approved by the IRB, it is a violation of the protocol not to comply with the established procedures and inclusion/exclusion criteria. [Note: Sponsors will usually provide the investigator with a final protocol. The investigator must decide in advance if he/she can comply with the entire document as written. There may be no opportunity for protocol input.]

Any deviations from the protocol should be documented and, for sponsored studies, the sponsor should be consulted in advance if a deviation is requested. Most industry sponsors will consider unauthorized deviations protocol violations and may not be willing to pay for these data.

If changes to the research design and/or the consent form are to be made, they must be approved by the IRB before they are implemented. The exception to this rule is that the investigator may deviate from the protocol to eliminate an immediate hazard to patients without prior IRB approval; in this case, the IRB must be notified within five days of the deviation occurrence. Changes in the consent form, particularly when new risks are added, usually require the re-consent of currently enrolled patients if the IRB deems it necessary. Re-consent is documented in study records through the use of a consent addendum or new consent form.

> **The investigator (or designee) should document and explain all deviations from the protocol, both to the sponsor (and the IRB, when required) and in the investigator study records.**

Investigators conducting industry-sponsored studies also should be aware that there also may be special circumstances (e.g., open label therapeutic use) under which the sponsor may allow a person into a clinical trial who does not meet the protocol's inclusion/exclusion criteria. This must be approved in advance by the sponsor and documented in the study records.

Some studies, such as industry-sponsored drug trials and cooperative group studies, include routine auditing or monitoring. The study monitor reviews adherence to the protocol at the monitoring visits. These reviews include, but are not limited to:

- Review of patient eligibility criteria to verify that no inclusion/exclusion violations occur

- Scheduling of patient visits and review of patient compliance for visits

- Evaluation procedures and primary outcome measures

- Safety parameters

- Follow-up of study dropouts for safety issues

- Records of disposition and use of the investigational agent

- Thoroughness of source documentation

- Accuracy of case report forms as compared to source documentation.

> **Discovery of major or repeated noncompliance with the protocol can result in termination of the investigator's participation in a trial, or even disqualification as an investigator.**

While most common in drug and medical device studies, adverse events can occur in almost any research study. Investigators have the responsibility to monitor research patients to detect difficulties, discomfort and other more severe reactions, whether or not related to the study intervention. Adverse events must be reported to the IRB, according to the IRB directions, and the protocol will explain the reporting requirements in sponsored studies. If the adverse events were expected and listed in the consent form, they usually can be reported to the IRB at the time of continuing review. If they are unexpected, especially if serious, adverse events should be reported when they occur both to the IRB and to the sponsor for review. IRBs have defined time limits for adverse event reporting by investigators. FDA regulations also set timelines for sponsor to report adverse events.

It is critical that investigators understand the requirements and mechanisms for reporting adverse events, especially serious events. It is important to note that in drug and device trials, patients are receiving treatments about which very little is known; it is part of the purpose of these trials to determine a safety profile for each investigative treatment.

References

1. Guidance for Industry, E6 Good Clinical Practice, section 4.3.1

CHAPTER FIVE

FDA-Regulated Research

At the conclusion of this chapter, readers will be able to:

- Describe the Food and Drug Administration (FDA) regulations as they apply to drugs/biologics and medical devices.

- Discuss the responsibilities of the sponsor in FDA-regulated research.

- Describe the study process for industry-sponsored studies.

- Discuss sponsor–investigator–institution interactions.

- Identify the responsibilities of the investigator who assumes the additional role of sponsor.

Introduction

The FDA regulates drugs, biologics and devices used in the diagnosis, cure, mitigation, treatment or prevention of disease in humans and animals. This section addresses FDA-regulated clinical research and the responsibilities of industry sponsors, the additional study processes industry sponsors may require and the additional responsibilities investigators take on when they choose to sponsor a study with an FDA-regulated drug, biologic or device.

The FDA conducts a thorough review of drugs, biologics and medical devices for safety and effectiveness for a given indication prior to granting approval for marketing. Before release to the marketplace, the FDA and the sponsor write the package insert (also referred to as the "labeling"). This document summarizes what the FDA has determined to be the safe and effective use of the product. The FDA then exempts further clinical studies conducted according to this labeling from the Investigational New Drug/Investigational Device Exemption (IND/IDE) regulations. The FDA does not, however, exempt such studies from the human subject protection regulations. All research studies with FDA-regulated products that involve human subjects are required to undergo review by an IRB, even if exempt from IND filing.

> **Exemption from IND/IDE regulations is NOT an exemption from IRB review.**

Drugs and Biologics/INDs

Research involving a drug or biologic that has not yet reached the market-place requires an IND. The FDA carefully and critically reviews these applications and will allow human exposure only if it feels the risks of exposure are reasonable. The IND application usually contains:

- Evidence of safety and tolerability in animals

- A controlled method of manufacture that assures the consistency of the final drug product

- Specific tests for significant toxins or toxic ingredients

- A well-developed research plan that minimizes the risks for human volunteers.

If the subject population is different from that indicated in the labeling, it becomes a clinical judgment and/or ethical question as to whether this new population is at greater risk of injury with the product than the indicated population. Examples of when an IND is warranted because of greater risk include:

- Increased dose

- Different route of administration

- Longer duration

- If the research population is "vulnerable"

- If there is reason to believe this population has different pharmacokinetic or pharmacodynamic responses from the indicated population.

> **Exemptions to the IND process apply only when the product is used according to the product labeling (dose, duration, patient population, etc.).**

Form FDA 1572 (Statement of Investigator)

Each investigator participating in a drug or biologic study subject to IND regulations is required to complete and sign a Form FDA 1572. The 1572 requires the submission of a curriculum vitae or other statement of qualifications. By signing the 1572, the investigator agrees to conduct the investigation according to the provisions listed on the form. These commitments come from the regulations that govern investigational drugs (i.e., 21 CFR 312). By signing the 1572, the investigator agrees to:

- Conduct the study(ies) in accordance with the relevant, current protocol(s) and make changes in a protocol only after notifying the sponsor, except when necessary to protect the safety, rights or welfare of subjects

- Personally conduct or supervise the described investigation(s)

- Inform any patients, or any persons used as controls, that the drugs are being used for investigational purposes

- Ensure the requirements relating to obtaining informed consent in 21 CFR Part 50 and institutional review board (IRB) review and approval in 21 CFR Part 56 are met

- Report to the sponsor adverse experiences that occur in the course of the investigation(s) in accordance with 21 CFR 312.64

- Read and understand the information in the investigator's brochure, including the potential risks and side effects of the drug

- Ensure all associates, colleagues and employees assisting in the conduct of the study(ies) are informed about their obligations in meeting the above commitments

- Maintain adequate and accurate records in accordance with 21 CFR 312.62 and make those records available for inspection in accordance with 21 CFR 312.68

- Ensure an IRB that complies with the requirements of 21 CFR Part 56 will be responsible for the initial and continuing review and approval of the clinical investigation

- Promptly report to the IRB all changes in the research activity and all unanticipated problems involving risks to human participants or others

- Not make any changes in the research without IRB approval, except when necessary to eliminate apparent immediate hazards to participants

- Comply with all other requirements regarding the obligations of clinical investigators and all other pertinent requirements in 21 CFR Part 312.

It is a criminal offense to sign the document if it contains false information or if commitments made within the signed document are ignored. These investigator commitments should be reviewed prior to signing this form. [Investigators have been prosecuted based on this signature in the past.]

Investigator

The name and address of the investigator is required on the 1572. If the study has co-principal investigators, each co-investigator completes and signs a separate form. The person/persons signing as the investigator assumes full responsibility for the proper conduct of the study.

Subinvestigator

The section of the form that often causes the most difficulty is Section 6, "Names of the subinvestigators (e.g., other investigators, research fellows, residents, specialists, associates) who will be assisting the investigator in the conduct of the investigation(s)." The issue of who should be listed as a subinvestigator frequently causes confusion. In May 2010, the FDA issued a guidance document titled *"Frequently Asked Questions–Statement of Investigator (Form FDA 1572),"* intended to help sponsors, clinical investigators and IRBs by discussing and clarifying how to complete the 1572 form. Over the years, there have been significant differences of opinion about who should (or should not) be included as subinvestigators on the 1572, and this guidance helps clarify this issue.

The guidance document states, "the purpose of Section #6 is to capture information about individuals who, as part of an investigative team, will assist the investigator and make a direct and significant contribution to the data."[1] Therefore, if a person is directly involved in performing study procedures or collecting data (as most study coordinators are), they should be listed on the 1572. Those people who provide ancillary or intermittent care, but do not make direct and significant contributions to the data (these could include nurses, fellows, residents, office staff) do not need to be listed. However, all individuals participating in the study, whether listed on the 1572 or not, should be listed on a delegation of authority log.

IRB

The 1572 requires the name and address of the IRB that will be responsible for review and approval of the study.

Clinical Laboratory

The form also requires the contact information for any laboratories that will be used in the study to provide results of lab tests, radiographic studies, etc.

The sponsor submits the completed, signed Form FDA 1572 to the FDA.

Medical Devices/IDEs

The regulations require all new devices have an FDA-approved IDE for use in clinical research. A system, unique to devices, to comply with this regulation requires determination by the reviewing IRB of whether the study presents a significant or non-significant risk to the participant population. A review of the list of typical non-significant risk devices published by the FDA shows they carry very little risk of harm or potential to have a negative impact on a volunteer's health status.

A non-significant risk device study is considered to have an approved IDE application (i.e., no application need be filed with the FDA). With this non-significant risk determination, the study can be conducted without prior FDA review as long as the device is properly labeled, it has IRB approval, investigators obtain and document informed consent, proper study monitoring is conducted and compliance is assured for all other IDE regulations.

A significant risk device is an investigational device that is intended as an implant and presents a potential for serious risk to the health, safety or welfare of a participant; is for use in supporting or sustaining human life and represents a potential for serious risk to the health, safety or welfare of a participant; is for a use of substantial importance in diagnosing, curing, mitigating or treating disease or otherwise preventing impairment of human health and presents a potential for serious risk to the health, safety or welfare of a participant; or otherwise presents a potential for serious risk to a participant. An FDA-approved IDE application is required prior to human subject exposure for all significant-risk device studies. Besides the IDE regulations, significant risk studies must also comply with the IRB, informed consent, monitoring and compliance regulations.

Although there is no Form FDA 1572 for device studies, documentation of similar commitments by the investigators is required in a signed agreement that the sponsor obtains from each investigator. This agreement includes the investigator's curriculum vitae and a statement of the investigator's commitment to conduct the research according to the investigational plan and applicable regulations, to supervise all testing of the device involving human volunteers and to ensure the requirements for obtaining informed consent are met. All investigators participating in studies with a significant risk device are listed in the IDE application.

Sponsor Responsibilities in FDA-Regulated Research

The sponsor can be an individual, company, institution or other organization that takes responsibility for the initiation, management and financing of a research project or study. Investigators who also take on the role of sponsor must comply with the responsibilities of both roles.

> **The responsibilities of the research sponsor can be divided into four main areas:**
> 1. Qualifying and informing investigators.
> 2. Monitoring study conduct.
> 3. Completing regulatory filings.
> 4. Control of product (drug, biologic or device) shipment and disposition.

1. Qualifying and Informing Investigators

The sponsor is responsible for selecting and qualifying investigators. This involves reviewing the investigator's training and experience and obtaining the investigator's commitment to:

- Conduct the study as agreed, including any IRB stipulations

- Supervise all testing

- Obtain informed consent.

Once investigators are selected, the sponsor is responsible for providing them with the necessary information to conduct the study, including reports of all prior investigations and the current investigational plan (protocol). For drugs, the sponsor must supply investigators with the most current investigator's brochure (IB), which contains results of animal studies, pharmacokinetic and pharmacodynamic information and any previous clinical studies. For a drug already on the market, the approved package insert takes the place of the IB. Any additional significant information learned during the course of the study, including reports of adverse events from other sites, is to be provided to all investigators in a timely manner. Information not critical to the conduct of a study may be provided at the time the investigator brochure is updated.

IRB Approval at Study Sites
A copy of the IRB approval letter should be obtained from each study site prior to the shipment of any investigational materials. For device studies, the determination of significant versus non-significant risk should be documented. Verbal assurances of submission to, or approval by, an IRB are not considered adequate.

2. Monitoring of Study Conduct

Monitoring of studies is viewed as a critical step in securing compliance of all investigators and assuring adequate participant informed consent is obtained. Any significant new safety information regarding study conduct must be provided to the reviewing IRB(s), the FDA and study investigators. It is the sponsor's responsibility to evaluate and terminate investigations if undue risks to study participants are observed.

For some NIH-funded studies, as well as for FDA-regulated studies, study monitors are appointed by the sponsor. The monitor reviews source documents to determine that reported data are accurate and complete. The monitor also audits the research to assure the investigator is in compliance with:

- The approved protocol and amendments

- Good Clinical Practices (GCPs)

- Applicable regulations.

3. Completing Regulatory Filings

The sponsor must determine whether an application for an IDE or IND is necessary for a specific project. Once an application is active, the sponsor is required to keep the FDA informed of any new significant adverse effects or risks, withdrawal of IRB approval for any reason, any recalls of test articles and any emergency use of test articles without informed consent, as well as submit investigator names, progress reports (usually submitted annually) and a final study report.

For significant risk devices, the sponsor must also supply the FDA with a current list of investigators, as well as any change in risk category.

Original Application

The sponsor is responsible for filing adequate information in the initial IND or IDE application to allow the FDA to make a decision on whether the study risks are acceptable. The sponsor is required to wait 30 days for FDA review prior to enrolling subjects in the study. If insufficient information is filed, the FDA may place a clinical hold on the application. If no notice is received within that 30-day period, the FDA has no concerns with the application and the IND or IDE is considered to be approved. It is advisable, however, to call the FDA to confirm it does not have any issues or concerns with the application. Absolutely no subjects are to be enrolled in the study until the FDA has removed all holds on an application. If the FDA denies the application, the project may not be initiated. It is possible to re-apply to the FDA for the same project if modified to be acceptable to the FDA.

Amendments to Documentation

Any new clinical study protocol must be submitted under the IND/IDE prior to study initiation. This is true for changes to any other information within an application that has an impact on subject safety. These can be filed at any time, but before any participants are exposed. Minor changes that do not affect patient safety may be submitted in the annual report.

IND Safety Reports

Sponsors are required to notify the FDA and all participating investigators in writing of any adverse experience associated with the drug that is serious and unexpected. This information may be submitted in a narrative format or on the FDA Form 3500A (MedWatch). The MedWatch form also is used to report post-marketing adverse event information. The sponsor also must determine if any safety reports previously had been filed that are similar to each new reportable event. The significance of the new report must be analyzed with regard to previous, similar reports. The report must be clearly marked "IND Safety Report" and must be filed with the FDA no more than 15 calendar days after the investigator-sponsor initially receives the information. These reports are sent directly to the division of the FDA responsible for reviewing the IND.

The sponsor is to notify the FDA by telephone or fax of any unexpected, fatal or life-threatening experience associated with the use of a drug in clinical studies conducted under the IND within seven calendar days after receiving the information. For this purpose only, the FDA defines life-threatening as the patient being at immediate risk of death from the reaction.

Note that sponsors of INDs for marketed drugs are NOT required to re-

> **Serious, related, unexpected adverse experiences must be reported promptly to the FDA.**

port adverse events associated with the use of the drug that occur outside of the studies conducted under their INDs (i.e., literature reports and events reported during patient care are not reportable to the IND, as there is a different reporting system for marketed drugs). However, if such information affects the perceived risks to participants in the clinical trials, the information must be shared with the investigators and their respective IRBs.

In 21 CFR 312.32(a), the FDA provides the following five definitions to be used when reporting adverse events:

- *Adverse event* means any untoward medical occurrence associated with the use of a drug in humans, whether or not considered drug related.

- *Life-threatening adverse event* or *life-threatening suspected adverse reaction*. An adverse event or suspected adverse reaction is considered "life-threatening" if, in the view of either the investigator or sponsor, its occurrence places the patient or subject at immediate risk of death. It does not include an adverse event or suspected adverse reaction that, had it occurred in a more severe form, might have caused death.

- *Serious adverse event* or *serious suspected adverse reaction*. An adverse event or suspected adverse reaction is considered "serious" if, in the view of either the investigator or sponsor, it results in any of the following outcomes: Death, a life-threatening adverse event, inpatient hospitalization or prolongation of existing hospitalization, a persistent or significant incapacity or substantial disruption of the ability to conduct normal life functions or a congenital anomaly/birth defect. Important medical events that may not result in death, be life threatening or require hospitalization may be considered serious when, based on appropriate medical judgment, they may jeopardize the patient or subject and may require medical or surgical intervention to prevent one of the outcomes listed above. Examples of such medical events include allergic bronchospasm requiring intensive treatment in an emergency room or at home, blood dyscrasias or convulsions that do not result in inpatient hospitalization or the development of drug dependency or drug abuse.

- *Suspected adverse reaction* means any adverse event for which there is a reasonable possibility that the drug caused the adverse event. For the purposes of IND safety reporting, "reasonable possibility" means there is evidence to suggest a causal relationship between the drug and the adverse event. Suspected adverse reaction implies a lesser degree of certainty about causality than adverse reaction, which means any adverse event caused by a drug.

- *Unexpected adverse event* or *unexpected suspected adverse reaction.* An adverse event or suspected adverse reaction is considered "unexpected" if it is not listed in the investigator brochure or is not listed at the specificity or severity that has been observed; or, if an investigator brochure is not required or available, is not consistent with the risk information described in the general investigational plan or elsewhere in the current application, as amended. For example, under this definition, hepatic necrosis would be unexpected (by virtue of greater severity) if the investigator brochure referred only to elevated hepatic enzymes or hepatitis. Similarly, cerebral thromboembolism and cerebral vasculitis would be unexpected (by virtue of greater specificity) if the investigator brochure listed only cerebral vascular accidents. "Unexpected," as used in this definition, also refers to adverse events or suspected adverse reactions mentioned in the investigator brochure as occurring with a class of drugs or as anticipated from the pharmacological properties of the drug, but are not specifically mentioned as occurring with the particular drug under investigation.

Unanticipated Adverse Device Effect (UADE) Reports

The reporting requirements for adverse device effects are different from those for drugs and biologics.

Sponsors are required to immediately conduct an evaluation of any unanticipated adverse device effect. If the sponsor determines an unanticipated adverse device effect presents an unreasonable risk to study participants, the sponsor must terminate all studies (or parts of the studies) that present that risk as soon as possible. This termination is to occur within five working days following sponsor determination, and no later than 15 working days after the sponsor first received notice of the effect.

Both the FDA and the IRB must be informed of unanticipated adverse device effects. Any terminated study must NOT be resumed without approval of both the FDA and the reviewing IRB.

Annual Reports

An annual report from the sponsor to the FDA is required for both INDs and IDEs. It is due no later than 60 calendar days after the anniversary date of an application going into effect.

The format for the annual report is provided in regulatory guidance documents. Critical components of these reports include:

- Protocol summaries for ongoing and completed studies, to document the total human exposure under the application

- All changes made to protocols or manufacturing information. This is the mechanism to report minor changes that occurred during the year that were not subject to amendments

- New pre-clinical (animal) and clinical (human) information. Any impact on participant safety should be addressed

- Changes to the investigational plan for the coming year

- Any information requested by the FDA but not received should also be documented.

Withdrawal of Application

Upon completion of studies, or when no additional work is envisioned, the investigator-sponsor should send a letter to the FDA requesting withdrawal of the IND/IDE. A sponsor may withdraw an IND at any time. If an IND is withdrawn for safety reasons, the sponsor must promptly inform the FDA, all investigators and all reviewing IRBs of the reason for the withdrawal.

4. Control of Product (Drug, Biologic or Device) Shipment and Disposition

It is the sponsor's responsibility to control the distribution and disposition of all investigational test articles. Prior to the initial shipment, there must be documentation indicating that any necessary IDE or IND is filed and active, and that the site's IRB has reviewed and approved the study. Test articles may be shipped only to qualified sites. Complete and accurate records are required for the shipment of test articles with an accounting of their final disposition.

The Study Process for Industry-Sponsored Studies

Clinical studies conducted on the behalf of industry sponsors are generally required to comply with Good Clinical Practices (GCPs), an international, ethical and scientific quality standard for designing, conducting, monitoring, recording, auditing, analyzing and reporting trials that involve participation of humans. The investigator responsibilities critical to the conduct of industry-sponsored studies include three additional processes.

1. Investigational Materials Handling and Accountability

For the purpose of this section, investigational materials are drugs or medical devices being tested in accordance with an approved protocol or investigational plan. The investigator is responsible for the accurate accountability and use of investigational materials provided to participants. By law, the investigator is required to maintain adequate records of the accountability and final disposition of the investigational drugs/devices.

Receipt, Handling and Storage of Investigational Materials
Upon receiving investigational materials, the investigator or appropriate staff member (e.g., investigational drug pharmacist) must adhere to the following:

- Verify the contents and integrity of each shipment against the packing slip and what materials were actually ordered.

- If no discrepancies are found, the investigator should acknowledge in writing to the sponsor the receipt of the materials. This is typically accomplished by signing the shipping document enclosed with the investigational materials. The investigator must notify the sponsor immediately if discrepancies are found.

- A copy of this receipt should be in the investigator's study file (or in the pharmacy if the drug is received and dispensed there).

- All investigational materials must be stored in a secure (locked) limited access area.

- Additionally, materials must be stored in accordance with the approved storage conditions (i.e., correct temperature, light and humidity).

Accountability Records

Drug or device accountability records are used to provide evidence that, at the conclusion of the investigation, all materials are accounted for and that their final disposition is controlled (i.e., the materials are returned to the sponsor or destroyed). The drug/device accountability records are customized documents tailored to the individual protocol. The following minimum information should be captured on each form:

- Protocol Identification (protocol # and/or title)

- Principal investigator's name

- Description of test article(s) received including batch or lot numbers

- Date (and time, if relevant) study drug/device was dispensed/used

- Amount dispensed (for drugs)

- Subject identification

- Signature and/or initials of person dispensing the drug(s)/device(s)

- Amount returned by the subject, if any

- Principal investigator's signature and date. [Note: The investigator should review, sign and date the forms at the conclusion of each subject's participation in the trial.]

Accountability records may be created to track individual subjects enrolled in a trial or may be customized to capture all participating subjects (usually with smaller trials or trials with single-dose dispensing). The main objective of the regulations is to require the investigator to maintain adequate records of the disposition of the drug or device.

Drug/Device Returns (Final Disposition)

At the conclusion, discontinuance or termination of the study, for both drugs and devices, the investigator is responsible for returning all unused investigational material to the sponsor. Return shipments should include a list of the contents, which must be reconciled with the amounts originally received and the amounts used by the participants.

Alternatively, after drug/device accountability records are complete, the sponsor may authorize alternative disposition for these materials (destruction by the investigator) provided the alternate disposition does not expose humans to risks from the drug. Any directive from the sponsor allowing destruction must be in writing before disposal. The investigator will be responsible for assuring that the destruction is carried out, and the investigator must maintain a written record of destruction.

2. Adverse Events

Drug and Biologic Requirements

New regulations for investigational new drug safety reporting requirements went into effect in September 2010. The revisions from previous regulations are expected to improve the FDA's ability to review critical safety information by ensuring the information received by the FDA is relevant and useful. Previously, there was an over-reporting of serious adverse events, for which there was little reason to believe the drug had caused the event, complicating or delaying the FDA's ability to detect a safety signal. The idea was to minimize reports that don't contribute to the safety profile of the drug and to decrease the number of uninterpretable reports ("noise") in the system.

The new regulations also require expedited reporting of certain safety information that was not previously required, including:

- Findings from clinical studies, epidemiological studies or pooled analyses of multiple studies that suggest a significant risk in humans exposed to the drug

- Serious, suspected adverse reactions that occur at a higher rate than the rate in the protocol or investigator brochure

- Serious adverse events from bioavailability and bioequivalence studies.

Definitions and reporting standards also were revised to be as consistent as possible with international definitions and standards. The previous phase "associated with the use of the drug" has been replaced by "suspected adverse drug reaction" (SADR). Investigators must report any serious SADR immediately to the sponsor, and any other SADRs are to be reported promptly, unless otherwise specified in the protocol or investigator brochure. These regulations are found in 21 CFR 312.32. Investigators also must report serious SADRs and other events to their IRBs, as required by the IRB.

Anyone involved in clinical trials should be aware of the regulations and definitions, keeping in mind the definitions are *regulatory* definitions, not *clinical* definitions. Each protocol should specify the relevant reporting requirements for each type of adverse event, including the time requirements.

Device Requirements

Regulations require that investigators prepare and submit complete, accurate and timely reports of unanticipated adverse device effects (UADEs) to the sponsor and to the reviewing IRB as soon as possible, but no later than 10 business days after the investigator learns of the effect. Sponsors immediately must conduct evaluations of any UADEs that occur in their clinical studies and must report the results of these evaluations to the FDA, all reviewing IRBs and participating investigators within 10 working days of receiving notice of the effect.

3. Documentation

Source Documentation

Investigators are required to prepare and maintain adequate and accurate records of all observations and other data pertinent to the study for each participant. Source documentation is the first recording of the information. These are the original documents, data and records (including medical records, lab reports and case report forms).

The investigator must maintain primary source documents supporting significant data for each subject in the case history records. These documents, considered "source data," should include documentation of the following:

- Demographic information
- Evidence supporting the diagnosis/condition for which the participant is being studied (i.e., compliance with inclusion criteria)
- General information or medical history demonstrating the participant meets the inclusion and exclusion criteria.
- Physical findings
- Hospital records (if appropriate)
- Each study visit by date
- Relevant findings/notes by the investigator
- Occurrence (or lack of) adverse events
- Changes in test article usage
- Information regarding the participant's exposure to test or control article
- Documentation that informed consent was obtained for each volunteer prior to participation in the study

- Other important study information.

The investigator also must retain all printouts/test reports/procedures/forms for each volunteer. Examples include:

- Original, signed and dated consent forms
- Diagnostic test results, X-rays and laboratory test results
- Subject diaries or evaluation checklists
- Clinical and office charts
- Consultations
- Drug and device receipt, accountability and return records
- Case report forms (CRFs)
- Test instruments.

Investigators also need to maintain the following study documents:

- Copies of all correspondence sent to or received by the sponsor and the monitor
- The protocol
- Protocol amendments
- Records of IRB communications, including protocol, informed consent and advertising approvals and re-approvals
- Materials used in recruiting subjects (e.g., flyers and advertisements)
- Materials used in obtaining informed consent
- Investigator brochure
- Any other relevant documents.

> **Source documentation is the first recording of information, including medical records and case report forms.**

Case Report Forms

These forms are critical study documents. Study results are a summary of the data reported to the sponsor on case report forms (CRFs). The case report forms will contain all information relevant to the study; in this regard, they mimic the requirements of the protocol. CRFs may be either printed or electronic documents, and will be provided by the sponsor. It is important that:

- The content captures all data required by the protocol

> **It is the responsibility of the investigator to ensure the accuracy of the data recorded on the case report form.**

- The investigator ensures the accuracy of the data recorded.

ICH GCP guidelines specify the protocol should identify any data to be recorded directly on the CRF and classify what is considered to be source data. For example, rating scale data might be recorded on the case report form as it is being collected. During monitoring visits, the monitor will validate data recorded on the CRF against source data.

Final Study Reports

Regulations require the investigator write and submit a final report to the sponsor for each completed clinical study. This report also should be submitted to the IRB.

Record Retention

Investigators are required to retain all study records in a secure and safe facility with limited access until one of the following time periods:

- At least two years after notification from the sponsor that the drug/device has been approved for the indication investigated

- Or, if not approved for such indication, at least two years after the investigation is completed or discontinued and the FDA has been notified by the sponsor.

> **Investigators are advised to contact the sponsor before any study records are destroyed to ensure compliance with regulatory requirements.**

Most sponsors will specify a records retention policy in the study contract; investigators should not dispose of study records without written approval from the sponsor.

The investigator should notify the sponsor of any change in the location, disposition or custody of the study files and is advised to contact the sponsor with any questions about the disposition of study records to ensure compliance with regulatory and contractual requirements.

Responsibilities of the Investigator-Sponsor

For FDA-regulated studies for which there is no company or other organization acting as sponsor, individuals may become a sponsor of a clinical research study by assuming the role and responsibilities of the study sponsor. By definition (21 CFR 312.3), a "sponsor-investigator means an individual who both initiates and conducts an investigation, and under whose immediate direction the investigational drug is administered or dispensed." The term does not include anyone other than an individual. This means one individual is assuming all responsibilities of both study sponsor and investigator. The additional tasks of the sponsor include all regulatory reporting (FDA) requirements and, if relevant, responsibility for drug manufacture and control issues (including proper labeling of the investigational product), the assessment of safety, ensuring IRB approval prior to shipping clinical supplies to sites and informing and monitoring all investigators.

The sponsor responsibilities discussed earlier in this chapter also apply to investigator-sponsors.

Additional Issues for Investigator-Sponsors to Consider

Liability Concerns
For industry-sponsored studies, the company, the institution and the investigator share responsibility for study-related injury to participants. For investigator-sponsored studies, the liability for research-related injury lies completely with the investigator and the associated institution.

Conflict of Interest
There may be a conflict of interest for investigator-sponsors, especially when financial or career enhancement benefits exist with a project. Documentation of all financial compensation is required by the FDA prior to approving products for market.

Contracts
Investigator-sponsors must have all contracts related to the conduct of research reviewed and approved by the appropriate institutional office.

Clinical Supplies
Obtaining appropriate clinical supplies for research is the responsibility of the sponsor. Manufacturing issues are of concern to the FDA when reviewing non-commercial or commercial applications. When pharmaceutical-grade material is not available, documentation of product identity, purity and lack of contamination is generally required. This usually involves the testing of each batch of clinical supplies by a qualified laboratory.

Sponsor–Investigator–Institution Interaction Issues

The interactions among the sponsor, investigator and institution (including the IRB) may be complex. Generally, sponsors and IRBs do not contact each other directly. Instead, communication flows through the site. This serves to keep the investigator aware of any issues and concerns, maintains the investigator's responsibility for the conduct of the study and can prevent any appearance of pressure by the sponsor on the IRB to approve a study. However, the FDA does not prohibit direct IRB–sponsor contact, and there are times when this is the most efficient method for resolving issues, e.g., questions about interpretation of sponsor policies, efficiencies over multi-center trials using a central IRB and reporting of suspected adverse reactions (SARs) seen by the sponsor over multiple sites.

An IRB is required to notify the investigator in writing of its decision to approve, disapprove or request modification to a research project. The investigator must provide the sponsor with a copy of this written decision, because the sponsor is also responsible for ensuring that studies are conducted in compliance with informed consent and IRB regulations. Most sponsors will not ship the investigational product until they have all institutional approvals and other required paperwork.

References

1. FDA guidance document, "Frequently Asked Questions–Statement of Investigator (Form FDA 1572)," issued May 2010, page 15.

CHAPTER SIX

Behavioral Research Issues

At the conclusion of this chapter, readers will be able to:

- Identify when studies qualify as human subject research.
- Describe potential risks associated with behavioral research.
- Indicate measures that can be taken to protect patients' privacy and confidentiality.
- Recognize when waivers of consent or of written consent may be appropriate.
- Explain issues related to deception.

Introduction

When people think of research, especially research risk, often they think only of medical research. This is due to the fact that much of the focus on research and research ethics has been on the dangers posed by biomedical research and the harms caused by the transgressions of researchers in that field. However, research with drugs, devices and other medical procedures is only a part of the total research endeavor. Many studies are also conducted in human behavior, social science, education, anthropology, epidemiology and similar areas. For brevity, these will be subsumed here under the broad label "behavioral research." The following issues also are important for biomedical researchers, as many of the concerns may be present to some extent in those studies as well.

Federal Regulations

The relationship between behavioral research and the IRB is sometimes perceived as an uneasy fit. Current academic literature is replete with references to behavioral scientists' struggles navigating federal human subject regulations and working with their IRBs. The regulations do focus primarily on the quantitative methods used for biomedical research; however, provisions are included to accommodate the qualitative aspects of behavioral research as well. The following provides a brief guide to federal regulations for investigators conducting behavioral research.

Colleges and universities that receive Department of Health and Human Services (DHHS) support must have a Federalwide Assurance (FWA). The FWA is a commitment to DHHS that the institution will comply with federal regulations 45 CFR part 46 for the protection of human subjects. Fifteen federal agencies and departments have adopted the "Common Rule" by including identical language in their separate regulations. The Departments of Defense, Energy and Justice, among others, may impose additional regulations on human subject research.

Investigators are encouraged to check with their IRBs to determine whether their institutions apply the Common Rule to non-federally funded research and if additional requirements apply for specific funding agencies. This chapter will provide guidance based on the Common Rule.

Types of IRB Review

The Common Rule allows for three levels of initial and ongoing review based on the degree of risk associated with the research. Research may qualify for exempt status, expedited or full board review. Information on the requirements for each of these categories can be helpful to investigators as they plan their studies and complete their IRB applications. One of the first steps to take, however, is to determine whether the planned study actually involves human subject research and is governed by the Common Rule.

Does the Study Qualify as Human Subject Research?

The Common Rule provides IRBs with the authority to review and oversee "human subject research." Thus, for a project to be subject to IRB review it must both qualify as "research" and involve "human subjects." Check with your IRB for its policies and procedures regarding research that does not involve human subjects.

Is the Project Research?

Federal regulations define "research" as a **systematic investigation**, including research development, testing and evaluation, designed to develop or contribute to **generalizable knowledge.**

As defined in the Belmont Report, "…'research' designates an activity designed to test a hypothesis, permit conclusions to be drawn and thereby to develop or contribute to generalizable knowledge (expressed, for example, in theories, principles and statements of relationships). Research is usually described in a formal protocol that that sets forth an objective and a set of procedures designed to reach that objective." Projects that are not intended to draw conclusions to address a hypothesis or to contribute to generalizable knowledge are not subject to the Common Rule.

Example: In recent years, the American Historical Association (AHA) and the Oral History Association (OHA) have questioned whether oral histories meet the federal definition of research and are subject to federally mandated IRB review. The Oral History Association defines oral history as "a method of gathering and preserving historical information through recorded interviews with participants in past events and ways of life." In 2003, OHRP released a statement that historians "do not reach for generalizable principals of historical or social development; nor do they seek underlying principles or laws of nature that have predictive value and can be applied to other circumstances for the purpose of controlling outcomes." Thus, many IRBs do not consider oral history activities, which serve only to document an individual's life history or memories of the past, to be research covered under the Common Rule.

Does the Project Involve Human Subjects?

If your project meets the definition of research per the Common Rule, the next step is to determine whether it involves human subjects.

Federal regulations define a human subject as a **living** individual **about whom** an investigator (whether professional or student) conducting research obtains: (1) data through **intervention or interaction** with the individual or (2) **identifiable private information**. Thus, a project can be considered to involve human subjects if it involves living individuals and at least one of the following conditions:

1. *An interaction or intervention with the individual(s).*
    Interactions involve communication or interpersonal contact between the investigator and subject, whether in person, by telephone, mail or other forms of communication. Interventions include physical procedures (for example, venipuncture), manipulation of the subject or manipulations of the subjects' environments for research procedures.

2. *The research involves identifiable private information.*
    "Identifiable" means that the identity of the subject is or may be ascertained readily by the investigator or associated with the information. Examples of direct identifiers include the subjects' name, social security number and phone number. In some cases, "identifiable" also refers to combinations of data that can be used to identify subjects; for example, a combination of a person's age, job title, employer and gender, or a combination of a code and key to the code that could allow the investigator to identify and link private information to an individual. Note: For more information on whether use of coded data is considered human subject research see: www.hhs.gov/ohrp/policy/cdebiol.html.

    Private information includes information about behavior that occurs in a context in which an individual can reasonably expect that no observation or recording is taking place, and information that has been provided for specific purposes by an individual and that the individual reasonably can expect will not be made public (for example, a school record).

If the project is research, but does not involve human subjects as defined in the Common Rule, it is not subject to IRB review.

Example: An investigator obtains an aggregate or secondary dataset that does not contain any identifiers.

The next three sections provide descriptions of the levels of review for projects that do meet the criteria for human subject research under federal regulations.

Exempt Research

The Common Rule defines specific categories of research that are exempt from human subject protection requirements. This usually means that once an exempt determination is made, annual IRB review is not required. At most institutions, however, investigators may not make the exempt determination themselves. If you think your research may be exempt, check with your IRB office for further information. The following exempt categories often apply to behavioral studies. **Note:** The exempt categories do not apply to research with prisoners.

- Research conducted in established or commonly accepted educational settings, involving normal educational practices such as instructional techniques, content of established curriculum and classroom management strategies

  Note: Even when research in an educational setting is exempt, it still may be subject to regulations through the U.S. Department of Education (ED), such as:

  a. The Family Educational Rights and Privacy Act (FERPA): FERPA protects the privacy of student education records. Further information is available at www2.ed.gov/policy/gen/guid/fpco/ferpa/index.html.

  b. Protection of Pupil Rights Amendment (PPRA): PPRA is intended to protect the rights of parents and students by ensuring that

     i. Parents can inspect instructional materials used in connection with ED funded surveys, analysis or evaluations in which their children participate, and

     ii. Written parental consent is obtained before minors participate in ED-funded surveys, analysis or evaluations that reveal specific data such as political affiliation, income or potentially embarrassing or stigmatizing information.

        Further information is available at: www2.ed.gov/policy/gen/guid/fpco/ppra/index.html.

- Research involving the use of educational tests (cognitive, diagnostic, aptitude, achievement), survey procedures, interview procedures or observation of public behavior. There are several conditions related to this exemption:

    a. Children: Research involving survey, interview procedures or observation of public behavior with children is **not** exempt, except for observations of public behavior in which the investigator does not participate in the activities being observed.

    b. Adults (who are not public officials or running for public office): Research involving information that is recorded in such a manner that human subjects can be identified, directly or through identifiers linked to the subjects, is not exempt **if** any disclosure of the human subjects' responses outside the research could reasonably place the subjects at risk of criminal or civil liability or be damaging to their financial standing, employability or reputation.
    Note: research with these characteristics may be exempt if federal statues require confidentiality without exception.

- Research involving the collection or study of existing data, documents, records, pathological specimens or diagnostic specimens, if these sources are publicly available or if the information is recorded by the investigator in such a manner that subjects cannot be identified, directly or through identifiers linked to the subjects. There are a few concepts related to this exemption that require explanation:

    a. Existing: The regulations use the term "existing" to refer to data, documents and records that already exist at the time the research is being proposed. Studies that propose to use materials that do not currently exist, or will be collected in the future, are not exempt. In many cases, however, these types of studies can be reviewed using expedited procedures.

    b. Publicly available: The term "publicly available" is not defined by the regulations. Many IRBs consider this to mean information available commercially and/or accessible to everyone (for example, telephone directories).
    Note: There are instances in which research involving coded materials is not considered human subject research. More information is available from the IRB or at www.hhs.gov/ohrp/policy/cdebiol.html.

- Research to study or evaluate public benefit and service programs conducted by, or subject to the approval of, department or agency heads. The following criteria must be satisfied for this type of research to be exempt:

    a. The program under study must provide a public benefit or service (for example, financial benefits provided by Social Security or social services provided by the Older American Act).

    b. The project must be conducted under specific federal statutory authority.

    c. There are no regulations requiring review by an IRB.

    d. The project does not involve significant physical intrusions or invasions of privacy with subjects.

Expedited Review

Per the Common Rule, research may be reviewed by the IRB chair, or by one or more experienced board members designated by the chair, if the research activities meet two criteria:

- Present no more than minimal risk to subjects. The Common Rule defines "minimal risk" as the probability and magnitude of harm or discomfort anticipated in the research not greater in and of themselves than those ordinarily encountered in daily life or during the performance of routine physical or psychological examinations or tests.

- Qualify for one or more of nine categories specified in the regulations.

This process is termed "expedited review." Expedited research receives a continuing review at least once a year for the life of the study. The following categories most often apply to behavioral studies:

- Research involving data, documents, records or specimens that have been collected or will be collected solely for nonresearch purposes

- Research on individual or group characteristics or behavior (including, but not limited to, research on perception, cognition, motivation, identity, language, communication, cultural beliefs or practices and social behavior) or research employing survey, interview, oral history, focus group, program evaluation, human factors evaluation or quality assurance methodologies
  Note: Some research in the above categories may be exempt.

- Collection of data from voice, video, digital or image recordings made for research purposes.

Several additional categories are worth mentioning for investigators conducting research on the relationships between physical and/or genetic characteristics and behavior:

- Collection of blood samples by finger stick, heel stick or venipuncture

- Prospective collection of biological specimens by noninvasive means

- Collection of data through non-invasive procedures routinely employed in clinical practice.
  Note: Restrictions apply to these expedited categories, such as the quantity of blood samples that may be collected, and acceptable mini-

mal risk procedures for collecting biological specimens and data. Information is available at: www.hhs.gov/ohrp/policy/expedited98.html.

Full Board Review

Research that does not qualify for exempt status or expedited review and/or involves more than minimal risk must be reviewed at a convened IRB meeting. Research approved by the full board receives continuing review at least once a year by the IRB, or more often depending on the risk of the study.

Research Risks

Because often there are no physical interventions, behavioral studies generally do not pose risks to physical well being, but they do carry risks of their own. Risks related to these studies most often are related to violations of privacy, breaches of confidentiality and other risks regarding study procedures, such as psychological harms. When assessing the risks presented by a study, investigators, IRBs and volunteers must consider a wide range of potential harms. Investigators should anticipate potential problem areas and design the study to provide an adequate level of protection. The traditional risk/benefit balance also is somewhat changed, as the benefits rarely accrue to the individual subject, but rather to science and/or society.

Privacy and Confidentiality

Privacy and confidentiality generally create more concern for behavioral research than for biomedical studies. In fact, these concerns often are the central considerations for behavioral research. Harms related to losses of privacy and/or confidentiality, depending on the focus of the research, may include social harms such as embarrassment, social stigma and loss of status, as well as similar effects on the volunteer's family and community. Economic and legal risks could include loss of employment, prosecution, arrest and civil or criminal liability. A major tenet, however, in the protection of human subjects is that persons can be wronged even if they are not harmed. This philosophy focuses upon rights, both individual and societal. We have a right to expect that our private actions will remain private and that information others have about us will be kept confidential and used only for their intended purposes.

Privacy refers to a volunteer's ability to control how other people see, touch or obtain information about the volunteers. The degree of privacy needed is related to the sensitivity of the information collected and the cultural norms of the patient population. Violations of privacy can involve being photographed or videotaped without consent, being asked personal questions in a public setting, being seen without clothing, being observed while conducting personal behavior or disclosing sensitive information about abortion, HIV status or illegal drug use. Good research design may include measures to protect patient privacy such as:

- Choosing recruitment measures that are respectful of potential volunteers' expectations for privacy

- Determining whether it would be more appropriate to collect certain types of data in an individual interview conducted in a private room rather than in a group setting

- Limiting collection of sensitive information to the minimal amount necessary to achieve the research aims

- Obtaining consent from a person who may be considered a secondary subject prior to collecting sensitive identifiable information about that person.

Confidentiality is an extension of the concept of privacy; it refers to the volunteer's understanding of, and agreement to, the ways identifiable information will be stored and shared. Identifiable information can be printed, electronic or visual information, such as photographs. Examples of precautions that can be taken to maintain the confidentiality of private information include:

- Requiring personnel to sign statements agreeing to protect the security and confidentiality of identifiable information

- Keeping paper-based records in a secure location and accessible only to personnel involved in the study

- Removing identifiers, whenever feasible, from study-related information

- Securing data collected through internet surveys by using passwords and encryption

- Using access privileges and passwords to secure computer-based files.

For further information on privacy and confidentiality see the WIRB submission forms at www.wirb.com.

Additional Measures to Protect Subject Information

Certificate of Confidentiality

A Certificate of confidentiality is an important mechanism to protect the privacy of research study participants. Certificates of Confidentiality are issued by the National Institutes of Health (NIH) and other DHHS agencies to protect the privacy of research subjects by protecting investigators and institutions from being compelled to release information (i.e., forced disclosure) that could be used to identify patients in a research project. They allow the investigator to refuse to disclose identifying information on research participants in any civil, criminal, administrative, legislative or other proceeding, whether at the federal, state or local level. Investigators are not prevented from the voluntary disclosure of matters such as child abuse, reportable communicable diseases or a patient's threatened violence to himself or others; however, the consent form must say if the investigator intends to make any voluntary disclosures. Additionally, investigators cannot rely on a Certificate of Confidentiality to withhold data when subjects agree in writing to the disclosure.

Certificates of Confidentiality do not protect against accidental or intentional breaches of confidentiality. Thus, investigators must ensure that appropriate measures are in place to protect patients' private information.

Certificates of Confidentiality are issued for behavioral, biomedical or other types of research that collect information that, if disclosed, could have adverse consequences for volunteers or damage their financial standing, employability, insurability or reputation (i.e., "sensitive" information), or could involve them in criminal or civil litigation. Examples of sensitive information include:

- Information on psychological well being of volunteers

- Information on volunteers' sexual attitudes, preferences or practices

- Data on substance abuse or other illegal behaviors

- Information on HIV, AIDs and other STDs

- Genetic information.

Some projects are not eligible for a Certificate of Confidentiality, including activities that are:

- Not research

- Not collecting personally identifiable information

- Not reviewed and approved by an IRB

- Collecting information that if disclosed would not significantly harm or damage the participant.

Certificates of Confidentiality are not limited to federally-funded research, but the subject of the study must be within the mission areas covered by NIH. Further information, including a list of contacts for other DHHS agencies, is available on the NIH web site at: http://grants1.nih.gov/grants/policy/coc/index.htm.

Privacy Certificates

The National Institute of Justice (NIJ) does not issue or accept Certificates of Confidentiality. Investigators receiving NIJ funding must apply for a Privacy Certificate per the Department of Justice Confidentiality statute (42 USC 3789g). This makes identifiable data collected during the course of the research immune from legal action. Further information is available on the NIJ web site at: www.nij.gov/nij/funding/humansubjects/privacy-certificate-guidance.htm.

Emotional and Other Risks Related to Study Procedures

Implementation of behavioral interventions or data collection instruments may involve risks of psychological harms such as anxiety, distress and precipitation of emotional or behavioral disorders. Symptoms may range from mild to severe. Investigators should consider the specific sensitivities of their patient populations when selecting and implementing data collection instruments or interventions. They should also ensure they know enough about the patient population to minimize potential risks and have the skills to handle problems, should they occur.

Although physical harms may not be common with behavioral studies, volunteers could be at risk for physical harm (e.g., from retaliation) if a confidentiality breach discloses they are participating in certain studies, such as those regarding gang activities or domestic abuse. The National Science Foundation, on its web site, points out the risk of potential harms when participation in research may inadvertently strengthen subjects' inclinations to behave unethically. This may include unintentional reinforcement of risky or other undesirable behaviors, for example, in a study of substance abuse.

Vulnerable Subjects

People are autonomous when they can deliberate personal goals and then act accordingly. The capacity for self-determination increases with maturity. Individuals may lose this capacity because of physical illness, mental disability or while under circumstances that severely restrict liberty. The regulations define as "vulnerable populations" those groups that may contain some individuals who have limited autonomy, i.e., they cannot give informed consent. Such groups include children, some mentally incapacitated, individuals with dementia and other cognitive disorders and prisoners. Many institutions also have included the elderly, students and employees in the definition of vulnerable populations deserving special consideration by investigators and IRBs. The regulations require IRBs treat pregnant women as a vulnerable population because of the need to avoid unnecessary risk to the fetus, and because of the additional health concerns during pregnancy. Additional protections when conducting research with these populations may include the use of witnesses, requiring consultants/advocates, formally renewing consent at specified stages and limiting the scope of research projects.

Informed Consent

A comprehensive discussion of written informed consent and the informed consent process is provided in Chapter 9. The general requirements for informed consent in the Common Rule may not be applicable to some behavioral studies. The IRB has authority to alter or waive some or all of the requirements for consent as described below.

Waiver of Written Consent

The IRB may waive the requirement for the investigator to obtain a signed consent form for some or all volunteers in either of the following circumstances:

- The only record linking the subject and the research would be the consent document, and the principal risk would be the potential harm resulting from a breach of confidentiality. Each subject will be asked whether the subject wants documentation linking the subject with the research, and the subject's wishes will govern.

Example: Research involving an in-person survey on risky sexual behaviors related to HIV transmission. Identifiers are not collected on the survey.

- The research presents no more than minimal risk to subjects and involves no procedures for which consent is normally required outside the research setting. IRBs sometimes require the investigator to provide them with a script of what subjects will be told about participation in the research or to provide subjects with a written information sheet about the research.

Example: A mail or telephone survey.

Alterations or Waivers of Consent

The IRB may approve a consent procedure that does not include, or that alters, some or all of the elements of informed consent or waive the requirements to obtain informed consent when:

- The research involves no more than minimal risk to the participants
- The waiver or alteration will not adversely affect the rights and welfare of the participants
- The research could not practicably be carried out without the waiver or alteration
- Whenever appropriate, the participants will be provided with additional pertinent information after participation.

Example: Research involving deception about the intent of the study. Subjects are debriefed after their participation about the actual purpose of the study.

Deception

Deception in research is intentionally misleading subjects or withholding full information about the purpose or procedures involved in the research. Deception should not be used when feasible alternatives are available. Deception may take the form of covert observation or not fully informing the patient when obtaining consent. Deception interferes with the patient's ability to give informed consent. As such, it can be thought of as a wrong in itself, as a limiting influence on the protection afforded by informed consent and a violation of the norms of trust and truthfulness. Ethical concerns are increased whenever the protection of informed consent is compromised in any way, because the research subjects are deprived of the opportunity to protect their own interests. Thus, many IRBs require the deception, or the research project as a whole, involve minimal risk and qualify for a waiver of some or all required elements of informed consent.

For certain types of behavioral inquiry deception is arguably necessary, because humans act differently depending on circumstances, and the participant's full knowledge would thus bias the results. Federal regulations permit, but establish limitations on, the use of deception. Use of deception must be scientifically and ethically justified and approved by an IRB. In cases in which the study can be conducted only with participants who are less than fully informed, the missing information should not increase the risks of the study. Volunteers should be fully debriefed at the end of their participation in the study or no later than the conclusion of data collection for the study. This can be a formal process that includes assessment of the volunteer's reaction to the deception, or an informal discussion.

In any event, participants must have the opportunity to ask questions about the new information and be given the opportunity to withdraw from the study and have their data removed as well. There are limited circumstances in which debriefing may not be appropriate; for example, concern that the debriefing may be harmful to the participants, or the design of the research makes debriefing impossible. Professional organizations such as the American Psychological Association (APA) and the American Sociological Association provide guidance on this topic in their ethical codes of conduct. See: www.apa.org/ethics/code/index.aspx#807 or http://asanet.org.

Conclusion

The diversity in research topics and the research methods appropriate to those studies are unique features in the field of behavioral research. Study methods used include surveys, interviews, questionnaires, record reviews, observation (participatory, overt or covert) and various psychological and social interventions in laboratory and field settings. Each method presents ethical and scientific considerations.

Laboratory and field experimentation may not pose concerns in the areas of privacy and confidentiality but may involve consent issues and the full range of research risks. Survey and interview research may be just the reverse, that is, no concerns regarding consent but possible confidentiality issues. Record reviews may raise both consent and privacy issues. The evolution of internet research challenges traditional definitions of privacy, confidentiality and the definitions of human subjects. Thus, investigators must design studies with an eye to minimizing the negative effects of the study's methods, including not only regulatory considerations but also their knowledge of the cultures and customs of those they choose to study.

Resources

1. Belmont Report; Ethical Principles and Guidelines for the Protection of Human Subjects Research. Federal Register Document 79-12065

2. Bankert EA and Amdur, RJ (eds): Institutional Review Board: Management and Function 2nd Edition; Boston Jones and Bartlett Publishers; 2006

3. National Science Foundation: Interpreting the Common Rule for the Protection of Human Subjects for Behavioral and Social Science Research www.nsf.gov/bfa/dias/policy/hsfaqs.jsp

4. 45 CFR Part 46

5. C.K. Gunsalus et al, The Illinois White Paper: Improving the System for Protecting Human Subjects: Counteracting "Mission Creep," Qualitative Inquiry 2007 13: 617.

6. Human Subject Regulations Decision Charts, The Office for Human Subjects Protections (2004) www.hhs.gov/ohrp/policy/checklists/decisioncharts.html

7. OHRP - Guidance on Research Involving Coded Private Information or Biological Specimens (2008) www.hhs.gov/ohrp/policy/cdebiol.html

8. Human Subjects Protection Resource Book, U.S. Department of Energy 2006 http://humansubjects.energy.gov/doe-resources/files/HumSubj Protect-ResourceBook.pdf

9. WIRB Investigator Handbook: A Guide for Researchers www.wirb.com/Pages/DownloadForms1d.aspx

10. WIRB Initial Review Submission Form www.wirb.com/Pages/DownloadForms.aspx

Professional Organizations

- American Anthropology Association:
  www.aaanet.org

- American Educational Research Association:
  www.aera.net

- American Folklore Society:
  www.afsnet.org

- American Historical Association:
  www.historians.org

- Association of Internet Researchers:
  http://aoir.org

- American Political Science Association:
  www.apsanet.org

- American Psychological Association:
  www.apa.org

- American Sociological Association:
  www.asanet.org

- Oral History Association:
  www.oralhistory.org

CHAPTER SEVEN

Publication of Study Results

At the conclusion of this chapter, readers will be able to:

- Explain why investigators, administrators, hospitals, universities and research sponsors may have different expectations for publishing and presenting data.

- Discuss the implications of publishing study results for the investigator, the sponsor, other researchers, hospitals, universities and the public.

- Identify and minimize potential areas of conflict before starting the study.

Introduction

Surveys show professionals at the graduate and post-graduate levels receive most of their new knowledge by reading, especially the current peer-reviewed periodicals. Thus, it is important that research is published in a timely manner in an appropriate venue, and that data be presented accurately and clearly. Most of the time, this is the case. However, scientific publication is not immune to fraud and misconduct.

In his book, *Stealing into Print* (1992), Marcel Latollette defines fraud in scientific communication as "when an author, editor or referee makes a false representation to obtain some unfair advantage or to injure deliberately the rights or interests of another person or group." This may include any of the following:

- Presenting data that do not exist or have been "made up"

- Misrepresenting or deliberately altering evidence

- Plagiarism

- Misrepresentation of authorship

- Unreasonably delaying review or publication for personal gain.

The underlying reasons for such actions may be personal (i.e., fame, career advancement, institutional pressure to publish) or financial (i.e., monetary gain, investment options, competitive advantage in the market). Another reason is the conflict of interest that may occur between the investigator and the source of funding for the research. This type of conflict directly challenges the accountability and independence of the investigator and can create considerable tension among the investigator, the sponsor and the institution at which the research is being conducted. This chapter reviews some of the key issues for scientific publication related to conflicts of interest between sponsor and investigator.

> **Professionals receive most of their new knowledge by reading, especially current peer-reviewed scholarly journals and periodicals. Research results should be published in a timely manner and in an appropriate venue.**

Examples of fraud in scientific publication can be found in all fields—from archaeology and psychology to engineering and medicine. However, in terms of press coverage, it is misconduct within the biomedical arena that receives the most attention, probably because of two factors: there is greater public awareness and interest in matters of health, and more sponsored funding is available from government agencies and from the pharmaceutical and biotechnology industries. Thus, the cases presented in this chapter focus on biomedical research, specifically research sponsored by industry. However, the issues and principles illustrated are not unique to medicine or biology but are applicable to any type of academic research funded by an outside source.

The requirement to publish clinical study results has gained widespread attention during the past decade in response to government- and industry-funded research sponsors failing to disclose, and even withhold, important safety information from the research community, the public and patients. In 2006, the International Committee of Medical Journal Editors (ICMJE) established requirements for authors when submitting manuscripts to top peer-review journals including the *British Medical Journal (BMJ), Journal of the American Medical Association (JAMA), the New England Journal of Medicine (NEJM)* and *The Lancet.* Since then, a number of other publishers of peer-reviewed biomedical research journals have established best practice guidelines and publications ethics that mirror the ICMJE requirements.

Some of the key requirements include:

Sponsorship disclosure: funding of any type in support of the research and publication should be transparent to disclose any interests that might appear to affect the objectivity and the integrity of the research results. In 2010, the ICMJE provided additional guidelines on a standardized reporting format for authors' conflicts of interest.

Contributing authorship disclosure: the list of authors should accurately reflect those individuals who made a material contribution to the manuscript. Greater authorship transparency may help discourage 'ghost writers' (i.e., individuals who qualify as authors but are not noted) and 'guest writers' (i.e., individuals who are listed but did not contribute enough to merit inclusion).

Publication of original research results: journal publishers generally wish to consider only original work that has not been published elsewhere. Meta analyses of scientific literature can be distorted, and a health decision influenced, by a research result published redundantly.

Clinical trial registration: Editors of biomedical journals require that clinical trials reported in manuscripts be posted in a freely accessible, public registry prior to publication. This measures helps ensure transparency of the results and the opportunity to review and analyze study findings.

In 2007, federal regulations governing the dissemination of clinical research results were enacted. The Food and Drug Administration Amendments Act (FDAAA), Section 801, mandated the submission of summary clinical trial results data for phase IIb–IV studies, whether the results are conclusive, inconclusive, published or not. The mandate stipulates that failure to comply may result in a substantial civil penalty of up to $10,000 per day or the withholding of NIH grant funding if noncompliance remains uncorrected 30 days after the violation has been cited. Research sponsors are permitted to delay reporting results for up to three years for clinical trials conducted before drugs are initially approved and for studies of unapproved new clinical indications for those drugs already approved. The National Institutes is responsible for maintaining a public registry of clinical study results on www.clinicaltrials.gov; the FDA is responsible for enforcing compliance with the statutory requirements.

The Declaration of Helsinki (2008; Guideline 33) similarly obligates sponsors and research professionals to provide clinical trial results to study volunteers. The European Medicines Agency (EMA) has not yet made summary results information publicly available for clinical trials of approved and unapproved drugs conducted in the European Union.

The FDA does not object to a pharmaceutical company providing financial support to an investigator to present data or to publish a manuscript, but notes there may be questions about investigator independence under such an arrangement. Will the investigator author actually write the article or will the research sponsor provide assistance with a medical writer? If so, how much input will the investigator actually have? There also may be issues around the timing of the publication: could the sponsor try to delay (or, in extreme cases, even stop) publication of the data if they are not "acceptable" to it? The answers are not always as straightforward as they might seem. Two cases can serve as illustrations.

> **FDA concerns about publishing industry-sponsored studies most frequently focus on independence and how the sponsor may affect independence.**

Case One: B. Dong v. Boots Pharmaceuticals

In the April 16, 1997, issue of the *Journal of the American Medical Association* *(JAMA)*, Dong et al. (University of California at San Francisco) reported a study of the bioequivalence of generic and branded levothyroxine products in the treatment of hypothyroidism. Two generic products (Geneva Generics, Rugby) were compared with two brand-name medications (Synthroid, Boots Pharmaceuticals [now Knoll Pharmaceuticals]; and Levoxine [now Levoxyl], Daniels Pharmaceuticals [now Jones Medical Industries]) using current FDA criteria for bioequivalence. The study was funded, in part, by Flint Laboratories (taken over by Boots Pharmaceuticals during the course of the study), the manufacturers of Synthroid. As is usual for this type of sponsorship, Dr. Betty Dong signed a contract with Flint Laboratories. Company representatives made regular site visits, and copies of the data were sent to the manufacturer.

Preliminary analysis of the data indicated all four medications were bioequivalent according to the FDA standards for oral preparations, thereby implying the products were clinically interchangeable. In reviewing the results, the investigators calculated that if the generics or the other brand-name preparation were substituted for Synthroid, $356 million might be saved annually. These results were obtained in 1990, yet the published report did not appear until 1997. What happened between 1990 and 1997 that delayed publication?

Obviously, the sponsor and the investigators had conflicting views about publishing the results. The investigators believed the results had important clinical implications and should be shared with the medical and academic community. The sponsor, on the other hand, was concerned the results would increase market share for the generic products at the expense of the brand-name product. In this case, the sponsor attempted to prevent publication. The company complained to administrators at UCSF that procedures were not carried out as detailed in the protocol, suggesting the results were flawed due to problems with patient selection, compliance, assay reliability and statistical analysis. UCSF responded to the complaints with an internal investigation that revealed no major problems with the study. It concluded the study was rigorously conducted in a way that complied fully with the contract, and it supported publication. Responding to the company after almost four years of review, UCSF noted all data had been open to the sponsor and the sponsor had monitored the study closely. Thus, the university concluded there was no reason to suppress the manuscript, and to do so would be "an unprecedented intrusion upon academic freedom."

Dr. Dong submitted the manuscript to *JAMA* in April 1994, along with a

> **Suppressing publication of study results can be viewed as an intrusion on academic freedom. However, industry sponsors may have other concerns (e.g. patent infringement, commercial interests, liability issues).**

letter disclosing the funding of the study and the criticism from the sponsor. Publication was originally intended for early 1995, but Dr. Dong then abruptly withdrew the manuscript from the journal due to "impending legal action by Boots Pharmaceutical, Inc. against UCSF and the investigators." The basis for the legal action was the following contract clause: "All information contained in this protocol is confidential and is to be used by the investigator only for the conduct of this study. Data obtained by the investigator while carrying out this study is also considered confidential and is not to be published or otherwise released without written consent from Flint Laboratories, Inc." UCSF did not have this permission, and a university attorney indicated the authors could not be defended if a suit ensued.

Interestingly, the University of California, like most U.S. universities, prohibits restrictions on publishing rights. In fact, the UCSF contract of employment (signed by Dr. Dong) stated that "The University will undertake research or studies only if the scientific results can be published or otherwise promptly disseminated." So, how did this happen? The fact is that protocol contracts with pharmaceutical sponsors often contain restrictive clauses, yet rarely have they prevented publication. Dr. Dong and her colleagues believed these contracts, regardless of content, could not prevent publication.

> **Protocol contracts with industry sponsors may contain restrictive clauses. Pay attention to confidentiality clauses that prohibit publication without permission from the sponsor.**

The issue came to the attention of the public on April 25, 1996, in an article in the *Wall Street Journal*. Carter Eckert, president of Boots Pharmaceuticals, was quoted saying, "I stopped a flawed study that would have put millions of patients at risk." Additionally, in 1994, Boots, now Knoll, had received a letter from the FDA stating a manuscript published by company researchers in 1992 was misleading, and that dissemination of the article by the company should cease. The conclusions of this paper opposed those of Dr. Dong, namely that in normal volunteers studied over 48 hours, the bioavailability of Synthroid was superior to Levoxine. The FDA said the study design was not appropriate for comparing bioequivalence, noting specifically that "A more complex design involving chronic administration in a well-controlled, hypothyroid population with the measurement of several endpoints would be required" (precisely the protocol used by Dong and her colleagues). In its response to the FDA, Knoll referred to the work by Dr. Dong but dismissed it as "worthless." However, the FDA took exception, writing that the Dong study was appropriate to test bioequivalence and cited Knoll for not previously disclosing the Dong results.

Under pressure from the FDA and scrutiny from the public, Knoll ultimately agreed to publication of the manuscript. *JAMA* published the paper along with letters from Knoll apologizing for the delay and objecting to the findings. Rebuttals from the investigator/authors also were published. The cost calculations were included in the discussion. The accompanying comments of the journal editors are of particular interest:

We do not claim that we are publishing a perfect study, just one of the best, made as good as expert review can make it. Experience has taught us that there are very few studies in which some reviewers cannot find flaws ...it is our belief that this is a good study carried out by highly competent workers following a sensible design that tried to answer an important question. It is hard to believe that the sponsors would have made such extraordinary efforts to delay and block publication of the study for such a very long time and for such an extraordinary number of specious reasons if the results had shown Synthroid to be better.

Case Two: D. Kern v. Microfibres Inc.

The second case involves a physician/investigator who investigated the outbreak of an occupational disease at an industrial facility. The physician/investigator was Dr. David Kern, an associate professor at Brown University School of Medicine and chief of general internal medicine, director of occupational and environmental health service (OEHS) at the Memorial Hospital of Rhode Island since 1986. In his latter role, Dr. Kern provided consultancy services, as needed, to local industry and agencies regarding occupational and environmental health hazards.

In 1994, a worker at a local textile plant, Microfibres in Pawtucket, R.I., developed worsening shortness of breath, apparently due to interstitial lung disease (ILD). Dr. Kern visited the plant with several medical students, in part to fulfill his commitment to the medical school to arrange for industrial site visits for medical students every six weeks. At the door of the plant, company officials asked Dr. Kern and the students to sign an agreement in which they promised not to reveal trade secrets. On this visit, Dr. Kern and the students found nothing at the plant that was clearly responsible for the patient's symptoms.

In early 1996, Dr. Kern learned of another worker at the plant with ILD. Dr. Kern notified the company and the National Institute for Occupational Health and Safety (NIOSH). Finding there had been a similar "outbreak" of ILD cases at the company's Canadian facility in 1990, Dr. Kern approached company officials, offering his services as a consultant to study the ILD outbreaks. The company agreed. According to Dr. Kern, at that time the company did not bring up the agreement about trade secrets that he had signed in 1994. Moreover, the company declined to sign a contract covering the new investigation, although it eventually paid the hospital more than $100,000 for Dr. Kern's services. Dr. Kern's ensuing investigation identified another six "work-related" cases of ILD among 150 employees.

Late in 1996, Dr. Kern prepared an abstract of his findings for submission to the 1997 annual meeting of the American Thoracic Society (ATS). Prior to submission, Dr. Kern shared copies of a draft of the abstract with both company and hospital officials. Microfibres asked that the draft not be submitted because it contained information about chemicals it used in manufacturing that it considered proprietary, stating publication of this information would violate the agreement regarding trade secrets that Kern had signed in 1994. Dr. Kern revised the abstract to make it difficult for readers to identify the company, but it still forbade publication. Kern notified administrators at both the hospital and the medical school.

> **Sponsors and investigators may have conflicting perspectives on what constitutes a "trade secret." Open communication BEFORE signing agreements is important.**

Lawyers and administrators at Memorial Hospital of Rhode Island, Kern's employer, expressed concern that Microfibres might sue the hospital. One university official suggested he should not publish, and another suggested that doing so would breach Kern's contract with Microfibres. Nevertheless, Kern submitted his abstract. A week later, hospital officials informed him his contract would not be renewed and the occupational medicine program he directed would be disbanded. In May 1997, Dr. Kern presented the data in a poster session at the ATS meeting.

University administrators defended the hospital's action because Dr. Kern failed to protect himself from pressure from Microfibres and failed to get written assurance that the company would not interfere with his right to publish his results.

Dr. Kern received support from the Rhode Island Medical Society, the Association of Occupational and Environmental Clinics, local physicians, public health advocates and several well-known occupational physicians. In particular, specialists in occupational medicine and environmental science challenged the idea that the trade secret protection agreement Dr. Kern had signed in 1994, a year before he had begun the investigation of the ILD outbreak at the hospital, had any bearing on his rights to publish the results of this investigation.

Dr. Kern's description of a case series of what is now called flock worker's lung was published in the *Annals of Internal Medicine*. It was accompanied by an editorial that described Dr. Kern's saga as "at best... A story of incorrect assumptions and mutual misunderstandings by well-intentioned persons on all sides, starting early in the investigation and leading, over time, to a self-reinforcing downward spiral of further misunderstandings and deepening mistrust. At worst, it is a story of narrow self interest getting in the way of public disclosure, responsibility to patients and academic freedom." Since then, more cases of the disease have been reported. Microfibres never filed a lawsuit against any of the involved parties. Dr. Kern left academic medicine and occupational health for a private general internal medicine practice.

Lessons to be Learned from these Cases

These two cases provide classic illustrations of the timeless tensions that can develop among industry sponsors, investigators, hospitals and universities about the publication and dissemination of research results, particularly when those results are in some sense undesirable to one of the parties involved.

> **Tension between investigators and industry may occur due to:**
> - Different interpretations of contractual text.
> - Different expectations of what will happen to the data.

The Research Contract

The dispute described in the first case could have been avoided if the investigator/consultant had carefully read the contract and asked for clarification of key points. The dispute described in the second case possibly could have been avoided if the researcher had not commenced the research in the absence of a contract that specifically protected his rights. Some takeaway messages that may be important for investigators/consultants:

- Before signing any contract, make sure you have the authority to do so for your institution and, if not, arrange for the appropriate person to deal with the contract.

- Read the contract! Know exactly what you are signing. Do not sign any contract without expert advice.

- Obtain the proper institutional reviews/approvals of the grant/contract prior to signing it.

- Ask the sponsor questions. Do not assume your interpretation of "trade secret," "proprietary information" or "confidential information" matches that of the sponsor. Ask the sponsor to define these terms explicitly. If your interpretation differs from the sponsor's, there should be an open discussion. Most industry sponsors are very open to these types of discussions and negotiations. If the sponsor is not willing to negotiate, obtain assistance with (or avoid) the agreement.

Even if you and the sponsor are in verbal agreement, do not assume any agreement that is not written is enforceable. Therefore, make sure any verbal understandings are fully reflected in the written contract.

- Know your rights. This means knowing your institution's policies. What is the perspective of the institution regarding industry sponsors? How vigorously is the university prepared to defend the academic freedom of its faculty, and/or the hospital prepared to defend the academic freedom of its employee investigators, if at all? If a lawsuit ensues between you and the sponsor, will the institution defend you? Are there any situations in which the institution may not legally be able to defend you?

- Before signing any agreement, review your employment contract. Specifically, look for any terms that negate points included in the company agreement.

- Recognize the different concerns of all parties involved—you, your colleagues who may be working with you on the project, your institution and the sponsor.

- Remember that if you sign a contract without carefully reviewing it, you may be signing away certain rights.

Three steps to prevent contract conflicts:

- Read the contract. Know exactly what you are signing.
- Ask questions. Clarify all issues and terminology.
- Know your rights.

The Data

It is important to clarify what data are and who controls the data. Different academic institutions have different definitions of data, for legal reasons. All contracts must be approved by the institution before you sign them. Research data may be created through programs funded by external sponsors (e.g., government agencies, industry, private foundations). However, regardless of the funding, it is the institution that usually holds title to, or "owns," the data produced. The "creator(s)" of the data (i.e., the investigators) and the sponsors of the research retain rights to access and use the data. To avoid situations such as those faced by Dr. Dong and her colleagues, know how your institution defines data and what the institution's perspective is regarding publication and presentation.

- Read the contract carefully, particularly terms that affect the publication and dissemination of the study results. Do not sign until any issues you have are addressed by the institution and the sponsor.

- Do not assume sponsors will encourage (or even permit) publication of unfavorable results, unless agreed to in the contract.

- Do not allow sponsors veto power for publication or presentation of data.

- Know the position of your institution regarding restrictive clauses in relation to the publication and dissemination of data.

- Do not assume your institution will defend your academic freedom and/or your right to publish in all situations.

- Ask questions about the intentions of the sponsor with regard to publication and dissemination of the results. Consider asking the following questions:

  - Will these data be published? Will they be published if they are equivocal or negative?

  - Who will write the publication?

  - What other studies has the sponsor recently completed? Were the data published? If so, where and how long after the study was conducted?

  - When will the data be published?

  - Will the publication be limited by any concerns regarding potential claims and fair balance?

  - Are there financial or commercial interests at stake in the results? Will publication of the data have potential impact on these interests?

- Be honest about your expectations regarding the presentation and publication of study results.

Sponsors come to researchers at academic institutions in order to establish mutually beneficial and cooperative relationships. They are attracted by an institution's reputation, credibility and prestige. Therefore, it is in the long-term interest of academic institutions to maintain their reputations by being vigorously proactive in preserving academic freedom.

Most sponsors also should know that academic investigators need to report study results, and that there is a high premium placed on publication. Sponsors should recognize that results may or may not support the initial hypothesis, and that researchers need to present and publish studies in a timely manner.

The investigator/consultant needs to recognize that the sponsor may have legitimate concerns regarding the timing of releasing data to publication: e.g., it may be awaiting FDA approval; there may be potential liability issues; publication might artificially inflate the stock price. Open discussion of the concerns of all parties before an agreement is signed will prevent situations that compromise the credibility of either.

Conflict of interest in the scientific publication of sponsored research is not limited to industry funding. There are published reports of similar cases involving professional societies and government agencies. A well-known example are the restrictions placed by the federal government on publishing data that might have an impact on national security. The conflict arises when the definition of national security and perceptions of "impacting data" are not clearly communicated. Again, open and clear discussion among the sponsor, the researcher and the institution prior to signing an agreement will reduce the likelihood of potential disputes.

Withholding Data

Withholding or delaying the publication or presentation of research results is defined as not publishing or presenting the data for a year or more after completion of the study. It is not only the sponsor that may attempt to delay the dissemination of research data. In fact, when data are withheld, most often it is the investigator who has chosen to do so. This was one of the conclusions of a survey of 3,394 life science faculty at 50 U.S. universities. The universities were identified as the top 50 recipients of NIH funding during the 1990s.

Approximately 20% of 2,100 researchers who responded to the survey indicated they had delayed the publication of study results in the past. The majority of the researchers had delayed publication in order to protect the commercial value of the data: 46% cited the time for patent application as a reason; 33% cited other proprietary and/or financial value of the data; and 26% had delayed publication due to the time needed for licensing. Other common reasons given were to protect their own scientific lead, reported by 46% of the researchers (and often attributed to increased competition for funding), and to delay the publication of "undesirable" results, reported by 28%.

Only 4% of the researchers reported that dissemination of study results had been delayed due to any formal agreement with an industry sponsor. Other reasons included avoiding potential liability issues.

Investigators and sponsors gave very similar reasons for withholding or delaying the dissemination of data. However, in addition, a company may delay publication in order to avoid artificial inflation of stock or to wait until FDA approval of a new product or new indication so claims of efficacy and safety can be made appropriately.

Two studies, one published in late 2011 and the other in early 2012, indicate very low levels of compliance with the FDAAA mandate, suggesting that government- and industry-funded research sponsors and investigators continue to withhold clinical study results. In the December 2011 issue of *Health Affairs*, Michael Law and colleagues presented very troublesome findings that of the 4,455 completed trials registered between September 1999 and May 2010, less than one in 10 (only 7.6%) sponsors eventually reported their results on clinicaltrials.gov. Law and colleagues found government agencies are nearly four times less likely to report results than are industry sponsors. The January 2012 issue of the *British Medical Journal* found that of the 738 clinical trials completed in 2009 for which reporting was mandatory, only 22% were published within the mandated time frame.

The results of these two recent studies point to a need for greater enforcement of, and accountability for, the timely publication of clinical study results.

CHAPTER EIGHT

Conflicts of Interest in Research

At the conclusion of this chapter, readers will be able to:

- Discuss why various types of conflicts of interest are ethically problematic in human subjects research.
- Recognize the situations that may contribute to conflicts of interest.
- Describe the various strategies for handling conflicts of interest.

Introduction

Since the death of Jesse Gelsinger in 1999 (see chapter 1), one of the main issues in clinical research ethics has been conflict of interest. Organizations such as the Office for Human Research Protection (OHRP), the Association of American Universities (AAU), the Association of American Medical Colleges (AAMC), the National Institutes of Health (NIH) and the Institute of Medicine (IOM) at the National Academy of Sciences, associations of academic journal editors and the General Accounting Office (GAO) have issued statements on conflict of interest. While Gelsinger's tragic death may have triggered this interest, it should not be surprising that an enterprise—in this case, our society's clinical research apparatus—that has become a multibillion-dollar activity remains in need of clarified and new regulation and public scrutiny.

Recent cases of researcher failure to disclose financial conflicts of interests—most notably the results of a comparison trial of Celebrex and ibuprofen (an over-the-counter non steroidal anti-inflammatory drug) published in the *Journal of the American Medical Association (JAMA)* in 2000—underscore the need for greater transparency and uniformity in reporting conflicts of interest.

The public's perception of academia (and of academics) as driven by an altruistic societal mission may be lagging behind the current reality, in part because investing great trust in researchers and their institutions has been increasingly questioned. Academia has evolved into a partnership with profit-conscious, if not profit-driven, companies in the exploration of science and the development of products and technology. Because mere compliance with the letter of the rules often falls short of meeting the proper ethical standards, this chapter will focus on enduring principles rather than on specific rules that are likely to change.

Financial Conflict of Interest

Money is a potent behavioral incentive, and there is no scientific reason to think researchers' motivational structures are different from those of most people. Further, the scale of such an incentive present in medical research today is a relatively new phenomenon. Other sources of potential conflict (e.g., personal fame, ambition, even the proverbial "thirst for knowledge") already may be factored into the public's perception of researchers. Of course, there is nothing intrinsically wrong with for-profit science. The question is whether the business of science should be exempted from the usual external regulations that other businesses tend to have. This chapter focuses on financial conflict of interest, recognizing that the discussion and ethical principles should be applicable to other domains of conflict of interest.

> **In addition to financial incentives, personal fame and ambition can be sources of conflict of interest.**

There are many non-financial sources of conflict of interest for an investigator, including conflicts of commitment. A common remark in surveys of study participants is that they would like to have seen the investigator more. Conflicts of commitment are not resolved by disclosure. Instead, avoidance and elimination are the most effective management techniques. Researchers should ensure they have sufficient time and interest to safely and properly conduct the study.

Patient Safety, Scientific Integrity and Academic Mission are Threatened by Conflict of Interest

Research cannot occur without the generosity and willingness of both healthy and ill human volunteers. Because research, by definition, limits individualized treatment, every volunteer is making some sacrifice by participating in a research protocol. As a society, we allow this to occur because the knowledge to be gained is deemed to outweigh the sacrifice. Conflicts of interest on the part of investigators and institutions cut to the core of this socially sanctioned risk-benefit compromise in two important ways: patients' safety may be compromised, and/or the "knowledge" produced may be biased to serve the interests of the few rather than those of society. This latter problem could have tremendous long-term unwanted effects.

Conflict of interest may also affect the academic mission, such as com-

> **An investigator's motivation for conducting a clinical study can affect patient safety.**

promising the career of a student or a fellow investigator who may have difficulty publishing or disseminating scientific work if there are contractual constraints on the project for business reasons.

Current Regulatory Framework

For individual financial conflict of interest, the Public Health Service and the National Science Foundation issued similar guidelines in 1995, entrusting the mechanism of oversight to local organizations (such as universities).

In 1998, the FDA issued rule 21 CFR 54 that requires disclosure of certain financial interests on the part of investigators participating in sponsored clinical trials leading to marketing applications. Sponsors must collect the following information from all persons listed on the Statement of Investigator form (1572) for each study, both at the beginning of the study and for one year following completion of the study. The information to be collected includes:

- Compensation made to the investigator in which the value of the compensation could be affected by study outcome

- A proprietary interest in the tested product including, but not limited to, a patent, trademark, copyright or licensing agreement

- Any equity interest in the sponsor of a covered study, i.e., any ownership interest, stock options or other financial interest whose value cannot be readily determined through reference to public prices

- Any equity interest in a publicly held company that exceeds $50,000 in value

- Significant payments of other sorts, which are payments that have a cumulative monetary value of $25,000 or more made by the sponsor of a covered study to the investigator or the investigator's institution to support activities of the investigator exclusive of the costs of conducting the clinical study or other clinical studies, (e.g., a grant to fund ongoing research, compensation in the form of equipment or retainers for ongoing consultation or honoraria).

Note that having a financial interest does not imply that the person cannot be involved in the trial, but serves to make participants aware of the potential for conflict of interest. None of these federal mechanisms is currently coordinated with human subject protections, such as IRB review or informed consent. In fact, the main motivation behind these federal mechanisms is to preserve scientific integrity (and marketing accuracy) rather than protection of human volunteers.

Since the early 2000s, a number of organizations have developed guidelines and policies for managing potential conflict of interest situations. Several of these are worth noting.

- In 2002, conflict of interest principles for institutions were issued by the Association of American Medical Colleges (AAMC). Its report, *"Protecting Subjects, Preserving Trust, Promoting Progress II,"* proposed a framework for the oversight of financial conflicts of interest at institutions that conduct human subjects research. In particular, this report addressed a research-conducting institution's conflicts of interest, such as financial relationships with commercial research sponsors or an indirect financial interest in the outcome of the research project itself. Its key recommendation was that institutions separate their financial and research management functions as cleanly as possible, as the welfare of human subjects and the objectivity of the research could be compromised whenever an institution holds a significant financial interest that might be affected by the research outcome.

- In May 2004 the Department of Health and Human Services (HHS) issued an official guidance document on managing conflicts of interest, developed because of concerns that financial conflicts of interest in research might affect the rights and welfare of the human volunteers. This document said financial interests are not prohibited, and that not all financial interests cause conflicts of interest, but that investigators, institutions and IRBs must consider these situations and the actions that may be necessary to protect participants. HHS suggested establishing conflict of interest committees (COICs) to deal with individual or institutional financial interests, or to verify the absence of such interests, and to address institutional financial interests in research. Among other items, it also suggested establishing clear channels of communication between COICs and IRBs, providing training to appropriate individuals regarding financial interest requirements and establishing policies regarding the types of financial relationships that may be held by parties involved in the research and circumstances under which those financial relationships and interests may or may not be held.

- During the mid-2000s organizations that provide continuing education credits and nursing credit hours established more stringent policies around issuing educational credits for training that was influenced by conflicts of interests.

- In 2006, policies were proposed by the American Medical Association (AMA) that focused on prohibiting certain pharmaceutical detailing practices, such as doctors receiving drug samples, gifts from industry (especially the pharmaceutical industry) and speaking grants. Among other things, these policies called for prohibiting sales representatives from giving small gifts (reminder items) such as pens, cups, clipboards, etc. and from providing restaurant meals to healthcare providers (but still allowed occasional in-office meals in conjunction with informational presentations). These practices had been common until this time and were thought to influence physicians' prescribing patterns for pharmaceutical products.

- The Association for the Accreditation of Human Research Protection Programs (AAHRPP) accredits IRBs, with the goal of helping ensure that all human research participants are respected and protected from harm. Nine principles govern its relationship with institutions and IRBs, one of which states that protecting research participants is the responsibility of everyone within an organization and is not limited to the IRB. The AAHRPP accreditation process has helped facilitate tighter and more expansive conflict of interest policies at institutions.

- In April 2009, the Institute of Medicine (IOM) issued its *Report on Conflicts of Interest in Medical Research, Education, and Practice.* This report examines COI in medicine and recommends steps to identify, limit and manage conflicts in interest without negatively affecting constructive collaboration. The report focuses specifically on financial conflicts of interest involving pharmaceutical, medical device and biotechnology companies. The report calls for: standardized and more widely adopted policies at institutions; a congressionally established national initiative requiring sponsors to report any and all payments to physicians, researchers and patient advocacy groups; and prohibition of any faculty, students, residents and fellows from receiving gifts of any form from industry.

- The Patient Protection and Affordable Health Care Act (H.R. 3590) was signed into law in March 2010 and includes the Physician Payment Sunshine Act (section 6002). The Sunshine Act requires pharmaceutical, medical device, biological and medical supply manufacturers to report to Health and Human Services (HHS) any "payment or other transfer of value" to physicians and teaching hospitals. The first reports will be due March 31, 2013 for the calendar year 2012 reporting period. These reports must include information about the amount of the payment, the date on which the payment was made, the form of payment and the nature of the payment (e.g., gift, consulting fees or entertainment). The details will be posted in a searchable database starting Sept. 30, 2013. Companies out of compliance can be fined from $10,000 to $100,000.

Surveys have shown the rules and policies of local institutions vary widely. Further, scientific journals and societies have issued their own requirements or guidelines on the financial conflict of interest issue. Therefore, investigators must learn and adhere to their own institution's requirements as well as pay close attention to the guidelines of other relevant organizations. Although these requirements and guidelines likely will undergo changes in the future, the principles of managing conflicts of interest will remain the same. The first principle in managing financial conflict of interest is to understand why it is a difficult problem to address.

The Self-perpetuating Nature of the Conflict-of-Interest Problem

Conflict-of-interest problems are difficult to solve because they require people under a conflict be able to rise above the limited perspective created by the conflict itself. Because this is the first, most difficult and most important ingredient in managing financial conflicts of interest, it is worth examining in some depth.

We care about conflicts of interest when they affect important decisions. People who make important decisions are people with power. Since people in power also influence policy—including policies regarding conflicts of interest—it is often the case that people with conflicts of interest have conflicts of interest about dealing with these conflicts. This can take the form of not seeing that there is a problem at all or denying or underestimating one's

Figure 1: A non-exhaustive list of types of financial conflicts of interest		
Type of conflict	**Institutional conflicts**	**Individual conflicts**
Equity ownership including stocks, stock options, etc.	X	X
Patent rights, licenses and royalties	X	X
Conflict of commitment	X[a]	X
Research funding	X	X
Institutional gifts (endowed chairs, other gifts)	X	X[b]
Gifts to laboratory or research group	X	X
Per capita fee for contracted clinical trial		X
Consultant or scientific advisory fees		X
Honoraria in CME activities including speaking at sponsored scientific sessions at professional meetings		X
Informal benefits and gifts (e.g., entertainment, even if done under the rubric of "scientific consultation")	X[c]	X
Informal (non-documented) compensation arrangements[d]		X
Recruitment incentives		X

a. May differ in nature between institutions and individuals. For institutions, it may mean effects on research focus. For individuals, it may mean a compromise of one's institutionally defined role.

b. If individual investigators play an active role in obtaining such gifts for the institution.

c. If it involves institutional leaders.

d. This is admittedly an elusive category and therefore especially worrisome.

Source: www.fda.gov

potential for becoming biased. Another complicating factor in tackling the problem of financial conflict of interest is that it can lead to diverse forms of biased behavior, ranging from outright fraud to subtle and complex bias on the part of well-meaning and honest scientists. Many researchers who would never dream of committing fraud may find it hard to believe the assertion that they are susceptible to acts that fall under the same description (i.e., bias due to financial incentives) and, therefore, resist and even resent the attempts to regulate their behavior. However, the issue is not about their character, but rather about situations and the workings of ordinary human nature. For instance, the social psychology principle of reciprocity (the conscious or unconscious returning of favors) is a powerful psychosocial mechanism necessary for sustained, collective coordination and behavior. This principle is routinely exploited by lobbyists in influencing politicians and by pharmaceutical companies in influencing physician behavior. It would be unscientific and unrealistic to think researchers are exempt from these principles of ordinary human motivation and behavior.

Thus, an ethically effective management of conflict of interest requires a genuine willingness on the part of the investigator (or the institution) to accept that he or she, when standing in a conflict situation, is susceptible to biased perception and action. Such internally motivated willingness to address the conflict of interest problem is an ethical imperative.

Types of Financial Conflicts of Interest: a Non-exhaustive List

A financial interest of any amount that could potentially bias the behavior of an investigator is a morally relevant conflict of interest. While institutions need to create thresholds for practical purposes, such thresholds are arbitrary. For a researcher committed to preserving objectivity and subject safety, it is better to scrutinize all sources of conflict regardless of amount. The table below summarizes the typical situations of financial conflict of interest; other situations may exist.

Strategies for Dealing with Financial Conflicts of Interest

Disclosure is the most often discussed strategy for dealing with financial conflicts of interest and is currently the only mandated federal step. Disclosure alerts others who have a stake in the matter to the potential for bias. Thus, there is a prima facie reason to disclose one's financial conflict of interest to a person or an institution who has a direct, substantial stake in the potential bias created by the financial conflict of interest. At minimum, this includes the investigator's IRB, the investigator's institution and those to whom the results are reported (journals, sponsors, FDA, etc.). Increasingly, statements about conflicts of interest are being added to consent forms for research participants.

It is also worth noting that in order for disclosure to serve its intended ethical function, it needs to occur in a system that can make use of the disclosure. Thus, within a university, for example, close coordination between the IRB and the conflict of interest committee (or official) is necessary. In some institutions the conflict of interest (COI) committee may turn selected information over to the IRB, which will then assume the responsibility for deciding what, if anything, should be disclosed to the participant.

> **Establishing a conflict of interest committee is one mechanism for dealing with COI issues.**

Other strategies for addressing financial conflicts of interest go beyond mere disclosure to actually limiting certain behaviors. For example, an investigator with a significant financial conflict of interest might have certain roles in a protocol curbed, e.g., not obtaining direct informed consent from potential volunteers. A position statement of the American Society for Gene Therapy prohibits certain integral personnel in clinical research from owning equity in the sponsor of the trial, for instance.

The exact application of these strategies will vary, depending on the institution.

Conflict of Interest: An Example to Think About

A physician at a large teaching hospital developed a new cardiology device. In conjunction with a family member, he started a small company to develop, test and market this drug.

The company started clinical trials with the drug, and one study site was at the hospital where the physician practiced. He planned to be the principal clinical investigator for the trial, but the IRB determined this was inappropriate because of the potential conflict of interest. The IRB decided, however, that it was acceptable for this physician to be a sub-investigator for the study, as long as another physician was the principal investigator (PI). The new principal investigator reported to the developing physician in the cardiology unit.

When the study began, the developing physician recommended patients for the trial, and saw patients for study visits, especially if they were his patients. He recommended the study to other doctors within the hospital and the community, telling them how beneficial this device would be for their patients.

What are some potential conflicts of interest in this situation?

- The main conflict of interest is the financial tie between the physician who invented the device and his family company that is developing it for marketing. One has to think about the difficulty in maintaining objectivity during the research.

- Having this physician as a sub-investigator is also a potential conflict, especially as he is the new PI's superior. Added to that, the inventor physician is recommending the trial not only to his own patients, but also to other doctors within the community.

- Having the company place a study at this hospital is not ideal. There would not be as large a potential conflict if the inventing physician were not involved in any way, but it could still be an issue since everyone knows of his involvement, and because of his stature at the hospital.

Points to Consider for Investigators

1. As a first step, the researcher should remain open to the possibility that his or her perceptions and behaviors are susceptible to external incentives. This is a statement about people in general and not about the researcher's character.

2. At minimum, the researcher must know and comply with his or her institution's conflict of interest standards. Researchers also should be aware of and comply with requirements of sponsors, professional societies, regulatory agencies and scientific journals.

3. Compliance with conflict of interest rules may not be sufficient to eliminate all or even most of the ethical concerns behind financial conflict of interest. For instance, one could comply with all the rules and still be biased due to financial incentives, even intentionally so.

4. Evaluate each sponsor-initiated protocol with a critical eye: what is the primary motivation for agreeing to be part of this project? What would the investigator's comfort level be with one of his or her loved ones being approached to enroll in the research? Are the proposed benefits of the research primarily for marketing advantage? Some researchers feel pressured to maintain their research infrastructure using commercial funding in the hopes of doing "discovery research" with federal or other non-commercial sources of funding.

As a final note, researchers should recognize that being sensitive to and complying with conflict of interest guidelines are not exercises in moral purity. Minimizing or eliminating conflicts of interest is ultimately beneficial to investigators and institutions, because loss of public trust will have a devastating effect on the research enterprise, to the loss of all.

CHAPTER NINE

Informed Consent—Beyond the Basics

At the conclusion of this chapter, readers will be able to:

- Describe the three qualities of valid consent as presented in the Belmont Report.

- Discuss techniques to decrease undue influences for potential volunteers.

- Discuss considerations for obtaining assent of children.

- Address issues pertaining to consent of patients with limited capacity.

- Discuss considerations for developing consents.

- Frame consent within the context of an ongoing process.

Introduction

The concept of informed consent is easy to understand but can be a challenge to carry out in practice. Informed consent is based on the principle of respect for persons described in the Belmont Report. This means patients are to be granted the right to freely choose what they want to do. As the Report states, the process requires three key components to be ethically valid: information, understanding and voluntary agreement.

The careful, complete application of these three elements sets consent in the context of an integrated, continuous process and helps delineate the difference between clinical practice and research. The Belmont Report discusses distinguishing clinical practice from research.

Much time is spent on the informational component of consent. This reflects the emphasis on the elements of information found in the Code of Federal Regulations (CFR) that regulates human subject research. Investigators and sponsors labor over consent documents that explain the research. The institutional review board (IRB) spends time reviewing and revising documents to ensure that they meet regulatory requirements for content and reflect local standards for readability and acceptability. Ultimately, volunteers are asked to read the final document, which may exceed 20 pages. Investigators then review the information with volunteers, addressing any questions they may have. Sometimes the consent process may even contain questions to ensure patient comprehension as a condition of enrollment.

The federal "Common Rule" regulations for human subject research require that the following information elements—as they apply to the study at hand—be conveyed as part of the consent process:

- Statement that the activity is research

- Purpose of study

- Description of study procedures (identifying those that are experimental)

- Duration of patient involvement

- Potential risks and discomforts of participation

- Potential benefits of participation (to the patient and others)

- Alternatives, if any

- Confidentiality of records description

- Compensation for injury statement (for greater than minimal risk studies)

- Contact persons for questions

- Statement of voluntary participation

- Unforeseen risks

- Reasons for involuntary termination of participation

- Additional costs to participate (if any)

- Consequences for withdrawal (e.g., adverse health/welfare effects)

- New findings to be provided, if relevant

- Number of patients (if it may have an impact on the decision).

As of March 2011, there is a new consent element:

- A description of this clinical trial will be available on www.ClinicalTrials.gov, as required by U.S. law. This web site will not include information that can identify you. At most, the web site will include a summary of the results. You can search this web site at any time.

This came about as part of the FDAAA (Food and Drug Administration Amendments Act of 2007), which requires that information, not including personally identifiable information, about each clinical trial will be entered into a government-operated clinical trial registry data bank, which contains registration, results and other information about registered clinical trials. The general public can access this database at www.ClinicalTrials.gov.

Neither the consent document nor the oral information should contain any language that causes the patient or legal representative to waive or appear to waive any legal rights or to release the investigator, institution, sponsor or their agents from liability for negligence.

Federal regulations require specific information be conveyed in the consent process; state or local laws and institutional policies may add other standard items. This information represents the "What" of informed consent. To address the other two components of valid consent—understanding and voluntary agreement—we need to consider "Who, Where, When and How"— or the context of the process. These elements, when properly executed, help ensure a consent that is knowledgeably given, voluntary and free of coercion and undue influence.

Context

To ensure the circumstances under which consent is obtained are free from undue influence, investigators and sponsors should address the following points when planning a study:

Who will Obtain Consent?

- While it is usually assumed the investigator will obtain consent, this is not always the case. Frequently, study coordinators or other team members are charged with this responsibility. In some cases, translators, witnesses, advocates and others can help ensure impartiality and enhance the decision-making process.

- The person or persons obtaining consent must be sufficiently trained and knowledgeable about the study to answer questions posed by patients. When principal investigators delegate this important task, they need to be sure that those who obtain consent are properly qualified and know when to refer questions that may exceed their expertise.

- An important issue in deciding who will obtain consent is whether or not the investigator has a pre-existing relationship with the potential patient. If the investigator is in a position of power, e.g., the patient's teacher or personal physician, it may be appropriate to delegate the consent responsibility to someone else. This technique helps avoid undue influence and the possibility—real or perceived—that the patient would feel pressured or obligated to agree to participate.

> **The individual obtaining consent can unintentionally influence a patient's decision to participate in research.**

Where will Consent be Obtained?

- Privacy is of paramount importance to the consent process. The consent process should not be conducted in areas that would permit others to overhear the discussion. The assurance of privacy is of even greater importance when the topic of the research is in sensitive areas of patients' lives. Typically, a private office or room helps ensure privacy.

- While consent is often obtained in the investigator's office or laboratory, settings may negatively influence the process. For example, a classroom setting may introduce peer pressure and/or inattention. The pre-operative area of the surgical suite likely adds an unwanted element of stress and anxiety. Also, the prospective patient may feel pressured to make an immediate decision. These situations reduce both comprehension and volunteerism, thus detracting from the decision-making process.

- A neutral setting, or one in which the potential patient feels comfortable and familiar, may help remove the "intimidation factor" caused by the power and/or knowledge imbalance present between the investigator and the participant.

- Occasionally, informed consent materials will be presented to a group of potential volunteers, especially if the consent is done in a video format. The individual giving the consent will be present to answer questions and explain anything that is not clear. However, it is still important to spend some time alone with each potential volunteer to allow him or her to ask questions and discuss issues he or she might not want to bring up in a group setting.

When will Consent be Obtained?

- The timing of the consent process also may have a negative impact on the potential patient's ability to make an informed decision. For example, if the research procedures follow immediately after the consent form is signed, there will be no time for the patient to reflect on potential consequences or ask questions that might come to mind later on. While this may be acceptable for minimal risk studies, for those posing greater risk or possible negative consequences lengthening the time between presentation of the consent and the final agreement to participate can help protect patients.

- Investigators should anticipate circumstances under which it would be difficult to have a satisfactory consent discussion. For example, when evaluating a new drug for the treatment of women during delivery, one should anticipate that once labor begins it will be relatively difficult to have a satisfactory consent discussion; therefore, this discussion should occur during a prenatal visit.

- Allowing patients sufficient time to read the consent and to consult with family, friends and others also may improve the quality of the process. According to several internet sources, the average reading speed for an American adult is around 200-250 words per minute (wpm), with a typical comprehension of about 60%. Given the length and complexity of current consent forms, it is a good idea, when possible, to allow potential patients to take the consent document home and consider it for a few days.

How will Consent be Obtained?

- While the traditional model is for the investigator to sit with the potential volunteer and read/discuss a written consent document, this may not be the best technique for all volunteers and for all types of studies. Some volunteers may respond better to different modes of presentation. Computer presentations of the consent have become relatively common, with various "point and click" enhancements to aid understanding. Investigators whose research involves mailed surveys may not interact with volunteers, making face-to-face consent not possible. Ethnographic research is another example for which alternate methods of seeking consent and providing information are useful.

- For complex studies, additional aids—e.g., videotapes, charts or brochures—may enhance the volunteer's understanding. Additionally, in long-term studies with many different elements, volunteers are likely to benefit from a "phased" consent. In this model, an initial explanation of the complete study is supplemented by renewed consent and/or information review prior to each new section.

- Under certain circumstances in research involving minimal risk, the consent process—or its documentation—may be waived. This often is the case for telephone surveys and interviews, for which the investigator may note in the study records that the patient gave consent but a signed document is not obtained.

When appropriate, the consent document may also contain information about:

- Incentive payments and expense reimbursements to volunteers
- Conflict of Interest declaration
- Institutional/investigator incentives and reimbursements.

The categories noted above provide a foundation on which the consent process is based.

Developing a Consent Document

As research protocols have become longer and more complex, the informed consent documents that accompany them have also become longer and more complex. This can make it very difficult for potential study volunteers to truly be informed about the research and makes it a challenge to develop a document that covers all of the essential elements and information, yet remains comprehensible to the volunteer.

The Institutional Review Board (IRB) is legally obligated to ensure that the elements of informed consent are "provided to each subject." Providing them in an unreadable form does not meet this requirement. One cannot have "informed" consent without fully comprehending information.

Consents must inform patients of all study activities in which they will be involved, yet care must be taken to keep the form as short as possible because people tend to lose concentration and comprehend less the longer they read.

The consent document must be written in a way and language understood by those being consented. Readability should be at about the 8th grade level. According to ProLiteracy, a nonprofit organization focused on combating illiteracy, 29% (63 million) of the U.S. population over age 16 do not read well enough to understand a newspaper article written at an 8th grade level, while an additional 14% (30 million) can read only at a 5th grade level or lower. These figures make it obvious that we need to do everything possible to construct informed consent documents in a simple, easy to comprehend format.

There are a number of techniques that can be used to make consent documents more "user friendly" for potential volunteers:

- Use commonly understood words. Terms such as "adverse," "bruising," "confidentiality," "protocol" and "unforeseen" appear less than once per million words in common usage

- Avoid words with more than three syllables

- Use bullets, headings, short paragraphs and lots of white space

- Use an easily readable font

- Justify the left margin and leave the right margin ragged

- Consider using columns

- Consider having a FAQ sheet to accompany the consent form

- Test it before using it (have a teenager, an older person, someone with no medical background each read it).

Spending the time to develop a good consent form will help ensure study volunteers truly are informed and able to make an educated decision about participation.

Vulnerable Subjects

The concept of vulnerable subjects is addressed at length in the Belmont Report. The "Common Rule" federal human subject protection regulations [sections 107(a) and 111(a)(3) and (b)] apply specific requirements to help ensure the proper treatment of patients who have limitations on their capacity or freedom. DHHS has three subparts (B, C and D), which provide additional protections for specific classes of vulnerable patients. (Note: the FDA and the Department of Education also subscribe to their own versions of the DHHS subpart D protections for children.) Special considerations are described below.

Children

Because children cannot legally give consent, federal regulations require the permission of their parents and, with the exception of very young children in some treatment protocols, the assent (the affirmative agreement) of the child-patient. In general, the considerations for parental permission are the same as for consent in adult patients.

Assent has generally been divided into three categories, depending on the age of the child-patient. Very young children have not developed decision-making skills, while older children may function at adult levels. The commonly accepted rule of thumb is that children under the age of 7 are too young to assent; children over the age of 12 should be capable of full participation in the consent process (i.e., giving assent and documenting that decision in writing); those children in between—ages 7 to 12—should be capable of assenting, but need not provide written documentation. When assent is to be used in a research study and a child capable of assenting says "no" to involvement in research, the child should not be intimidated or enrolled in the research. The investigator's professional judgment and expertise are vital in determining individual variations on this theme to assure an adequate consent process.

> **It is the responsibility of the investigator to decide the level of understanding of the child.**

An additional concern is the potential for conflicts of interest when parents enroll their children in research studies. Researchers need to be cognizant of parental conflicts when designing the consent process for studies involving children.

Adults with Limited Capacity to Consent

There are no separate federal regulations for this category of human subject research, although state laws may apply. Investigators and IRBs have developed general restrictions and consent techniques when enrolling these patients:

- *Assent:* As in research involving children, many institutions require the affirmative agreement of the patient. Thus, those patients who object or who fail to object, but do not affirmatively agree, are not enrolled.

- *Legally Authorized Representative (LAR):* The federal regulations allow for the use of an LAR. The LAR is asked to represent the incompetent patient's previously demonstrated values in enrolling that patient in research, i.e., substituted judgment standard. If they aren't known, then the LAR should use the best interest standard. Again, institutions have established policies to guide investigators when involving patients who cannot give their own consent for research. Investigators should be sure to comply with these policies, particularly when using family, caregivers and advocates to give permission for enrollment. The ICH guidelines (4.8.12) require assent for all who are entered by an LAR. State law determines who qualifies as an LAR for research. Note that this issue is unsettled in most states.

- *Staged consent:* Investigators and IRBs have made use of phased consent, or staged consent, when patients' abilities to retain information may be compromised.

- *Continuing evaluations of capacity and consent understanding:* Depending upon the specific study, formal or informal evaluations of capacity may be helpful to ensure adequate protection is provided by the consent process. There is an inherent conflict of interest/judgment when the investigator determines the capacity of a potential patient to consent or assent to research.

> **Investigators should be aware of any state laws or institutional policies regarding legally authorized representatives.**

Prisoners

Federal regulations note special considerations in both participation in and consent to research studies involving prisoners. Clearly, for research conducted in prison settings, investigators must take extra steps to ensure the voluntary nature of consent is maintained and volunteers understand the research and its effect on them. Consent forms must explain that participation will not affect the prisoner's consideration for parole. Special attention is mandated by the regulations to ensure the information is presented in language understandable to this group of potential volunteers.

Additional Consent Considerations

Deception

To achieve the objectives of certain studies, particularly those in the behavioral and social sciences, volunteers may need to be intentionally misled. The regulations allow deception only in research that presents no greater than minimal risk. When deception is used, obtaining informed consent is problematic because, by definition, not all of the information is provided. To address this concern, some institutions have used a "consent to research procedures" to enroll volunteers into the study initially, followed after the volunteer's participation by a "consent to the use of research data"—a debriefing form that divulges the true nature of the study and offers volunteers the opportunity to decline participation.

Non-English-speaking Patients

Federal regulations require that consent be in language understandable to the patient. This pertains not only to English-speaking patients, but also to potential volunteers for whom English is not their first language. When patients who do not speak English are anticipated to be in the study population, a certified translation of the consent, including all required elements, should be submitted to the IRB for review and approval. Federal regulations also permit a "short-form" document to be used in this instance. It is particularly important to remember that consent is a process, i.e., once the form is signed, study personnel fluent in the patient's language are needed to ensure ongoing understanding.

Consent Renewal

Patients need to know about new information that may affect their willingness to continue participating in the research. Such information might include new data concerning efficacy, the need to extend the duration of the study, adverse events, previously undocumented toxicities or additional tests or measurements. New information may be conveyed to current/previous patients through an addendum to the original consent form or in a new consent form. New patients enrolled would receive a new consent form (as approved by the IRB) with the additional information listed.

> **The consent process does not end after the patient's initial consent to participate; it is an ongoing process.**

Study protocols often are changed during the course of a study. When these changes require revision of the informed consent document, a system must identify the revised consent document to preclude continued use of the older version, and identify file copies. If the consent must be amended, the new consent (or summary of changes) must be approved by the IRB. All patients still in the study must sign the new consent (or a summary of the changes). New patients will sign the new consent but do not need to sign older versions. Patients who already have completed the study usually will not need to sign the new consent.

In long and complex studies, renewal of consent also may be desirable to ensure patient understanding and voluntary agreement to participate. This may consist of an informal review of the study and its procedures, or a formal process with forms and signatures ("phased consent"). Again, investigator judgment and discussion with the IRB are important to ensure an effective consent process.

Conclusion

Honoring a person's right to make decisions is the basis for obtaining consent in the research context. Because many studies involve benefits that are either nonexistent or unsure, the volunteer's participation represents a societal good. Investigators need to ensure that the process of consent—the information in the consent form, the setting, the timing and the manner—shows respect for patients and gives them the opportunity to choose what is best for them. In this way we continue to earn the trust the public and our patients have placed in us as researchers.

CHAPTER TEN

Community-Based Qualitative Research

At the conclusion of this chapter, readers will be able to:

- Identify the unique aspects of human subject protection involved in community-based qualitative research.

- Appropriately apply guidelines for the protection of study communities to specific research contexts.

- Recognize the need to actively engage the community during all stages of the research including formulation of the study question and design, data collection and synthesis and dissemination of the findings.

Introduction

Increasingly at academic medical centers, universities and colleges, hospital based-systems and other institutions, investigators have begun to use community-based qualitative research to explore public health problems, design programs and policies and evaluate effectiveness. While many of the ethical principles for the protection of human subjects already discussed in this book also apply to community-based qualitative research (CBQR), some issues are unique to this approach.

Philosophical Assumptions Unique to CBQR and the Implications for Practice

Assumption #1
The community is the authority on its own situation, strengths, needs and potential solutions.

Practice implication—Community engagement at every stage of research through regular meetings with community representatives. This may involve convening a special community advisory board representing all of the project's major stakeholders.

Assumption #2

Cultural biases of the research team may unduly skew the formulation of the research questions, the collection of data and the interpretation of the findings.

Practice implication—A continual process of critical self-reflection that makes explicit the research team's own cultural values and how they may differ from the cultural values of the study community.

Defining Community-Based Qualitative Research (CBQR)

CBQR is defined as research conducted at a site away from research centers, engaging people on their own territory. This can include their homes, community centers, work sites, places of worship or schools. It also may occur online through social networking sites, email, chat rooms, list serves and bulletin boards, or over the telephone. The data generated are in the form of textual descriptions of human experience rather than numbers, and they involve understanding issues from the point of view of those people most affected. The notion of community is flexible.

Communities may be bounded by geography (e.g., certain census tracts), or they may be defined socially, culturally, by economic status or by disorder (e.g., Alzheimer's, caregivers or diabetics). Communities may be included in the process of how they would like to be identified. This may take researchers beyond the traditional categories of "white, black, Hispanic" to a more nuanced sense of community and belonging. Some Hispanic communities, for example, may prefer to be identified more specifically as Puerto Rican, Mexican-American or Cuban-American.

> **Researchers need to understand the cultural values of the community under study.**

Maintaining Confidentiality

Responsibility for maintaining confidentiality rests with the researcher; however, study participants may want to be identified. If the participant so desires, and with his or her permission, the participant's real name can be used. This is sometimes the case in a specific type of CBQR known as Participatory Action Research (PAR). PAR partners researchers with communities for the explicit purpose of social change. Community partners in PAR, such as community leaders and grass-roots activists, may prefer their real names be used in the publication of study findings to make themselves available for advancing the process of social change. Identification may be done by attribution of direct quotes, citing ideas, in the description of activities and/or in explanations of the research collaboration.

Alternatively, in protecting community and/or individual identities, the researcher and the participants may elect to avoid gathering or reporting identifying information. Masking identities with pseudonyms and gathering only general information such as gender and age group allow for composite descriptions when reporting while maintaining anonymity. Community identities also may be masked, giving the location a fictional name and locating it in broad geographic terms such as "mid-sized, northeastern city." Masking can be undone if acknowledgements specify a cooperating agency in the community.

> **As in other types of research with human subjects, maintaining the confidentiality of the community is important.**

Stigmatizing topics (e.g., HIV status or drug use) or sensitive social identities (e.g gay/lesbian, transgender, hate groups, prostitution) usually involve masking names, and accurate data might be difficult to collect unless assurances of confidentiality can be made. In such cases, written informed consent may threaten participants' desire to remain anonymous. For these situations, the researcher may request a waiver of documentation of consent from the IRB so participants may provide verbal rather than written consent, indicating their understanding of the purposes of the research, how their information will be stored and used and their rights as research participants. Also, Certificates of Confidentiality may be obtained from the Department of Health and Human Services to protect study data from involuntary disclosure through subpoena.

Study Methods

CBQR may make use of a variety of data collection tools within a single project, including participant observations, in-depth interviews (both structured and unstructured), focus groups and examination of public documents. Data collected using these tools may be captured by videotape, audiotape, field notes (handwritten or on a laptop) or any combination of these. All of these approaches require approval from the institution's review board, but often they are considered eligible for expedited review as they generally are of minimal risk.

Particular Points to be Considered

Audio and Videotaping
In research situations in which audio or videotapes are necessary, there are some special ethical and regulatory requirements.

In the case of individual interviews, the participant is informed in advance that the researcher wishes to tape the interview. The interviewee's consent can be taped to provide confirmation of his or her willingness to be taped. A participant being taped should be told that the tape can be stopped at any time during the interview at his or her request. For groups being taped, all participants should agree to be taped. Similarly, any participant has the prerogative to stop the tape at any time.

How the information on the tapes will be used and the protections provided to the taped information (e.g., secured for researcher use, transcribed and then destroyed; access limited to researcher only or research staff, etc.) need to be specified.

The decision about how taped material will be handled is made at the outset of the research and, along with the procedure for obtaining consent (usually a script), must be specified in the application to the IRB.

Written Notes

Although the above stipulations apply to the researcher's written notes as well, a few other points must be considered when taking notes. Investigators might want to consider using only pseudonyms in the notes themselves. If the notes are to be entered into a computer, a decision must be made as to whether to destroy the handwritten notes or store them in a secure place.

Focus Group Participants

Focus groups are group interviews conducted and facilitated by a moderator. The goal is to generate discussion among focus group members, record their comments and observe their interactions.

Because topics may generate heated debate, special steps must be taken to protect focus group members from the potential ire of others. Explicating ground rules for participation at the beginning of the group provides a method to clarify how members are expected to conduct themselves during the group and the expectation of maintaining confidentiality afterward. Because topics discussed in some focus groups may evoke strong emotional reactions, a referral sheet should be distributed at the conclusion of the group that provides each participant with references and resources should they want to further discuss their feelings or concerns. Moderators may want to suggest participants can contact their healthcare provider, therapist or case worker. Participants also may want advice on specific problems they have related to the topic area. While such problems cannot be resolved within the context of a focus group, information sheets can be made available to direct them to other resources. Information that should be provided varies based on the focus group topic but commonly includes community referral numbers, hot line numbers and web sites.

Occasionally, the focus group moderator must confront the behavior of a particular participant. Whether the topic of discussion has raised issues that are upsetting to the individual or a conflict has arisen between group members, the moderator ought to intervene. Most often, the upset or disruptive individual is asked to leave, thanked for participation, provided the above-mentioned information and referral sheets and given the agreed-to incentive or payment.

In addition, the researcher should consider what to do in the event a subject discloses that he is a threat to himself or others during the focus group session and outline the procedures for how this situation will be handled in the protocol, if appropriate.

Disclosure

The investigator also may be faced with ethical dilemmas. Hearing information about illegal activities, such as domestic violence, drug use, child abuse or sexual assault, for example, cannot be treated simply as research data. The researcher's obligation necessitates further action if certain conditions apply. Sometimes information already has been reported by the participant to the proper authorities. In this case, the researcher need only clarify if the participant has taken this action. Reporting activities to the police or other governmental agency requires a level of detail (date/time, place, activity), not just suspicions or vague references. Again, the researcher also must ensure the participant is not currently in an unsafe situation. In both cases, the written information sheets provided by the researcher to the participant can be useful. Certificates of Confidentiality may be issued to protect sensitive data from release under subpoena, etc. If reports will be made, for example, of child abuse, the moderator should advise participants of that fact.

In anticipation of possible disclosures that indicate the participant is in some danger or distress, it is wise to consult with the study communities ahead of time about what they would like to see happen. The community might prefer notifying clergy, healthcare providers, a case worker, parents, teachers or guidance counselors.

Payment/Incentives

Study participants provide their time and effort to benefit the research or project. Covering transportation costs (e.g., bus or taxi fare) or providing a meal or child care may reduce the burden of participating and improve recruitment. Acknowledging their time can be accomplished through monetary payment such as cash or a gift card. Consultation with the community can help establish what would be considered fair, legitimate compensation. This could range from cash to food or clothing coupons.

Resources for Participants

It is helpful for researchers to keep a list of community resources that participants can access should the need arise. The list may include hot line numbers, contact information for free clinics, community support groups or community-based centers.

Participant Observation

Less intrusive qualitative research includes observing and/or participating at community gatherings or public events. In the case of small gatherings, it is important that the researcher identify him or herself as being there to collect data with the permission of the organizers. Of course, only individuals themselves can give consent for research participation, and researchers must be prepared if some people decline participation/observation. This may mean people are free to ignore the researcher or not speak with him or her. It may mean data on/about certain individuals cannot be collected or recorded. It may even mean the research must withdraw from the event. When the setting is a large public event, which assures subject anonymity, no special measures usually need to be taken.

Secondary Subjects

In some cases, the researcher may obtain information about another person (i.e. a third party) from the primary subject during the course of the community-based research. If the researcher obtains information about a third party that is both private and individually identifiable, then the third party becomes a secondary subject. Secondary subjects meet the definition of a human subject under federal regulations. As a result, the researcher must obtain informed consent from the secondary subject and ensure that appropriate procedures are in place to protect his or her privacy and confidentiality. In some cases, the IRB may grant a waiver of informed consent for secondary subjects if the regulatory criteria are met.

Disenfranchised Populations

The information on the protection of vulnerable populations (children, pregnant women, etc.) applies during CBQR. However, some communities under study represent disenfranchised populations such as the economically disadvantaged or the incarcerated. These communities may be suspicious of researchers or projects seeking to use their information without a benefit to them or the community. The researcher must be clear about the intent of the research and the potential benefits to the community, if any. It is important not to overstate the potential benefits or promise resources that are not directly under the authority of the researcher. Communities that believe their participation will result in a guaranteed service that is not forthcoming will generally feel exploited. Researchers should clearly describe the contingent nature of any benefits. A good rule is not to promise anything that you cannot guarantee.

Dissemination of Study Findings

Researchers should carefully consider how the findings are written for publication and who the audience will be. One of the goals of dissemination is to render accounts that present an empathetic understanding of the study community's circumstances and the logic that informs decision making and actions. Explaining the "other" to outsiders may be difficult, especially in cases in which the values and social conditions of the study community are radically different from those of the outside reading audience. Researchers should avoid promoting stereotypes or stigmatizing individuals/communities. Study communities might want to review written accounts and be allowed to comment on them prior to publication or presentation. Think carefully about any unintended consequences that might result from publication of sensitive, embarrassing or divisive information.

Further Resources

The American Anthropological Association's Code of Ethics (www.Aaanet. org) and the American Public Health Association guidelines (www.apha.org) are helpful in considering how CBQR can be conducted in a way that "preserves the confidentiality and dignity of the study community, while promoting trustful, non-exploitive relationships needed for continued study by other researchers."

CHAPTER ELEVEN

Ethical Issues in Genetic Research

> **At the conclusion of this chapter, readers will be able to:**
>
> - Define the term "genetic research" and discuss the complexities of the definition.
>
> - Discuss the human subject protection issues related to conducting genetic research.
>
> - Define the term "gene transfer" and discuss the complexities of this concept.
>
> - Address the human subject protection issues related to conducting research with gene transfer.

Introduction

Over the past two decades, human genetic research has focused mainly on rare genetic diseases attributable to single (mendelian) genes, such as cystic fibrosis or Huntington's disease. With the sequencing of the human genome and definition of the estimated 30,000 genes it is believed to contain, the research focus in medical genetics is rapidly changing. For mendelian disorders with known genes and mutations, the research is shifting to the examination of efficient diagnostic testing (including genetic screening), the search for "modifier genes" that may determine the course and prognosis of the disease and novel interventions, including gene therapy.

A major effort has been initiated to study the genetic contributions to common disorders that have complex inheritance patterns and significant environmental causes. The study of these complex disorders generally requires a combined genetic and epidemiological approach. Consequently, much larger numbers of volunteers usually are needed, and the study data collected often involve extensive personal information over long periods of time, including clinical and demographic data, occupational, dietary and other environmental exposure, socioeconomic data and behavioral characteristics. Because these complex disorders have multi-genetic causation, the nature and number of genes to be tested often are unclear at the outset of the research study, resulting in a realistic potential of unintended or undesired genetic testing results.

The high prevalence of these common complex disorders—including

131

coronary heart disease, hypertension, cancer, psychiatric disorders, addictions, diabetes mellitus, allergy or asthma—also means research data, tissue samples and overall study results have enormous commercial potential. The eventual ability to identify predisposition to a large number of diseases, while having enormous prevention potentials, is also redefining the boundary of what we consider a "patient" and a "non-patient." Thus, modern genetic research, often accompanied by its many ethical, legal and social issues, is challenging the way we interpret what are considered risks and benefits of research, how we deal with privacy, confidentiality and anonymity, how we define conflicts of interest and the consent process itself.

Federal and State Regulations

Currently, no comprehensive federal regulation addresses all facets of genetic research. Previously existing federal regulations on human subject protection is being used to guide how these research studies are conducted, subject to interpretation by individual IRBs. New legislation at the federal and state level is mainly concerned with protection of patients against genetic discrimination (in insurance or employment) or loss of privacy where genetic testing is concerned. Some of these regulations also are being applied to the protection of human subjects when research genetic testing is involved, sometimes with rather awkward limitations for research and researchers.

Some Points to Consider

There are many different kinds of genetic research and different contexts under which the term "genetic" is used. Being clear about these concepts is an important key to understanding what issues must be addressed in the protection of human subjects in genetic research.

> **Genetic research is rapidly changing. Investigators need to keep their IRB informed of new developments.**

What Does "Genetic" Mean?

Often "genetic" means that which pertains to DNA and/or RNA ("molecular genetics") in the cells within a tissue, organ or the entire individual (e.g., as in the statement: "Genetic changes in a cancer cell result in abnormal cell growth."). In other situations, "genetic" is taken to mean that which passes from one generation to another through DNA, the hereditary material (e.g., as in the statement: "There is a genetic condition running through that family."). This latter use of the term also carries the connotation of "familial" and "hereditary." All of these terms should be distinguished from the term "congenital," which simply refers to that which an individual is born with, regardless of whether it is from environmental, genetic, hereditary or familial factors.

What are the Different Kinds of Genetic Variations?

Genetic variations include what are commonly called genetic mutations and genetic polymorphisms. Genetic mutations are of two broad categories. Molecular genetic alterations present in all cells of an individual mean that such alterations are present within the first cell (i.e., the fertilized egg) that gave rise to the individual. These genetic mutations are considered "constitutional" (or "germ-line") and are generally inherited from one or both parents. They likewise can be passed on to the next generation. Sometimes genetic mutations are present only in certain cells, tissues or organs of an individual, and not in the majority of his or her body cells. These individuals most often are born with a normal "constitution," with the genetic mutation taking place later in life. These more confined genetic mutations are called "somatic" mutations. Somatic genetic mutations are not inherited and likewise are not generally passed on to the next generation.

Of course, these two categories of genetic mutations are not always mutually exclusive. For example, an individual may inherit a constitutional mutation that predisposes him or her to more easily develop a somatic mutation. This is the basis for many familial cancer predisposition syndromes. Alternatively, somatic mutations may take place in the gonads of an individual, such that these mutations may be passed on to the next generation through the eggs or sperm.

Genetic polymorphisms represent naturally occurring variations in the general population of an individual's genetic makeup, as manifested in DNA, RNA or protein sequences. A good example of genetic polymorphism is that of ABO blood group differences among individuals. These polymorphisms are generally not thought to be directly disease causing. However, much of the current human genetic research on common complex disorders seeks to establish associations between specific genetic polymorphisms and predisposition to disease states. A good example of this is the association of apoe4 polymorphism with an increased risk of Alzheimer's disease.

Other genetic polymorphisms are believed to modify an individual's resistance to known pathogens, highlighting the genetic-environmental interaction of many common diseases. A good example of this is the association of mutations in the chemokine gene CCR5 and resistance to HIV infection. Genetic polymorphisms are part of an individual's genetic constitution and, as such, are passed on from parents to their children following the known rules of inheritance. They provide a particular challenge in the determination of the risks and benefits of study results to participants.

Compounding the difficulty in dealing with genetic research protocols is the fact that knowledge about the implications for specific genetic mutations and polymorphisms is constantly evolving, making constant reassessment of protocol a necessary part of the IRB re-approval process. Consultation with individuals who have some expertise in the area is essential. Researchers should assist their IRB to stay current with the field, for example, by including review articles with progress reports or offering a brief update to the board.

Genetic Research and Genetic Testing

Much of the concern and anxiety surrounding human subject protection in modern genetic studies involve genetic testing. Before discussing what constitutes a "genetic test," it is important to point out that there are many genetic studies that do not involve genetic testing. For example, a study published in 1990 in the *Journal of Human Genetics* by McGuffin and Huckle examined whether attending medical school is a genetic trait. This was a survey-based study that utilized family histories on medical school attendance. The pedigree information was analyzed by statistical genetic methods and a specific mode of inheritance was proposed. This was a genetic study but did not involve any genetic testing. There are many more serious investigations of this type, including twin studies, sibling studies and extended family history analysis.

The question of what constitutes a "genetic test" cannot easily be answered. One definition of a "genetic test" is "a test that involves looking at the genes." This definition emphasizes the laboratory technique used in the testing process and includes any DNA testing. However, it does not discriminate between the detection of somatic and constitutional genetic variations, even though somatic mutations usually are not familial or heritable. Another possible definition of a "genetic test" is a test that "determines the genetic status of an individual with respect to a certain trait." This definition focuses on the intent of why a test is done, as opposed to the actual technique employed. This definition can be overly inclusive in that many commonly used non-DNA-based tests can determine an individual status, such as a sweat chloride determination for cystic fibrosis.

In New York State, the Civil Rights Law (section 79-l) defines a "genetic test" as "any laboratory test of human DNA, chromosomes, genes or gene products to diagnose the presence of a genetic variation linked to a predisposition to a genetic disease or disability in the individual or the individual's offspring; such term shall also include DNA profile analysis." It does provide exclusions, in that genetic tests do not include "any test of blood or other medically prescribed test in routine use that has been or may be hereafter found to be associated with a genetic variation, unless conducted purposely to identify such genetic variation." While the exclusion still contains some ambiguity as to what "purposely" means, this definition is a reasonable compromise given the complexity of the issues. The larger question is that as more diseases are found to have a genetic contribution, it will become increasingly difficult to define a "genetic disease or disability." This will be a challenge for future human subject protection.

Common Kinds of Genetic Studies and Things to Watch Out for

There are four main kinds of genetic research in which testing of gene or gene products is included. They will be discussed with respect to whether they are "genetic research involving genetic testing," using the definition of "genetic testing" as stated above.

1. *Studies that deal exclusively with the molecular genetic alterations in DNA or RNA in specific cells, tissues or organs involved in the disease process, without any intent to address whether that change is inherited or that it represents a predisposition to the disease or disability.*

This is common in many oncology studies, in which a tumor is analyzed for specific genetic changes related to the biology or treatment response of the tumor. However, to show that these genetic changes in tumor cells are indeed somatic mutations, one often has to establish that similar mutations do not exist in the normal tissues of the patient. This is why a sample from the normal (non-cancerous) tissue, most commonly blood, from the affected subjects is often required as a "control" in most genetic studies on cancer patients. The exceptions perhaps are leukemia or lymphoma, because blood is the tissue involved in the disease process. Also, unaffected volunteers may be needed to serve as additional controls, though testing on these volunteers often can be done anonymously. Thus, these kinds of studies technically do not involve genetic testing as defined above. However, if a cancer study looks at the "normal" non-tumor tissues for additional constitutional genetic mutations, it is testing for a predisposition to the disease and thus involves "genetic testing." The results of these studies would have an entirely different set of implications for the subjects and their families.

> **The results of genetic testing affects not only the subjects but also their families.**

A sub-category of this kind of genetic research often is seen in anthropologic or population genetic studies. These studies aim to use genetic markers to trace the genetic origin, population behavior (e.g., migration, admixture and mating with other populations) and characteristics (e.g., frequencies of specific genes in different populations). The genetic markers being studied can include genes associated with disease states. An example of this is a study to compare the frequency of specific mutations of a certain gene in different ethnic populations to understand the history of that population or to provide better ethnic-based genetic counseling. Even though these kinds of studies invoke the concept of genetic heritability in the data analysis, the intent usually is not to identify predisposition to diseases in individual subjects or families, and as such usually are allowed some flexibility in consent form requirements. Investigators for studies like these should be encouraged to perform data collection and genetic testing in an anonymous manner to protect subjects against further unintended harm.

2. *Studies involving the detection of mutations in one or more specified gene(s) known to harbor causative mutations in individuals affected with a certain disease.*

For example, a study that examines the association of disease severity with specific mutations in the gene for cystic fibrosis (CFTR gene) in known CF patients falls into this category. Generally speaking, this kind of study does involve genetic testing. However, prior to genetic testing, the subjects already have been determined to have the genetic disorder based on clinical grounds, such that the incremental "risk" associated with genetic testing in these studies is small. In other words, since the genetic test does not reveal a new genetic predisposition and would confirm only the disease status of the patient, it would change little of the psychosocial makeup of the subject.

3. *Studies involving the detection of mutations or DNA polymorphisms in one or more gene regions in which a gene responsible for the disease is suspected to reside. These studies are generally known as "genetic mapping" studies.*

This kind of study generally focuses on patients known to have the disease under study, as well as their affected or unaffected family members. The clinical information (i.e., disease status and family history) is therefore used to establish that a specific gene is indeed the cause for the disease, or that the causative gene(s) resides in a certain gene region. Even though these studies often involve DNA testing, they do not involve "genetic testing" per se.

There are two points to keep in mind about studies of this kind. First, to ascertain the disease status of every family member, it is not unusual that individuals formerly thought to be unaffected may become diagnosed with the disease. This may represent either a "risk" or a "benefit," depending on the particpant's perspective. Second, as the study progresses, new findings may arise that could lead one to conclude that the causative gene(s) has indeed been identified, and from that point on any testing of a new study participant with respect to that gene would constitute true "genetic testing." This point emphasizes the ongoing assessment of what is known about the disease under study and the importance of expert consultation over the course of the study.

4. *Studies involving known mutations or DNA polymorphisms in one or more gene regions either known or suspected to predispose to a disease. These types of studies are often referred to as "genetic association studies."*

An important distinction is made here between genetic variations that cause disease and those that predispose a person to a disease or disability. For example, mutations in the CFTR gene cause cystic fibrosis, whereas having two copies of the apoe4 gene greatly increases the likelihood for an individual to develop Alzheimer's disease, but this may not happen.

There is some confusion about genetic association studies because, to some, it seems that as long as the testing is not diagnostic of the disease state, it should not be considered "genetic testing." However, it should be clear that testing for a genetic predisposition to a disease does constitute genetic testing.

Association studies are the most common approach to identifying genetic contributions to common complex disorders. Depending on the status of knowledge about these various genetic contributions, and whether subjects with known, suspected or unknown disease status are involved, considerations similar to those discussed in categories two and three above may be relevant.

An Example

The above categorizations of genetic studies are not mutually exclusive. The following is a slightly more complicated example that illustrates the complexity of the issues. A disease is caused by mutations in one of at least two genes, one of which is already identified (Gene A), but the remaining one (Gene B) is yet to be discovered. A study is designed to find (or "map") Gene B. To do this, one would have to collect blood samples from individuals affected with the disease, as well from their affected and unaffected family members. In order to show that the affected individual has a mutation in Gene B, you would have to show that the disease is not caused by a mutation in Gene A. Therefore, genetic testing of Gene A is necessary. This testing of Gene A is considered genetic testing, although the risk associated with the testing is low because the subject already is known to have the disease.

When an affected patient tests negative for mutation in Gene A, the patient and his or her family will be used to map Gene B. This part of the study does not constitute genetic testing because the location of Gene B still is hypothetical. A study like this, which is not uncommon, involves genetic studies of both categories two and three above. If the study is completed and Gene B has been found, any testing of subsequent subjects for Gene B also constitutes true "genetic testing" (Category two).

Suppose that after the gene mapping study is completed, it is found that a significant number of patients with the disease do not have severe and deleterious mutations in either Gene A or Gene B. Instead, these patients have mild variants of Genes A and/or B, which by themselves would not cause the disease but when coupled with variants of an additional number of genes, say C, D and E, the disease will be manifested under the right environmental input (e.g., poor diet or lack of exercise). In this case, testing patients with the disease for Genes A and B falls in Categories two and three as described above, and in Category four as well, depending on what is currently known about the gene's relation to the disease. This example highlights how the evolving nature of new information may change how a genetic study must be assessed.

Behavioral Genetic Studies

A special kind of genetic study concerns an individual's behavioral characteristics. The behaviors being studied may range from those traditionally considered to be medical problems (such as schizophrenia or manic-depressive illness) to those more recently accepted as partly organic in nature (such as drug addiction or alcoholism) and those that may be considered "normal" variations in the general population (such as personality traits, sexual orientation or intelligence). Many of these behavioral characteristics carry a social stigma and therefore deserve special attention with respect to confidentiality and many other consent issues. The sensitivity of behavioral issues is particularly heightened when a "genetic" component also is being examined. For example, a study that tries to determine the genetic predisposition to drug addiction in an "unaffected" individual may have significant impact on an individual's self-image, social status, employability and insurability. Therefore, behavioral genetics studies deserve a high degree of alertness when being designed and reviewed. A Certificate of Confidentiality should always be considered to further protect subjects against forced disclosure of study data concerning individual subjects (see Chapter 6).

Special Considerations in Protocols and Consent Forms

The basic principles of human subject protection embodied in the Belmont Report apply to genetic research. As a result, the usual protocol and consent form elements required for genetic research are similar to those for other human research. However, because genetic information is inherently different than other personal information in many ways, special considerations are needed for some protocol and consent form items.

Risks and Benefits

For most genetic studies, the physical risk to individuals is minimal, often involving no more than a blood draw, cheek scraping or use of biological tissues obtained in the course of clinical care. However, the risks that are psychosocial or financial in nature are far more insidious. For gene mapping or association studies, clarification of disease status through clinical evaluation or genetic testing as part of the research may result in some individuals being diagnosed with the disease or found to be at a significantly increased risk of developing the disease. To some, this information constitutes a risk in that it is unexpected and undesired and may have an impact on their self image, insurability or employability. To other individuals, however, this may represent a benefit because it may lead to early treatment, preventive care and knowledge about future genetic risk to the patients and their families. In this case, the study protocol should include some provision for referral to genetic counseling and clinical management services, should a patient receive a previously unknown diagnosis. The possibility of false-positive and false-negative results in making the diagnosis also may need to be addressed.

For some multi-site research studies, the genetic testing is performed at a site different from the one at which the patients were recruited. Some of these studies would not provide genetic testing results to individuals despite providing such information to the principal investigator at the recruitment site. Occasionally, this results in an ethical dilemma for the principal investigators at the recruitment site, because they may feel a professional obligation to inform the patients of a potential risk to their health. This is particularly true in studies in which the principal investigators are physicians and the participants are their patients. In fact, the American Society of Human Genetics has issued clear guidelines specifying that physicians have a duty to inform patients they have previously seen of potential risks to their health due to newly available information. This may compel some investigators to regret the pledge not to provide genetic testing results to their patients. Because of this, in the initial design of a genetic research study investigators should consider this possibility carefully, and not simply decide against providing genetic testing results out of expediency.

Identifiers, Anonymity and Confidentiality

Genetic research adds complexity to the definition of what is generally considered "identifying" information. As a result, the protection of confidentiality may require one to address a number of questions in addition to those asked in non-genetic studies.

In general, information such as names, addresses, medical record numbers, social security numbers, telephone numbers, fingerprints, photographs and video recordings are considered complete or partial identifiers. As illustrated by the extensive use of DNA testing in forensic medicine, one might argue that DNA embodies the ultimate identifier of an individual, as suggested by such a term as the "DNA fingerprint" of an individual. As yet, however, most individuals cannot be readily identified through DNA testing results because there is no extensive bank of DNA data on individuals to make it a truly good "identifier." In other words, the DNA "code" on any given individual may not exist or is not easily accessible. This may be different for some participants who, due to their profession or legal status, may have information concerning their DNA stored in an electronic database, such as criminals or armed services personnel. Therefore, genetic research involving genetic testing needs to be carefully evaluated with respect to this issue.

For rare genetic diseases, a positive disease status often is, by itself, a powerful identifier. For example, a participant who is the only patient ever to be diagnosed with a certain disease at a medical center usually will be known by virtue of his or her diagnosis. Thus even "anonymous" study records on a participant with this rare diagnosis actually may be identifying information. In family studies, the specific pattern of different kinds of relatives in a pedigree drawing may betray the identity of an individual, especially when linked to the disease being studied. This is common in genetic mapping studies involving large pedigrees. For example, a subject with myotonic dystrophy, who has two affected sisters and one affected brother out of a total of 10 siblings, sometimes can be readily identified within a support group community. Thus, when genetic research studies are published in medical journals, there may be a significant likelihood family and friends reading the articles may be able to identify the individuals who have been studied, even though no names or other obvious identifiers have been given. This could be a particularly difficult problem if the published report contains sensitive information not previously known to friends and family, such as non-paternity, previous abortions or history of drug addiction.

In general, it is very difficult to maintain confidentiality of genetic testing results among family members participating in a genetic study as a group. Sometimes the genetic testing results of one individual may lead one to draw certain conclusions about the results of another individual. There can be significant coercion concerning participation in a study and sharing of testing results in an extended family. Investigators and reviewers of study protocols must be sensitive to these issues. In addition, the complex and sometimes unpredictable relationships among family members make it important to protect against disclosure of genetic testing information through legal proceedings. One is encouraged to seriously consider obtaining a Certificate of Confidentiality to protect against such disclosure.

Data and Tissue Storage

Any genetic testing protocol should prompt a list of questions concerning tissue and data storage for future research. It is important to explicitly mention in the consent form the duration of tissue and data storage, how such tissue and data will be used in the future and whether such uses will be limited to studying only diseases for which the tissue was obtained. The issues of whether and how future genetic testing results will be conveyed to study participants also will need to be addressed. Often, tissue samples and data may be distributed to investigators outside of the study during future research. It is important the specific points about confidentiality be addressed.

The Consent Process and Genetic Counseling

The complexity of the issues concerning genetic research can make consent forms extremely difficult to comprehend. For this reason, some have suggested genetic counseling should be offered to participants before or during the consent process. While some states including New York have made this an explicit requirement for research involving genetic testing, in other, more permissive settings, this should be an issue for IRBs to consider. There is no generally agreed upon definition of who is qualified to provide genetic research counseling, other than that such genetic counseling should be provided by a "professional," which can be interpreted to include the investigators or support personnel for the study. How such genetic counseling must be documented also is unclear and as such is left to local investigators and IRBs.

Points to Consider

It is impossible to have a single protocol or consent form template that can cover all kinds of genetic research. In general, however, a list of questions must be considered when designing and reviewing genetic research protocols, in addition to those usually considered for any human subject studies:

- Does the genetic research protocol involve genetic testing? If so, does the genetic testing establish a cause or predisposition to a disease?

- Is the disease status of the participants undergoing genetic testing established, unclear or unknown?

- Will the results of genetic testing be available to the principal investigator at the site of the study?

- Will the results of genetic testing be available to the participants?

- If the results of genetic testing will not be available to the participants, but are available to the principal investigator at the study site, will the non-communication of results to the participant infringe on the ethical duty of the investigator to inform participants of potentially serious harm, particularly if the investigator is a physician and the participant is his or her patient?

- If the results of genetic testing are available to the participants, will they constitute a risk (e.g., unintended result, false-positive diagnosis, loss of insurability and employment potential) or a benefit (e.g., early diagnosis resulting in early treatment or prevention, determination of future risk to the individual or family)?

- If an individual receives a previously unknown or unsuspected diagnosis as a result of participating in the study, are there any provisions for referral to genetic counseling or to a clinical management service?

- Who else will have access to the genetic testing results?

- Will other partially identifying information, such as that concerning an individual's genetic variation, disease status and family history be disclosed during publication of research data?

- Will a Certificate of Confidentiality be needed to increase the assurance that the participants' privacy will be protected against disclosure?

- How long will tissue and/or data be retained? Where will tissue and data be stored? Will tissue and data be discarded at the conclusion of the current study? Or will tissue and data be retained for future research, including genetic testing?

- Will there be secondary distribution of tissue and/or data and how will participants' confidentiality be protected?

- How will the results of future genetic testing be handled with respect to the above issues?

- Will genetic counseling be necessary prior to a participant signing the consent document? Who will provide such genetic counseling and what are his or her qualifications for doing so?

- When withdrawing from participation in a study, can patients request that samples be destroyed or anonymized or require data not be used?

Gene Transfer Research

Clinical gene transfer research has grown significantly since the first human recombinant DNA experiment in 1980, particularly in the area of cancer clinical trials. To date, the vast majority of human gene transfer protocols registered with the NIH involve the use of gene transfer in an oncology-related diagnosis and have primarily been phase I and phase I/II trials.

Interest in human gene transfer (HGT) research, by both the scientific community and the public, has grown, with an increase in both knowledge and misunderstandings about disease-related genes and associated treatment strategies. This research has raised uniquely complex scientific, medical, ethical and social issues that warrant special monitoring.

This section focuses on the regulatory and informed consent issues specific to gene transfer. The roles of the NIH, Recombinant DNA Advisory Committee (also known as RAC) and the FDA in the oversight of HGT studies are briefly discussed. The role of the Institutional Biosafety Committee (IBC) and some special consent considerations associated with gene transfer are summarized.

Background

Since the advent of genetic engineering over 25 years ago, recombinant DNA technology has made possible the manufacture of therapeutic proteins, such as human insulin and human growth hormone, the sequencing of the human genome and the ability to discern the genetic basis of many diseases. Gene transfer, however, is a relatively recent and still experimental clinical application of recombinant DNA technology that has captured the public's attention—partly because of its promise, but also because of the ethical and social implications of this research.

Gene transfer is a technique to substitute absent or faulty genes causing diseases with working genes, so that cells make the correct enzyme or protein. The transfer is accomplished by carrying the gene fragment to the cells by use of "vectors" (usually of viral or bacterial origin). Gene transfer has been limited to somatic cells in contrast to germline cells, which would have the potential to affect not only the individual being treated but also future offspring. The ethical concern (changing the genetic pool of the entire human species) and certain technical considerations make it unlikely germline experiments will be tried on humans in the near future.

Human gene transfer research, as with clinical research in general, is not without risk. Efforts to minimize and manage risks both known and unforeseen are paramount. The unexpected death of Jesse Gelsinger, a young man enrolled in a University of Pennsylvania gene transfer study, underscored the need for constant vigilance by researchers, federal agencies, IRBs and IBCs in the oversight and conduct of clinical gene transfer research. While IRBs exist to protect the rights and well-being of trial participants, IBCs have evolved to play a role in protecting the public from the potentially broader consequences of gene transfer.

All clinical gene transfer trials, regardless of funding source or research site, are subject to FDA regulations (21 CFR 312) as biological products. The FDA has statutory authority to allow a gene transfer clinical study to proceed after review or, if necessary, to place a study on clinical hold to ensure the safety of participants. The FDA has issued a "Points to Consider" document (available on the FDA web site) directed primarily at the aspects of good manufacturing practices. FDA requirements for clinical trials involving gene transfer essentially are no different than for other biologics, with the focus primarily on sponsor requirements.

> **All gene transfer trials are subject to FDA regulations as biological products.**

Additionally, researchers conducting basic or applied gene transfer research—either funded by the NIH or carried out at an institution that receives NIH support for recombinant DNA research of any type—are also expected to comply with the NIH Guidelines. Appendix M of the NIH Guidelines, also known as the "Points to Consider in the Design and Submissions of Protocols for the Transfer of rDNA Molecules Into One or More Human Subjects" specifically addresses the requirements for human gene transfer. It is intended to assist the principal investigator, the institution, the IBC, the biological safety officer and the IRB in determining safeguards that should be implemented for these studies. Failure to comply with the requirements set forth in the NIH Guidelines can result in the limitation, suspension or withdrawal of all NIH support to the institution. The NIH also can impose a requirement for prior NIH approval of any or all recombinant DNA projects at an institution.

Privately funded gene transfer research conducted at a site that does not receive federal funds for recombinant DNA research is not mandated to follow NIH Guidelines, but many sponsors and investigative sites choose to voluntarily comply because of the enhanced human subject protections outlined by the Guidelines.

Each institution, through the IBC, is responsible for ensuring all recombinant DNA research conducted at, or sponsored by, that institution is conducted in accordance with NIH Guidelines. The questions the IBC asks the investigator include scientific issues such as how the vector construct was prepared and how the agent will be contained. Additionally, the IBC also is concerned with how the consent process will be conducted. In other words, the IBC must address not only protection issues for the public at large, but also protections of the individual research subject.

> **The IBC is responsible for ensuring recombinant DNA research is conducted according to NIH Guidelines.**

The roles of the IBC and IRB overlap when considering human subject protections. While many IBCs have minimal experience with clinical settings, many IRBs have little knowledge of the technical issues associated with gene transfer. Therefore, it is essential communication exists between these committees.

Some general concepts investigators, IBCs and IRBs should keep in mind for consent forms associated with gene transfer trials include:

- What measures have been taken to minimize the risks of transmission to non-participants?

- If transmission were to occur, what would be the consequences?

- The use of the terms "therapy/treatment/drug" should be avoided; "agent" is preferred

- The use of recombinant DNA should be clearly stated

- The potential for recombinant DNA remaining in the body should be addressed

- What are the risks for the vector to activate an oncogene or inactivate a tumor suppressor gene leading to vector-related malignancy?

- Are there any special issues related to this gene transfer trial, such as uncertainty associated with short- or long-term risks and benefits or the possibility of media attention?

- The possibility that subjects may be contacted for lifelong follow-up should be clear (Appendix M, III, B, 2, b)

- Use of contraception should be explicitly stated for both males and females

- Potential need for confinement should be outlined

- Potential exposure for family members should be noted
- Risk of media exposure should be explained
- Subjects should be informed that an autopsy will be requested.

Gene transfer, if successful, will constitute a revolution in medical science. However, gene transfer research has raised uniquely complex scientific, medical, ethical and social issues that warrant special monitoring. Striking the balance between protections of trial participants and communities while advancing promising research will continue to be a challenging task.

CHAPTER TWELVE

Special Ethical Concerns in Clinical Research

At the conclusion of this chapter, readers will be able to:

- Discuss the ethical issues with the use of placebos in clinical research.

- Describe guidelines for using placebos in clinical trials.

- Describe the use, roles and responsibilities of DMCs and how the DMC interacts with IRBs, investigators, sponsors and external regulatory bodies.

- Describe the process by which DMCs make recommendations to modify the conduct of ongoing clinical trials.

The Use of Placebo

The fifth revision of the Declaration of Helsinki included a principle that stated, "The benefits, risks, burdens and effectiveness of a new method should be tested against the best current prophylactic, diagnostic and therapeutic method." This seemed to preclude the use of placebo in clinical research whenever standard treatment is available. Although this statement was subsequently clarified to not preclude all uses of placebo, it intensified the long-standing discussion of and concern about placebo use and the ethical review of clinical research.

A central ethical question with the use of placebo is whether the patients in placebo control groups of a research study are being unfairly denied a medical benefit. The concern becomes even more important when the use of placebo might imply the risk of irreversible harm or major discomfort. On the other hand, the degree of placebo response in certain conditions and the effectiveness of comparator treatments raise questions about the validity of the use of standard treatments as comparators.

Internationally sponsored research using placebo in developing countries has raised concerns regarding justice and the relationship between the welfare of individual patients and the benefit to society. Some of these studies would have been considered unethical in most developed countries, but were justified on the basis of a different local standard of care. This raises the ques-

> **Use of placebo dilemma: potential patient harm and the scientific validity of the study.**

tion of whether ethics require practices in all parts of the world be identical.

The range of opinions regarding the use of placebo in clinical research varies between two extreme positions:

1. The insistence on placebo-controlled trials, which considers that placebo is the preferred comparator unless it exposes the patient to death or irreversible, severe damage, and provided that the patient consents to participate and tolerate the risks and discomforts of the investigation.

2. The categorical objection to the use of placebo, which maintains that whenever standard treatment exists the use of placebo is unethical, and in such situations, research treatments should be compared with standard treatments.

All parties agree that the use of placebo is unacceptable in life-threatening diseases or in case of potential irreversible damage when there is effective treatment available, but the dilemma persists as to whether it is ethical to deprive patients of standard treatment and expose them to a lesser degree to risks and discomforts. Some bioethicists agree that if placebo is required for scientific validity in a research study, this constitutes one ethical argument in favor, though not the full justification, of the use of placebo. An appeal to the patient's autonomy is another justification for the use of placebo. This argument relies heavily upon the disclosure of the risks of placebo in the process of informed consent; however, some believe this just transfers the ethical burden to the patient. The ethical acceptability of disclosure as a justification for the use of placebo depends on the patient's capacity to understand the implications of participating in a research study.

Federal regulations and international guidelines rely on independent ethical review to help ensure research volunteers are not exposed to unnecessary risks including those presented by the use of placebo. They also recommend additional safeguards be taken in research involving vulnerable populations, so studies that have been judged ethical for autonomous adult patients may not be acceptable for children or people with mental incapacities. Strictly speaking, because placebo is inactive, it does not exert any physiological effect. Patients' expectations of the encounter with the healing setting (doctor or drug), however, have been shown to produce objective signs of improvement in several medical conditions that, in the absence of a placebo arm, could be inaccurately attributed to the research treatment. The placebo arm also is used to measure the side effect profile of the treatment under study. The magnitude of placebo response can be measured only by comparing the experimental group with a placebo-controlled group.

On the other hand, the validity of the use of an active comparator depends heavily on the efficacy of the treatment for a certain condition. Unless the efficacy of a standard treatment has been consistently and unequivocally proven, the omission of a placebo arm in the evaluation of a research treatment may be disadvantageous. For scientific validity, the choice of active comparator would eventually have to be supported by previous studies against placebo; however, limitations to comparability will persist, since placebo response for the same condition may vary geographically and historically depending on the population under study, the medical care environment and the assessment methods. Also, the definition of standard treatment may not be universal, and research outcomes using different local practice comparators would be difficult to interpret and compare.

The use of placebo in clinical research has several purposes:

1. To measure subjective response to the research treatment caused by the patients' expectations of improvement as opposed to therapeutic effect

2. To differentiate improvement attributable to the study treatment from improvement due to other factors, such as spontaneous remission, diet, local care and supplements

3. To determine the baseline (no treatment) improvement

4. To distinguish the adverse events related to the investigational treatment from those caused by chance or concomitant treatments, and from complications of the disease

5. To make the volunteers in the control group indistinguishable from those who receive the experimental treatment and, thus, to blind the assessment of therapeutic effects and adverse events

6. To help pursue the possibility that while a new drug might be less effective on average than the standard, the new drug is at least better than nothing and some individuals might find the new drug better than the standard.

The complexity and variety of ethical and scientific concerns regarding the use of placebo requires that its ethical acceptability be determined on a case-by-case basis. The assessment of the risks and benefits of placebo use versus use of standard treatment is a required step for investigators and IRBs. Although ethical principles are deemed to be universal, potential risks and benefits apply to a concrete time and population, and the ethical acceptability of study designs, including those that use placebo, differs depending on the particular circumstances of each research study.

Points to Consider

To facilitate and systematize the ethical review of placebo use, algorithms and guidelines have been published. In general, they include the following aspects:

The Scientific Justification for the Use of Placebo

References to the expected spontaneous remission in diseases such as viral respiratory tract infections or bacterial conjunctivitis and the magnitude of the "placebo effect" in conditions such as depression and anxiety are valuable to evaluate the scientific need for the use of placebo. The "state of the art" in the use of active comparators, the effectiveness and consistency of the standard treatment and the existence of "gold standards" of efficacy should also be addressed. Additionally, the therapeutic role of concurrent interventions that constitute "standard of care" ought to be considered.

The Evaluation of the Potential Risks of Placebo Use as Compared to the Risks and Benefits of Standard Treatment

The risks of irreversible harm or severe discomfort due to the use of placebo are unacceptable if proven therapeutic methods exist. Less severe risks should be evaluated relative to potential benefits. The risks and benefits of the active treatment should be stated.

Risk Management in the Research Protocol

Per federal regulations and ethical standards, the inherent risks of placebo use and other research procedures should be minimized in the research protocol. For instance, high-risk subjects, such as diabetic patients with a history of ketoacidosis, should not be enrolled in placebo-controlled trials of oral hypoglycemia. The use of placebo should be restricted to the minimum time required to show medical benefit, and adequate risk monitoring and stopping rules should be in place to identify and manage deterioration in early stages. Should there be a risk of an acute crisis, as in asthma, or the possibility of severe pain, rescue medication should be available.

Whether the Use of Placebo and its Potential Risks have been Adequately Addressed in the Consent Form

Once the risk/benefit assessment has determined that the research study does not expose patients to excessive, unnecessary risks, the investigator should ensure that the use of placebo and the risks and burdens it implies are appropriately described in the consent form. Any change in the standard of care that might occur during the conduct of the study and might affect the willingness of the patient to remain in the study should be promptly communicated to the patient. The inclusion of overly reassuring language should be avoided. The patient must be adequately informed of the risks involved in participating in a placebo-controlled study.

Cases

Case #1
Newly depressed patients were recruited for an eight-week, double-blind study of an investigational antidepressant versus placebo. Treatment-resistant, suicidal and severely depressed subjects were excluded. Assessment visits were planned at weeks one, two, four, six and eight, with follow-up visits at weeks 10 and 12. The IRB requested discontinuation criteria for relapse or deterioration be clearly defined and emergency treatment be available. The protocol was approved once amended.

Case #2
A double-blind, 12-week study of an investigational inhaled antiasthmatic steroid versus placebo in mild-to-moderate persistent asthma in teenagers. The parents' permission and the patient's assent would be obtained, and the personal physician would be informed of the patient's participation in the study. After washout, spirometric parameters would be evaluated and high-risk subjects excluded. A personal peak flow meter would be provided for daily monitoring of the expiratory flow. Rescue medication (a beta2-adrenergic bronchodilator) would be available, and discontinuation criteria for clinical deterioration were clearly defined. The IRB approved the protocol.

Case #3
Patients undergoing chemotherapy with the potential to develop mucositis would be enrolled in a double-blind, placebo-controlled study. If they developed mucositis grade ≥3, they would be randomized to receive, in addition to standard mucositis care, the investigational drug or placebo. The IRB approved the study.

In conclusion, the use of placebo in clinical research is ethically acceptable if: (1) placebo is necessary for scientific reasons, (2) the use of placebo does not expose the patient to excessive or unnecessary risks, and (3) the patient is adequately informed of the risks and burdens of placebo use and freely consents to participate. Placebo use with vulnerable patients also may be ethically acceptable if they receive additional appropriate protection and the corresponding permission and assent signatures, as applicable, are obtained.

Data Monitoring Committees

Introduction

When researchers think of the responsibility for human subject protection in clinical trials, they often think of the Institutional Review Board (IRB). The fact is that human subject protection in clinical trials is shared among the IRB, the principal investigator, clinical trial sponsors and oversight boards/committees. One such committee is the Data Monitoring Committee (DMC). This chapter provides an overview of the federal guidelines relating to DMCs, when and how they should be formed and the responsibilities of the DMC, investigator, IRB, trial sponsor and regulatory bodies charged with oversight of clinical research.

DMCs Defined

A DMC is a group of individuals with clinical expertise in the areas pertinent to the disease state and treatments being studied in controlled clinical trials. DMCs typically also include a biostatistician who possesses a background and knowledge relevant to the conduct of clinical trials and analysis of clinical trial data, and they also may include an ethicist. As a group, the DMC acts as an independent review/advisory board whose primary mission is to measure and report on the continuing safety of current research volunteers as well as patients who have not yet enrolled. The DMC accomplishes this through meeting on a regular basis and reviewing the accumulating data in an ongoing clinical trial. Through this process, the DMC also is assessing the continuing validity and scientific merit of the trial.

Background and History of DMCs

National Institutes of Health (NIH) Sponsored Studies

The use of DMCs was first established in the early 1960s, primarily in large, multi-center trials in which the study endpoints were to assess improved survival or risk of major morbidity. NIH established these committees to conduct in-process monitoring of these studies to ensure the safety of the trial participants. Until 2001, DMCs were largely referred to as Data Safety Monitoring Boards (DSMBs). The name was changed to coincide with the proposed wording from the International Conference on Harmonization. This section outlines the history and evolution of significant regulations that form the basis for both current and future use of DMCs.

- In 1979, the NIH Clinical Trials Committee issued recommendations that "every clinical trial should have provision for data and safety monitoring." The NIH acknowledged that in some cases, the principal investigator (PI) might be expected to perform the monitoring function.

- In June 1998, the NIH issued a policy for data and safety monitoring. The policy was a result of the Office of Extramural Research's Committee on Clinical Trial Monitoring recommendation that "all trials, even those that pose little likelihood of harm, should consider an external monitoring body." It stated that all clinical trials require monitoring, and that the method and degree of monitoring required should be related to the degree of risk involved.

- Additional guidance was issued in June 1999. This guidance directed that all multi-site trials with data monitoring boards must forward summary reports of adverse events to IRBs. The guidance specifically addressed the need for communication between the DMC and the IRB.

- The most recent guidance on data and safety monitoring was issued in March 2006. The purpose of this guidance is to assist clinical trial sponsors in determining when a DMC might be useful for study monitoring and how such committees should operate.

FDA-regulated Studies

In March 2006, the FDA issued the *Guideline for Clinical Trial Sponsors on the Establishment and Operation of Clinical Trial Data Monitoring Committees*. The guidance document was intended to assist sponsors in determining when a DMC may be necessary and explain how the agency believes such committees should operate. Prior to this guidance, FDA guidelines did not require the use of DMCs except for those studies that allowed the informed consent requirement to be waived, i.e., studies conducted in emergency situations. Further, it should be noted that the references in this guidance confer DMC responsibility on any individual or group to which the sponsor has delegated relevant management responsibility (CROs, for example). This is the first FDA document to thoroughly explore DMCs and provide the public with the agency's current thinking on this topic.

When a DMC is Needed

All clinical trials require safety monitoring, but not all trials require a DMC. The FDA draft guidance specifically states DMCs should be established for controlled trials in which mortality and major morbidity serve as the primary or secondary end points. Other major factors to consider regarding the establishment of a DMC are outlined below. Patient safety is of the utmost importance. The following bulleted points are presented in a "points-to-consider" format to allow investigators and sponsors to deliberate the necessity of establishing a DMC:

Patient Safety

- Is mortality or major morbidity an endpoint?

- Would positive or negative results during the study require termination for ethical reasons?

- Is there little knowledge regarding the safety of the intervention (drug/ device) or is there knowledge of safety concerns (potential toxicity)?

- Is the targeted study population fragile, e.g., elderly, children, pregnant women, for whom there may be an increased risk?

- Is the study a large, multi-center trial, with a long duration, in which subjects would have greater exposure possibly resulting in adverse events that would not as easily be identified in single-center studies with shorter durations?

The FDA guidance suggests that if the answer to any or all of the above is yes, then the use of a DMC may be warranted.

> **A DMC should be established in trials in which mortality and morbidity serve as endpoints.**

Practicality

- Is the study a short-term trial in which a DMC would not have adequate time to respond?
- If the study is a short-term trial in which patient safety is a concern, are there mechanisms in place for a DMC to be notified quickly of unexpected events/results?

The guidance recognizes that many clinical trials evaluate interventions to relieve symptoms. These studies are usually of short duration and smaller than major outcome studies. DMCs usually have not been established to monitor these types of trials.

Scientific Validity

- Is the study of long duration over which changes in the understanding of the disease process, the target population or new treatment discoveries would warrant changes to the trial as it progresses?

The guideline recognizes that a DMC may be useful in that it is correctly positioned to monitor changes to a trial, over time, in an unbiased and patient-protective manner. Major implications could arise, however, if this process is not carefully managed, i.e., sponsor exposure to unblinded, interim data. This issue is also addressed in the guideline.

Composition and Administration of DMCs

Committee Composition

A tremendous amount of responsibility is placed on the DMC in terms of its power to make recommendations based on the data it receives from the trial itself, as well as from external sources. Usually the trial sponsor or trial steering committee appoints DMC members. The FDA guidance suggests that the following factors be used to consider the selection of DMC members:

- Relevant expertise (clinical specialty, biostatistician, pharmacologist, toxicologist, bioethicist)

- Previous DMC experience

- Clinical trial experience

- In all cases, DMC members should be free of conflicts of interest or any perceived conflicts that can be financial, scientific or intellectual in nature.

Administration

Each DMC should establish procedures up front on how it will operate. Factors to consider are:

- Meeting schedule/frequency (based on expected rates of accrual/risks to patients)

- Meeting structure—open session to allow investigator and sponsor attendance versus closed session in which blinded and confidential information is discussed

- Format of the interim reports that the sponsor provides to the DMC

- Statistical methods to be used for the interim analyses.

DMC Responsibilities

The main responsibility of a DMC is to review accumulating data from an ongoing clinical trial on a regular basis. After thorough analysis of the accumulated data, the DMC may advise the sponsor and/or IRB regarding the continuing safety of patients in the trial and of those yet to be recruited, as well as the continuing validity and scientific safety of the trial.

> **The DMC is responsible for recommending trial termination when patient safety is jeopardized.**

The DMC Accomplishes this by:

- Safety monitoring

  - Interim review of adverse events in each arm of the study

  - Making judgments on early termination of a trial when based on the types and extent of adverse events if the risks outweigh the benefits.

- Monitoring for effectiveness

  - It is important in studies with serious outcomes that any treatment advance is made available as soon as possible but only when based on the predetermined statistical monitoring plan

- It is just as important to terminate a study when the predetermined benefit has no chance of being achieved.

- Monitoring study conduct
  - Reviewing and assuring that rates of recruitment are adequate, when appropriate
  - Assessing whether eligibility requirements are being met
  - Reviewing any excessive protocol violations
  - Verifying completeness and timeliness of the data accumulated
  - Evaluating excessive dropout rates (could affect interpretation of study results).

- Monitoring external data
  - Reviewing results of related studies, which may affect the design of the ongoing study or its continuation.

- Making recommendations
  - The primary responsibility of a DMC is to make recommendations to the sponsor and/or IRB regarding the continuation of the study. These recommendations could include continuation with modification, temporary suspension of enrollment or intervention.
  - Recommendations, supported by a rationale, should be documented in a clear, concise manner for review by the sponsor, IRB or regulatory agency.

- Maintenance of records
  - Keep minutes of all meetings and issue the sponsor a report based on the minutes
  - Minutes should contain two parts, depending on confidential information (unblinded comparative data) being discussed, i.e., the open and closed parts of the meetings are kept separate.

Regulatory Safety Reporting Requirements

Studies conducted under an Investigational New Drug application (IND) or Investigational Device Exemption (IDE) are subject to safety reporting requirements. These requirements include the reporting of serious unexpected events to the FDA by the sponsor. There may be instances in which a DMC may detect a greater frequency of serious adverse events in one arm of a controlled study. This finding, reported to the sponsor as part of a recommendation to modify the study, would be considered serious and unexpected, and the sponsor would be required to report this to the FDA as well as to all other study investigators.

Investigator Responsibilities

In studies in which DMCs are involved, the investigator is still responsible for identifying potential adverse events experienced by patients and reporting them to the sponsor.

When the investigator is the sponsor of the clinical research study, the investigator assumes all of the roles of sponsor in addition to those of the investigator. Refer to "Sponsor responsibilities" below for the sponsor investigator responsibilities when a DMC is involved.

IRB Responsibilities

After its initial approval of studies, the IRB is responsible for reviewing all available information from both the study site and external sources to ensure the continued acceptability of the trial. The IRB may take actions based on the recommendations of the DMC to the sponsor.

Sponsor Responsibilities

The trial sponsor is responsible for thoroughly reviewing the recommendations of the DMC and taking appropriate actions regarding modifications or termination of the study. In addition to determining when a DMC is needed and the appointment of individuals to serve on the DMC, the following procedures usually are undertaken by the sponsor:

- Appointing the committee chair

- Establishing procedures to assess potential conflicts of interests of potential members

- Ensuring the confidentiality of the interim data analyses

- Establishing or approving DMC Standard Operating Procedures (SOPs), i.e., meeting schedules, format of reports, statistical methods

- Submitting to the FDA all DMC meeting records and interim reports

- Notifying the FDA and responsible IRBs of any recommendations or requests made by the DMC regarding the safety of the participants

- Consulting with the FDA before accessing interim data, terminating the study or modifying the protocol (could affect the validity of the study).

Other Oversight Groups

There may be additional individuals or groups that assume or share the responsibility of clinical trial monitoring or oversight.

Clinical Trial Steering Committees

A sponsor may appoint a steering committee to design the study, ensure the quality of the study conduct and write the final study report. The committee usually comprises investigators, sponsor representatives and experts not directly involved in the study. If a steering committee is in place, the sponsor may have the DMC communicate directly with the committee.

Site Monitoring

Monitoring of study sites usually is conducted by the sponsor, either by the sponsor's clinical research associates (CRAs) or by a CRO retained by the sponsor. NIH Institute Centers also perform site monitoring. Sites are monitored for adherence to Good Clinical Practices (GCPs), which include following the protocol, informed consent compliance, reporting of all adverse events, using appropriate source documents (case histories) and data accuracy (case report form entries).

CHAPTER THIRTEEN

Participant Recruitment and Retention in Clinical Trials

At the conclusion of this chapter, readers will be able to:

- Identify special populations for inclusion in clinical trials.

- Describe a variety of recruitment methods and the potential benefits and disadvantages of each.

- Define the IRB role in the review of advertising materials.

- Understand the need to set realistic recruitment and retention goals for clinical trials.

Introduction

In 2010, pharmaceutical and biotechnology companies spent more than $60 billion on research and development, including a large amount for clinical studies.[1] The average cost of developing one new drug has increased to over $1.24 billion, and the development process time from the pre-clinical stage to FDA approval averages about seven years.[1] Around the world, more than 80,000 study sites a year are involved in carrying out research, based on 5,000 to 6,000 unique protocols. More than one million volunteers will participate in these trials. The largest numbers of volunteers are needed for phase III programs.

Given the enormous development costs, companies obviously want to speed the process as much as possible, allowing for more marketing time before their patent protection for the product expires. The timely enrollment of appropriate participants into trials is critical to managing the timelines for a development program. Finding, enrolling and retaining study participants are some of the largest and costliest challenges facing clinical research professionals today.

The majority (nearly 86%) of clinical trials fail to enroll the desired number of patients within the contract specified enrollment period. This failure rate is up from 80% of trials in the late 1990s.[1] Clearly, these enrollment delays result in significant direct development costs for the study sponsor and, even more importantly, they delay the introduction of promising new therapies for patients' unmet needs. Recruitment efforts fail for a number of reasons including poor protocol design, conflicting clinical trials for similar treatments, new and competing products becoming available on the market, workload of the study investigator and staff and negative public perception of and lack of trust in clinical research.

> **The investigator should be realistic when determining the feasibility of recruiting participants prior to conducting a study.**

Education of Potential Participants

One of the key components of successful recruitment stems from educated patients who understand clinical trials, their roles in the clinical trial and how they may or may not personally benefit from participation. Educating potential participants takes time, resources and patience.

In past years, there have been reports of negative occurrences in clinical trials, including deaths and injuries, undermining public confidence in research and making it more difficult for investigators to recruit participants. Ultimately it is the investigator's responsibility to address any safety concerns a potential participant may have. This is best done by ensuring the study design does everything possible to protect the safety and welfare of research participants.

Why Patients Join Clinical Trials

Patients join clinical trials for myriad reasons, including wanting to help advance the science of their diseases, a lack of available therapies, a desire to obtain improved medical care, lack of health insurance, advice from a primary care physician or financial or other reasons. The decision whether to participate is a very complex process that involves not only what is known about a drug, but also the patient's reaction to his disease, his relationship with his doctor and his cultural roots. Understanding why a patient chooses to participate is helpful and will aid with both recruitment and retention of participants for the full duration of the trial.

The well-discussed phenomenon of "therapeutic misconception" must be considered among the reasons patients volunteer for trials. Simply put, despite cautions about lack of direct benefit in the consent forms and verbal statements from investigators confirming the questionable nature of benefits, many patients still believe clinical trials are "treatment." This is particularly evident when patients have serious diseases, such as cancer or AIDS. Investigators must guard against overstating the benefits of research and should ensure that patients make a realistic assessment of benefits and risks before volunteering.

The most frequently mentioned concern as to why people do not participate in clinical trials is the fear of receiving placebo instead of the active drug. Another concern is the fear that study drugs may cause risky side effects. With increased effort focused on education regarding clinical trials, individuals who agree to join should have a better understanding of the risks and benefits of participation.

Recruitment of Special Populations

It is important to include a representative population in most clinical trials. This generally means the study should include men, women, minorities and age-appropriate participants, in keeping with the proportion of individuals afflicted with the disease or condition being studied. In many cases, including a representative population is not only important but also mandatory. For example, the National Institutes of Health (NIH) has made the inclusion of appropriate numbers of women and minorities an explicit criterion to be considered when reviewing grant applications. Similarly, the FDA now requires data being submitted in support of a new drug application (NDA) include an appropriate number of female and minority participants, and that the data are analyzed to determine differing effects on these populations.

The following are specific considerations for recruitment of various populations:

Minorities

Much has been written about the lack of participation by minorities in clinical trials in the U.S. Barriers include economic factors, mistrust and lack of awareness about clinical research. These barriers often can be surmounted with careful planning, including efforts to address minority participant concerns prior to participation via educational materials, the availability of transportation, meals and child care services as needed, the use of home visits or study centers with convenient locations, participation by minority researchers and research staff, the use of study materials in other languages, investigator or other study staff of the same ethnicity and efforts to educate and develop trust with potential participants.

> **Barriers to recruiting minorities can be surmounted with careful planning, time and effort upfront to better understand the needs and concerns of the targeted populations.**

Women

Today, in many studies, women make up 50% or more of the study cohort. This has not always been the case. As recently as the early 1990s, it was the

FDA's stated guideline that women of childbearing potential were to be excluded from phase I and early phase II studies. Unfortunately, this policy, enacted in the early 1970s due to concerns over possible pregnancy and potential toxicity of experimental medications on the developing fetus, had the unintended effect of restricting participation by women not only in early trials, but also in later trials. In 1993, the FDA reversed that rule by publishing its *"Guideline for the Study and Evaluation of Gender Differences in the Clinical Evaluation of Drugs."* The NIH also has published guidelines about the inclusion of women in NIH-sponsored clinical trials (Outreach Notebook for the NIH Guidelines on Inclusion of Women and Minorities as Subjects in Clinical Research).

The overarching rationales behind the NIH and FDA guidance and regulations apply to most clinical studies; i.e., to ensure that populations at risk for particular disease or receiving treatment are represented in relevant clinical trials, and to assess possible differences in the effects of treatment on women and men, based on factors such as variations in body size and composition and the effects of hormones. For these reasons, it is important recruitment plans include mechanisms to ensure appropriate representation among both women and men.

Children

In 1998, the FDA issued a new rule designed to encourage, and in some cases mandate, the testing of new products in children. In the preamble to this rule, the FDA said a number of medications were very commonly prescribed for children, despite the absence of pediatric clinical trial data. The FDA concluded the absence of pediatric labeling information posed significant risks for children.

Recruitment of children for clinical trials poses a variety of challenges, including the fact that children legally are not able to consent to the treatments or procedures being conducted during the clinical trial. For pediatric trials, it is important to assure a proper balance between the need to recruit children and the need to protect their rights as human subjects. For more information on children in clinical trials, see 45 CFR 46.

Elderly

Participation of the elderly in clinical trials, as with other special populations, presents unique challenges; however, inclusion of adult participants in research should not be age restricted unless there is valid scientific and/or medical justification. Without recruitment methods directed specifically to the elderly, enrollment of seniors in certain clinical trials may be significantly less than expected. The reasons for this may include misconceptions about the benefits of enrollment in clinical trials, stringent eligibility criteria, coexisting medical conditions and logistical barriers.

To overcome some of these hurdles, recruitment initiatives directed to encourage participation by the elderly have included conducting study visits at locations easily accessible by the study population (e.g., senior centers); providing transportation; targeting advertising to newspapers, periodicals and other media more typically read or seen by seniors; recruitment via physician offices; and community-based initiatives that target locations frequented by seniors.

Recruiting Study Participants

Once the appropriate study population has been identified, a number of recruitment mechanisms are available to investigators. Regardless of the method used (print, radio, television, internet, etc.), the IRB must review the methods and the content of the message. IRB review is necessary to ensure the information is not misleading or coercive to potential participants, does not state a certainty of favorable outcome and does not imply benefit beyond what is outlined in the consent document and protocol.

Recruitment methods include public relations and direct advertising. Critical to the success of direct advertisement or any other alternative is ensuring that a correct and factual message is delivered to interest the targeted population in making the initial contact with the site. The following venues are commonly used: TV, radio, newspaper, magazines, posters, flyers, brochures, internet, social media, mass mailings, advocacy group newsletters, support group meetings, formal referrals or informal word-of-mouth, health workshops, screenings, health fairs, chart/record review, etc. A few of the most popular recruitment tools are described in further detail below.

Advertising

In general, advertising is anything directed toward potential study participants with the goal of recruiting them into a study. It may consist of radio or TV spots, newspaper ads, posters on bulletin boards, flyers or any other items intended to directly reach prospective subjects. The FDA considers advertising for study subjects the start of the informed consent process. Consequently, all advertising should be reviewed and approved by the IRB before use.

Making claims either explicitly or implicitly that the test article is safe or effective for the purpose under investigation, or that it is known to be equivalent or superior to any other treatments, is misleading to participants and also is a violation of FDA regulations [21 CFR 312.7(a) and 21 CFR 812.7(d)]. In general, the FDA believes advertisements should be limited to the information the prospective participants need to determine their eligibility and interest.

Advertising material for clinical trials should not use terms such as "new treatment," "new medication" or "new drug" without explaining that the test article is investigational; such characterizations may lead study participants to believe they will be receiving newly improved products of proven worth. Additionally, advertisements should not promise "free medical treatment," when the intent is that participants will not be charged for taking part in the investigation. The promise of treatment without charge may be coercive to financially constrained participants; therefore, advertisements may state that participants will be paid but should not emphasize the payment or the amount.

When setting up a recruitment campaign, the best approach is to utilize several recruitment tactics concurrently and measure the success rate of each. The investigator should be prepared to change the recruitment campaign mid-stream if some or all of the components are not successful.

Advertising pointers:

1. Avoid acronyms. They may not be understood by the target audience.

2. Place the ad carefully to reach the appropriate audience.

3. Advertise frequently in the right places.

4. Measure the effectiveness of the advertising technique.

5. Modify tactics as needed.

Recruitment from Practice and Databases

In some studies, the majority of participants recruited come from the investigator's own practice or through recruitment initiatives that utilize hospital medical records or other databases. The advantage to this recruitment method is that it allows the study staff to review records to pre-select potentially eligible subjects. An important factor to consider when utilizing practice or hospital medical record databases, however, is the Health Insurance Portability and Accountability Act (HIPAA) Privacy Rule, which imposes strict privacy requirements for medical record information. (See Chapter 15 to learn more about HIPAA's impact on recruitment).

Call Centers

In the pharmaceutical industry, call centers may be utilized to improve subject identification, study participant management, compliance assistance and study follow-up. These call centers help minimize burden at investigative sites by referring only pre-screened patients to sites. Services offered include inbound patient screening, outbound calling to recruit patients, scheduling of participant visits, advertising and medical placement assistance and feedback during the trial.

New Strategies for Subject Recruitment

Internet Searches

Today, it is very common for potential study subjects to search the internet using Google, BING, or other search engines for information on their medical conditions, or to look for possible clinical trials in which they might participate.

When advertising on the internet, it is important the web page is carefully and professionally designed for each trial, with the appropriate keywords and information to both attract potential subjects and aid in achieving a higher search level. As with other advertising, internet advertising must be approved by an IRB before use.

Social Networks

There has been an explosion in the growth and use of social networks, such as Facebook, Twitter, and MySpace, and this has created new opportunities for recruiting patients into clinical trials. Used correctly, social networking can be an effective method for generating pre-qualified patient referrals.

Ads can run on social networks, as well as on Google. Since people have chosen to belong to these networks, they are more inclined to accept and act on messages received on these sites than they are to unsolicited advertising. Messages also are shared exponentially, without huge cost to the messenger.

Social networking sites have the ability to target ads to individual user pages based on information in the user profile, including location. Because these networks are global in scope, geo-targeting can be used for specifying areas for desired recruitment of study participants.

Advertising on social networks is no different than any other IRB-approved ads; just the location of the ad is different (online). Using social networks is simply a new tool to reach a broader population and to help with the always difficult task of recruiting enough patients for a clinical trial.

Other Recruitment Methods

Many potential participants hear about a trial by word of mouth, perhaps from a friend in the trial. Sites that conduct a number of trials often have "free advertising" from current or past study volunteers spreading the word. Participants also find clinical trials by talking to people, contacting organizations, including disease-related groups and pharmaceutical companies, and searching the web.

Many web sites that list trials in process or about to start are available to potential study participants.. CenterWatch, for example, has an online database listing of clinical trials that is easily accessible (www.centerwatch.com).

Other web sites, particularly through the NIH, list active trials with information for potential participants. An example can be found at www.cancer.

gov/clinicaltrials. The U.S. Food and Drug Administration Modernization Act (FDAMA) legislation of 1997 contains a provision requiring that information about clinical trials for serious or life-threatening diseases be accessible to potential volunteers.

Information for Potential Study Participants

Potential study participants often are not very knowledgeable about clinical trials and the clinical trial process. They tend to think receiving treatment in a clinical trial is the same as receiving treatment as a regular patient in a medical practice. This is not true. Clinical trials are designed to answer scientific questions, not to provide medical treatment. Anyone who is considering participation needs to understand the difference between participating in a clinical trial and receiving treatment at a doctor's private practice. It is the responsibility of investigators to help educate their potential patients about the differences between these activities.

Participant Recruitment/Retention Incentives

Payments to Volunteers for Participation

It is quite common for trial participants to be compensated for participation, especially in the early phases of development. When subjects are compensated, however, it is viewed by the FDA as a recruitment incentive, not as a study benefit. All compensation schedules must be approved by the IRB before the study, or in advance of being used. The IRB will look at both the compensation amounts and the timing of the compensation to be sure they are not coercive and would not present an undue influence on the participant's trial-related decisions.

Participants usually are compensated on a regular basis throughout the trial, most commonly for each completed visit, although they do not have to be compensated at each visit. It is rarely appropriate to compensate volunteers only if they complete the entire trial; this might encourage them to continue with the trial even if they otherwise would have discontinued due to side effects or other reasons.

The amount of compensation to volunteers varies with respect to their involvement and the complexity of the study. Compensation usually is designed to cover any costs participants might incur, such as transportation, parking, lunch and childcare. Compensation must not be so large as to be

> **Payments to participants are not considered a benefit but a recruitment incentive.**

coercive; that is, participants should not be entering a trial only because of the compensation. Before approving compensation, the IRB also will take into account where the study is being conducted and the patient population.

Retention Incentives

While recruiting the participant into a clinical trial is the most difficult component of study conduct, maintaining a participant for the full study period also can prove to be challenging. Participants prematurely withdraw from studies for various reasons (e.g., perceived lack of efficacy, interference with work or family schedule, travel becomes burdensome, family members or primary care physician advises against continued participation, adverse experience, etc.). Too many premature withdrawals potentially can have a negative impact on study results. The investigator and study staff should make a concerted effort to maintain participants in a study for the full study period, while not compromising their rights, safety or welfare. Retention of participants requires both selective screening and a good relationship among the subject, investigator and coordinator. Contacting the participant via phone between in-person visits, sending newsletters to participants about study progress or updating them with new information about their disease have been successfully used to keep participants vested in a study.

Recruitment Strategies by Sponsors

In an effort to enhance recruitment, sponsors may offer financial and other incentives to sites that meet or exceed enrollment goals. Certain financial incentives, however, may compromise the integrity of studies or may give an appearance of affecting the judgment of the investigator/research team. In some cases, such payments may violate professional ethics codes, federal regulations and/or institutional policies. Examples of commonly prohibited incentives include:

- *Finder's fees*—payment for referring potential participants to investigators

- *Bonus payments*—additional payments to the investigator, study coordinator, enrollers or the institution for enhanced enrollment, when the payments are not related to increased trial costs.

Other types of payments, such as increased payment for additional expenses incurred by the site, and supplemental payments based on costs of enrollment not originally anticipated, are usually permissible. For example, added visits, or additional procedures at each visit (e.g., added ECG, diary, blood draw, efficacy evaluation, etc.), are permissible. In all cases in which additional payments are made, such payments should be incorporated into the contract with the study sponsor.

Setting the Proper Tone in Recruiting Patients

In designing recruitment strategies, investigators and sponsors must balance their enthusiasm for the research with the need to maintain an atmosphere that minimizes the possibility of coercion or undue influence (21 CFR 50.20 and 45 CFR 46.116). The FDA's *Guidance for IRBs and Clinical Investigators,* September 1998, offers additional guidance on recruitment practices.

Communicating an excessive or unrealistic enthusiasm about the possible benefits of the research to potential volunteers, either consciously or subconsciously, may unduly influence their enrollment decisions. Both the atmosphere of the consent conference and the language of the consent document must enhance the prospective volunteer's ability to make a truly informed and objective decision about whether to participate.

All recruitment programs must be free of advertising strategies or incentive arrangements that unduly influence participants' enrollment decisions. IRBs must review and approve the methods and materials investigators propose to use in recruiting patients to ensure they do not present patients with coercive or other undue influences that could compromise their right to exercise free, autonomous and informed consent.

Conclusion

In general, a successful recruitment strategy requires early planning, with multiple strategies for recruitment, and tracking the success or lack of success of each strategy used, reviewing the progress, revising the plan as necessary and treating participants well. For successful patient recruitment, the site should have the ability to draw from a broad population, a cohesive staff that can respond to a large number of calls generated by advertising campaigns, continuous meetings with staff to ensure everyone understands the goals of the study and the ability to shift quickly from unsuccessful recruitment strategies. Addressing barriers to enrollment is important, and considerations include appropriate payment for time and effort. The object of recruitment strategies is to enroll interested, eligible and informed participants in a manner that respects their privacy and autonomy.

References

1. "Drug Development: Economic and Operating Realities," R&D Leadership Summit, Getz, Ken. Feb. 3, 2011.

CHAPTER FOURTEEN

Research with Secondary Subjects, Tissue Studies and Records Reviews

At the conclusion of this chapter, readers will be able to:

- Understand the concept of "secondary subjects" and the regulatory basis for this concept.

- Discuss human subject protection issues related to conducting research with human tissues.

- Address human subject protection issues related to conducting research with collections of data.

Introduction

While the greater part of this book addresses research involving direct intervention with volunteers, there also are several categories of research that involve the collection of information about individuals from sources other than through direct intervention. The examples discussed in this chapter are the collection of information about the family members of an individual subject with whom the investigator has direct contact ("secondary" or "third party" subjects), the study of human tissue samples and the study of collected "data sets" such as medical records.

The principal risks involved in these types of research are a breach of confidentiality and a violation of privacy. Confidentiality and privacy are supported by two of the three principles identified in the Belmont Report—respect for persons and beneficence. Respect for persons requires that volunteers be allowed to exercise their autonomy, including the autonomy to maintain their privacy and to have private information that identifies them kept confidential. Beneficence requires that risks to volunteers are minimized, benefits are maximized and that risks to volunteers do not outweigh the benefits to them and others. The maintenance of confidentiality and privacy helps to protect volunteers from a variety of potential harms, including psychological distress, loss of insurance, loss of employment and damage to social standing.

> **Secondary subjects' confidentiality and privacy must be protected.**

Secondary Subjects

The concept of "secondary" or "third party" subjects has come to light primarily through genetics research, which relies on family history and the creation of pedigrees for critical information and validity. The issue of whether to obtain consent from secondary subjects has a potential impact on genetics research as well as on other types of research. The definition of a research subject is provided in the DHHS regulations [45 CFR 46.102(f)] and the "Common Rule":

- *Human subject* means a living individual about whom an investigator (whether professional or student) conducting research obtains (1) data through intervention or interaction with the individual, or (2) identifiable private information.

- *Intervention* includes both physical procedures by which data are gathered (e.g., venipuncture) and manipulations of the individual or the individual's environment that are performed for research purposes. Interaction includes communication or interpersonal contact between investigator and subject.

- *Private information* includes information about a behavior that occurs in a context in which an individual can reasonably expect that no observation or recording is taking place, and information that has been provided for specific purposes by an individual and that the individual can reasonably expect will not be made public (e.g., a medical record). Private information must be individually identifiable (i.e., the identity of the subject is or may readily be ascertained by the investigator or associated with the information) in order for information to constitute research involving human subjects.

There are four key elements of this definition of a human subject:

- A living individual

- An individual about whom an investigator obtains data in a research context

- The investigator obtains the data through intervention or interaction with the individual

- The investigator otherwise obtains identifiable private information.

According to the federal definition, "identifiable private information" includes information about an individual:

- That occurs in a context with no expectation of observation or recording

- That is provided for specific purposes by an individual

- About which there is a reasonable expectation it will not be made public

- That is individually identifiable or that the identity may be readily ascertained.

It is from this definition of a human research subject that the concept of secondary subjects arises. When a detailed family history is obtained from a subject enrolled in a research study, with private information obtained on specific family members, those family members also may to be considered subjects in the research study. The determination of who is a human subject rests with the IRB.

For example, in a genetic study of acne, an investigator wishes to track possible genetic inheritance patterns of this disorder and potential co-morbidities. The investigator obtains appropriate informed consent from an individual with acne, and then asks him or her for detailed family medical histories to construct a pedigree and identify family members with the same co-morbidities. The investigator and the IRB must consider first whether the information obtained about the family members will be "identifiable private information." If so, those family members are also subjects in the research. Consent from the family members (secondary subjects) then must be obtained prior to soliciting the information from the primary subject, or consent may be waived or altered for these subjects, in accordance with federal regulations.

Obviously, one of the contested issues regarding secondary subjects is what is considered "private" information. For example, many researchers argue information freely shared and known within a family is not "private" information but belongs to each member of that family. Others counter this is an example of information sharing that an individual "can reasonably expect will not be made public."

This issue becomes more critical and problematic when very sensitive information is being obtained. In research in areas such as mental illness, behavioral disorders, substance abuse and dependence or seizure disorders, obtaining personal identifiable information on third parties can have significant consequences for those individuals. As required by federal regulation, potential harm to subjects resulting from the disclosure of private information, and not just the potential physical risks of research, must be a part of the risk/benefit analysis of the research and its impact on individuals. Prior consent becomes a crucial consideration in such instances.

The definition of "identifiable information" is also a contested issue. If family member names are not used but reference is made to specific members of the participant's family—such as "mother," "father," "maternal grandfather"—the identity of these un-named family members still may be "readily ascertained by the investigator" in relation to the subject, and therefore be identifiable.

> **Disclosing personal identifiable information about third parties can potentially cause harm to these individuals.**

Research Involving Human Tissues

Human tissue samples have long been stored for a variety of purposes, including research, and they can serve as a valuable source of information. There are thousands of collections of stored human tissue samples, which can be referred to generically as tissue banks, maintained in a wide variety of settings. Examples include pathology collections, newborn screening collections, blood banks, umbilical cord blood banks, organ banks, forensic DNA banks, military DNA banks and dedicated tissue storage facilities. They can be located in government, nonprofit and for-profit institutions. Many of these tissue banks were not created for research purposes, but often they become a source of research material. Research with human tissues involves several unique considerations regarding subject confidentiality and privacy, regulatory interpretation and IRB oversight.

Research with tissues may require informed consent from volunteers, or it may qualify for a waiver of consent. It even may qualify as exempt from IRB review. A key issue in the ethical and regulatory analysis of research with tissues is whether and how easily the person who provided the tissue can be identified. As with secondary subjects, the federal definition of "human subject" determines when IRB review is required for research under Common Rule jurisdiction. If an investigator conducting research with tissue obtains "identifiable private information," then the individuals who provided the tissues are human subjects who must consent to the research use of the tissue, unless the IRB finds it acceptable to waive consent.

When consent must be obtained, several issues need to be addressed in the consent process, such as:

- What tissue samples will be collected and how they will be collected

- What type(s) of research will, or may, be conducted using the tissue sample, including whether genetic analysis will be performed

- Potential risks of disclosure of the information, such as negative effects on insurance coverage, employment status, emotional discomfort, familial strife or even harm to a cultural group

- The potential benefits, including whether any results will be provided to the subject

- What types of processes are in place to protect confidentiality and privacy; for instance, whether direct identifiers will be kept with the sample or whether a code will be used. If a code is used, who will maintain the linking information, and how will that information be stored and protected?

- With whom the sample may be shared, if known

- Whether the sample will eventually be anonymized (i.e., made unidentifiable) and, if so, how and when

- Whether there will be any commercial applications of the research

- Whether the subject can have the sample destroyed if he or she decides to withdraw from the research

- How long the samples will be kept.

There can be a great deal of variability in specific circumstances, and the consent process and format will need to be tailored to the specific situation. Research with tissues may qualify for a waiver of consent for the use of the tissue under 45 CFR 46.116(d), if four conditions are met:

1. The research involves no more than minimal risk to the participants.

2. The waiver or alteration will not adversely affect the rights and welfare of the participants.

3. The research could not practicably be carried out without the waiver or alteration.

4. Whenever appropriate, participants will be provided with additional pertinent information after participation.

The application of these four criteria often is difficult. While most IRBs have traditionally felt research with human tissues is of minimal risk for the purposes of the first criterion, the recent explosion of genetic research and its possible implications for insurance and employment have caused some IRBs to consider at least some tissue research to involve more than minimal risk. For the second criterion, there often is debate as to whether the use of tissue in research without consent violates the rights and welfare of the participants. This may be a particularly important consideration when the tissues derive from a distinct cultural community such as Native Americans. Finally, the definition of "practicably" in the third criterion is often disputed. For tissue samples being collected prospectively, it often is inconvenient but still practicable to get consent from the research participants.

Research with tissues also may be exempt from IRB review and informed consent requirements if the research involves the collection or study of existing pathological or diagnostic specimens, and if they are publicly available or if the information is recorded by the investigator in such a manner that participants cannot be identified (45 CFR 56.101(b)(4)). For this exemption, the ability to identify the individual from whom the tissue was taken is a key feature. If all identifiers are severed, so no one including the investigator can link the identity of the person providing the tissue to the sample, then that specimen is effectively unidentified and any research using that sample may be exempt from Common Rule requirements. However, if there is an identifying link between the individual donor and the sample kept by, or accessible to, any party, the subject could be identified and the use of the sample for research falls under Common Rule requirements.

Furthermore, the research is exempt under 45 CFR 46.101(b)(4) only if the tissue collection is existing, i.e., it has already been collected and stored. If the tissue is going to be collected prospectively, the exemption does not apply and the research must undergo IRB review. Very often, tissue banks are created for non-research purposes, and therefore already exist at the time the research is initiated. If new tissues will continue to be added to the tissue bank after initiation of research, separate analyses need to be applied to those tissue samples already stored and those that will be collected prospectively. It may be possible to waive consent for the existing samples, or even for their use to be exempt, while at the same time obtaining consent for the prospectively collected samples.

OHRP also has issued guidance stating that if the tissue was not collected for the currently proposed research subject, and the investigator cannot readily identify the individuals to whom the tissues pertain, there are no human subjects in the research and the research does not need IRB review or informed consent. Unlike the exemption described above, the tissues can be collected prospectively under this guidance.[1]

Publishing Policies

The publishing policies of medical journals are another factor that may influence an investigator's decision whether to have IRB review for research performed on tissue samples. Approximately half the medical journals require IRB approval as a prerequisite for the publication of results of research involving human subjects. Therefore, an investigator conducting research with tissues for which the Common Rule requirement for IRB review does not apply may still need IRB review to publish the results.

FDA Regulations

Research with human tissue also can fall under FDA jurisdiction. When human tissues are used to test a device, such as an in vitro diagnostic device, and the sponsor intends to submit the data to the FDA as an application for marketing, the research involves a clinical investigation and human subjects. Under certain limited criteria, the FDA will exercise enforcement discretion and not require consent for such research. However, when research is conducted under FDA regulations and these criteria are not met, the waiver of consent under 45 CFR 46.116(d) is not applicable and investigators must obtain full consent, including notice that the FDA may review the participant's identifiable research and medical records.

Multiple IRB Reviews

Another difficult matter in tissue research is that multiple IRBs often become involved in the oversight of the research. Often, tissue is collected at one institution, then stored at a tissue bank at a second institution and, finally, transferred to a third institution for research purposes. The respective

IRB for each of these institutions is responsible for overseeing compliance with federal regulations for the collection, storage and/or use of the tissues at that institution. However, it often is difficult for the IRB at an institution to determine whether there are identifiers linking the tissue to the individual who provided it, and whether proper consent was obtained for the use of the tissue in research. An investigator who will be using samples stored elsewhere can assist the IRB in its review of tissue research by gathering, in advance, the relevant documents, such as prior IRB approvals, consent forms and privacy policies from the institutions at which the tissue was collected or handled.

Research Involving Record Reviews

Another source of research information that does not involve direct intervention with research participants is the review of collected information in various media. For the purposes of this book, any type of stored data will be referred to as "data sets" and can include educational records, medical records (including images such as X-rays and photographs), billing records, disease registries, records created for Quality Assurance (QA) purposes, government databases such as prison or driving records and employment records. These data sets may be confidential or public and can be created and maintained by a wide variety of institutions.

Research with data sets may require informed consent from individuals, may qualify for a waiver of consent or may be exempt from IRB review. A key issue is how easily the person whose information is in the data set can be identified. Another important consideration is whether the person performing the research has access to the data sets as part of his or her employment duties. For instance, if an investigator does not have access privileges to medical records that he or she wishes to review for research purposes, the issues of a breach of confidentiality and an invasion of privacy are concerns that must be addressed in the protocol and in any consent process.

As with secondary subjects and tissue research, the definition of "human subject" determines whether research with data sets is considered human subject research that requires IRB review. If the investigator is obtaining "identifiable private information" about individuals, IRB review is required and participants must consent to the research use of the data set unless the IRB finds it acceptable to waive consent.

When consent is required, there are several issues to address. However, the consent form usually can be quite short and still include all of the required elements. General issues that need to be addressed on a case-by-case basis include:

- What data sets will be used for research purposes

- To whom the data set will be released

- What types of processes are in place to protect confidentiality and privacy. For example, will direct identifiers will be kept with the data set, or will a code be used? If a code is used, who will maintain the linking information, and how will that information be stored and protected?

- Whether the data set will be made unidentifiable and, if so, how and when.

Research with data sets also may qualify for a waiver of consent under the four criteria listed in 45 CFR 46.116(d).

For research with data sets, the most controversial of these criteria is the third—the definition of "practicably." It often is inconvenient but still practicable to get consent from the research subjects, particularly if they continue to come to the institution for ongoing interventions and/or services.

Like tissue research, some research involving the review of data sets may qualify for exemption from Common Rule requirements if the data sets are already in existence prior to the initiation of the research and the information is recorded/provided in such a way that there is no link between the data set and individuals. It may qualify as research that does not include human subjects.

The federal government and many states have statutes and case law regarding the privacy of data sets, such as educational, employment and medical records, and these must be taken into account. Also, the federal Health Insurance Portability and Accountability Act (HIPAA) Privacy Rule affects research involving medical records. (See Chapter 15 to learn about the impact HIPAA has on research databases and repositories.)

References

1. "Guidance on Research Involving Coded Private Information or Biological Specimens," available at www.hhs.gov/ohrp/policy/cdebiol.html

CHAPTER FIFTEEN

Implementing the HIPAA Privacy Rule in Research

At the conclusion of this chapter, readers will be able to:

- Describe the circumstances when the HIPAA Privacy Rule applies to research.

- Distinguish a covered entity from a non-covered entity under the HIPAA Privacy Rule.

- Discuss the general requirements for uses and disclosures of protected health information (PHI) for research.

- Describe the required elements and statements for authorizations.

Introduction

The Health Insurance Portability and Accountability Act of 1996 (HIPAA) requires parties who participate in certain healthcare transactions to conduct the transactions electronically using standardized formats and code sets. For example, insurance plans must accept claims electronically and healthcare providers must use a standard format and set of codes when submitting a claim for payment. The intent of HIPAA is to facilitate these transactions and create efficiencies.

When Congress enacted HIPAA, it recognized that facilitating the electronic exchange of health information would pose challenges to the privacy and security of the information. To address these concerns, the Department of Health and Human Services (HHS) issued standards to protect the security and privacy of identifiable health information in 2003. These standards are referred to as the Privacy Rule and the Security Rule. The Privacy Rule restricts the use and disclosure of identifiable health information maintained by individuals or organizations covered by the regulation. The Security Rule requires appropriate administrative, physical and technical safeguards to ensure the confidentiality, integrity and security of identifiable health information maintained in an electronic format.

The rules introduced two phrases that are important to understanding the scope and applicability of the standards. The first phrase is "covered entity," which refers to the individuals and organizations that must comply with the standards. The second phrase is "protected health information (PHI)," which refers to identifiable health information maintained by a covered entity. These phrases are more clearly defined in detail later in this chapter.

The scope of both the Privacy Rule and the Security Rule was expanded in 2009, when Congress enacted the Health Information Technology for Economic and Clinical Health Act (HITECH Act), which is part of the American Recovery and Reinvestment Act of 2009 (ARRA). The HITECH Act includes incentives for healthcare providers who adopt electronic health records (EHR). The act also expands the scope of HIPAA so that it applies directly to "business associates" of covered entities, increases the penalties for noncompliance and mandates governmental enforcement activities.

The Privacy Rule is not intended to interfere with access to and exchange of PHI for traditional healthcare purposes—treatment, payment for healthcare or healthcare operations ("TPO"). However, the Privacy Rule imposes restrictions on the use or disclosure by covered entities of PHI for non-TPO purposes, including research. The Privacy Rule has had a substantial impact on medical research involving human volunteers, including studies of existing information and/or biological specimens obtained from human volunteers. Clinical research typically involves the exchange of information among multiple parties, including research sites, CROs, site management organizations (SMOs), data safety monitoring boards (DSMBs), institutional review boards (IRBs) and sponsors. All of these parties are affected, even though only some are directly regulated by HIPAA as covered entities or business associates. Covered entities and business associates are the "gatekeepers" of PHI; they must obtain some form of permission under HIPAA to receive, use or disclose PHI for any research purpose.

For research to proceed efficiently under HIPAA, all parties involved in medical research—regardless of whether they are directly regulated by the standards —must understand how the Privacy Rule affects the flow of PHI to and from the gatekeepers of PHI. Individuals and organizations directly subject to the rules must understand their responsibilities to avoid legal liability. Compliance with the standards usually requires constraints on the use and disclosure of PHI, and these constraints often are included in agreements with research partners, who are not directly subject to the standards. Thus, non-covered entities engaged in medical research must understand the Privacy Rule's requirements to ensure research contracts include procedures for obtaining the HIPAA permissions or waivers necessary for access to necessary PHI. Commercial sponsors who draft research protocols will need to determine the Privacy Rule requirements that apply to their studies and include procedures in the protocols to meet those requirements.

It is important to note that the scope of research affected by the HIPAA Privacy Rule is different from the scope of both the Common Rule (45 CFR 46, Subpart A) and FDA regulations (21 CFR Parts 50 and 56). The HIPAA Privacy Rule affects any research use or disclosure of PHI, including subject screening and recruitment; accessing medical records and other existing health information; collecting, creating or receiving PHI; creating new databases or tissue repositories; secondary uses of existing databases and repositories; site monitoring; management of multi-site studies and publication of results.

Implementation of the standards for either the Privacy or Security Rule in research is procedurally complex. Different procedures may apply to a particular research activity, such as subject recruitment, depending on who is involved. A comprehensive explanation of the standards and their application to research is beyond the scope of this chapter. Instead, the goal here is to provide some practical understanding and basic tools necessary to design and conduct research efficiently and in compliance with the Privacy Rule.

Since the Security Rule applies mainly to computer security and maintaining or transmitting PHI electronically, this rule will not be discussed here in any depth. Additional guidance on the Security Rule can be found at www. hhs.gov/ocr/privacy/hipaa/administrative/securityrule/securityruleguidance.html.

While there are some basic rules researchers can use to resolve questions about the Privacy Rule, many questions will be fact-specific and answers will depend on the types of organizations, individuals and data involved. Readers should seek guidance from their institutions' Privacy Officers, research administrators or legal counsel regarding the implementation of the standards in their research activities.

Integration with State and Federal Laws

Implementation of the Privacy Rule is, by itself, complex. The fact that the Privacy Rule's requirements must be integrated with related state and federal laws adds another layer of complexity that often will require legal analysis. At the state level, the Privacy Rule preempts (overrides) state privacy laws that are contrary and provide less protection. Thus, the Privacy Rule provides a federal "floor" of medical privacy protection, but individual state laws may provide more stringent protections. State law protection of medical information related to highly sensitive and potentially damaging information (e.g., HIV/AIDS, drug use, mental illness) often exceeds that of the Privacy Rule and will, therefore, control the use of such information in research. Those engaged in such research should seek advice from legal counsel to determine whether state law or the Privacy Rule applies. This state "preemption" analysis can be complicated, particularly for multi-site studies.

At the federal level, the Privacy Rule does not preempt either the Common Rule or the FDA's regulations governing use of human volunteers in research. Researchers must comply with all applicable laws. There are significant procedural and analytical differences between the Common Rule and the Privacy Rule, especially regarding research involving existing data or tissue, patient screening and patient recruitment. These differences are discussed in more detail later in this chapter.

Entities Regulated by the Privacy Rule

The Privacy Rule regulates the flow of PHI to and from covered entities. The first step in understanding how the Privacy Rule affects research is to determine which parties involved in the research are covered entities. Determining who is and is not a covered entity can be very complicated, especially when organizationally and functionally complex institutions (e.g., universities and academic medical centers) are involved.

HIPAA directly regulates the use and disclosure of PHI by four groups of entities involved in treatment, payment for healthcare or healthcare operations (TPO) activities. The first three groups include healthcare providers, healthcare clearinghouses and health plans. HIPAA refers to these parties as "covered entities." As stated above, HITECH HIPAA expanded the scope such that business associates of covered entities are also directly regulated by HIPAA. Of the groups directly responsible for compliance with the standards, healthcare providers are the ones most typically involved in clinical research. However, not all healthcare providers involved in research are covered entities. Only healthcare providers that transmit health information electronically as part of a HIPAA "transaction" are covered entities. Essentially, a HIPAA "transaction" involves financial or administrative activities related to healthcare (e.g., processing healthcare claims and administration of healthcare benefits). In general terms, payment to a healthcare provider that involves electronic transmission of health information between two parties makes the provider a covered entity under HIPAA. "Electronic" transmissions include those conducted over the internet, extranet, leased lines, dial-up lines and private networks, and those involving physical relocation by magnetic tape, CD or floppy disk. Payment by third-party insurers (health plans) typically involves electronic transmission of health information. In contrast, merely maintaining billing and payment records on a computer would not be a "transmission" and would not make the provider a covered entity.

A covered entity may be an individual (e.g., a physician) or an institution (e.g., a hospital). For an institution that is a covered entity, all members of the institution's workforce are part of the covered entity. "Workforce" is broadly defined under HIPAA and includes all paid and unpaid persons (employees, volunteers, trainees, etc.) who work under the direct control of the covered entity.

Institutional Covered Entities

There are several types of organizational structures for institutional covered entities under HIPAA. Each structure has significant implications for the implementation of the Privacy Rule in research because whether, and how, research at an institution is subject to the Privacy Rule depends on the functional unit in which the institution has chosen to place research. The implementation of the Privacy Rule in research must be examined through the lens of each institution's organizational structure to determine which requirements, if any, apply. There is no "one size fits all" Privacy Rule for research.

Hybrid Entities

An organization or institution that is a single legal entity that performs both covered and non-covered functions may elect to be a "hybrid entity" under HIPAA. Designation as a hybrid entity can simplify the implementation of the Privacy Rule at an institution because the Privacy Rule would apply only to the components of the institution that conduct covered functions. A "covered function" is any function that makes the entity a healthcare provider, health plan or healthcare clearinghouse. For example, a hospital may functionally divide itself into one or more healthcare components and non-healthcare components. The hospital must designate all covered functions as part of a healthcare component and may include non-covered functions in either the healthcare or non-healthcare component.

Organizations that elect to become hybrid entities must determine which functions within the entity are covered functions and which are not. The organization should prepare a document stating (1) its decision to become a hybrid entity; (2) which functions are covered and which are not; and (3) the components responsible for the functions. The organization should also implement physical and procedural safeguards between covered and non-covered components that prevent unauthorized exchange of PHI between the components. The procedural safeguards should be in the form of standard operating procedures (SOPs) and often are referred to as "firewalls." Many organizationally complex research institutions such as universities, multi-component hospitals and nonprofit research organizations have designated themselves hybrid entities. When engaging in research with hybrid entities, outside researchers must determine whether research is part of the healthcare component. If so, the entity's researchers are covered entities.

Affiliated Covered Entities

HIPAA also provides inter-institutional strategies for implementing the Privacy Rule. Legally separate but affiliated institutions may choose to designate themselves or their healthcare components as a single covered entity under HIPAA if they are under common ownership or control. Organizing as an "affiliated covered entity" (ACE) can create some administrative efficiencies by allowing the institutions that make up the ACE to share solutions (e.g., a common notice of privacy practices). However, each legally distinct covered entity is separately liable for HIPAA noncompliance.

There are advantages and disadvantages associated with designation as an ACE. A research-related benefit of an ACE is that PHI shared among an ACE's healthcare components is a "use" rather than a "disclosure," thereby avoiding the disclosure tracking requirement (discussed in more detail under the section "Individual Rights"). However, as with hybrid entities, the Privacy Rule still applies to the exchange (disclosure from or receipt by) of PHI between the healthcare component(s) and non-healthcare components of the

ACE. This creates administrative burdens for researchers who are in the non-healthcare component but wish to obtain PHI from colleagues in the healthcare component at their own (or affiliated) institution. Also, this exchange would be a disclosure that must be tracked by the healthcare component.

Organized Healthcare Arrangements

Organized healthcare arrangements (OHCA) are another inter-institutional organization under the Privacy Rule. Multiple independent covered entities that hold themselves out to the public as participating in a joint arrangement to provide a clinically integrated care setting may choose to operate as an OHCA. The covered entities in an OHCA must participate in joint activities such as utilization review, quality assessment and improvement or payment. As with affiliated covered entities, members of an OHCA may use one notice of privacy practices.

Business Associates

A business associate is a person or organization providing a service or function on behalf of a covered entity that involves use of the covered entity's PHI. Examples of functions performed by business associates include claims processing, medical transcription, data analysis, accreditation and quality assurance. Business associates must comply with the provisions of the HIPAA Privacy Rule and must have written SOPs to help ensure compliance.

A covered entity may disclose PHI to a business associate under an agreement that, among other things, requires the business associate to use appropriate safeguards to prevent use or disclosure not permitted under the agreement.

There has been some confusion as to who is a business associate in the context of research. Any party hired by sponsors or their agents (e.g., CROs, call centers and recruitment services) are not business associates because they are acting on behalf of the sponsor—not the covered entity. Research collaborators (e.g., researchers at other sites) also are not business associates because sharing PHI for research purposes does not create a business associate relationship. However, individuals hired to de-identify data or create limited data sets for research purposes would be considered business associates under the Privacy Rule.

Categories of Information Under the Privacy Rule

Protected Health Information

The Privacy Rule's regulations apply to PHI, which is (1) "health information" that is (2) "individually identifiable" and (3) created or received by a covered entity. The first step in determining whether research involves PHI is to determine whether the research involves any covered entities. If there are no covered entities involved, either as researchers or as sources of data (e.g., holder of medical records), there is no PHI. If there are covered entities involved, the second question is whether "health information" is involved, and if so, whether it is "individually identifiable."

What is "Health Information"?

"Health information" is information in any form or medium (paper, electronic, oral and images such as x-rays or sonograms) that relates to a living or deceased individual's past, present or future physical or mental health or condition, the provision or payment of healthcare to an individual. Note that unlike the Common Rule, the Privacy Rule also applies to deceased persons.

Importantly, biological specimens (e.g., blood and tissue) by themselves are not PHI. According to HHS, biological specimens are not "information" in and of themselves. In practice, however, biological specimens typically are collected and/or stored with diagnostic information (e.g., breast cancer tissue repository), which is "health information." If the associated health information includes any of the HIPAA identifiers listed in Table 1, the data are "individually identifiable" and, therefore, constitute individually identifiable health information (IIHI). In the hands of a covered entity, the IIHI becomes PHI. Determining when biological material is or is not PHI is a critical part of creating or maintaining repositories and studies of existing material. These issues are discussed in more detail in this chapter under "Research databases and repositories."

What Health Information is "Individually Identifiable?"

Health information is "individually identifiable" under the Privacy Rule if it directly identifies an individual or reasonably could be used to identify an individual. The Privacy Rule provides two ways to determine whether information is individually identifiable. One method is to obtain certification by a knowledgeable statistician that there is a very small risk the information could be used alone or in combination with other reasonably available information to identify the individual who is the subject of the information.

The other method of establishing whether information is individually identifiable is to determine if the information includes any of 18 identifiers of the individual, his or her relatives, employers or household members. These identifiers are listed in Figure 1. Importantly, these identifiers that are part of PHI are subject to all of the protections of the Privacy Rule and may be disclosed for research only in compliance with the Privacy Rule's requirements.

Item 18 is an important "catchall" category that deserves additional explanation for two reasons. First, it covers any identifier not specified in items 1-17 that could be used to identify an individual. Thus, if a covered entity knew certain information included with health information could be used to re-identify an individual, even if the information is not a specified HIPAA identifier, it would render the data PHI. Item 18 requires covered entities to make reasonable subjective determinations of what information qualifies as "uniquely identifying."

Figure 1: The 18 HIPAA identifiers

1. Names

2. All geographic subdivisions smaller than a state, including ZIP Code (except for the first three digits of the ZIP Code if the region contains more than 20,000 people, or the last two digits if the region contains fewer than 20,000 people)

3. All elements of dates (except year), including birth, death admission and discharge dates; all ages over 89 years (may include ages younger than 89 years)

4. Telephone numbers

5. Fax numbers

6. Email addresses

7. Social Security numbers

8. Medical record numbers

9. Health plan beneficiary numbers

10. Account numbers

11. Certificate/license numbers

12. Vehicle identifiers and serial numbers, including license plate numbers

13. Device identifiers and serial numbers

14. Web Universal Resource Locators (URLs)

15. Internet Protocol (IP) address numbers

16. Biometric identifiers, including finger and voice prints

17. Full face photographic images and any comparable images

18. Any other unique identifying number, characteristic or code

Coded Data

Item 18 also is important because it includes an "identifying code." Understanding which types of codes would be an identifying code is important and requires some explanation. Part of the confusion in understanding which types of codes would make health information PHI stems from the different nomenclature used in the research community and by federal agencies. Adding to the confusion is the fact that HHS does not provide neat labels for identifying versus non-identifying codes. In this chapter, the term "identifying code" is used to mean a code that could be used in combination with other information to identify the individual subject of the associated health information. Such codes link the health information to an individual's health information and are sometimes referred to as a "code-link." Identifying codes typically are derived from some other identifier. Examples of identifying codes include the last four digits of a person's Social Security number or a clinical trial record number.

In contrast, "non-identifying" code is one that provides no information about the identity of the individual subject of the associated health information. Under the Privacy Rule, a non-identifying code is not derived from the data or another identifier. An example would be a randomly assigned code or one that uses the sequential number of subjects entered into a study. In addition, the covered entity may not use or disclose the code for any other purpose and may not disclose the "key" that can be used to re-link the information to an individual's identity. Thus, without the linking "key," the identity of the individuals in the data set could not be determined. If a covered entity holding PHI creates a new data set in which all identifiers in the list of HIPAA identifiers are removed and individual records are coded with a non-identifying code, the new data set is not PHI and release by the covered entity to a researcher would not be subject to the Privacy Rule. This is called de-identifying PHI.

Use this simple formula as a guide to determine if your research involves PHI:

IIHI + Covered Entity = PHI

De-identified Data

The Privacy Rule does not apply to de-identified data. PHI may be de-identified by one of the two methods discussed above. Also, de-identified data may contain a code or other means of record re-identification if that code is not derived from or related to the information about the individual, and is not otherwise capable of being translated to identify the individual. Because de-identified data are not subject to the Privacy Rule and may be shared freely by covered entities, researchers who do not need identifying information should consider using de-identified data instead of PHI, especially for studies of existing data or biological specimens. Figure 2 illustrates an example in which a researcher obtains de-identified data from a covered entity. The covered entity maintains a database of PHI (Step 1 in Figure 2). The covered entity de-identifies the PHI in the database to create a de-identified database (Step 2). If the covered entity discloses PHI from the PHI Database to a researcher, the disclosure will be subject to the Privacy Rule (Step 3). However, if the covered entity discloses de-identified data from the De-identified Database, the disclosure is not subject to the Privacy Rule (Step 4). In this scenario, the covered entity is responsible for ensuring the data meet the Privacy Rule's definition of "de-identified." Nonetheless, to facilitate cooperation by the disclosing covered entity, researchers who request de-identified data should carefully review the data fields included in their request to make sure no HIPAA identifiers are included.

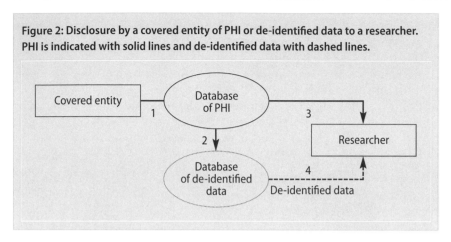

Figure 2: Disclosure by a covered entity of PHI or de-identified data to a researcher. PHI is indicated with solid lines and de-identified data with dashed lines.

Limited Data Sets

There is a third type of data recognized under the Privacy Rule with which researchers should be familiar. Recognizing some research—epidemiological research, for example—requires minimal identifying information, the HIPAA Privacy Rule provides an alternative to the extremes of de-identified data and PHI. A limited data set is a subset of PHI that excludes all HIPAA identifiers in Figure 1 except for addresses, dates and indirect identifiers. Regarding the postal address, all information except the street address may be included in a limited data set. HHS attempted to strike a balance between protecting privacy and facilitating highly valuable epidemiological research. Thus, limited data sets do not have a "free pass" like de-identified data, but they also do not require the approval necessary for PHI. The requirements that apply for use or disclosure of limited data sets are discussed later in the chapter.

Case Report Forms

Under the Privacy Rule, case report forms (CRFs) must be screened carefully for HIPAA identifiers that would make the data PHI. If the study is being conducted under an authorization in which subjects have given their permission for their PHI to be disclosed by the researchers to outside parties such as a CRO or a sponsor, the CRF may include PHI. In this situation, the CRF and the authorization must be consistent; any PHI included on the CRF must be specified on the authorization. Similarly, if only limited data sets will be disclosed by a covered entity to outside researchers, the CRF needs to be screened to make sure it complies with the restrictions imposed on limited data sets.

Many commercial sponsors, as a matter of company policy, do not want to receive PHI from research sites. If a study is designed so outside parties will receive only de-identified data, the CRF must be screened carefully to make sure it does not include any HIPAA identifiers. Data fields that have caused problems and may not be included in de-identified CRFs include dates (e.g., birth, treatment, surgical), medical record numbers and five-digit ZIP codes.

General Requirements for Uses and Disclosures of PHI

Some general requirements apply to the use or disclosure of PHI for any non-TPO purpose that also affects research. While these requirements are the responsibility of covered entities, they affect how PHI may be obtained, used or disclosed by any party involved in research. Therefore, all parties involved in research should be familiar with them.

Notice of Privacy Practices

The Privacy Rule requires covered entities to provide notice to individuals of how the covered entity may use or disclose the individual's PHI, the individual's rights afforded by the Privacy Rule and the covered entity's legal duties. This notice is called a "Notice of Privacy Practices (NPP)." There are many detailed requirements regarding the content and provision of the NPP, including some research-related issues that deserve mentioning.

The first issue involves content of the NPP. Among other required content, the NPP must include a description of each purpose for which the covered entity might use or disclose PHI without the individual's authorization. Several research-related uses or disclosures do not require an individual's authorization, including subject screening and recruitment or analysis of existing databases and tissue repositories. These research activities may be conducted under a review preparatory to research or a waiver of authorization. To comply with the Privacy Rule's requirements, covered entities that engage in research using PHI should include references to these activities in their NPP.

The second issue involves the provision of the NPP to research volunteers. At some research institutions, especially those with a hospital or physician clinics, many of the volunteers will be the institution's patients. As patients, they should receive the NPP from the covered entity the first time they receive service. The NPP must be presented only once. Research volunteers who have received the covered entity's NPP already do not need to be presented with it again. However, if an individual's first healthcare interaction with a covered entity is as a research volunteer, the researcher-provider must present the volunteer with the covered entity's NPP. Thus, as a practical matter, clinical researchers at a covered entity should query volunteers during their first meeting as to whether they previously have been presented with the institution's NPP.

Minimum Necessary Rule

Before HITECH HIPAA, covered entities were required to take reasonable steps to limit the use or disclosure of PHI to the minimum necessary to accomplish the intended purpose whenever use or disclosure is made without any authorization. However, there was no clear guidance defining "minimum necessary." HITECH HIPAA sought to remedy any confusion over this issue by requiring HHS to issue guidance defining "minimum necessary." Until the guidance is issued, HITECH HIPAA requires covered entities and business associates to limit uses and disclosures of PHI without an authorization to a limited data set or, if needed, to the minimum necessary to accomplish the intended purpose. To date, HHS had not issued the guidance. Since HITECH HIPAA places the responsibility of determining "minimum necessary" on the entity using or disclosing the PHI, it is important that covered entities and business associates be prepared to justify any uses or disclosures of PHI made without an authorization and which exceed the restrictions of a limited data set.

Individual Rights

The Privacy Rule provides individuals with a number of individual rights including the right to access and amend their PHI and to know to whom the covered entity has disclosed their PHI. These rights create administrative responsibilities for covered entities and business associates involved in research.

Right to Access and Amend PHI
Individuals have a right to access and amend their PHI that is maintained in a "designated record set." A designated record set is the set of medical records, billing records or other records used by the covered entity to make decisions about the individual. Whenever research data are held by a covered entity, maintained in a record and used to make decisions about the subject, the data would be a designated record set and the subject would have the right to access and amend the records. Additionally, under HITECH HIPAA, the covered entity must provide the record to the individual in an electronic format whenever an electronic health record is maintained.

There are a few exceptions to the individual's right to access or amend their record. The first allows a covered entity to deny a request for access to PHI if the entity determines that receipt of the information is reasonably likely to endanger the life or physical safety of the individual or of another person. Covered entities also are permitted to deny an individual's access to psychotherapy notes and to deny the individual's right to amend a record if the covered entity determines the record is accurate and complete.

An important exception for the research community allows a covered entity to suspend a research participant's right to access a research record until the end of the study. To use this exception, the covered entity must obtain the participant's agreement to the suspension at the time the investigator obtains his or her consent to participate in the research. This exception is intended to protect the scientific integrity of the data by preventing participants from breaking blinds associated with various treatment or placebo arms of a study. In many instances, an investigator will obtain the required agreement by including language in the research participant's consent form through which the participant agrees to the suspension. According to the requirements of the Rule, participants must be informed that the right to access their records will be re-instated when the research is completed.

Right to an Accounting of Disclosures

Under the Privacy Rule, individuals have the right to know who has had access to their PHI. The Privacy Rule requires covered entities and business associates to account for unauthorized disclosures made for purposes other than treatment, payment or healthcare operations (TPO) and disclosures in a limited data set. The individual has a right to receive an accounting for disclosures made within six years of the request. HITECH HIPAA expanded this right to include disclosures of PHI made for TPO if the records were maintained in an electronic health record. However, the individual's right to an accounting of disclosures made for TPO is limited to disclosures made within three years of the request.

Currently, covered entities and business associates are required to include in the accounting the date of disclosure, name and (if known) address of the recipient, a brief description of the type of PHI disclosed and a brief statement of the purpose of the disclosure. HITECH HIPAA allows covered entities to report the disclosures made by both the covered entity and all business associates or report the disclosures made only by the covered entity along with all business associates' contact information.

On May 31, 2011, HHS published a Notice of Proposed Rule Making (NPRM) entitled, *HIPAA Privacy Rule Accounting of Disclosures Under the Health Information Technology for Economic and Clinical Health Act* that explains HHS's intentions with respect to the HITECH HIPAA revisions to the requirements for accounting for disclosures. The proposed rule simplifies the reporting requirements by requiring covered entities and business associates to provide individuals with an "access report" within 30 days of a request. The access report must include accesses of electronic health occurring within three years of the date of the request, but the report can exclude some types of access including accesses that were done under an authorization or a waiver of authorization. The proposed rule also reduces the amount of information that must be provided in the accounting and requires the access to the report to include the date (or approximate date) of disclosure, the name and address (if known) of the recipient and a brief description of the type of PHI disclosed. It is not clear whether the proposed regulation will take effect as originally proposed or with changes. In either event, covered entities and business associates should begin to consider and develop processes to comply with these requirements. In addition, researchers must determine and follow the procedures used at their institutions and collaborating sites.

Uses and Disclosures of PHI for Research

Different Rules for "Uses" and "Disclosures"

Under the Privacy Rule, different requirements apply to "uses" and "disclosures" of PHI. To determine which Privacy Rule requirements apply, researchers must understand the difference between a "use" and a "disclosure."

A use occurs when a covered entity or members of its workforce utilize (collect, review, analyze, etc.) PHI within the covered entity. A disclosure occurs when a covered entity shares, releases or transfers PHI to a person or entity outside the covered entity.

An institution's organizational structure can have a significant impact on the procedural implementation of the Privacy Rule in research. As shown in Figure 3, what constitutes a use or a disclosure is different in a hybrid entity, an ACE or an OHCA. A hybrid entity is a single legal entity that has been functionally segregated into healthcare components and non-healthcare components. If there are multiple healthcare components, they function as a single covered entity. PHI that is shared within the hybrid entity's healthcare component is a use; sharing PHI with the non-healthcare component is a disclosure. In an ACE, multiple institutions function as a single covered entity. Thus, sharing PHI within the ACE is a use even if the PHI is exchanged across institutions. Sharing PHI outside the ACE is a disclosure. Because the members of an OHCA remain separate covered entities, research uses and disclosures of PHI are treated the same as if they were individual covered entities. Sharing PHI with another member of the OHCA for a research purpose is a disclosure that must be tracked and must comply with other Privacy Rule requirements.

In some instances, the requirements of the Privacy Rule will differ from the requirements of the Common Rule. For example, the Common Rule exempts research from the regulatory requirement for IRB approval and informed consent when the research involves only the review of existing identifiable medical records and the investigator does not record any direct or indirect identifiers during the research [45 CFR 46 101(b)(4)]. At the same time, the Privacy Rule imposes regulatory requirements on this type of research because it involves a use of PHI. Therefore, researchers who may be

Figure 3: Uses and disclosures in different HIPAA organizational structures			
	Hybrid entity	**Affiliated Covered Entity (ACE)**	**Organized Health Care Arrangement (OHCA)**
Ownership status	A single legal entity	Separate legal entities	Separate legal entities
Covered entity status	Health care component (HCC) and non-health care components (non-HCC)	Single covered entity	Separate covered entities
"Use" of PHI	Within the HCC	Within the ACE	Within each member institution
"Disclosure" of PHI	Outside of the HCC	Outside of the ACE	Outside of each member institution

experienced in determining activities regulated as research under the Common Rule cannot rely on the same analysis to determine what research activities trigger Privacy Rule requirements.

Authorizations to Use or Disclose PHI for Research

For clinical research, de-identified data or limited data sets usually are not sufficient to obtain access to PHI needed for the study. With a few exceptions, the Privacy Rule requires a covered entity to obtain an authorization before the covered entity can use or disclose PHI for research. An authorization is a formal permission (either in a separate document or as part of the research consent form) granted by the subject for his or her PHI to be used and disclosed. The required elements in research authorizations go beyond the elements for consent forms required by the Common Rule and FDA regulations, because the HIPAA Privacy Rule protects the privacy of information, whereas the Common Rule and FDA regulations protect the safety and well-being, including privacy, of participants.

Oversight of authorizations to make sure they are valid under the Privacy Rule is a matter of institutional policy. The Privacy Rule does not require IRB review or approval of research authorizations; but if the authorization is combined with the informed consent form, IRB review is required under the Common Rule and FDA regulations. To optimize compliance, some institutions have adopted a policy requiring IRB review and approval of all authorizations. Others require the use of an institutionally approved template form that contains all required elements. A covered entity also may choose to use an outside party's authorization form. Sponsors and investigators should determine each covered entity's institutional requirements for authorizations. For multi-site studies, sponsors must plan adequate time to determine the policies and procedures for authorization at each research site.

Revocation of Research Authorizations

Under the Common Rule, subjects may withdraw from a study at any time simply by ceasing to participate; written notice of withdrawal is not required. Under the HIPAA Privacy Rule, subjects may revoke their authorization to use or disclose PHI for research at any time, but this request must be made in writing. The authorization should explain how to revoke the authorization and any exceptions to the subjects' right to revoke. One exception to consider is that a revocation would not apply to PHI collected for the research prior to the subject's revocation. This exception should be included if it would affect the integrity of the research study. As a practical matter, subjects may want or need to withdraw from a clinical trial but are willing to allow their PHI to be used and collected. Therefore, investigators conducting clinical trials should consider giving withdrawing subjects the option of allowing researchers to continue to use and/or collect their PHI.

Figure 4: Required elements and statements in authorizations

Under the HIPAA Privacy Rule research authorizations must include the following:

- Specific, meaningful description of PHI to be used or disclosed
- Identification of persons (or classes of persons) authorized to request use or disclosure of PHI
- Identification of persons (or classes of persons) to whom the covered entity may disclose PHI
- Description of each purpose of the use/disclosure
    - Blanket authorizations are not permitted for future unspecified research, e.g., "We will use your PHI for future studies." (This prohibition also affects research databases and repositories.)
- Expiration date or event
    - The "event" may be "the end of research" or equivalent, or
    - "None."
- Subject's signature and date
    - If signed by a personal representative, include a statement of representative's authority.
- Notice that the subject has the right to revoke the authorization in writing at any time, the exceptions to the right to revoke and instructions on how the subject may revoke the authorization
- A warning that PHI disclosed under the authorization could be re-disclosed by the recipient and no longer protected by HIPAA
- The consequences to the individual if he or she refuses to sign the authorization, which for clinical trials is usually a statement that the individual will not able to participate in the trial
- The authorization must be written in plain language and a copy of the signed authorization must be given to the participant

Under the Privacy Rule, investigators may continue to use or disclose PHI after a revocation if needed "to protect the integrity of a research study." This standard is open to interpretation but, in general, a covered entity may continue to analyze PHI collected prior to a revocation but may disclose PHI only under limited circumstances. Acceptable disclosures would include notifying sponsors of a subject's withdrawal, notifying the IRB, sponsor and FDA of adverse events and including the PHI in a pre-marketing application to the FDA. Disclosures and uses made prior to a revocation would not be affected.

Waivers of Authorization

Under the HIPAA Privacy Rule, a covered entity may use or disclose PHI for research without an authorization if an IRB or privacy board determines the requirements for the waiver are met.

A privacy board is a review body that may be established to review and approve requests for waivers of authorization. The boards are similar to IRBs in membership.

IRBs and privacy boards can waive all requirements for an authorization or waive only one or more requirements. For example, if an IRB approves a waiver of documentation of consent, a researcher might also request the IRB to waive the requirement for the signature and date on the authorization. Likewise, the IRB can waive the requirement for an authorization for use and disclosure of PHI for the entire study, for one arm of the study or for specific protocol procedures. For example, if a study includes a historical control arm, the investigator could request the IRB to waive the requirement for an authorization from the control subjects because these subjects might not be available to sign an authorization.

An important use for waivers of authorization is for reviewing PHI for subject screening and recruitment. Investigators might request a partial waiver of authorization to conduct screening and recruitment activities. The regulations require the IRB or privacy board to make specific determinations before it can waive the requirement for an authorization. The first determination involves risk to the privacy of the individuals. The IRB must determine that such risk is no more than minimal, based on the investigator's plan to protect and destroy the identifiers and written assurances that the PHI will not be reused or re-disclosed except as allowed by law or by the Privacy Rule. The IRB or privacy board also must determine that the research could not be done practicably without the waiver and with the access to and use of the PHI. It is expected that the IRB will limit the investigator's use and disclosure of the PHI to only the PHI necessary to conduct the research.

Reviews Preparatory to Research

The Privacy Rule permits covered entities to disclose PHI to researchers for research activities that are "preparatory to research," such as protocol development and screening for subjects without an authorization or a waiver of authorization. This exception often is used to determine protocol feasibility and identify potential participants.

If the researcher is not part of the covered entity's workforce, the researcher cannot contact participants or remove any PHI from the covered entity's site. However, researchers who are part of the covered entity's workforce may use PHI to identify participants under a review preparatory to research exception and then may contact potential participants under the covered entity's healthcare operations exception.

Access to PHI under a review preparatory to research does not need to be approved by an IRB or privacy board. Instead, the researcher must make a "representation" to the covered entity that the PHI:

- will be used to develop a research protocol or for a similar purpose

- is necessary for the research purpose

- will not be removed from the covered entity's site.

For operational reasons, covered entities may require "representations" to access PHI under a review preparatory to research to be in writing even though it is not required by the HIPAA Privacy Rule.

Remember, a "disclosure" of PHI to screen for potential participants and for recruitment requires covered entities to maintain tracking records, even if the covered entity is not otherwise involved in the research. For example, if a CRO wishes to use a hospital's medical records to screen for potential participants, the hospital must ensure the tracking of the disclosure of each record to the CRO.

PHI of Deceased Persons

The Privacy Rule protects the privacy of PHI from deceased persons. However, procedurally the PHI of decedents is relatively easy to access for research. A covered entity may use or disclose a decedent's PHI for research if the researcher provides a "representation" that the PHI will be used for research only and is necessary for the research. Also, if requested, the researcher must provide documentation of the individual's death. The Privacy Rule does not specify the form of the "representation." Because this is a disclosure the covered entity must track, the representation typically will be in written form.

Use or Disclosure of Limited Data Sets

The Privacy Rule permits a covered entity to disclose a limited data set with a "data use agreement." Data use agreements must contain certain required elements, including:

- Description of how the limited data set will be used

- Identification of those who will have access to the limited data set

- Listing of the recipient's responsibilities, including:

  - to not use the limited data set to contact individuals (for recruitment) or to identify individuals to others

  - to report to the covered entity any improper uses/disclosures of the limited data set

- to use appropriate safeguards to prevent uses/disclosures outside of the data use agreement

- to ensure downstream compliance from those who receive the limited data set.

Patient Screening

Patient screening typically involves reviewing existing PHI in medical records, a database or a tissue repository to determine the approximate number of potential patients who might be available from a pool of patients and/or the clinical profile of prospective participants. As used in this chapter, patient screening does not involve contacting prospective participants.

Several HIPAA mechanisms may be used to obtain or use PHI for patient screening. Depending on institutional policy, researchers may be able to access a covered entity's PHI under either a review preparatory to research or a partial waiver of authorization.

Limited data sets also may be used to screen participants. A researcher, CRO or sponsor outside the covered entity may obtain a limited data set from a covered entity with a data use agreement and use the information off-site for patient screening. Remember, limited data sets may not include contact information, so they cannot be used to contact individuals. Thus, they may be used for patient screening but not patient recruitment.

Patient Recruitment

Recruitment involves contacting prospective participants. Targeted contacts (e.g., letters, emails or phone calls to pre-screened individuals) may require access to PHI. In contrast, newspaper or radio ads (non-targeted contacts) do not require access to PHI.

Targeted Contacts

Unlike patient screening, different requirements apply to "inside" and "outside" researchers seeking a covered entity's PHI for patient recruitment. A researcher who is a member of the covered entity's workforce may use that covered entity's PHI to screen patients under a review preparatory to research. Members of the workforce also may contact patients under the exception for healthcare operations. Researchers outside the covered entity may identify potential patients under the preparatory to research provision, but they may not remove PHI from a covered entity or contact potential patients. If a researcher who is not a member of a covered entity's workforce wishes to obtain PHI to contact potential patients, the researcher could request a waiver of authorization from an IRB or privacy board.

One way to minimize confidentiality concerns is to ensure that potential patients are contacted by people they would expect to have access to their PHI. For example, a potential patient would expect his or her healthcare provider or an employee of that healthcare provider to have access to PHI. Consequently, the provider or staff member could make the initial contact. If the healthcare provider is not otherwise involved in the research study, the provider could be given recruitment letters to send to prospective patients. The letter should contain a brief description of the study and provide contact information for the research team. There is no restriction under the Privacy Rule on the exchange of PHI between a covered entity and its patients. So it is acceptable for healthcare providers to discuss participation in a research study with their own patients. This means investigator-providers may communicate directly to their patients, informing them of a study and inviting them to participate.

Non-targeted Contacts

Non-targeted contacts, such as ads, do not involve PHI in making the initial contact, but PHI may be collected as part of the follow-up screening process. Covered entity interactive internet sites (those that solicit information from people who visit) may also collect PHI as part of the recruitment process and, therefore, must comply with the HIPAA Privacy Rule.

Typically, ads announcing a clinical trial provide a telephone number for interested individuals to call, an email address or a web site so the investigator can obtain more information. Often, screening information (related to the inclusion/exclusion criteria for the trial) is collected from these prospective subjects. If this screening information includes individually identifiable health information (IIHI), it becomes PHI once it is given to a covered entity. If the call-in number is to a covered entity, PHI will be collected as part of patient recruitment and the investigator must comply with the requirements of the HIPAA Privacy Rule. The provision for activities preparatory to research allows a researcher who is a member of the covered entity's workforce to collect and use this PHI for recruitment purposes.

If the call-in number is not to a covered entity (e.g., a call center or site management organization), the information collected over the phone is not PHI. If the screening information is then given to a clinical investigator who is a covered entity, it becomes PHI. The researcher would then be obligated to obtain an authorization from the individual or a waiver of authorization from an IRB or privacy board before using the PHI for any research activity, unless an exception to the requirement for an authorization (e.g. activity preparatory to research) applies.

Some institutions and research sites require researchers to obtain a waiver of authorization before using or sharing information for recruitment purposes. It is important researchers understand the requirements of their institutions and their standard operating procedures.

As a reminder, if the research is subject to the Common Rule, and the recruitment process involves obtaining private identifiable information about living individuals, the requirements of the Common Rule must be satisfied.

Research Databases and Repositories

The creation and use of databases and repositories of biological specimens are affected by the Privacy Rule. Researchers who are covered entities must comply with the Privacy Rule when PHI is included in the database or repository and again when PHI is removed from the database or repository.

Creating Databases and Repositories

Unless an exception to the requirement for an authorization is applicable, a covered entity must obtain an authorization from the patient before the entity can maintain that patient's PHI in a database or repository. If obtaining the data or specimens involves an interaction with the patient, the covered entity usually will need to obtain the patient's authorization to include the data or specimen in the database or repository.

In some cases a database or repository receives specimens without interacting with patients because the data and specimens were collected for another purpose, such as treatment or for a different protocol. In these cases, an authorization from the patient might not be required. For example, the covered entity could elect to obtain only de-identified material, or the covered entity could enter into a data use agreement and accept only PHI that meets the requirements for a limited data set. Another alternative would be to obtain the specimens or data under a waiver of authorization.

If the specimens were collected prior to April 14, 2003, and some form of legal permission was obtained to collect and store the tissue for research, use of the material to create a research repository could be exempt from authorization requirements under the Privacy Rule's transition provisions.

When an authorization is required to collect data or specimens to create or maintain a research database or repository, the covered entity should ensure authorization is drafted so the use of the PHI is limited to creation of the database or repository. The Privacy Rule prohibits authorizations for unspecified future research. This means the authorization must be limited to use or disclosure of PHI for defined study and/or storing the PHI in a database or repository. This is why creating databases and repositories must be separated from subsequent use of research databases or repositories under the Privacy Rule whenever the exact purpose of future use is unknown. Subsequent use of existing PHI in databases or repositories often can be conducted under a waiver of authorization.

Using PHI in Research Databases and Repositories

Researchers who wish to use existing data or tissue in databases or repositories maintained by a covered entity have several alternatives under the Privacy Rule. First, if the researcher does not need identifiable data, the researcher could request the covered entity to provide only de-identified data or tissue. De-identified data is not subject to the Privacy Rule. Second, the researcher could request only a limited data set from the covered entity. The covered entity may provide the limited data set to the researcher, but only with a data use agreement.

Third, if the researcher needs PHI beyond that available in a limited data set, the researcher may request a waiver of authorization from an IRB or Privacy Board. If the use or disclosure of the PHI for the stated research purpose does not pose more than a minimal risk to the patients' privacy and meets the other waiver criteria, the research most likely would qualify for a waiver of authorization.

Recruitment Databases

Covered entities also could use PHI to create a database of potential research participants under the "preparatory to research" exception to the requirement for an authorization. This exception allows a covered entity to permit a researcher to identify but not contact potential study participants or remove PHI from the covered entity. If the researcher is a member of the workforce of the covered entity, the researcher may contact potential patients as part of the covered entity's healthcare operations. As an alternative, if the covered entity obtains documentation that an IRB or privacy board has waived the requirement for an authorization for use of the PHI for recruitment, the covered entity may disclose the PHI necessary for the researcher to contact the potential patients. However, if creation of the database of potential research participants in future research is subject to 45 CFR Part 46, this activity must be approved by an IRB and informed consent from potential patients must be obtained, unless the IRB waives the requirement for informed consent.

Breach Notification Requirements, Liability and Enforcement

Breach Notification Requirements

Covered entities and business associates promptly must notify affected individuals, the HHS Secretary and the media when of a breach of unsecured PHI affects more than 500 individuals. Breaches of unsecured PHI affecting fewer than 500 individuals must be reported to the HHS secretary annually. Business associates must notify the covered entity of breaches by the business associate.

Whether or not notifications are required needs a careful analysis by the covered entity or business associate and readers should seek guidance from their institution's Privacy Officer, research administrator or legal counsel regarding any suspected breach occurring at their research site.

Liability for Noncompliance

Following the promulgation of HIPAA's Privacy Rule, the opinion of the healthcare industry was that HIPAA was not rigorously enforced. The HI-TECH Act includes provisions that significantly increased enforcement activities and also increased penalties for noncompliance. In 2009, DHHS enacted an Enforcement Interim Final Rule, which imposed a tiered penalty structure for violating HIPAA. Monetary penalty ranges from $100 to $50,000 per violation, with a maximum of $1.5 million for repeat violations. The penalty is based on the nature and extent of the violation and the nature and extent of the harm resulting from the violation. Covered entities and business associates who "knowingly" obtain and disclose PHI in violation of HIPAA also may face criminal fines and imprisonment.

Enforcement of HIPAA falls under the Office of Civil Rights (OCR), and any civil penalties collected for privacy and security violations of HIPAA are turned over to OCR to fund its enforcement activities. In addition, State Attorneys General can bring civil actions on behalf of state residents for violations of the HIPAA Privacy and Security Rules, and penalties resulting from these actions are turned over to the state.

The Secretary of DHHS is required to conduct periodic audits of covered entities and of business associates to ensure they are complying with the provisions of both The Privacy Rule and The Security Rule.

Conclusion

Conducting research under HIPAA's Privacy Rule requires more than just forms and additional compliance concerns for covered entities. Successful and efficient research under the Privacy Rule requires coordinated efforts by all parties involved, including participants, investigators, IRBs, privacy boards, CROs, SMOs and sponsors. All parties—not just covered entities—that conduct research involving PHI need to understand the Privacy Rule requirements that apply to each research activity, including subject screening, recruitment, data collection and exchange and the creation and use of research databases and repositories.

References, Resources and Suggested Readings

Chapter 1: Historical Perspectives on Human Subject Research

Annas G, Grodin M, eds. *The Nazi Doctors and the Nuremberg Code: Human Rights in Human Experimentation*. New York, NY: Oxford University Press, 1992.

Beecher HK. *Ethics and Clinical Research*. N Engl J Med 1996;274: 1354-60.

Caplan A, ed. *When Medicine Went Mad: Bioethics and the Holocaust*. Totowa, NJ: Humanna Press, 1992.

Ethical and Policy Issues in International Research: Clinical Trials in developing Countries. NBAC. April 2001

Faden R, ed. *Human Radiation Experiments: Final Report of the President's Advisory Committee*. New York, NY: Oxford University Press, 1996.

Faden R, Beauchamp T. *A History and Theory of Informed Consent*. New York, NY: Oxford University Press, 1986.

Jones J. *Bad Blood: The Tuskegee Syphilis Experiment*. New York, NY: Free Press, 1993.

Milgram S. *Obedience to Authority*. New York, NY: Harper & Row Publishers, Inc., 1974.

Research Involving Human Biological Materials: Ethical Issues and Policy Guidance. NBAC January 2000

Research Involving Persons with Mental Disorders That May Affect Decisionmaking Capacity. NBAC. December 1998

Third Report of the Attorney General's Research Working Group. Office of the Maryland Attorney General, Annapolis MD: Office of the Attorney General, August 1997.

Chapter 2: Ethics and Federal Regulations

Belmont Report: Ethical Principles and Guidelines for the Protection of Human Subjects of Research. Federal Register Document 79-12065 (see: http://ohsr.od.nih.gov/guidelines/belmont.html).

Beauchamp TL, Childress JF. *Principles of Biomedical Ethics (5th ed.)*. New York, NY: Oxford University Press, 2001.

Food, Drug, & Cosmetic Act (see: www.fda.gov).

Levine RJ. *Ethics and Regulation of Clinical Research (2nd ed.)*. New Haven, CT: Yale University Press, 1986.

Office of Research Integrity (see: www.hhs.gov/ohrp).

Office for Human Research Protection (see http://ohrp.osophs.dhhs.gov).

Vanderpool, HY. *The Ethics of Research Involving Human Subjects*. Frederick (MD): University Publishing Group, 1996

Gina Kolata, *"How Bright Promise in Cancer Testing Fell Apart."* New York Times, July 7, 2011

New York Times
  (see: www.nytimes.com/2011/07/08/health/research/08genes.html).

The Economist (see: www.economist.com/node/21528593).

New England Journal of Medicine
  (see: www.nejm.org/doi/full/10.1056/NEJMp078032).

Lawyersandsettlements.com
  (see: www.lawyersandsettlements.com/articles/drugs-medical/
  ketek-scandal-00680.html).

42 CFR 50.102

FDA warning letter Ref. 07-HFD-45-0501

Chapter 3: Roles and Responsibilities of Institutions in Human Subject Research

21 Code of Federal Regulations (CFR) 312, 314, 600, 812 and 814.

Department of Health and Human Services 45 CFR

Amdur, R. & Bankert, E. *Institutional Review Board: Management and Function*. Sudbury, MA: Jones and Bartlett Publishers, 2002

Food and Drug Administration (see: www.fda.gov).

Food, Drug and Cosmetic Act (see: www.fda.gov).

National Institutes of Health (see: www.nih.gov).

Research Subjects Review Board (see: www.rochester.edu/rsrb).

"Undercover tests show the institutional review board system is vulnerable to unethical manipulation." GAO, March 26, 2009.

Chapter 4: The Roles and Responsibilities of the Investigator and the Study Process

FDA Clinical Investigator and IRB Information Sheets (see: www.fda.gov).

Harwood F. *A Professional's Guide to ACP's Certification Program For Clinical Research Associates and Clinical Research Coordinators*. Washington, DC: Associates of Clinical Research Professionals (ACRP).

ICH Harmonized Tripartite Guideline: Guideline For Good Clinical Practice. (see: www.ich.org/fileadmin/Public_Web_Site/ICH_Products/

Guidelines/Efficacy/E6_R1/Step4/E6_R1__Guideline.pdf).

Mackintosh DR, Zepp VJ. *GCP Responsibilities of Investigators—Beyond the 1572*. Appl Clin Trials. 1996; 5:32-40. 183 References, Resources and Suggested Reading

Sayre JE. *GCP Quality Audit Manual (1st ed.)*. Buffalo Grove, IL: Interpharm Press; 1990.

Stephen L, Papke A. *Certified Clinical Research Coordinators*. Appl Clin Trials 1995; 4:58-63.

Guidance for Industry E6, Good Clinical Practice, section 4.3.1.

Chapter 5: FDA-Regulated Research Issues

21 CFR 312, 314, 600, 812 and 814.

21 CFR 803 (Investigational Devices), 600 (Postmarketing), 310 (Investigational Drugs and Biologics).

Food and Drug Administration (see: www.fda.gov).

Mackintosh DR, Zepp VJ. *GCP Responsibilities of Investigators—Beyond the 1572*. Appl Clin Trials. 1996; 5:32-40.

MEDWATCH: *The FDA Medical Products Reporting Program*

O'Donnell P. *Closer to Harmonized GCP*. Appl Clin Trials 1995; 4:48-53.

FDA Guidance document *"FAQ—Statement of Investigator (Form FDA1572)."* Issued May 2010, p. 15.

Chapter 6: Behavioral Research Issues

Beauchamp, TL, Faden RR, Wallace RJ, et al. *Ethical Issues in Social Science Research*. Baltimore, MD: Johns Hopkins University Press.

OPRR IRB Guidebook: Protecting Human Research Subjects. Washington, DC: Government Printing Office, 1993.

Belmont Report; Ethical Principles and Guidelines for the Protection of Human Subjects Research. Federal Register Document 79-12065

Bankert EA and Amdur, RJ (eds): *Institutional Review Board: Management and Function 2nd Edition*; Boston Jones and Bartlett Publishers; 2006

National Science Foundation: Interpreting the Common Rule for the Protection of Human Subjects for Behavioral and Social Science Research www.nsf.gov/bfa/dias/policy/hsfaqs.jsp

45 CFR Part 46

C.K. Gunsalus et al, *The Illinois White Paper: Improving the System for Protecting Human Subjects: Counteracting "Mission Creep,"* Qualitative Inquiry 2007 13: 617.

Human Subject Regulations Decision Charts, The Office for Human Subjects Protections (2004) www.hhs.gov/ohrp/policy/checklists/decisioncharts.html

OHRP - Guidance on Research Involving Coded Private Information or Biological Specimens (2008)

www.hhs.gov/ohrp/policy/cdebiol.html
Human Subjects Protection Resource Book, U.S. Department of Energy 2006
http://humansubjects.energy.gov/doe-resources/files/HumSubj
Protect-ResourceBook.pdf
WIRB Investigator Handbook: A Guide for Researchers
www.wirb.com/Pages/DownloadForms1d.aspx
WIRB Initial Review Submission Form
www.wirb.com/Pages/DownloadForms.aspx

Professional organizations:

American Anthropology Association:
www.aaanet.org
American Educational Research Association:
www.aera.net
American Folklore Society:
www.afsnet.org
American Historical Association:
www.historians.org
Association of Internet Researchers:
http://aoir.org
American Political Science Association:
www.apsanet.org
American Psychological Association:
www.apa.org
American Sociological Association:
www.asanet.org
Oral History Association:
www.oralhistory.org

Chapter 7: Publication of Study Results

Berg JA, Mayor GH. *A study in normal human volunteers to compare the rate and extent of levothyroxine absorption from Synthroid and Levoxine.* J Clin Pharmacol 1992; 32:1135-40.

Blumenthal D, Campbell EG, Anderson MS, et al. *Withholding research results by academic life scientists: evidence from a national survey of faculty.* JAMA 1997; 277:1224-1228.

Cohen W, Florida R, Goe WR. *University-industry research centers in the United States.* Pittsburgh, PA: Carnegie Mellon University Press, 1994.

Committee on Science, Engineering, and Public Policy. *On Being A Scientist: Responsible Conduct in Research, (2nd edition).* Washington, DC: National Academy of Sciences, National Academy of Engineering, Institute of Medicine, National Academy Press, 1995.

Dong BJ, Harck WW, Gambertoglio JG, et al. *Bioequivalence of generic and brand-name levothyroxine products in the treatment of hypothyroidism.* JAMA 1997; 277:1205-1213.

King R. *Bitter pill: how a drug company paid for university study, then undermined it.* Wall Street Journal. April 25, 1996:1

Lafollette MC. *Stealing into Print.* Los Angeles, CA: University of California Press, 1992.

Rennie D. *Thyroid storm.* JAMA 1997; 277:1238-1243.

Chapter 8: Conflicts of Interest in Research

Office for Human Research Protection. *Draft Interim guidelines: Financial relationships in clinical research: Issues for institutions, clinical investigators, and irbs to consider when dealing with issues of financial interests and human subject protection.* 1-10-2001 (see: www.hhs.gov/ohrp/archive/humansubjects/finreltn/fguid.pdf).

American Society of Gene Therapy. *Policy of The American Society of Gene Therapy on Financial Conflict of Interest in Clinical Research.* American Society of Gene Therapy. 4-5-2000.

Task Force on Research Accountability: Report on individual and institutional financial conflict of interest. Association of American Universities, 2001

Task Force on Financial Conflicts of Interest in Clinical Research: Protecting subjects, preserving trust, promoting progress—policy and guidelines for the oversight of individual financial interest in human subjects research. Association of American Medical Colleges, 2001.

21 CFR 54 Financial Disclosure by Clinical Investigators, 63 Federal Register 5250, Feb. 2, 1998.

Chapter 9: Informed Consent

A History and Theory of Informed Consent; Faden & Beauchamp; Oxford University Press; New York; 1986

Medical Research and the Principle of Respect for Persons in Non-Western Cultures; ijsselmuiden & Faden; in The Ethics of Research Involving Human Subjects; Vanderpool; University Publishing Group; Frederick, MD

Chapter 10: Community-Based Qualitative Research

The American Anthropological Association's Code of Ethics (see: www.aaanet.org).

American Public Health Association guidelines (see: www.apha.org).

Chapter 11: Ethical Issues in Genetic Studies

Genetic Testing and Screening in the Age of Genomic Medicine by the New York State Task Force on Life and the Law, 2001

NIH Guidelines for Research Involving Recombinant DNA Molecules [NIH Guidelines]
(see: http://oba.od.nih.gov/rdna/nih_guidelines_oba.html).

President's Council on Bioethics (see: http://bioethics.gov).

Chapter 12: Special Ethical Concerns in Clinical Research

WMA. *5th Revision of the Declaration of Helsinki.* General Assembly. Edinburgh, Scotland; October 2000

Temple R, Ellenberg S. *Placebo controlled trials and active-control trials in the evaluation of new treatments. Part 1: Ethical and scientific issues.* Ann Intern Med. 2000; 133: 455-63.

Ellenberg S, Temple R. *Placebo controlled trials and active-control trials in the evaluation of new treatments. Part 2: Practical Issues and Specific Cases.* Ann Intern Med. 2000; 133: 464-70.

Rothman KJ, Michels KB. *The continuing unethical use of placebo controls.* N Engl J Med. 1994; 331:394-8.

Chapter 13: Participant Recruitment and Retention in Clinical Trials

A Word From Study Volunteers, Opinions and Experiences of Clinical Trial Participants, CenterWatch survey of 1,050 study volunteers 1999/2000, p.1-5.

W.M. Vollmer et. Al., *Recruiting Children and Their Families for Clinical Trials: A Case Study.* Controlled Clinical Trials 1992; 13(4): 315-20.

Gorelick, et. Al., *The Recruitment Triangle: reasons why African Americans Enroll, Refuse to Enroll, or voluntarily withdraw from a Clinical Trial,* JAMA, 90(3) 141-5, 1998 Mar.

Gorelick, fn.6; El Sadr, et. Al, *The Challenges of Minority Recruitment in Clinical Trials for AIDS,* JAMA 1992; 267 (7): 954-7.

Guideline for the Study and Evaluation of Gender Differences in the Clinical Evaluation of Drugs, 58 FR 139, 39406-39416, July 22, 1993.

National Institutes of Health, *Outreach Notebook for the NIH Guidelines on Inclusion of women and Minorities as Subjects in Clinical Research,* 1994.

21 CFR 312.7(a) (promotion of investigational drugs); 21 CFR 812.7(d) (promotion of investigational devices).

21 CFR 50.20

45 CFR 46.116

FDA IRB Information Sheets, *Recruiting Study Subjects,* 9/98.

Silagy, et al, *Comparison of Recruitment Strategies for a Large-Scale Clinical Trial in the Elderly,* J. Clinical Epidemiology, Vol, 33, No 10, 1105-1114, 1991.

Health Insurance Portability and Accountability Act of 1996, Public Law 104-191, August 21, 1996.

Good Clinical Practice Monthly Bulletin, August 2000, p6.

Zisson, S., *Call Centers Dial Up for Patients,* CenterWatch 2001;8(3):1-10.

Nathan, RA, *How Important is Patient Recruitment in Performing Clinical Trials?,* J. Of Asthma 1999: 36 (3), 213-216.

A Guide to Patient Recruitment and Retention, edited by Diana L. Anderson-Foster, Ph.D.

"Drug Development: Economic and Operating Realities." R&D Leadership Summit, Getz, Ken. Feb. 3, 2011.

FDA *Guidance for IRBs and Clinical Investigators,* September 1998.

Chapter 14: Secondary Subjects, Tissue Studies and Records Reviews

45 CFR Part 46.101 (b)(4)

45 CFR Part 46.116 (d)

45 CFR Part 56.101 (b)(4)

21 CFR Parts 50 and 56

21 CFR 812

Botkin, *Protecting the Privacy of Family Members in Survey and Pedigree Research,* 285(2) JAMA 207-211 (January 10, 2001).

National Human Research Protections Advisory Committee (NHRPAC), *Clarification of the Status of Third Parties when Referenced by Human Subjects in Research,* January 2002.

National Bioethics Advisory Committee, *Research Involving Human Biological Materials: Ethical Issues and Policy Guidance,* Volumes I and II, August 1999.

Amdur and Biddle, *Institutional Review Board Approval and Publication of Human Research Results,* 277(11) JAMA 909-914 (March 19, 1997).

Moore v. Regents of the University of California, 793 P.2d 479 (Cal. 1990).

Colorado Revised Statute 10-3-1104.7, *Genetic Testing—declaration—limitations of disclosure of information—liability—legislative declaration,"* 1994.

Office for Protection from Research Risks (OPRR), *"Exculpatory Language" in Informed Consents,* November 15, 1996, accessed April 29, 2002 (see: www.hhs.gov/ohrp/policy/exculp.html).

Food and Drug Administration, *Information Sheets: Guidance for Investigators and irbs, Frequently Asked Questions,* 14, 1998, accessed April 29, 2002 (see: www.fda.gov/oc/ohrt/irbs/faqs.html#InformedConsent DocumentContent).

Institute of Medicine, *Protecting Data Privacy in Health Services Research,* 2000, accessed online May 1, 2002 (see: www.nap.edu/catalog/9952. html).

"Guidance on Research Involving Coded Private Information or Biological Specimens" (see: www.hhs.gov/ohrp/policy/cdebiol.html).

Chapter 15: Implementing the HIPAA Privacy Rule in Research

45 CFR Parts 160 and 164

Barnes, Mark; Kulynych, Jennifer, *HIPAA and Human Subjects Research: A Question & Answer Reference Guide*, March 2003, Barnett International

Information For Covered Entities And Researchers On Authorizations For Research Uses Or Disclosures Of Protected Health Information
(see http://privacyruleandresearch.nih.gov/authorization.asp).

Clinical Research and the HIPAA Privacy Rule
(see http://privacyruleandresearch.nih.gov/clin_research.asp).

Protecting Personal Health Information in Research: Understanding the HIPAA Privacy Rule
(see http://privacyruleandresearch.nih.gov/pr_02.asp).

Institutional Review Boards and the HIPAA Privacy Rule
(see http://privacyruleandresearch.nih.gov/irbandprivacyrule.asp).

Privacy Boards and the HIPAA Privacy Rule
(see http://privacyruleandresearch.nih.gov/irbandprivacyrule.asp).

Research Repositories, Databases, and the HIPAA Privacy Rule
(see http://privacyruleandresearch.nih.gov/research_repositories.asp).

The Belmont Report

Ethical Principles & Guidelines for Research Involving Human Subjects

Scientific research has produced substantial social benefits. It has also posed some troubling ethical questions. Public attention was drawn to these questions by reported abuses of human subjects in biomedical experiments, especially during the second world war. During the Nuremberg war Crime Trials, the Nuremberg code was drafted as a set of standards for judging physicians and scientists who had conducted biomedical experiments on concentration camp prisoners. This code became the prototype of many later codes[1] intended to assure that research involving human subjects would be carried out in an ethical manner.

The codes consist of rules, some general, others specific, that guide the investigators or the reviewers of research in their work. Such rules often are inadequate to cover complex situations; at times they come into conflict, and they are frequently difficult to interpret or apply. Broader ethical principles will provide a basis on which specific rules may be formulated, criticized and interpreted.

Three principles, or general prescriptive judgments, that are relevant to research involving human subjects are identified in this statement. Other principles may also be relevant. These three are comprehensive, however, and are stated at a level of generalization that should assist scientists, subjects, reviewers and interested citizens to understand the ethical issues inherent in research involving human subjects. These principles cannot always be applied so as to resolve beyond dispute particular ethical problems. The objective is to provide an analytical framework that will guide the resolution of ethical problems arising from research involving human subjects.

This statement consists of a distinction between research and practice, a discussion of the three basic ethical principles, and remarks about the application of these principles.

Part A: Boundaries Between Practice & Research

A. Boundaries Between Practice and Research

It is important to distinguish between biomedical and behavioral research, on the one hand, and the practice of accepted therapy on the other, in order to know what activities ought to undergo review for the protection of human subjects of research. The distinction between research and practice is blurred partly because both often occur together (as in research designed to evaluate a therapy) and partly because notable departures from standard practice are often called "experimental" when the terms "experimental" and "research" are not carefully defined.

For the most part, the term "practice" refers to interventions that are designed solely to enhance the well-being of an individual patient or client and that have a reasonable expectation of success. The purpose of medical or behavioral practice is to provide diagnosis, preventive treatment or therapy to particular individuals.[2] By contrast, the term "research" designates an activity designed to test an hypothesis, permit conclusions to be drawn, and thereby to develop or contribute to generalizable knowledge (expressed, for example, in theories, principles, and statements of relationships). Research is usually described in a formal protocol that sets forth an objective and a set of procedures designed to reach that objective.

When a clinician departs in a significant way from standard or accepted practice, the innovation does not, in and of itself, constitute research. The fact that a procedure is "experimental," in the sense of new, untested or different, does not automatically place it in the category of research. Radically new procedures of this description should, however, be made the object of formal research at an early stage in order to determine whether they are safe and effective. Thus, it is the responsibility of medical practice committees, for example, to insist that a major innovation be incorporated into a formal research project.[3]

Research and practice may be carried on together when research is designed to evaluate the safety and efficacy of a therapy. This need not cause any confusion regarding whether or not the activity requires review; the general rule is that if there is any element of research in an activity, that activity should undergo review for the protection of human subjects.

Part B: Basic Ethical Principles

B. Basic Ethical Principles

The expression "basic ethical principles" refers to those general judgments that serve as a basic justification for the many particular ethical prescriptions and evaluations of human actions. Three basic principles, among those generally accepted in our cultural tradition, are particularly relevant to the ethics of research involving human subjects: the principles of respect of persons, beneficence and justice.

1. Respect for Persons.—Respect for persons incorporates at least two ethical convictions: first, that individuals should be treated as autonomous agents, and second, that persons with diminished autonomy are entitled to protection. The principle of respect for persons thus divides into two separate moral requirements: the requirement to acknowledge autonomy and the requirement to protect those with diminished autonomy.

An autonomous person is an individual capable of deliberation about personal goals and of acting under the direction of such deliberation. To respect autonomy is to give weight to autonomous persons' considered opinions and choices while refraining from obstructing their actions unless they are clearly detrimental to others. To show lack of respect for an autonomous agent is to repudiate that person's considered judgments, to deny an individual the freedom to act on those considered judgments, or to withhold information necessary to make a considered judgment, when there are no compelling reasons to do so.

However, not every human being is capable of self-determination. The capacity for self-determination matures during an individual's life, and some individuals lose this capacity wholly or in part because of illness, mental disability, or circumstances that severely restrict liberty. Respect for the immature and the incapacitated may require protecting them as they mature or while they are incapacitated.

Some persons are in need of extensive protection, even to the point of excluding them from activities which may harm them; other persons require little protection beyond making sure they undertake activities freely and with awareness of possible adverse consequence. The extent of protection afforded should depend upon the risk of harm and the likelihood of benefit. The judgment that any individual lacks autonomy should be periodically re-evaluated and will vary in different situations.

In most cases of research involving human subjects, respect for persons demands that subjects enter into the research voluntarily and with adequate information. In some situations, however, application of the principle is not obvious. The involvement of prisoners as subjects of research provides an instructive example. On the one hand, it would seem that the principle of respect for persons requires that prisoners not be deprived of the opportunity to volunteer for research. On the other hand, under prison conditions they may be subtly coerced or unduly influenced to engage in research activities for which they would not otherwise volunteer. Respect for persons would then dictate that prisoners be protected. Whether to allow prisoners to "volunteer" or to "protect" them presents a dilemma. Respecting persons, inmost hard cases, is often a matter of balancing competing claims urged by the principle of respect itself.

2. Beneficence.—Persons are treated in an ethical manner not only by respecting their decisions and protecting them from harm, but also by making efforts to secure their well-being. Such treatment falls under the principle of beneficence. The term "beneficence" is often understood to cover acts of kindness or charity that go beyond strict obligation. In this document, beneficence is understood in a stronger sense, as an obligation. Two general rules have been formulated as complementary expressions of beneficent actions in this sense: (1) do not harm and (2) maximize possible benefits and minimize possible harms.

The Hippocratic maxim "do no harm" has long been a fundamental principle of medical ethics. Claude Bernard extended it to the realm of research, saying that one should not injure one person regardless of the benefits that might come to others. However, even avoiding harm requires learning what is harmful; and, in the process of obtaining this information, persons may be exposed to risk of harm. Further, the Hippocratic Oath requires physicians to benefit their patients "according to their best judgment." Learning what will in fact benefit may require exposing persons to risk. The problem posed by these imperatives is to decide when it is justifiable to seek certain benefits despite the risks involved, and when the benefits should be foregone because of the risks.

The obligations of beneficence affect both individual investigators and society at large, because they extend both to particular research projects and to the entire enterprise of research. In the case of particular projects, investigators and members of their institutions are obliged to give forethought to the maximization of benefits and the reduction of risk that might occur from the research investigation. In the case of scientific research in general, members of the larger society are obliged to recognize the longer term benefits and risks that may result from the improvement of knowledge and from the development of novel medical, psychotherapeutic, and social procedures.

The principle of beneficence often occupies a well-defined justifying role in many areas of research involving human subjects. An example is found in research involving children. Effective ways of treating childhood diseases and fostering healthy development are benefits that serve to justify research involving children—even when individual research subjects are not direct beneficiaries. Research also makes it possible to avoid the harm that may result from the application of previously accepted routine practices that on closer investigation turn out to be dangerous. But the role of the principle of beneficence is not always so unambiguous. A difficult ethical problem remains, for example, about research that presents more than minimal risk without immediate prospect of direct benefit to the children involved. Some have argued that such research is inadmissible, while others have pointed out that this limit would rule out much research promising great benefit to children in the future. Here again, as with all hard cases, the different claims covered by the principle of beneficence may come into conflict and force difficult choices.

3. Justice.—Who ought to receive the benefits of research and bear its burdens? This is a question of justice, in the sense of "fairness in distribution" or "what is deserved." An injustice occurs when some benefit to which a person is entitled is denied without good reason or when some burden is imposed unduly. Another way of conceiving the principle of justice is that equals ought to be treated equally. However, this statement requires explication. Who is equal and who is unequal? What considerations justify departure from equal distribution? Almost all commentators allow that distinctions based on experience, age, deprivation, competence, merit and position do sometimes constitute criteria justifying differential treatment for certain purposes. It is necessary, then, to explain in what respects people should be treated equally. There are several widely accepted formulations of just ways to distribute burdens and benefits. Each formulation mentions some relevant property on the basis of which burdens and benefits should be distributed. These formulations are (1) to each person an equal share, (2) to each person according to individual need, (3) to each person according to individual effort, (4) to each person according to societal contribution, and (5) to each person according to merit.

Questions of justice have long been associated with social practices such as punishment, taxation and political representation. Until recently these questions have not generally been associated with scientific research. However, they are foreshadowed even in the earliest reflections on the ethics of research involving human subjects. For example, during the 19th and early 20th centuries the burdens of serving as research subjects fell largely upon poor ward patients, while the benefits of improved medical care flowed primarily to private patients. Subsequently, the exploitation of unwilling prisoners as research subjects in Nazi concentration camps was condemned as a particularly flagrant injustice. In this country, in the 1940s, the Tuskegee syphilis study used disadvantaged, rural black men to study the untreated course of a disease that is by no means confined to that population. These subjects were deprived of demonstrably effective treatment in order not to interrupt the project, long after such treatment became generally available.

Against this historical background, it can be seen how conceptions of justice are relevant to research involving human subjects. For example, the selection of research subjects needs to be scrutinized in order to determine whether some classes (e.g., welfare patients, particular racial and ethnic minorities, or persons confined to institutions) are being systematically selected simply because of their easy availability, their compromised position, or their manipulability, rather than for reasons directly related to the problem being studied. Finally, whenever research supported by public funds leads to the development of therapeutic devices and procedures, justice demands both that these not provide advantages only to those who can afford them and that such research should not unduly involve persons from groups unlikely to be among the beneficiaries of subsequent applications of the research.

Part C: Applications

C. Applications

Applications of the general principles to the conduct of research leads to consideration of the following requirements: informed consent, risk/benefit assessment, and the selection of subjects of research.

1. Informed Consent.—Respect for persons requires that subjects, to the degree that they are capable, be given the opportunity to choose what shall or shall not happen to them. This opportunity is provided when adequate standards for informed consent are satisfied.

While the importance of informed consent is unquestioned, controversy prevails over the nature and possibility of an informed consent. Nonetheless, there is widespread agreement that the consent process can be analyzed as containing three elements: information, comprehension and voluntariness.

Information. Most codes of research establish specific items for disclosure intended to assure that subjects are given sufficient information. These items generally include: the research procedure, their purposes, risks and anticipated benefits, alternative procedures (where therapy is involved), and a statement offering the subject the opportunity to ask questions and to withdraw at any time from the research. Additional items have been proposed, including how subjects are selected, the person responsible for the research, etc.

However, a simple listing of items does not answer the question of what the standard should be for judging how much and what sort of information should be provided. One standard frequently invoked in medical practice, namely the information commonly provided by practitioners in the field or in the locale, is inadequate since research takes place precisely when a common understanding does not exist. Another standard, currently popular in malpractice law, requires the practitioner to reveal the information that reasonable persons would wish to know in order to make a decision regarding their care. This, too, seems insufficient since the research subject, being in essence a volunteer, may wish to know considerably more about risks gratuitously undertaken than do patients who deliver themselves into the hand of a clinician for needed care. It may be that a standard of "the reasonable volunteer" should be proposed: the extent and nature of information should be such that persons, knowing that the procedure is neither necessary for their care nor perhaps fully understood, can decide whether they wish to participate in the furthering of knowledge. Even when some direct benefit to them is anticipated, the subjects should understand clearly the range of risk and the voluntary nature of participation.

A special problem of consent arises where informing subjects of some pertinent aspect of the research is likely to impair the validity of the research. In many cases, it is sufficient to indicate to subjects that they are being invited to participate in research of which some features will not be revealed until the research is concluded. In all cases of research involving incomplete disclosure, such research is justified only if it is clear that (1) incomplete disclosure is truly necessary to accomplish the goals of the research, (2) there are no undisclosed risks to subjects that are more than minimal, and (3) there is an adequate plan for debriefing subjects, when appropriate, and for dissemination of research results to them. Information about risks should never be withheld for the purpose of eliciting the cooperation of subjects, and truthful answers should always be given to direct questions about the research. Care should be taken to distinguish cases in which disclosure would destroy or invalidate the research from cases in which disclosure would simply inconvenience the investigator.

Comprehension. The manner and context in which information is conveyed is as important as the information itself. For example, presenting information in a disorganized and rapid fashion, allowing too little time for consideration or curtailing opportunities for questioning, all may adversely affect a subject's ability to make an informed choice.

Because the subject's ability to understand is a function of intelligence, rationality, maturity and language, it is necessary to adapt the presentation of the information to the subject's capacities. Investigators are responsible for ascertaining that the subject has comprehended the information. While there is always an obligation to ascertain that the information about risk to subjects is complete and adequately comprehended, when the risks are more serious, that obligation increases. On occasion, it may be suitable to give some oral or written tests of comprehension.

Special provision may need to be made when comprehension is severely limited—for example, by conditions of immaturity or mental disability. Each class of subjects that one might consider as incompetent (e.g., infants and young children, mentally disable patients, the terminally ill and the comatose) should be considered on its own terms. Even for these persons, however, respect requires giving them the opportunity to choose to the extent they are able, whether or not to participate in research. The objections of these subjects to involvement should be honored, unless the research entails providing them a therapy unavailable elsewhere. Respect for persons also requires seeking the permission of other parties in order to protect the subjects from harm. Such persons are thus respected both by acknowledging their own wishes and by the use of third parties to protect them from harm.

The third parties chosen should be those who are most likely to understand the incompetent subject's situation and to act in that person's best interest. The person authorized to act on behalf of the subject should be given an opportunity to observe the research as it proceeds in order to be able to withdraw the subject from the research, if such action appears in the subject's best interest.

Voluntariness. An agreement to participate in research constitutes a valid consent only if voluntarily given. This element of informed consent requires conditions free of coercion and undue influence. Coercion occurs when an overt threat of harm is intentionally presented by one person to another in order to obtain compliance. Undue influence, by contrast, occurs through an offer of an excessive, unwarranted, inappropriate or improper reward or other overture in order to obtain compliance. Also, inducements that would ordinarily be acceptable may become undue influences if the subject is especially vulnerable.

Unjustifiable pressures usually occur when persons in positions of authority or commanding influence—especially where possible sanctions are involved—urge a course of action for a subject. A continuum of such influencing factors exists, however, and it is impossible to state precisely where justifiable persuasion ends and undue influence begins. But undue influence would include actions such as manipulating a person's choice through the controlling influence of a close relative and threatening to withdraw health services to which an individual would otherwise be entitle.

2. Assessment of Risks and Benefits.—The assessment of risks and benefits requires a careful arrayal of relevant data, including, in some cases, alternative ways of obtaining the benefits sought in the research. Thus, the assessment presents both an opportunity and a responsibility to gather systematic and comprehensive information about proposed research. For the investigator, it is a means to examine whether the proposed research is properly designed. For a review committee, it is a method for determining whether the risks that will be presented to subjects are justified. For prospective subjects, the assessment will assist the determination whether or not to participate.

The Nature and Scope of Risks and Benefits. The requirement that research be justified on the basis of a favorable risk/benefit assessment bears a close relation to the principle of beneficence, just as the moral requirement that informed consent be obtained is derived primarily from the principle of respect for persons. The term "risk" refers to a possibility that harm may occur. However, when expressions such as "small risk" or "high risk" are used, they usually refer (often ambiguously) both to the chance (probability) of experiencing a harm and the severity (magnitude) of the envisioned harm.

The term "benefit" is used in the research context to refer to something of positive value related to health or welfare. Unlike, "risk," "benefit" is not a term that expresses probabilities. Risk is properly contrasted to probability of benefits, and benefits are properly contrasted with harms rather than risks of harm. Accordingly, so-called risk/benefit assessments are concerned with the probabilities and magnitudes of possible harm and anticipated benefits. Many kinds of possible harms and benefits need to be taken into account. There are, for example, risks of psychological harm, physical harm, legal harm, social harm and economic harm and the corresponding benefits. While the most likely types of harms to research subjects are those of psychological or physical pain or injury, other possible kinds should not be overlooked.

Risks and benefits of research may affect the individual subjects, the families of the individual subjects, and society at large (or special groups of subjects in society). Previous codes and Federal regulations have required that risks to subjects be outweighed by the sum of both the anticipated benefit to the subject, if any, and the anticipated benefit to society in the form of knowledge to be gained from the research. In balancing these different elements, the risks and benefits affecting the immediate research subject will normally carry special weight. On the other hand, interests other than those of the subject may on some occasions be sufficient by themselves to justify the risks involved in the research, so long as the subjects' rights have been protected. Beneficence thus requires that we protect against risk of harm to subjects and also that we be concerned about the loss of the substantial benefits that might be gained from research.

The Systematic Assessment of Risks and Benefits. It is commonly said that benefits and risks must be "balanced" and shown to be "in a favorable ratio." The metaphorical character of these terms draws attention to the difficulty of making precise judgments. Only on rare occasions will quantitative techniques be available for the scrutiny of research protocols. However, the idea of systematic, non-arbitrary analysis of risks and benefits should be emulated insofar as possible. This ideal requires those making decisions about the justifiability of research to be thorough in the accumulation and assessment of information about all aspects of the research, and to consider alternatives systematically. This procedure renders the assessment of research more rigorous and precise, while making communication between review board members and investigators less subject to misinterpretation, misinformation and conflicting judgments. Thus, there should first be a determination of the validity of the presuppositions of the research; then the nature, probability and magnitude of risk should be distinguished with as much clarity as possible. The method of ascertaining risks should be explicit, especially where there is no alternative to the use of such vague categories as small or slight risk. It should also be determined whether an investigator's estimates of the probability of harm or benefits are reasonable, as judged by known facts or other available studies.

Finally, assessment of the justifiability of research should reflect at least the following considerations: (i) Brutal or inhumane treatment of human subjects is never morally justified. (ii) Risks should be reduced to those necessary to achieve the research objective. It should be determined whether it is in fact necessary to use human subjects at all. Risk can perhaps never be entirely eliminated, but it can often be reduced by careful attention to alternative procedures. (iii) When research involves significant risk of serious impairment, review committees should be extraordinarily insistent on the justification of the risk (looking usually to the likelihood of benefit to the subject—or, in some rare cases, to the manifest voluntariness of the participation). (iv) When vulnerable populations are involved in research, the appropriateness of involving them should itself be demonstrated. A number of variables go into such judgments, including the nature and degree of risk, the condition of the particular population involved, and the nature and level of the anticipated benefits. (v) Relevant risks and benefits must be thoroughly arrayed in documents and procedures used in the informed consent process.

3. Selection of Subjects.—Just as the principle of respect for persons finds expression in the requirements for consent, and the principle of beneficence in risk/benefit assessment, the principle of justice gives rise to moral requirements that there be fair procedures and outcomes in the selection of research subjects.

Justice is relevant to the selection of subjects of research at two levels: the social and the individual. Individual justice in the selection of subjects would require that researchers exhibit fairness: thus, they should not offer potentially beneficial research only to some patients who are in their favor or select only "undesirable" persons for risky research. Social justice requires that distinction be drawn between classes of subjects that ought, and ought not, to participate in any particular kind of research, based on the ability of members of that class to bear burdens and on the appropriateness of placing further burdens on already burdened persons. Thus, it can be considered a matter of social justice that there is an order of preference in the selection of classes of subjects (e.g., adults before children) and that some classes of potential subjects (e.g., the institutionalized mentally infirm or prisoners) may be involved as research subjects, if at all, only on certain conditions.

Injustice may appear in the selection of subjects, even if individual subjects are selected fairly by investigators and treated fairly in the course of research. Thus injustice arises from social, racial, sexual and cultural biases institutionalized in society. Thus, even if individual researchers are treating their research subjects fairly, and even if IRBs are taking care to assure that subjects are selected fairly within a particular institution, unjust social patterns may nevertheless appear in the overall distribution of the burdens and benefits of research. Although individual institutions or investigators may not be able to resolve a problem that is pervasive in their social setting, they can consider distributive justice in selecting research subjects.

Some populations, especially institutionalized ones, are already burdened in many ways by their infirmities and environments. When research is proposed that involves risks and does not include a therapeutic component, other less burdened classes of persons should be called upon first to accept these risks of research, except where the research is directly related to the specific conditions of the class involved. Also, even though public funds for research may often flow in the same directions as public funds for health care, it seems unfair that populations dependent on public health care constitute a pool of preferred research subjects if more advantaged populations are likely to be the recipients of the benefits.

One special instance of injustice results from the involvement of vulnerable subjects. Certain groups, such as racial minorities, the economically disadvantaged, the very sick, and the institutionalized may continually be sought as research subjects, owing to their ready availability in settings where research is conducted. Given their dependent status and their frequently compromised capacity for free consent, they should be protected against the danger of being involved in research solely for administrative convenience, or because they are easy to manipulate as a result of their illness or socioeconomic condition.

1. Since 1945, various codes for the proper and responsible conduct of human experimentation in medical research have been adopted by different organizations. The best known of these codes are the Nuremberg Code of 1947, the Helsinki Declaration of 1964 (revised in 1975), and the 1971 Guidelines (codified into Federal Regulations in 1974) issued by the U.S. Department of Health, Education, and Welfare Codes for the conduct of social and behavioral research have also been adopted, the best known being that of the American Psychological Association, published in 1973.

2. Although practice usually involves interventions designed solely to enhance the well-being of a particular individual, interventions are sometimes applied to one individual for the enhancement of the well-being of another (e.g., blood donation, skin grafts, organ transplants) or an intervention may have the dual purpose of enhancing the well-being of a particular individual, and, at the same time, providing some benefit to others (e.g., vaccination, which protects both the person who is vaccinated and society generally). The fact that some forms of practice have elements other than immediate benefit to the individual receiving an intervention, however, should not confuse the general distinction between research and practice. Even when a procedure applied in practice may benefit some other person, it remains an intervention designed to enhance the well-being of a particular individual or groups of individuals; thus, it is practice and need not be reviewed as research.

3. Because the problems related to social experimentation may differ substantially from those of biomedical and behavioral research, the Commission specifically declines to make any policy determination regarding such research at this time. Rather, the Commission believes that the problem ought to be addressed by one of its successor bodies.

Code of Federal Regulations
Title 21—Food and Drugs

Chapter 1
Food and Drug Administration,
Department of Health and Human Services

Subchapter A—General

Part 11—Electronic Records; Electronic Signatures

Authority:
21 U.S.C. 321-393; 42 U.S.C. 262.

Source:
62 FR 13464, Mar. 20, 1997, unless otherwise noted.

Subpart A—General Provisions

§ 11.1   Scope.

(a) The regulations in this part set forth the criteria under which the agency considers electronic records, electronic signatures, and handwritten signatures executed to electronic records to be trustworthy, reliable, and generally equivalent to paper records and handwritten signatures executed on paper.

(b) This part applies to records in electronic form that are created, modified, maintained, archived, retrieved, or transmitted, under any records requirements set forth in agency regulations. This part also applies to electronic records submitted to the agency under requirements of the Federal Food, Drug, and Cosmetic Act and the Public Health Service Act, even if such records are not specifically identified in agency regulations. However, this part does not apply to paper records that are, or have been, transmitted by electronic means.

(c) Where electronic signatures and their associated electronic records meet the requirements of this part, the agency will consider the electronic signatures to be equivalent to full handwritten signatures, initials, and other general signings as required by agency regulations, unless specifically excepted by regulation(s) effective on or after August 20, 1997.

(d) Electronic records that meet the requirements of this part may be used in lieu of paper records, in accordance with § 11.2, unless paper records are specifically required.

(e) Computer systems (including hardware and software), controls, and attendant documentation maintained under this part shall be readily available for, and subject to, FDA inspection.

(f) This part does not apply to records required to be established or maintained by §§ 1.326 through 1.368 of this chapter. Records that satisfy the requirements of part 1, subpart J of this chapter, but that also are required under other applicable statutory provisions or regulations, remain subject to this part.

[62 FR 13464, Mar. 20, 1997, as amended at 69 FR 71655, Dec. 9, 2004]

§ 11.2   Implementation.

(a) For records required to be maintained but not submitted to the agency, persons may use electronic records in lieu of paper records or electronic signatures in lieu of traditional signatures, in whole or in part, provided that the requirements of this part are met.

(b) For records submitted to the agency, persons may use electronic records in lieu of paper records or electronic signatures in lieu of traditional signatures, in whole or in part, provided that:

(1) The requirements of this part are met; and

(2) The document or parts of a document to be submitted have been identified in public docket No. 92S-0251 as being the type of submission the agency accepts in electronic form. This docket will identify specifically what types of documents or parts of documents are acceptable for submission in electronic form without paper records and the agency receiving unit(s) (e.g., specific center, office, division, branch) to which such submissions may be made. Documents to agency receiving unit(s) not specified in the public docket will not be considered as official if they are submitted in electronic form; paper forms of such documents will be considered as official and must accompany any electronic records. Persons are expected to consult with the intended agency receiving unit for details on how (e.g., method of transmission, media, file formats, and technical protocols) and whether to proceed with the electronic submission.

§ 11.3 Definitions.

(a) The definitions and interpretations of terms contained in section 201 of the act apply to those terms when used in this part.

(b) The following definitions of terms also apply to this part:

(1) Act means the Federal Food, Drug, and Cosmetic Act (secs. 201-903 (21 U.S.C. 321-393)).

(2) Agency means the Food and Drug Administration.

(3) Biometrics means a method of verifying an individual's identity based on measurement of the individual's physical feature(s) or repeatable action(s) where those features and/or actions are both unique to that individual and measurable.

(4) Closed system means an environment in which system access is controlled by persons who are responsible for the content of electronic records that are on the system.

(5) Digital signature means an electronic signature based upon cryptographic methods of originator authentication, computed by using a set of rules and a set of parameters such that the identity of the signer and the integrity of the data can be verified.

(6) Electronic record means any combination of text, graphics, data, audio, pictorial, or other information representation in digital form that is created, modified, maintained, archived, retrieved, or distributed by a computer system.

(7) Electronic signature means a computer data compilation of any symbol or series of symbols executed, adopted, or authorized by an individual to be the legally binding equivalent of the individual's handwritten signature.

(8) Handwritten signature means the scripted name or legal mark of an individual handwritten by that individual and executed or adopted with the present intention to authenticate a writing in a permanent form. The act of signing with a writing or marking instrument such as a pen or stylus is preserved. The scripted name or legal mark, while conventionally applied to paper, may also be applied to other devices that capture the name or mark.

(9) Open system means an environment in which system access is not controlled by persons who are responsible for the content of electronic records that are on the system.

Subpart B—Electronic Records

§ 11.10   Controls for closed systems.

Persons who use closed systems to create, modify, maintain, or transmit electronic records shall employ procedures and controls designed to ensure the authenticity, integrity, and, when appropriate, the confidentiality of electronic records, and to ensure that the signer cannot readily repudiate the signed record as not genuine. Such procedures and controls shall include the following:

(a) Validation of systems to ensure accuracy, reliability, consistent intended performance, and the ability to discern invalid or altered records.

(b) The ability to generate accurate and complete copies of records in both human readable and electronic form suitable for inspection, review, and copying by the agency. Persons should contact the agency if there are any questions regarding the ability of the agency to perform such review and copying of the electronic records.

(c) Protection of records to enable their accurate and ready retrieval throughout the records retention period.

(d) Limiting system access to authorized individuals.

(e) Use of secure, computer-generated, time-stamped audit trails to independently record the date and time of operator entries and actions that create, modify, or delete electronic records. Record changes shall not obscure previously recorded information. Such audit trail documentation shall be retained for a period at least as long as that required for the subject electronic records and shall be available for agency review and copying.

(f) Use of operational system checks to enforce permitted sequencing of steps and events, as appropriate.

(g) Use of authority checks to ensure that only authorized individuals can use the system, electronically sign a record, access the operation or

computer system input or output device, alter a record, or perform the operation at hand.

(h) Use of device (e.g., terminal) checks to determine, as appropriate, the validity of the source of data input or operational instruction.

(i) Determination that persons who develop, maintain, or use electronic record/electronic signature systems have the education, training, and experience to perform their assigned tasks.

(j) The establishment of, and adherence to, written policies that hold individuals accountable and responsible for actions initiated under their electronic signatures, in order to deter record and signature falsification.

(k) Use of appropriate controls over systems documentation including:

(1) Adequate controls over the distribution of, access to, and use of documentation for system operation and maintenance.

(2) Revision and change control procedures to maintain an audit trail that documents time-sequenced development and modification of systems documentation.

§ 11.30   Controls for open systems.

Persons who use open systems to create, modify, maintain, or transmit electronic records shall employ procedures and controls designed to ensure the authenticity, integrity, and, as appropriate, the confidentiality of electronic records from the point of their creation to the point of their receipt. Such procedures and controls shall include those identified in § 11.10, as appropriate, and additional measures such as document encryption and use of appropriate digital signature standards to ensure, as necessary under the circumstances, record authenticity, integrity, and confidentiality.

§ 11.50   Signature manifestations.

(a) Signed electronic records shall contain information associated with the signing that clearly indicates all of the following:

(1) The printed name of the signer;

(2) The date and time when the signature was executed; and

(3) The meaning (such as review, approval, responsibility, or authorship) associated with the signature.

(b) The items identified in paragraphs (a)(1), (a)(2), and (a)(3) of this section shall be subject to the same controls as for electronic records and shall be included as part of any human readable form of the electronic record (such as electronic display or printout).

§ 11.70   Signature/record linking.

Electronic signatures and handwritten signatures executed to electronic records shall be linked to their respective electronic records to ensure that the signatures cannot be excised, copied, or otherwise transferred to falsify an electronic record by ordinary means.

Subpart C—Electronic Signatures

§ 11.100   General requirements.

(a) Each electronic signature shall be unique to one individual and shall not be reused by, or reassigned to, anyone else.

(b) Before an organization establishes, assigns, certifies, or otherwise sanctions an individual's electronic signature, or any element of such electronic signature, the organization shall verify the identity of the individual.

(c) Persons using electronic signatures shall, prior to or at the time of such use, certify to the agency that the electronic signatures in their system, used on or after August 20, 1997, are intended to be the legally binding equivalent of traditional handwritten signatures.

(1) The certification shall be submitted in paper form and signed with a traditional handwritten signature, to the Office of Regional Operations (HFC-100), 5600 Fishers Lane, Rockville, MD 20857.

(2) Persons using electronic signatures shall, upon agency request, provide additional certification or testimony that a specific electronic signature is the legally binding equivalent of the signer's handwritten signature.

§ 11.200   Electronic signature components and controls.

(a) Electronic signatures that are not based upon biometrics shall:

(1) Employ at least two distinct identification components such as an identification code and password.

(i) When an individual executes a series of signings during a single, continuous period of controlled system access, the first signing shall be executed using all electronic signature components; subsequent signings shall be executed using at least one electronic signature component that is only executable by, and designed to be used only by, the individual.

(ii) When an individual executes one or more signings not performed during a single, continuous period of controlled system access, each signing shall be executed using all of the electronic signature components.

(2) Be used only by their genuine owners; and

(3) Be administered and executed to ensure that attempted use of an individual's electronic signature by anyone other than its genuine owner requires collaboration of two or more individuals.

(b) Electronic signatures based upon biometrics shall be designed to ensure that they cannot be used by anyone other than their genuine owners.

§ 11.300   Controls for identification codes/passwords.

Persons who use electronic signatures based upon use of identification codes in combination with passwords shall employ controls to ensure their security and integrity. Such controls shall include:

(a) Maintaining the uniqueness of each combined identification code and password, such that no two individuals have the same combination of identification code and password.

(b) Ensuring that identification code and password issuances are periodically checked, recalled, or revised (e.g., to cover such events as password aging).

(c) Following loss management procedures to electronically deauthorize lost, stolen, missing, or otherwise potentially compromised tokens, cards, and other devices that bear or generate identification code or password information, and to issue temporary or permanent replacements using suitable, rigorous controls.

(d) Use of transaction safeguards to prevent unauthorized use of passwords and/or identification codes, and to detect and report in an immediate and urgent manner any attempts at their unauthorized use to the system security unit, and, as appropriate, to organizational management.

(e) Initial and periodic testing of devices, such as tokens or cards, that bear or generate identification code or password information to ensure that they function properly and have not been altered in an unauthorized manner.

Part 50—Protection of Human Subjects
Subpart A—General Provisions

Authority:
21 U.S.C 321, 343, 346, 346a, 348, 350a, 350b, 352, 353, 355, 360, 360c-360f, 360h-360j, 371, 379e, 381; 42 U.S.C. 216, 241, 262, 263b-263n.

Source:
45 FR 36390, May 30, 1980, unless otherwise noted.

Subpart A—General Provisions

§ 50.1   Scope.

(a) This part applies to all clinical investigations regulated by the Food and Drug Administration under sections 505(i) and 520(g) of the Federal Food, Drug, and Cosmetic Act, as well as clinical investigations that support applications for research or marketing permits for products regulated by the Food and Drug Administration, including foods, including dietary supplements, that bear a nutrient content claim or a health claim, infant formulas, food and color additives, drugs for human use, medical devices for human use, biological products for human use, and electronic products. Additional specific obligations and commitments of, and standards of conduct for, persons who sponsor or monitor clinical investigations involving particular test articles may also be found in other parts (e.g., parts 312 and 812). Compliance with these parts is intended to protect the rights and safety of subjects involved in investigations filed with the Food and Drug Administration pursuant to sections 403, 406, 409, 412, 413, 502, 503, 505, 510, 513-516, 518-520, 721, and 801 of the Federal Food, Drug, and Cosmetic Act and sections 351 and 354-360F of the Public Health Service Act.

(b) References in this part to regulatory sections of the Code of Federal Regulations are to chapter I of title 21, unless otherwise noted.

[45 FR 36390, May 30, 1980; 46 FR 8979, Jan. 27, 1981, as amended at 63 FR 26697, May 13, 1998; 64 FR 399, Jan. 5, 1999; 66 FR 20597, Apr. 24, 2001]

§ 50.3   Definitions.

As used in this part:

(a) Act means the Federal Food, Drug, and Cosmetic Act, as amended (secs. 201-902, 52 Stat. 1040 et seq. as amended (21 U.S.C. 321-392)).

(b) Application for research or marketing permit includes:

(1) A color additive petition, described in part 71.

(2) A food additive petition, described in parts 171 and 571.

(3) Data and information about a substance submitted as part of the procedures for establishing that the substance is generally recognized as safe for use that results or may reasonably be expected to result, directly or indirectly, in its becoming a component or otherwise affecting the characteristics of any food, described in §§ 170.30 and 570.30.

(4) Data and information about a food additive submitted as part of the procedures for food additives permitted to be used on an interim basis pending additional study, described in § 180.1.

(5) Data and information about a substance submitted as part of the procedures for establishing a tolerance for unavoidable contaminants in food and food-packaging materials, described in section 406 of the act.

(6) An investigational new drug application, described in part 312 of this chapter.

(7) A new drug application, described in part 314.

(8) Data and information about the bioavailability or bioequivalence of drugs for human use submitted as part of the procedures for issuing, amending, or repealing a bioequivalence requirement, described in part 320.

(9) Data and information about an over-the-counter drug for human use submitted as part of the procedures for classifying these drugs as generally recognized as safe and effective and not misbranded, described in part 330.

(10) Data and information about a prescription drug for human use submitted as part of the procedures for classifying these drugs as generally recognized as safe and effective and not misbranded, described in this chapter.

(11) [Reserved]

(12) An application for a biologics license, described in part 601 of this chapter.

(13) Data and information about a biological product submitted as part of the procedures for

determining that licensed biological products are safe and effective and not misbranded, described in part 601.

(14) Data and information about an *in vitro* diagnostic product submitted as part of the procedures for establishing, amending, or repealing a standard for these products, described in part 809.

(15) An Application for an Investigational Device Exemption, described in part 812.

(16) Data and information about a medical device submitted as part of the procedures for classifying these devices, described in section 513.

(17) Data and information about a medical device submitted as part of the procedures for establishing, amending, or repealing a standard for these devices, described in section 514.

(18) An application for premarket approval of a medical device, described in section 515.

(19) A product development protocol for a medical device, described in section 515.

(20) Data and information about an electronic product submitted as part of the procedures for establishing, amending, or repealing a standard for these products, described in section 358 of the Public Health Service Act.

(21) Data and information about an electronic product submitted as part of the procedures for obtaining a variance from any electronic product performance standard, as described in § 1010.4.

(22) Data and information about an electronic product submitted as part of the procedures for granting, amending, or extending an exemption from a radiation safety performance standard, as described in § 1010.5.

(23) Data and information about a clinical study of an infant formula when submitted as part of an infant formula notification under section 412(c) of the Federal Food, Drug, and Cosmetic Act.

(24) Data and information submitted in a petition for a nutrient content claim, described in § 101.69 of this chapter, or for a health claim, described in § 101.70 of this chapter.

(25) Data and information from investigations involving children submitted in a new dietary ingredient notification, described in § 190.6 of this chapter.

(c) Clinical investigation means any experiment that involves a test article and one or more human subjects and that either is subject to requirements for prior submission to the Food and Drug Administration under section 505(i) or 520(g) of the act, or is not subject to requirements for prior submission to the Food and Drug Administration under these sections of the act, but the results of which are intended to be submitted later to, or held for inspection by, the Food and Drug Administration as part of an application for a research or marketing permit. The term does not include experiments that are subject to the provisions of part 58 of this chapter, regarding nonclinical laboratory studies.

(d) Investigator means an individual who actually conducts a clinical investigation, i.e., under whose immediate direction the test article is administered or dispensed to, or used involving, a subject, or, in the event of an investigation conducted by a team of individuals, is the responsible leader of that team.

(e) Sponsor means a person who initiates a clinical investigation, but who does not actually conduct the investigation, i.e., the test article is administered or dispensed to or used involving, a subject under the immediate direction of another individual. A person other than an individual (e.g., corporation or agency) that uses one or more of its own employees to conduct a clinical investigation it has initiated is considered to be a sponsor (not a sponsor-investigator), and the employees are considered to be investigators.

(f) Sponsor-investigator means an individual who both initiates and actually conducts, alone or with others, a clinical investigation, i.e., under whose immediate direction the test article is administered or dispensed to, or used involving, a subject. The term does not include any person other than an individual, e.g., corporation or agency.

(g) Human subject means an individual who is or becomes a participant in research, either as a recipient of the test article or as a control. A subject may be either a healthy human or a patient.

(h) Institution means any public or private entity or agency (including Federal, State, and other agencies). The word facility as used in section 520(g) of the act is deemed to be synonymous with the term institution for purposes of this part.

(i) Institutional review board (IRB) means any board, committee, or other group formally designated by an institution to review biomedical research involving humans as subjects, to approve the initiation of and conduct periodic review of such research. The term has the same meaning as the phrase institutional review committee as used in section 520(g) of the act.

(j) Test article means any drug (including a biological product for human use), medical device for human use, human food additive, color additive, electronic product, or any other article subject to regulation under the act or under sections 351 and 354-360F of the Public Health Service Act (42 U.S.C. 262 and 263b-263n).

(k) Minimal risk means that the probability and magnitude of harm or discomfort anticipated in the research are not greater in and of themselves than those ordinarily encountered in daily life or during the performance of routine physical or psychological examinations or tests.

(l) Legally authorized representative means an individual or judicial or other body authorized under applicable law to consent on behalf of a prospective subject to the subject's participation in the procedure(s) involved in the research.

(m) Family member means any one of the following legally competent persons: Spouse; parents; children (including adopted children); brothers, sisters, and spouses of brothers and sisters; and any individual related by blood or affinity whose close association with the subject is the equivalent of a family relationship.

(n) Assent means a child's affirmative agreement to participate in a clinical investigation. Mere failure to object may not, absent affirmative agreement, be construed as assent.

(o) Children means persons who have not attained the legal age for consent to treatments or procedures involved in clinical investigations, under the applicable law of the jurisdiction in which the clinical investigation will be conducted.

(p) Parent means a child's biological or adoptive parent.

(q) Ward means a child who is placed in the legal custody of the State or other agency, institution, or entity, consistent with applicable Federal, State, or local law.

(r) Permission means the agreement of parent(s) or guardian to the participation of their child or ward in a clinical investigation. Permission must be obtained in compliance with subpart B of this part and must include the elements of informed consent described in § 50.25.

(s) Guardian means an individual who is authorized under applicable State or local law to consent on behalf of a child to general medical care when general medical care includes participation in research. For purposes of subpart D of this part, a guardian also means an individual who is authorized to consent on behalf of a child to participate in research.

[45 FR 36390, May 30, 1980, as amended at 46 FR 8950, Jan. 27, 1981; 54 FR 9038, Mar. 3, 1989; 56 FR 28028, June 18, 1991; 61 FR 51528, Oct. 2, 1996; 62 FR 39440, July 23, 1997; 64 FR 399, Jan. 5, 1999; 64 FR 56448, Oct. 20, 1999; 66 FR 20597, Apr. 24, 2001]

Subpart B—Informed Consent of Human Subjects

Source:

46 FR 8951, Jan. 27, 1981, unless otherwise noted.

§ 50.20   General requirements for informed consent.

Except as provided in §§ 50.23 and 50.24, no investigator may involve a human being as a subject in research covered by these regulations unless the investigator has obtained the legally effective informed consent of the subject or the subject's legally authorized representative. An investigator shall seek such consent only under circumstances that provide the prospective subject or the representative sufficient opportunity to consider whether or not to participate and that minimize the possibility of coercion or undue influence. The information that is given to the subject or the representative shall be in language understandable to the subject or the representative. No informed consent, whether oral or written, may include any exculpatory language through which the subject or the representative is made to waive or appear to waive any of the subject's legal rights, or releases or appears to release the investigator, the sponsor, the institution, or its agents from liability for negligence.

[46 FR 8951, Jan. 27, 1981, as amended at 64 FR 10942, Mar. 8, 1999]

§ 50.23   Exception from general requirements.

(a) The obtaining of informed consent shall be deemed feasible unless, before use of the test article (except as provided in paragraph (b) of this section), both the investigator and a physician who is not otherwise participating in the clinical investigation certify in writing all of the following:

(1) The human subject is confronted by a life-

threatening situation necessitating the use of the test article.

(2) Informed consent cannot be obtained from the subject because of an inability to communicate with, or obtain legally effective consent from, the subject.

(3) Time is not sufficient to obtain consent from the subject's legal representative.

(4) There is available no alternative method of approved or generally recognized therapy that provides an equal or greater likelihood of saving the life of the subject.

(b) If immediate use of the test article is, in the investigator's opinion, required to preserve the life of the subject, and time is not sufficient to obtain the independent determination required in paragraph (a) of this section in advance of using the test article, the determinations of the clinical investigator shall be made and, within 5 working days after the use of the article, be reviewed and evaluated in writing by a physician who is not participating in the clinical investigation.

(c) The documentation required in paragraph (a) or (b) of this section shall be submitted to the IRB within 5 working days after the use of the test article.

(d)(1) Under 10 U.S.C. 1107(f) the President may waive the prior consent requirement for the administration of an investigational new drug to a member of the armed forces in connection with the member's participation in a particular military operation. The statute specifies that only the President may waive informed consent in this connection and the President may grant such a waiver only if the President determines in writing that obtaining consent: Is not feasible; is contrary to the best interests of the military member; or is not in the interests of national security. The statute further provides that in making a determination to waive prior informed consent on the ground that it is not feasible or the ground that it is contrary to the best

interests of the military members involved, the President shall apply the standards and criteria that are set forth in the relevant FDA regulations for a waiver of the prior informed consent requirements of section 505(i)(4) of the Federal Food, Drug, and Cosmetic Act (21 U.S.C. 355(i)(4)). Before such a determination may be made that obtaining informed consent from military personnel prior to the use of an investigational drug (including an antibiotic or biological product) in a specific protocol under an investigational new drug application (IND) sponsored by the Department of Defense (DOD) and limited to specific military personnel involved in a particular military operation is not feasible or is contrary to the best interests of the military members involved the Secretary of Defense must first request such a determination from the President, and certify and document to the President that the following standards and criteria contained in paragraphs (d)(1) through (d)(4) of this section have been met.

(i) The extent and strength of evidence of the safety and effectiveness of the investigational new drug in relation to the medical risk that could be encountered during the military operation supports the drug's administration under an IND.

(ii) The military operation presents a substantial risk that military personnel may be subject to a chemical, biological, nuclear, or other exposure likely to produce death or serious or life-threatening injury or illness.

(iii) There is no available satisfactory alternative therapeutic or preventive treatment in relation to the intended use of the investigational new drug.

(iv) Conditioning use of the investigational new drug on the voluntary participation of each member could significantly risk the safety and health of any individual member who would decline its use, the safety of other military personnel, and the accomplishment of the military mission.

(v) A duly constituted institutional review board (IRB) established and operated in accordance with the requirements of paragraphs (d)(2) and (d)(3) of this section, responsible for review of the study, has reviewed and approved the investigational new drug protocol and the administration of the investigational new drug without informed consent. DOD's request is to include the documentation required by § 56.115(a)(2) of this chapter.

(vi) DOD has explained:

(A) The context in which the investigational drug will be administered, e.g., the setting or whether it will be self-administered or it will be administered by a health professional;

(B) The nature of the disease or condition for which the preventive or therapeutic treatment is intended; and

(C) To the extent there are existing data or information available, information on conditions that could alter the effects of the investigational drug.

(vii) DOD's recordkeeping system is capable of tracking and will be used to track the proposed treatment from supplier to the individual recipient.

(viii) Each member involved in the military operation will be given, prior to the administration of the investigational new drug, a specific written information sheet (including information required by 10 U.S.C. 1107(d)) concerning the investigational new drug, the risks and benefits of its use, potential side effects, and other pertinent information about the appropriate use of the product.

(ix) Medical records of members involved in the military operation will accurately document the receipt by members of the notification required by paragraph (d)(1)(viii) of this section.

(x) Medical records of members involved in the military operation will accurately document the receipt by members of any investigational

new drugs in accordance with FDA regulations including part 312 of this chapter.

(xi) DOD will provide adequate followup to assess whether there are beneficial or adverse health consequences that result from the use of the investigational product.

(xii) DOD is pursuing drug development, including a time line, and marketing approval with due diligence.

(xiii) FDA has concluded that the investigational new drug protocol may proceed subject to a decision by the President on the informed consent waiver request.

(xiv) DOD will provide training to the appropriate medical personnel and potential recipients on the specific investigational new drug to be administered prior to its use.

(xv) DOD has stated and justified the time period for which the waiver is needed, not to exceed one year, unless separately renewed under these standards and criteria.

(xvi) DOD shall have a continuing obligation to report to the FDA and to the President any changed circumstances relating to these standards and criteria (including the time period referred to in paragraph (d)(1)(xv) of this section) or that otherwise might affect the determination to use an investigational new drug without informed consent.

(xvii) DOD is to provide public notice as soon as practicable and consistent with classification requirements through notice in the Federal Register describing each waiver of informed consent determination, a summary of the most updated scientific information on the products used, and other pertinent information.

(xviii) Use of the investigational drug without informed consent otherwise conforms with applicable law.

(2) The duly constituted institutional review board, described in paragraph (d)(1)(v) of this

section, must include at least 3 nonaffiliated members who shall not be employees or officers of the Federal Government (other than for purposes of membership on the IRB) and shall be required to obtain any necessary security clearances. This IRB shall review the proposed IND protocol at a convened meeting at which a majority of the members are present including at least one member whose primary concerns are in nonscientific areas and, if feasible, including a majority of the nonaffiliated members. The information required by § 56.115(a)(2) of this chapter is to be provided to the Secretary of Defense for further review.

(3) The duly constituted institutional review board, described in paragraph (d)(1)(v) of this section, must review and approve:

(i) The required information sheet;

(ii) The adequacy of the plan to disseminate information, including distribution of the information sheet to potential recipients, on the investigational product (e.g., in forms other than written);

(iii) The adequacy of the information and plans for its dissemination to health care providers, including potential side effects, contraindications, potential interactions, and other pertinent considerations; and

(iv) An informed consent form as required by part 50 of this chapter, in those circumstances in which DOD determines that informed consent may be obtained from some or all personnel involved.

(4) DOD is to submit to FDA summaries of institutional review board meetings at which the proposed protocol has been reviewed.

(5) Nothing in these criteria or standards is intended to preempt or limit FDA's and DOD's authority or obligations under applicable statutes and regulations.

(e)(1) Obtaining informed consent for investigational *in vitro* diagnostic devices used to identify chemical, biological, radiological, or nuclear agents will be deemed feasible unless, before use of the test article, both the investigator (e.g., clinical laboratory director or other responsible individual) and a physician who is not otherwise participating in the clinical investigation make the determinations and later certify in writing all of the following:

(i) The human subject is confronted by a life-threatening situation necessitating the use of the investigational *in vitro* diagnostic device to identify a chemical, biological, radiological, or nuclear agent that would suggest a terrorism event or other public health emergency.

(ii) Informed consent cannot be obtained from the subject because:

(A) There was no reasonable way for the person directing that the specimen be collected to know, at the time the specimen was collected, that there would be a need to use the investigational *in vitro* diagnostic device on that subject's specimen; and

(B) Time is not sufficient to obtain consent from the subject without risking the life of the subject.

(iii) Time is not sufficient to obtain consent from the subject's legally authorized representative.

(iv) There is no cleared or approved available alternative method of diagnosis, to identify the chemical, biological, radiological, or nuclear agent that provides an equal or greater likelihood of saving the life of the subject.

(2) If use of the investigational device is, in the opinion of the investigator (e.g., clinical laboratory director or other responsible person), required to preserve the life of the subject, and time is not sufficient to obtain the independent determination required in paragraph (e)(1) of this section in advance of using the investigational device, the determinations of the investigator shall be made and, within 5 working days after the use of the device, be reviewed and evaluated in writing by a physician who is not

participating in the clinical investigation.

(3) The investigator must submit the documentation required in paragraph (e)(1) or (e)(2) of this section to the IRB within 5 working days after the use of the device.

(4) An investigator must disclose the investigational status of the *in vitro* diagnostic device and what is known about the performance characteristics of the device in the report to the subject's health care provider and in any report to public health authorities. The investigator must provide the IRB with the information required in § 50.25 (except for the information described in § 50.25(a)(8)) and the procedures that will be used to provide this information to each subject or the subject's legally authorized representative at the time the test results are provided to the subject's health care provider and public health authorities.

(5) The IRB is responsible for ensuring the adequacy of the information required in section 50.25 (except for the information described in § 50.25(a)(8)) and for ensuring that procedures are in place to provide this information to each subject or the subject's legally authorized representative.

(6) No State or political subdivision of a State may establish or continue in effect any law, rule, regulation or other requirement that informed consent be obtained before an investigational *in vitro* diagnostic device may be used to identify chemical, biological, radiological, or nuclear agent in suspected terrorism events and other potential public health emergencies that is different from, or in addition to, the requirements of this regulation.

[46 FR 8951, Jan. 27, 1981, as amended at 55 FR 52817, Dec. 21, 1990; 64 FR 399, Jan. 5, 1999; 64 FR 54188, Oct. 5, 1999; 71 FR 32833, June 7, 2006]

§ 50.24   Exception from informed consent requirements for emergency research.

(a) The IRB responsible for the review, approval, and continuing review of the clinical investigation described in this section may approve that investigation without requiring that informed consent of all research subjects be obtained if the IRB (with the concurrence of a licensed physician who is a member of or consultant to the IRB and who is not otherwise participating in the clinical investigation) finds and documents each of the following:

(1) The human subjects are in a life-threatening situation, available treatments are unproven or unsatisfactory, and the collection of valid scientific evidence, which may include evidence obtained through randomized placebo-controlled investigations, is necessary to determine the safety and effectiveness of particular interventions.

(2) Obtaining informed consent is not feasible because:

(i) The subjects will not be able to give their informed consent as a result of their medical condition;

(ii) The intervention under investigation must be administered before consent from the subjects' legally authorized representatives is feasible; and

(iii) There is no reasonable way to identify prospectively the individuals likely to become eligible for participation in the clinical investigation.

(3) Participation in the research holds out the prospect of direct benefit to the subjects because:

(i) Subjects are facing a life-threatening situation that necessitates intervention;

(ii) Appropriate animal and other preclinical studies have been conducted, and the information derived from those studies and related evidence support the potential for the intervention to provide a direct benefit to the individual subjects; and

(iii) Risks associated with the investigation are reasonable in relation to what is known about the medical condition of the potential class of subjects, the risks and benefits of standard therapy, if any, and what is known about the risks and benefits of the proposed intervention or activity.

(4) The clinical investigation could not practicably be carried out without the waiver.

(5) The proposed investigational plan defines the length of the potential therapeutic window based on scientific evidence, and the investigator has committed to attempting to contact a legally authorized representative for each subject within that window of time and, if feasible, to asking the legally authorized representative contacted for consent within that window rather than proceeding without consent. The investigator will summarize efforts made to contact legally authorized representatives and make this information available to the IRB at the time of continuing review.

(6) The IRB has reviewed and approved informed consent procedures and an informed consent document consistent with § 50.25. These procedures and the informed consent document are to be used with subjects or their legally authorized representatives in situations where use of such procedures and documents is feasible. The IRB has reviewed and approved procedures and information to be used when providing an opportunity for a family member to object to a subject's participation in the clinical investigation consistent with paragraph (a) (7)(v) of this section.

(7) Additional protections of the rights and welfare of the subjects will be provided, including, at least:

(i) Consultation (including, where appropriate, consultation carried out by the IRB) with representatives of the communities in which the clinical investigation will be conducted and from which the subjects will be drawn;

(ii) Public disclosure to the communities in which the clinical investigation will be conducted and from which the subjects will be drawn, prior to initiation of the clinical investigation, of plans for the investigation and its risks and expected benefits;

(iii) Public disclosure of sufficient information following completion of the clinical investigation to apprise the community and researchers of the study, including the demographic characteristics of the research population, and its results;

(iv) Establishment of an independent data monitoring committee to exercise oversight of the clinical investigation; and

(v) If obtaining informed consent is not feasible and a legally authorized representative is not reasonably available, the investigator has committed, if feasible, to attempting to contact within the therapeutic window the subject's family member who is not a legally authorized representative, and asking whether he or she objects to the subject's participation in the clinical investigation. The investigator will summarize efforts made to contact family members and make this information available to the IRB at the time of continuing review.

(b) The IRB is responsible for ensuring that procedures are in place to inform, at the earliest feasible opportunity, each subject, or if the subject remains incapacitated, a legally authorized representative of the subject, or if such a representative is not reasonably available, a family member, of the subject's inclusion in the clinical investigation, the details of the investigation and other information contained in the informed consent document. The IRB shall also ensure that there is a procedure to inform the subject, or if the subject remains incapacitated, a legally authorized representative of the subject, or if such a representative is not reasonably available, a family member, that he or she may discontinue the subject's participation at any time without penalty or loss of benefits to which the subject is otherwise entitled. If a legally authorized representative or family member is told about the clinical investigation and the subject's condition improves, the subject is also to be informed as soon as feasible. If a subject is entered into a clinical investigation with waived consent and the subject dies before a legally authorized representative or family member can be contacted, information about the clinical investigation is to be provided to the subject's legally authorized representative or family member, if feasible.

(c) The IRB determinations required by paragraph (a) of this section and the documentation required by paragraph (e) of this section are to be retained by the IRB for at least 3 years after completion of the clinical investigation, and the records shall be accessible for inspection and copying by FDA in accordance with § 56.115(b) of this chapter.

(d) Protocols involving an exception to the informed consent requirement under this section must be performed under a separate investigational new drug application (IND) or investigational device exemption (IDE) that clearly identifies such protocols as protocols that may include subjects who are unable to consent. The submission of those protocols in a separate IND/IDE is required even if an IND for the same drug product or an IDE for the same device already exists. Applications for investigations under this section may not be submitted as amendments under §§ 312.30 or 812.35 of this chapter.

(e) If an IRB determines that it cannot approve a clinical investigation because the investigation does not meet the criteria in the exception provided under paragraph (a) of this section or because of other relevant ethical concerns, the IRB must document its findings and provide these findings promptly in writing to the clinical investigator and to the sponsor of the clinical investigation. The sponsor of the clinical investigation must promptly disclose this information to FDA and to the sponsor's clinical investigators who are participating or are asked to partic-

ipate in this or a substantially equivalent clinical investigation of the sponsor, and to other IRB's that have been, or are, asked to review this or a substantially equivalent investigation by that sponsor.

[61 FR 51528, Oct. 2, 1996]

§ 50.25 Elements of informed consent.

(a) Basic elements of informed consent. In seeking informed consent, the following information shall be provided to each subject:

(1) A statement that the study involves research, an explanation of the purposes of the research and the expected duration of the subject's participation, a description of the procedures to be followed, and identification of any procedures which are experimental.

(2) A description of any reasonably foreseeable risks or discomforts to the subject.

(3) A description of any benefits to the subject or to others which may reasonably be expected from the research.

(4) A disclosure of appropriate alternative procedures or courses of treatment, if any, that might be advantageous to the subject.

(5) A statement describing the extent, if any, to which confidentiality of records identifying the subject will be maintained and that notes the possibility that the Food and Drug Administration may inspect the records.

(6) For research involving more than minimal risk, an explanation as to whether any compensation and an explanation as to whether any medical treatments are available if injury occurs and, if so, what they consist of, or where further information may be obtained.

(7) An explanation of whom to contact for answers to pertinent questions about the research and research subjects' rights, and whom to contact in the event of a research-related injury to the subject.

(8) A statement that participation is voluntary, that refusal to participate will involve no penalty or loss of benefits to which the subject is otherwise entitled, and that the subject may discontinue participation at any time without penalty or loss of benefits to which the subject is otherwise entitled.

(b) Additional elements of informed consent. When appropriate, one or more of the following elements of information shall also be provided to each subject:

(1) A statement that the particular treatment or procedure may involve risks to the subject (or to the embryo or fetus, if the subject is or may become pregnant) which are currently unforeseeable.

(2) Anticipated circumstances under which the subject's participation may be terminated by the investigator without regard to the subject's consent.

(3) Any additional costs to the subject that may result from participation in the research.

(4) The consequences of a subject's decision to withdraw from the research and procedures for orderly termination of participation by the subject.

(5) A statement that significant new findings developed during the course of the research which may relate to the subject's willingness to continue participation will be provided to the subject.

(6) The approximate number of subjects involved in the study.

(c) The informed consent requirements in these regulations are not intended to preempt any applicable Federal, State, or local laws which require additional information to be disclosed for informed consent to be legally effective.

(d) Nothing in these regulations is intended to limit the authority of a physician to provide emergency medical care to the extent the physician is permitted to do so under applicable Federal, State, or local law.

§ 50.27   Documentation of informed consent.

(a) Except as provided in § 56.109(c), informed consent shall be documented by the use of a written consent form approved by the IRB and signed and dated by the subject or the subject's legally authorized representative at the time of consent. A copy shall be given to the person signing the form.

(b) Except as provided in § 56.109(c), the consent form may be either of the following:

(1) A written consent document that embodies the elements of informed consent required by § 50.25. This form may be read to the subject or the subject's legally authorized representative, but, in any event, the investigator shall give either the subject or the representative adequate opportunity to read it before it is signed.

(2) A short form written consent document stating that the elements of informed consent required by § 50.25 have been presented orally to the subject or the subject's legally authorized representative. When this method is used, there shall be a witness to the oral presentation. Also, the IRB shall approve a written summary of what is to be said to the subject or the representative. Only the short form itself is to be signed by the subject or the representative. However, the witness shall sign both the short form and a copy of the summary, and the person actually obtaining the consent shall sign a copy of the summary. A copy of the summary shall be given to the subject or the representative in addition to a copy of the short form.

[46 FR 8951, Jan. 27, 1981, as amended at 61 FR 57280, Nov. 5, 1996]

Subpart C [Reserved]
Subpart D—Additional Safeguards for Children in Clinical Investigations

Source:

66 FR 20598, Apr. 24, 2001, unless otherwise noted.

§ 50.50   IRB duties.

In addition to other responsibilities assigned to IRBs under this part and part 56 of this chapter, each IRB must review clinical investigations involving children as subjects covered by this subpart D and approve only those clinical investigations that satisfy the criteria described in § 50.51, § 50.52, or § 50.53 and the conditions of all other applicable sections of this subpart D.

§ 50.51   Clinical investigations not involving greater than minimal risk.

Any clinical investigation within the scope described in §§ 50.1 and 56.101 of this chapter in which no greater than minimal risk to children is presented may involve children as subjects only if the IRB finds and documents that adequate provisions are made for soliciting the assent of the children and the permission of their parents or guardians as set forth in § 50.55.

§ 50.52   Clinical investigations involving greater than minimal risk but presenting the prospect of direct benefit to individual subjects.

Any clinical investigation within the scope described in §§ 50.1 and 56.101 of this chapter in which more than minimal risk to children is presented by an intervention or procedure that holds out the prospect of direct benefit for the individual subject, or by a monitoring procedure that is likely to contribute to the subject's well-being, may involve children as subjects only if the IRB finds and documents that:

(a) The risk is justified by the anticipated benefit to the subjects;

(b) The relation of the anticipated benefit to the risk is at least as favorable to the subjects as that presented by available alternative approaches; and

(c) Adequate provisions are made for soliciting the assent of the children and permission of their parents or guardians as set forth in § 50.55.

§ 50.53   Clinical investigations involving greater than minimal risk and no prospect of direct benefit to individual subjects, but likely to yield generalizable knowledge about the subjects' disorder or condition.

Any clinical investigation within the scope described in §§ 50.1 and 56.101 of this chapter in which more than minimal risk to children is presented by an intervention or procedure that does not hold out the prospect of direct benefit for the individual subject, or by a monitoring procedure that is not likely to contribute to the well-being of the subject, may involve children as subjects only if the IRB finds and documents that:

(a) The risk represents a minor increase over minimal risk;

(b) The intervention or procedure presents experiences to subjects that are reasonably commensurate with those inherent in their actual or expected medical, dental, psychological, social, or educational situations;

(c) The intervention or procedure is likely to yield generalizable knowledge about the subjects' disorder or condition that is of vital importance for the understanding or amelioration of the subjects' disorder or condition; and

(d) Adequate provisions are made for soliciting the assent of the children and permission of their parents or guardians as set forth in § 50.55.

§ 50.54   Clinical investigations not otherwise approvable that present an opportunity to understand, prevent, or alleviate a serious problem affecting the health or welfare of children.

If an IRB does not believe that a clinical investigation within the scope described in §§ 50.1 and 56.101 of this chapter and involving children as subjects meets the requirements of § 50.51, § 50.52, or § 50.53, the clinical investigation may proceed only if:

(a) The IRB finds and documents that the clinical investigation presents a reasonable opportunity to further the understanding, prevention, or alleviation of a serious problem affecting the health or welfare of children; and

(b) The Commissioner of Food and Drugs, after consultation with a panel of experts in pertinent disciplines (for example: science, medicine, education, ethics, law) and following opportunity for public review and comment, determines either:

(1) That the clinical investigation in fact satisfies the conditions of § 50.51, § 50.52, or § 50.53, as applicable, or

(2) That the following conditions are met:

(i) The clinical investigation presents a reasonable opportunity to further the understanding, prevention, or alleviation of a serious problem affecting the health or welfare of children;

(ii) The clinical investigation will be conducted in accordance with sound ethical principles; and

(iii) Adequate provisions are made for soliciting the assent of children and the permission of their parents or guardians as set forth in § 50.55.

§ 50.55   Requirements for permission by parents or guardians and for assent by children.

(a) In addition to the determinations required under other applicable sections of this subpart D, the IRB must determine that adequate provisions are made for soliciting the assent of the children when in the judgment of the IRB the children are capable of providing assent.

(b) In determining whether children are capable of providing assent, the IRB must take into account the ages, maturity, and psychological state of the children involved. This judgment may be made for all children to be involved in clinical investigations under a particular protocol, or for each child, as the IRB deems appropriate.

(c) The assent of the children is not a necessary condition for proceeding with the clinical investigation if the IRB determines:

(1) That the capability of some or all of the children is so limited that they cannot reasonably be consulted, or

(2) That the intervention or procedure involved in the clinical investigation holds out a prospect of direct benefit that is important to the health or well-being of the children and is available only in the context of the clinical investigation.

(d) Even where the IRB determines that the subjects are capable of assenting, the IRB may still waive the assent requirement if it finds and documents that:

(1) The clinical investigation involves no more than minimal risk to the subjects;

(2) The waiver will not adversely affect the rights and welfare of the subjects;

(3) The clinical investigation could not practicably be carried out without the waiver; and

(4) Whenever appropriate, the subjects will be provided with additional pertinent information after participation.

(e) In addition to the determinations required under other applicable sections of this subpart D, the IRB must determine that the permission of each child's parents or guardian is granted.

(1) Where parental permission is to be obtained, the IRB may find that the permission of one parent is sufficient, if consistent with State law, for clinical investigations to be conducted under § 50.51 or § 50.52.

(2) Where clinical investigations are covered by § 50.53 or § 50.54 and permission is to be obtained from parents, both parents must give their permission unless one parent is deceased, unknown, incompetent, or not reasonably available, or when only one parent has legal responsibility for the care and custody of the child if consistent with State law.

(f) Permission by parents or guardians must be documented in accordance with and to the extent required by § 50.27.

(g) When the IRB determines that assent is required, it must also determine whether and how assent must be documented.

§ 50.56   Wards.

(a) Children who are wards of the State or any other agency, institution, or entity can be included in clinical investigations approved under § 50.53 or § 50.54 only if such clinical investigations are:

(1) Related to their status as wards; or

(2) Conducted in schools, camps, hospitals, institutions, or similar settings in which the majority of children involved as subjects are not wards.

(b) If the clinical investigation is approved under paragraph (a) of this section, the IRB must require appointment of an advocate for each child who is a ward.

(1) The advocate will serve in addition to any other individual acting on behalf of the child as guardian or in loco parentis.

(2) One individual may serve as advocate for more than one child.

(3) The advocate must be an individual who has the background and experience to act in, and agrees to act in, the best interest of the child for the duration of the child's participation in the clinical investigation.

(4) The advocate must not be associated in any way (except in the role as advocate or member of the IRB) with the clinical investigation, the investigator(s), or the guardian organization.

Part 54—Financial Disclosure by Clinical Investigators
Authority:
21 U.S.C. 321, 331, 351, 352, 353, 355, 360, 360c-360j, 371, 372, 373, 374, 375, 376, 379; 42 U.S.C. 262.

Source:
63 FR 5250, Feb. 2, 1998, unless otherwise noted.

§ 54.1   Purpose.

(a) The Food and Drug Administration (FDA) evaluates clinical studies submitted in marketing applications, required by law, for new human drugs and biological products and marketing applications and reclassification petitions for medical devices.

(b) The agency reviews data generated in these clinical studies to determine whether the applications are approvable under the statutory requirements. FDA may consider clinical studies inadequate and the data inadequate if, among other things, appropriate steps have not been taken in the design, conduct, reporting, and analysis of the studies to minimize bias. One potential source of bias in clinical studies is a financial interest of the clinical investigator in the outcome of the study because of the way payment is arranged (e.g., a royalty) or because the investigator has a proprietary interest in the product (e.g., a patent) or because the investigator has an equity interest in the sponsor of the covered study. This section and conforming regulations require an applicant whose submission relies in part on clinical data to disclose certain financial arrangements between sponsor(s) of the covered studies and the clinical investigators and certain interests of the clinical investigators in the product under study or in the sponsor of the covered studies. FDA will use this information, in conjunction with information about the design and purpose of the study, as well as information obtained through on-site inspections, in the agency's assessment of the reliability of the data.

§ 54.2   Definitions.

For the purposes of this part:

(a) Compensation affected by the outcome of

clinical studies means compensation that could be higher for a favorable outcome than for an unfavorable outcome, such as compensation that is explicitly greater for a favorable result or compensation to the investigator in the form of an equity interest in the sponsor of a covered study or in the form of compensation tied to sales of the product, such as a royalty interest.

(b) Significant equity interest in the sponsor of a covered study means any ownership interest, stock options, or other financial interest whose value cannot be readily determined through reference to public prices (generally, interests in a nonpublicly traded corporation), or any equity interest in a publicly traded corporation that exceeds $50,000 during the time the clinical investigator is carrying out the study and for 1 year following completion of the study.

(c) Proprietary interest in the tested product means property or other financial interest in the product including, but not limited to, a patent, trademark, copyright or licensing agreement.

(d) Clinical investigator means only a listed or identified investigator or subinvestigator who is directly involved in the treatment or evaluation of research subjects. The term also includes the spouse and each dependent child of the investigator.

(e) Covered clinical study means any study of a drug or device in humans submitted in a marketing application or reclassification petition subject to this part that the applicant or FDA relies on to establish that the product is effective (including studies that show equivalence to an effective product) or any study in which a single investigator makes a significant contribution to the demonstration of safety. This would, in general, not include phase I tolerance studies or pharmacokinetic studies, most clinical pharmacology studies (unless they are critical to an efficacy determination), large open safety studies conducted at multiple sites, treatment protocols, and parallel track protocols. An applicant may consult with FDA as to which clinical studies constitute "covered clinical studies" for purposes of complying with financial disclosure requirements.

(f) Significant payments of other sorts means payments made by the sponsor of a covered study to the investigator or the institution to support activities of the investigator that have a monetary value of more than $25,000, exclusive of the costs of conducting the clinical study or other clinical studies, (e.g., a grant to fund ongoing research, compensation in the form of equipment or retainers for ongoing consultation or honoraria) during the time the clinical investigator is carrying out the study and for 1 year following the completion of the study.

(g) Applicant means the party who submits a marketing application to FDA for approval of a drug, device, or biologic product. The applicant is responsible for submitting the appropriate certification and disclosure statements required in this part.

(h) Sponsor of the covered clinical study means the party supporting a particular study at the time it was carried out.

[63 FR 5250, Feb. 2, 1998, as amended at 63 FR 72181, Dec. 31, 1998]

§ 54.3 Scope.

The requirements in this part apply to any applicant who submits a marketing application for a human drug, biological product, or device and who submits covered clinical studies. The applicant is responsible for making the appropriate certification or disclosure statement where the applicant either contracted with one or more clinical investigators to conduct the studies or submitted studies conducted by others not under contract to the applicant.

§ 54.4 Certification and disclosure requirements.

For purposes of this part, an applicant must submit a list of all clinical investigators who conducted covered clinical studies to determine whether the applicant's product meets FDA's marketing requirements, identifying those clinical investigators who are full-time or part-time employees of the sponsor of each covered study. The applicant must also completely and accurately disclose or certify information concerning the financial interests of a clinical investigator who is not a full-time or part-time employee of the sponsor for each covered clinical study. Clinical investigators subject to investigational new drug or investigational device exemption regulations must provide the sponsor of the study with sufficient accurate information needed to allow subsequent disclosure or certification. The applicant is required to submit for each clinical investigator who participates in a covered study, either a certification that none of the financial arrangements described in § 54.2 exist, or disclose the nature of those arrangements to the agency. Where the applicant acts with due diligence to obtain the information required in this section but is unable to do so, the applicant shall certify that despite the applicant's due diligence in attempting to obtain the information, the applicant was unable to obtain the information and shall include the reason.

(a) The applicant (of an application submitted under sections 505, 506, 510(k), 513, or 515 of the Federal Food, Drug, and Cosmetic Act, or section 351 of the Public Health Service Act) that relies in whole or in part on clinical studies shall submit, for each clinical investigator who participated in a covered clinical study, either a certification described in paragraph (a)(1) of this section or a disclosure statement described in paragraph (a)(3) of this section.

(1) Certification: The applicant covered by this section shall submit for all clinical investigators (as defined in § 54.2(d)), to whom the certification applies, a completed Form FDA 3454 attesting to the absence of financial interests and arrangements described in paragraph (a)(3) of this section. The form shall be dated and signed by the chief financial officer or other responsible corporate official or representative.

(2) If the certification covers less than all covered clinical data in the application, the applicant shall include in the certification a list of the studies covered by this certification.

(3) Disclosure Statement: For any clinical investigator defined in § 54.2(d) for whom the applicant does not submit the certification described in paragraph (a)(1) of this section, the applicant shall submit a completed Form FDA 3455 disclosing completely and accurately the following:

(i) Any financial arrangement entered into between the sponsor of the covered study and the clinical investigator involved in the conduct of a covered clinical trial, whereby the value of the compensation to the clinical investigator for conducting the study could be influenced by the outcome of the study;

(ii) Any significant payments of other sorts from the sponsor of the covered study, such as a grant to fund ongoing research, compensation in the form of equipment, retainer for ongoing consultation, or honoraria;

(iii) Any proprietary interest in the tested product held by any clinical investigator involved in a study;

(iv) Any significant equity interest in the sponsor of the covered study held by any clinical investigator involved in any clinical study; and

(v) Any steps taken to minimize the potential for bias resulting from any of the disclosed arrangements, interests, or payments.

(b) The clinical investigator shall provide to the sponsor of the covered study sufficient accurate financial information to allow the sponsor to submit complete and accurate certification or disclosure statements as required in paragraph (a) of this section. The investigator shall promptly update this information if any relevant changes occur in the course of the investigation or for 1 year following completion of the study.

(c) Refusal to file application. FDA may refuse

to file any marketing application described in paragraph (a) of this section that does not contain the information required by this section or a certification by the applicant that the applicant has acted with due diligence to obtain the information but was unable to do so and stating the reason.

[63 FR 5250, Feb. 2, 1998; 63 FR 35134, June 29, 1998, as amended at 64 FR 399, Jan. 5, 1999]

§ 54.5   Agency evaluation of financial interests.

(a) Evaluation of disclosure statement. FDA will evaluate the information disclosed under § 54.4(a)(2) about each covered clinical study in an application to determine the impact of any disclosed financial interests on the reliability of the study. FDA may consider both the size and nature of a disclosed financial interest (including the potential increase in the value of the interest if the product is approved) and steps that have been taken to minimize the potential for bias.

(b) Effect of study design. In assessing the potential of an investigator's financial interests to bias a study, FDA will take into account the design and purpose of the study. Study designs that utilize such approaches as multiple investigators (most of whom do not have a disclosable interest), blinding, objective endpoints, or measurement of endpoints by someone other than the investigator may adequately protect against any bias created by a disclosable financial interest.

(c) Agency actions to ensure reliability of data. If FDA determines that the financial interests of any clinical investigator raise a serious question about the integrity of the data, FDA will take any action it deems necessary to ensure the reliability of the data including:

(1) Initiating agency audits of the data derived from the clinical investigator in question;

(2) Requesting that the applicant submit further analyses of data, e.g., to evaluate the effect of the clinical investigator's data on overall study outcome;

(3) Requesting that the applicant conduct additional independent studies to confirm the results of the questioned study; and

(4) Refusing to treat the covered clinical study as providing data that can be the basis for an agency action.

§ 54.6   Recordkeeping and record retention.

(a) Financial records of clinical investigators to be retained. An applicant who has submitted a marketing application containing covered clinical studies shall keep on file certain information pertaining to the financial interests of clinical investigators who conducted studies on which the application relies and who are not full or part-time employees of the applicant, as follows:

(1) Complete records showing any financial interest or arrangement as described in § 54.4(a) (3)(i) paid to such clinical investigators by the sponsor of the covered study.

(2) Complete records showing significant payments of other sorts, as described in § 54.4(a)(3) (ii), made by the sponsor of the covered clinical study to the clinical investigator.

(3) Complete records showing any financial interests held by clinical investigators as set forth in § 54.4(a)(3)(iii) and (a)(3)(iv).

(b) Requirements for maintenance of clinical investigators' financial records. (1) For any application submitted for a covered product, an applicant shall retain records as described in paragraph (a) of this section for 2 years after the date of approval of the application.

(2) The person maintaining these records shall, upon request from any properly authorized officer or employee of FDA, at reasonable times, permit such officer or employee to have access to and copy and verify these records.

Part 56—Institutional Review Boards
Subpart A—General Provisions

Authority:

21 U.S.C. 321, 343, 346, 346a, 348, 350a, 350b, 351, 352, 353, 355, 360, 360c-360f, 360h-360j, 371, 379e, 381; 42 U.S.C. 216, 241, 262, 263b-263n.

Source:

46 FR 8975, Jan. 27, 1981, unless otherwise noted.

Subpart A—General Provisions

§ 56.101   Scope.

(a) This part contains the general standards for the composition, operation, and responsibility of an Institutional Review Board (IRB) that reviews clinical investigations regulated by the Food and Drug Administration under sections 505(i) and 520(g) of the act, as well as clinical investigations that support applications for research or marketing permits for products regulated by the Food and Drug Administration, including foods, including dietary supplements, that bear a nutrient content claim or a health claim, infant formulas, food and color additives, drugs for human use, medical devices for human use, biological products for human use, and electronic products. Compliance with this part is intended to protect the rights and welfare of human subjects involved in such investigations.

(b) References in this part to regulatory sections of the Code of Federal Regulations are to chapter I of title 21, unless otherwise noted.

[46 FR 8975, Jan. 27, 1981, as amended at 64 FR 399, Jan. 5, 1999; 66 FR 20599, Apr. 24, 2001]

§ 56.102   Definitions.

As used in this part:

(a) Act means the Federal Food, Drug, and Cosmetic Act, as amended (secs. 201-902, 52 Stat. 1040 et seq., as amended (21 U.S.C. 321-392)).

(b) Application for research or marketing permit includes:

(1) A color additive petition, described in part 71.

(2) Data and information regarding a substance submitted as part of the procedures for establishing that a substance is generally recognized as safe for a use which results or may reasonably be expected to result, directly or indirectly, in its becoming a component or otherwise affecting the characteristics of any food, described in § 170.35.

(3) A food additive petition, described in part 171.

(4) Data and information regarding a food additive submitted as part of the procedures regarding food additives permitted to be used on an interim basis pending additional study, described in § 180.1.

(5) Data and information regarding a substance submitted as part of the procedures for establishing a tolerance for unavoidable contaminants in food and food-packaging materials, described in section 406 of the act.

(6) An investigational new drug application, described in part 312 of this chapter.

(7) A new drug application, described in part 314.

(8) Data and information regarding the bioavailability or bioequivalence of drugs for human use submitted as part of the procedures for issuing, amending, or repealing a bioequivalence requirement, described in part 320.

(9) Data and information regarding an over-the-counter drug for human use submitted as part of the procedures for classifying such drugs as generally recognized as safe and effective and not misbranded, described in part 330.

(10) An application for a biologics license, described in part 601 of this chapter.

(11) Data and information regarding a biological product submitted as part of the procedures

for determining that licensed biological products are safe and effective and not misbranded, as described in part 601 of this chapter.

(12) An Application for an Investigational Device Exemption, described in part 812.

(13) Data and information regarding a medical device for human use submitted as part of the procedures for classifying such devices, described in part 860.

(14) Data and information regarding a medical device for human use submitted as part of the procedures for establishing, amending, or repealing a standard for such device, described in part 861.

(15) An application for premarket approval of a medical device for human use, described in section 515 of the act.

(16) A product development protocol for a medical device for human use, described in section 515 of the act.

(17) Data and information regarding an electronic product submitted as part of the procedures for establishing, amending, or repealing a standard for such products, described in section 358 of the Public Health Service Act.

(18) Data and information regarding an electronic product submitted as part of the procedures for obtaining a variance from any electronic product performance standard, as described in § 1010.4.

(19) Data and information regarding an electronic product submitted as part of the procedures for granting, amending, or extending an exemption from a radiation safety performance standard, as described in § 1010.5.

(20) Data and information regarding an electronic product submitted as part of the procedures for obtaining an exemption from notification of a radiation safety defect or failure of compliance with a radiation safety performance standard, described in subpart D of part 1003.

(21) Data and information about a clinical study of an infant formula when submitted as part of an infant formula notification under section 412(c) of the Federal Food, Drug, and Cosmetic Act.

(22) Data and information submitted in a petition for a nutrient content claim, described in § 101.69 of this chapter, and for a health claim, described in § 101.70 of this chapter.

(23) Data and information from investigations involving children submitted in a new dietary ingredient notification, described in § 190.6 of this chapter.

(c) Clinical investigation means any experiment that involves a test article and one or more human subjects, and that either must meet the requirements for prior submission to the Food and Drug Administration under section 505(i) or 520(g) of the act, or need not meet the requirements for prior submission to the Food and Drug Administration under these sections of the act, but the results of which are intended to be later submitted to, or held for inspection by, the Food and Drug Administration as part of an application for a research or marketing permit. The term does not include experiments that must meet the provisions of part 58, regarding nonclinical laboratory studies. The terms research, clinical research, clinical study, study, and clinical investigation are deemed to be synonymous for purposes of this part.

(d) Emergency use means the use of a test article on a human subject in a life-threatening situation in which no standard acceptable treatment is available, and in which there is not sufficient time to obtain IRB approval.

(e) Human subject means an individual who is or becomes a participant in research, either as a recipient of the test article or as a control. A subject may be either a healthy individual or a patient.

(f) Institution means any public or private entity or agency (including Federal, State, and other agencies). The term facility as used in section 520(g) of the act is deemed to be synonymous with the term institution for purposes of this part.

(g) Institutional Review Board (IRB) means any board, committee, or other group formally designated by an institution to review, to approve the initiation of, and to conduct periodic review of, biomedical research involving human subjects. The primary purpose of such review is to assure the protection of the rights and welfare of the human subjects. The term has the same meaning as the phrase institutional review committee as used in section 520(g) of the act.

(h) Investigator means an individual who actually conducts a clinical investigation (i.e., under whose immediate direction the test article is administered or dispensed to, or used involving, a subject) or, in the event of an investigation conducted by a team of individuals, is the responsible leader of that team.

(i) Minimal risk means that the probability and magnitude of harm or discomfort anticipated in the research are not greater in and of themselves than those ordinarily encountered in daily life or during the performance of routine physical or psychological examinations or tests.

(j) Sponsor means a person or other entity that initiates a clinical investigation, but that does not actually conduct the investigation, i.e., the test article is administered or dispensed to, or used involving, a subject under the immediate direction of another individual. A person other than an individual (e.g., a corporation or agency) that uses one or more of its own employees to conduct an investigation that it has initiated is considered to be a sponsor (not a sponsor-investigator), and the employees are considered to be investigators.

(k) Sponsor-investigator means an individual who both initiates and actually conducts, alone or with others, a clinical investigation, i.e., under whose immediate direction the test article

is administered or dispensed to, or used involving, a subject. The term does not include any person other than an individual, e.g., it does not include a corporation or agency. The obligations of a sponsor-investigator under this part include both those of a sponsor and those of an investigator.

(l) Test article means any drug for human use, biological product for human use, medical device for human use, human food additive, color additive, electronic product, or any other article subject to regulation under the act or under sections 351 or 354-360F of the Public Health Service Act.

(m) IRB approval means the determination of the IRB that the clinical investigation has been reviewed and may be conducted at an institution within the constraints set forth by the IRB and by other institutional and Federal requirements.

[46 FR 8975, Jan. 27, 1981, as amended at 54 FR 9038, Mar. 3, 1989; 56 FR 28028, June 18, 1991; 64 FR 399, Jan. 5, 1999; 64 FR 56448, Oct. 20, 1999; 65 FR 52302, Aug. 29, 2000; 66 FR 20599, Apr. 24, 2001; 74 FR 2368, Jan. 15, 2009]

§ 56.103　Circumstances in which IRB review is required.

(a) Except as provided in §§ 56.104 and 56.105, any clinical investigation which must meet the requirements for prior submission (as required in parts 312, 812, and 813) to the Food and Drug Administration shall not be initiated unless that investigation has been reviewed and approved by, and remains subject to continuing review by, an IRB meeting the requirements of this part.

(b) Except as provided in §§ 56.104 and 56.105, the Food and Drug Administration may decide not to consider in support of an application for a research or marketing permit any data or information that has been derived from a clinical investigation that has not been approved by, and that was not subject to initial and continuing review by, an IRB meeting the requirements of this part. The determination that a clinical investigation may not be considered in support of an application for a research or marketing permit does not, however, relieve the applicant for such a permit of any obligation under any other applicable regulations to submit the results of the investigation to the Food and Drug Administration.

(c) Compliance with these regulations will in no way render inapplicable pertinent Federal, State, or local laws or regulations.

[46 FR 8975, Jan. 27, 1981; 46 FR 14340, Feb. 27, 1981]

§ 56.104   Exemptions from IRB requirement.

The following categories of clinical investigations are exempt from the requirements of this part for IRB review:

(a) Any investigation which commenced before July 27, 1981 and was subject to requirements for IRB review under FDA regulations before that date, provided that the investigation remains subject to review of an IRB which meets the FDA requirements in effect before July 27, 1981.

(b) Any investigation commenced before July 27, 1981 and was not otherwise subject to requirements for IRB review under Food and Drug Administration regulations before that date.

(c) Emergency use of a test article, provided that such emergency use is reported to the IRB within 5 working days. Any subsequent use of the test article at the institution is subject to IRB review.

(d) Taste and food quality evaluations and consumer acceptance studies, if wholesome foods without additives are consumed or if a food is consumed that contains a food ingredient at or below the level and for a use found to be safe, or agricultural, chemical, or environmental contaminant at or below the level found to be safe, by the Food and Drug Administration

or approved by the Environmental Protection Agency or the Food Safety and Inspection Service of the U.S. Department of Agriculture.

[46 FR 8975, Jan. 27, 1981, as amended at 56 FR 28028, June 18, 1991]

§ 56.105   Waiver of IRB requirement.

On the application of a sponsor or sponsor-investigator, the Food and Drug Administration may waive any of the requirements contained in these regulations, including the requirements for IRB review, for specific research activities or for classes of research activities, otherwise covered by these regulations.

Subpart B—Organization and Personnel

§ 56.106   Registration.

(a) Who must register? Each IRB in the United States that reviews clinical investigations regulated by FDA under sections 505(i) or 520(g) of the act and each IRB in the United States that reviews clinical investigations that are intended to support applications for research or marketing permits for FDA-regulated products must register at a site maintained by the Department of Health and Human Services (HHS). (A research permit under section 505(i) of the act is usually known as an investigational new drug application (IND), while a research permit under section 520(g) of the act is usually known as an investigational device exemption (IDE).) An individual authorized to act on the IRB's behalf must submit the registration information. All other IRBs may register voluntarily.

(b) What information must an IRB register? Each IRB must provide the following information:

(1) The name, mailing address, and street address (if different from the mailing address) of the institution operating the IRB and the name, mailing address, phone number, facsimile number, and electronic mail address of the senior officer of that institution who is responsible for overseeing activities performed by the IRB;

(2) The IRB's name, mailing address, street address (if different from the mailing address), phone number, facsimile number, and electronic mail address; each IRB chairperson's name, phone number, and electronic mail address; and the name, mailing address, phone number, facsimile number, and electronic mail address of the contact person providing the registration information.

(3) The approximate number of active protocols involving FDA-regulated products reviewed. For purposes of this rule, an "active protocol" is any protocol for which an IRB conducted an initial review or a continuing review at a convened meeting or under an expedited review procedure during the preceding 12 months; and

(4) A description of the types of FDA-regulated products (such as biological products, color additives, food additives, human drugs, or medical devices) involved in the protocols that the IRB reviews.

(c) When must an IRB register? Each IRB must submit an initial registration. The initial registration must occur before the IRB begins to review a clinical investigation described in paragraph (a) of this section. Each IRB must renew its registration every 3 years. IRB registration becomes effective after review and acceptance by HHS.

(d) Where can an IRB register? Each IRB may register electronically through http://ohrp.cit.nih.gov/efile. If an IRB lacks the ability to register electronically, it must send its registration information, in writing, to the Good Clinical Practice Program (HF-34), Office of Science and Health Coordination, Food and Drug Administration, 5600 Fishers Lane, Rockville, MD 20857.

(e) How does an IRB revise its registration information? If an IRB's contact or chair person information changes, the IRB must revise its registration information by submitting any changes in that information within 90 days of the change. An IRB's decision to review new types of FDA-regulated products (such as a decision to review studies pertaining to food additives whereas the IRB previously reviewed studies pertaining to drug products), or to discontinue reviewing clinical investigations regulated by FDA is a change that must be reported within 30 days of the change. An IRB's decision to disband is a change that must be reported within 30 days of permanent cessation of the IRB's review of research. All other information changes may be reported when the IRB renews its registration. The revised information must be sent to FDA either electronically or in writing in accordance with paragraph (d) of this section.

[74 FR 2368, Jan. 15, 2009]

§ 56.107   IRB membership.

(a) Each IRB shall have at least five members, with varying backgrounds to promote complete and adequate review of research activities commonly conducted by the institution. The IRB shall be sufficiently qualified through the experience and expertise of its members, and the diversity of the members, including consideration of race, gender, cultural backgrounds, and sensitivity to such issues as community attitudes, to promote respect for its advice and counsel in safeguarding the rights and welfare of human subjects. In addition to possessing the professional competence necessary to review the specific research activities, the IRB shall be able to ascertain the acceptability of proposed research in terms of institutional commitments and regulations, applicable law, and standards or professional conduct and practice. The IRB shall therefore include persons knowledgeable in these areas. If an IRB regularly reviews research that involves a vulnerable category of subjects, such as children, prisoners, pregnant women, or handicapped or mentally disabled persons, consideration shall be given to the inclusion of one or more individuals who are knowledgeable about and experienced in working with those subjects.

(b) Every nondiscriminatory effort will be made to ensure that no IRB consists entirely of men or entirely of women, including the instituton's consideration of qualified persons of both sexes, so long as no selection is made to the IRB on the basis of gender. No IRB may consist entirely of members of one profession.

(c) Each IRB shall include at least one member whose primary concerns are in the scientific area and at least one member whose primary concerns are in nonscientific areas.

(d) Each IRB shall include at least one member who is not otherwise affiliated with the institution and who is not part of the immediate family of a person who is affiliated with the institution.

(e) No IRB may have a member participate in the IRB's initial or continuing review of any project in which the member has a conflicting interest, except to provide information requested by the IRB.

(f) An IRB may, in its discretion, invite individuals with competence in special areas to assist in the review of complex issues which require expertise beyond or in addition to that available on the IRB. These individuals may not vote with the IRB.

[46 FR 8975, Jan 27, 1981, as amended at 56 FR 28028, June 18, 1991; 56 FR 29756, June 28, 1991]

Subpart C—IRB Functions and Operations

§ 56.108   IRB functions and operations.

In order to fulfill the requirements of these regulations, each IRB shall:

(a) Follow written procedures: (1) For conducting its initial and continuing review of research and for reporting its findings and actions to the investigator and the institution; (2) for determining which projects require review more often than annually and which projects need verification from sources other than the investigator that no material changes have occurred since previous IRB review; (3) for ensuring prompt reporting to the IRB of changes in research activity; and (4) for ensuring that changes in approved research, during the period for which IRB approval has already been given, may not be initiated without IRB review and approval except where necessary to eliminate apparent immediate hazards to the human subjects.

(b) Follow written procedures for ensuring prompt reporting to the IRB, appropriate institutional officials, and the Food and Drug Administration of: (1) Any unanticipated problems involving risks to human subjects or others; (2) any instance of serious or continuing noncompliance with these regulations or the requirements or determinations of the IRB; or (3) any suspension or termination of IRB approval.

(c) Except when an expedited review procedure is used (see § 56.110), review proposed research at convened meetings at which a majority of the members of the IRB are present, including at least one member whose primary concerns are in nonscientific areas. In order for the research to be approved, it shall receive the approval of a majority of those members present at the meeting.

[46 FR 8975, Jan. 27, 1981, as amended at 56 FR 28028, June 18, 1991; 67 FR 9585, Mar. 4, 2002]

§ 56.109   IRB review of research.

(a) An IRB shall review and have authority to approve, require modifications in (to secure approval), or disapprove all research activities covered by these regulations.

(b) An IRB shall require that information given to subjects as part of informed consent is in accordance with § 50.25. The IRB may require that information, in addition to that specifically mentioned in § 50.25, be given to the subjects when in the IRB's judgment the information would meaningfully add to the protection of the rights and welfare of subjects.

(c) An IRB shall require documentation of informed consent in accordance with § 50.27 of this chapter, except as follows:

(1) The IRB may, for some or all subjects, waive the requirement that the subject, or the subject's legally authorized representative, sign a written consent form if it finds that the research presents no more than minimal risk of harm to subjects and involves no procedures for which written consent is normally required outside the research context; or

(2) The IRB may, for some or all subjects, find that the requirements in § 50.24 of this chapter for an exception from informed consent for emergency research are met.

(d) In cases where the documentation requirement is waived under paragraph (c)(1) of this section, the IRB may require the investigator to provide subjects with a written statement regarding the research.

(e) An IRB shall notify investigators and the institution in writing of its decision to approve or disapprove the proposed research activity, or of modifications required to secure IRB approval of the research activity. If the IRB decides to disapprove a research activity, it shall include in its written notification a statement of the reasons for its decision and give the investigator an opportunity to respond in person or in writing. For investigations involving an exception to informed consent under § 50.24 of this chapter, an IRB shall promptly notify in writing the investigator and the sponsor of the research when an IRB determines that it cannot approve the research because it does not meet the criteria in the exception provided under § 50.24(a) of this chapter or because of other relevant ethical concerns. The written notification shall include a statement of the reasons for the IRB's determination.

(f) An IRB shall conduct continuing review of research covered by these regulations at intervals appropriate to the degree of risk, but not less than once per year, and shall have authority to observe or have a third party observe the consent process and the research.

(g) An IRB shall provide in writing to the sponsor of research involving an exception to informed consent under § 50.24 of this chapter a copy of information that has been publicly disclosed under § 50.24(a)(7)(ii) and (a)(7)(iii) of this chapter. The IRB shall provide this information to the sponsor promptly so that the sponsor is aware that such disclosure has occurred. Upon receipt, the sponsor shall provide copies of the information disclosed to FDA.

(h) When some or all of the subjects in a study are children, an IRB must determine that the research study is in compliance with part 50, subpart D of this chapter, at the time of its initial review of the research. When some or all of the subjects in a study that is ongoing on April 30, 2001 are children, an IRB must conduct a review of the research to determine compliance with part 50, subpart D of this chapter, either at the time of continuing review or, at the discretion of the IRB, at an earlier date.

[46 FR 8975, Jan. 27, 1981, as amended at 61 FR 51529, Oct. 2, 1996; 66 FR 20599, Apr. 24, 2001]

§ 56.110 Expedited review procedures for certain kinds of research involving no more than minimal risk, and for minor changes in approved research.

(a) The Food and Drug Administration has established, and published in the Federal Register, a list of categories of research that may be reviewed by the IRB through an expedited review procedure. The list will be amended, as appropriate, through periodic republication in the Federal Register.

(b) An IRB may use the expedited review procedure to review either or both of the following: (1) Some or all of the research appearing on the list and found by the reviewer(s) to involve no more than minimal risk, (2) minor changes in previously approved research during the period (of 1 year or less) for which approval is authorized. Under an expedited review procedure, the review may be carried out by the IRB chairperson or by one or more experienced reviewers designated by the IRB chairperson from among the members of the IRB. In reviewing the research, the reviewers may exercise all of the authorities of the IRB except that the reviewers may not disapprove the research. A research activity may be disapproved only after review in accordance with the nonexpedited review procedure set forth in § 56.108(c).

(c) Each IRB which uses an expedited review procedure shall adopt a method for keeping all members advised of research proposals which have been approved under the procedure.

(d) The Food and Drug Administration may restrict, suspend, or terminate an institution's or IRB's use of the expedited review procedure when necessary to protect the rights or welfare of subjects.

[46 FR 8975, Jan. 27, 1981, as amended at 56 FR 28029, June 18, 1991]

§ 56.111   Criteria for IRB approval of research.

(a) In order to approve research covered by these regulations the IRB shall determine that all of the following requirements are satisfied:

(1) Risks to subjects are minimized: (i) By using procedures which are consistent with sound research design and which do not unnecessarily expose subjects to risk, and (ii) whenever appropriate, by using procedures already being performed on the subjects for diagnostic or treatment purposes.

(2) Risks to subjects are reasonable in relation to anticipated benefits, if any, to subjects, and the importance of the knowledge that may be expected to result. In evaluating risks and benefits, the IRB should consider only those risks and benefits that may result from the research (as distinguished from risks and benefits of therapies that subjects would receive even if not participating in the research). The IRB should not consider possible long-range effects of applying knowledge gained in the research (for example, the possible effects of the research on public policy) as among those research risks that fall within the purview of its responsibility.

(3) Selection of subjects is equitable. In making this assessment the IRB should take into account the purposes of the research and the setting in which the research will be conducted and should be particularly cognizant of the special problems of research involving vulnerable populations, such as children, prisoners, pregnant women, handicapped, or mentally disabled persons, or economically or educationally disadvantaged persons.

(4) Informed consent will be sought from each prospective subject or the subject's legally authorized representative, in accordance with and to the extent required by part 50.

(5) Informed consent will be appropriately documented, in accordance with and to the extent required by § 50.27.

(6) Where appropriate, the research plan makes adequate provision for monitoring the data collected to ensure the safety of subjects.

(7) Where appropriate, there are adequate provisions to protect the privacy of subjects and to maintain the confidentiality of data.

(b) When some or all of the subjects, such as children, prisoners, pregnant women, handicapped, or mentally disabled persons, or economically or educationally disadvantaged persons, are likely to be vulnerable to coercion or undue influence additional safeguards have been included in the study to protect the rights and welfare of these subjects.

(c) In order to approve research in which some or all of the subjects are children, an IRB must determine that all research is in compliance with part 50, subpart D of this chapter.

[46 FR 8975, Jan. 27, 1981, as amended at 56 FR 28029, June 18, 1991; 66 FR 20599, Apr. 24, 2001]

§ 56.112   Review by institution.

Research covered by these regulations that has been approved by an IRB may be subject to further appropriate review and approval or disapproval by officials of the institution. However, those officials may not approve the research if it has not been approved by an IRB.

§ 56.113   Suspension or termination of IRB approval of research.

An IRB shall have authority to suspend or terminate approval of research that is not being conducted in accordance with the IRB's requirements or that has been associated with unexpected serious harm to subjects. Any suspension or termination of approval shall include a statement of the reasons for the IRB's action and shall be reported promptly to the investigator, appropriate institutional officials, and the Food and Drug Administration.

§ 56.114   Cooperative research.

In complying with these regulations, institutions involved in multi-institutional studies may use joint review, reliance upon the review of another qualified IRB, or similar arrangements aimed at avoidance of duplication of effort.

Subpart D—Records and Reports

§ 56.115   IRB records.

(a) An institution, or where appropriate an IRB, shall prepare and maintain adequate documentation of IRB activities, including the following:

(1) Copies of all research proposals reviewed, scientific evaluations, if any, that accompany the proposals, approved sample consent documents, progress reports submitted by investigators, and reports of injuries to subjects.

(2) Minutes of IRB meetings which shall be in sufficient detail to show attendance at the meetings; actions taken by the IRB; the vote on these actions including the number of members voting for, against, and abstaining; the basis for requiring changes in or disapproving

research; and a written summary of the discussion of controverted issues and their resolution.

(3) Records of continuing review activities.

(4) Copies of all correspondence between the IRB and the investigators.

(5) A list of IRB members identified by name; earned degrees; representative capacity; indications of experience such as board certifications, licenses, etc., sufficient to describe each member's chief anticipated contributions to IRB deliberations; and any employment or other relationship between each member and the institution; for example: full-time employee, part-time employee, a member of governing panel or board, stockholder, paid or unpaid consultant.

(6) Written procedures for the IRB as required by § 56.108 (a) and (b).

(7) Statements of significant new findings provided to subjects, as required by § 50.25.

(b) The records required by this regulation shall be retained for at least 3 years after completion of the research, and the records shall be accessible for inspection and copying by authorized representatives of the Food and Drug Administration at reasonable times and in a reasonable manner.

(c) The Food and Drug Administration may refuse to consider a clinical investigation in support of an application for a research or marketing permit if the institution or the IRB that reviewed the investigation refuses to allow an inspection under this section.

[46 FR 8975, Jan. 27, 1981, as amended at 56 FR 28029, June 18, 1991; 67 FR 9585, Mar. 4, 2002]

Subpart E—Administrative Actions for Non-compliance

§ 56.120   Lesser administrative actions.

(a) If apparent noncompliance with these regulations in the operation of an IRB is observed by an FDA investigator during an inspection, the inspector will present an oral or written summary of observations to an appropriate representative of the IRB. The Food and Drug Administration may subsequently send a letter describing the noncompliance to the IRB and to the parent institution. The agency will require that the IRB or the parent institution respond to this letter within a time period specified by FDA and describe the corrective actions that will be taken by the IRB, the institution, or both to achieve compliance with these regulations.

(b) On the basis of the IRB's or the institution's response, FDA may schedule a reinspection to confirm the adequacy of corrective actions. In addition, until the IRB or the parent institution takes appropriate corrective action, the agency may:

(1) Withhold approval of new studies subject to the requirements of this part that are conducted at the institution or reviewed by the IRB;

(2) Direct that no new subjects be added to ongoing studies subject to this part;

(3) Terminate ongoing studies subject to this part when doing so would not endanger the subjects; or

(4) When the apparent noncompliance creates a significant threat to the rights and welfare of human subjects, notify relevant State and Federal regulatory agencies and other parties with a direct interest in the agency's action of the deficiencies in the operation of the IRB.

(c) The parent institution is presumed to be responsible for the operation of an IRB, and the Food and Drug Administration will ordinarily direct any administrative action under this subpart against the institution. However, depending on the evidence of responsibility for deficiencies, determined during the investigation, the Food and Drug Administration may restrict its administrative actions to the IRB or to a component of the parent institution determined to be responsible for formal designation of the IRB.

§ 56.121   Disqualification of an IRB or an institution.

(a) Whenever the IRB or the institution has failed to take adequate steps to correct the noncompliance stated in the letter sent by the agency under § 56.120(a), and the Commissioner of Food and Drugs determines that this noncompliance may justify the disqualification of the IRB or of the parent institution, the Commissioner will institute proceedings in accordance with the requirements for a regulatory hearing set forth in part 16.

(b) The Commissioner may disqualify an IRB or the parent institution if the Commissioner determines that:

(1) The IRB has refused or repeatedly failed to comply with any of the regulations set forth in this part, and

(2) The noncompliance adversely affects the rights or welfare of the human subjects in a clinical investigation.

(c) If the Commissioner determines that disqualification is appropriate, the Commissioner will issue an order that explains the basis for the determination and that prescribes any actions to be taken with regard to ongoing clinical research conducted under the review of the IRB. The Food and Drug Administration will send notice of the disqualification to the IRB and the parent institution. Other parties with a direct interest, such as sponsors and clinical investigators, may also be sent a notice of the disqualification. In addition, the agency may elect to publish a notice of its action in the Federal Register.

(d) The Food and Drug Administration will not approve an application for a research permit for a clinical investigation that is to be under the review of a disqualified IRB or that is to be conducted at a disqualified institution, and it may refuse to consider in support of a marketing permit the data from a clinical investigation that was reviewed by a disqualified IRB as conducted at a disqualified institution, unless the IRB or the parent institution is reinstated as provided in § 56.123.

§ 56.122 Public disclosure of information regarding revocation.

A determination that the Food and Drug Administration has disqualified an institution and the administrative record regarding that determination are disclosable to the public under part 20.

§ 56.123 Reinstatement of an IRB or an institution.

An IRB or an institution may be reinstated if the Commissioner determines, upon an evaluation of a written submission from the IRB or institution that explains the corrective action that the institution or IRB plans to take, that the IRB or institution has provided adequate assurance that it will operate in compliance with the standards set forth in this part. Notification of reinstatement shall be provided to all persons notified under § 56.121(c).

§ 56.124 Actions alternative or additional to disqualification.

Disqualification of an IRB or of an institution is independent of, and neither in lieu of nor a precondition to, other proceedings or actions authorized by the act. The Food and Drug Administration may, at any time, through the Department of Justice institute any appropriate judicial proceedings (civil or criminal) and any other appropriate regulatory action, in addition to or in lieu of, and before, at the time of, or after, disqualification. The agency may also refer pertinent matters to another Federal, State, or local government agency for any action that that agency determines to be appropriate.

Subchapter D—Drugs for Human Use

Part 312—Investigational New Drug Application

Authority:
21 U.S.C. 321, 331, 351, 352, 353, 355, 360bbb, 371; 42 U.S.C. 262.

Source:
52 FR 8831, Mar. 19, 1987, unless otherwise noted.

Editorial Note:
Nomenclature changes to part 312 can be found at 69 FR 13717, Mar. 24, 2004.

Subpart A—General Provisions

§ 312.1 Scope.

(a) This part contains procedures and requirements governing the use of investigational new drugs, including procedures and requirements for the submission to, and review by, the Food and Drug Administration of investigational new drug applications (IND's). An investigational new drug for which an IND is in effect in accordance with this part is exempt from the premarketing approval requirements that are otherwise applicable and may be shipped lawfully for the purpose of conducting clinical investigations of that drug.

(b) References in this part to regulations in the Code of Federal Regulations are to chapter I of title 21, unless otherwise noted.

§ 312.2 Applicability.

(a) Applicability. Except as provided in this section, this part applies to all clinical investigations of products that are subject to section 505 of the Federal Food, Drug, and Cosmetic Act or to the licensing provisions of the Public Health Service Act (58 Stat. 632, as amended (42 U.S.C. 201 et seq.)).

(b) Exemptions. (1) The clinical investigation of a drug product that is lawfully marketed in the United States is exempt from the requirements of this part if all the following apply:

(i) The investigation is not intended to be reported to FDA as a well-controlled study in support of a new indication for use nor intended to be used to support any other significant change in the labeling for the drug;

(ii) If the drug that is undergoing investigation is lawfully marketed as a prescription drug product, the investigation is not intended to support a significant change in the advertising for the product;

(iii) The investigation does not involve a route of administration or dosage level or use in a patient population or other factor that significantly increases the risks (or decreases the acceptability of the risks) associated with the use of the drug product;

(iv) The investigation is conducted in compliance with the requirements for institutional review set forth in part 56 and with the requirements for informed consent set forth in part 50; and

(v) The investigation is conducted in compliance with the requirements of § 312.7.

(2)(i) A clinical investigation involving an *in vitro* diagnostic biological product listed in paragraph (b)(2)(ii) of this section is exempt from the requirements of this part if (a) it is intended to be used in a diagnostic procedure that confirms the diagnosis made by another, medically established, diagnostic product or procedure and (b) it is shipped in compliance with § 312.160.

(ii) In accordance with paragraph (b)(2)(i) of this section, the following products are exempt from the requirements of this part: (a) blood grouping serum; (b) reagent red blood cells; and (c) anti-human globulin.

(3) A drug intended solely for tests *in vitro* or in laboratory research animals is exempt from the requirements of this part if shipped in accordance with § 312.160.

(4) FDA will not accept an application for an in-

vestigation that is exempt under the provisions of paragraph (b)(1) of this section.

(5) A clinical investigation involving use of a placebo is exempt from the requirements of this part if the investigation does not otherwise require submission of an IND.

(6) A clinical investigation involving an exception from informed consent under § 50.24 of this chapter is not exempt from the requirements of this part.

(c) Bioavailability studies. The applicability of this part to *in vivo* bioavailability studies in humans is subject to the provisions of § 320.31.

(d) Unlabeled indication. This part does not apply to the use in the practice of medicine for an unlabeled indication of a new drug product approved under part 314 or of a licensed biological product.

(e) Guidance. FDA may, on its own initiative, issue guidance on the applicability of this part to particular investigational uses of drugs. On request, FDA will advise on the applicability of this part to a planned clinical investigation.

[52 FR 8831, Mar. 19, 1987, as amended at 61 FR 51529, Oct. 2, 1996; 64 FR 401, Jan. 5, 1999]

§ 312.3   Definitions and interpretations.

(a) The definitions and interpretations of terms contained in section 201 of the Act apply to those terms when used in this part:

(b) The following definitions of terms also apply to this part:

Act means the Federal Food, Drug, and Cosmetic Act (secs. 201-902, 52 Stat. 1040 et seq., as amended (21 U.S.C. 301-392)).

Clinical investigation means any experiment in which a drug is administered or dispensed to, or used involving, one or more human subjects. For the purposes of this part, an experiment is any use of a drug except for the use of a marketed drug in the course of medical practice.

Contract research organization means a person that assumes, as an independent contractor with the sponsor, one or more of the obligations of a sponsor, e.g., design of a protocol, selection or monitoring of investigations, evaluation of reports, and preparation of materials to be submitted to the Food and Drug Administration.

FDA means the Food and Drug Administration.

IND means an investigational new drug application. For purposes of this part, "IND" is synonymous with "Notice of Claimed Investigational Exemption for a New Drug."

Independent ethics committee (IEC) means a review panel that is responsible for ensuring the protection of the rights, safety, and well-being of human subjects involved in a clinical investigation and is adequately constituted to provide assurance of that protection. An institutional review board (IRB), as defined in § 56.102(g) of this chapter and subject to the requirements of part 56 of this chapter, is one type of IEC.

Investigational new drug means a new drug or biological drug that is used in a clinical investigation. The term also includes a biological product that is used in vitro for diagnostic purposes. The terms "investigational drug" and "investigational new drug" are deemed to be synonymous for purposes of this part.

Investigator means an individual who actually conducts a clinical investigation (i.e., under whose immediate direction the drug is administered or dispensed to a subject). In the event an investigation is conducted by a team of individuals, the investigator is the responsible leader of the team. "Subinvestigator" includes any other individual member of that team.

Marketing application means an application for a new drug submitted under section 505(b) of the act or a biologics license application for a biological product submitted under the Public Health Service Act.

Sponsor means a person who takes responsibility for and initiates a clinical investigation. The sponsor may be an individual or pharmaceutical company, governmental agency, academic institution, private organization, or other organization. The sponsor does not actually conduct the investigation unless the sponsor is a sponsor-investigator. A person other than an individual that uses one or more of its own employees to conduct an investigation that it has initiated is a sponsor, not a sponsor-investigator, and the employees are investigators.

Sponsor-Investigator means an individual who both initiates and conducts an investigation, and under whose immediate direction the investigational drug is administered or dispensed. The term does not include any person other than an individual. The requirements applicable to a sponsor-investigator under this part include both those applicable to an investigator and a sponsor.

Subject means a human who participates in an investigation, either as a recipient of the investigational new drug or as a control. A subject may be a healthy human or a patient with a disease.

[52 FR 8831, Mar. 19, 1987, as amended at 64 FR 401, Jan. 5, 1999; 64 FR 56449, Oct. 20, 1999; 73 FR 22815, Apr. 28, 2008]

§ 312.6   Labeling of an investigational new drug.

(a) The immediate package of an investigational new drug intended for human use shall bear a label with the statement "Caution: New Drug— Limited by Federal (or United States) law to investigational use."

(b) The label or labeling of an investigational new drug shall not bear any statement that is false or misleading in any particular and shall not represent that the investigational new drug is safe or effective for the purposes for which it is being investigated.

(c) The appropriate FDA Center Director, according to the procedures set forth in §§ 201.26 or

610.68 of this chapter, may grant an exception or alternative to the provision in paragraph (a) of this section, to the extent that this provision is not explicitly required by statute, for specified lots, batches, or other units of a human drug product that is or will be included in the Strategic National Stockpile.

[52 FR 8831, Mar. 19, 1987, as amended at 72 FR 73599, Dec. 28, 2007]

§ 312.7   Promotion of investigational drugs.

(a) Promotion of an investigational new drug. A sponsor or investigator, or any person acting on behalf of a sponsor or investigator, shall not represent in a promotional context that an investigational new drug is safe or effective for the purposes for which it is under investigation or otherwise promote the drug. This provision is not intended to restrict the full exchange of scientific information concerning the drug, including dissemination of scientific findings in scientific or lay media. Rather, its intent is to restrict promotional claims of safety or effectiveness of the drug for a use for which it is under investigation and to preclude commercialization of the drug before it is approved for commercial distribution.

(b) Commercial distribution of an investigational new drug. A sponsor or investigator shall not commercially distribute or test market an investigational new drug.

(c) Prolonging an investigation. A sponsor shall not unduly prolong an investigation after finding that the results of the investigation appear to establish sufficient data to support a marketing application.

[52 FR 8831, Mar. 19, 1987, as amended at 52 FR 19476, May 22, 1987; 67 FR 9585, Mar. 4, 2002; 74 FR 40899, Aug. 13, 2009]

§ 312.8   Charging for investigational drugs under an IND.

(a) General criteria for charging. (1) A sponsor must meet the applicable requirements in paragraph (b) of this section for charging in a clinical trial or paragraph (c) of this section for charging for expanded access to an investigational drug for treatment use under subpart I of this part, except that sponsors need not fulfill the requirements in this section to charge for an approved drug obtained from another entity not affiliated with the sponsor for use as part of the clinical trial evaluation (e.g., in a clinical trial of a new use of the approved drug, for use of the approved drug as an active control).

(2) A sponsor must justify the amount to be charged in accordance with paragraph (d) of this section.

(3) A sponsor must obtain prior written authorization from FDA to charge for an investigational drug.

(4) FDA will withdraw authorization to charge if it determines that charging is interfering with the development of a drug for marketing approval or that the criteria for the authorization are no longer being met.

(b) Charging in a clinical trial—(1) Charging for a sponsor's drug. A sponsor who wishes to charge for its investigational drug, including investigational use of its approved drug, must·

(i) Provide evidence that the drug has a potential clinical benefit that, if demonstrated in the clinical investigations, would provide a significant advantage over available products in the diagnosis, treatment, mitigation, or prevention of a disease or condition;

(ii) Demonstrate that the data to be obtained from the clinical trial would be essential to establishing that the drug is effective or safe for the purpose of obtaining initial approval of a drug, or would support a significant change in the labeling of an approved drug (e.g., new indication, inclusion of comparative safety information); and

(iii) Demonstrate that the clinical trial could not be conducted without charging because the cost of the drug is extraordinary to the sponsor. The cost may be extraordinary due to manufacturing complexity, scarcity of a natural resource, the large quantity of drug needed (e.g., due to the size or duration of the trial), or some combination of these or other extraordinary circumstances (e.g., resources available to a sponsor).

(2) Duration of charging in a clinical trial. Unless FDA specifies a shorter period, charging may continue for the length of the clinical trial.

(c) Charging for expanded access to investigational drug for treatment use. (1) A sponsor who wishes to charge for expanded access to an investigational drug for treatment use under subpart I of this part must provide reasonable assurance that charging will not interfere with developing the drug for marketing approval.

(2) For expanded access under § 312.320 (treatment IND or treatment protocol), such assurance must include:

(i) Evidence of sufficient enrollment in any ongoing clinical trial(s) needed for marketing approval to reasonably assure FDA that the trial(s) will be successfully completed as planned;

(ii) Evidence of adequate progress in the development of the drug for marketing approval; and

(iii) Information submitted under the general investigational plan (§ 312.23(a)(3)(iv)) specifying the drug development milestones the sponsor plans to meet in the next year.

(3) The authorization to charge is limited to the number of patients authorized to receive the drug under the treatment use, if there is a limitation.

(4) Unless FDA specifies a shorter period, charging for expanded access to an investigational drug for treatment use under subpart I of this part may continue for 1 year from the time of FDA authorization. A sponsor may request that FDA reauthorize charging for additional periods.

(d) Costs recoverable when charging for an investigational drug. (1) A sponsor may recover only the direct costs of making its investigational drug available.

(i) Direct costs are costs incurred by a sponsor that can be specifically and exclusively attributed to providing the drug for the investigational use for which FDA has authorized cost recovery. Direct costs include costs per unit to manufacture the drug (e.g., raw materials, labor, and nonreusable supplies and equipment used to manufacture the quantity of drug needed for the use for which charging is authorized) or costs to acquire the drug from another manufacturing source, and direct costs to ship and handle (e.g., store) the drug.

(ii) Indirect costs include costs incurred primarily to produce the drug for commercial sale (e.g., costs for facilities and equipment used to manufacture the supply of investigational drug, but that are primarily intended to produce large quantities of drug for eventual commercial sale) and research and development, administrative, labor, or other costs that would be incurred even if the clinical trial or treatment use for which charging is authorized did not occur.

(2) For expanded access to an investigational drug for treatment use under §§ 312.315 (intermediate-size patient populations) and 312.320 (treatment IND or treatment protocol), in addition to the direct costs described in paragraph (d)(1)(i) of this section, a sponsor may recover the costs of monitoring the expanded access IND or protocol, complying with IND reporting requirements, and other administrative costs directly associated with the expanded access IND.

(3) To support its calculation for cost recovery, a sponsor must provide supporting documentation to show that the calculation is consistent with the requirements of paragraphs (d) (1) and, if applicable, (d)(2) of this section. The documentation must be accompanied by a statement that an independent certified public accountant has reviewed and approved the

calculations.

[74 FR 40899, Aug. 13, 2009]

§ 312.10   Waivers.

(a) A sponsor may request FDA to waive applicable requirement under this part. A waiver request may be submitted either in an IND or in an information amendment to an IND. In an emergency, a request may be made by telephone or other rapid communication means. A waiver request is required to contain at least one of the following:

(1) An explanation why the sponsor's compliance with the requirement is unnecessary or cannot be achieved;

(2) A description of an alternative submission or course of action that satisfies the purpose of the requirement; or

(3) Other information justifying a waiver.

(b) FDA may grant a waiver if it finds that the sponsor's noncompliance would not pose a significant and unreasonable risk to human subjects of the investigation and that one of the following is met:

(1) The sponsor's compliance with the requirement is unnecessary for the agency to evaluate the application, or compliance cannot be achieved;

(2) The sponsor's proposed alternative satisfies the requirement; or

(3) The applicant's submission otherwise justifies a waiver.

[52 FR 8831, Mar. 19, 1987, as amended at 52 FR 23031, June 17, 1987; 67 FR 9585, Mar. 4, 2002]

Subpart B—Investigational New Drug Application (IND)

§ 312.20   Requirement for an IND.

(a) A sponsor shall submit an IND to FDA if the sponsor intends to conduct a clinical investigation with an investigational new drug that is subject to § 312.2(a).

(b) A sponsor shall not begin a clinical investigation subject to § 312.2(a) until the investigation is subject to an IND which is in effect in accordance with § 312.40.

(c) A sponsor shall submit a separate IND for any clinical investigation involving an exception from informed consent under § 50.24 of this chapter. Such a clinical investigation is not permitted to proceed without the prior written authorization from FDA. FDA shall provide a written determination 30 days after FDA receives the IND or earlier.

[52 FR 8831, Mar. 19, 1987, as amended at 61 FR 51529, Oct. 2, 1996; 62 FR 32479, June 16, 1997]

§ 312.21   Phases of an investigation.

An IND may be submitted for one or more phases of an investigation. The clinical investigation of a previously untested drug is generally divided into three phases. Although in general the phases are conducted sequentially, they may overlap. These three phases of an investigation are as follows:

(a) Phase 1. (1) Phase 1 includes the initial introduction of an investigational new drug into humans. Phase 1 studies are typically closely monitored and may be conducted in patients or normal volunteer subjects. These studies are designed to determine the metabolism and pharmacologic actions of the drug in humans, the side effects associated with increasing doses, and, if possible, to gain early evidence on effectiveness. During Phase 1, sufficient information about the drug's pharmacokinetics and pharmacological effects should be obtained to permit the design of well-controlled, scientifically valid, Phase 2 studies. The total number of subjects and patients included in Phase 1 studies varies with the drug, but is generally in the range of 20 to 80.

(2) Phase 1 studies also include studies of drug metabolism, structure-activity relationships, and mechanism of action in humans, as well as studies in which investigational drugs are used as research tools to explore biological phenomena or disease processes.

(b) Phase 2. Phase 2 includes the controlled clinical studies conducted to evaluate the effectiveness of the drug for a particular indication or indications in patients with the disease or condition under study and to determine the common short-term side effects and risks associated with the drug. Phase 2 studies are typically well controlled, closely monitored, and conducted in a relatively small number of patients, usually involving no more than several hundred subjects.

(c) Phase 3. Phase 3 studies are expanded controlled and uncontrolled trials. They are performed after preliminary evidence suggesting effectiveness of the drug has been obtained, and are intended to gather the additional information about effectiveness and safety that is needed to evaluate the overall benefit-risk relationship of the drug and to provide an adequate basis for physician labeling. Phase 3 studies usually include from several hundred to several thousand subjects.

§ 312.22   General principles of the IND submission.

(a) FDA's primary objectives in reviewing an IND are, in all phases of the investigation, to assure the safety and rights of subjects, and, in Phase 2 and 3, to help assure that the quality of the scientific evaluation of drugs is adequate to permit an evaluation of the drug's effectiveness and safety. Therefore, although FDA's review of Phase 1 submissions will focus on assessing the safety of Phase 1 investigations, FDA's review of Phases 2 and 3 submissions will also include an assessment of the scientific quality of the clinical investigations and the likelihood that the investigations will yield data capable of meeting statutory standards for marketing approval.

(b) The amount of information on a particular drug that must be submitted in an IND to assure the accomplishment of the objectives described in paragraph (a) of this section depends upon such factors as the novelty of the drug, the extent to which it has been studied previously, the known or suspected risks, and the developmental phase of the drug.

(c) The central focus of the initial IND submission should be on the general investigational plan and the protocols for specific human studies. Subsequent amendments to the IND that contain new or revised protocols should build logically on previous submissions and should be supported by additional information, including the results of animal toxicology studies or other human studies as appropriate. Annual reports to the IND should serve as the focus for reporting the status of studies being conducted under the IND and should update the general investigational plan for the coming year.

(d) The IND format set forth in § 312.23 should be followed routinely by sponsors in the interest of fostering an efficient review of applications. Sponsors are expected to exercise considerable discretion, however, regarding the content of information submitted in each section, depending upon the kind of drug being studied and the nature of the available information. Section 312.23 outlines the information needed for a commercially sponsored IND for a new molecular entity. A sponsor-investigator who uses, as a research tool, an investigational new drug that is already subject to a manufacturer's IND or marketing application should follow the same general format, but ordinarily may, if authorized by the manufacturer, refer to the manufacturer's IND or marketing application in providing the technical information supporting the proposed clinical investigation. A sponsor-investigator who uses an investigational drug not subject to a manufacturer's IND or marketing application is ordinarily required to submit all technical information supporting the IND, unless such information may be referenced from the scientific literature.

§ 312.23   IND content and format.

(a) A sponsor who intends to conduct a clinical investigation subject to this part shall submit an "Investigational New Drug Application" (IND) including, in the following order:

(1) Cover sheet (Form FDA-1571). A cover sheet for the application containing the following:

(i) The name, address, and telephone number of the sponsor, the date of the application, and the name of the investigational new drug.

(ii) Identification of the phase or phases of the clinical investigation to be conducted.

(iii) A commitment not to begin clinical investigations until an IND covering the investigations is in effect.

(iv) A commitment that an Institutional Review Board (IRB) that complies with the requirements set forth in part 56 will be responsible for the initial and continuing review and approval of each of the studies in the proposed clinical investigation and that the investigator will report to the IRB proposed changes in the research activity in accordance with the requirements of part 56.

(v) A commitment to conduct the investigation in accordance with all other applicable regulatory requirements.

(vi) The name and title of the person responsible for monitoring the conduct and progress of the clinical investigations.

(vii) The name(s) and title(s) of the person(s) responsible under § 312.32 for review and evaluation of information relevant to the safety of the drug.

(viii) If a sponsor has transferred any obligations for the conduct of any clinical study to a contract research organization, a statement containing the name and address of the contract research organization, identification of the clinical study, and a listing of the obligations transferred. If all obligations governing the conduct of the study have been transferred, a general statement of this transfer—in lieu of a listing of the specific obligations transferred—may be submitted.

(ix) The signature of the sponsor or the sponsor's authorized representative. If the person signing the application does not reside or have a place of business within the United States, the IND is required to contain the name and address of, and be countersigned by, an attorney, agent, or other authorized official who resides or maintains a place of business within the United States.

(2) A table of contents.

(3) Introductory statement and general investigational plan. (i) A brief introductory statement giving the name of the drug and all active ingredients, the drug's pharmacological class, the structural formula of the drug (if known), the formulation of the dosage form(s) to be used, the route of administration, and the broad objectives and planned duration of the proposed clinical investigation(s).

(ii) A brief summary of previous human experience with the drug, with reference to other IND's if pertinent, and to investigational or marketing experience in other countries that may be relevant to the safety of the proposed clinical investigation(s).

(iii) If the drug has been withdrawn from investigation or marketing in any country for any reason related to safety or effectiveness, identification of the country(ies) where the drug was withdrawn and the reasons for the withdrawal.

(iv) A brief description of the overall plan for investigating the drug product for the following year. The plan should include the following: (a) The rationale for the drug or the research study; (b) the indication(s) to be studied; (c) the general approach to be followed in evaluating the drug; (d) the kinds of clinical trials to be conducted in the first year following the submission (if plans are not developed for the entire year, the sponsor should so indicate); (e) the estimated number of patients to be given the drug in those studies; and (f) any risks of particular severity or seriousness anticipated on the basis of the toxicological data in animals or prior studies in humans with the drug or related drugs.

(4) [Reserved]

(5) Investigator's brochure. If required under § 312.55, a copy of the investigator's brochure, containing the following information:

(i) A brief description of the drug substance and the formulation, including the structural formula, if known.

(ii) A summary of the pharmacological and toxicological effects of the drug in animals and, to the extent known, in humans.

(iii) A summary of the pharmacokinetics and biological disposition of the drug in animals and, if known, in humans.

(iv) A summary of information relating to safety and effectiveness in humans obtained from prior clinical studies. (Reprints of published articles on such studies may be appended when useful.)

(v) A description of possible risks and side effects to be anticipated on the basis of prior experience with the drug under investigation or with related drugs, and of precautions or special monitoring to be done as part of the investigational use of the drug.

(6) Protocols. (i) A protocol for each planned study. (Protocols for studies not submitted initially in the IND should be submitted in accordance with § 312.30(a).) In general, protocols for Phase 1 studies may be less detailed and more flexible than protocols for Phase 2 and 3 studies. Phase 1 protocols should be directed primarily at providing an outline of the investigation—an estimate of the number of patients to be involved, a description of safety exclusions, and a description of the dosing plan including duration, dose, or method to be used in determining dose—and should specify in detail only those elements of the study that are critical to safety, such as necessary monitoring of vital signs and blood chemistries. Modifications of the experimental design of Phase 1 studies that do not affect critical safety assessments are required to be reported to FDA only in the annual report.

(ii) In Phases 2 and 3, detailed protocols describing all aspects of the study should be submitted. A protocol for a Phase 2 or 3 investigation should be designed in such a way that, if the sponsor anticipates that some deviation from the study design may become necessary as the investigation progresses, alternatives or contingencies to provide for such deviation are built into the protocols at the outset. For example, a protocol for a controlled short-term study might include a plan for an early crossover of nonresponders to an alternative therapy.

(iii) A protocol is required to contain the following, with the specific elements and detail of the protocol reflecting the above distinctions depending on the phase of study:

(a) A statement of the objectives and purpose of the study.

(b) The name and address and a statement of the qualifications (curriculum vitae or other statement of qualifications) of each investigator, and the name of each subinvestigator (e.g., research fellow, resident) working under the supervision of the investigator; the name and address of the research facilities to be used; and the name and address of each reviewing Institutional Review Board.

(c) The criteria for patient selection and for exclusion of patients and an estimate of the number of patients to be studied.

(d) A description of the design of the study, including the kind of control group to be used, if any, and a description of methods to be used to minimize bias on the part of subjects, investigators, and analysts.

(e) The method for determining the dose(s) to be administered, the planned maximum dosage, and the duration of individual patient exposure to the drug.

(f) A description of the observations and measurements to be made to fulfill the objectives of the study.

(g) A description of clinical procedures, laboratory tests, or other measures to be taken to monitor the effects of the drug in human subjects and to minimize risk.

(7) Chemistry, manufacturing, and control information. (i) As appropriate for the particular investigations covered by the IND, a section describing the composition, manufacture, and control of the drug substance and the drug product. Although in each phase of the investigation sufficient information is required to be submitted to assure the proper identification, quality, purity, and strength of the investigational drug, the amount of information needed to make that assurance will vary with the phase of the investigation, the proposed duration of the investigation, the dosage form, and the amount of information otherwise available. FDA recognizes that modifications to the method of preparation of the new drug substance and dosage form and changes in the dosage form itself are likely as the investigation progresses. Therefore, the emphasis in an initial Phase 1 submission should generally be placed on the identification and control of the raw materials and the new drug substance. Final specifications for the drug substance and drug product are not expected until the end of the investigational process.

(ii) It should be emphasized that the amount of information to be submitted depends upon the scope of the proposed clinical investigation. For example, although stability data are required in all phases of the IND to demonstrate that the new drug substance and drug product are within acceptable chemical and physical limits for the planned duration of the proposed clinical investigation, if very short-term tests are proposed, the supporting stability data can be correspondingly limited.

(iii) As drug development proceeds and as the scale or production is changed from the pilot-scale production appropriate for the limited initial clinical investigations to the larger-scale production needed for expanded clinical trials, the sponsor should submit information amendments to supplement the initial information submitted on the chemistry, manufacturing, and control processes with information appropriate to the expanded scope of the investigation.

(iv) Reflecting the distinctions described in this paragraph (a)(7), and based on the phase(s) to be studied, the submission is required to contain the following:

(a) Drug substance. A description of the drug substance, including its physical, chemical, or biological characteristics; the name and address of its manufacturer; the general method of preparation of the drug substance; the acceptable limits and analytical methods used to assure the identity, strength, quality, and purity of the drug substance; and information sufficient to support stability of the drug substance during the toxicological studies and the planned clinical studies. Reference to the current edition of the United States Pharmacopeia—National Formulary may satisfy relevant requirements in this paragraph.

(b) Drug product. A list of all components, which may include reasonable alternatives for inactive compounds, used in the manufacture of the investigational drug product, including both those components intended to appear in the drug product and those which may not appear but which are used in the manufacturing process, and, where applicable, the quantitative composition of the investigational drug product, including any reasonable variations that may be expected during the investigational stage; the name and address of the drug product manufacturer; a brief general description of the manufacturing and packaging procedure as appropriate for the product; the acceptable limits and analytical methods used to assure the identity, strength, quality, and purity of the drug product; and information sufficient to assure the product's stability during the planned clinical studies. Reference to the current edition of the United States Pharmacopeia—National Formulary may satisfy certain requirements in this paragraph.

(c) A brief general description of the composition, manufacture, and control of any placebo used in a controlled clinical trial.

(d) Labeling. A copy of all labels and labeling to be provided to each investigator.

(e) Environmental analysis requirements. A claim for categorical exclusion under § 25.30 or 25.31 or an environmental assessment under § 25.40.

(8) Pharmacology and toxicology information. Adequate information about pharmacological and toxicological studies of the drug involving laboratory animals or in vitro, on the basis of which the sponsor has concluded that it is reasonably safe to conduct the proposed clinical investigations. The kind, duration, and scope of animal and other tests required varies with the duration and nature of the proposed clinical investigations. Guidance documents are available from FDA that describe ways in which these requirements may be met. Such information is required to include the identification and qualifications of the individuals who evaluated the results of such studies and concluded that it is reasonably safe to begin the proposed investigations and a statement of where the investigations were conducted and where the records are available for inspection. As drug development proceeds, the sponsor is required to submit informational amendments, as appropriate, with additional information pertinent to safety.

(i) Pharmacology and drug disposition. A section describing the pharmacological effects and mechanism(s) of action of the drug in animals, and information on the absorption, distribution, metabolism, and excretion of the drug, if known.

(ii) Toxicology. (a) An integrated summary of the toxicological effects of the drug in animals and in vitro. Depending on the nature of the drug and the phase of the investigation, the description is to include the results of acute, subacute, and chronic toxicity tests; tests of the drug's effects on reproduction and the developing fetus; any special toxicity test related to the drug's particular mode of administration or conditions of use (e.g., inhalation, dermal, or ocular toxicology); and any in vitro studies intended to evaluate drug toxicity.

(b) For each toxicology study that is intended primarily to support the safety of the proposed clinical investigation, a full tabulation of data suitable for detailed review.

(iii) For each nonclinical laboratory study subject to the good laboratory practice regulations under part 58, a statement that the study was conducted in compliance with the good laboratory practice regulations in part 58, or, if the study was not conducted in compliance with those regulations, a brief statement of the reason for the noncompliance.

(9) Previous human experience with the investigational drug. A summary of previous human experience known to the applicant, if any, with the investigational drug. The information is required to include the following:

(i) If the investigational drug has been investigated or marketed previously, either in the United States or other countries, detailed information about such experience that is relevant to the safety of the proposed investigation or to the investigation's rationale. If the drug has been the subject of controlled trials, detailed information on such trials that is relevant to an assessment of the drug's effectiveness for the proposed investigational use(s) should also be provided. Any published material that is relevant to the safety of the proposed investigation or to an assessment of the drug's effectiveness for its proposed investigational use should be provided in full. Published material that is less directly relevant may be supplied by a bibliography.

(ii) If the drug is a combination of drugs previously investigated or marketed, the information required under paragraph (a)(9)(i) of this section should be provided for each active drug component. However, if any component in such combination is subject to an approved marketing application or is otherwise lawfully marketed in the United States, the sponsor is not required to submit published material concerning that active drug component unless such material relates directly to the proposed investigational use (including publications relevant to component-component interaction).

(iii) If the drug has been marketed outside the United States, a list of the countries in which the drug has been marketed and a list of the countries in which the drug has been withdrawn from marketing for reasons potentially related to safety or effectiveness.

(10) Additional information. In certain applications, as described below, information on special topics may be needed. Such information shall be submitted in this section as follows:

(i) Drug dependence and abuse potential. If the drug is a psychotropic substance or otherwise has abuse potential, a section describing relevant clinical studies and experience and studies in test animals.

(ii) Radioactive drugs. If the drug is a radioactive drug, sufficient data from animal or human studies to allow a reasonable calculation of radiation-absorbed dose to the whole body and critical organs upon administration to a human subject. Phase 1 studies of radioactive drugs must include studies which will obtain sufficient data for dosimetry calculations.

(iii) Pediatric studies. Plans for assessing pediatric safety and effectiveness.

(iv) Other information. A brief statement of any other information that would aid evaluation of the proposed clinical investigations with respect to their safety or their design and potential as controlled clinical trials to support marketing of the drug.

(11) Relevant information. If requested by FDA, any other relevant information needed for review of the application.

(b) Information previously submitted. The sponsor ordinarily is not required to resubmit information previously submitted, but may incorporate the information by reference. A reference to information submitted previously must identify the file by name, reference number, volume, and page number where the information can be found. A reference to information submitted to the agency by a person other than the sponsor is required to contain a written statement that authorizes the reference and that is signed by the person who submitted the information.

(c) Material in a foreign language. The sponsor shall submit an accurate and complete English translation of each part of the IND that is not in English. The sponsor shall also submit a copy of each original literature publication for which an English translation is submitted.

(d) Number of copies. The sponsor shall submit an original and two copies of all submissions to the IND file, including the original submission and all amendments and reports.

(e) Numbering of IND submissions. Each submission relating to an IND is required to be numbered serially using a single, three-digit serial number. The initial IND is required to be numbered 000; each subsequent submission (e.g., amendment, report, or correspondence) is required to be numbered chronologically in sequence.

(f) Identification of exception from informed consent. If the investigation involves an exception from informed consent under § 50.24 of this chapter, the sponsor shall prominently identify on the cover sheet that the investigation is subject to the requirements in § 50.24 of this chapter.

[52 FR 8831, Mar. 19, 1987, as amended at 52 FR 23031, June 17, 1987; 53 FR 1918, Jan. 25, 1988; 61 FR 51529, Oct. 2, 1996; 62 FR 40599, July 29, 1997; 63 FR 66669, Dec. 2, 1998; 65 FR 56479, Sept. 19, 2000; 67 FR 9585, Mar. 4, 2002]

§ 312.30   Protocol amendments.

Once an IND is in effect, a sponsor shall amend it as needed to ensure that the clinical investigations are conducted according to protocols included in the application. This section sets forth the provisions under which new protocols may be submitted and changes in previously submitted protocols may be made. Whenever a sponsor intends to conduct a clinical investigation with an exception from informed consent for emergency research as set forth in § 50.24 of this chapter, the sponsor shall submit a separate IND for such investigation.

(a) New protocol. Whenever a sponsor intends to conduct a study that is not covered by a protocol already contained in the IND, the sponsor shall submit to FDA a protocol amendment containing the protocol for the study. Such study may begin provided two conditions are met: (1) The sponsor has submitted the protocol to FDA for its review; and (2) the protocol has been approved by the Institutional Review Board (IRB) with responsibility for review and approval of the study in accordance with the requirements of part 56. The sponsor may comply with these two conditions in either order.

(b) Changes in a protocol. (1) A sponsor shall submit a protocol amendment describing any change in a Phase 1 protocol that significantly affects the safety of subjects or any change in a Phase 2 or 3 protocol that significantly affects the safety of subjects, the scope of the investigation, or the scientific quality of the study. Examples of changes requiring an amendment under this paragraph include:

(i) Any increase in drug dosage or duration of exposure of individual subjects to the drug beyond that in the current protocol, or any significant increase in the number of subjects under study.

(ii) Any significant change in the design of a protocol (such as the addition or dropping of a control group).

(iii) The addition of a new test or procedure that is intended to improve monitoring for, or reduce the risk of, a side effect or adverse event; or the dropping of a test intended to monitor safety.

(2)(i) A protocol change under paragraph (b)(1) of this section may be made provided two conditions are met:

(a) The sponsor has submitted the change to FDA for its review; and

(b) The change has been approved by the IRB with responsibility for review and approval of the study. The sponsor may comply with these two conditions in either order.

(ii) Notwithstanding paragraph (b)(2)(i) of this section, a protocol change intended to eliminate an apparent immediate hazard to subjects may be implemented immediately provided FDA is subsequently notified by protocol amendment and the reviewing IRB is notified in accordance with § 56.104(c).

(c) New investigator. A sponsor shall submit a protocol amendment when a new investigator is added to carry out a previously submitted protocol, except that a protocol amendment is not required when a licensed practitioner is added in the case of a treatment protocol under § 312.315 or § 312.320. Once the investigator is added to the study, the investigational drug may be shipped to the investigator and the investigator may begin participating in the study. The sponsor shall notify FDA of the new investigator within 30 days of the investigator being added.

(d) Content and format. A protocol amendment is required to be prominently identified as such (i.e., "Protocol Amendment: New Protocol",

"Protocol Amendment: Change in Protocol", or "Protocol Amendment: New Investigator"), and to contain the following:

(1)(i) In the case of a new protocol, a copy of the new protocol and a brief description of the most clinically significant differences between it and previous protocols.

(ii) In the case of a change in protocol, a brief description of the change and reference (date and number) to the submission that contained the protocol.

(iii) In the case of a new investigator, the investigator's name, the qualifications to conduct the investigation, reference to the previously submitted protocol, and all additional information about the investigator's study as is required under § 312.23(a)(6)(iii)(b).

(2) Reference, if necessary, to specific technical information in the IND or in a concurrently submitted information amendment to the IND that the sponsor relies on to support any clinically significant change in the new or amended protocol. If the reference is made to supporting information already in the IND, the sponsor shall identify by name, reference number, volume, and page number the location of the information.

(3) If the sponsor desires FDA to comment on the submission, a request for such comment and the specific questions FDA's response should address.

(e) When submitted. A sponsor shall submit a protocol amendment for a new protocol or a change in protocol before its implementation. Protocol amendments to add a new investigator or to provide additional information about investigators may be grouped and submitted at 30-day intervals. When several submissions of new protocols or protocol changes are anticipated during a short period, the sponsor is encouraged, to the extent feasible, to include these all in a single submission.

[52 FR 8831, Mar. 19, 1987, as amended at 52 FR 23031, June 17, 1987; 53 FR 1918, Jan. 25, 1988; 61 FR 51530, Oct. 2, 1996; 67 FR 9585, Mar. 4, 2002; 74 FR 40942, Aug. 13, 2009]

§ 312.31   Information amendments.

(a) Requirement for information amendment. A sponsor shall report in an information amendment essential information on the IND that is not within the scope of a protocol amendment, IND safety reports, or annual report. Examples of information requiring an information amendment include:

(1) New toxicology, chemistry, or other technical information; or

(2) A report regarding the discontinuance of a clinical investigation.

(b) Content and format of an information amendment. An information amendment is required to bear prominent identification of its contents (e.g., "Information Amendment: Chemistry, Manufacturing, and Control", "Information Amendment: Pharmacology-Toxicology", "Information Amendment: Clinical"), and to contain the following:

(1) A statement of the nature and purpose of the amendment.

(2) An organized submission of the data in a format appropriate for scientific review.

(3) If the sponsor desires FDA to comment on an information amendment, a request for such comment.

(c) When submitted. Information amendments to the IND should be submitted as necessary but, to the extent feasible, not more than every 30 days.

[52 FR 8831, Mar. 19, 1987, as amended at 52 FR 23031, June 17, 1987; 53 FR 1918, Jan. 25, 1988; 67 FR 9585, Mar. 4, 2002]

§ 312.32   IND safety reports.

(a) Definitions. The following definitions of

terms apply to this section:-

Associated with the use of the drug. There is a reasonable possibility that the experience may have been caused by the drug.

Disability. A substantial disruption of a person's ability to conduct normal life functions.

Life-threatening adverse drug experience. Any adverse drug experience that places the patient or subject, in the view of the investigator, at immediate risk of death from the reaction as it occurred, i.e., it does not include a reaction that, had it occurred in a more severe form, might have caused death.

Serious adverse drug experience: Any adverse drug experience occurring at any dose that results in any of the following outcomes: Death, a life-threatening adverse drug experience, inpatient hospitalization or prolongation of existing hospitalization, a persistent or significant disability/incapacity, or a congenital anomaly/ birth defect. Important medical events that may not result in death, be life-threatening, or require hospitalization may be considered a serious adverse drug experience when, based upon appropriate medical judgment, they may jeopardize the patient or subject and may require medical or surgical intervention to prevent one of the outcomes listed in this definition. Examples of such medical events include allergic bronchospasm requiring intensive treatment in an emergency room or at home, blood dyscrasias or convulsions that do not result in inpatient hospitalization, or the development of drug dependency or drug abuse.

Unexpected adverse drug experience: Any adverse drug experience, the specificity or severity of which is not consistent with the current investigator brochure; or, if an investigator brochure is not required or available, the specificity or severity of which is not consistent with the risk information described in the general investigational plan or elsewhere in the current application, as amended. For example, under this definition, hepatic necrosis would be unexpected (by virtue of greater severity) if the investigator brochure only referred to elevated hepatic enzymes or hepatitis. Similarly, cerebral thromboembolism and cerebral vasculitis would be unexpected (by virtue of greater specificity) if the investigator brochure only listed cerebral vascular accidents. "Unexpected," as used in this definition, refers to an adverse drug experience that has not been previously observed (e.g., included in the investigator brochure) rather than from the perspective of such experience not being anticipated from the pharmacological properties of the pharmaceutical product.

(b) Review of safety information. The sponsor shall promptly review all information relevant to the safety of the drug obtained or otherwise received by the sponsor from any source, foreign or domestic, including information derived from any clinical or epidemiological investigations, animal investigations, commercial marketing experience, reports in the scientific literature, and unpublished scientific papers, as well as reports from foreign regulatory authorities that have not already been previously reported to the agency by the sponsor.

(c) IND safety reports—(1) Written reports—(i) The sponsor shall notify FDA and all participating investigators in a written IND safety report of:

(A) Any adverse experience associated with the use of the drug that is both serious and unexpected; or

(B) Any finding from tests in laboratory animals that suggests a significant risk for human subjects including reports of mutagenicity, teratogenicity, or carcinogenicity. Each notification shall be made as soon as possible and in no event later than 15 calendar days after the sponsor's initial receipt of the information. Each written notification may be submitted on FDA Form 3500A or in a narrative format (foreign events may be submitted either on an FDA Form 3500A or, if preferred, on a CIOMS I form;

reports from animal or epidemiological studies shall be submitted in a narrative format) and shall bear prominent identification of its contents, i.e., "IND Safety Report." Each written notification to FDA shall be transmitted to the FDA new drug review division in the Center for Drug Evaluation and Research or the product review division in the Center for Biologics Evaluation and Research that has responsibility for review of the IND. If FDA determines that additional data are needed, the agency may require further data to be submitted.

(ii) In each written IND safety report, the sponsor shall identify all safety reports previously filed with the IND concerning a similar adverse experience, and shall analyze the significance of the adverse experience in light of the previous, similar reports.

(2) Telephone and facsimile transmission safety reports. The sponsor shall also notify FDA by telephone or by facsimile transmission of any unexpected fatal or life-threatening experience associated with the use of the drug as soon as possible but in no event later than 7 calendar days after the sponsor's initial receipt of the information. Each telephone call or facsimile transmission to FDA shall be transmitted to the FDA new drug review division in the Center for Drug Evaluation and Research or the product review division in the Center for Biologics Evaluation and Research that has responsibility for review of the IND.

(3) Reporting format or frequency. FDA may request a sponsor to submit IND safety reports in a format or at a frequency different than that required under this paragraph. The sponsor may also propose and adopt a different reporting format or frequency if the change is agreed to in advance by the director of the new drug review division in the Center for Drug Evaluation and Research or the director of the products review division in the Center for Biologics Evaluation and Research which is responsible for review of the IND.

(4) A sponsor of a clinical study of a marketed drug is not required to make a safety report for any adverse experience associated with use of the drug that is not from the clinical study itself.

(d) Followup. (1) The sponsor shall promptly investigate all safety information received by it.

(2) Followup information to a safety report shall be submitted as soon as the relevant information is available.

(3) If the results of a sponsor's investigation show that an adverse drug experience not initially determined to be reportable under paragraph (c) of this section is so reportable, the sponsor shall report such experience in a written safety report as soon as possible, but in no event later than 15 calendar days after the determination is made.

(4) Results of a sponsor's investigation of other safety information shall be submitted, as appropriate, in an information amendment or annual report.

(e) Disclaimer. A safety report or other information submitted by a sponsor under this part (and any release by FDA of that report or information) does not necessarily reflect a conclusion by the sponsor or FDA that the report or information constitutes an admission that the drug caused or contributed to an adverse experience. A sponsor need not admit, and may deny, that the report or information submitted by the sponsor constitutes an admission that the drug caused or contributed to an adverse experience.

[52 FR 8831, Mar. 19, 1987, as amended at 52 FR 23031, June 17, 1987; 55 FR 11579, Mar. 29, 1990; 62 FR 52250, Oct. 7, 1997; 67 FR 9585, Mar. 4, 2002]

§ 312.33   Annual reports.

A sponsor shall within 60 days of the anniversary date that the IND went into effect, submit a brief report of the progress of the investigation that includes:

(a) Individual study information. A brief summary of the status of each study in progress and each study completed during the previous year. The summary is required to include the following information for each study:

(1) The title of the study (with any appropriate study identifiers such as protocol number), its purpose, a brief statement identifying the patient population, and a statement as to whether the study is completed.

(2) The total number of subjects initially planned for inclusion in the study; the number entered into the study to date, tabulated by age group, gender, and race; the number whose participation in the study was completed as planned; and the number who dropped out of the study for any reason.

(3) If the study has been completed, or if interim results are known, a brief description of any available study results.

(b) Summary information. Information obtained during the previous year's clinical and nonclinical investigations, including:

(1) A narrative or tabular summary showing the most frequent and most serious adverse experiences by body system.

(2) A summary of all IND safety reports submitted during the past year.

(3) A list of subjects who died during participation in the investigation, with the cause of death for each subject.

(4) A list of subjects who dropped out during the course of the investigation in association with any adverse experience, whether or not thought to be drug related.

(5) A brief description of what, if anything, was obtained that is pertinent to an understanding of the drug's actions, including, for example, information about dose response, information from controlled trials, and information about bioavailability.

(6) A list of the preclinical studies (including animal studies) completed or in progress during the past year and a summary of the major preclinical findings.

(7) A summary of any significant manufacturing or microbiological changes made during the past year.

(c) A description of the general investigational plan for the coming year to replace that submitted 1 year earlier. The general investigational plan shall contain the information required under § 312.23(a)(3)(iv).

(d) If the investigator brochure has been revised, a description of the revision and a copy of the new brochure.

(e) A description of any significant Phase 1 protocol modifications made during the previous year and not previously reported to the IND in a protocol amendment.

(f) A brief summary of significant foreign marketing developments with the drug during the past year, such as approval of marketing in any country or withdrawal or suspension from marketing in any country.

(g) If desired by the sponsor, a log of any outstanding business with respect to the IND for which the sponsor requests or expects a reply, comment, or meeting.

[52 FR 8831, Mar. 19, 1987, as amended at 52 FR 23031, June 17, 1987; 63 FR 6862, Feb. 11, 1998; 67 FR 9585, Mar. 4, 2002]

§ 312.38 Withdrawal of an IND.

(a) At any time a sponsor may withdraw an effective IND without prejudice.

(b) If an IND is withdrawn, FDA shall be so notified, all clinical investigations conducted under the IND shall be ended, all current investigators notified, and all stocks of the drug returned to the sponsor or otherwise disposed of at the request of the sponsor in accordance with § 312.59.

(c) If an IND is withdrawn because of a safety reason, the sponsor shall promptly so inform FDA, all participating investigators, and all reviewing Institutional Review Boards, together with the reasons for such withdrawal.

[52 FR 8831, Mar. 19, 1987, as amended at 52 FR 23031, June 17, 1987; 67 FR 9586, Mar. 4, 2002]

Subpart C—Administrative Actions

§ 312.40   General requirements for use of an investigational new drug in a clinical investigation.

(a) An investigational new drug may be used in a clinical investigation if the following conditions are met:

(1) The sponsor of the investigation submits an IND for the drug to FDA; the IND is in effect under paragraph (b) of this section; and the sponsor complies with all applicable requirements in this part and parts 50 and 56 with respect to the conduct of the clinical investigations; and

(2) Each participating investigator conducts his or her investigation in compliance with the requirements of this part and parts 50 and 56.

(b) An IND goes into effect:

(1) Thirty days after FDA receives the IND, unless FDA notifies the sponsor that the investigations described in the IND are subject to a clinical hold under § 312.42; or

(2) On earlier notification by FDA that the clinical investigations in the IND may begin. FDA will notify the sponsor in writing of the date it receives the IND.

(c) A sponsor may ship an investigational new drug to investigators named in the IND:

(1) Thirty days after FDA receives the IND; or

(2) On earlier FDA authorization to ship the drug.

(d) An investigator may not administer an investigational new drug to human subjects until the IND goes into effect under paragraph (b) of this section.

§ 312.41   Comment and advice on an IND.

(a) FDA may at any time during the course of the investigation communicate with the sponsor orally or in writing about deficiencies in the IND or about FDA's need for more data or information.

(b) On the sponsor's request, FDA will provide advice on specific matters relating to an IND. Examples of such advice may include advice on the adequacy of technical data to support an investigational plan, on the design of a clinical trial, and on whether proposed investigations are likely to produce the data and information that is needed to meet requirements for a marketing application.

(c) Unless the communication is accompanied by a clinical hold order under § 312.42, FDA communications with a sponsor under this section are solely advisory and do not require any modification in the planned or ongoing clinical investigations or response to the agency.

[52 FR 8831, Mar. 19, 1987, as amended at 52 FR 23031, June 17, 1987; 67 FR 9586, Mar. 4, 2002]

§ 312.42   Clinical holds and requests for modification.

(a) General. A clinical hold is an order issued by FDA to the sponsor to delay a proposed clinical investigation or to suspend an ongoing investigation. The clinical hold order may apply to one or more of the investigations covered by an IND. When a proposed study is placed on clinical hold, subjects may not be given the investigational drug. When an ongoing study is placed on clinical hold, no new subjects may be recruited to the study and placed on the investigational drug; patients already in the study should be taken off therapy involving the investigational drug unless specifically permitted by FDA in the interest of patient safety.

(b) Grounds for imposition of clinical hold—(1)

269

Clinical hold of a Phase 1 study under an IND. FDA may place a proposed or ongoing Phase 1 investigation on clinical hold if it finds that:

(i) Human subjects are or would be exposed to an unreasonable and significant risk of illness or injury;

(ii) The clinical investigators named in the IND are not qualified by reason of their scientific training and experience to conduct the investigation described in the IND;

(iii) The investigator brochure is misleading, erroneous, or materially incomplete; or

(iv) The IND does not contain sufficient information required under § 312.23 to assess the risks to subjects of the proposed studies.

(v) The IND is for the study of an investigational drug intended to treat a life-threatening disease or condition that affects both genders, and men or women with reproductive potential who have the disease or condition being studied are excluded from eligibility because of a risk or potential risk from use of the investigational drug of reproductive toxicity (i.e., affecting reproductive organs) or developmental toxicity (i.e., affecting potential offspring). The phrase "women with reproductive potential" does not include pregnant women. For purposes of this paragraph, "life-threatening illnesses or diseases" are defined as "diseases or conditions where the likelihood of death is high unless the course of the disease is interrupted." The clinical hold would not apply under this paragraph to clinical studies conducted:

(A) Under special circumstances, such as studies pertinent only to one gender (e.g., studies evaluating the excretion of a drug in semen or the effects on menstrual function);

(B) Only in men or women, as long as a study that does not exclude members of the other gender with reproductive potential is being conducted concurrently, has been conducted, or will take place within a reasonable time

agreed upon by the agency; or

(C) Only in subjects who do not suffer from the disease or condition for which the drug is being studied.

(2) Clinical hold of a Phase 2 or 3 study under an IND. FDA may place a proposed or ongoing Phase 2 or 3 investigation on clinical hold if it finds that:

(i) Any of the conditions in paragraphs (b)(1)(i) through (b)(1)(v) of this section apply; or

(ii) The plan or protocol for the investigation is clearly deficient in design to meet its stated objectives.

(3) Clinical hold of an expanded access IND or expanded access protocol. FDA may place an expanded access IND or expanded access protocol on clinical hold under the following conditions:

(i) Final use. FDA may place a proposed expanded access IND or treatment use protocol on clinical hold if it is determined that:

(A) The pertinent criteria in subpart I of this part for permitting the expanded access use to begin are not satisfied; or

(B) The expanded access IND or expanded access protocol does not comply with the requirements for expanded access submissions in subpart I of this part.

(ii) Ongoing use. FDA may place an ongoing expanded access IND or expanded access protocol on clinical hold if it is determined that the pertinent criteria in subpart I of this part for permitting the expanded access are no longer satisfied.

(4) Clinical hold of any study that is not designed to be adequate and well-controlled. FDA may place a proposed or ongoing investigation that is not designed to be adequate and well-controlled on clinical hold if it finds that:

(i) Any of the conditions in paragraph (b)(1) or (b)(2) of this section apply; or

(ii) There is reasonable evidence the investigation that is not designed to be adequate and well-controlled is impeding enrollment in, or otherwise interfering with the conduct or completion of, a study that is designed to be an adequate and well-controlled investigation of the same or another investigational drug; or

(iii) Insufficient quantities of the investigational drug exist to adequately conduct both the investigation that is not designed to be adequate and well-controlled and the investigations that are designed to be adequate and well-controlled; or

(iv) The drug has been studied in one or more adequate and well-controlled investigations that strongly suggest lack of effectiveness; or

(v) Another drug under investigation or approved for the same indication and available to the same patient population has demonstrated a better potential benefit/risk balance; or

(vi) The drug has received marketing approval for the same indication in the same patient population; or

(vii) The sponsor of the study that is designed to be an adequate and well-controlled investigation is not actively pursuing marketing approval of the investigational drug with due diligence; or

(viii) The Commissioner determines that it would not be in the public interest for the study to be conducted or continued. FDA ordinarily intends that clinical holds under paragraphs (b)(4)(ii), (b)(4)(iii) and (b)(4)(v) of this section would only apply to additional enrollment in nonconcurrently controlled trials rather than eliminating continued access to individuals already receiving the investigational drug.

(5) Clinical hold of any investigation involving an exception from informed consent under § 50.24 of this chapter. FDA may place a proposed or ongoing investigation involving an exception from informed consent under § 50.24 of this chapter on clinical hold if it is determined that:

(i) Any of the conditions in paragraphs (b)(1) or (b)(2) of this section apply; or

(ii) The pertinent criteria in § 50.24 of this chapter for such an investigation to begin or continue are not submitted or not satisfied.

(6) Clinical hold of any investigation involving an exception from informed consent under § 50.23(d) of this chapter. FDA may place a proposed or ongoing investigation involving an exception from informed consent under § 50.23(d) of this chapter on clinical hold if it is determined that:

(i) Any of the conditions in paragraphs (b)(1) or (b)(2) of this section apply; or

(ii) A determination by the President to waive the prior consent requirement for the administration of an investigational new drug has not been made.

(c) Discussion of deficiency. Whenever FDA concludes that a deficiency exists in a clinical investigation that may be grounds for the imposition of clinical hold FDA will, unless patients are exposed to immediate and serious risk, attempt to discuss and satisfactorily resolve the matter with the sponsor before issuing the clinical hold order.

(d) Imposition of clinical hold. The clinical hold order may be made by telephone or other means of rapid communication or in writing. The clinical hold order will identify the studies under the IND to which the hold applies, and will briefly explain the basis for the action. The clinical hold order will be made by or on behalf of the Division Director with responsibility for review of the IND. As soon as possible, and no more than 30 days after imposition of the clinical hold, the Division Director will provide the sponsor a written explanation of the basis for the hold.

(e) Resumption of clinical investigations. An investigation may only resume after FDA (usually the Division Director, or the Director's designee, with responsibility for review of the IND) has notified the sponsor that the investigation may proceed. Resumption of the affected investigation(s) will be authorized when the sponsor corrects the deficiency(ies) previously cited or otherwise satisfies the agency that the investigation(s) can proceed. FDA may notify a sponsor of its determination regarding the clinical hold by telephone or other means of rapid communication. If a sponsor of an IND that has been placed on clinical hold requests in writing that the clinical hold be removed and submits a complete response to the issue(s) identified in the clinical hold order, FDA shall respond in writing to the sponsor within 30-calendar days of receipt of the request and the complete response. FDA's response will either remove or maintain the clinical hold, and will state the reasons for such determination. Notwithstanding the 30-calendar day response time, a sponsor may not proceed with a clinical trial on which a clinical hold has been imposed until the sponsor has been notified by FDA that the hold has been lifted.

(f) Appeal. If the sponsor disagrees with the reasons cited for the clinical hold, the sponsor may request reconsideration of the decision in accordance with § 312.48.

(g) Conversion of IND on clinical hold to inactive status. If all investigations covered by an IND remain on clinical hold for 1 year or more, the IND may be placed on inactive status by FDA under § 312.45.

[52 FR 8831, Mar. 19, 1987, as amended at 52 FR 19477, May 22, 1987; 57 FR 13249, Apr. 15, 1992; 61 FR 51530, Oct. 2, 1996; 63 FR 68678, Dec. 14, 1998; 64 FR 54189, Oct. 5, 1999; 65 FR 34971, June 1, 2000; 74 FR 40942, Aug. 13, 2009]

§ 312.44   Termination.

(a) General. This section describes the procedures under which FDA may terminate an IND. If an IND is terminated, the sponsor shall end all clinical investigations conducted under the IND and recall or otherwise provide for the disposi-

tion of all unused supplies of the drug. A termination action may be based on deficiencies in the IND or in the conduct of an investigation under an IND. Except as provided in paragraph (d) of this section, a termination shall be preceded by a proposal to terminate by FDA and an opportunity for the sponsor to respond. FDA will, in general, only initiate an action under this section after first attempting to resolve differences informally or, when appropriate, through the clinical hold procedures described in § 312.42.

(b) Grounds for termination—(1) Phase 1. FDA may propose to terminate an IND during Phase 1 if it finds that:

(i) Human subjects would be exposed to an unreasonable and significant risk of illness or unjury.

(ii) The IND does not contain sufficient information required under § 312.23 to assess the safety to subjects of the clinical investigations.

(iii) The methods, facilities, and controls used for the manufacturing, processing, and packing of the investigational drug are inadequate to establish and maintain appropriate standards of identity, strength, quality, and purity as needed for subject safety.

(iv) The clinical investigations are being conducted in a manner substantially different than that described in the protocols submitted in the IND.

(v) The drug is being promoted or distributed for commercial purposes not justified by the requirements of the investigation or permitted by § 312.7.

(vi) The IND, or any amendment or report to the IND, contains an untrue statement of a material fact or omits material information required by this part.

(vii) The sponsor fails promptly to investigate and inform the Food and Drug Administration and all investigators of serious and unexpected adverse experiences in accordance with § 312.32 or fails to make any other report required under this part.

(viii) The sponsor fails to submit an accurate annual report of the investigations in accordance with § 312.33.

(ix) The sponsor fails to comply with any other applicable requirement of this part, part 50, or part 56.

(x) The IND has remained on inactive status for 5 years or more.

(xi) The sponsor fails to delay a proposed investigation under the IND or to suspend an ongoing investigation that has been placed on clinical hold under § 312.42(b)(4).

(2) Phase 2 or 3. FDA may propose to terminate an IND during Phase 2 or Phase 3 if FDA finds that:

(i) Any of the conditions in paragraphs (b)(1)(i) through (b)(1)(xi) of this section apply; or

(ii) The investigational plan or protocol(s) is not reasonable as a bona fide scientific plan to determine whether or not the drug is safe and effective for use; or

(iii) There is convincing evidence that the drug is not effective for the purpose for which it is being investigated.

(3) FDA may propose to terminate a treatment IND if it finds that:

(i) Any of the conditions in paragraphs (b)(1)(i) through (x) of this section apply; or

(ii) Any of the conditions in § 312.42(b)(3) apply.

(c) Opportunity for sponsor response. (1) If FDA proposes to terminate an IND, FDA will notify the sponsor in writing, and invite correction or explanation within a period of 30 days.

(2) On such notification, the sponsor may provide a written explanation or correction or may request a conference with FDA to provide the requested explanation or correction. If the sponsor does not respond to the notification

within the allocated time, the IND shall be terminated.

(3) If the sponsor responds but FDA does not accept the explanation or correction submitted, FDA shall inform the sponsor in writing of the reason for the nonacceptance and provide the sponsor with an opportunity for a regulatory hearing before FDA under part 16 on the question of whether the IND should be terminated. The sponsor's request for a regulatory hearing must be made within 10 days of the sponsor's receipt of FDA's notification of nonacceptance.

(d) Immediate termination of IND. Notwithstanding paragraphs (a) through (c) of this section, if at any time FDA concludes that continuation of the investigation presents an immediate and substantial danger to the health of individuals, the agency shall immediately, by written notice to the sponsor from the Director of the Center for Drug Evaluation and Research or the Director of the Center for Biologics Evaluation and Research, terminate the IND. An IND so terminated is subject to reinstatement by the Director on the basis of additional submissions that eliminate such danger. If an IND is terminated under this paragraph, the agency will afford the sponsor an opportunity for a regulatory hearing under part 16 on the question of whether the IND should be reinstated.

[52 FR 8831, Mar. 19, 1987, as amended at 52 FR 23031, June 17, 1987; 55 FR 11579, Mar. 29, 1990; 57 FR 13249, Apr. 15, 1992; 67 FR 9586, Mar. 4, 2002]

§ 312.45   Inactive status.

(a) If no subjects are entered into clinical studies for a period of 2 years or more under an IND, or if all investigations under an IND remain on clinical hold for 1 year or more, the IND may be placed by FDA on inactive status. This action may be taken by FDA either on request of the sponsor or on FDA's own initiative. If FDA seeks to act on its own initiative under this section, it shall first notify the sponsor in writing of the proposed inactive status. Upon receipt of such notification, the sponsor shall have 30 days to respond as to why the IND should continue to remain active.

(b) If an IND is placed on inactive status, all investigators shall be so notified and all stocks of the drug shall be returned or otherwise disposed of in accordance with § 312.59.

(c) A sponsor is not required to submit annual reports to an IND on inactive status. An inactive IND is, however, still in effect for purposes of the public disclosure of data and information under § 312.130.

(d) A sponsor who intends to resume clinical investigation under an IND placed on inactive status shall submit a protocol amendment under § 312.30 containing the proposed general investigational plan for the coming year and appropriate protocols. If the protocol amendment relies on information previously submitted, the plan shall reference such information. Additional information supporting the proposed investigation, if any, shall be submitted in an information amendment. Notwithstanding the provisions of § 312.30, clinical investigations under an IND on inactive status may only resume (1) 30 days after FDA receives the protocol amendment, unless FDA notifies the sponsor that the investigations described in the amendment are subject to a clinical hold under § 312.42, or (2) on earlier notification by FDA that the clinical investigations described in the protocol amendment may begin.

(e) An IND that remains on inactive status for 5 years or more may be terminated under § 312.44.

[52 FR 8831, Mar. 19, 1987, as amended at 52 FR 23031, June 17, 1987; 67 FR 9586, Mar. 4, 2002]

§ 312.47   Meetings.

(a) General. Meetings between a sponsor and the agency are frequently useful in resolving questions and issues raised during the course of a clinical investigation. FDA encourages such meetings to the extent that they aid in the evaluation of the drug and in the solution of scientific problems concerning the drug, to the extent that FDA's resources permit. The general principle underlying the conduct of such meetings is that there should be free, full, and open communication about any scientific or medical question that may arise during the clinical investigation. These meetings shall be conducted and documented in accordance with part 10.

(b) "End-of-Phase 2" meetings and meetings held before submission of a marketing application. At specific times during the drug investigation process, meetings between FDA and a sponsor can be especially helpful in minimizing wasteful expenditures of time and money and thus in speeding the drug development and evaluation process. In particular, FDA has found that meetings at the end of Phase 2 of an investigation (end-of-Phase 2 meetings) are of considerable assistance in planning later studies and that meetings held near completion of Phase 3 and before submission of a marketing application ("pre-NDA" meetings) are helpful in developing methods of presentation and submission of data in the marketing application that facilitate review and allow timely FDA response.

(1) End-of-Phase 2 meetings—(i) Purpose. The purpose of an end-of-phase 2 meeting is to determine the safety of proceeding to Phase 3, to evaluate the Phase 3 plan and protocols and the adequacy of current studies and plans to assess pediatric safety and effectiveness, and to identify any additional information necessary to support a marketing application for the uses under investigation.

(ii) Eligibility for meeting. While the end-of-Phase 2 meeting is designed primarily for IND's involving new molecular entities or major new uses of marketed drugs, a sponsor of any IND may request and obtain an end-of-Phase 2 meeting.

(iii) Timing. To be most useful to the sponsor, end-of-Phase 2 meetings should be held before major commitments of effort and resources to specific Phase 3 tests are made. The scheduling of an end-of-Phase 2 meeting is not, however, intended to delay the transition of an investigation from Phase 2 to Phase 3.

(iv) Advance information. At least 1 month in advance of an end-of-Phase 2 meeting, the sponsor should submit background information on the sponsor's plan for Phase 3, including summaries of the Phase 1 and 2 investigations, the specific protocols for Phase 3 clinical studies, plans for any additional nonclinical studies, plans for pediatric studies, including a time line for protocol finalization, enrollment, completion, and data analysis, or information to support any planned request for waiver or deferral of pediatric studies, and, if available, tentative labeling for the drug. The recommended contents of such a submission are described more fully in FDA Staff Manual Guide 4850.7 that is publicly available under FDA's public information regulations in part 20.

(v) Conduct of meeting. Arrangements for an end-of-Phase 2 meeting are to be made with the division in FDA's Center for Drug Evaluation and Research or the Center for Biologics Evaluation and Research which is responsible for review of the IND. The meeting will be scheduled by FDA at a time convenient to both FDA and the sponsor. Both the sponsor and FDA may bring consultants to the meeting. The meeting should be directed primarily at establishing agreement between FDA and the sponsor of the overall plan for Phase 3 and the objectives and design of particular studies. The adequacy of the technical information to support Phase 3 studies and/or a marketing application may also be discussed. FDA will also provide its best judgment, at that time, of the pediatric studies that will be required for the drug product and whether their submission will be deferred until after approval. Agreements reached at the meeting on these matters will be recorded in minutes of the conference that will be taken by FDA in accordance with § 10.65 and provided to the sponsor. The minutes along with any other written material provided to the sponsor will serve as a permanent record of any agreements reached. Barring a significant scientific development that requires otherwise, studies conducted in accordance with the agreement shall be presumed to be sufficient in objective and design for the purpose of obtaining marketing approval for the drug.

(2) "Pre-NDA" and "pre-BLA" meetings. FDA has found that delays associated with the initial review of a marketing application may be reduced by exchanges of information about a proposed marketing application. The primary purpose of this kind of exchange is to uncover any major unresolved problems, to identify those studies that the sponsor is relying on as adequate and well-controlled to establish the drug's effectiveness, to identify the status of ongoing or needed studies adequate to assess pediatric safety and effectiveness, to acquaint FDA reviewers with the general information to be submitted in the marketing application (including technical information), to discuss appropriate methods for statistical analysis of the data, and to discuss the best approach to the presentation and formatting of data in the marketing application. Arrangements for such a meeting are to be initiated by the sponsor with the division responsible for review of the IND. To permit FDA to provide the sponsor with the most useful advice on preparing a marketing application, the sponsor should submit to FDA's reviewing division at least 1 month in advance of the meeting the following information:

(i) A brief summary of the clinical studies to be submitted in the application.

(ii) A proposed format for organizing the submission, including methods for presenting the data.

(iii) Information on the status of needed or ongoing pediatric studies.

(iv) Any other information for discussion at the meeting.

[52 FR 8831, Mar. 19, 1987, as amended at 52 FR 23031, June 17, 1987; 55 FR 11580, Mar. 29, 1990; 63 FR 66669, Dec. 2, 1998; 67 FR 9586, Mar. 4, 2002]

§ 312.48   Dispute resolution.

(a) General. The Food and Drug Administration is committed to resolving differences between sponsors and FDA reviewing divisions with respect to requirements for IND's as quickly and amicably as possible through the cooperative exchange of information and views.

(b) Administrative and procedural issues. When administrative or procedural disputes arise, the sponsor should first attempt to resolve the matter with the division in FDA's Center for Drug Evaluation and Research or Center for Biologics Evaluation and Research which is responsible for review of the IND, beginning with the consumer safety officer assigned to the application. If the dispute is not resolved, the sponsor may raise the matter with the person designated as ombudsman, whose function shall be to investigate what has happened and to facilitate a timely and equitable resolution. Appropriate issues to raise with the ombudsman include resolving difficulties in scheduling meetings and obtaining timely replies to inquiries. Further details on this procedure are contained in FDA Staff Manual Guide 4820.7 that is publicly available under FDA's public information regulations in part 20.

(c) Scientific and medical disputes. (1) When scientific or medical disputes arise during the drug investigation process, sponsors should discuss the matter directly with the responsible reviewing officials. If necessary, sponsors may request a meeting with the appropriate reviewing officials and management representatives in order to seek a resolution. Requests for such meetings shall be directed to the director of the division in FDA's Center for Drug Evaluation and Research

or Center for Biologics Evaluation and Research which is responsible for review of the IND. FDA will make every attempt to grant requests for meetings that involve important issues and that can be scheduled at mutually convenient times.

(2) The "end-of-Phase 2" and "pre-NDA" meetings described in § 312.47(b) will also provide a timely forum for discussing and resolving scientific and medical issues on which the sponsor disagrees with the agency.

(3) In requesting a meeting designed to resolve a scientific or medical dispute, applicants may suggest that FDA seek the advice of outside experts, in which case FDA may, in its discretion, invite to the meeting one or more of its advisory committee members or other consultants, as designated by the agency. Applicants may rely on, and may bring to any meeting, their own consultants. For major scientific and medical policy issues not resolved by informal meetings, FDA may refer the matter to one of its standing advisory committees for its consideration and recommendations.

[52 FR 8831, Mar. 19, 1987, as amended at 55 FR 11580, Mar. 29, 1990]

Subpart D—Responsibilities of Sponsors and Investigators

§ 312.50   General responsibilities of sponsors.

Sponsors are responsibile for selecting qualified investigators, providing them with the information they need to conduct an investigation properly, ensuring proper monitoring of the investigation(s), ensuring that the investigation(s) is conducted in accordance with the general investigational plan and protocols contained in the IND, maintaining an effective IND with respect to the investigations, and ensuring that FDA and all participating investigators are promptly informed of significant new adverse effects or risks with respect to the drug. Additional specific responsibilities of sponsors are described elsewhere in this part.

§ 312.52   Transfer of obligations to a contract research organization.

(a) A sponsor may transfer responsibility for any or all of the obligations set forth in this part to a contract research organization. Any such transfer shall be described in writing. If not all obligations are transferred, the writing is required to describe each of the obligations being assumed by the contract research organization. If all obligations are transferred, a general statement that all obligations have been transferred is acceptable. Any obligation not covered by the written description shall be deemed not to have been transferred.

(b) A contract research organization that assumes any obligation of a sponsor shall comply with the specific regulations in this chapter applicable to this obligation and shall be subject to the same regulatory action as a sponsor for failure to comply with any obligation assumed under these regulations. Thus, all references to "sponsor" in this part apply to a contract research organization to the extent that it assumes one or more obligations of the sponsor.

§ 312.53   Selecting investigators and monitors.

(a) Selecting investigators. A sponsor shall select only investigators qualified by training and experience as appropriate experts to investigate the drug.

(b) Control of drug. A sponsor shall ship investigational new drugs only to investigators participating in the investigation.

(c) Obtaining information from the investigator. Before permitting an investigator to begin participation in an investigation, the sponsor shall obtain the following:

(1) A signed investigator statement (Form FDA-1572) containing:

(i) The name and address of the investigator;

(ii) The name and code number, if any, of the protocol(s) in the IND identifying the study(ies) to be conducted by the investigator;

(iii) The name and address of any medical school, hospital, or other research facility where the clinical investigation(s) will be conducted;

(iv) The name and address of any clinical laboratory facilities to be used in the study;

(v) The name and address of the IRB that is responsible for review and approval of the study(ies);

(vi) A commitment by the investigator that he or she:

(a) Will conduct the study(ies) in accordance with the relevant, current protocol(s) and will only make changes in a protocol after notifying the sponsor, except when necessary to protect the safety, the rights, or welfare of subjects;

(b) Will comply with all requirements regarding the obligations of clinical investigators and all other pertinent requirements in this part;

(c) Will personally conduct or supervise the described investigation(s);

(d) Will inform any potential subjects that the drugs are being used for investigational purposes and will ensure that the requirements relating to obtaining informed consent (21 CFR part 50) and institutional review board review and approval (21 CFR part 56) are met;

(e) Will report to the sponsor adverse experiences that occur in the course of the investigation(s) in accordance with § 312.64;

(f) Has read and understands the information in the investigator's brochure, including the potential risks and side effects of the drug; and

(g) Will ensure that all associates, colleagues, and employees assisting in the conduct of the study(ies) are informed about their obligations in meeting the above commitments.

(vii) A commitment by the investigator that, for an investigation subject to an institutional review requirement under part 56, an IRB that complies with the requirements of that part will be responsible for the initial and continuing review and approval of the clinical investigation and that the investigator will promptly report to the IRB all changes in the research activity and all unanticipated problems involving risks to human subjects or others, and will not make any changes in the research without IRB approval, except where necessary to eliminate apparent immediate hazards to the human subjects.

(viii) A list of the names of the subinvestigators (e.g., research fellows, residents) who will be assisting the investigator in the conduct of the investigation(s).

(2) Curriculum vitae. A curriculum vitae or other statement of qualifications of the investigator showing the education, training, and experience that qualifies the investigator as an expert in the clinical investigation of the drug for the use under investigation.

(3) Clinical protocol. (i) For Phase 1 investigations, a general outline of the planned investigation including the estimated duration of the study and the maximum number of subjects that will be involved.

(ii) For Phase 2 or 3 investigations, an outline of the study protocol including an approximation of the number of subjects to be treated with the drug and the number to be employed as controls, if any; the clinical uses to be investigated; characteristics of subjects by age, sex, and condition; the kind of clinical observations and laboratory tests to be conducted; the estimated duration of the study; and copies or a description of case report forms to be used.

(4) Financial disclosure information. Sufficient accurate financial information to allow the sponsor to submit complete and accurate certification or disclosure statements required under part 54 of this chapter. The sponsor shall obtain a commitment from the clinical investigator to promptly update this information if any relevant changes occur during the course of the investigation and for 1 year following the completion of the study.

(d) Selecting monitors. A sponsor shall select a monitor qualified by training and experience to monitor the progress of the investigation.

[52 FR 8831, Mar. 19, 1987, as amended at 52 FR 23031, June 17, 1987; 61 FR 57280, Nov. 5, 1996; 63 FR 5252, Feb. 2, 1998; 67 FR 9586, Mar. 4, 2002]

§ 312.54 Emergency research under § 50.24 of this chapter.

(a) The sponsor shall monitor the progress of all investigations involving an exception from informed consent under § 50.24 of this chapter. When the sponsor receives from the IRB information concerning the public disclosures required by § 50.24(a)(7)(ii) and (a)(7)(iii) of this chapter, the sponsor promptly shall submit to the IND file and to Docket Number 95S-0158 in the Division of Dockets Management (HFA-305), Food and Drug Administration, 5630 Fishers Lane, rm. 1061, Rockville, MD 20852, copies of the information that was disclosed, identified by the IND number.

(b) The sponsor also shall monitor such investigations to identify when an IRB determines that it cannot approve the research because it does not meet the criteria in the exception in § 50.24(a) of this chapter or because of other relevant ethical concerns. The sponsor promptly shall provide this information in writing to FDA, investigators who are asked to participate in this or a substantially equivalent clinical investigation, and other IRB's that are asked to review this or a substantially equivalent investigation.

[61 FR 51530, Oct. 2, 1996, as amended at 68 FR 24879, May 9, 2003]

§ 312.55 Informing investigators.

(a) Before the investigation begins, a sponsor (other than a sponsor-investigator) shall give each participating clinical investigator an investigator brochure containing the information described in § 312.23(a)(5).

(b) The sponsor shall, as the overall investigation proceeds, keep each participating investigator informed of new observations discovered by or reported to the sponsor on the drug, particularly with respect to adverse effects and safe use. Such information may be distributed to investigators by means of periodically revised investigator brochures, reprints or published studies, reports or letters to clinical investigators, or other appropriate means. Important safety information is required to be relayed to investigators in accordance with § 312.32.

[52 FR 8831, Mar. 19, 1987, as amended at 52 FR 23031, June 17, 1987; 67 FR 9586, Mar. 4, 2002]

§ 312.56   Review of ongoing investigations.

(a) The sponsor shall monitor the progress of all clinical investigations being conducted under its IND.

(b) A sponsor who discovers that an investigator is not complying with the signed agreement (Form FDA-1572), the general investigational plan, or the requirements of this part or other applicable parts shall promptly either secure compliance or discontinue shipments of the investigational new drug to the investigator and end the investigator's participation in the investigation. If the investigator's participation in the investigation is ended, the sponsor shall require that the investigator dispose of or return the investigational drug in accordance with the requirements of § 312.59 and shall notify FDA.

(c) The sponsor shall review and evaluate the evidence relating to the safety and effectiveness of the drug as it is obtained from the investigator. The sponsors shall make such reports to FDA regarding information relevant to the safety of the drug as are required under § 312.32. The sponsor shall make annual reports on the progress of the investigation in accordance with § 312.33.

(d) A sponsor who determines that its investigational drug presents an unreasonable and significant risk to subjects shall discontinue those investigations that present the risk, notify FDA, all institutional review boards, and all investigators who have at any time participated in the investigation of the discontinuance, assure the disposition of all stocks of the drug outstanding as required by § 312.59, and furnish FDA with a full report of the sponsor's actions. The sponsor shall discontinue the investigation as soon as possible, and in no event later than 5 working days after making the determination that the investigation should be discontinued. Upon request, FDA will confer with a sponsor on the need to discontinue an investigation.

[52 FR 8831, Mar. 19, 1987, as amended at 52 FR 23031, June 17, 1987; 67 FR 9586, Mar. 4, 2002]

§ 312.57   Recordkeeping and record retention.

(a) A sponsor shall maintain adequate records showing the receipt, shipment, or other disposition of the investigational drug. These records are required to include, as appropriate, the name of the investigator to whom the drug is shipped, and the date, quantity, and batch or code mark of each such shipment.

(b) A sponsor shall maintain complete and accurate records showing any financial interest in § 54.4(a)(3)(i), (a)(3)(ii), (a)(3)(iii), and (a)(3)(iv) of this chapter paid to clinical investigators by the sponsor of the covered study. A sponsor shall also maintain complete and accurate records concerning all other financial interests of investigators subject to part 54 of this chapter.

(c) A sponsor shall retain the records and reports required by this part for 2 years after a marketing application is approved for the drug; or, if an application is not approved for the drug, until 2 years after shipment and delivery of the drug for investigational use is discontinued and FDA has been so notified.

(d) A sponsor shall retain reserve samples of any

279

test article and reference standard identified in, and used in any of the bioequivalence or bio-availability studies described in, § 320.38 or § 320.63 of this chapter, and release the reserve samples to FDA upon request, in accordance with, and for the period specified in § 320.38.

[52 FR 8831, Mar. 19, 1987, as amended at 52 FR 23031, June 17, 1987; 58 FR 25926, Apr. 28, 1993; 63 FR 5252, Feb. 2, 1998; 67 FR 9586, Mar. 4, 2002]

§ 312.58   Inspection of sponsor's records and reports.

(a) FDA inspection. A sponsor shall upon re-quest from any properly authorized officer or employee of the Food and Drug Administra-tion, at reasonable times, permit such officer or employee to have access to and copy and verify any records and reports relating to a clinical investigation conducted under this part. Upon written request by FDA, the sponsor shall sub-mit the records or reports (or copies of them) to FDA. The sponsor shall discontinue shipments of the drug to any investigator who has failed to maintain or make available records or reports of the investigation as required by this part.

(b) Controlled substances. If an investigational new drug is a substance listed in any schedule of the Controlled Substances Act (21 U.S.C. 801; 21 CFR part 1308), records concerning ship-ment, delivery, receipt, and disposition of the drug, which are required to be kept under this part or other applicable parts of this chapter shall, upon the request of a properly authorized employee of the Drug Enforcement Administra-tion of the U.S. Department of Justice, be made available by the investigator or sponsor to whom the request is made, for inspection and copying. In addition, the sponsor shall assure that adequate precautions are taken, including storage of the investigational drug in a securely locked, substantially constructed cabinet, or other securely locked, substantially constructed enclosure, access to which is limited, to prevent theft or diversion of the substance into illegal channels of distribution.

§ 312.59   Disposition of unused supply of investigational drug.

The sponsor shall assure the return of all unused supplies of the investigational drug from each individual investigator whose participation in the investigation is discontinued or terminated. The sponsor may authorize alternative disposi-tion of unused supplies of the investigational drug provided this alternative disposition does not expose humans to risks from the drug. The sponsor shall maintain written records of any disposition of the drug in accordance with § 312.57.

[52 FR 8831, Mar. 19, 1987, as amended at 52 FR 23031, June 17, 1987; 67 FR 9586, Mar. 4, 2002]

§ 312.60   General responsibilities of investigators.

An investigator is responsible for ensuring that an investigation is conducted according to the signed investigator statement, the investiga-tional plan, and applicable regulations; for pro-tecting the rights, safety, and welfare of subjects under the investigator's care; and for the control of drugs under investigation. An investigator shall, in accordance with the provisions of part 50 of this chapter, obtain the informed consent of each human subject to whom the drug is administered, except as provided in §§ 50.23 or 50.24 of this chapter. Additional specific respon-sibilities of clinical investigators are set forth in this part and in parts 50 and 56 of this chapter.

[52 FR 8831, Mar. 19, 1987, as amended at 61 FR 51530, Oct. 2, 1996]

§ 312.61   Control of the investigational drug.

An investigator shall administer the drug only to subjects under the investigator's personal supervision or under the supervision of a sub-investigator responsible to the investigator. The investigator shall not supply the investigational drug to any person not authorized under this part to receive it.

§ 312.62   Investigator recordkeeping and record retention.

(a) Disposition of drug. An investigator is required to maintain adequate records of the disposition of the drug, including dates, quantity, and use by subjects. If the investigation is terminated, suspended, discontinued, or completed, the investigator shall return the unused supplies of the drug to the sponsor, or otherwise provide for disposition of the unused supplies of the drug under § 312.59.

(b) Case histories. An investigator is required to prepare and maintain adequate and accurate case histories that record all observations and other data pertinent to the investigation on each individual administered the investigational drug or employed as a control in the investigation. Case histories include the case report forms and supporting data including, for example, signed and dated consent forms and medical records including, for example, progress notes of the physician, the individual's hospital chart(s), and the nurses' notes. The case history for each individual shall document that informed consent was obtained prior to participation in the study.

(c) Record retention. An investigator shall retain records required to be maintained under this part for a period of 2 years following the date a marketing application is approved for the drug for the indication for which it is being investigated; or, if no application is to be filed or if the application is not approved for such indication, until 2 years after the investigation is discontinued and FDA is notified.

[52 FR 8831, Mar. 19, 1987, as amended at 52 FR 23031, June 17, 1987; 61 FR 57280, Nov. 5, 1996; 67 FR 9586, Mar. 4, 2002]

§ 312.64   Investigator reports.

(a) Progress reports. The investigator shall furnish all reports to the sponsor of the drug who is responsible for collecting and evaluating the results obtained. The sponsor is required under § 312.33 to submit annual reports to FDA on the progress of the clinical investigations.

(b) Safety reports. An investigator shall promptly report to the sponsor any adverse effect that may reasonably be regarded as caused by, or probably caused by, the drug. If the adverse effect is alarming, the investigator shall report the adverse effect immediately.

(c) Final report. An investigator shall provide the sponsor with an adequate report shortly after completion of the investigator's participation in the investigation.

(d) Financial disclosure reports. The clinical investigator shall provide the sponsor with sufficient accurate financial information to allow an applicant to submit complete and accurate certification or disclosure statements as required under part 54 of this chapter. The clinical investigator shall promptly update this information if any relevant changes occur during the course of the investigation and for 1 year following the completion of the study.

[52 FR 8831, Mar. 19, 1987, as amended at 52 FR 23031, June 17, 1987; 63 FR 5252, Feb. 2, 1998; 67 FR 9586, Mar. 4, 2002]

§ 312.66   Assurance of IRB review.

An investigator shall assure that an IRB that complies with the requirements set forth in part 56 will be responsible for the initial and continuing review and approval of the proposed clinical study. The investigator shall also assure that he or she will promptly report to the IRB all changes in the research activity and all unanticipated problems involving risk to human subjects or others, and that he or she will not make any changes in the research without IRB approval, except where necessary to eliminate apparent immediate hazards to human subjects.

[52 FR 8831, Mar. 19, 1987, as amended at 52 FR 23031, June 17, 1987; 67 FR 9586, Mar. 4, 2002]

§ 312.68   Inspection of investigator's records and reports.

An investigator shall upon request from any properly authorized officer or employee of FDA, at reasonable times, permit such officer or employee to have access to, and copy and verify any records or reports made by the investigator pursuant to § 312.62. The investigator is not required to divulge subject names unless the records of particular individuals require a more detailed study of the cases, or unless there is reason to believe that the records do not represent actual case studies, or do not represent actual results obtained.

§ 312.69   Handling of controlled substances.

If the investigational drug is subject to the Controlled Substances Act, the investigator shall take adequate precautions, including storage of the investigational drug in a securely locked, substantially constructed cabinet, or other securely locked, substantially constructed enclosure, access to which is limited, to prevent theft or diversion of the substance into illegal channels of distribution.

§ 312.70   Disqualification of a clinical investigator.

(a) If FDA has information indicating that an investigator (including a sponsor-investigator) has repeatedly or deliberately failed to comply with the requirements of this part, part 50, or part 56 of this chapter, or has submitted to FDA or to the sponsor false information in any required report, the Center for Drug Evaluation and Research or the Center for Biologics Evaluation and Research will furnish the investigator written notice of the matter complained of and offer the investigator an opportunity to explain the matter in writing, or, at the option of the investigator, in an informal conference. If an explanation is offered but not accepted by the Center for Drug Evaluation and Research or the Center for Biologics Evaluation and Research, the investigator will be given an opportunity for a regulatory hearing under part 16 on the question of whether the investigator is entitled to receive investigational new drugs.

(b) After evaluating all available information, including any explanation presented by the investigator, if the Commissioner determines that the investigator has repeatedly or deliberately failed to comply with the requirements of this part, part 50, or part 56 of this chapter, or has deliberately or repeatedly submitted false information to FDA or to the sponsor in any required report, the Commissioner will notify the investigator and the sponsor of any investigation in which the investigator has been named as a participant that the investigator is not entitled to receive investigational drugs. The notification will provide a statement of basis for such determination.

(c) Each IND and each approved application submitted under part 314 containing data reported by an investigator who has been determined to be ineligible to receive investigational drugs will be examined to determine whether the investigator has submitted unreliable data that are essential to the continuation of the investigation or essential to the approval of any marketing application.

(d) If the Commissioner determines, after the unreliable data submitted by the investigator are eliminated from consideration, that the data remaining are inadequate to support a conclusion that it is reasonably safe to continue the investigation, the Commissioner will notify the sponsor who shall have an opportunity for a regulatory hearing under part 16. If a danger to the public health exists, however, the Commissioner shall terminate the IND immediately and notify the sponsor of the determination. In such case, the sponsor shall have an opportunity for a regulatory hearing before FDA under part 16 on the question of whether the IND should be reinstated.

(e) If the Commissioner determines, after the unreliable data submitted by the investigator are eliminated from consideration, that the continued approval of the drug product for which the data were submitted cannot be justified, the Commissioner will proceed to withdraw approval of the drug product in accordance with the applicable provisions of the act.

(f) An investigator who has been determined to be ineligible to receive investigational drugs may be reinstated as eligible when the Commissioner determines that the investigator has presented adequate assurances that the investigator will employ investigational drugs solely in compliance with the provisions of this part and of parts 50 and 56.

[52 FR 8831, Mar. 19, 1987, as amended at 52 FR 23031, June 17, 1987; 55 FR 11580, Mar. 29, 1990; 62 FR 46876, Sept. 5, 1997; 67 FR 9586, Mar. 4, 2002]

Subpart E—Drugs Intended to Treat Life-threatening and Severely-debilitating Illnesses

Authority:

21 U.S.C. 351, 352, 353, 355, 371; 42 U.S.C. 262.

Source:

53 FR 41523, Oct. 21, 1988, unless otherwise noted.

§ 312.80   Purpose.

The purpose of this section is to establish procedures designed to expedite the development, evaluation, and marketing of new therapies intended to treat persons with life-threatening and severely-debilitating illnesses, especially where no satisfactory alternative therapy exists. As stated § 314.105(c) of this chapter, while the statutory standards of safety and effectiveness apply to all drugs, the many kinds of drugs that are subject to them, and the wide range of uses for those drugs, demand flexibility in applying

the standards. The Food and Drug Administration (FDA) has determined that it is appropriate to exercise the broadest flexibility in applying the statutory standards, while preserving appropriate guarantees for safety and effectiveness. These procedures reflect the recognition that physicians and patients are generally willing to accept greater risks or side effects from products that treat life-threatening and severely-debilitating illnesses, than they would accept from products that treat less serious illnesses. These procedures also reflect the recognition that the benefits of the drug need to be evaluated in light of the severity of the disease being treated. The procedure outlined in this section should be interpreted consistent with that purpose.

§ 312.81   Scope.

This section applies to new drug and biological products that are being studied for their safety and effectiveness in treating life-threatening or severely-debilitating diseases.

(a) For purposes of this section, the term "life-threatening" means:

(1) Diseases or conditions where the likelihood of death is high unless the course of the disease is interrupted; and

(2) Diseases or conditions with potentially fatal outcomes, where the end point of clinical trial analysis is survival.

(b) For purposes of this section, the term "severely debilitating" means diseases or conditions that cause major irreversible morbidity.

(c) Sponsors are encouraged to consult with FDA on the applicability of these procedures to specific products.

[53 FR 41523, Oct. 21, 1988, as amended at 64 FR 401, Jan. 5, 1999]

§ 312.82   Early consultation.

For products intended to treat life-threatening or severely-debilitating illnesses, sponsors may request to meet with FDA-reviewing officials early in the drug development process to review and reach agreement on the design of necessary preclinical and clinical studies. Where appropriate, FDA will invite to such meetings one or more outside expert scientific consultants or advisory committee members. To the extent FDA resources permit, agency reviewing officials will honor requests for such meetings

(a) Pre-investigational new drug (IND) meetings. Prior to the submission of the initial IND, the sponsor may request a meeting with FDA-reviewing officials. The primary purpose of this meeting is to review and reach agreement on the design of animal studies needed to initiate human testing. The meeting may also provide an opportunity for discussing the scope and design of phase 1 testing, plans for studying the drug product in pediatric populations, and the best approach for presentation and formatting of data in the IND.

(b) End-of-phase 1 meetings. When data from phase 1 clinical testing are available, the sponsor may again request a meeting with FDA-reviewing officials. The primary purpose of this meeting is to review and reach agreement on the design of phase 2 controlled clinical trials, with the goal that such testing will be adequate to provide sufficient data on the drug's safety and effectiveness to support a decision on its approvability for marketing, and to discuss the need for, as well as the design and timing of, studies of the drug in pediatric patients. For drugs for life-threatening diseases, FDA will provide its best judgment, at that time, whether pediatric studies will be required and whether their submission will be deferred until after approval. The procedures outlined in § 312.47(b) (1) with respect to end-of-phase 2 conferences, including documentation of agreements reached, would also be used for end-of-phase 1 meetings.

[53 FR 41523, Oct. 21, 1988, as amended at 63 FR 66669, Dec. 2, 1998]

§ 312.83   Treatment protocols.

If the preliminary analysis of phase 2 test results appears promising, FDA may ask the sponsor to submit a treatment protocol to be reviewed under the procedures and criteria listed in §§ 312.34 and 312.35. Such a treatment protocol, if requested and granted, would normally remain in effect while the complete data necessary for a marketing application are being assembled by the sponsor and reviewed by FDA (unless grounds exist for clinical hold of ongoing protocols, as provided in § 312.42(b)(3)(ii)).

§ 312.84   Risk-benefit analysis in review of marketing applications for drugs to treat life-threatening and severely-debilitating illnesses.

(a) FDA's application of the statutory standards for marketing approval shall recognize the need for a medical risk-benefit judgment in making the final decision on approvability. As part of this evaluation, consistent with the statement of purpose in § 312.80, FDA will consider whether the benefits of the drug outweigh the known and potential risks of the drug and the need to answer remaining questions about risks and benefits of the drug, taking into consideration the severity of the disease and the absence of satisfactory alternative therapy.

(b) In making decisions on whether to grant marketing approval for products that have been the subject of an end-of-phase 1 meeting under § 312.82, FDA will usually seek the advice of outside expert scientific consultants or advisory committees. Upon the filing of such a marketing application under § 314.101 or part 601 of this chapter, FDA will notify the members of the relevant standing advisory committee of the application's filing and its availability for review.

(c) If FDA concludes that the data presented are not sufficient for marketing approval, FDA will issue a complete response letter under § 314.110 of this chapter or the biological product licensing procedures. Such letter, in describing the deficiencies in the application, will address why the results of the research design agreed to under § 312.82, or in subsequent meetings, have not provided sufficient evidence for marketing approval. Such letter will also describe any recommendations made by the advisory committee regarding the application.

(d) Marketing applications submitted under the procedures contained in this section will be subject to the requirements and procedures contained in part 314 or part 600 of this chapter, as well as those in this subpart.

[53 FR 41523, Oct. 21, 1988, as amended at 73 FR 39607, July 10, 2008]

§ 312.85   Phase 4 studies.

Concurrent with marketing approval, FDA may seek agreement from the sponsor to conduct certain postmarketing (phase 4) studies to delineate additional information about the drug's risks, benefits, and optimal use. These studies could include, but would not be limited to, studying different doses or schedules of administration than were used in phase 2 studies, use of the drug in other patient populations or other stages of the disease, or use of the drug over a longer period of time.

§ 312.86   Focused FDA regulatory research.

At the discretion of the agency, FDA may undertake focused regulatory research on critical rate-limiting aspects of the preclinical, chemical/manufacturing, and clinical phases of drug development and evaluation. When initiated, FDA will undertake such research efforts as a means for meeting a public health need in facilitating the development of therapies to treat life-threatening or severely debilitating illnesses.

§ 312.87   Active monitoring of conduct and evaluation of clinical trials.

For drugs covered under this section, the Commissioner and other agency officials will monitor the progress of the conduct and evaluation of clinical trials and be involved in facilitating their appropriate progress.

§ 312.88   Safeguards for patient safety.

All of the safeguards incorporated within parts 50, 56, 312, 314, and 600 of this chapter designed to ensure the safety of clinical testing and the safety of products following marketing approval apply to drugs covered by this section. This includes the requirements for informed consent (part 50 of this chapter) and institutional review boards (part 56 of this chapter). These safeguards further include the review of animal studies prior to initial human testing (§ 312.23), and the monitoring of adverse drug experiences through the requirements of IND safety reports (§ 312.32), safety update reports during agency review of a marketing application (§ 314.50 of this chapter), and postmarketing adverse reaction reporting (§ 314.80 of this chapter).

Subpart F—Miscellaneous

§ 312.110   Import and export requirements.

(a) Imports. An investigational new drug offered for import into the United States complies with the requirements of this part if it is subject to an IND that is in effect for it under § 312.40 and: (1) The consignee in the United States is the sponsor of the IND; (2) the consignee is a qualified investigator named in the IND; or (3) the consignee is the domestic agent of a foreign sponsor, is responsible for the control and distribution of the investigational drug, and the IND identifies the consignee and describes what, if any, actions the consignee will take with respect to the investigational drug.

(b) Exports. An investigational new drug may be exported from the United States for use in a clinical investigation under any of the following conditions:

(1) An IND is in effect for the drug under § 312.40, the drug complies with the laws of the country to which it is being exported, and each person who receives the drug is an investigator in a study submitted to and allowed to proceed

under the IND; or

(2) The drug has valid marketing authorization in Australia, Canada, Israel, Japan, New Zealand, Switzerland, South Africa, or in any country in the European Union or the European Economic Area, and complies with the laws of the country to which it is being exported, section 802(b)(1)(A), (f), and (g) of the act, and § 1.101 of this chapter; or

(3) The drug is being exported to Australia, Canada, Israel, Japan, New Zealand, Switzerland, South Africa, or to any country in the European Union or the European Economic Area, and complies with the laws of the country to which it is being exported, the applicable provisions of section 802(c), (f), and (g) of the act, and § 1.101 of this chapter. Drugs exported under this paragraph that are not the subject of an IND are exempt from the label requirement in § 312.6(a); or

(4) Except as provided in paragraph (b)(5) of this section, the person exporting the drug sends a written certification to the Office of International Programs (HFG-1), Food and Drug Administration, 5600 Fishers Lane, Rockville, MD 20857, at the time the drug is first exported and maintains records documenting compliance with this paragraph. The certification shall describe the drug that is to be exported (i.e., trade name (if any), generic name, and dosage form), identify the country or countries to which the drug is to be exported, and affirm that:

(i) The drug is intended for export;

(ii) The drug is intended for investigational use in a foreign country;

(iii) The drug meets the foreign purchaser's or consignee's specifications;

(iv) The drug is not in conflict with the importing country's laws;

(v) The outer shipping package is labeled to show that the package is intended for export from the United States;

(vi) The drug is not sold or offered for sale in the United States;

(vii) The clinical investigation will be conducted in accordance with § 312.120;

(viii) The drug is manufactured, processed, packaged, and held in substantial conformity with current good manufacturing practices;

(ix) The drug is not adulterated within the meaning of section 501(a)(1), (a)(2)(A), (a)(3), (c), or (d) of the act;

(x) The drug does not present an imminent hazard to public health, either in the United States, if the drug were to be reimported, or in the foreign country; and

(xi) The drug is labeled in accordance with the foreign country's laws.

(5) In the event of a national emergency in a foreign country, where the national emergency necessitates exportation of an investigational new drug, the requirements in paragraph (b)(4) of this section apply as follows:

(i) Situations where the investigational new drug is to be stockpiled in anticipation of a national emergency. There may be instances where exportation of an investigational new drug is needed so that the drug may be stockpiled and made available for use by the importing country if and when a national emergency arises. In such cases:

(A) A person may export an investigational new drug under paragraph (b)(4) of this section without making an affirmation with respect to any one or more of paragraphs (b)(4)(i), (b)(4)(iv), (b)(4)(vi), (b)(4)(vii), (b)(4)(viii), and/or (b)(4)(ix) of this section, provided that he or she:

(1) Provides a written statement explaining why compliance with each such paragraph is not feasible or is contrary to the best interests of the individuals who may receive the investigational new drug;

(2) Provides a written statement from an autho-

rized official of the importing country's government. The statement must attest that the official agrees with the exporter's statement made under paragraph (b)(5)(i)(A)(1) of this section; explain that the drug is to be stockpiled solely for use of the importing country in a national emergency; and describe the potential national emergency that warrants exportation of the investigational new drug under this provision; and

(3) Provides a written statement showing that the Secretary of Health and Human Services (the Secretary), or his or her designee, agrees with the findings of the authorized official of the importing country's government. Persons who wish to obtain a written statement from the Secretary should direct their requests to Secretary's Operations Center, Office of Emergency Operations and Security Programs, Office of Public Health Emergency Preparedness, Office of the Secretary, Department of Health and Human Services, 200 Independence Ave, SW., Washington, DC 20201. Requests may be also be sent by FAX: 202-619 7870 or by e-mail: HHS.SOC@hhs.gov.

(B) Exportation may not proceed until FDA has authorized exportation of the investigational new drug. FDA may deny authorization if the statements provided under paragraphs (b)(5)(i)(A)(1) or (b)(5)(i)(A)(2) of this section are inadequate or if exportation is contrary to public health.

(ii) Situations where the investigational new drug is to be used for a sudden and immediate national emergency. There may be instances where exportation of an investigational new drug is needed so that the drug may be used in a sudden and immediate national emergency that has developed or is developing. In such cases:

(A) A person may export an investigational new drug under paragraph (b)(4) of this section without making an affirmation with respect to any one or more of paragraphs (b)(4)(i), (b)(4)(iv), (b)(4)(v), (b)(4)(vi), (b)(4)(vii), (b)(4)(viii), (b)(4)(ix), and/or (b)(4)(xi), provided that he or she:

(1) Provides a written statement explaining why compliance with each such paragraph is not feasible or is contrary to the best interests of the individuals who are expected to receive the investigational new drug and

(2) Provides sufficient information from an authorized official of the importing country's government to enable the Secretary, or his or her designee, to decide whether a national emergency has developed or is developing in the importing country, whether the investigational new drug will be used solely for that national emergency, and whether prompt exportation of the investigational new drug is necessary. Persons who wish to obtain a determination from the Secretary should direct their requests to Secretary's Operations Center, Office of Emergency Operations and Security Programs, Office of Public Health Emergency Preparedness, Office of the Secretary, Department of Health and Human Services, 200 Independence Ave. SW., Washington, DC 20201. Requests may be also be sent by FAX: 202-619-7870 or by e-mail: HHS.SOC@hhs.gov.

(B) Exportation may proceed without prior FDA authorization.

(c) Limitations. Exportation under paragraph (b) of this section may not occur if:

(1) For drugs exported under paragraph (b)(1) of this section, the IND pertaining to the clinical investigation is no longer in effect;

(2) For drugs exported under paragraph (b)(2) of this section, the requirements in section 802(b)(1), (f), or (g) of the act are no longer met;

(3) For drugs exported under paragraph (b)(3) of this section, the requirements in section 802(c), (f), or (g) of the act are no longer met;

(4) For drugs exported under paragraph (b)(4) of this section, the conditions underlying the certification or the statements submitted under paragraph (b)(5) of this section are no

longer met; or

(5) For any investigational new drugs under this section, the drug no longer complies with the laws of the importing country.

(d) Insulin and antibiotics. New insulin and antibiotic drug products may be exported for investigational use in accordance with section 801(e)(1) of the act without complying with this section.

[52 FR 8831, Mar. 19, 1987, as amended at 52 FR 23031, June 17, 1987; 64 FR 401, Jan. 5, 1999; 67 FR 9586, Mar. 4, 2002; 70 FR 70729, Nov. 23, 2005]

§ 312.120   Foreign clinical studies not conducted under an IND.

(a) Acceptance of studies. (1) FDA will accept as support for an IND or application for marketing approval (an application under section 505 of the act or section 351 of the Public Health Service Act (the PHS Act) (42 U.S.C. 262)) a well-designed and well-conducted foreign clinical study not conducted under an IND, if the following conditions are met:

(i) The study was conducted in accordance with good clinical practice (GCP). For the purposes of this section, GCP is defined as a standard for the design, conduct, performance, monitoring, auditing, recording, analysis, and reporting of clinical trials in a way that provides assurance that the data and reported results are credible and accurate and that the rights, safety, and well-being of trial subjects are protected. GCP includes review and approval (or provision of a favorable opinion) by an independent ethics committee (IEC) before initiating a study, continuing review of an ongoing study by an IEC, and obtaining and documenting the freely given informed consent of the subject (or a subject's legally authorized representative, if the subject is unable to provide informed consent) before initiating a study. GCP does not require informed consent in life-threatening situations when the IEC reviewing the study finds, before initiation of the

study, that informed consent is not feasible and either that the conditions present are consistent with those described in § 50.23 or § 50.24(a) of this chapter, or that the measures described in the study protocol or elsewhere will protect the rights, safety, and well-being of subjects; and

(ii) FDA is able to validate the data from the study through an onsite inspection if the agency deems it necessary.

(2) Although FDA will not accept as support for an IND or application for marketing approval a study that does not meet the conditions of paragraph (a)(1) of this section, FDA will examine data from such a study.

(3) Marketing approval of a new drug based solely on foreign clinical data is governed by § 314.106 of this chapter.

(b) Supporting information. A sponsor or applicant who submits data from a foreign clinical study not conducted under an IND as support for an IND or application for marketing approval must submit to FDA, in addition to information required elsewhere in parts 312, 314, or 601 of this chapter, a description of the actions the sponsor or applicant took to ensure that the research conformed to GCP as described in paragraph (a)(1)(i) of this section. The description is not required to duplicate information already submitted in the IND or application for marketing approval. Instead, the description must provide either the following information or a cross-reference to another section of the submission where the information is located:

(1) The investigator's qualifications;

(2) A description of the research facilities;

(3) A detailed summary of the protocol and results of the study and, should FDA request, case records maintained by the investigator or additional background data such as hospital or other institutional records;

(4) A description of the drug substance and drug product used in the study, including a de-

scription of the components, formulation, specifications, and, if available, bioavailability of the specific drug product used in the clinical study;

(5) If the study is intended to support the effectiveness of a drug product, information showing that the study is adequate and well controlled under § 314.126 of this chapter;

(6) The name and address of the IEC that reviewed the study and a statement that the IEC meets the definition in § 312.3 of this chapter. The sponsor or applicant must maintain records supporting such statement, including records of the names and qualifications of IEC members, and make these records available for agency review upon request;

(7) A summary of the IEC's decision to approve or modify and approve the study, or to provide a favorable opinion;

(8) A description of how informed consent was obtained;

(9) A description of what incentives, if any, were provided to subjects to participate in the study;

(10) A description of how the sponsor(s) monitored the study and ensured that the study was carried out consistently with the study protocol; and

(11) A description of how investigators were trained to comply with GCP (as described in paragraph (a)(1)(i) of this section) and to conduct the study in accordance with the study protocol, and a statement on whether written commitments by investigators to comply with GCP and the protocol were obtained. Any signed written commitments by investigators must be maintained by the sponsor or applicant and made available for agency review upon request.

(c) Waivers. (1) A sponsor or applicant may ask FDA to waive any applicable requirements under paragraphs (a)(1) and (b) of this section. A waiver request may be submitted in an IND or in an information amendment to an IND, or in an

application or in an amendment or supplement to an application submitted under part 314 or 601 of this chapter. A waiver request is required to contain at least one of the following:

(i) An explanation why the sponsor's or applicant's compliance with the requirement is unnecessary or cannot be achieved;

(ii) A description of an alternative submission or course of action that satisfies the purpose of the requirement; or

(iii) Other information justifying a waiver.

(2) FDA may grant a waiver if it finds that doing so would be in the interest of the public health.

(d) Records. A sponsor or applicant must retain the records required by this section for a foreign clinical study not conducted under an IND as follows:

(1) If the study is submitted in support of an application for marketing approval, for 2 years after an agency decision on that application;

(2) If the study is submitted in support of an IND but not an application for marketing approval, for 2 years after the submission of the IND.

[73 FR 22815, Apr. 28, 2008]

§ 312.130   Availability for public disclosure of data and information in an IND.

(a) The existence of an investigational new drug application will not be disclosed by FDA unless it has previously been publicly disclosed or acknowledged.

(b) The availability for public disclosure of all data and information in an investigational new drug application for a new drug will be handled in accordance with the provisions established in § 314.430 for the confidentiality of data and information in applications submitted in part 314. The availability for public disclosure of all data and information in an investigational new drug application for a biological product will be governed by the provisions of §§ 601.50 and

601.51.

(c) Notwithstanding the provisions of § 314.430, FDA shall disclose upon request to an individual to whom an investigational new drug has been given a copy of any IND safety report relating to the use in the individual.

(d) The availability of information required to be publicly disclosed for investigations involving an exception from informed consent under § 50.24 of this chapter will be handled as follows: Persons wishing to request the publicly disclosable information in the IND that was required to be filed in Docket Number 95S-0158 in the Division of Dockets Management (HFA-305), Food and Drug Administration, 5630 Fishers Lane, rm. 1061, Rockville, MD 20852, shall submit a request under the Freedom of Information Act.

[52 FR 8831, Mar. 19, 1987. Redesignated at 53 FR 41523, Oct. 21, 1988, as amended at 61 FR 51530, Oct. 2, 1996; 64 FR 401, Jan. 5, 1999; 68 FR 24879, May 9, 2003]

§ 312.140   Address for correspondence.

(a) A sponsor must send an initial IND submission to the Center for Drug Evaluation and Research (CDER) or to the Center for Biologics Evaluation and Research (CBER), depending on the Center responsible for regulating the product as follows:

(1) For drug products regulated by CDER. Send the IND submission to the Central Document Room, Center for Drug Evaluation and Research, Food and Drug Administration, 5901-B Ammendale Rd., Beltsville, MD 20705-1266; except send an IND submission for an *in vivo* bioavailability or bioequivalence study in humans to support an abbreviated new drug application to the Office of Generic Drugs (HFD-600), Center for Drug Evaluation and Research, Food and Drug Administration, Metro Park North II, 7500 Standish Pl., Rockville, MD 20855.

(2) For biological products regulated by CDER. Send the IND submission to the CDER Thera-

peutic Biological Products Document Room, Center for Drug Evaluation and Research, Food and Drug Administration, 12229 Wilkins Ave., Rockville, MD 20852.

(3) For biological products regulated by CBER. Send the IND submission to the Document Control Center (HFM-99), Center for Biologics Evaluation and Research, Food and Drug Administration, 1401 Rockville Pike, suite 200N, Rockville, MD 20852-1448.

(b) On receiving the IND, the responsible Center will inform the sponsor which one of the divisions in CDER or CBER is responsible for the IND. Amendments, reports, and other correspondence relating to matters covered by the IND should be sent to the appropriate center at the address indicated in this section and marked to the attention of the responsible division. The outside wrapper of each submission shall state what is contained in the submission, for example, "IND Application", "Protocol Amendment", etc.

(c) All correspondence relating to export of an investigational drug under § 312.110(b)(2) shall be submitted to the International Affairs Staff (HFY-50), Office of Health Affairs, Food and Drug Administration, 5600 Fishers Lane, Rockville, MD 20857.

[70 FR 14981, Mar. 24, 2005, as amended at 74 FR 13113, Mar. 26, 2009; 74 FR 55771, Oct. 29, 2009]

§ 312.145   Guidance documents.

(a) FDA has made available guidance documents under § 10.115 of this chapter to help you to comply with certain requirements of this part.

(b) The Center for Drug Evaluation and Research (CDER) and the Center for Biologics Evaluation and Research (CBER) maintain lists of guidance documents that apply to the centers' regulations. The lists are maintained on the Internet and are published annually in the Federal Register. A request for a copy of the CDER list should be directed to the Office of Training and Communications, Division of Drug Information, Center for Drug Evaluation and Research, Food and Drug Administration, 10903 New Hampshire Ave., Silver Spring, MD 20993-0002. A request for a copy of the CBER list should be directed to the Office of Communication, Training, and Manufacturers Assistance (HFM-40), Center for Biologics Evaluation and Research, Food and Drug Administration, 1401 Rockville Pike, Rockville, MD 20852-1448.

[65 FR 56479, Sept. 19, 2000, as amended at 74 FR 13113, Mar. 26, 2009]

Subpart G—Drugs for Investigational Use in Laboratory Research Animals or *In Vitro* Tests

§ 312.160   Drugs for investigational use in laboratory research animals or *in vitro* tests.

(a) Authorization to ship. (1)(i) A person may ship a drug intended solely for tests *in vitro* or in animals used only for laboratory research purposes if it is labeled as follows:

CAUTION: Contains a new drug for investigational use only in laboratory research animals, or for tests *in vitro*. Not for use in humans.

(ii) A person may ship a biological product for investigational *in vitro* diagnostic use that is listed in § 312.2(b)(2)(ii) if it is labeled as follows:

CAUTION: Contains a biological product for investigational *in vitro* diagnostic tests only.

(2) A person shipping a drug under paragraph (a) of this section shall use due diligence to assure that the consignee is regularly engaged in conducting such tests and that the shipment of the new drug will actually be used for tests *in vitro* or in animals used only for laboratory research.

(3) A person who ships a drug under paragraph (a) of this section shall maintain adequate records showing the name and post office address of the expert to whom the drug is shipped

and the date, quantity, and batch or code mark of each shipment and delivery. Records of shipments under paragraph (a)(1)(i) of this section are to be maintained for a period of 2 years after the shipment. Records and reports of data and shipments under paragraph (a)(1)(ii) of this section are to be maintained in accordance with § 312.57(b). The person who ships the drug shall upon request from any properly authorized officer or employee of the Food and Drug Administration, at reasonable times, permit such officer or employee to have access to and copy and verify records required to be maintained under this section.

(b) Termination of authorization to ship. FDA may terminate authorization to ship a drug under this section if it finds that:

(1) The sponsor of the investigation has failed to comply with any of the conditions for shipment established under this section, or

(2) The continuance of the investigation is unsafe or otherwise contrary to the public interest or the drug is used for purposes other than bona fide scientific investigation. FDA will notify the person shipping the drug of its finding and invite immediate correction. If correction is not immediately made, the person shall have an opportunity for a regulatory hearing before FDA pursuant to part 16.

(c) Disposition of unused drug. The person who ships the drug under paragraph (a) of this section shall assure the return of all unused supplies of the drug from individual investigators whenever the investigation discontinues or the investigation is terminated. The person who ships the drug may authorize in writing alternative disposition of unused supplies of the drug provided this alternative disposition does not expose humans to risks from the drug, either directly or indirectly (e.g., through food-producing animals). The shipper shall maintain records of any alternative disposition.

[52 FR 8831, Mar. 19, 1987, as amended at 52

FR 23031, June 17, 1987. Redesignated at 53 FR 41523, Oct. 21, 1988; 67 FR 9586, Mar. 4, 2002]

Subpart H [Reserved]

Subpart I—Expanded Access to Investigational Drugs for Treatment Use

Source:

74 FR 40942, Aug. 13, 2009, unless otherwise noted.

§ 312.300   General.

(a) Scope. This subpart contains the requirements for the use of investigational new drugs and approved drugs where availability is limited by a risk evaluation and mitigation strategy (REMS) when the primary purpose is to diagnose, monitor, or treat a patient's disease or condition. The aim of this subpart is to facilitate the availability of such drugs to patients with serious diseases or conditions when there is no comparable or satisfactory alternative therapy to diagnose, monitor, or treat the patient's disease or condition.

(b) Definitions. The following definitions of terms apply to this subpart:

Immediately life-threatening disease or condition means a stage of disease in which there is reasonable likelihood that death will occur within a matter of months or in which premature death is likely without early treatment.

Serious disease or condition means a disease or condition associated with morbidity that has substantial impact on day-to-day functioning. Short-lived and self-limiting morbidity will usually not be sufficient, but the morbidity need not be irreversible, provided it is persistent or recurrent. Whether a disease or condition is serious is a matter of clinical judgment, based on its impact on such factors as survival, day-to-day functioning, or the likelihood that the disease, if left untreated, will progress from a less severe condition to a more serious one.

§ 312.305   Requirements for all expanded access uses.

The criteria, submission requirements, safeguards, and beginning treatment information set out in this section apply to all expanded access uses described in this subpart. Additional criteria, submission requirements, and safeguards that apply to specific types of expanded access are described in §§ 312.310 through 312.320.

(a) Criteria. FDA must determine that:

(1) The patient or patients to be treated have a serious or immediately life-threatening disease or condition, and there is no comparable or satisfactory alternative therapy to diagnose, monitor, or treat the disease or condition;

(2) The potential patient benefit justifies the potential risks of the treatment use and those potential risks are not unreasonable in the context of the disease or condition to be treated; and

(3) Providing the investigational drug for the requested use will not interfere with the initiation, conduct, or completion of clinical investigations that could support marketing approval of the expanded access use or otherwise compromise the potential development of the expanded access use.

(b) Submission. (1) An expanded access submission is required for each type of expanded access described in this subpart. The submission may be a new IND or a protocol amendment to an existing IND. Information required for a submission may be supplied by referring to pertinent information contained in an existing IND if the sponsor of the existing IND grants a right of reference to the IND.

(2) The expanded access submission must include:

(i) A cover sheet (Form FDA 1571) meeting the requirements of § 312.23(a);

(ii) The rationale for the intended use of the drug, including a list of available therapeutic options that would ordinarily be tried before resorting to the investigational drug or an explanation of why the use of the investigational drug is preferable to the use of available therapeutic options;

(iii) The criteria for patient selection or, for an individual patient, a description of the patient's disease or condition, including recent medical history and previous treatments of the disease or condition;

(iv) The method of administration of the drug, dose, and duration of therapy;

(v) A description of the facility where the drug will be manufactured;

(vi) Chemistry, manufacturing, and controls information adequate to ensure the proper identification, quality, purity, and strength of the investigational drug;

(vii) Pharmacology and toxicology information adequate to conclude that the drug is reasonably safe at the dose and duration proposed for expanded access use (ordinarily, information that would be adequate to permit clinical testing of the drug in a population of the size expected to be treated); and

(viii) A description of clinical procedures, laboratory tests, or other monitoring necessary to evaluate the effects of the drug and minimize its risks.

(3) The expanded access submission and its mailing cover must be plainly marked "EXPANDED ACCESS SUBMISSION." If the expanded access submission is for a treatment IND or treatment protocol, the applicable box on Form FDA 1571 must be checked.

(c) Safeguards. The responsibilities of sponsors and investigators set forth in subpart D of this part are applicable to expanded access use under this subpart as described in this paragraph.

(1) A licensed physician under whose immediate direction an investigational drug is adminis-

tered or dispensed for an expanded access use under this subpart is considered an investigator, for purposes of this part, and must comply with the responsibilities for investigators set forth in subpart D of this part to the extent they are applicable to the expanded access use.

(2) An individual or entity that submits an expanded access IND or protocol under this subpart is considered a sponsor, for purposes of this part, and must comply with the responsibilities for sponsors set forth in subpart D of this part to the extent they are applicable to the expanded access use.

(3) A licensed physician under whose immediate direction an investigational drug is administered or dispensed, and who submits an IND for expanded access use under this subpart is considered a sponsor-investigator, for purposes of this part, and must comply with the responsibilities for sponsors and investigators set forth in subpart D of this part to the extent they are applicable to the expanded access use.

(4) Investigators. In all cases of expanded access, investigators are responsible for reporting adverse drug events to the sponsor, ensuring that the informed consent requirements of part 50 of this chapter are met, ensuring that IRB review of the expanded access use is obtained in a manner consistent with the requirements of part 56 of this chapter, and maintaining accurate case histories and drug disposition records and retaining records in a manner consistent with the requirements of § 312.62. Depending on the type of expanded access, other investigator responsibilities under subpart D may also apply.

(5) Sponsors. In all cases of expanded access, sponsors are responsible for submitting IND safety reports and annual reports (when the IND or protocol continues for 1 year or longer) to FDA as required by §§ 312.32 and 312.33, ensuring that licensed physicians are qualified to administer the investigational drug for the expanded access use, providing licensed physicians with the information needed to minimize

the risk and maximize the potential benefits of the investigational drug (the investigator's brochure must be provided if one exists for the drug), maintaining an effective IND for the expanded access use, and maintaining adequate drug disposition records and retaining records in a manner consistent with the requirements of § 312.57. Depending on the type of expanded access, other sponsor responsibilities under subpart D may also apply.

(d) Beginning treatment—(1) INDs. An expanded access IND goes into effect 30 days after FDA receives the IND or on earlier notification by FDA that the expanded access use may begin.

(2) Protocols. With the following exceptions, expanded access use under a protocol submitted under an existing IND may begin as described in § 312.30(a).

(i) Expanded access use under the emergency procedures described in § 312.310(d) may begin when the use is authorized by the FDA reviewing official.

(ii) Expanded access use under § 312.320 may begin 30 days after FDA receives the protocol or upon earlier notification by FDA that use may begin.

(3) Clinical holds. FDA may place any expanded access IND or protocol on clinical hold as described in § 312.42.

§ 312.310   Individual patients, including for emergency use.

Under this section, FDA may permit an investigational drug to be used for the treatment of an individual patient by a licensed physician.

(a) Criteria. The criteria in § 312.305(a) must be met; and the following determinations must be made:

(1) The physician must determine that the probable risk to the person from the investigational drug is not greater than the probable risk from the disease or condition; and

(2) FDA must determine that the patient cannot obtain the drug under another IND or protocol.

(b) Submission. The expanded access submission must include information adequate to demonstrate that the criteria in § 312.305(a) and paragraph (a) of this section have been met. The expanded access submission must meet the requirements of § 312.305(b).

(1) If the drug is the subject of an existing IND, the expanded access submission may be made by the sponsor or by a licensed physician.

(2) A sponsor may satisfy the submission requirements by amending its existing IND to include a protocol for individual patient expanded access.

(3) A licensed physician may satisfy the submission requirements by obtaining from the sponsor permission for FDA to refer to any information in the IND that would be needed to support the expanded access request (right of reference) and by providing any other required information not contained in the IND (usually only the information specific to the individual patient).

(c) Safeguards. (1) Treatment is generally limited to a single course of therapy for a specified duration unless FDA expressly authorizes multiple courses or chronic therapy.

(2) At the conclusion of treatment, the licensed physician or sponsor must provide FDA with a written summary of the results of the expanded access use, including adverse effects.

(3) FDA may require sponsors to monitor an individual patient expanded access use if the use is for an extended duration.

(4) When a significant number of similar individual patient expanded access requests have been submitted, FDA may ask the sponsor to submit an IND or protocol for the use under § 312.315 or § 312.320.

(d) Emergency procedures. If there is an emergency that requires the patient to be treated before a written submission can be made, FDA may authorize the expanded access use to begin without a written submission. The FDA reviewing official may authorize the emergency use by telephone.

(1) Emergency expanded access use may be requested by telephone, facsimile, or other means of electronic communications. For investigational biological drug products regulated by the Center for Biologics Evaluation and Research, the request should be directed to the Office of Communication, Outreach and Development, Center for Biologics Evaluation and Research, 301-827-1800 or 1-800-835-4709, e-mail: ocod@fda.hhs.gov. For all other investigational drugs, the request for authorization should be directed to the Division of Drug Information, Center for Drug Evaluation and Research, 301-796-3400, e-mail: druginfo@fda.hhs.gov. After normal working hours, the request should be directed to the FDA Office of Emergency Operations, 301-443-1240, e-mail: emergency.operations@fda.hhs.gov.

(2) The licensed physician or sponsor must explain how the expanded access use will meet the requirements of §§ 312.305 and 312.310 and must agree to submit an expanded access submission within 15 working days of FDA's authorization of the use.

§ 312.315   Intermediate-size patient populations.

Under this section, FDA may permit an investigational drug to be used for the treatment of a patient population smaller than that typical of a treatment IND or treatment protocol. FDA may ask a sponsor to consolidate expanded access under this section when the agency has received a significant number of requests for individual patient expanded access to an investigational drug for the same use.

(a) Need for expanded access. Expanded access under this section may be needed in the following situations:

(1) Drug not being developed. The drug is not being developed, for example, because the disease or condition is so rare that the sponsor is unable to recruit patients for a clinical trial.

(2) Drug being developed. The drug is being studied in a clinical trial, but patients requesting the drug for expanded access use are unable to participate in the trial. For example, patients may not be able to participate in the trial because they have a different disease or stage of disease than the one being studied or otherwise do not meet the enrollment criteria, because enrollment in the trial is closed, or because the trial site is not geographically accessible.

(3) Approved or related drug. (i) The drug is an approved drug product that is no longer marketed for safety reasons or is unavailable through marketing due to failure to meet the conditions of the approved application, or

(ii) The drug contains the same active moiety as an approved drug product that is unavailable through marketing due to failure to meet the conditions of the approved application or a drug shortage.

(b) Criteria. The criteria in § 312.305(a) must be met; and FDA must determine that·

(1) There is enough evidence that the drug is safe at the dose and duration proposed for expanded access use to justify a clinical trial of the drug in the approximate number of patients expected to receive the drug under expanded access; and

(2) There is at least preliminary clinical evidence of effectiveness of the drug, or of a plausible pharmacologic effect of the drug to make expanded access use a reasonable therapeutic option in the anticipated patient population.

(c) Submission. The expanded access submission must include information adequate to satisfy FDA that the criteria in § 312.305(a) and paragraph (b) of this section have been met.

The expanded access submission must meet the requirements of § 312.305(b). In addition:

(1) The expanded access submission must state whether the drug is being developed or is not being developed and describe the patient population to be treated.

(2) If the drug is not being actively developed, the sponsor must explain why the drug cannot currently be developed for the expanded access use and under what circumstances the drug could be developed.

(3) If the drug is being studied in a clinical trial, the sponsor must explain why the patients to be treated cannot be enrolled in the clinical trial and under what circumstances the sponsor would conduct a clinical trial in these patients.

(d) Safeguards. (1) Upon review of the IND annual report, FDA will determine whether it is appropriate for the expanded access to continue under this section.

(i) If the drug is not being actively developed or if the expanded access use is not being developed (but another use is being developed), FDA will consider whether it is possible to conduct a clinical study of the expanded access use.

(ii) If the drug is being actively developed, FDA will consider whether providing the investigational drug for expanded access use is interfering with the clinical development of the drug.

(iii) As the number of patients enrolled increases, FDA may ask the sponsor to submit an IND or protocol for the use under § 312.320.

(2) The sponsor is responsible for monitoring the expanded access protocol to ensure that licensed physicians comply with the protocol and the regulations applicable to investigators.

§ 312.320   Treatment IND or treatment protocol.

Under this section, FDA may permit an investigational drug to be used for widespread treatment use.

(a) Criteria. The criteria in § 312.305(a) must be met, and FDA must determine that:

(1) Trial status. (i) The drug is being investigated in a controlled clinical trial under an IND designed to support a marketing application for the expanded access use, or

(ii) All clinical trials of the drug have been completed; and

(2) Marketing status. The sponsor is actively pursuing marketing approval of the drug for the expanded access use with due diligence; and

(3) Evidence. (i) When the expanded access use is for a serious disease or condition, there is sufficient clinical evidence of safety and effectiveness to support the expanded access use. Such evidence would ordinarily consist of data from phase 3 trials, but could consist of compelling data from completed phase 2 trials; or

(ii) When the expanded access use is for an immediately life-threatening disease or condition, the available scientific evidence, taken as a whole, provides a reasonable basis to conclude that the investigational drug may be effective for the expanded access use and would not expose patients to an unreasonable and significant risk of illness or injury. This evidence would ordinarily consist of clinical data from phase 3 or phase 2 trials, but could be based on more preliminary clinical evidence.

(b) Submission. The expanded access submission must include information adequate to satisfy FDA that the criteria in § 312.305(a) and paragraph (a) of this section have been met. The expanded access submission must meet the requirements of § 312.305(b).

(c) Safeguard. The sponsor is responsible for monitoring the treatment protocol to ensure that licensed physicians comply with the protocol and the regulations applicable to investigators.

Part 314—Applications for FDA Approval to market a new drug

Authority:

21 U.S.C. 321, 331, 351, 352, 353, 355, 356, 356a, 356b, 356c, 371, 374, 379e.

Source:

50 FR 7493, Feb. 22, 1985, unless otherwise noted.

Editorial Note:

Nomenclature changes to part 314 can be found at 69 FR 13717, Mar. 24, 2004.

Subpart A—General Provisions

§ 314.1   Scope of this part.

(a) This part sets forth procedures and requirements for the submission to, and the review by, the Food and Drug Administration of applications and abbreviated applications to market a new drug under section 505 of the Federal Food, Drug, and Cosmetic Act, as well as amendments, supplements, and postmarketing reports to them.

(b) This part does not apply to drug products subject to licensing by FDA under the Public Health Service Act (58 Stat. 632 as amended (42 U.S.C. 201 et seq.)) and subchapter F of chapter I of title 21 of the Code of Federal Regulations.

(c) References in this part to regulations in the Code of Federal Regulations are to chapter I of title 21, unless otherwise noted.

[50 FR 7493, Feb. 22, 1985, as amended at 57 FR 17981, Apr. 28, 1992; 64 FR 401, Jan. 5, 1999]

§ 314.2   Purpose.

The purpose of this part is to establish an efficient and thorough drug review process in order to: (a) Facilitate the approval of drugs shown to be safe and effective; and (b) ensure the disapproval of drugs not shown to be safe and effective. These regulations are also intended to establish an effective system for FDA's surveillance of marketed drugs. These regulations shall be construed in light of these objectives.

§ 314.3   Definitions.

(a) The definitions and interpretations contained in section 201 of the act apply to those terms when used in this part.

(b) The following definitions of terms apply to this part:

Abbreviated application means the application described under § 314.94, including all amendments and supplements to the application. "Abbreviated application" applies to both an abbreviated new drug application and an abbreviated antibiotic application.

Act means the Federal Food, Drug, and Cosmetic Act (sections 201-901 (21 U.S.C. 301-392)).

Applicant means any person who submits an application or abbreviated application or an amendment or supplement to them under this part to obtain FDA approval of a new drug or an antibiotic drug and any person who owns an approved application or abbreviated application.

Application means the application described under § 314.50, including all amendements and supplements to the application.

505(b)(2) Application means an application submitted under section 505(b)(1) of the act for a drug for which the investigations described in section 505(b)(1)(A) of the act and relied upon by the applicant for approval of the application were not conducted by or for the applicant and for which the applicant has not obtained a right of reference or use from the person by or for whom the investigations were conducted.

Approval letter means a written communication to an applicant from FDA approving an application or an abbreviated application.

Assess the effects of the change means to evaluate the effects of a manufacturing change on the identity, strength, quality, purity, and potency of a drug product as these factors may relate to the safety or effectiveness of the drug product.

Authorized generic drug means a listed drug, as defined in this section, that has been approved under section 505(c) of the act and is marketed, sold, or distributed directly or indirectly to retail class of trade with labeling, packaging (other than repackaging as the listed drug in blister packs, unit doses, or similar packaging for use in institutions), product code, labeler code, trade name, or trademark that differs from that of the listed drug.

Class 1 resubmission means the resubmission of an application or efficacy supplement, following receipt of a complete response letter, that contains one or more of the following: Final printed labeling, draft labeling, certain safety updates, stability updates to support provisional or final dating periods, commitments to perform postmarketing studies (including proposals for such studies), assay validation data, final release testing on the last lots used to support approval, minor reanalyses of previously submitted data, and other comparatively minor information.

Class 2 resubmission means the resubmission of an application or efficacy supplement, following receipt of a complete response letter, that includes any item not specified in the definition of "Class 1 resubmission," including any item that would require presentation to an advisory committee.

Complete response letter means a written communication to an applicant from FDA usually describing all of the deficiencies that the agency has identified in an application or abbreviated application that must be satisfactorily addressed before it can be approved.

Drug product means a finished dosage form, for example, tablet, capsule, or solution, that contains a drug substance, generally, but not necessarily, in association with one or more other ingredients.

Drug substance means an active ingredient that is intended to furnish pharmacological activity or other direct effect in the diagnosis, cure, mitigation, treatment, or prevention of disease or to affect the structure or any function of the human body, but does not include intermediates use in the synthesis of such ingredient.

Efficacy supplement means a supplement to an approved application proposing to make one or more related changes from among the following changes to product labeling:

(1) Add or modify an indication or claim;

(2) Revise the dose or dose regimen;

(3) Provide for a new route of administration;

(4) Make a comparative efficacy claim naming another drug product;

(5) Significantly alter the intended patient population;

(6) Change the marketing status from prescription to over-the-counter use;

(7) Provide for, or provide evidence of effectiveness necessary for, the traditional approval of a product originally approved under subpart H of part 314; or

(8) Incorporate other information based on at least one adequate and well-controlled clinical study.

FDA means the Food and Drug Administration.

Listed drug means a new drug product that has an effective approval under section 505(c) of the act for safety and effectiveness or under section 505(j) of the act, which has not been withdrawn or suspended under section 505(e) (1) through (e)(5) or (j)(5) of the act, and which has not been withdrawn from sale for what FDA has determined are reasons of safety or effectiveness. Listed drug status is evidenced by the drug product's identification as a drug with an effective approval in the current edition of FDA's "Approved Drug Products with Therapeutic

Equivalence Evaluations" (the list) or any current supplement thereto, as a drug with an effective approval. A drug product is deemed to be a listed drug on the date of effective approval of the application or abbreviated application for that drug product.

Newly acquired information means data, analyses, or other information not previously submitted to the agency, which may include (but are not limited to) data derived from new clinical studies, reports of adverse events, or new analyses of previously submitted data (e.g., meta-analyses) if the studies, events or analyses reveal risks of a different type or greater severity or frequency than previously included in submissions to FDA.

Original application means a pending application for which FDA has never issued a complete response letter or approval letter, or an application that was submitted again after FDA had refused to file it or after it was withdrawn without being approved.

Reference listed drug means the listed drug identified by FDA as the drug product upon which an applicant relies in seeking approval of its abbreviated application.

Resubmission means submission by the applicant of all materials needed to fully address all deficiencies identified in the complete response letter. An application or abbreviated application for which FDA issued a complete response letter, but which was withdrawn before approval and later submitted again, is not a resubmission.

Right of reference or use means the authority to rely upon, and otherwise use, an investigation for the purpose of obtaining approval of an application, including the ability to make available the underlying raw data from the investigation for FDA audit, if necessary.

Specification means the quality standard (i.e., tests, analytical procedures, and acceptance criteria) provided in an approved application to confirm the quality of drug substances, drug products, intermediates, raw materials, reagents, components, in-process materials, container closure systems, and other materials used in the production of a drug substance or drug product. For the purpose of this definition, acceptance criteria means numerical limits, ranges, or other criteria for the tests described.

The list means the list of drug products with effective approvals published in the current edition of FDA's publication "Approved Drug Products with Therapeutic Equivalence Evaluations" and any current supplement to the publication.

[50 FR 7493, Feb. 22, 1985, as amended at 57 FR 17981, Apr. 28, 1992; 69 FR 18763, Apr. 8, 2004; 73 FR 39607, July 10, 2008; 73 FR 49609, Aug. 22, 2008; 74 FR 37167, July 28, 2009]

Subpart B—Applications

§ 314.50   Content and format of an application.

Applications and supplements to approved applications are required to be submitted in the form and contain the information, as appropriate for the particular submission, required under this section. Three copies of the application are required: An archival copy, a review copy, and a field copy. An application for a new chemical entity will generally contain an application form, an index, a summary, five or six technical sections, case report tabulations of patient data, case report forms, drug samples, and labeling, including, if applicable, any Medication Guide required under part 208 of this chapter. Other applications will generally contain only some of those items, and information will be limited to that needed to support the particular submission. These include an application of the type described in section 505(b)(2) of the act, an amendment, and a supplement. The application is required to contain reports of all investigations of the drug product sponsored by the applicant, and all other information about the drug pertinent to an evaluation of the application that is received or otherwise obtained by the applicant from any source. FDA will maintain guidance documents on the format and content of applications to assist applicants in their preparation.

(a) Application form. The applicant shall submit a completed and signed application form that contains the following:

(1) The name and address of the applicant; the date of the application; the application number if previously issued (for example, if the application is a resubmission, an amendment, or a supplement); the name of the drug product, including its established, proprietary, code, and chemical names; the dosage form and strength; the route of administration; the identification numbers of all investigational new drug applications that are referenced in the application; the identification numbers of all drug master files and other applications under this part that are referenced in the application; and the drug product's proposed indications for use.

(2) A statement whether the submission is an original submission, a 505(b)(2) application, a resubmission, or a supplement to an application under § 314.70.

(3) A statement whether the applicant proposes to market the drug product as a prescription or an over-the-counter product.

(4) A check-list identifying what enclosures required under this section the applicant is submitting.

(5) The applicant, or the applicant's attorney, agent, or other authorized official shall sign the application. If the person signing the application does not reside or have a place of business within the United States, the application is required to contain the name and address of, and be countersigned by, an attorney, agent, or other authorized official who resides or maintains a place of business within the United States.

(b) Index. The archival copy of the application is required to contain a comprehensive index by

volume number and page number to the summary under paragraph (c) of this section, the technical sections under paragraph (d) of this section, and the supporting information under paragraph (f) of this section.

(c) Summary. (1) An application is required to contain a summary of the application in enough detail that the reader may gain a good general understanding of the data and information in the application, including an understanding of the quantitative aspects of the data. The summary is not required for supplements under § 314.70. Resubmissions of an application should contain an updated summary, as appropriate. The summary should discuss all aspects of the application, and synthesize the information into a well-structured and unified document. The summary should be written at approximately the level of detail required for publication in, and meet the editorial standards generally applied by, refereed scientific and medical journals. In addition to the agency personnel reviewing the summary in the context of their review of the application, FDA may furnish the summary to FDA advisory committee members and agency officials whose duties require an understanding of the application. To the extent possible, data in the summary should be presented in tabular and graphic forms. FDA has prepared a guideline under § 10.90(b) that provides information about how to prepare a summary. The summary required under this paragraph may be used by FDA or the applicant to prepare the Summary Basis of Approval document for public disclosure (under § 314.430(e)(2)(ii)) when the application is approved.

(2) The summary is required to contain the following information:

(i) The proposed text of the labeling, including, if applicable, any Medication Guide required under part 208 of this chapter, for the drug, with annotations to the information in the summary and technical sections of the application that support the inclusion of each statement in the labeling, and, if the application is for a prescription drug, statements describing the reasons for omitting a section or subsection of the labeling format in § 201.57 of this chapter.

(ii) A statement identifying the pharmacologic class of the drug and a discussion of the scientific rationale for the drug, its intended use, and the potential clinical benefits of the drug product.

(iii) A brief description of the marketing history, if any, of the drug outside the United States, including a list of the countries in which the drug has been marketed, a list of any countries in which the drug has been withdrawn from marketing for any reason related to safety or effectiveness, and a list of countries in which applications for marketing are pending. The description is required to describe both marketing by the applicant and, if known, the marketing history of other persons.

(iv) A summary of the chemistry, manufacturing, and controls section of the application.

(v) A summary of the nonclinical pharmacology and toxicology section of the application.

(vi) A summary of the human pharmacokinetics and bioavailability section of the application.

(vii) A summary of the microbiology section of the application (for anti-infective drugs only).

(viii) A summary of the clinical data section of the application, including the results of statistical analyses of the clinical trials.

(ix) A concluding discussion that presents the benefit and risk considerations related to the drug, including a discussion of any proposed additional studies or surveillance the applicant intends to conduct postmarketing.

(d) Technical sections. The application is required to contain the technical sections described below. Each technical section is required to contain data and information in sufficient detail to permit the agency to make a knowledgeable judgment about whether to approve

the application or whether grounds exist under section 505(d) of the act to refuse to approve the application. The required technical sections are as follows:

(1) Chemistry, manufacturing, and controls section. A section describing the composition, manufacture, and specification of the drug substance and the drug product, including the following:

(i) Drug substance. A full description of the drug substance including its physical and chemical characteristics and stability; the name and address of its manufacturer; the method of synthesis (or isolation) and purification of the drug substance; the process controls used during manufacture and packaging; and the specifications necessary to ensure the identity, strength, quality, and purity of the drug substance and the bioavailability of the drug products made from the substance, including, for example, tests, analytical procedures, and acceptance criteria relating to stability, sterility, particle size, and crystalline form. The application may provide additionally for the use of alternatives to meet any of these requirements, including alternative sources, process controls, and analytical procedures. Reference to the current edition of the U.S. Pharmacopeia and the National Formulary may satisfy relevant requirements in this paragraph.

(ii)(a) Drug product. A list of all components used in the manufacture of the drug product (regardless of whether they appear in the drug product) and a statement of the composition of the drug product; the specifications for each component; the name and address of each manufacturer of the drug product; a description of the manufacturing and packaging procedures and in-process controls for the drug product; the specifications necessary to ensure the identity, strength, quality, purity, potency, and bioavailability of the drug product, including, for example, tests, analytical procedures, and acceptance criteria relating to sterility, dissolution rate, container closure systems; and stability data with proposed expiration dating. The application may provide additionally for the use of alternatives to meet any of these requirements, including alternative components, manufacturing and packaging procedures, in-process controls, and analytical procedures. Reference to the current edition of the U.S. Pharmacopeia and the National Formulary may satisfy relevant requirements in this paragraph.

(b) Unless provided by paragraph (d)(1)(ii)(a) of this section, for each batch of the drug product used to conduct a bioavailability or bioequivalence study described in § 320.38 or § 320.63 of this chapter or used to conduct a primary stability study: The batch production record; the specification for each component and for the drug product; the names and addresses of the sources of the active and noncompendial inactive components and of the container and closure system for the drug product; the name and address of each contract facility involved in the manufacture, processing, packaging, or testing of the drug product and identification of the operation performed by each contract facility; and the results of any test performed on the components used in the manufacture of the drug product as required by § 211.84(d) of this chapter and on the drug product as required by § 211.165 of this chapter.

(c) The proposed or actual master production record, including a description of the equipment, to be used for the manufacture of a commercial lot of the drug product or a comparably detailed description of the production process for a representative batch of the drug product.

(iii) Environmental impact. The application is required to contain either a claim for categorical exclusion under § 25.30 or 25.31 of this chapter or an environmental assessment under § 25.40 of this chapter.

(iv) The applicant may, at its option, submit a complete chemistry, manufacturing, and controls section 90 to 120 days before the anticipated submission of the remainder of the application. FDA will review such early submissions as resources permit.

(v) The applicant shall include a statement certifying that the field copy of the application has been provided to the applicant's home FDA district office.

(2) Nonclinical pharmacology and toxicology section. A section describing, with the aid of graphs and tables, animal and *in vitro* studies with drug, including the following:

(i) Studies of the pharmacological actions of the drug in relation to its proposed therapeutic indication and studies that otherwise define the pharmacologic properties of the drug or are pertinent to possible adverse effects.

(ii) Studies of the toxicological effects of the drug as they relate to the drug's intended clinical uses, including, as appropriate, studies assessing the drug's acute, subacute, and chronic toxicity; carcinogenicity; and studies of toxicities related to the drug's particular mode of administration or conditions of use.

(iii) Studies, as appropriate, of the effects of the drug on reproduction and on the developing fetus.

(iv) Any studies of the absorption, distribution, metabolism, and excretion of the drug in animals.

(v) For each nonclinical laboratory study subject to the good laboratory practice regulations under part 58 a statement that it was conducted in compliance with the good laboratory practice regulations in part 58, or, if the study was not conducted in compliance with those regulations, a brief statement of the reason for the noncompliance.

(3) Human pharmacokinetics and bioavailability section. A section describing the human pharmacokinetic data and human bioavailability data, or information supporting a waiver of the submission of *in vivo* bioavailability data under

subpart B of part 320, including the following:

(i) A description of each of the bioavailability and pharmacokinetic studies of the drug in humans performed by or on behalf of the applicant that includes a description of the analytical procedures and statistical methods used in each study and a statement with respect to each study that it either was conducted in compliance with the institutional review board regulations in part 56, or was not subject to the regulations under § 56.104 or § 56.105, and that it was conducted in compliance with the informed consent regulations in part 50.

(ii) If the application describes in the chemistry, manufacturing, and controls section tests, analytical procedures, and acceptance criteria needed to assure the bioavailability of the drug product or drug substance, or both, a statement in this section of the rationale for establishing the tests, analytical procedures, and acceptance criteria, including data and information supporting the rationale.

(iii) A summarizing discussion and analysis of the pharmacokinetics and metabolism of the active ingredients and the bioavailability or bioequivalence, or both, of the drug product.

(4) Microbiology section. If the drug is an anti-infective drug, a section describing the microbiology data, including the following·

(i) A description of the biochemical basis of the drug's action on microbial physiology.

(ii) A description of the antimicrobial spectra of the drug, including results of *in vitro* preclinical studies to demonstrate concentrations of the drug required for effective use.

(iii) A description of any known mechanisms of resistance to the drug, including results of any known epidemiologic studies to demonstrate prevalence of resistance factors.

(iv) A description of clinical microbiology laboratory procedures (for example, *in vitro* sensitivity discs) needed for effective use of the drug.

(5) Clinical data section. A section describing the clinical investigations of the drug, including the following:

(i) A description and analysis of each clinical pharmacology study of the drug, including a brief comparison of the results of the human studies with the animal pharmacology and toxicology data.

(ii) A description and analysis of each controlled clinical study pertinent to a proposed use of the drug, including the protocol and a description of the statistical analyses used to evaluate the study. If the study report is an interim analysis, this is to be noted and a projected completion date provided. Controlled clinical studies that have not been analyzed in detail for any reason (e.g., because they have been discontinued or are incomplete) are to be included in this section, including a copy of the protocol and a brief description of the results and status of the study.

(iii) A description of each uncontrolled clinical study, a summary of the results, and a brief statement explaining why the study is classified as uncontrolled.

(iv) A description and analysis of any other data or information relevant to an evaluation of the safety and effectiveness of the drug product obtained or otherwise received by the applicant from any source, foreign or domestic, including information derived from clinical investigations, including controlled and uncontrolled studies of uses of the drug other than those proposed in the application, commercial marketing experience, reports in the scientific literature, and unpublished scientific papers.

(v) An integrated summary of the data demonstrating substantial evidence of effectiveness for the claimed indications. Evidence is also required to support the dosage and administration section of the labeling, including support for the dosage and dose interval recommended. The effectiveness data shall be presented by gender, age, and racial subgroups and shall identify any modifications of dose or dose interval needed for specific subgroups. Effectiveness data from other subgroups of the population of patients treated, when appropriate, such as patients with renal failure or patients with different levels of severity of the disease, also shall be presented.

(vi) A summary and updates of safety information, as follows:

(a) The applicant shall submit an integrated summary of all available information about the safety of the drug product, including pertinent animal data, demonstrated or potential adverse effects of the drug, clinically significant drug/drug interactions, and other safety considerations, such as data from epidemiological studies of related drugs. The safety data shall be presented by gender, age, and racial subgroups. When appropriate, safety data from other subgroups of the population of patients treated also shall be presented, such as for patients with renal failure or patients with different levels of severity of the disease. A description of any statistical analyses performed in analyzing safety data should also be included, unless already included under paragraph (d)(5)(ii) of this section.

(b) The applicant shall, under section 505(i) of the act, update periodically its pending application with new safety information learned about the drug that may reasonably affect the statement of contraindications, warnings, precautions, and adverse reactions in the draft labeling and, if applicable, any Medication Guide required under part 208 of this chapter. These "safety update reports" are required to include the same kinds of information (from clinical studies, animal studies, and other sources) and are required to be submitted in the same format as the integrated summary in paragraph (d)(5) (vi)(a) of this section. In addition, the reports are required to include the case report forms for each patient who died during a clinical study or who did not complete the study because of an adverse event (unless this requirement is waived). The applicant shall submit these reports (1) 4 months after the initial submission; (2) in a resubmission following receipt of a complete response letter; and (3) at other times as requested by FDA. Prior to the submission of the first such report, applicants are encouraged to consult with FDA regarding further details on its form and content.

(vii) If the drug has a potential for abuse, a description and analysis of studies or information related to abuse of the drug, including a proposal for scheduling under the Controlled Substances Act. A description of any studies related to overdosage is also required, including information on dialysis, antidotes, or other treatments, if known.

(viii) An integrated summary of the benefits and risks of the drug, including a discussion of why the benefits exceed the risks under the conditions stated in the labeling.

(ix) A statement with respect to each clinical study involving human subjects that it either was conducted in compliance with the institutional review board regulations in part 56, or was not subject to the regulations under § 56.104 or § 56.105, and that it was conducted in compliance with the informed consent regulations in part 50.

(x) If a sponsor has transferred any obligations for the conduct of any clinical study to a contract research organization, a statement containing the name and address of the contract research organization, identification of the clinical study, and a listing of the obligations transferred. If all obligations governing the conduct of the study have been transferred, a general statement of this transfer—in lieu of a listing of the specific obligations transferred—may be submitted.

(xi) If original subject records were audited or reviewed by the sponsor in the course of monitoring any clinical study to verify the accuracy of the case reports submitted to the sponsor, a list identifying each clinical study so audited or reviewed.

(6) Statistical section. A section describing the statistical evaluation of clinical data, including the following:

(i) A copy of the information submitted under paragraph (d)(5)(ii) of this section concerning the description and analysis of each controlled clinical study, and the documentation and supporting statistical analyses used in evaluating the controlled clinical studies.

(ii) A copy of the information submitted under paragraph (d)(5)(vi)(a) of this section concerning a summary of information about the safety of the drug product, and the documentation and supporting statistical analyses used in evaluating the safety information.

(7) Pediatric use section. A section describing the investigation of the drug for use in pediatric populations, including an integrated summary of the information (the clinical pharmacology studies, controlled clinical studies, or uncontrolled clinical studies, or other data or information) that is relevant to the safety and effectiveness and benefits and risks of the drug in pediatric populations for the claimed indications, a reference to the full descriptions of such studies provided under paragraphs (d)(3) and (d)(5) of this section, and information required to be submitted under § 314.55.

(e) Samples and labeling. (1) Upon request from FDA, the applicant shall submit the samples described below to the places identified in the agency's request. FDA will generally ask applicants to submit samples directly to two or more agency laboratories that will perform all necessary tests on the samples and validate the applicant's analytical procedures.

(i) Four representative samples of the following, each sample in sufficient quantity to permit FDA to perform three times each test described in the application to determine whether the drug substance and the drug product meet the specifications given in the application:

(a) The drug product proposed for marketing;

(b) The drug substance used in the drug product from which the samples of the drug product were taken; and

(c) Reference standards and blanks (except that reference standards recognized in an official compendium need not be submitted).

(ii) Samples of the finished market package, if requested by FDA.

(2) The applicant shall submit the following in the archival copy of the application:

(i) Three copies of the analytical procedures and related descriptive information contained in the chemistry, manufacturing, and controls section under paragraph (d)(1) of this section for the drug substance and the drug product that are necessary for FDA's laboratories to perform all necessary tests on the samples and to validate the applicant's analytical procedures. The related descriptive information includes a description of each sample; the proposed regulatory specifications for the drug; a detailed description of the methods of analysis; supporting data for accuracy, specificity, precision and ruggedness; and complete results of the applicant's tests on each sample.

(ii) Copies of the label and all labeling for the drug product (including, if applicable, any Medication Guide required under part 208 of this chapter) for the drug product (4 copies of draft labeling or 12 copies of final printed labeling).

(f) Case report forms and tabulations. The archival copy of the application is required to contain the following case report tabulations and case report forms:

(1) Case report tabulations. The application is required to contain tabulations of the data from each adequate and well-controlled study under § 314.126 (Phase 2 and Phase 3 studies as described in §§ 312.21 (b) and (c) of this chapter), tabulations of the data from the earliest clinical pharmacology studies (Phase 1 studies as

described in § 312.21(a) of this chapter), and tabulations of the safety data from other clinical studies. Routine submission of other patient data from uncontrolled studies is not required. The tabulations are required to include the data on each patient in each study, except that the applicant may delete those tabulations which the agency agrees, in advance, are not pertinent to a review of the drug's safety or effectiveness. Upon request, FDA will discuss with the applicant in a "pre-NDA" conference those tabulations that may be appropriate for such deletion. Barring unforeseen circumstances, tabulations agreed to be deleted at such a conference will not be requested during the conduct of FDA's review of the application. If such unforeseen circumstances do occur, any request for deleted tabulations will be made by the director of the FDA division responsible for reviewing the application, in accordance with paragraph (f)(3) of this section.

(2) Case report forms. The application is required to contain copies of individual case report forms for each patient who died during a clinical study or who did not complete the study because of an adverse event, whether believed to be drug related or not, including patients receiving reference drugs or placebo. This requirement may be waived by FDA for specific studies if the case report forms are unnecessary for a proper review of the study.

(3) Additional data. The applicant shall submit to FDA additional case report forms and tabulations needed to conduct a proper review of the application, as requested by the director of the FDA division responsible for reviewing the application. The applicant's failure to submit information requested by FDA within 30 days after receipt of the request may result in the agency viewing any eventual submission as a major amendment under § 314.60 and extending the review period as necessary. If desired by the applicant, the FDA division director will verify in writing any request for additional data that was made orally.

(4) Applicants are invited to meet with FDA before submitting an application to discuss the presentation and format of supporting information. If the applicant and FDA agree, the applicant may submit tabulations of patient data and case report forms in a form other than hard copy, for example, on microfiche or computer tapes.

(g) Other. The following general requirements apply to the submission of information within the summary under paragraph (c) of this section and within the technical sections under paragraph (d) of this section.

(1) The applicant ordinarily is not required to resubmit information previously submitted, but may incorporate the information by reference. A reference to information submitted previously is required to identify the file by name, reference number, volume, and page number in the agency's records where the information can be found. A reference to information submitted to the agency by a person other than the applicant is required to contain a written statement that authorizes the reference and that is signed by the person who submitted the information.

(2) The applicant shall submit an accurate and complete English translation of each part of the application that is not in English. The applicant shall submit a copy of each original literature publication for which an English translation is submitted.

(3) If an applicant who submits a new drug application under section 505(b) of the act obtains a "right of reference or use," as defined under § 314.3(b), to an investigation described in clause (A) of section 505(b)(1) of the act, the applicant shall include in its application a written statement signed by the owner of the data from each such investigation that the applicant may rely on in support of the approval of its application, and provide FDA access to, the underlying raw data that provide the basis for the report of the investigation submitted in its application.

(h) Patent information. The application is required to contain the patent information described under § 314.53.

(i) Patent certification—(1) Contents. A 505(b)(2) application is required to contain the following:

(i) Patents claiming drug, drug product, or method of use. (A) Except as provided in paragraph (i)(2) of this section, a certification with respect to each patent issued by the United States Patent and Trademark Office that, in the opinion of the applicant and to the best of its knowledge, claims a drug (the drug product or drug substance that is a component of the drug product) on which investigations that are relied upon by the applicant for approval of its application were conducted or that claims an approved use for such drug and for which information is required to be filed under section 505(b) and (c) of the act and § 314.53. For each such patent, the applicant shall provide the patent number and certify, in its opinion and to the best of its knowledge, one of the following circumstances:

(1) That the patent information has not been submitted to FDA. The applicant shall entitle such a certification "Paragraph I Certification";

(2) That the patent has expired. The applicant shall entitle such a certification "Paragraph II Certification";

(3) The date on which the patent will expire. The applicant shall entitle such a certification "Paragraph III Certification"; or

(4) That the patent is invalid, unenforceable, or will not be infringed by the manufacture, use, or sale of the drug product for which the application is submitted. The applicant shall entitle such a certification "Paragraph IV Certification". This certification shall be submitted in the following form:

I, (name of applicant), certify that Patent No. _____ (is invalid, unenforceable, or will not be infringed by the manufacture, use, or sale of) (name of proposed drug product) for which this application is submitted.

The certification shall be accompanied by a statement that the applicant will comply with the requirements under § 314.52(a) with respect to providing a notice to each owner of the patent or their representatives and to the holder of the approved application for the drug product which is claimed by the patent or a use of which is claimed by the patent and with the requirements under § 314.52(c) with respect to the content of the notice.

(B) If the drug on which investigations that are relied upon by the applicant were conducted is itself a licensed generic drug of a patented drug first approved under section 505(b) of the act, the appropriate patent certification under this section with respect to each patent that claims the first-approved patented drug or that claims an approved use for such a drug.

(ii) No relevant patents. If, in the opinion of the applicant and to the best of its knowledge, there are no patents described in paragraph (i)(1)(i) of this section, a certification in the following form:

In the opinion and to the best knowledge of (name of applicant), there are no patents that claim the drug or drugs on which investigations that are relied upon in this application were conducted or that claim a use of such drug or drugs.

(iii) Method of use patent. (A) If information that is submitted under section 505(b) or (c) of the act and § 314.53 is for a method of use patent, and the labeling for the drug product for which the applicant is seeking approval does not include any indications that are covered by the use patent, a statement explaining that the method of use patent does not claim any of the proposed indications.

(B) If the labeling of the drug product for which the applicant is seeking approval includes an indication that, according to the patent information submitted under section 505(b) or (c) of the act and § 314.53 or in the opinion of the applicant, is claimed by a use patent, the applicant shall submit an applicable certification under paragraph (i)(1)(i) of this section.

(2) Method of manufacturing patent. An applicant is not required to make a certification with respect to any patent that claims only a method of manufacturing the drug product for which the applicant is seeking approval.

(3) Licensing agreements. If a 505(b)(2) application is for a drug or method of using a drug claimed by a patent and the applicant has a licensing agreement with the patent owner, the applicant shall submit a certification under paragraph (i)(1)(i)(A)(4) of this section ("Paragraph IV Certification") as to that patent and a statement that it has been granted a patent license. If the patent owner consents to an immediate effective date upon approval of the 505(b)(2) application, the application shall contain a written statement from the patent owner that it has a licensing agreement with the applicant and that it consents to an immediate effective date.

(4) Late submission of patent information. If a patent described in paragraph (i)(1)(i)(A) of this section is issued and the holder of the approved application for the patented drug does not submit the required information on the patent within 30 days of issuance of the patent, an applicant who submitted a 505(b)(2) application that, before the submission of the patent information, contained an appropriate patent certification is not required to submit an amended certification. An applicant whose 505(b)(2) application is filed after a late submission of patent information or whose 505(b)(2) application was previously filed but did not contain an appropriate patent certification at the time of the patent submission shall submit a certification under paragraph (i)(1)(i) or (i)(1)(ii) of this section or a statement under paragraph (i)(1)(iii) of this section as to that patent.

(5) Disputed patent information. If an applicant disputes the accuracy or relevance of patent information submitted to FDA, the applicant

may seek a confirmation of the correctness of the patent information in accordance with the procedures under § 314.53(f). Unless the patent information is withdrawn or changed, the applicant must submit an appropriate certification for each relevant patent.

(6) Amended certifications. A certification submitted under paragraphs (i)(1)(i) through (i)(1)(iii) of this section may be amended at any time before the effective date of the approval of the application. An applicant shall submit an amended certification as an amendment to a pending application or by letter to an approved application. If an applicant with a pending application voluntarily makes a patent certification for an untimely filed patent, the applicant may withdraw the patent certification for the untimely filed patent. Once an amendment or letter for the change in certification has been submitted, the application will no longer be considered to be one containing the prior certification.

(i) After finding of infringement. An applicant who has submitted a certification under paragraph (i)(1)(i)(A)(4) of this section and is sued for patent infringement within 45 days of the receipt of notice sent under § 314.52 shall amend the certification if a final judgment in the action is entered finding the patent to be infringed unless the final judgment also finds the patent to be invalid. In the amended certification, the applicant shall certify under paragraph (i)(1)(i)(A)(3) of this section that the patent will expire on a specific date.

(ii) After removal of a patent from the list. If a patent is removed from the list, any applicant with a pending application (including a tentatively approved application with a delayed effective date) who has made a certification with respect to such patent shall amend its certification. The applicant shall certify under paragraph (i)(1)(ii) of this section that no patents described in paragraph (i)(1)(i) of this section claim the drug or, if other relevant patents claim the drug, shall amend the certification to refer only to those relevant patents. In the amendment, the applicant shall state the reason for the change in certification (that the patent is or has been removed from the list). A patent that is the subject of a lawsuit under § 314.107(c) shall not be removed from the list until FDA determines either that no delay in effective dates of approval is required under that section as a result of the lawsuit, that the patent has expired, or that any such period of delay in effective dates of approval is ended. An applicant shall submit an amended certification as an amendment to a pending application. Once an amendment for the change has been submitted, the application will no longer be considered to be one containing a certification under paragraph (i)(1)(i)(A)(4) of this section.

(iii) Other amendments. (A) Except as provided in paragraphs (i)(4) and (i)(6)(iii)(B) of this section, an applicant shall amend a submitted certification if, at any time before the effective date of the approval of the application, the applicant learns that the submitted certification is no longer accurate.

(B) An applicant is not required to amend a submitted certification when information on an otherwise applicable patent is submitted after the effective date of approval for the 505(b)(2) application.

(j) Claimed exclusivity. A new drug product, upon approval, may be entitled to a period of marketing exclusivity under the provisions of § 314.108. If an applicant believes its drug product is entitled to a period of exclusivity, it shall submit with the new drug application prior to approval the following information:

(1) A statement that the applicant is claiming exclusivity.

(2) A reference to the appropriate paragraph under § 314.108 that supports its claim.

(3) If the applicant claims exclusivity under § 314.108(b)(2), information to show that, to the best of its knowledge or belief, a drug has

not previously been approved under section 505(b) of the act containing any active moiety in the drug for which the applicant is seeking approval.

(4) If the applicant claims exclusivity under § 314.108(b)(4) or (b)(5), the following information to show that the application contains "new clinical investigations" that are "essential to approval of the application or supplement" and were "conducted or sponsored by the applicant:"

(i) "New clinical investigations." A certification that to the best of the applicant's knowledge each of the clinical investigations included in the application meets the definition of "new clinical investigation" set forth in § 314.108(a).

(ii) "Essential to approval." A list of all published studies or publicly available reports of clinical investigations known to the applicant through a literature search that are relevant to the conditions for which the applicant is seeking approval, a certification that the applicant has thoroughly searched the scientific literature and, to the best of the applicant's knowledge, the list is complete and accurate and, in the applicant's opinion, such published studies or publicly available reports do not provide a sufficient basis for the approval of the conditions for which the applicant is seeking approval without reference to the new clinical investigation(s) in the application, and an explanation as to why the studies or reports are insufficient.

(iii) "Conducted or sponsored by." If the applicant was the sponsor named in the Form FDA-1571 for an investigational new drug application (IND) under which the new clinical investigation(s) that is essential to the approval of its application was conducted, identification of the IND by number. If the applicant was not the sponsor of the IND under which the clinical investigation(s) was conducted, a certification that the applicant or its predecessor in interest provided substantial support for the clinical investigation(s) that is essential to the approval of its application, and information supporting the certification. To demonstrate "substantial support," an applicant must either provide a certified statement from a certified public accountant that the applicant provided 50 percent or more of the cost of conducting the study or provide an explanation of why FDA should consider the applicant to have conducted or sponsored the study if the applicant's financial contribution to the study is less than 50 percent or the applicant did not sponsor the investigational new drug. A predecessor in interest is an entity, e.g., a corporation, that the applicant has taken over, merged with, or purchased, or from which the applicant has purchased all rights to the drug. Purchase of nonexclusive rights to a clinical investigation after it is completed is not sufficient to satisfy this definition.

(k) Financial certification or disclosure statement. The application shall contain a financial certification or disclosure statement or both as required by part 54 of this chapter.

(l) Format of an original application—(1) Archival copy. The applicant must submit a complete archival copy of the application that contains the information required under paragraphs (a) through (f) of this section. FDA will maintain the archival copy during the review of the application to permit individual reviewers to refer to information that is not contained in their particular technical sections of the application, to give other agency personnel access to the application for official business, and to maintain in one place a complete copy of the application. Except as required by paragraph (l)(1)(i) of this section, applicants may submit the archival copy on paper or in electronic format provided that electronic submissions are made in accordance with part 11 of this chapter.

(i) Labeling. The content of labeling required under § 201.100(d)(3) of this chapter (commonly referred to as the package insert or professional labeling), including all text, tables, and figures, must be submitted to the agency in electronic format as described in paragraph (l)(5) of this section. This requirement is in addition to the requirements of paragraph (e)(2)(ii) of this section that copies of the formatted label and all labeling be submitted. Submissions under this paragraph must be made in accordance with part 11 of this chapter, except for the requirements of § 11.10(a), (c) through (h), and (k), and the corresponding requirements of § 11.30.

(ii) [Reserved]

(2) Review copy. The applicant must submit a review copy of the application. Each of the technical sections, described in paragraphs (d)(1) through (d)(6) of this section, in the review copy is required to be separately bound with a copy of the application form required under paragraph (a) of this section and a copy of the summary required under paragraph (c) of this section.

(3) Field copy. The applicant must submit a field copy of the application that contains the technical section described in paragraph (d)(1) of this section, a copy of the application form required under paragraph (a) of this section, a copy of the summary required under paragraph (c) of this section, and a certification that the field copy is a true copy of the technical section described in paragraph (d)(1) of this section contained in the archival and review copies of the application.

(4) Binding folders. The applicant may obtain from FDA sufficient folders to bind the archival, the review, and the field copies of the application.

(5) Electronic format submissions. Electronic format submissions must be in a form that FDA can process, review, and archive. FDA will periodically issue guidance on how to provide the electronic submission (e.g., method of transmission, media, file formats, preparation and organization of files).

[50 FR 7493, Feb. 22, 1985]

Editorial Note:

For Federal Register citations affecting § 314.50,

see the List of CFR Sections Affected, which appears in the Finding Aids section of the printed volume and on GPO Access.

§ 314.52   Notice of certification of invalidity or noninfringement of a patent.

(a) Notice of certification. For each patent which claims the drug or drugs on which investigations that are relied upon by the applicant for approval of its application were conducted or which claims a use for such drug or drugs and which the applicant certifies under § 314.50(i)(1)(i)(A)(4) that a patent is invalid, unenforceable, or will not be infringed, the applicant shall send notice of such certification by registered or certified mail, return receipt requested to each of the following persons:

(1) Each owner of the patent that is the subject of the certification or the representative designated by the owner to receive the notice. The name and address of the patent owner or its representative may be obtained from the United States Patent and Trademark Office; and

(2) The holder of the approved application under section 505(b) of the act for each drug product which is claimed by the patent or a use of which is claimed by the patent and for which the applicant is seeking approval, or, if the application holder does not reside or maintain a place of business within the United States, the application holder's attorney, agent, or other authorized official. The name and address of the application holder or its attorney, agent, or authorized official may be obtained from the Orange Book Staff, Office of Generic Drugs, 7500 Standish Pl., Rockville, MD 20855.

(3) This paragraph does not apply to a use patent that claims no uses for which the applicant is seeking approval.

(b) Sending the notice. The applicant shall send the notice required by paragraph (a) of this section when it receives from FDA an acknowledgment letter stating that its application has been filed. At the same time, the applicant shall

amend its application to include a statement certifying that the notice has been provided to each person identified under paragraph (a) of this section and that the notice met the content requirement under paragraph (c) of this section.

(c) Content of a notice. In the notice, the applicant shall cite section 505(b)(3)(B) of the act and shall include, but not be limited to, the following information:

(1) A statement that a 505(b)(2) application submitted by the applicant has been filed by FDA.

(2) The application number.

(3) The established name, if any, as defined in section 502(e)(3) of the act, of the proposed drug product.

(4) The active ingredient, strength, and dosage form of the proposed drug product.

(5) The patent number and expiration date, as submitted to the agency or as known to the applicant, of each patent alleged to be invalid, unenforceable, or not infringed.

(6) A detailed statement of the factual and legal basis of the applicant's opinion that the patent is not valid, unenforceable, or will not be infringed. The applicant shall include in the detailed statement:

(I) For each claim of a patent alleged not to be infringed, a full and detailed explanation of why the claim is not infringed.

(ii) For each claim of a patent alleged to be invalid or unenforceable, a full and detailed explanation of the grounds supporting the allegation.

(7) If the applicant does not reside or have a place of business in the United States, the name and address of an agent in the United States authorized to accept service of process for the applicant.

(d) Amendment to an application. If an application is amended to include the certification described in § 314.50(i), the applicant shall send the notice required by paragraph (a) of this section at the same time that the amendment to the application is submitted to FDA.

(e) Documentation of receipt of notice. The applicant shall amend its application to document receipt of the notice required under paragraph (a) of this section by each person provided the notice. The applicant shall include a copy of the return receipt or other similar evidence of the date the notification was received. FDA will accept as adequate documentation of the date of receipt a return receipt or a letter acknowledging receipt by the person provided the notice. An applicant may rely on another form of documentation only if FDA has agreed to such documentation in advance. A copy of the notice itself need not be submitted to the agency.

(f) Approval. If the requirements of this section are met, the agency will presume the notice to be complete and sufficient, and it will count the day following the date of receipt of the notice by the patent owner or its representative and by the approved application holder as the first day of the 45-day period provided for in section 505(c)(3)(C) of the act. FDA may, if the applicant amends its application with a written statement that a later date should be used, count from such later date.

[59 FR 50362, Oct. 3, 1994, as amended at 68 FR 36703, June 18, 2003; 69 FR 11310, Mar. 10, 2004; 74 FR 9766, Mar. 6, 2009; 74 FR 36605, July 24, 2009]

§ 314.53   Submission of patent information.

(a) Who must submit patent information. This section applies to any applicant who submits to FDA a new drug application or an amendment to it under section 505(b) of the act and § 314.50 or a supplement to an approved application under § 314.70, except as provided in paragraph (d)(2) of this section.

(b) Patents for which information must be submitted and patents for which information must not be submitted—(1) General requirements. An applicant described in paragraph (a) of this section shall submit the required information on the declaration form set forth in paragraph (c) of this section for each patent that claims the drug or a method of using the drug that is the subject of the new drug application or amendment or supplement to it and with respect to which a claim of patent infringement could reasonably be asserted if a person not licensed by the owner of the patent engaged in the manufacture, use, or sale of the drug product. For purposes of this part, such patents consist of drug substance (active ingredient) patents, drug product (formulation and composition) patents, and method-of-use patents. For patents that claim the drug substance, the applicant shall submit information only on those patents that claim the drug substance that is the subject of the pending or approved application or that claim a drug substance that is the same as the active ingredient that is the subject of the approved or pending application. For patents that claim a polymorph that is the same as the active ingredient described in the approved or pending application, the applicant shall certify in the declaration forms that the applicant has test data, as set forth in paragraph (b)(2) of this section, demonstrating that a drug product containing the polymorph will perform the same as the drug product described in the new drug application. For patents that claim a drug product, the applicant shall submit information only on those patents that claim a drug product, as is defined in § 314.3, that is described in the pending or approved application. For patents that claim a method of use, the applicant shall submit information only on those patents that claim indications or other conditions of use that are described in the pending or approved application. The applicant shall separately identify each pending or approved method of use and related patent claim. For approved applications, the applicant submitting the method-of-use patent shall identify with specificity the section of the approved labeling that corresponds to the method of use claimed by the patent submitted. Process patents, patents claiming packaging, patents claiming metabolites, and patents claiming intermediates are not covered by this section, and information on these patents must not be submitted to FDA.

(2) Test Data for Submission of Patent Information for Patents That Claim a Polymorph. The test data, referenced in paragraph (b)(1) of this section, must include the following:

(i) A full description of the polymorphic form of the drug substance, including its physical and chemical characteristics and stability; the method of synthesis (or isolation) and purification of the drug substance; the process controls used during manufacture and packaging; and such specifications and analytical methods as are necessary to assure the identity, strength, quality, and purity of the polymorphic form of the drug substance;

(ii) The executed batch record for a drug product containing the polymorphic form of the drug substance and documentation that the batch was manufactured under current good manufacturing practice requirements;

(iii) Demonstration of bioequivalence between the executed batch of the drug product that contains the polymorphic form of the drug substance and the drug product as described in the NDA;

(iv) A list of all components used in the manufacture of the drug product containing the polymorphic form and a statement of the composition of the drug product; a statement of the specifications and analytical methods for each component; a description of the manufacturing and packaging procedures and in-process controls for the drug product; such specifications and analytical methods as are necessary to assure the identity, strength, quality, purity, and bioavailability of the drug product, including release and stability data complying with the approved product specifications to demonstrate

pharmaceutical equivalence and comparable product stability; and

(v) Comparative *in vitro* dissolution testing on 12 dosage units each of the executed test batch and the new drug application product.

(c) Reporting requirements—(1) General requirements. An applicant described in paragraph (a) of this section shall submit the required patent information described in paragraph (c)(2) of this section for each patent that meets the requirements described in paragraph (b) of this section. We will not accept the patent information unless it is complete and submitted on the appropriate forms, FDA Forms 3542 or 3542a. These forms may be obtained on the Internet at http://www.fda.gov by searching for "forms".

(2) Drug substance (active ingredient), drug product (formulation or composition), and method-of-use patents—(i) Original Declaration. For each patent that claims a drug substance (active ingredient), drug product (formulation and composition), or method of use, the applicant shall submit FDA Form 3542a. The following information and verification is required:

(A) New drug application number;

(B) Name of new drug application sponsor;

(C) Trade name (or proposed trade name) of new drug;

(D) Active ingredient(s) of new drug;

(E) Strength(s) of new drug;

(F) Dosage form of new drug;

(G) United States patent number, issue date, and expiration date of patent submitted;

(H) The patent owner's name, full address, phone number and, if available, fax number and e-mail address;

(I) The name, full address, phone number and, if available, fax number and e-mail address of an agent or representative who resides or maintains a place of business within the United States authorized to receive notice of patent certification under sections 505(b)(3) and 505(j) (2)(B) of the act and §§ 314.52 and 314.95 (if patent owner or new drug application applicant or holder does not reside or have a place of business within the United States);

(J) Information on whether the patent has been submitted previously for the new drug application;

(K) Information on whether the expiration date is a new expiration date if the patent had been submitted previously for listing;

(L) Information on whether the patent is a product-by-process patent in which the product claimed is novel;

(M) Information on the drug substance (active ingredient) patent including the following:

(1) Whether the patent claims the drug substance that is the active ingredient in the drug product described in the new drug application or supplement;

(2) Whether the patent claims a polymorph that is the same active ingredient that is described in the pending application or supplement;

(3) Whether the applicant has test data, described in paragraph (b)(2) of this section, demonstrating that a drug product containing the polymorph will perform the same as the drug product described in the new drug application or supplement, and a description of the polymorphic form(s) claimed by the patent for which such test data exist;

(4) Whether the patent claims only a metabolite of the active ingredient; and

(5) Whether the patent claims only an intermediate;

(N) Information on the drug product (composition/formulation) patent including the following:

(1) Whether the patent claims the drug product for which approval is being sought, as defined in § 314.3; and

(2) Whether the patent claims only an intermediate;

(O) Information on each method-of-use patent including the following:

(1) Whether the patent claims one or more methods of using the drug product for which use approval is being sought and a description of each pending method of use or related indication and related patent claim of the patent being submitted; and

(2) Identification of the specific section of the proposed labeling for the drug product that corresponds to the method of use claimed by the patent submitted;

(P) Whether there are no relevant patents that claim the drug substance (active ingredient), drug product (formulation or composition) or method(s) of use, for which the applicant is seeking approval and with respect to which a claim of patent infringement could reasonably be asserted if a person not licensed by the owner of the patent engaged in the manufacture, use, or sale of the drug product;

(Q) A signed verification which states:

"The undersigned declares that this is an accurate and complete submission of patent information for the NDA, amendment or supplement pending under section 505 of the Federal Food, Drug, and Cosmetic Act. This time-sensitive patent information is submitted pursuant to 21 CFR 314.53. I attest that I am familiar with 21 CFR 314.53 and this submission complies with the requirements of the regulation. I verify under penalty of perjury that the foregoing is true and correct."; and

(R) Information on whether the applicant, patent owner or attorney, agent, representative or other authorized official signed the form; the name of the person; and the full address, phone number and, if available, the fax number and e-mail address.

(ii) Submission of patent information upon and after approval. Within 30 days after the date of approval of its application or supplement, the applicant shall submit FDA Form 3542 for each patent that claims the drug substance (active ingredient), drug product (formulation and composition), or approved method of use. FDA will rely only on the information submitted on this form and will not list or publish patent information if the patent declaration is incomplete or indicates the patent is not eligible for listing. Patent information must also be submitted for patents issued after the date of approval of the new drug application as required in paragraph (c)(2)(ii) of this section. As described in paragraph (d)(4) of this section, patent information must be submitted to FDA within 30 days of the date of issuance of the patent. If the applicant submits the required patent information within the 30 days but we notify an applicant that a declaration form is incomplete or shows that the patent is not eligible for listing, the applicant must submit an acceptable declaration form within 15 days of FDA notification to be considered timely filed. The following information and verification statement is required:

(A) New drug application number;

(B) Name of new drug application sponsor;

(C) Trade name of new drug;

(D) Active ingredient(s) of new drug;

(E) Strength(s) of new drug;

(F) Dosage form of new drug;

(G) Approval date of new drug application or supplement;

(H) United States patent number, issue date, and expiration date of patent submitted;

(I) The patent owner's name, full address, phone number and, if available, fax number and e-mail address;

(J) The name, full address, phone number and, if available, fax number and e-mail address of an agent or representative who resides or maintains a place of business within the United States authorized to receive notice of patent certification under sections 505(b)(3) and 505(j)(2)(B) of the act and §§ 314.52 and 314.95 (if patent owner or new drug application applicant or holder does not reside or have a place of business within the United States);

(K) Information on whether the patent has been submitted previously for the new drug application;

(L) Information on whether the expiration date is a new expiration date if the patent had been submitted previously for listing;

(M) Information on whether the patent is a product-by-process patent in which the product claimed is novel;

(N) Information on the drug substance (active ingredient) patent including the following:

(1) Whether the patent claims the drug substance that is the active ingredient in the drug product described in the approved application;

(2) Whether the patent claims a polymorph that is the same as the active ingredient that is described in the approved application;

(3) Whether the applicant has test data, described at paragraph (b)(2) of this section, demonstrating that a drug product containing the polymorph will perform the same as the drug product described in the approved application and a description of the polymorphic form(s) claimed by the patent for which such test data exist;

(4) Whether the patent claims only a metabolite of the active ingredient; and

(5) Whether the patent claims only an intermediate;

(O) Information on the drug product (composition/formulation) patent including the following:

(1) Whether the patent claims the approved drug product as defined in § 314.3; and

(2) Whether the patent claims only an intermediate;

(P) Information on each method-of-use patent including the following:

(1) Whether the patent claims one or more approved methods of using the approved drug product and a description of each approved method of use or indication and related patent claim of the patent being submitted;

(2) Identification of the specific section of the approved labeling for the drug product that corresponds to the method of use claimed by the patent submitted; and

(3) The description of the patented method of use as required for publication;

(Q) Whether there are no relevant patents that claim the approved drug substance (active ingredient), the approved drug product (formulation or composition) or approved method(s) of use and with respect to which a claim of patent infringement could reasonably be asserted if a person not licensed by the owner of the patent engaged in the manufacture, use, or sale of the drug product;

(R) A signed verification which states: "The undersigned declares that this is an accurate and complete submission of patent information for the NDA, amendment or supplement approved under section 505 of the Federal Food, Drug, and Cosmetic Act. This time-sensitive patent information is submitted pursuant to 21 CFR 314.53. I attest that I am familiar with 21 CFR 314.53 and this submission complies with the requirements of the regulation. I verify under penalty of perjury that the foregoing is true and correct."; and

(S) Information on whether the applicant, patent owner or attorney, agent, representative or other authorized official signed the form; the name of the person; and the full address, phone number and, if available, the fax number and e-mail address.

(3) No relevant patents. If the applicant believes that there are no relevant patents that claim the drug substance (active ingredient), drug product (formulation or composition), or the method(s) of use for which the applicant has received approval, and with respect to which a claim of patent infringement could reasonably be asserted if a person not licensed by the owner of the patent engaged in the manufacture, use, or sale of the drug product, the applicant will verify this information in the appropriate forms, FDA Forms 3542 or 3542a.

(4) Authorized signature. The declarations required by this section shall be signed by the applicant or patent owner, or the applicant's or patent owner's attorney, agent (representative), or other authorized official.

(d) When and where to submit patent information—(1) Original application. An applicant shall submit with its original application submitted under this part, including an application described in section 505(b)(2) of the act, the information described in paragraph (c) of this section on each drug (ingredient), drug product (formulation and composition), and method of use patent issued before the application is filed with FDA and for which patent information is required to be submitted under this section. If a patent is issued after the application is filed with FDA but before the application is approved, the applicant shall, within 30 days of the date of issuance of the patent, submit the required patent information in an amendment to the application under § 314.60.

(2) Supplements. (i) An applicant shall submit patent information required under paragraph (c) of this section for a patent that claims the drug, drug product, or method of use for which approval is sought in any of the following supplements:

(A) To change the formulation;

(B) To add a new indication or other condition of use, including a change in route of administration;

(C) To change the strength;

(D) To make any other patented change regarding the drug, drug product, or any method of use.

(ii) If the applicant submits a supplement for one of the changes listed under paragraph (d) (2)(i) of this section and existing patents for which information has already been submitted to FDA claim the changed product, the applicant shall submit a certification with the supplement identifying the patents that claim the changed product.

(iii) If the applicant submits a supplement for one of the changes listed under paragraph (d) (2)(i) of this section and no patents, including previously submitted patents, claim the changed product, it shall so certify.

(iv) The applicant shall comply with the requirements for amendment of formulation or composition and method of use patent information under paragraphs (c)(2)(ii) and (d)(3) of this section.

(3) Patent information deadline. If a patent is issued for a drug, drug product, or method of use after an application is approved, the applicant shall submit to FDA the required patent information within 30 days of the date of issuance of the patent.

(4) Copies. The applicant shall submit two copies of each submission of patent information, an archival copy and a copy for the chemistry, manufacturing, and controls section of the review copy, to the Central Document Room, Center for Drug Evaluation and Research, Food and Drug Administration, 5901-B Ammendale Rd., Beltsville, MD 20705-1266. The applicant shall submit the patent information by letter separate from, but at the same time as, submission of the supplement.

(5) Submission date. Patent information shall be considered to be submitted to FDA as of the date the information is received by the Central Document Room.

(6) Identification. Each submission of patent information, except information submitted with an original application, and its mailing cover shall bear prominent identification as to its contents, i.e., "Patent Information," or, if submitted after approval of an application, "Time Sensitive Patent Information."

(e) Public disclosure of patent information. FDA will publish in the list the patent number and expiration date of each patent that is required to be, and is, submitted to FDA by an applicant, and for each use patent, the approved indications or other conditions of use covered by a patent. FDA will publish such patent information upon approval of the application, or, if the patent information is submitted by the applicant after approval of an application as provided under paragraph (d)(2) of this section, as soon as possible after the submission to the agency of the patent information. Patent information submitted by the last working day of a month will be published in that month's supplement to the list. Patent information received by the agency between monthly publication of supplements to the list will be placed on public display in FDA's Freedom of Information Staff. A request for copies of the file shall be sent in writing to the Freedom of Information Staff (HFI-35), Food and Drug Administration, rm. 12A-16, 5600 Fishers Lane, Rockville, MD 20857.

(f) Correction of patent information errors. If any person disputes the accuracy or relevance of patent information submitted to the agency under this section and published by FDA in the list, or believes that an applicant has failed to submit required patent information, that person must first notify the agency in writing stating the grounds for disagreement. Such notification should be directed to the Office of Generic Drugs, OGD Document Room, Attention:

Orange Book Staff, 7500 Standish Pl., Rockville, MD 20855. The agency will then request of the applicable new drug application holder that the correctness of the patent information or omission of patent information be confirmed. Unless the application holder withdraws or amends its patent information in response to FDA's request, the agency will not change the patent information in the list. If the new drug application holder does not change the patent information submitted to FDA, a 505(b)(2) application or an abbreviated new drug application under section 505(j) of the act submitted for a drug that is claimed by a patent for which information has been submitted must, despite any disagreement as to the correctness of the patent information, contain an appropriate certification for each listed patent.

[59 FR 50363, Oct. 3, 1994, as amended at 68 FR 36703, June 18, 2003; 69 FR 13473, Mar. 23, 2004; 74 FR 9766, Mar. 6, 2009; 74 FR 36605, July 24, 2009]

§ 314.54   Procedure for submission of an application requiring investigations for approval of a new indication for, or other change from, a listed drug.

(a) The act does not permit approval of an abbreviated new drug application for a new indication, nor does it permit approval of other changes in a listed drug if investigations, other than bioavailability or bioequivalence studies, are essential to the approval of the change. Any person seeking approval of a drug product that represents a modification of a listed drug (e.g., a new indication or new dosage form) and for which investigations, other than bioavailability or bioequivalence studies, are essential to the approval of the changes may, except as provided in paragraph (b) of this section, submit a 505(b)(2) application. This application need contain only that information needed to support the modification(s) of the listed drug.

(1) The applicant shall submit a complete archival copy of the application that contains the

following:

(i) The information required under § 314.50(a), (b), (c), (d)(1), (d)(3), (e), and (g), except that § 314.50(d)(1)(ii)(c) shall contain the proposed or actual master production record, including a description of the equipment, to be used for the manufacture of a commercial lot of the drug product.

(ii) The information required under § 314.50 (d)(2), (d)(4) (if an anti-infective drug), (d)(5), (d)(6), and (f) as needed to support the safety and effectiveness of the drug product.

(iii) Identification of the listed drug for which FDA has made a finding of safety and effectiveness and on which finding the applicant relies in seeking approval of its proposed drug product by established name, if any, proprietary name, dosage form, strength, route of administration, name of listed drug's application holder, and listed drug's approved application number.

(iv) If the applicant is seeking approval only for a new indication and not for the indications approved for the listed drug on which the applicant relies, a certification so stating.

(v) Any patent information required under section 505(b)(1) of the act with respect to any patent which claims the drug for which approval is sought or a method of using such drug and to which a claim of patent infringement could reasonably be asserted if a person not licensed by the owner of the patent engaged in the manufacture, use, or sale of the drug product.

(vi) Any patent certification or statement required under section 505(b)(2) of the act with respect to any relevant patents that claim the listed drug or that claim any other drugs on which investigations relied on by the applicant for approval of the application were conducted, or that claim a use for the listed or other drug.

(vii) If the applicant believes the change for which it is seeking approval is entitled to a period of exclusivity, the information required under § 314.50(j).

(2) The applicant shall submit a review copy that contains the technical sections described in § 314.50(d)(1), except that § 314.50(d)(1)(ii)(c) shall contain the proposed or actual master production record, including a description of the equipment, to be used for the manufacture of a commercial lot of the drug product, and paragraph (d)(3), and the technical sections described in paragraphs (d)(2), (d)(4), (d)(5), (d)(6), and (f) when needed to support the modification. Each of the technical sections in the review copy is required to be separately bound with a copy of the information required under § 314.50 (a), (b), and (c) and a copy of the proposed labeling.

(3) The information required by § 314.50 (d)(2), (d)(4) (if an anti-infective drug), (d)(5), (d)(6), and (f) for the listed drug on which the applicant relies shall be satisfied by reference to the listed drug under paragraph (a)(1)(iii) of this section.

(4) The applicant shall submit a field copy of the application that contains the technical section described in § 314.50(d)(1), a copy of the information required under § 314.50(a) and (c), and certification that the field copy is a true copy of the technical section described in § 314.50(d)(1) contained in the archival and review copies of the application.

(b) An application may not be submitted under this section for a drug product whose only difference from the reference listed drug is that:

(1) The extent to which its active ingredient(s) is absorbed or otherwise made available to the site of action is less than that of the reference listed drug; or

(2) The rate at which its active ingredient(s) is absorbed or otherwise made available to the site of action is unintentionally less than that of the reference listed drug.

[57 FR 17982, Apr. 28, 1992; 57 FR 61612, Dec. 28, 1992, as amended at 58 FR 47351, Sept. 8, 1993; 59 FR 50364, Oct. 3, 1994]

§ 314.55   Pediatric use information.

(a) Required assessment. Except as provided in paragraphs (b), (c), and (d) of this section, each application for a new active ingredient, new indication, new dosage form, new dosing regimen, or new route of administration shall contain data that are adequate to assess the safety and effectiveness of the drug product for the claimed indications in all relevant pediatric subpopulations, and to support dosing and administration for each pediatric subpopulation for which the drug is safe and effective. Where the course of the disease and the effects of the drug are sufficiently similar in adults and pediatric patients, FDA may conclude that pediatric effectiveness can be extrapolated from adequate and well-controlled studies in adults usually supplemented with other information obtained in pediatric patients, such as pharmacokinetic studies. Studies may not be needed in each pediatric age group, if data from one age group can be extrapolated to another. Assessments of safety and effectiveness required under this section for a drug product that represents a meaningful therapeutic benefit over existing treatments for pediatric patients must be carried out using appropriate formulations for each age group(s) for which the assessment is required.

(b) Deferred submission. (1) FDA may, on its own initiative or at the request of an applicant, defer submission of some or all assessments of safety and effectiveness described in paragraph (a) of this section until after approval of the drug product for use in adults. Deferral may be granted if, among other reasons, the drug is ready for approval in adults before studies in pediatric patients are complete, or pediatric studies should be delayed until additional safety or effectiveness data have been collected. If an applicant requests deferred submission, the request must provide a certification from the applicant of the grounds for delaying pediatric studies, a description of the planned or ongoing studies, and evidence that the studies are being or will be conducted with due diligence and at the earliest possible time.

(2) If FDA determines that there is an adequate justification for temporarily delaying the submission of assessments of pediatric safety and effectiveness, the drug product may be approved for use in adults subject to the requirement that the applicant submit the required assessments within a specified time.

(c) Waivers—(1) General. FDA may grant a full or partial waiver of the requirements of paragraph (a) of this section on its own initiative or at the request of an applicant. A request for a waiver must provide an adequate justification.

(2) Full waiver. An applicant may request a waiver of the requirements of paragraph (a) of this section if the applicant certifies that:

(i) The drug product does not represent a meaningful therapeutic benefit over existing treatments for pediatric patients and is not likely to be used in a substantial number of pediatric patients;

(ii) Necessary studies are impossible or highly impractical because, e.g., the number of such patients is so small or geographically dispersed; or

(iii) There is evidence strongly suggesting that the drug product would be ineffective or unsafe in all pediatric age groups.

(3) Partial waiver. An applicant may request a waiver of the requirements of paragraph (a) of this section with respect to a specified pediatric age group, if the applicant certifies that:

(i) The drug product does not represent a meaningful therapeutic benefit over existing treatments for pediatric patients in that age group, and is not likely to be used in a substantial number of patients in that age group;

(ii) Necessary studies are impossible or highly

impractical because, e.g., the number of patients in that age group is so small or geographically dispersed;

(iii) There is evidence strongly suggesting that the drug product would be ineffective or unsafe in that age group; or

(iv) The applicant can demonstrate that reasonable attempts to produce a pediatric formulation necessary for that age group have failed.

(4) FDA action on waiver. FDA shall grant a full or partial waiver, as appropriate, if the agency finds that there is a reasonable basis on which to conclude that one or more of the grounds for waiver specified in paragraphs (c)(2) or (c)(3) of this section have been met. If a waiver is granted on the ground that it is not possible to develop a pediatric formulation, the waiver will cover only those pediatric age groups requiring that formulation. If a waiver is granted because there is evidence that the product would be ineffective or unsafe in pediatric populations, this information will be included in the product's labeling.

(5) Definition of "meaningful therapeutic benefit". For purposes of this section and § 201.23 of this chapter, a drug will be considered to offer a meaningful therapeutic benefit over existing therapies if FDA estimates that:

(i) If approved, the drug would represent a significant improvement in the treatment, diagnosis, or prevention of a disease, compared to marketed products adequately labeled for that use in the relevant pediatric population. Examples of how improvement might be demonstrated include, for example, evidence of increased effectiveness in treatment, prevention, or diagnosis of disease, elimination or substantial reduction of a treatment-limiting drug reaction, documented enhancement of compliance, or evidence of safety and effectiveness in a new subpopulation; or

(ii) The drug is in a class of drugs or for an indication for which there is a need for additional therapeutic options.

(d) Exemption for orphan drugs. This section does not apply to any drug for an indication or indications for which orphan designation has been granted under part 316, subpart C, of this chapter.

[63 FR 66670, Dec. 2, 1998]

§ 314.60   Amendments to an unapproved application, supplement, or resubmission.

(a) FDA generally assumes that when an original application, supplement to an approved application, or resubmission of an application or supplement is submitted to the agency for review, the applicant believes that the agency can approve the application, supplement, or resubmission as submitted. However, the applicant may submit an amendment to an application that has been filed under § 314.101 but is not yet approved.

(b)(1) Submission of a major amendment to an original application, efficacy supplement, or resubmission of an application or efficacy supplement within 3 months of the end of the initial review cycle constitutes an agreement by the applicant under section 505(c) of the act to extend the initial review cycle by 3 months. (For references to a resubmission of an application or efficacy supplement in paragraph (b) of this section, the timeframe for reviewing the resubmission is the "review cycle" rather than the "initial review cycle.") FDA may instead defer review of the amendment until the subsequent review cycle. If the agency extends the initial review cycle for an original application, efficacy supplement, or resubmission under this paragraph, the division responsible for reviewing the application, supplement, or resubmission will notify the applicant of the extension. The initial review cycle for an original application, efficacy supplement, or resubmission of an application or efficacy supplement may be extended only once due to submission of a major amendment. FDA may, at its discretion, review

any subsequent major amendment during the initial review cycle (as extended) or defer review until the subsequent review cycle.

(2) Submission of a major amendment to an original application, efficacy supplement, or resubmission of an application or efficacy supplement more than 3 months before the end of the initial review cycle will not extend the cycle. FDA may, at its discretion, review such an amendment during the initial review cycle or defer review until the subsequent review cycle.

(3) Submission of an amendment to an original application, efficacy supplement, or resubmission of an application or efficacy supplement that is not a major amendment will not extend the initial review cycle. FDA may, at its discretion, review such an amendment during the initial review cycle or defer review until the subsequent review cycle.

(4) Submission of a major amendment to a manufacturing supplement within 2 months of the end of the initial review cycle constitutes an agreement by the applicant under section 505(c) of the act to extend the initial review cycle by 2 months. FDA may instead defer review of the amendment until the subsequent review cycle. If the agency extends the initial review cycle for a manufacturing supplement under this paragraph, the division responsible for reviewing the supplement will notify the applicant of the extension. The initial review cycle for a manufacturing supplement may be extended only once due to submission of a major amendment. FDA may, at its discretion, review any subsequent major amendment during the initial review cycle (as extended) or defer review until the subsequent review cycle.

(5) Submission of an amendment to a supplement other than an efficacy or manufacturing supplement will not extend the initial review cycle. FDA may, at its discretion, review such an amendment during the initial review cycle or defer review until the subsequent review cycle.

(6) A major amendment may not include data to support an indication or claim that was not included in the original application, supplement, or resubmission, but it may include data to support a minor modification of an indication or claim that was included in the original application, supplement, or resubmission.

(7) When FDA defers review of an amendment until the subsequent review cycle, the agency will notify the applicant of the deferral in the complete response letter sent to the applicant under § 314.110 of this part.

(c)(1) An unapproved application may not be amended if all of the following conditions apply:

(i) The unapproved application is for a drug for which a previous application has been approved and granted a period of exclusivity in accordance with section 505(c)(3)(D)(ii) of the act that has not expired;

(ii) The applicant seeks to amend the unapproved application to include a published report of an investigation that was conducted or sponsored by the applicant entitled to exclusivity for the drug;

(iii) The applicant has not obtained a right of reference to the investigation described in paragraph (c)(1)(ii) of this section; and

(iv) The report of the investigation described in paragraph (c)(1)(ii) of this section would be essential to the approval of the unapproved application.

(2) The submission of an amendment described in paragraph (c)(1) of this section will cause the unapproved application to be deemed to be withdrawn by the applicant under § 314.65 on the date of receipt by FDA of the amendment. The amendment will be considered a resubmission of the application, which may not be accepted except as provided in accordance with section 505(c)(3)(D)(ii) of the act.

(d) The applicant shall submit a field copy of each amendment to § 314.50(d)(1). The appli-

cant shall include in its submission of each such amendment to FDA a statement certifying that a field copy of the amendment has been sent to the applicant's home FDA district office.

[50 FR 7493, Feb. 22, 1985, as amended at 57 FR 17983, Apr. 28, 1992; 58 FR 47352, Sept. 8, 1993; 63 FR 5252, Feb. 2, 1998; 69 FR 18764, Apr. 8, 2004; 73 FR 39608, July 10, 2008]

§ 314.65   Withdrawal by the applicant of an unapproved application.

An applicant may at any time withdraw an application that is not yet approved by notifying the Food and Drug Administration in writing. If, by the time it receives such notice, the agency has identified any deficiencies in the application, we will list such deficiencies in the letter we send the applicant acknowledging the withdrawal. A decision to withdraw the application is without prejudice to refiling. The agency will retain the application and will provide a copy to the applicant on request under the fee schedule in § 20.45 of FDA's public information regulations.

[50 FR 7493, Feb. 22, 1985, as amended at 68 FR 25287, May 12, 2003; 73 FR 39609, July 10, 2008]

§ 314.70   Supplements and other changes to an approved application.

(a) Changes to an approved application.

(1)(i) Except as provided in paragraph (a)(1) (ii) of this section, the applicant must notify FDA about each change in each condition established in an approved application beyond the variations already provided for in the application. The notice is required to describe the change fully. Depending on the type of change, the applicant must notify FDA about the change in a supplement under paragraph (b) or (c) of this section or by inclusion of the information in the annual report to the application under paragraph (d) of this section.

(ii) The submission and grant of a written request for an exception or alternative under §

201.26 of this chapter satisfies the applicable requirements in paragraphs (a) through (c) of this section. However, any grant of a request for an exception or alternative under § 201.26 of this chapter must be reported as part of the annual report to the application under paragraph (d) of this section.

(2) The holder of an approved application under section 505 of the act must assess the effects of the change before distributing a drug product made with a manufacturing change.

(3) Notwithstanding the requirements of paragraphs (b) and (c) of this section, an applicant must make a change provided for in those paragraphs in accordance with a regulation or guidance that provides for a less burdensome notification of the change (for example, by submission of a supplement that does not require approval prior to distribution of the product or in an annual report).

(4) The applicant must promptly revise all promotional labeling and advertising to make it consistent with any labeling change implemented in accordance with paragraphs (b) and (c) of this section.

(5) Except for a supplement providing for a change in the labeling, the applicant must include in each supplement and amendment to a supplement providing for a change under paragraph (b) or (c) of this section a statement certifying that a field copy has been provided in accordance with § 314.440(a)(4).

(6) A supplement or annual report must include a list of all changes contained in the supplement or annual report. For supplements, this list must be provided in the cover letter.

(b) Changes requiring supplement submission and approval prior to distribution of the product made using the change (major changes). (1) A supplement must be submitted for any change in the drug substance, drug product, production process, quality controls, equipment, or facilities that has a substantial poten-

tial to have an adverse effect on the identity, strength, quality, purity, or potency of the drug product as these factors may relate to the safety or effectiveness of the drug product.

(2) These changes include, but are not limited to:

(i) Except those described in paragraphs (c) and (d) of this section, changes in the qualitative or quantitative formulation of the drug product, including inactive ingredients, or in the specifications provided in the approved application;

(ii) Changes requiring completion of studies in accordance with part 320 of this chapter to demonstrate the equivalence of the drug product to the drug product as manufactured without the change or to the reference listed drug;

(iii) Changes that may affect drug substance or drug product sterility assurance, such as changes in drug substance, drug product, or component sterilization method(s) or an addition, deletion, or substitution of steps in an aseptic processing operation;

(iv) Changes in the synthesis or manufacture of the drug substance that may affect the impurity profile and/or the physical, chemical, or biological properties of the drug substance;

(v) The following labeling changes:

(A) Changes in labeling, except those described in paragraphs (c)(6)(iii), (d)(2)(ix), or (d)(2)(x) of this section;

(B) If applicable, any change to a Medication Guide required under part 208 of this chapter, except for changes in the information specified in § 208.20(b)(8)(iii) and (b)(8)(iv) of this chapter; and

(C) Any change to the information required by § 201.57(a) of this chapter, with the following exceptions that may be reported in an annual report under paragraph (d)(2)(x) of this section:

(1) Removal of a listed section(s) specified in § 201.57(a)(5) of this chapter; and

(2) Changes to the most recent revision date of the labeling as specified in § 201.57(a)(15) of this chapter.

(vi) Changes in a drug product container closure system that controls the drug product delivered to a patient or changes in the type (e.g., glass to high density polyethylene (HDPE), HDPE to polyvinyl chloride, vial to syringe) or composition (e.g., one HDPE resin to another HDPE resin) of a packaging component that may affect the impurity profile of the drug product.

(vii) Changes solely affecting a natural product, a recombinant DNA-derived protein/polypeptide, or a complex or conjugate of a drug substance with a monoclonal antibody for the following:

(A) Changes in the virus or adventitious agent removal or inactivation method(s);

(B) Changes in the source material or cell line; and

(C) Establishment of a new master cell bank or seed.

(viii) Changes to a drug product under an application that is subject to a validity assessment because of significant questions regarding the integrity of the data supporting that application.

(3) The applicant must obtain approval of a supplement from FDA prior to distribution of a drug product made using a change under paragraph (b) of this section. Except for submissions under paragraph (e) of this section, the following information must be contained in the supplement:

(i) A detailed description of the proposed change;

(ii) The drug product(s) involved;

(iii) The manufacturing site(s) or area(s) affected;

(iv) A description of the methods used and studies performed to assess the effects of the change;

(v) The data derived from such studies;

(vi) For a natural product, a recombinant DNA-derived protein/polypeptide, or a complex or conjugate of a drug substance with a monoclonal antibody, relevant validation protocols and a list of relevant standard operating procedures must be provided in addition to the requirements in paragraphs (b)(3)(iv) and (b)(3)(v) of this section; and

(vii) For sterilization process and test methodologies related to sterilization process validation, relevant validation protocols and a list of relevant standard operating procedures must be provided in addition to the requirements in paragraphs (b)(3)(iv) and (b)(3)(v) of this section.

(4) An applicant may ask FDA to expedite its review of a supplement for public health reasons or if a delay in making the change described in it would impose an extraordinary hardship on the applicant. Such a supplement and its mailing cover should be plainly marked: "Prior Approval Supplement-Expedited Review Requested."

(c) Changes requiring supplement submission at least 30 days prior to distribution of the drug product made using the change (moderate changes). (1) A supplement must be submitted for any change in the drug substance, drug product, production process, quality controls, equipment, or facilities that has a moderate potential to have an adverse effect on the identity, strength, quality, purity, or potency of the drug product as these factors may relate to the safety or effectiveness of the drug product. If the supplement provides for a labeling change under paragraph (c)(6)(iii) of this section, 12 copies of the final printed labeling must be included.

(2) These changes include, but are not limited to:

(i) A change in the container closure system that does not affect the quality of the drug product, except those described in paragraphs (b) and (d) of this section; and

(ii) Changes solely affecting a natural protein, a

recombinant DNA-derived protein/polypeptide or a complex or conjugate of a drug substance with a monoclonal antibody, including:

(A) An increase or decrease in production scale during finishing steps that involves different equipment; and

(B) Replacement of equipment with that of a different design that does not affect the process methodology or process operating parameters.

(iii) Relaxation of an acceptance criterion or deletion of a test to comply with an official compendium that is consistent with FDA statutory and regulatory requirements.

(3) A supplement submitted under paragraph (c)(1) of this section is required to give a full explanation of the basis for the change and identify the date on which the change is to be made. The supplement must be labeled "Supplement—Changes Being Effected in 30 Days" or, if applicable under paragraph (c)(6) of this section, "Supplement—Changes Being Effected."

(4) Pending approval of the supplement by FDA, except as provided in paragraph (c)(6) of this section, distribution of the drug product made using the change may begin not less than 30 days after receipt of the supplement by FDA. The information listed in paragraphs (b)(3)(i) through (b)(3)(vii) of this section must be contained in the supplement.

(5) The applicant must not distribute the drug product made using the change if within 30 days following FDA's receipt of the supplement, FDA informs the applicant that either:

(i) The change requires approval prior to distribution of the drug product in accordance with paragraph (b) of this section; or

(ii) Any of the information required under paragraph (c)(4) of this section is missing; the applicant must not distribute the drug product made using the change until the supplement has been amended to provide the missing information.

(6) The agency may designate a category of changes for the purpose of providing that, in the case of a change in such category, the holder of an approved application may commence distribution of the drug product involved upon receipt by the agency of a supplement for the change. These changes include, but are not limited to:

(i) Addition to a specification or changes in the methods or controls to provide increased assurance that the drug substance or drug product will have the characteristics of identity, strength, quality, purity, or potency that it purports or is represented to possess;

(ii) A change in the size and/or shape of a container for a nonsterile drug product, except for solid dosage forms, without a change in the labeled amount of drug product or from one container closure system to another;

(iii) Changes in the labeling to reflect newly acquired information, except for changes to the information required in § 201.57(a) of this chapter (which must be made under paragraph (b)(2)(v)(C) of this section), to accomplish any of the following:

(A) To add or strengthen a contraindication, warning, precaution, or adverse reaction for which the evidence of a causal association satisfies the standard for inclusion in the labeling under § 201.57(c) of this chapter;

(B) To add or strengthen a statement about drug abuse, dependence, psychological effect, or overdosage;

(C) To add or strengthen an instruction about dosage and administration that is intended to increase the safe use of the drug product;

(D) To delete false, misleading, or unsupported indications for use or claims for effectiveness; or

(E) Any labeling change normally requiring a supplement submission and approval prior to distribution of the drug product that FDA specifically requests be submitted under this provision.

(7) If the agency disapproves the supplemental application, it may order the manufacturer to cease distribution of the drug product(s) made with the manufacturing change.

(d) Changes to be described in an annual report (minor changes). (1) Changes in the drug substance, drug product, production process, quality controls, equipment, or facilities that have a minimal potential to have an adverse effect on the identity, strength, quality, purity, or potency of the drug product as these factors may relate to the safety or effectiveness of the drug product must be documented by the applicant in the next annual report in accordance with § 314.81(b)(2).

(2) These changes include, but are not limited to:

(i) Any change made to comply with a change to an official compendium, except a change described in paragraph (c)(2)(iii) of this section, that is consistent with FDA statutory and regulatory requirements.

(ii) The deletion or reduction of an ingredient intended to affect only the color of the drug product;

(iii) Replacement of equipment with that of the same design and operating principles except those equipment changes described in paragraph (c) of this section;

(iv) A change in the size and/or shape of a container containing the same number of dosage units for a nonsterile solid dosage form drug product, without a change from one container closure system to another;

(v) A change within the container closure system for a nonsterile drug product, based upon a showing of equivalency to the approved system under a protocol approved in the application or published in an official compendium;

(vi) An extension of an expiration dating period based upon full shelf life data on production batches obtained from a protocol approved in the application;

(vii) The addition or revision of an alternative analytical procedure that provides the same or increased assurance of the identity, strength, quality, purity, or potency of the material being tested as the analytical procedure described in the approved application, or deletion of an alternative analytical procedure;

(viii) The addition by embossing, debossing, or engraving of a code imprint to a solid oral dosage form drug product other than a modified release dosage form, or a minor change in an existing code imprint;

(ix) A change in the labeling concerning the description of the drug product or in the information about how the drug product is supplied, that does not involve a change in the dosage strength or dosage form; and

(x) An editorial or similar minor change in labeling, including a change to the information allowed by paragraphs (b)(2)(v)(C)(1) and (2) of this section.

(3) For changes under this category, the applicant is required to submit in the annual report:

(i) A statement by the holder of the approved application that the effects of the change have been assessed;

(ii) A full description of the manufacturing and controls changes, including the manufacturing site(s) or area(s) involved;

(iii) The date each change was implemented;

(iv) Data from studies and tests performed to assess the effects of the change; and,

(v) For a natural product, recombinant DNA-derived protein/polypeptide, complex or conjugate of a drug substance with a monoclonal antibody, sterilization process or test methodology related to sterilization process validation, a cross-reference to relevant validation protocols and/or standard operating procedures.

(e) Protocols. An applicant may submit one or more protocols describing the specific tests and studies and acceptance criteria to be achieved to demonstrate the lack of adverse effect for specified types of manufacturing changes on the identity, strength, quality, purity, and potency of the drug product as these factors may relate to the safety or effectiveness of the drug product. Any such protocols, if not included in the approved application, or changes to an approved protocol, must be submitted as a supplement requiring approval from FDA prior to distribution of a drug product produced with the manufacturing change. The supplement, if approved, may subsequently justify a reduced reporting category for the particular change because the use of the protocol for that type of change reduces the potential risk of an adverse effect.

(f) Patent information. The applicant must comply with the patent information requirements under section 505(c)(2) of the act.

(g) Claimed exclusivity. If an applicant claims exclusivity under § 314.108 upon approval of a supplement for change to its previously approved drug product, the applicant must include with its supplement the information required under § 314.50(j).

[69 FR 18764, Apr. 8, 2004, as amended at 71 FR 3997, Jan. 24, 2006; 72 FR 73600, Dec. 28, 2007; 73 FR 49609, Aug. 22, 2008]

§ 314.71   Procedures for submission of a supplement to an approved application.

(a) Only the applicant may submit a supplement to an application.

(b) All procedures and actions that apply to an application under § 314.50 also apply to supplements, except that the information required in the supplement is limited to that needed to support the change. A supplement is required to contain an archival copy and a review copy that include an application form and appropriate technical sections, samples, and labeling; except that a supplement for a change other than a change in labeling is required also to contain a field copy.

(c) All procedures and actions that apply to applications under this part, including actions by applicants and the Food and Drug Administration, also apply to supplements except as specified otherwise in this part.

[50 FR 7493, Feb. 22, 1985, as amended at 50 FR 21238, May 23, 1985; 58 FR 47352, Sept. 8, 1993; 67 FR 9586, Mar. 4, 2002; 73 FR 39609, July 10, 2008]

§ 314.72   Change in ownership of an application.

(a) An applicant may transfer ownership of its application. At the time of transfer the new and former owners are required to submit information to the Food and Drug Administration as follows:

(1) The former owner shall submit a letter or other document that states that all rights to the application have been transferred to the new owner.

(2) The new owner shall submit an application form signed by the new owner and a letter or other document containing the following:

(i) The new owner's commitment to agreements, promises, and conditions made by the former owner and contained in the application;

(ii) The date that the change in ownership is effective; and

(iii) Either a statement that the new owner has a complete copy of the approved application, including supplements and records that are required to be kept under § 314.81, or a request for a copy of the application from FDA's files. FDA will provide a copy of the application to the new owner under the fee schedule in § 20.45 of FDA's public information regulations.

(b) The new owner shall advise FDA about any change in the conditions in the approved application under § 314.70, except the new owner may advise FDA in the next annual report about a change in the drug product's label or labeling to change the product's brand or the name of its manufacturer, packer, or distributor.

[50 FR 7493, Feb. 22, 1985; 50 FR 14212, Apr. 11, 1985, as amended at 50 FR 21238, May 23, 1985; 67 FR 9586, Mar. 4, 2002; 68 FR 25287, May 12, 2003]

§ 314.80 Postmarketing reporting of adverse drug experiences.

(a) Definitions. The following definitions of terms apply to this section:-

Adverse drug experience. Any adverse event associated with the use of a drug in humans, whether or not considered drug related, including the following: An adverse event occurring in the course of the use of a drug product in professional practice; an adverse event occurring from drug overdose whether accidental or intentional; an adverse event occurring from drug abuse; an adverse event occurring from drug withdrawal; and any failure of expected pharmacological action.

Disability. A substantial disruption of a person's ability to conduct normal life functions.

Life-threatening adverse drug experience. Any adverse drug experience that places the patient, in the view of the initial reporter, at immediate risk of death from the adverse drug experience as it occurred, i.e., it does not include an adverse drug experience that, had it occurred in a more severe form, might have caused death.

Serious adverse drug experience. Any adverse drug experience occurring at any dose that results in any of the following outcomes: Death, a life-threatening adverse drug experience, inpatient hospitalization or prolongation of existing hospitalization, a persistent or significant disability/incapacity, or a congenital anomaly/birth defect. Important medical events that may not result in death, be life-threatening, or

require hospitalization may be considered a serious adverse drug experience when, based upon appropriate medical judgment, they may jeopardize the patient or subject and may require medical or surgical intervention to prevent one of the outcomes listed in this definition. Examples of such medical events include allergic bronchospasm requiring intensive treatment in an emergency room or at home, blood dyscrasias or convulsions that do not result in inpatient hospitalization, or the development of drug dependency or drug abuse.

Unexpected adverse drug experience. Any adverse drug experience that is not listed in the current labeling for the drug product. This includes events that may be symptomatically and pathophysiologically related to an event listed in the labeling, but differ from the event because of greater severity or specificity. For example, under this definition, hepatic necrosis would be unexpected (by virtue of greater severity) if the labeling only referred to elevated hepatic enzymes or hepatitis. Similarly, cerebral thromboembolism and cerebral vasculitis would be unexpected (by virtue of greater specificity) if the labeling only listed cerebral vascular accidents. "Unexpected," as used in this definition, refers to an adverse drug experience that has not been previously observed (i.e., included in the labeling) rather than from the perspective of such experience not being anticipated from the pharmacological properties of the pharmaceutical product.

(b) Review of adverse drug experiences. Each applicant having an approved application under § 314.50 or, in the case of a 505(b)(2) application, an effective approved application, shall promptly review all adverse drug experience information obtained or otherwise received by the applicant from any source, foreign or domestic, including information derived from commercial marketing experience, postmarketing clinical investigations, postmarketing epidemiological/surveillance studies, reports in the scientific literature, and unpublished scientific papers. Applicants are not required to re-submit to FDA adverse drug experience reports forwarded to the applicant by FDA; however, applicants must submit all followup informa-tion on such reports to FDA. Any person subject to the reporting requirements under paragraph (c) of this section shall also develop written pro-cedures for the surveillance, receipt, evaluation, and reporting of postmarketing adverse drug experiences to FDA.

(c) Reporting requirements. The applicant shall report to FDA adverse drug experience informa-tion, as described in this section. The applicant shall submit two copies of each report de-scribed in this section to the Central Document Room, 5901-B Ammendale Rd., Beltsville, MD 20705-1266. FDA may waive the requirement for the second copy in appropriate instances.

(1)(i) Postmarketing 15-day "Alert reports". The applicant shall report each adverse drug ex-perience that is both serious and unexpected, whether foreign or domestic, as soon as possible but in no case later than 15 calendar days of ini-tial receipt of the information by the applicant.

(ii) Postmarketing 15-day "Alert reports"—fol-lowup. The applicant shall promptly investigate all adverse drug experiences that are the sub-ject of these postmarketing 15-day Alert re-ports and shall submit followup reports within 15 calendar days of receipt of new information or as requested by FDA. If additional informa-tion is not obtainable, records should be main-tained of the unsuccessful steps taken to seek additional information. Postmarketing 15-day Alert reports and followups to them shall be submitted under separate cover.

(iii) Submission of reports. The requirements of paragraphs (c)(1)(i) and (c)(1)(ii) of this section, concerning the submission of postmarketing 15-day Alert reports, shall also apply to any person other than the applicant (nonapplicant) whose name appears on the label of an ap-proved drug product as a manufacturer, packer, or distributor. To avoid unnecessary duplication

in the submission to FDA of reports required by paragraphs (c)(1)(i) and (c)(1)(ii) of this sec-tion, obligations of a nonapplicant may be met by submission of all reports of serious adverse drug experiences to the applicant. If a nonappli-cant elects to submit adverse drug experience reports to the applicant rather than to FDA, the nonapplicant shall submit each report to the applicant within 5 calendar days of receipt of the report by the nonapplicant, and the appli-cant shall then comply with the requirements of this section. Under this circumstance, the non-applicant shall maintain a record of this action which shall include:

(A) A copy of each adverse drug experience re-port;

(B) The date the report was received by the non-applicant;

(C) The date the report was submitted to the ap-plicant; and

(D) The name and address of the applicant.

(iv) Report identification. Each report submit-ted under this paragraph shall bear prominent identification as to its contents, i.e., "15-day Alert report," or "15-day Alert report-followup."

(2) Periodic adverse drug experience reports. (i) The applicant shall report each adverse drug ex-perience not reported under paragraph (c)(1)(i) of this section at quarterly intervals, for 3 years from the date of approval of the application, and then at annual intervals. The applicant shall submit each quarterly report within 30 days of the close of the quarter (the first quarter begin-ning on the date of approval of the application) and each annual report within 60 days of the anniversary date of approval of the applica-tion. Upon written notice, FDA may extend or reestablish the requirement that an applicant submit quarterly reports, or require that the ap-plicant submit reports under this section at dif-ferent times than those stated. For example, the agency may reestablish a quarterly reporting requirement following the approval of a major

supplement. Followup information to adverse drug experiences submitted in a periodic report may be submitted in the next periodic report.

(ii) Each periodic report is required to contain: (a) a narrative summary and analysis of the information in the report and an analysis of the 15-day Alert reports submitted during the reporting interval (all 15-day Alert reports being appropriately referenced by the applicant's patient identification number, adverse reaction term(s), and date of submission to FDA); (b) a FDA Form 3500A (Adverse Reaction Report) for each adverse drug experience not reported under paragraph (c)(1)(i) of this section (with an index consisting of a line listing of the applicant's patient identification number and adverse reaction term(s)); and (c) a history of actions taken since the last report because of adverse drug experiences (for example, labeling changes or studies initiated).

(iii) Periodic reporting, except for information regarding 15-day Alert reports, does not apply to adverse drug experience information obtained from postmarketing studies (whether or not conducted under an investigational new drug application), from reports in the scientific literature, and from foreign marketing experience.

(d) Scientific literature. (1) A 15-day Alert report based on information from the scientific literature is required to be accompanied by a copy of the published article. The 15-day reporting requirements in paragraph (c)(1)(i) of this section (i.e., serious, unexpected adverse drug experiences) apply only to reports found in scientific and medical journals either as case reports or as the result of a formal clinical trial.

(2) As with all reports submitted under paragraph (c)(1)(i) of this section, reports based on the scientific literature shall be submitted on FDA Form 3500A or comparable format as prescribed by paragraph (f) of this section. In cases where the applicant believes that preparing the FDA Form 3500A constitutes an undue hardship, the applicant may arrange with the Office

of Surveillance and Epidemiology for an acceptable alternative reporting format.

(e) Postmarketing studies. (1) An applicant is not required to submit a 15-day Alert report under paragraph (c) of this section for an adverse drug experience obtained from a postmarketing study (whether or not conducted under an investigational new drug application) unless the applicant concludes that there is a reasonable possibility that the drug caused the adverse experience.

(2) The applicant shall separate and clearly mark reports of adverse drug experiences that occur during a postmarketing study as being distinct from those experiences that are being reported spontaneously to the applicant.

(f) Reporting FDA Form 3500A. (1) Except as provided in paragraph (f)(3) of this section, the applicant shall complete FDA Form 3500A for each report of an adverse drug experience (foreign events may be submitted either on an FDA Form 3500A or, if preferred, on a CIOMS I form).

(2) Each completed FDA Form 3500A should refer only to an individual patient or a single attached publication.

(3) Instead of using FDA Form 3500A, an applicant may use a computer-generated FDA Form 3500A or other alternative format (e.g., a computer-generated tape or tabular listing) provided that:

(i) The content of the alternative format is equivalent in all elements of information to those specified in FDA Form 3500A; and

(ii) The format is agreed to in advance by the Office of Surveillance and Epidemiology.

(4) FDA Form 3500A and instructions for completing the form are available on the Internet at http://www.fda.gov/medwatch/index.html.

(g) Multiple reports. An applicant should not include in reports under this section any adverse drug experiences that occurred in clinical trials if they were previously submitted as part of the approved application. If a report applies to a drug for which an applicant holds more than one approved application, the applicant should submit the report to the application that was first approved. If a report refers to more than one drug marketed by an applicant, the applicant should submit the report to the application for the drug listed first in the report.

(h) Patient privacy. An applicant should not include in reports under this section the names and addresses of individual patients; instead, the applicant should assign a unique code number to each report, preferably not more than eight characters in length. The applicant should include the name of the reporter from whom the information was received. Names of patients, health care professionals, hospitals, and geographical identifiers in adverse drug experience reports are not releasable to the public under FDA's public information regulations in part 20.

(i) Recordkeeping. The applicant shall maintain for a period of 10 years records of all adverse drug experiences known to the applicant, including raw data and any correspondence relating to adverse drug experiences.

(j) Withdrawal of approval. If an applicant fails to establish and maintain records and make reports required under this section, FDA may withdraw approval of the application and, thus, prohibit continued marketing of the drug product that is the subject of the application.

(k) Disclaimer. A report or information submitted by an applicant under this section (and any release by FDA of that report or information) does not necessarily reflect a conclusion by the applicant or FDA that the report or information constitutes an admission that the drug caused or contributed to an adverse effect. An applicant need not admit, and may deny, that the report or information submitted under this section constitutes an admission that the drug caused or contributed to an adverse effect. For

purposes of this provision, the term "applicant" also includes any person reporting under paragraph (c)(1)(iii) of this section.

[50 FR 7493, Feb. 22, 1985; 50 FR 14212, Apr. 11, 1985, as amended at 50 FR 21238, May 23, 1985; 51 FR 24481, July 3, 1986; 52 FR 37936, Oct. 13, 1987; 55 FR 11580, Mar. 29, 1990; 57 FR 17983, Apr. 28, 1992; 62 FR 34168, June 25, 1997; 62 FR 52251, Oct. 7, 1997; 63 FR 14611, Mar. 26, 1998; 67 FR 9586, Mar. 4, 2002; 69 FR 13473, Mar. 23, 2004; 74 FR 13113, Mar. 26, 2009]

§ 314.81   Other postmarketing reports.

(a) Applicability. Each applicant shall make the reports for each of its approved applications and abbreviated applications required under this section and section 505(k) of the act.

(b) Reporting requirements. The applicant shall submit to the Food and Drug Administration at the specified times two copies of the following reports.

(1) NDA—Field alert report. The applicant shall submit information of the following kinds about distributed drug products and articles to the FDA district office that is responsible for the facility involved within 3 working days of receipt by the applicant. The information may be provided by telephone or other rapid communication means, with prompt written followup. The report and its mailing cover should be plainly marked: "NDA—Field Alert Report."

(i) Information concerning any incident that causes the drug product or its labeling to be mistaken for, or applied to, another article.

(ii) Information concerning any bacteriological contamination, or any significant chemical, physical, or other change or deterioration in the distributed drug product, or any failure of one or more distributed batches of the drug product to meet the specification established for it in the application.

(2) Annual report. The applicant shall submit each year within 60 days of the anniversary date

of U.S. approval of the application, two copies of the report to the FDA division responsible for reviewing the application. Each annual report is required to be accompanied by a completed transmittal Form FDA 2252 (Transmittal of Periodic Reports for Drugs for Human Use), and must include all the information required under this section that the applicant received or otherwise obtained during the annual reporting interval that ends on the U.S. anniversary date. The report is required to contain in the order listed:

(i) Summary. A brief summary of significant new information from the previous year that might affect the safety, effectiveness, or labeling of the drug product. The report is also required to contain a brief description of actions the applicant has taken or intends to take as a result of this new information, for example, submit a labeling supplement, add a warning to the labeling, or initiate a new study. The summary shall briefly state whether labeling supplements for pediatric use have been submitted and whether new studies in the pediatric population to support appropriate labeling for the pediatric population have been initiated. Where possible, an estimate of patient exposure to the drug product, with special reference to the pediatric population (neonates, infants, children, and adolescents) shall be provided, including dosage form.

(ii)(a) Distribution data. Information about the quantity of the drug product distributed under the approved application, including that distributed to distributors. The information is required to include the National Drug Code (NDC) number, the total number of dosage units of each strength or potency distributed (e.g., 100,000/5 milligram tablets, 50,000/10 milliliter vials), and the quantities distributed for domestic use and the quantities distributed for foreign use. Disclosure of financial or pricing data is not required.

(b) Authorized generic drugs. If applicable, the date each authorized generic drug (as defined in § 314.3) entered the market, the date each

authorized generic drug ceased being distributed, and the corresponding trade or brand name. Each dosage form and/or strength is a different authorized generic drug and should be listed separately. The first annual report submitted on or after January 25, 2010 must include the information listed in this paragraph for any authorized generic drug that was marketed during the time period covered by an annual report submitted after January 1, 1999. If information is included in the annual report with respect to any authorized generic drug, a copy of that portion of the annual report must be sent to the Food and Drug Administration, Center for Drug Evaluation and Research, Office of New Drug Quality Assessment, Bldg. 21, rm. 2562, 10903 New Hampshire Ave., Silver Spring, MD 20993-0002, and marked "Authorized Generic Submission" or, by e-mail, to the Authorized Generics electronic mailbox at AuthorizedGenerics@fda. hhs.gov with "Authorized Generic Submission" indicated in the subject line. However, at such time that FDA has required that annual reports be submitted in an electronic format, the information required by this paragraph must be submitted as part of the annual report, in the electronic format specified for submission of annual reports at that time, and not as a separate submission under the preceding sentence in this paragraph.

(iii) Labeling. (a) Currently used professional labeling, patient brochures or package inserts (if any), and a representative sample of the package labels.

(b) The content of labeling required under § 201.100(d)(3) of this chapter (i.e., the package insert or professional labeling), including all text, tables, and figures, must be submitted in electronic format. Electronic format submissions must be in a form that FDA can process, review, and archive. FDA will periodically issue guidance on how to provide the electronic submission (e.g., method of transmission, media, file formats, preparation and organization of files). Submissions under this paragraph must be made in accordance with part 11 of this chapter, except for the requirements of § 11.10(a), (c) through (h), and (k), and the corresponding requirements of § 11.30.

(c) A summary of any changes in labeling that have been made since the last report listed by date in the order in which they were implemented, or if no changes, a statement of that fact.

(iv) Chemistry, manufacturing, and controls changes. (a) Reports of experiences, investigations, studies, or tests involving chemical or physical properties, or any other properties of the drug (such as the drug's behavior or properties in relation to microorganisms, including both the effects of the drug on microorganisms and the effects of microorganisms on the drug). These reports are only required for new information that may affect FDA's previous conclusions about the safety or effectiveness of the drug product.

(b) A full description of the manufacturing and controls changes not requiring a supplemental application under § 314.70 (b) and (c), listed by date in the order in which they were implemented.

(v) Nonclinical laboratory studies. Copies of unpublished reports and summaries of published reports of new toxicological findings in animal studies and *in vitro* studies (e.g., mutagenicity) conducted by, or otherwise obtained by, the applicant concerning the ingredients in the drug product. The applicant shall submit a copy of a published report if requested by FDA.

(vi) Clinical data. (a) Published clinical trials of the drug (or abstracts of them), including clinical trials on safety and effectiveness; clinical trials on new uses; biopharmaceutic, pharmacokinetic, and clinical pharmacology studies; and reports of clinical experience pertinent to safety (for example, epidemiologic studies or analyses of experience in a monitored series of patients) conducted by or otherwise obtained by the applicant. Review articles, papers describing the use of the drug product in medical practice, papers and abstracts in which the drug is used as a research tool, promotional articles, press clippings, and papers that do not contain tabulations or summaries of original data should not be reported.

(b) Summaries of completed unpublished clinical trials, or prepublication manuscripts if available, conducted by, or otherwise obtained by, the applicant. Supporting information should not be reported. (A study is considered completed 1 year after it is concluded.)

(c) Analysis of available safety and efficacy data in the pediatric population and changes proposed in the labeling based on this information. An assessment of data needed to ensure appropriate labeling for the pediatric population shall be included.

(vii) Status reports of postmarketing study commitments. A status report of each postmarketing study of the drug product concerning clinical safety, clinical efficacy, clinical pharmacology, and nonclinical toxicology that is required by FDA (e.g., accelerated approval clinical benefit studies, pediatric studies) or that the applicant has committed, in writing, to conduct either at the time of approval of an application for the drug product or a supplement to an application, or after approval of the application or a supplement. For pediatric studies, the status report shall include a statement indicating whether postmarketing clinical studies in pediatric populations were required by FDA under § 201.23 of this chapter. The status of these postmarketing studies shall be reported annually until FDA notifies the applicant, in writing, that the agency concurs with the applicant's determination that the study commitment has been fulfilled or that the study is either no longer feasible or would no longer provide useful information.

(a) Content of status report. The following information must be provided for each postmarketing study reported under this paragraph:

(1) Applicant's name.

(2) Product name. Include the approved drug product's established name and proprietary name, if any.

(3) NDA, ANDA, and supplement number.

(4) Date of U.S. approval of NDA or ANDA.

(5) Date of postmarketing study commitment.

(6) Description of postmarketing study commitment. The description must include sufficient information to uniquely describe the study. This information may include the purpose of the study, the type of study, the patient population addressed by the study and the indication(s) and dosage(s) that are to be studied.

(7) Schedule for completion and reporting of the postmarketing study commitment. The schedule should include the actual or projected dates for submission of the study protocol to FDA, completion of patient accrual or initiation of an animal study, completion of the study, submission of the final study report to FDA, and any additional milestones or submissions for which projected dates were specified as part of the commitment. In addition, it should include a revised schedule, as appropriate. If the schedule has been previously revised, provide both the original schedule and the most recent, previously submitted revision.

(8) Current status of the postmarketing study commitment. The status of each postmarketing study should be categorized using one of the following terms that describes the study's status on the anniversary date of U.S. approval of the application or other agreed upon date:

(i) Pending. The study has not been initiated, but does not meet the criterion for delayed.

(ii) Ongoing. The study is proceeding according to or ahead of the original schedule described under paragraph (b)(2)(vii)(a)(7) of this section.

(iii) Delayed. The study is behind the original schedule described under paragraph (b)(2)(vii)

(a)(7) of this section.

(iv) Terminated. The study was ended before completion but a final study report has not been submitted to FDA.

(v) Submitted. The study has been completed or terminated and a final study report has been submitted to FDA.

(9) Explanation of the study's status. Provide a brief description of the status of the study, including the patient accrual rate (expressed by providing the number of patients or subjects enrolled to date, and the total planned enrollment), and an explanation of the study's status identified under paragraph (b)(2)(vii)(a)(8) of this section. If the study has been completed, include the date the study was completed and the date the final study report was submitted to FDA, as applicable. Provide a revised schedule, as well as the reason(s) for the revision, if the schedule under paragraph (b)(2)(vii)(a)(7) of this section has changed since the last report.

(b) Public disclosure of information. Except for the information described in this paragraph, FDA may publicly disclose any information described in paragraph (b)(2)(vii) of this section, concerning a postmarketing study, if the agency determines that the information is necessary to identify the applicant or to establish the status of the study, including the reasons, if any, for failure to conduct, complete, and report the study. Under this section, FDA will not publicly disclose trade secrets, as defined in § 20.61 of this chapter, or information, described in § 20.63 of this chapter, the disclosure of which would constitute an unwarranted invasion of personal privacy.

(viii) Status of other postmarketing studies. A status report of any postmarketing study not included under paragraph (b)(2)(vii) of this section that is being performed by, or on behalf of, the applicant. A status report is to be included for any chemistry, manufacturing, and controls studies that the applicant has agreed to perform and for all product stability studies.

(ix) Log of outstanding regulatory business. To facilitate communications between FDA and the applicant, the report may, at the applicant's discretion, also contain a list of any open regulatory business with FDA concerning the drug product subject to the application (e.g., a list of the applicant's unanswered correspondence with the agency, a list of the agency's unanswered correspondence with the applicant).

(3) Other reporting—(i) Advertisements and promotional labeling. The applicant shall submit specimens of mailing pieces and any other labeling or advertising devised for promotion of the drug product at the time of initial dissemination of the labeling and at the time of initial publication of the advertisement for a prescription drug product. Mailing pieces and labeling that are designed to contain samples of a drug product are required to be complete, except the sample of the drug product may be omitted. Each submission is required to be accompanied by a completed transmittal Form FDA-2253 (Transmittal of Advertisements and Promotional Labeling for Drugs for Human Use) and is required to include a copy of the product's current professional labeling. Form FDA-2253 is available on the Internet at http://www.fda.gov/opacom/morechoices/fdaforms/cder.html.

(ii) Special reports. Upon written request the agency may require that the applicant submit the reports under this section at different times than those stated.

(iii) Notification of discontinuance. (a) An applicant who is the sole manufacturer of an approved drug product must notify FDA in writing at least 6 months prior to discontinuing manufacture of the drug product if:

(1) The drug product is life supporting, life sustaining, or intended for use in the prevention of a serious disease or condition; and

(2) The drug product was not originally derived from human tissue and replaced by a recombi-

nant product.

(b) For drugs regulated by the Center for Drug Evaluation and Research (CDER) or the Center for Biologics Evaluation and Research (CBER), one copy of the notification required by paragraph (b)(3)(iii)(a) of this section must be sent to the CDER Drug Shortage Coordinator, at the address of the Director of CDER; one copy to the CDER Drug Registration and Listing Team, Division of Compliance Risk Management and Surveillance; and one copy to either the director of the review division in CDER that is responsible for reviewing the application, or the director of the office in CBER that is responsible for reviewing the application.

(c) FDA will publicly disclose a list of all drug products to be discontinued under paragraph (b)(3)(iii)(a) of this section. If the notification period is reduced under § 314.91, the list will state the reason(s) for such reduction and the anticipated date that manufacturing will cease.

(iv) Withdrawal of approved drug product from sale. (a) The applicant shall submit on Form FDA 2657 (Drug Product Listing), within 15 working days of the withdrawal from sale of a drug product, the following information:

(1) The National Drug Code (NDC) number.

(2) The identity of the drug product by established name and by proprietary name.

(3) The new drug application or abbreviated application number.

(4) The date of withdrawal from sale. It is requested but not required that the reason for withdrawal of the drug product from sale be included with the information.

(b) The applicant shall submit each Form FDA-2657 to the Records Repository Team (HFD-143), Center for Drug Evaluation and Research, Food and Drug Administration, 5600 Fishers Lane, Rockville, MD 20857.

(c) Reporting under paragraph (b)(3)(iv) of this

section constitutes compliance with the requirements under § 207.30(a) of this chapter to report "at the discretion of the registrant when the change occurs."

(c) General requirements—(1) Multiple applications. For all reports required by this section, the applicant shall submit the information common to more than one application only to the application first approved, and shall not report separately on each application. The submission is required to identify all the applications to which the report applies.

(2) Patient identification. Applicants should not include in reports under this section the names and addresses of individual patients; instead, the applicant should code the patient names whenever possible and retain the code in the applicant's files. The applicant shall maintain sufficient patient identification information to permit FDA, by using that information alone or along with records maintained by the investigator of a study, to identify the name and address of individual patients; this will ordinarily occur only when the agency needs to investigate the reports further or when there is reason to believe that the reports do not represent actual results obtained.

(d) Withdrawal of approval. If an applicant fails to make reports required under this section, FDA may withdraw approval of the application and, thus, prohibit continued marketing of the drug product that is the subject of the application.

(Collection of information requirements approved by the Office of Management and Budget under control number 0910-0001)

[50 FR 7493, Feb. 22, 1985; 50 FR 14212, Apr. 11, 1985, as amended at 50 FR 21238, May 23, 1985; 55 FR 11580, Mar. 29, 1990; 57 FR 17983, Apr. 28, 1992; 63 FR 66670, Dec. 2, 1998; 64 FR 401, Jan. 5, 1999; 65 FR 64617, Oct. 30, 2000; 66 FR 10815, Feb. 20, 2001; 68 FR 69019, Dec. 11, 2003; 69 FR 18766, Apr. 8, 2004; 69 FR 48775, Aug. 11, 2004; 72 FR 58999, Oct. 18, 2007; 74 FR 13113, Mar. 26, 2009; 74 FR 37167, July 28, 2009]

§ 314.90 Waivers.

(a) An applicant may ask the Food and Drug Administration to waive under this section any requirement that applies to the applicant under §§ 314.50 through 314.81. An applicant may ask FDA to waive under § 314.126(c) any criteria of an adequate and well-controlled study described in § 314.126(b). A waiver request under this section is required to be submitted with supporting documentation in an application, or in an amendment or supplement to an application. The waiver request is required to contain one of the following:

(1) An explanation why the applicant's compliance with the requirement is unnecessary or cannot be achieved;

(2) A description of an alternative submission that satisfies the purpose of the requirement; or

(3) Other information justifying a waiver.

(b) FDA may grant a waiver if it finds one of the following:

(1) The applicant's compliance with the requirement is unnecessary for the agency to evaluate the application or compliance cannot be achieved;

(2) The applicant's alternative submission satisfies the requirement; or

(3) The applicant's submission otherwise justifies a waiver.

[50 FR 7493, Feb. 22, 1985, as amended at 50 FR 21238, May 23, 1985; 67 FR 9586, Mar. 4, 2002]

§ 314.91 Obtaining a reduction in the discontinuance notification period.

(a) What is the discontinuance notification period? The discontinuance notification period is the 6-month period required under § 314.81(b)(3)(iii)(a). The discontinuance notification period begins when an applicant who is the sole manufacturer of certain products notifies FDA that it will discontinue manufacturing the product. The discontinuance notification period ends when manufacturing ceases.

(b) When can FDA reduce the discontinuance notification period? FDA can reduce the 6-month discontinuance notification period when it finds good cause exists for the reduction. FDA may find good cause exists based on information certified by an applicant in a request for a reduction of the discontinuance notification period. In limited circumstances, FDA may find good cause exists based on information already known to the agency. These circumstances can include the withdrawal of the drug from the market based upon formal FDA regulatory action (e.g., under the procedures described in § 314.150 for the publication of a notice of opportunity for a hearing describing the basis for the proposed withdrawal of a drug from the market) or resulting from the applicant's consultations with the agency.

(c) How can an applicant request a reduction in the discontinuance notification period? (1) The applicant must certify in a written request that, in its opinion and to the best of its knowledge, good cause exists for the reduction. The applicant must submit the following certification:

The undersigned certifies that good cause exists for a reduction in the 6-month notification period required in § 314.81(b)(3)(iii)(a) for discontinuing the manufacture of (name of the drug product). The following circumstances establish good cause (one or more of the circumstances in paragraph (d) of this section).

(2) The certification must be signed by the applicant or the applicant's attorney, agent (representative), or other authorized official. If the person signing the certification does not reside or have a place of business within the United States, the certification must contain the name and address of, and must also be signed by, an attorney, agent, or other authorized official who resides or maintains a place of business within the United States.

(3) For drugs regulated by the Center for Drug Evaluation and Research (CDER) or the Center for Biologics Evaluation and Research (CBER), one copy of the certification must be submitted to the Drug Shortage Coordinator at the address of the Director of CDER, one copy to the CDER Drug Registration and Listing Team, Division of Compliance Risk Management and Surveillance in CDER, and one copy to either the director of the review division in CDER responsible for reviewing the application, or the director of the office in CBER responsible for reviewing the application.

(d) What circumstances and information can establish good cause for a reduction in the discontinuance notification period? (1) A public health problem may result from continuation of manufacturing for the 6-month period. This certification must include a detailed description of the potential threat to the public health.

(2) A biomaterials shortage prevents the continuation of the manufacturing for the 6-month period. This certification must include a detailed description of the steps taken by the applicant in an attempt to secure an adequate supply of biomaterials to enable manufacturing to continue for the 6-month period and an explanation of why the biomaterials could not be secured.

(3) A liability problem may exist for the manufacturer if the manufacturing is continued for the 6-month period. This certification must include a detailed description of the potential liability problem.

(4) Continuation of the manufacturing for the 6-month period may cause substantial economic hardship for the manufacturer. This certification must include a detailed description of the financial impact of continuing to manufacture the drug product over the 6-month period.

(5) The manufacturer has filed for bankruptcy under chapter 7 or 11 of title 11, United States Code (11 U.S.C. 701 et seq. and 1101 et seq.). This certification must be accompanied by doc-

umentation of the filing or proof that the filing occurred.

(6) The manufacturer can continue distribution of the drug product to satisfy existing market need for 6 months. This certification must include a detailed description of the manufacturer's processes to ensure such distribution for the 6-month period.

(7) Other good cause exists for the reduction. This certification must include a detailed description of the need for a reduction.

[72 FR 58999, Oct. 18, 2007]

Subpart C—Abbreviated Applications

Source:

57 FR 17983, Apr. 28, 1992, unless otherwise noted.

§ 314.92 Drug products for which abbreviated applications may be submitted.

(a) Abbreviated applications are suitable for the following drug products within the limits set forth under § 314.93:

(1) Drug products that are the same as a listed drug. A "listed drug" is defined in § 314.3. For determining the suitability of an abbreviated new drug application, the term "same as" means identical in active ingredient(s), dosage form, strength, route of administration, and conditions of use, except that conditions of use for which approval cannot be granted because of exclusivity or an existing patent may be omitted. If a listed drug has been voluntarily withdrawn from or not offered for sale by its manufacturer, a person who wishes to submit an abbreviated new drug application for the drug shall comply with § 314.122.

(2) [Reserved]

(3) Drug products that have been declared suitable for an abbreviated new drug application submission by FDA through the petition procedures set forth under § 10.30 of this chapter

and § 314.93.

(b) FDA will publish in the list listed drugs for which abbreviated applications may be submitted. The list is available from the Superintendent of Documents, U.S. Government Printing Office, Washington, DC 20402, 202-783-3238.

[57 FR 17983, Apr. 28, 1992, as amended at 64 FR 401, Jan. 5, 1999]

§ 314.93 Petition to request a change from a listed drug.

(a) The only changes from a listed drug for which the agency will accept a petition under this section are those changes described in paragraph (b) of this section. Petitions to submit abbreviated new drug applications for other changes from a listed drug will not be approved.

(b) A person who wants to submit an abbreviated new drug application for a drug product which is not identical to a listed drug in route of administration, dosage form, and strength, or in which one active ingredient is substituted for one of the active ingredients in a listed combination drug, must first obtain permission from FDA to submit such an abbreviated application.

(c) To obtain permission to submit an abbreviated new drug application for a change described in paragraph (b) of this section, a person must submit and obtain approval of a petition requesting the change. A person seeking permission to request such a change from a reference listed drug shall submit a petition in accordance with § 10.20 of this chapter and in the format specified in § 10.30 of this chapter. The petition shall contain the information specified in § 10.30 of this chapter and any additional information required by this section. If any provision of § 10.20 or § 10.30 of this chapter is inconsistent with any provision of this section, the provisions of this section apply.

(d) The petitioner shall identify a listed drug and include a copy of the proposed labeling for the drug product that is the subject of the petition and a copy of the approved labeling for the listed drug. The petitioner may, under limited circumstances, identify more than one listed drug, for example, when the proposed drug product is a combination product that differs from the combination reference listed drug with regard to an active ingredient, and the different active ingredient is an active ingredient of a listed drug. The petitioner shall also include information to show that:

(1) The active ingredients of the proposed drug product are of the same pharmacological or therapeutic class as those of the reference listed drug.

(2) The drug product can be expected to have the same therapeutic effect as the reference listed drug when administered to patients for each condition of use in the reference listed drug's labeling for which the applicant seeks approval.

(3) If the proposed drug product is a combination product with one different active ingredient, including a different ester or salt, from the reference listed drug, that the different active ingredient has previously been approved in a listed drug or is a drug that does not meet the definition of "new drug" in section 201(b) of the act.

(e) No later than 90 days after the date a petition that is permitted under paragraph (a) of this section is submitted, FDA will approve or disapprove the petition.

(1) FDA will approve a petition properly submitted under this section unless it finds that:

(i) Investigations must be conducted to show the safety and effectiveness of the drug product or of any of its active ingredients, its route of administration, dosage form, or strength which differs from the reference listed drug; or

(ii) For a petition that seeks to change an active ingredient, the drug product that is the subject of the petition is not a combination drug; or

(iii) For a combination drug product that is the subject of the petition and has an active ingredient different from the reference listed drug:

(A) The drug product may not be adequately evaluated for approval as safe and effective on the basis of the information required to be submitted under § 314.94; or

(B) The petition does not contain information to show that the different active ingredient of the drug product is of the same pharmacological or therapeutic class as the ingredient of the reference listed drug that is to be changed and that the drug product can be expected to have the same therapeutic effect as the reference listed drug when administered to patients for each condition of use in the listed drug's labeling for which the applicant seeks approval; or

(C) The different active ingredient is not an active ingredient in a listed drug or a drug that meets the requirements of section 201(p) of the act; or

(D) The remaining active ingredients are not identical to those of the listed combination drug; or

(iv) Any of the proposed changes from the listed drug would jeopardize the safe or effective use of the product so as to necessitate significant labeling changes to address the newly introduced safety or effectiveness problem; or

(v) FDA has determined that the reference listed drug has been withdrawn from sale for safety or effectiveness reasons under § 314.161, or the reference listed drug has been voluntarily withdrawn from sale and the agency has not determined whether the withdrawal is for safety or effectiveness reasons.

(2) For purposes of this paragraph, "investigations must be conducted" means that information derived from animal or clinical studies is necessary to show that the drug product is safe or effective. Such information may be contained in published or unpublished reports.

(3) If FDA approves a petition submitted under this section, the agency's response may de-

scribe what additional information, if any, will be required to support an abbreviated new drug application for the drug product. FDA may, at any time during the course of its review of an abbreviated new drug application, request additional information required to evaluate the change approved under the petition.

(f) FDA may withdraw approval of a petition if the agency receives any information demonstrating that the petition no longer satisfies the conditions under paragraph (e) of this section.

§ 314.94 Content and format of an abbreviated application.

Abbreviated applications are required to be submitted in the form and contain the information required under this section. Three copies of the application are required, an archival copy, a review copy, and a field copy. FDA will maintain guidance documents on the format and content of applications to assist applicants in their preparation.

(a) Abbreviated new drug applications. Except as provided in paragraph (b) of this section, the applicant shall submit a complete archival copy of the abbreviated new drug application that includes the following:

(1) Application form. The applicant shall submit a completed and signed application form that contains the information described under § 314.50(a)(1), (a)(3), (a)(4), and (a)(5). The applicant shall state whether the submission is an abbreviated application under this section or a supplement to an abbreviated application under § 314.97.

(2) Table of contents. the archival copy of the abbreviated new drug application is required to contain a table of contents that shows the volume number and page number of the contents of the submission.

(3) Basis for abbreviated new drug application submission. An abbreviated new drug application must refer to a listed drug. Ordinarily, that listed drug will be the drug product selected by the agency as the reference standard for conducting bioequivalence testing. The application shall contain:

(i) The name of the reference listed drug, including its dosage form and strength. For an abbreviated new drug application based on an approverd petition under § 10.30 of this chapter or § 314.93, the reference listed drug must be the same as the listed drug approved in the petition.

(ii) A statement as to whether, according to the information published in the list, the reference listed drug is entitled to a period of marketing exclusivity under section 505(j)(4)(D) of the act.

(iii) For an abbreviated new drug application based on an approved petition under § 10.30 of this chapter or § 314.93, a reference to FDA-assigned docket number for the petition and a copy of FDA's correspondence approving the petition.

(4) Conditions of use. (i) A statement that the conditions of use prescribed, recommended, or suggested in the labeling proposed for the drug product have been previously approved for the reference listed drug.

(ii) A reference to the applicant's annotated proposed labeling and to the currently approved labeling for the reference listed drug provided under paragraph (a)(8) of this section.

(5) Active ingredients. (i) For a single-active-ingredient drug product, information to show that the active ingredient is the same as that of the reference single-active-ingredient listed drug, as follows:

(A) A statement that the active ingredient of the proposed drug product is the same as that of the reference listed drug.

(B) A reference to the applicant's annotated proposed labeling and to the currently approved labeling for the reference listed drug provided under paragraph (a)(8) of this section.

(ii) For a combination drug product, information to show that the active ingredients are the same as those of the reference listed drug except for any different active ingredient that has been the subject of an approved petition, as follows:

(A) A statement that the active ingredients of the proposed drug product are the same as those of the reference listed drug, or if one of the active ingredients differs from one of the active ingredients of the reference listed drug and the abbreviated application is submitted under the approval of a petition under § 314.93 to vary such active ingredient, information to show that the other active ingredients of the drug product are the same as the other active ingredients of the reference listed drug, information to show that the different active ingredient is an active ingredient of another listed drug or of a drug that does not meet the definition of "new drug" in section 201(p) of the act, and such other information about the different active ingredient that FDA may require.

(B) A reference to the applicant's annotated proposed labeling and to the currently approved labeling for the reference listed drug provided under paragraph (a)(8) of this section.

(6) Route of administration, dosage form, and strength. (i) Information to show that the route of administration, dosage form, and strength of the drug product are the same as those of the reference listed drug except for any differences that have been the subject of an approved petition, as follows:

(A) A statement that the route of administration, dosage form, and strength of the proposed drug product are the same as those of the reference listed drug.

(B) A reference to the applicant's annotated proposed labeling and to the currently approved labeling for the reference listed drug provided under paragraph (a)(8) of this section.

(ii) If the route of administration, dosage form, or strength of the drug product differs from the reference listed drug and the abbreviated application is submitted under an approved petition under § 314.93, such information about the different route of administration, dosage form, or strength that FDA may require.

(7) Bioequivalence. (i) Information that shows that the drug product is bioequivalent to the reference listed drug upon which the applicant relies. A complete study report must be submitted for the bioequivalence study upon which the applicant relies for approval. For all other bioequivalence studies conducted on the same drug product formulation as defined in § 320.1(g) of this chapter, the applicant must submit either a complete or summary report. If a summary report of a bioequivalence study is submitted and FDA determines that there may be bioequivalence issues or concerns with the product, FDA may require that the applicant submit a complete report of the bioequivalence study to FDA; or

(ii) If the abbreviated new drug application is submitted under a petition approved under § 314.93, the results of any bioavailability of bioequivalence testing required by the agency, or any other information required by the agency to show that the active ingredients of the proposed drug product are of the same pharmacological or therapeutic class as those in the reference listed drug and that the proposed drug product can be expected to have the same therapeutic effect as the reference listed drug. If the proposed drug product contains a different active ingredient than the reference listed drug, FDA will consider the proposed drug product to have the same therapeutic effect as the reference listed drug if the applicant provides information demonstrating that:

(A) There is an adequate scientific basis for determining that substitution of the specific proposed dose of the different active ingredient for the dose of the member of the same pharmacological or therapeutic class in the reference listed drug will yield a resulting drug product whose safety and effectiveness have not been adversely affected.

(B) The unchanged active ingredients in the proposed drug product are bioequivalent to those in the reference listed drug.

(C) The different active ingredient in the proposed drug product is bioequivalent to an approved dosage form containing that ingredient and approved for the same indication as the proposed drug product or is bioequivalent to a drug product offered for that indication which does not meet the definition of "new drug" under section 201(p) of the act.

(iii) For each *in vivo* bioequivalence study contained in the abbreviated new drug application, a description of the analytical and statistical methods used in each study and a statement with respect to each study that it either was conducted in compliance with the institutional review board regulations in part 56 of this chapter, or was not subject to the regulations under § 56.104 or § 56.105 of this chapter and that each study was conducted in compliance with the informed consent regulations in part 50 of this chapter.

(8) Labeling—(i) Listed drug labeling. A copy of the currently approved labeling (including, if applicable, any Medication Guide required under part 208 of this chapter) for the listed drug referred to in the abbreviated new drug application, if the abbreviated new drug application relies on a reference listed drug.

(ii) Copies of proposed labeling. Copies of the label and all labeling for the drug product including, if applicable, any Medication Guide required under part 208 of this chapter (4 copies of draft labeling or 12 copies of final printed labeling).

(iii) Statement on proposed labeling. A statement that the applicant's proposed labeling including, if applicable, any Medication Guide required under part 208 of this chapter is the same as the labeling of the reference listed drug except for differences annotated and explained under paragraph (a)(8)(iv) of this section.

(iv) Comparison of approved and proposed labeling. A side-by-side comparison of the applicant's proposed labeling including, if applicable, any Medication Guide required under part 208 of this chapter with the approved labeling for the reference listed drug with all differences annotated and explained. Labeling (including the container label, package insert, and, if applicable, Medication Guide) proposed for the drug product must be the same as the labeling approved for the reference listed drug, except for changes required because of differences approved under a petition filed under § 314.93 or because the drug product and the reference listed drug are produced or distributed by different manufacturers. Such differences between the applicant's proposed labeling and labeling approved for the reference listed drug may include differences in expiration date, formulation, bioavailability, or pharmacokinetics, labeling revisions made to comply with current FDA labeling guidelines or other guidance, or omission of an indication or other aspect of labeling protected by patent or accorded exclusivity under section 505(j)(4)(D) of the act.

(9) Chemistry, manufacturing, and controls. (i) The information required under § 314.50(d)(1), except that § 314.50(d)(1)(ii)(c) shall contain the proposed or actual master production record, including a description of the equipment, to be used for the manufacture of a commercial lot of the drug product.

(ii) Inactive ingredients. Unless otherwise stated in paragraphs (a)(9)(iii) through (a)(9)(v) of this section, an applicant shall identify and characterize the inactive ingredients in the proposed drug product and provide information demonstrating that such inactive ingredients do not affect the safety or efficacy of the proposed drug product.

(iii) Inactive ingredient changes permitted in drug products intended for parenteral use. Generally, a drug product intended for parenteral use shall contain the same inactive ingredients and in the same concentration as the reference listed drug identified by the applicant under paragraph (a)(3) of this section. However, an applicant may seek approval of a drug product that differs from the reference listed drug in preservative, buffer, or antioxidant provided that the applicant identifies and characterizes the differences and provides information demonstrating that the differences do not affect the safety or efficacy of the proposed drug product.

(iv) Inactive ingredient changes permitted in drug products intended for ophthalmic or otic use. Generally, a drug product intended for ophthalmic or otic use shall contain the same inactive ingredients and in the same concentration as the reference listed drug identified by the applicant under paragraph (a)(3) of this section. However, an applicant may seek approval of a drug product that differs from the reference listed drug in preservative, buffer, substance to adjust tonicity, or thickening agent provided that the applicant identifies and characterizes the differences and provides information demonstrating that the differences do not affect the safety or efficacy of the proposed drug product, except that, in a product intended for ophthalmic use, an applicant may not change a buffer or substance to adjust tonicity for the purpose of claiming a therapeutic advantage over or difference from the listed drug, e.g., by using a balanced salt solution as a diluent as opposed to an isotonic saline solution, or by making a significant change in the pH or other change that may raise questions of irritability.

(v) Inactive ingredient changes permitted in drug products intended for topical use. Generally, a drug product intended for topical use, solutions for aerosolization or nebulization, and nasal solutions shall contain the same inactive ingredients as the reference listed drug identified by the applicant under paragraph (a)(3) of this section. However, an abbreviated application may include different inactive ingredients

provided that the applicant identifies and characterizes the differences and provides information demonstrating that the differences do not affect the safety or efficacy of the proposed drug product.

(10) Samples. The information required under § 314.50(e)(1) and (e)(2)(i). Samples need not be submitted until requested by FDA.

(11) Other. The information required under § 314.50(g).

(12) Patent certification—(i) Patents claiming drug, drug product, or method of use. (A) Except as provided in paragraph (a)(12)(iv) of this section, a certification with respect to each patent issued by the United States Patent and Trademark Office that, in the opinion of the applicant and to the best of its knowledge, claims the reference listed drug or that claims a use of such listed drug for which the applicant is seeking approval under section 505(j) of the act and for which information is required to be filed under section 505(b) and (c) of the act and § 314.53. For each such patent, the applicant shall provide the patent number and certify, in its opinion and to the best of its knowledge, one of the following circumstances:

(1) That the patent information has not been submitted to FDA. The applicant shall entitle such a certification "Paragraph I Certification";

(2) That the patent has expired. The applicant shall entitle such a certification "Paragraph II Certification";

(3) The date on which the patent will expire. The applicant shall entitle such a certification "Paragraph III Certification"; or

(4) That the patent is invalid, unenforceable, or will not be infringed by the manufacture, use, or sale of the drug product for which the abbreviated application is submitted. The applicant shall entitle such a certification "Paragraph IV Certification". This certification shall be submitted in the following form:

I, (name of applicant), certify that Patent No. _____ (is invalid, unenforceable, or will not be infringed by the manufacture, use, or sale of) (name of proposed drug product) for which this application is submitted.

The certification shall be accompanied by a statement that the applicant will comply with the requirements under § 314.95(a) with respect to providing a notice to each owner of the patent or their representatives and to the holder of the approved application for the listed drug, and with the requirements under § 314.95(c) with respect to the content of the notice.

(B) If the abbreviated new drug application refers to a listed drug that is itself a licensed generic product of a patented drug first approved under section 505(b) of the act, the appropriate patent certification under paragraph (a)(12)(i) of this section with respect to each patent that claims the first-approved patented drug or that claims a use for such drug.

(ii) No relevant patents. If, in the opinion of the applicant and to the best of its knowledge, there are no patents described in paragraph (a)(12)(i) of this section, a certification in the following form:

In the opinion and to the best knowledge of (name of applicant), there are no patents that claim the listed drug referred to in this application or that claim a use of the listed drug.

(iii) Method of use patent. (A) If patent information is submitted under section 505(b) or (c) of the act and § 314.53 for a patent claiming a method of using the listed drug, and the labeling for the drug product for which the applicant is seeking approval does not include any indications that are covered by the use patent, a statement explaining that the method of use patent does not claim any of the proposed indications.

(B) If the labeling of the drug product for which the applicant is seeking approval includes an indication that, according to the patent information submitted under section 505(b) or (c) of the act and § 314.53 or in the opinion of the applicant, is claimed by a use patent, an applicable certification under paragraph (a)(12)(i) of this section.

(iv) Method of manufacturing patent. An applicant is not required to make a certification with respect to any patent that claims only a method of manufacturing the listed drug.

(v) Licensing agreements. If the abbreviated new drug application is for a drug or method of using a drug claimed by a patent and the applicant has a licensing agreement with the patent owner, a certification under paragraph (a)(12)(i)(A)(4) of this section ("Paragraph IV Certification") as to that patent and a statement that it has been granted a patent license.

(vi) Late submission of patent information. If a patent on the listed drug is issued and the holder of the approved application for the listed drug does not submit the required information on the patent within 30 days of issuance of the patent, an applicant who submitted an abbreviated new drug application for that drug that contained an appropriate patent certification before the submission of the patent information is not required to submit an amended certification. An applicant whose abbreviated new drug application is submitted after a late submission of patent information, or whose pending abbreviated application was previously submitted but did not contain an appropriate patent certification at the time of the patent submission, shall submit a certification under paragraph (a)(12)(i) of this section or a statement under paragraph (a)(12)(iii) of this section as to that patent.

(vii) Disputed patent information. If an applicant disputes the accuracy or relevance of patent information submitted to FDA, the applicant may seek a confirmation of the correctness of the patent information in accordance with the procedures under § 314.53(f). Unless the patent information is withdrawn or changed, the applicant shall submit an appropriate certification for each relevant patent.

(viii) Amended certifications. A certification submitted under paragraphs (a)(12)(i) through (a)(12)(iii) of this section may be amended at any time before the effective date of the approval of the application. However, an applicant who has submitted a paragraph IV patent certification may not change it to a paragraph III certification if a patent infringement suit has been filed against another paragraph IV applicant unless the agency has determined that no applicant is entitled to 180-day exclusivity or the patent expires before the lawsuit is resolved or expires after the suit is resolved but before the end of the 180-day exclusivity period. If an applicant with a pending application voluntarily makes a patent certification for an untimely filed patent, the applicant may withdraw the patent certification for the untimely filed patent. An applicant shall submit an amended certification by letter or as an amendment to a pending application or by letter to an approved application. Once an amendment or letter is submitted, the application will no longer be considered to contain the prior certification.

(A) After finding of infringement. An applicant who has submitted a certification under paragraph (a)(12)(i)(A)(4) of this section and is sued for patent infringement within 45 days of the receipt of notice sent under § 314.95 shall amend the certification if a final judgment in the action against the applicant is entered finding the patent to be infringed. In the amended certification, the applicant shall certify under paragraph (a)(12)(i)(A)(3) of this section that the patent will expire on a specific date. Once an amendment or letter for the change has been submitted, the application will no longer be considered to be one containing a certification under paragraph (a)(12)(i)(A)(4) of this section. If a final judgment finds the patent to be invalid and infringed, an amended certification is not required.

(B) After removal of a patent from the list. If a

patent is removed from the list, any applicant with a pending application (including a tentatively approved application with a delayed effective date) who has made a certification with respect to such patent shall amend its certification. The applicant shall certify under paragraph (a)(12)(ii) of this section that no patents described in paragraph (a)(12)(i) of this section claim the drug or, if other relevant patents claim the drug, shall amend the certification to refer only to those relevant patents. In the amendment, the applicant shall state the reason for the change in certification (that the patent is or has been removed from the list). A patent that is the subject of a lawsuit under § 314.107(c) shall not be removed from the list until FDA determines either that no delay in effective dates of approval is required under that section as a result of the lawsuit, that the patent has expired, or that any such period of delay in effective dates of approval is ended. An applicant shall submit an amended certification. Once an amendment or letter for the change has been submitted, the application will no longer be considered to be one containing a certification under paragraph (a)(12)(i)(A)(4) of this section.

(C) Other amendments. (1) Except as provided in paragraphs (a)(12)(vi) and (a)(12)(viii)(C)(2) of this section, an applicant shall amend a submitted certification if, at any time before the effective date of the approval of the application, the applicant learns that the submitted certification is no longer accurate.

(2) An applicant is not required to amend a submitted certification when information on a patent on the listed drug is submitted after the effective date of approval of the abbreviated application.

(13) Financial certification or disclosure statement. An abbreviated application shall contain a financial certification or disclosure statement as required by part 54 of this chapter.

(b) Drug products subject to the Drug Efficacy Study Implementation (DESI) review. If the abbreviated new drug application is for a duplicate of a drug product that is subject to FDA's DESI review (a review of drug products approved as safe between 1938 and 1962) or other DESI-like review and the drug product evaluated in the review is a listed drug, the applicant shall comply with the provisions of paragraph (a) of this section.

(c) [Reserved]

(d) Format of an abbreviated application. (1) The applicant must submit a complete archival copy of the abbreviated application as required under paragraphs (a) and (c) of this section. FDA will maintain the archival copy during the review of the application to permit individual reviewers to refer to information that is not contained in their particular technical sections of the application, to give other agency personnel access to the application for official business, and to maintain in one place a complete copy of the application.

(i) Format of submission. An applicant may submit portions of the archival copy of the abbreviated application in any form that the applicant and FDA agree is acceptable, except as provided in paragraph (d)(1)(ii) of this section.

(ii) Labeling. The content of labeling required under § 201.100(d)(3) of this chapter (commonly referred to as the package insert or professional labeling), including all text, tables, and figures, must be submitted to the agency in electronic format as described in paragraph (d)(1)(iii) of this section. This requirement applies to the content of labeling for the proposed drug product only and is in addition to the requirements of paragraph (a)(8)(ii) of this section that copies of the formatted label and all proposed labeling be submitted. Submissions under this paragraph must be made in accordance with part 11 of this chapter, except for the requirements of § 11.10(a), (c) through (h), and (k), and the corresponding requirements of § 11.30.

(iii) Electronic format submissions. Electronic format submissions must be in a form that FDA can process, review, and archive. FDA will periodically issue guidance on how to provide the electronic submission (e.g., method of transmission, media, file formats, preparation and organization of files).

(2) For abbreviated new drug applications, the applicant shall submit a review copy of the abbreviated application that contains two separate sections. One section shall contain the information described under paragraphs (a)(2) through (a)(6), (a)(8), and (a)(9) of this section 505(j)(2)(A)(vii) of the act and one copy of the analytical procedures and descriptive information needed by FDA's laboratories to perform tests on samples of the proposed drug product and to validate the applicant's analytical procedures. The other section shall contain the information described under paragraphs (a)(3), (a)(7), and (a)(8) of this section. Each of the sections in the review copy is required to contain a copy of the application form described under § 314.50(a).

(3) [Reserved]

(4) The applicant may obtain from FDA sufficient folders to bind the archival, the review, and the field copies of the abbreviated application.

(5) The applicant shall submit a field copy of the abbreviated application that contains the technical section described in paragraph (a)(9) of this section, a copy of the application form required under paragraph (a)(1) of this section, and a certification that the field copy is a true copy of the technical section described in paragraph (a)(9) of this section contained in the archival and review copies of the abbreviated application.

[57 FR 17983, Apr. 28, 1992; 57 FR 29353, July 1, 1992, as amended at 58 FR 47352, Sept. 8, 1993; 59 FR 50364, Oct. 3, 1994; 63 FR 5252, Feb. 2, 1998; 63 FR 66399, Dec. 1, 1998; 64 FR 401, Jan. 5, 1999; 65 FR 56479, Sept. 19, 2000; 67 FR 77672, Dec. 19, 2002; 68 FR 69019, Dec.

11, 2003; 69 FR 18766, Apr. 8, 2004; 74 FR 2861, Jan. 16, 2009]

§ 314.95   Notice of certification of invalidity or noninfringement of a patent.

(a) Notice of certification. For each patent that claims the listed drug or that claims a use for such listed drug for which the applicant is seeking approval and that the applicant certifies under § 314.94(a)(12) is invalid, unenforceable, or will not be infringed, the applicant shall send notice of such certification by registered or certified mail, return receipt requested to each of the following persons:

(1) Each owner of the patent which is the subject of the certification or the representative designated by the owner to receive the notice. The name and address of the patent owner or its representative may be obtained from the United States Patent and Trademark Office; and

(2) The holder of the approved application under section 505(b) of the act for the listed drug that is claimed by the patent and for which the applicant is seeking approval, or, if the application holder does not reside or maintain a place of business within the United States, the application holder's attorney, agent, or other authorized official. The name and address of the application holder or its attorney, agent, or authorized official may be obtained from the Orange Book Staff, Office of Generic Drugs, 7500 Standish Pl., Rockville, MD 20855.

(3) This paragraph does not apply to a use patent that claims no uses for which the applicant is seeking approval.

(b) Sending the notice. The applicant shall send the notice required by paragraph (a) of this section when it receives from FDA an acknowledgment letter stating that its abbreviated new drug application is sufficiently complete to permit a substantive review. At the same time, the applicant shall amend its abbreviated new drug application to include a statement certifying that the notice has been provided to each person identified under paragraph (a) of this section and that the notice met the content requirements under paragraph (c) of this section.

(c) Contents of a notice. In the notice, the applicant shall cite section 505(j)(2)(B)(ii) of the act and shall include, but not be limited to, the following information:

(1) A statement that FDA has received an abbreviated new drug application submitted by the applicant containing any required bioavailability or bioequivalence data or information.

(2) The abbreviated application number.

(3) The established name, if any, as defined in section 502(e)(3) of the act, of the proposed drug product.

(4) The active ingredient, strength, and dosage form of the proposed drug product.

(5) The patent number and expiration date, as submitted to the agency or as known to the applicant, of each patent alleged to be invalid, unenforceable, or not infringed.

(6) A detailed statement of the factual and legal basis of the applicant's opinion that the patent is not valid, unenforceable, or will not be infringed. The applicant shall include in the detailed statement:

(i) For each claim of a patent alleged not to be infringed, a full and detailed explanation of why the claim is not infringed.

(ii) For each claim of a patent alleged to be invalid or unenforceable, a full and detailed explanation of the grounds supporting the allegation.

(7) If the applicant does not reside or have a place of business in the United States, the name and address of an agent in the United States authorized to accept service of process for the applicant.

(d) Amendment to an abbreviated application. If an abbreviated application is amended to include the certification described in § 314.94(a)

(12)(i)(A)(4), the applicant shall send the notice required by paragraph (a) of this section at the same time that the amendment to the abbreviated application is submitted to FDA.

(e) Documentation of receipt of notice. The applicant shall amend its abbreviated application to document receipt of the notice required under paragraph (a) of this section by each person provided the notice. The applicant shall include a copy of the return receipt or other similar evidence of the date the notification was received. FDA will accept as adequate documentation of the date of receipt a return receipt or a letter acknowledging receipt by the person provided the notice. An applicant may rely on another form of documentation only if FDA has agreed to such documentation in advance. A copy of the notice itself need not be submitted to the agency.

(f) Approval. If the requirements of this section are met, FDA will presume the notice to be complete and sufficient, and it will count the day following the date of receipt of the notice by the patent owner or its representative and by the approved application holder as the first day of the 45-day period provided for in section 505(j)(4)(B)(iii) of the act. FDA may, if the applicant provides a written statement to FDA that a later date should be used, count from such later date.

[59 FR 50366, Oct. 3, 1994, as amended at 68 FR 36705, June 18, 2003; 69 FR 11310, Mar. 10, 2004; 74 FR 9766, Mar. 6, 2009; 74 FR 36605, July 24, 2009]

§ 314.96   Amendments to an unapproved abbreviated application.

(a) Abbreviated new drug application. (1) An applicant may amend an abbreviated new drug application that is submitted under § 314.94, but not yet approved, to revise existing information or provide additional information. Amendments containing bioequivalence studies must contain reports of all bioequivalence studies conducted by the applicant on the same drug product formulation, unless the information has previously been submitted to FDA in the abbreviated new drug application. A complete study report must be submitted for any bioequivalence study upon which the applicant relies for approval. For all other bioequivalence studies conducted on the same drug product formulation as defined in § 320.1(g) of this chapter, the applicant must submit either a complete or summary report. If a summary report of a bioequivalence study is submitted and FDA determines that there may be bioequivalence issues or concerns with the product, FDA may require that the applicant submit a complete report of the bioequivalence study to FDA.

(2) Submission of an amendment containing significant data or information before the end of the initial review cycle constitutes an agreement between FDA and the applicant to extend the initial review cycle only for the time necessary to review the significant data or information and for no more than 180 days.

(b) The applicant shall submit a field copy of each amendment to § 314.94(a)(9). The applicant, other than a foreign applicant, shall include in its submission of each such amendment to FDA a statement certifying that a field copy of the amendment has been sent to the applicant's home FDA district office.

[57 FR 17983, Apr. 28, 1992, as amended at 58 FR 47352, Sept. 8, 1993; 64 FR 401, Jan. 5, 1999; 73 FR 39609, July 10, 2008; 74 FR 2861, Jan. 16, 2009]

§ 314.97   Supplements and other changes to an approved abbreviated application.

The applicant shall comply with the requirements of §§ 314.70 and 314.71 regarding the submission of supplemental applications and other changes to an approved abbreviated application.

§ 314.98   Postmarketing reports.

(a) Except as provided in paragraph (b) of this

section, each applicant having an approved abbreviated new drug application under § 314.94 that is effective shall comply with the requirements of § 314.80 regarding the reporting and recordkeeping of adverse drug experiences.

(b) Each applicant shall submit one copy of each report required under § 314.80 to the Central Document Room, Center for Drug Evaluation and Research, Food and Drug Administration, 5901-B Ammendale Rd., Beltsville, MD 20705-1266.

(c) Each applicant shall make the reports required under § 314.81 and section 505(k) of the act for each of its approved abbreviated applications.

[57 FR 17983, Apr. 28, 1992, as amended at 64 FR 401, Jan. 5, 1999; 74 FR 13113, Mar. 26, 2009]

§ 314.99   Other responsibilities of an applicant of an abbreviated application.

(a) An applicant shall comply with the requirements of § 314.65 regarding withdrawal by the applicant of an unapproved abbreviated application and § 314.72 regarding a change in ownership of an abbreviated application.

(b) An applicant may ask FDA to waive under this section any requirement that applies to the applicant under §§ 314.92 through 314.99. The applicant shall comply with the requirements for a waiver under § 314.90.

Subpart D—FDA Action on Applications and Abbreviated Applications

Source:

50 FR 7493, Feb. 22, 1985, unless otherwise noted. Redesignated at 57 FR 17983, Apr. 28, 1992.

§ 314.100   Timeframes for reviewing applications and abbreviated applications.

(a) Except as provided in paragraph (c) of this section, within 180 days of receipt of an application for a new drug under section 505(b) of the act or an abbreviated application for a new drug

under section 505(j) of the act, FDA will review it and send the applicant either an approval letter under § 314.105 or a complete response letter under § 314.110. This 180-day period is called the "initial review cycle."

(b) At any time before approval, an applicant may withdraw an application under § 314.65 or an abbreviated application under § 314.99 and later submit it again for consideration.

(c) The initial review cycle may be adjusted by mutual agreement between FDA and an applicant or as provided in §§ 314.60 and 314.96, as the result of a major amendment.

[73 FR 39609, July 10, 2008]

§ 314.101   Filing an application and receiving an abbreviated new drug application.

(a)(1) Within 60 days after FDA receives an application, the agency will determine whether the application may be filed. The filing of an application means that FDA has made a threshold determination that the application is sufficiently complete to permit a substantive review.

(2) If FDA finds that none of the reasons in paragraphs (d) and (e) of this section for refusing to file the application apply, the agency will file the application and notify the applicant in writing. The date of filing will be the date 60 days after the date FDA received the application. The date of filing begins the 180-day period described in section 505(c) of the act. This 180-day period is called the "filing clock."

(3) If FDA refuses to file the application, the agency will notify the applicant in writing and state the reason under paragraph (d) or (e) of this section for the refusal. If FDA refuses to file the application under paragraph (d) of this section, the applicant may request in writing within 30 days of the date of the agency's notification an informal conference with the agency about whether the agency should file the application. If, following the informal conference, the

applicant requests that FDA file the application (with or without amendments to correct the deficiencies), the agency will file the application over protest under paragraph (a)(2) of this section, notify the applicant in writing, and review it as filed. If the application is filed over protest, the date of filing will be the date 60 days after the date the applicant requested the informal conference. The applicant need not resubmit a copy of an application that is filed over protest. If FDA refuses to file the application under paragraph (e) of this section, the applicant may amend the application and resubmit it, and the agency will make a determination under this section whether it may be filed.

(b)(1) An abbreviated new drug application will be reviewed after it is submitted to determine whether the abbreviated application may be received. Receipt of an abbreviated new drug application means that FDA has made a threshold determination that the abbreviated application is sufficiently complete to permit a substantive review.

(2) If FDA finds that none of the reasons in paragraphs (d) and (e) of this section for considering the abbreviated new drug application not to have been received applies, the agency will receive the abbreviated new drug application and notify the applicant in writing.

(3) If FDA considers the abbreviated new drug application not to have been received under paragraph (d) or (e) of this section, FDA will notify the applicant, ordinarily by telephone. The applicant may then:

(i) Withdraw the abbreviated new drug application under § 314.99; or

(ii) Amend the abbreviated new drug application to correct the deficiencies; or

(iii) Take no action, in which case FDA will refuse to receive the abbreviated new drug application.

(c) [Reserved]

(d) FDA may refuse to file an application or may

not consider an abbreviated new drug application to be received if any of the following applies:

(1) The application does not contain a completed application form.

(2) The application is not submitted in the form required under § 314.50 or § 314.94.

(3) The application or abbreviated application is incomplete because it does not on its face contain information required under section 505(b), section 505(j), or section 507 of the act and § 314.50 or § 314.94.

(4) The applicant fails to submit a complete environmental assessment, which addresses each of the items specified in the applicable format under § 25.40 of this chapter or fails to provide sufficient information to establish that the requested action is subject to categorical exclusion under § 25.30 or § 25.31 of this chapter.

(5) The application or abbreviated application does not contain an accurate and complete English translation of each part of the application that is not in English.

(6) The application does not contain a statement for each nonclinical laboratory study that it was conducted in compliance with the requirements set forth in part 58 of this chapter, or, for each study not conducted in compliance with part 58 of this chapter, a brief statement of the reason for the noncompliance.

(7) The application does not contain a statement for each clinical study that it was conducted in compliance with the institutional review board regulations in part 56 of this chapter, or was not subject to those regulations, and that it was conducted in compliance with the informed consent regulations in part 50 of this chapter, or, if the study was subject to but was not conducted in compliance with those regulations, the application does not contain a brief statement of the reason for the noncompliance.

(8) The drug product that is the subject of the submission is already covered by an approved

application or abbreviated application and the applicant of the submission:

(i) Has an approved application or abbreviated application for the same drug product; or

(ii) Is merely a distributor and/or repackager of the already approved drug product.

(9) The application is submitted as a 505(b)(2) application for a drug that is a duplicate of a listed drug and is eligible for approval under section 505(j) of the act.

(e) The agency will refuse to file an application or will consider an abbreviated new drug application not to have been received if any of the following applies:

(1) The drug product is subject to licensing by FDA under the Public Health Service Act (42 U.S.C. 201 et seq.) and subchapter F of this chapter.

(2) In the case of a 505(b)(2) application or an abbreviated new drug application, the drug product contains the same active moiety as a drug that:

(i) Was approved after September 24, 1984, in an application under section 505(b) of the act, and

(ii) Is entitled to a 5-year period of exclusivity under section 505(c)(3)(D)(ii) and (j)(4)(D)(ii) of the act and § 314.108(b)(2), unless the 5-year exclusivity period has elapsed or unless 4 years of the 5-year period have elapsed and the application or abbreviated application contains a certification of patent invalidity or noninfringement described in § 314.50(i)(1)(i)(A)(4) or § 314.94(a)(12)(i)(A)(4).

(f)(1) Within 180 days after the date of filing, plus the period of time the review period was extended (if any), FDA will either:

(i) Approve the application; or

(ii) Issue a notice of opportunity for a hearing if the applicant asked FDA to provide it an opportunity for a hearing on an application in re-

sponse to a complete response letter.

(2) Within 180 days after the date of receipt, plus the period of time the review clock was extended (if any), FDA will either approve or disapprove the abbreviated new drug application. If FDA disapproves the abbreviated new drug application, FDA will issue a notice of opportunity for hearing if the applicant asked FDA to provide it an opportunity for a hearing on an abbreviated new drug application in response to a complete response letter.

(3) This paragraph does not apply to applications or abbreviated applications that have been withdrawn from FDA review by the applicant.

[57 FR 17987, Apr. 28, 1992; 57 FR 29353, July 1, 1992, as amended at 59 FR 50366, Oct. 3, 1994; 62 FR 40599, July 29, 1997; 64 FR 402, Jan. 5, 1999; 73 FR 39609, July 10, 2008]

§ 314.102   Communications between FDA and applicants.

(a) General principles. During the course of reviewing an application or an abbreviated application, FDA shall communicate with applicants about scientific, medical, and procedural issues that arise during the review process. Such communication may take the form of telephone conversations, letters, or meetings, whichever is most appropriate to discuss the particular issue at hand. Communications shall be appropriately documented in the application in accordance with § 10.65 of this chapter. Further details on the procedures for communication between FDA and applicants are contained in a staff manual guide that is publicly available.

(b) Notification of easily correctable deficiencies. FDA reviewers shall make every reasonable effort to communicate promptly to applicants easily correctable deficiencies found in an application or an abbreviated application when those deficiencies are discovered, particularly deficiencies concerning chemistry, manufacturing, and controls issues. The agency will also inform applicants promptly of its need for more data or information or for technical changes in the application or the abbreviated application needed to facilitate the agency's review. This early communication is intended to permit applicants to correct such readily identified deficiencies relatively early in the review process and to submit an amendment before the review period has elapsed. Such early communication would not ordinarily apply to major scientific issues, which require consideration of the entire pending application or abbreviated application by agency managers as well as reviewing staff. Instead, major scientific issues will ordinarily be addressed in a complete response letter.

(c) Ninety-day conference. Approximately 90 days after the agency receives the application, FDA will provide applicants with an opportunity to meet with agency reviewing officials. The purpose of the meeting will be to inform applicants of the general progress and status of their applications, and to advise applicants of deficiencies that have been identified by that time and that have not already been communicated. This meeting will be available on applications for all new chemical entities and major new indications of marketed drugs. Such meetings will be held at the applicant's option, and may be held by telephone if mutually agreed upon. Such meetings would not ordinarily be held on abbreviated applications because they are not submitted for new chemical entities or new indications.

(d) End-of-review conference. At the conclusion of FDA's review of an NDA as designated by the issuance of a complete response letter, FDA will provide the applicant with an opportunity to meet with agency reviewing officials. The purpose of the meeting will be to discuss what further steps need to be taken by the applicant before the application can be approved. Requests for such meetings must be directed to the director of the division responsible for reviewing the application.

(e) Other meetings. Other meetings between FDA and applicants may be held, with advance notice, to discuss scientific, medical, and other issues that arise during the review process. Requests for meetings shall be directed to the director of the division responsible for reviewing the application or abbreviated application. FDA will make every attempt to grant requests for meetings that involve important issues and that can be scheduled at mutually convenient times. However, "drop-in" visits (i.e., an unannounced and unscheduled visit by a company representative) are discouraged except for urgent matters, such as to discuss an important new safety issue.

[57 FR 17988, Apr. 28, 1992; 57 FR 29353, July 1, 1992, as amended at 73 FR 39609, July 10, 2008]

§ 314.103   Dispute resolution.

(a) General. FDA is committed to resolving differences between applicants and FDA reviewing divisions with respect to technical requirements for applications or abbreviated applications as quickly and amicably as possible through the cooperative exchange of information and views.

(b) Administrative and procedural issues. When administrative or procedural disputes arise, the applicant should first attempt to resolve the matter with the division responsible for reviewing the application or abbreviated application, beginning with the consumer safety officer assigned to the application or abbreviated application. If resolution is not achieved, the applicant may raise the matter with the person designated as ombudsman, whose function shall be to investigate what has happened and to facilitate a timely and equitable resolution. Appropriate issues to raise with the ombudsman include resolving difficulties in scheduling meetings, obtaining timely replies to inquiries, and obtaining timely completion of pending reviews. Further details on this procedure are contained in a staff manual guide that is publicly available under FDA's public information regulations in part 20.

(c) Scientific and medical disputes. (1) Because major scientific issues are ordinarily communicated to applicants in a complete response letter pursuant to § 314.110, the "end-of-review conference" described in § 314.102(d) will provide a timely forum for discussing and resolving, if possible, scientific and medical issues on which the applicant disagrees with the agency. In addition, the "ninety-day conference" described in § 314.102(c) will provide a timely forum for discussing and resolving, if possible, issues identified by that date.

(2) When scientific or medical disputes arise at other times during the review process, applicants should discuss the matter directly with the responsible reviewing officials. If necessary, applicants may request a meeting with the appropriate reviewing officials and management representatives in order to seek a resolution. Ordinarily, such meetings would be held first with the Division Director, then with the Office Director, and finally with the Center Director if the matter is still unresolved. Requests for such meetings shall be directed to the director of the division responsible for reviewing the application or abrreviated application. FDA will make every attempt to grant requests for meetings that involve important issues and that can be scheduled at mutually convenient times.

(3) In requesting a meeting designed to resolve a scientific or medical dispute, applicants may suggest that FDA seek the advice of outside experts, in which case FDA may, in its discretion, invite to the meeting one or more of its advisory committee members or other consultants, as designated by the agency. Applicants may also bring their own consultants. For major scientific and medical policy issues not resolved by informal meetings, FDA may refer the matter to one of its standing advisory committees for its consideration and recommendations.

[50 FR 7493, Feb. 22, 1985; 50 FR 14212, Apr. 11, 1985, as amended at 57 FR 17989, Apr. 28, 1992; 73 FR 39609, July 10, 2008]

§ 314.104   Drugs with potential for abuse.

The Food and Drug Administration will inform the Drug Enforcement Administration under section 201(f) of the Controlled Substances Act (21 U.S.C. 801) when an application or abbreviated application is submitted for a drug that appears to have an abuse potential.

[57 FR 17989, Apr. 28, 1992]

§ 314.105   Approval of an application and an abbreviated application.

(a) The Food and Drug Administration will approve an application and send the applicant an approval letter if none of the reasons in § 314.125 for refusing to approve the application applies. An approval becomes effective on the date of the issuance of the approval letter, except with regard to an approval under section 505(b)(2) of the act with a delayed effective date. An approval with a delayed effective date is tentative and does not become final until the effective date. A new drug product or antibiotic approved under this paragraph may not be marketed until an approval is effective.

(b) FDA will approve an application and issue the applicant an approval letter on the basis of draft labeling if the only deficiencies in the application concern editorial or similar minor deficiencies in the draft labeling. Such approval will be conditioned upon the applicant incorporating the specified labeling changes exactly as directed, and upon the applicant submitting to FDA a copy of the final printed labeling prior to marketing.

(c) FDA will approve an application after it determines that the drug meets the statutory standards for safety and effectiveness, manufacturing and controls, and labeling, and an abbreviated application after it determines that the drug meets the statutory standards for manufacturing and controls, labeling, and, where applicable, bioequivalence. While the statutory standards apply to all drugs, the many kinds of drugs that are subject to the statutory standards and the wide range of uses for those drugs demand flexibility in applying the standards. Thus FDA is required to exercise its scientific judgment to determine the kind and quantity of data and information an applicant is required to provide for a particular drug to meet the statutory standards. FDA makes its views on drug products and classes of drugs available through guidance documents, recommendations, and other statements of policy.

(d) FDA will approve an abbreviated new drug application and send the applicant an approval letter if none of the reasons in § 314.127 for refusing to approve the abbreviated new drug application applies. The approval becomes effective on the date of the issuance of the agency's approval letter unless the approval letter provides for a delayed effective date. An approval with a delayed effective date is tentative and does not become final until the effective date. A new drug product approved under this paragraph may not be introduced or delivered for introduction into interstate commerce until approval of the abbreviated new drug application is effective. Ordinarily, the effective date of approval will be stated in the approval letter.

[57 FR 17989, Apr. 28, 1992, as amended at 64 FR 402, Jan. 5, 1999; 65 FR 56479, Sept. 19, 2000; 73 FR 39609, July 10, 2008]

§ 314.106   Foreign data.

(a) General. The acceptance of foreign data in an application generally is governed by § 312.120 of this chapter.

(b) As sole basis for marketing approval. An application based solely on foreign clinical data meeting U.S. criteria for marketing approval may be approved if: (1) The foreign data are applicable to the U.S. population and U.S. medical practice; (2) the studies have been performed by clinical investigators of recognized competence; and (3) the data may be considered valid without the need for an on-site inspection by FDA or, if FDA considers such an inspection to

be necessary, FDA is able to validate the data through an on-site inspection or other appropriate means. Failure of an application to meet any of these criteria will result in the application not being approvable based on the foreign data alone. FDA will apply this policy in a flexible manner according to the nature of the drug and the data being considered.

(c) Consultation between FDA and applicants. Applicants are encouraged to meet with agency officials in a "presubmission" meeting when approval based solely on foreign data will be sought.

[50 FR 7493, Feb. 22, 1985, as amended at 55 FR 11580, Mar. 29, 1990]

§ 314.107   Effective date of approval of a 505(b)(2) application or abbreviated new drug application under section 505(j) of the act.

(a) General. A drug product may be introduced or delivered for introduction into interstate commerce when approval of the application or abbreviated application for the drug product becomes effective. Except as provided in this section, approval of an application or abbreviated application for a drug product becomes effective on the date FDA issues an approval letter under § 314.105 for the application or abbreviated application.

(b) Effect of patent on the listed drug. If approval of an abbreviated new drug application submitted under section 505(j) of the act or of a 505(b)(2) application is granted, that approval will become effective in accordance with the following:

(1) Date of approval letter. Except as provided in paragraphs (b)(3), (b)(4), and (c) of this section, approval will become effective on the date FDA issues an approval letter under § 314.105 if the applicant certifies under § 314.50(i) or § 314.94(a)(12) that:

(i) There are no relevant patents; or

(ii) The applicant is aware of a relevant patent but the patent information required under section 505 (b) or (c) of the act has not been submitted to FDA; or

(iii) The relevant patent has expired; or

(iv) The relevant patent is invalid, unenforceable, or will not be infringed.

(2) Patent expiration. If the applicant certifies under § 314.50(i) or § 314.94(a)(12) that the relevant patent will expire on a specified date, approval will become effective on the specified date.

(3) Disposition of patent litigation. (i)(A) Except as provided in paragraphs (b)(3)(ii), (b)(3)(iii), and (b)(3)(iv) of this section, if the applicant certifies under § 314.50(i) or § 314.94(a)(12) that the relevant patent is invalid, unenforceable, or will not be infringed, and the patent owner or its representative or the exclusive patent licensee brings suit for patent infringement within 45 days of receipt by the patent owner of the notice of certification from the applicant under § 314.52 or § 314.95, approval may be made effective 30 months after the date of the receipt of the notice of certification by the patent owner or by the exclusive licensee (or their representatives) unless the court has extended or reduced the period because of a failure of either the plaintiff or defendant to cooperate reasonably in expediting the action; or

(B) If the patented drug product qualifies for 5 years of exclusive marketing under § 314.108(b)(2) and the patent owner or its representative or the exclusive patent licensee brings suit for patent infringement during the 1-year period beginning 4 years after the date the patented drug was approved and within 45 days of receipt by the patent owner of the notice of certification, the approval may be made effective at the expiration of the 71/2 years from the date of approval of the application for the patented drug product.

(ii) If before the expiration of the 30-month pe-

riod, or 71/2 years where applicable, the court issues a final order that the patent is invalid, unenforceable, or not infringed, approval may be made effective on the date the court enters judgment;

(iii) If before the expiration of the 30-month period, or 71/2 years where applicable, the court issues a final order or judgment that the patent has been infringed, approval may be made effective on the date the court determines that the patent will expire or otherwise orders; or

(iv) If before the expiration of the 30-month period, or 71/2 years where applicable, the court grants a preliminary injunction prohibiting the applicant from engaging in the commercial manufacture or sale of the drug product until the court decides the issues of patent validity and infringement, and if the court later decides that the patent is invalid, unenforceable, or not infringed, approval may be made effective on the date the court enters a final order or judgment that the patent is invalid, unenforceable, or not infringed.

(v) FDA will issue a tentative approval letter when tentative approval is appropriate in accordance with paragraph (b)(3) of this section. In order for an approval to be made effective under paragraph (b)(3) of this section, the applicant must receive an approval letter from the agency indicating that the application has received final approval. Tentative approval of an application does not constitute "approval" of an application and cannot, absent a final approval letter from the agency, result in an effective approval under paragraph (b)(3) of this section.

(4) Multiple certifications. If the applicant has submitted certifications under § 314.50(i) or § 314.94(a)(12) for more than one patent, the date of approval will be calculated for each certification, and the approval will become effective on the last applicable date.

(c) Subsequent abbreviated new drug application submission. (1) If an abbreviated new drug application contains a certification that a relevant patent is invalid, unenforceable, or will not be infringed and the application is for a generic copy of the same listed drug for which one or more substantially complete abbreviated new drug applications were previously submitted containing a certification that the same patent was invalid, unenforceable, or would not be infringed, approval of the subsequent abbreviated new drug application will be made effective no sooner than 180 days from whichever of the following dates is earlier:

(i) The date the applicant submitting the first application first commences commercial marketing of its drug product; or

(ii) The date of a decision of the court holding the relevant patent invalid, unenforceable, or not infringed.

(2) For purposes of paragraph (c)(1) of this section, the "applicant submitting the first application" is the applicant that submits an application that is both substantially complete and contains a certification that the patent was invalid, unenforceable, or not infringed prior to the submission of any other application for the same listed drug that is both substantially complete and contains the same certification. A "substantially complete" application must contain the results of any required bioequivalence studies, or, if applicable, a request for a waiver of such studies.

(3) For purposes of paragraph (c)(1) of this section, if FDA concludes that the applicant submitting the first application is not actively pursuing approval of its abbreviated application, FDA will make the approval of subsequent abbreviated applications immediately effective if they are otherwise eligible for an immediately effective approval.

(4) For purposes of paragraph (c)(1)(i) of this section, the applicant submitting the first application shall notify FDA of the date that it commences commercial marketing of its drug product. Commercial marketing commences

with the first date of introduction or delivery for introduction into interstate commerce outside the control of the manufacturer of a drug product, except for investigational use under part 312 of this chapter, but does not include transfer of the drug product for reasons other than sale within the control of the manufacturer or application holder. If an applicant does not promptly notify FDA of such date, the effective date of approval shall be deemed to be the date of the commencement of first commercial marketing.

(d) Delay due to exclusivity. The agency will also delay the effective date of the approval of an abbreviated new drug application under section 505(j) of the act or a 505(b)(2) application if delay is required by the exclusivity provisions in § 314.108. When the effective date of an application is delayed under both this section and § 314.108, the effective date will be the later of the 2 days specified under this section and § 314.108.

(e) Notification of court actions. The applicant shall submit a copy of the entry of the order or judgment to the Office of Generic Drugs (HFD-600), or to the appropriate division in the Office of New Drugs within 10 working days of a final judgment.

(f) Computation of 45-day time clock. (1) The 45-day clock described in paragraph (b)(3) of this section begins on the day after the date of receipt of the applicant's notice of certification by the patent owner or its representative, and by the approved application holder. When the 45th day falls on Saturday, Sunday, or a Federal holiday, the 45th day will be the next day that is not a Saturday, Sunday, or a Federal holiday.

(2) The abbreviated new drug applicant or the 505(b)(2) applicant shall notify FDA immediately of the filing of any legal action filed within 45 days of receipt of the notice of certification. If the applicant submitting the abbreviated new drug application or the 505(b)(2) application or patent owner or its representative does

not notify FDA in writing before the expiration of the 45-day time period or the completion of the agency's review of the application, whichever occurs later, that a legal action for patent infringement was filed within 45 days of receipt of the notice of certification, approval of the abbreviated new drug application or the 505(b)(2) application will be made effective immediately upon expiration of the 45 days or upon completion of the agency's review and approval of the application, whichever is later. The notification to FDA of the legal action shall include:

(i) The abbreviated new drug application or 505(b)(2) application number.

(ii) The name of the abbreviated new drug or 505(b)(2) application applicant.

(iii) The established name of the drug product or, if no established name exists, the name(s) of the active ingredient(s), the drug product's strength, and dosage form.

(iv) A certification that an action for patent infringement identified by number, has been filed in an appropriate court on a specified date.

The applicant of an abbreviated new drug application shall send the notification to FDA's Office of Generic Drugs (HFD-600). A 505(b)(2) applicant shall send the notification to the appropriate division in the Office of New Drugs reviewing the application. A patent owner or its representative may also notify FDA of the filing of any legal action for patent infringement. The notice should contain the information and be sent to the offices or divisions described in this paragraph.

(3) If the patent owner or approved application holder who is an exclusive patent licensee waives its opportunity to file a legal action for patent infringement within 45 days of a receipt of the notice of certification and the patent owner or approved application holder who is an exclusive patent licensee submits to FDA a valid waiver before the 45 days elapse, approval of the abbreviated new drug application or the

505(b)(2) application will be made effective upon completion of the agency's review and approval of the application. FDA will only accept a waiver in the following form:

(Name of patent owner or exclusive patent licensee) has received notice from (name of applicant) under (section 505(b)(3) or 505(j)(2)(B) of the act) and does not intend to file an action for patent infringement against (name of applicant) concerning the drug (name of drug) before (date on which 45 days elapses. (Name of patent owner or exclusive patent licensee) waives the opportunity provided by (section 505(c)(3)(C) or 505(j)(B)(iii) of the act) and does not object to FDA's approval of (name of applicant)'s (505(b)(2) or abbreviated new drug application) for (name of drug) with an immediate effective date on or after the date of this letter.

[59 FR 50367, Oct. 3, 1994, as amended at 63 FR 59712, Nov. 5, 1998; 65 FR 43235, July 13, 2000; 73 FR 39609, July 10, 2008; 74 FR 9766, Mar. 6, 2009]

§ 314.108   New drug product exclusivity.

(a) Definitions. The following definitions of terms apply to this section:

Active moiety means the molecule or ion, excluding those appended portions of the molecule that cause the drug to be an ester, salt (including a salt with hydrogen or coordination bonds), or other noncovalent derivative (such as a complex, chelate, or clathrate) of the molecule, responsible for the physiological or pharmacological action of the drug substance.

Approved under section 505(b) means an application submitted under section 505(b) and approved on or after October 10, 1962, or an application that was "deemed approved" under section 107(c)(2) of Pub. L. 87-781.

Clinical investigation means any experiment other than a bioavailability study in which a drug is administered or dispensed to, or used on, human subjects.

Conducted or sponsored by the applicant with regard to an investigation means that before or during the investigation, the applicant was named in Form FDA-1571 filed with FDA as the sponsor of the investigational new drug application under which the investigation was conducted, or the applicant or the applicant's predecessor in interest, provided substantial support for the investigation. To demonstrate "substantial support," an applicant must either provide a certified statement from a certified public accountant that the applicant provided 50 percent or more of the cost of conducting the study or provide an explanation why FDA should consider the applicant to have conducted or sponsored the study if the applicant's financial contribution to the study is less than 50 percent or the applicant did not sponsor the investigational new drug. A predecessor in interest is an entity, e.g., a corporation, that the applicant has taken over, merged with, or purchased, or from which the applicant has purchased all rights to the drug. Purchase of nonexclusive rights to a clinical investigation after it is completed is not sufficient to satisfy this definition.

Date of approval means the date on the letter from FDA stating that the new drug application is approved, whether or not final printed labeling or other materials must yet be submitted as long as approval of such labeling or materials is not expressly required. "Date of approval" refers only to a final approval and not to a tentative approval that may become effective at a later date.

Essential to approval means, with regard to an investigation, that there are no other data available that could support approval of the application.

FDA means the Food and Drug Administration.

New chemical entity means a drug that contains no active moiety that has been approved by FDA in any other application submitted under section 505(b) of the act.

New clinical investigation means an investigation in humans the results of which have not been relied on by FDA to demonstrate substantial evidence of effectiveness of a previously approved drug product for any indication or of safety for a new patient population and do not duplicate the results of another investigation that was relied on by the agency to demonstrate the effectiveness or safety in a new patient population of a previously approved drug product. For purposes of this section, data from a clinical investigation previously submitted for use in the comprehensive evaluation of the safety of a drug product but not to support the effectiveness of the drug product would be considered new.

(b) Submission of and effective date of approval of an abbreviated new drug application submitted under section 505(j) of the act or a 505(b)(2) application. (1) [Reserved]

(2) If a drug product that contains a new chemical entity was approved after September 24, 1984, in an application submitted under section 505(b) of the act, no person may submit a 505(b)(2) application or abbreviated new drug application under section 505(j) of the act for a drug product that contains the same active moiety as in the new chemical entity for a period of 5 years from the date of approval of the first approved new drug application, except that the 505(b)(2) application or abbreviated application may be submitted after 4 years if it contains a certification of patent invalidity or noninfringement described in § 314.50(i)(1)(i)(A)(4) or § 314.94(a)(12)(i)(A)(4).

(3) The approval of a 505(b)(2) application or abbreviated application described in paragraph (b)(2) of this section will become effective as provided in § 314.107(b)(1) or (b)(2), unless the owner of a patent that claims the drug, the patent owner's representative, or exclusive licensee brings suit for patent infringement against the applicant during the 1-year period beginning 48 months after the date of approval of the new

drug application for the new chemical entity and within 45 days after receipt of the notice described at § 314.52 or § 314.95, in which case, approval of the 505(b)(2) application or abbreviated application will be made effective as provided in § 314.107(b)(3).

(4) If an application:

(i) Was submitted under section 505(b) of the act;

(ii) Was approved after September 24, 1984;

(iii) Was for a drug product that contains an active moiety that has been previously approved in another application under section 505(b) of the act; and

(iv) Contained reports of new clinical investigations (other than bioavailability studies) conducted or sponsored by the applicant that were essential to approval of the application, the agency will not make effective for a period of 3 years after the date of approval of the application the approval of a 505(b)(2) application or an abbreviated new drug application for the conditions of approval of the original application, or an abbreviated new drug application submitted pursuant to an approved petition under section 505(j)(2)(C) of the act that relies on the information supporting the conditions of approval of an original new drug application.

(5) If a supplemental application:

(i) Was approved after September 24, 1984; and

(ii) Contained reports of new clinical investigations (other than bioavailability studies) that were conducted or sponsored by the applicant that were essential to approval of the supplemental application, the agency will not make effective for a period of 3 years after the date of approval of the supplemental application the approval of a 505(b)(2) application or an abbreviated new drug application for a change, or an abbreviated new drug application submitted pursuant to an approved petition under section 505(j)(2)(C) of the act that relies on the infor-

mation supporting a change approved in the supplemental new drug application.

[59 FR 50368, Oct. 3, 1994]

§ 314.110   Complete response letter to the applicant.

(a) Complete response letter. FDA will send the applicant a complete response letter if the agency determines that we will not approve the application or abbreviated application in its present form for one or more of the reasons given in § 314.125 or § 314.127, respectively.

(1) Description of specific deficiencies. A complete response letter will describe all of the specific deficiencies that the agency has identified in an application or abbreviated application, except as stated in paragraph (a)(3) of this section.

(2) Complete review of data. A complete response letter reflects FDA's complete review of the data submitted in an original application or abbreviated application (or, where appropriate, a resubmission) and any amendments that the agency has reviewed. The complete response letter will identify any amendments that the agency has not yet reviewed.

(3) Inadequate data. If FDA determines, after an application is filed or an abbreviated application is received, that the data submitted are inadequate to support approval, the agency might issue a complete response letter without first conducting required inspections and/or reviewing proposed product labeling.

(4) Recommendation of actions for approval. When possible, a complete response letter will recommend actions that the applicant might take to place the application or abbreviated application in condition for approval.

(b) Applicant actions. After receiving a complete response letter, the applicant must take one of following actions:

(1) Resubmission. Resubmit the application or abbreviated application, addressing all de-

ficiencies identified in the complete response letter.

(i) A resubmission of an application or efficacy supplement that FDA classifies as a Class 1 resubmission constitutes an agreement by the applicant to start a new 2-month review cycle beginning on the date FDA receives the resubmission.

(ii) A resubmission of an application or efficacy supplement that FDA classifies as a Class 2 resubmission constitutes an agreement by the applicant to start a new 6-month review cycle beginning on the date FDA receives the resubmission.

(iii) A resubmission of an NDA supplement other than an efficacy supplement constitutes an agreement by the applicant to start a new review cycle the same length as the initial review cycle for the supplement (excluding any extension due to a major amendment of the initial supplement), beginning on the date FDA receives the resubmission.

(iv) A major resubmission of an abbreviated application constitutes an agreement by the applicant to start a new 6-month review cycle beginning on the date FDA receives the resubmission.

(v) A minor resubmission of an abbreviated application constitutes an agreement by the applicant to start a new review cycle beginning on the date FDA receives the resubmission.

(2) Withdrawal. Withdraw the application or abbreviated application. A decision to withdraw an application or abbreviated application is without prejudice to a subsequent submission.

(3) Request opportunity for hearing. Ask the agency to provide the applicant an opportunity for a hearing on the question of whether there are grounds for denying approval of the application or abbreviated application under section 505(d) or (j)(4) of the act, respectively. The applicant must submit the request to the Associate Director for Policy, Center for Drug Evaluation and Research, Food and Drug Administration, 10903 New Hampshire Ave., Silver Spring, MD 20993. Within 60 days of the date of the request for an opportunity for a hearing, or within a different time period to which FDA and the applicant agree, the agency will either approve the application or abbreviated application under § 314.105, or refuse to approve the application under § 314.125 or abbreviated application under § 314.127 and give the applicant written notice of an opportunity for a hearing under § 314.200 and section 505(c)(1)(B) or (j)(5)(c) of the act on the question of whether there are grounds for denying approval of the application or abbreviated application under section 505(d) or (j)(4) of the act, respectively.

(c) Failure to take action. (1) An applicant agrees to extend the review period under section 505(c)(1) or (j)(5)(A) of the act until it takes any of the actions listed in paragraph (b) of this section. For an application or abbreviated application, FDA may consider an applicant's failure to take any of such actions within 1 year after issuance of a complete response letter to be a request by the applicant to withdraw the application, unless the applicant has requested an extension of time in which to resubmit the application. FDA will grant any reasonable request for such an extension. FDA may consider an applicant's failure to resubmit the application within the extended time period or to request an additional extension to be a request by the applicant to withdraw the application.

(2) If FDA considers an applicant's failure to take action in accordance with paragraph (c)(1) of this section to be a request to withdraw the application, the agency will notify the applicant in writing. The applicant will have 30 days from the date of the notification to explain why the application should not be withdrawn and to request an extension of time in which to resubmit the application. FDA will grant any reasonable request for an extension. If the applicant does not respond to the notification within 30 days, the application will be deemed to be withdrawn.

[73 FR 39609, July 10, 2008]

§ 314.120   [Reserved]

§ 314.122   Submitting an abbreviated application for, or a 505(j)(2)(C) petition that relies on, a listed drug that is no longer marketed.

(a) An abbreviated new drug application that refers to, or a petition under section 505(j)(2)(C) of the act and § 314.93 that relies on, a listed drug that has been voluntarily withdrawn from sale in the United States must be accompanied by a petition seeking a determination whether the listed drug was withdrawn for safety or effectiveness reasons. The petition must be submitted under §§ 10.25(a) and 10.30 of this chapter and must contain all evidence available to the petitioner concerning the reasons for the withdrawal from sale.

(b) When a petition described in paragraph (a) of this section is submitted, the agency will consider the evidence in the petition and any other evidence before the agency, and determine whether the listed drug is withdrawn from sale for safety or effectiveness reasons, in accordance with the procedures in § 314.161.

(c) An abbreviated new drug application described in paragraph (a) of this section will be disapproved, under § 314.127(a)(11), and a 505(j)(2)(C) petition described in paragraph (a) of this section will be disapproved, under § 314.93(e)(1)(iv), unless the agency determines that the withdrawal of the listed drug was not for safety or effectiveness reasons.

(d) Certain drug products approved for safety and effectiveness that were no longer marketed on September 24, 1984, are not included in the list. Any person who wishes to obtain marketing approval for such a drug product under an abbreviated new drug application must petition FDA for a determination whether the drug product was withdrawn from the market for safety or effectiveness reasons and request that the list be amended to include the drug prod-uct. A person seeking such a determination shall use the petition procedures established in § 10.30 of this chapter. The petitioner shall include in the petition information to show that the drug product was approved for safety and effectiveness and all evidence available to the petitioner concerning the reason that marketing of the drug product ceased.

[57 FR 17990, Apr. 28, 1992; 57 FR 29353, July 1, 1992]

§ 314.125   Refusal to approve an application.

(a) The Food and Drug Administration will refuse to approve the application and for a new drug give the applicant written notice of an opportunity for a hearing under § 314.200 on the question of whether there are grounds for denying approval of the application under section 505(d) of the act, if:

(1) FDA sends the applicant a complete response letter under § 314.110;

(2) The applicant requests an opportunity for hearing for a new drug on the question of whether the application is approvable; and

(3) FDA finds that any of the reasons given in paragraph (b) of this section apply.

(b) FDA may refuse to approve an application for any of the following reasons:

(1) The methods to be used in, and the facilities and controls used for, the manufacture, processing, packing, or holding of the drug substance or the drug product are inadequate to preserve its identity, strength, quality, purity, stability, and bioavailability.

(2) The investigations required under section 505(b) of the act do not include adequate tests by all methods reasonably applicable to show whether or not the drug is safe for use under the conditions prescribed, recommended, or suggested in its proposed labeling.

(3) The results of the tests show that the drug is

unsafe for use under the conditions prescribed, recommended, or suggested in its proposed labeling or the results do not show that the drug product is safe for use under those conditions.

(4) There is insufficient information about the drug to determine whether the product is safe for use under the conditions prescribed, recommended, or suggested in its proposed labeling.

(5) There is a lack of substantial evidence consisting of adequate and well-controlled investigations, as defined in § 314.126, that the drug product will have the effect it purports or is represented to have under the conditions of use prescribed, recommended, or suggested in its proposed labeling.

(6) The proposed labeling is false or misleading in any particular.

(7) The application contains an untrue statement of a material fact.

(8) The drug product's proposed labeling does not comply with the requirements for labels and labeling in part 201.

(9) The application does not contain bioavailability or bioequivalence data required under part 320 of this chapter.

(10) A reason given in a letter refusing to file the application under § 314.101(d), if the deficiency is not corrected.

(11) The drug will be manufactured or processed in whole or in part in an establishment that is not registered and not exempt from registration under section 510 of the act and part 207.

(12) The applicant does not permit a properly authorized officer or employee of the Department of Health and Human Services an adequate opportunity to inspect the facilities, controls, and any records relevant to the application.

(13) The methods to be used in, and the facilities and controls used for, the manufacture, processing, packing, or holding of the drug substance or the drug product do not comply with the current good manufacturing practice regulations in parts 210 and 211.

(14) The application does not contain an explanation of the omission of a report of any investigation of the drug product sponsored by the applicant, or an explanation of the omission of other information about the drug pertinent to an evaluation of the application that is received or otherwise obtained by the applicant from any source.

(15) A nonclinical laboratory study that is described in the application and that is essential to show that the drug is safe for use under the conditions prescribed, recommended, or suggested in its proposed labeling was not conducted in compliance with the good laboratory practice regulations in part 58 of this chapter and no reason for the noncompliance is provided or, if it is, the differences between the practices used in conducting the study and the good laboratory practice regulations do not support the validity of the study.

(16) Any clinical investigation involving human subjects described in the application, subject to the institutional review board regulations in part 56 of this chapter or informed consent regulations in part 50 of this chapter, was not conducted in compliance with those regulations such that the rights or safety of human subjects were not adequately protected.

(17) The applicant or contract research organization that conducted a bioavailability or bioequivalence study described in § 320.38 or § 320.63 of this chapter that is contained in the application refuses to permit an inspection of facilities or records relevant to the study by a properly authorized officer or employee of the Department of Health and Human Services or refuses to submit reserve samples of the drug products used in the study when requested by FDA.

(18) For a new drug, the application failed to contain the patent information required by sec-

tion 505(b)(1) of the act.

(c) For drugs intended to treat life-threatening or severely-debilitating illnesses that are developed in accordance with §§ 312.80 through 312.88 of this chapter, the criteria contained in paragraphs (b) (3), (4), and (5) of this section shall be applied according to the considerations contained in § 312.84 of this chapter.

[50 FR 7493, Feb. 22, 1985, as amended at 53 FR 41524, Oct. 21, 1988; 57 FR 17991, Apr. 28, 1992; 58 FR 25926, Apr. 28, 1993; 64 FR 402, Jan. 5, 1999; 73 FR 39610, July 10, 2008; 74 FR 9766, Mar. 6, 2009]

§ 314.126   Adequate and well-controlled studies.

(a) The purpose of conducting clinical investigations of a drug is to distinguish the effect of a drug from other influences, such as spontaneous change in the course of the disease, placebo effect, or biased observation. The characteristics described in paragraph (b) of this section have been developed over a period of years and are recognized by the scientific community as the essentials of an adequate and well-controlled clinical investigation. The Food and Drug Administration considers these characteristics in determining whether an investigation is adequate and well-controlled for purposes of section 505 of the act. Reports of adequate and well-controlled investigations provide the primary basis for determining whether there is "substantial evidence" to support the claims of effectiveness for new drugs. Therefore, the study report should provide sufficient details of study design, conduct, and analysis to allow critical evaluation and a determination of whether the characteristics of an adequate and well-controlled study are present.

(b) An adequate and well-controlled study has the following characteristics:

(1) There is a clear statement of the objectives of the investigation and a summary of the proposed or actual methods of analysis in the pro-

tocol for the study and in the report of its results. In addition, the protocol should contain a description of the proposed methods of analysis, and the study report should contain a description of the methods of analysis ultimately used. If the protocol does not contain a description of the proposed methods of analysis, the study report should describe how the methods used were selected.

(2) The study uses a design that permits a valid comparison with a control to provide a quantitative assessment of drug effect. The protocol for the study and report of results should describe the study design precisely; for example, duration of treatment periods, whether treatments are parallel, sequential, or crossover, and whether the sample size is predetermined or based upon some interim analysis. Generally, the following types of control are recognized:

(i) Placebo concurrent control. The test drug is compared with an inactive preparation designed to resemble the test drug as far as possible. A placebo-controlled study may include additional treatment groups, such as an active treatment control or a dose-comparison control, and usually includes randomization and blinding of patients or investigators, or both.

(ii) Dose-comparison concurrent control. At least two doses of the drug are compared. A dose-comparison study may include additional treatment groups, such as placebo control or active control. Dose-comparison trials usually include randomization and blinding of patients or investigators, or both.

(iii) No treatment concurrent control. Where objective measurements of effectiveness are available and placebo effect is negligible, the test drug is compared with no treatment. No treatment concurrent control trials usually include randomization.

(iv) Active treatment concurrent control. The test drug is compared with known effective therapy; for example, where the condition treated is such that administration of placebo or no treatment would be contrary to the interest of the patient. An active treatment study may include additional treatment groups, however, such as a placebo control or a dose-comparison control. Active treatment trials usually include randomization and blinding of patients or investigators, or both. If the intent of the trial is to show similarity of the test and control drugs, the report of the study should assess the ability of the study to have detected a difference between treatments. Similarity of test drug and active control can mean either that both drugs were effective or that neither was effective. The analysis of the study should explain why the drugs should be considered effective in the study, for example, by reference to results in previous placebo-controlled studies of the active control drug.

(v) Historical control. The results of treatment with the test drug are compared with experience historically derived from the adequately documented natural history of the disease or condition, or from the results of active treatment, in comparable patients or populations. Because historical control populations usually cannot be as well assessed with respect to pertinent variables as can concurrent control populations, historical control designs are usually reserved for special circumstances. Examples include studies of diseases with high and predictable mortality (for example, certain malignancies) and studies in which the effect of the drug is self-evident (general anesthetics, drug metabolism).

(3) The method of selection of subjects provides adequate assurance that they have the disease or condition being studied, or evidence of susceptibility and exposure to the condition against which prophylaxis is directed.

(4) The method of assigning patients to treatment and control groups minimizes bias and is intended to assure comparability of the groups with respect to pertinent variables such as age,

sex, severity of disease, duration of disease, and use of drugs or therapy other than the test drug. The protocol for the study and the report of its results should describe how subjects were assigned to groups. Ordinarily, in a concurrently controlled study, assignment is by randomization, with or without stratification.

(5) Adequate measures are taken to minimize bias on the part of the subjects, observers, and analysts of the data. The protocol and report of the study should describe the procedures used to accomplish this, such as blinding.

(6) The methods of assessment of subjects' response are well-defined and reliable. The protocol for the study and the report of results should explain the variables measured, the methods of observation, and criteria used to assess response.

(7) There is an analysis of the results of the study adequate to assess the effects of the drug. The report of the study should describe the results and the analytic methods used to evaluate them, including any appropriate statistical methods. The analysis should assess, among other things, the comparability of test and control groups with respect to pertinent variables, and the effects of any interim data analyses performed.

(c) The Director of the Center for Drug Evaluation and Research may, on the Director's own initiative or on the petition of an interested person, waive in whole or in part any of the criteria in paragraph (b) of this section with respect to a specific clinical investigation, either prior to the investigation or in the evaluation of a completed study. A petition for a waiver is required to set forth clearly and concisely the specific criteria from which waiver is sought, why the criteria are not reasonably applicable to the particular clinical investigation, what alternative procedures, if any, are to be, or have been employed, and what results have been obtained. The petition is also required to state why the clinical investigations so conducted will yield, or have yielded, substantial evidence of effectiveness, notwithstanding nonconformance with the criteria for which waiver is requested.

(d) For an investigation to be considered adequate for approval of a new drug, it is required that the test drug be standardized as to identity, strength, quality, purity, and dosage form to give significance to the results of the investigation.

(e) Uncontrolled studies or partially controlled studies are not acceptable as the sole basis for the approval of claims of effectiveness. Such studies carefully conducted and documented, may provide corroborative support of well-controlled studies regarding efficacy and may yield valuable data regarding safety of the test drug. Such studies will be considered on their merits in the light of the principles listed here, with the exception of the requirement for the comparison of the treated subjects with controls. Isolated case reports, random experience, and reports lacking the details which permit scientific evaluation will not be considered.

[50 FR 7493, Feb. 22, 1985, as amended at 50 FR 21238, May 23, 1985; 55 FR 11580, Mar. 29, 1990; 64 FR 402, Jan. 5, 1999; 67 FR 9586, Mar. 4, 2002]

§ 314.127   Refusal to approve an abbreviated new drug application.

(a) FDA will refuse to approve an abbreviated application for a new drug under section 505(j) of the act for any of the following reasons:

(1) The methods used in, or the facilities and controls used for, the manufacture, processing, and packing of the drug product are inadequate to ensure and preserve its identity, strength, quality, and purity.

(2) Information submitted with the abbreviated new drug application is insufficient to show that each of the proposed conditions of use has been previously approved for the listed drug referred to in the application.

(3)(i) If the reference listed drug has only one active ingredient, information submitted with the abbreviated new drug application is insufficient to show that the active ingredient is the same as that of the reference listed drug;

(ii) If the reference listed drug has more than one active ingredient, information submitted with the abbreviated new drug application is insufficient to show that the active ingredients are the same as the active ingredients of the reference listed drug; or

(iii) If the reference listed drug has more than one active ingredient and if the abbreviated new drug application is for a drug product that has an active ingredient different from the reference listed drug:

(A) Information submitted with the abbreviated new drug application is insufficient to show:

(1) That the other active ingredients are the same as the active ingredients of the reference listed drug; or

(2) That the different active ingredient is an active ingredient of a listed drug or a drug that does not meet the requirements of section 201(p) of the act; or

(B) No petition to submit an abbreviated application for the drug product with the different active ingredient was approved under § 314.93.

(4)(i) If the abbreviated new drug application is for a drug product whose route of administration, dosage form, or strength purports to be the same as that of the listed drug referred to in the abbreviated new drug application, information submitted in the abbreviated new drug application is insufficient to show that the route of administration, dosage form, or strength is the same as that of the reference listed drug; or

(ii) If the abbreviated new drug application is for a drug product whose route of administration, dosage form, or strength is different from that of the listed drug referred to in the application, no petition to submit an abbreviated new drug application for the drug product with the different route of administration, dosage form, or strength was approved under § 314.93.

(5) If the abbreviated new drug application was submitted under the approval of a petition under § 314.93, the abbreviated new drug application did not contain the information required by FDA with respect to the active ingredient, route of administration, dosage form, or strength that is not the same as that of the reference listed drug.

(6)(i) Information submitted in the abbreviated new drug application is insufficient to show that the drug product is bioequivalent to the listed drug referred to in the abbreviated new drug application; or

(ii) If the abbreviated new drug application was submitted under a petition approved under § 314.93, information submitted in the abbreviated new drug application is insufficient to show that the active ingredients of the drug product are of the same pharmacological or therapeutic class as those of the reference listed drug and that the drug product can be expected to have the same therapeutic effect as the reference listed drug when administered to patients for each condition of use approved for the reference listed drug.

(7) Information submitted in the abbreviated new drug application is insufficient to show that the labeling proposed for the drug is the same as the labeling approved for the listed drug referred to in the abbreviated new drug application except for changes required because of differences approved in a petition under § 314.93 or because the drug product and the reference listed drug are produced or distributed by different manufacturers or because aspects of the listed drug's labeling are protected by patent, or by exclusivity, and such differences do not render the proposed drug product less safe or effective than the listed drug for all remaining, nonprotected conditions of use.

(8)(i) Information submitted in the abbreviated

new drug application of any other information available to FDA shows that:

(A) The inactive ingredients of the drug product are unsafe for use, as described in paragraph (a)(8)(ii) of this section, under the conditions prescribed, recommended, or suggested in the labeling proposed for the drug product; or

(B) The composition of the drug product is unsafe, as described in paragraph (a)(8)(ii) of this section, under the conditions prescribed, recommended, or suggested in the proposed labeling because of the type or quantity of inactive ingredients included or the manner in which the inactive ingredients are included.

(ii)(A) FDA will consider the inactive ingredients or composition of a drug product unsafe and refuse to approve an abbreviated new drug application under paragraph (a)(8)(i) of this section if, on the basis of information available to the agency, there is a reasonable basis to conclude that one or more of the inactive ingredients of the proposed drug or its composition raises serious questions of safety or efficacy. From its experience with reviewing inactive ingredients, and from other information available to it, FDA may identify changes in inactive ingredients or composition that may adversely affect a drug product's safety or efficacy. The inactive ingredients or composition of a proposed drug product will be considered to raise serious questions of safety or efficacy if the product incorporates one or more of these changes. Examples of the changes that may raise serious questions of safety or efficacy include, but are not limited to, the following:

(1) A change in an inactive ingredient so that the product does not comply with an official compendium.

(2) A change in composition to include an inactive ingredient that has not been previously approved in a drug product for human use by the same route of administration.

(3) A change in the composition of a parenteral

drug product to include an inactive ingredient that has not been previously approved in a parenteral drug product.

(4) A change in composition of a drug product for ophthalmic use to include an inactive ingredient that has not been previously approved in a drug for ophthalmic use.

(5) The use of a delivery or a modified release mechanism never before approved for the drug.

(6) A change in composition to include a significantly greater content of one or more inactive ingredients than previously used in the drug product.

(7) If the drug product is intended for topical administration, a change in the properties of the vehicle or base that might increase absorption of certain potentially toxic active ingredients thereby affecting the safety of the drug product, or a change in the lipophilic properties of a vehicle or base, e.g., a change from an oleaglnous to a water soluble vehicle or base.

(B) FDA will consider an inactive ingredient in, or the composition of, a drug product intended for parenteral use to be unsafe and will refuse to approve the abbreviated new drug application unless it contains the same inactive ingredients, other than preservatives, buffers, and antioxidants, in the same concentration as the listed drug, and, if it differs from the listed drug in a preservative, buffer, or antioxidant, the application contains sufficient information to demonstrate that the difference does not affect the safety or efficacy of the drug product.

(C) FDA will consider an inactive ingredient in, or the composition of, a drug product intended for ophthalmic or otic use unsafe and will refuse to approve the abbreviated new drug application unless it contains the same inactive ingredients, other than preservatives, buffers, substances to adjust tonicity, or thickening agents, in the same concentration as the listed drug, and if it differs from the listed drug in a preservative, buffer, substance to adjust tonicity, or thicken-

ing agent, the application contains sufficient information to demonstrate that the difference does not affect the safety or efficacy of the drug product and the labeling does not claim any therapeutic advantage over or difference from the listed drug.

(9) Approval of the listed drug referred to in the abbreviated new drug application has been withdrawn or suspended for grounds described in § 314.150(a) or FDA has published a notice of opportunity for hearing to withdraw approval of the reference listed drug under § 314.150(a).

(10) Approval of the listed drug referred to in the abbreviated new drug application has been withdrawn under § 314.151 or FDA has proposed to withdraw approval of the reference listed drug under § 314.151(a).

(11) FDA has determined that the reference listed drug has been withdrawn from sale for safety or effectiveness reasons under § 314.161, or the reference listed drug has been voluntarily withdrawn from sale and the agency has not determined whether the withdrawal is for safety or effectiveness reasons, or approval of the reference listed drug has been suspended under § 314.153, or the agency has issued an initial decision proposing to suspend the reference listed drug under § 314.153(a)(1).

(12) The abbreviated new drug application does not meet any other requirement under section 505(j)(2)(A) of the act.

(13) The abbreviated new drug application contains an untrue statement of material fact.

(b) FDA may refuse to approve an abbreviated application for a new drug if the applicant or contract research organization that conducted a bioavailability or bioequivalence study described in § 320.63 of this chapter that is contained in the abbreviated new drug application refuses to permit an inspection of facilities or records relevant to the study by a properly authorized officer of employee of the Department of Health and Human Services or refuses to submit reserve samples of the drug products used in the study when requested by FDA.

[57 FR 17991, Apr. 28, 1992; 57 FR 29353, July 1, 1992, as amended at 58 FR 25927, Apr. 28, 1993; 67 FR 77672, Dec. 19, 2002]

§ 314.150   Withdrawal of approval of an application or abbreviated application.

(a) The Food and Drug Administration will notify the applicant, and, if appropriate, all other persons who manufacture or distribute identical, related, or similar drug products as defined in §§ 310.6 and 314.151(a) of this chapter and for a new drug afford an opportunity for a hearing on a proposal to withdraw approval of the application or abbreviated new drug application under section 505(e) of the act and under the procedure in § 314.200, if any of the following apply:

(1) The Secretary of Health and Human Services has suspended the approval of the application or abbreviated application for a new drug on a finding that there is an imminent hazard to the public health. FDA will promptly afford the applicant an expedited hearing following summary suspension on a finding of imminent hazard to health.

(2) FDA finds:

(i) That clinical or other experience, tests, or other scientific data show that the drug is unsafe for use under the conditions of use upon the basis of which the application or abbreviated application was approved; or

(ii) That new evidence of clinical experience, not contained in the application or not available to FDA until after the application or abbreviated application was approved, or tests by new methods, or tests by methods not deemed reasonably applicable when the application or abbreviated application was approved, evaluated together with the evidence available when the application or abbreviated application was approved, reveal that the drug is not shown to be safe for use under the conditions of use upon

the basis of which the application or abbreviated application was approved; or

(iii) Upon the basis of new information before FDA with respect to the drug, evaluated together with the evidence available when the application or abbreviated application was approved, that there is a lack of substantial evidence from adequate and well-controlled investigations as defined in § 314.126, that the drug will have the effect it is purported or represented to have under the conditions of use prescribed, recommended, or suggested in its labeling; or

(iv) That the application or abbreviated application contains any untrue statement of a material fact; or

(v) That the patent information prescribed by section 505(c) of the act was not submitted within 30 days after the receipt of written notice from FDA specifying the failure to submit such information; or

(b) FDA may notify the applicant, and, if appropriate, all other persons who manufacture or distribute identical, related, or similar drug products as defined in § 310.6, and for a new drug afford an opportunity for a hearing on a proposal to withdraw approval of the application or abbreviated new drug application under section 505(e) of the act and under the procedure in § 314.200, if the agency finds:

(1) That the applicant has failed to establish a system for maintaining required records, or has repeatedly or deliberately failed to maintain required records or to make required reports under section 505(k) or 507(g) of the act and § 314.80, § 314.81, or § 314.98, or that the applicant has refused to permit access to, or copying or verification of, its records.

(2) That on the basis of new information before FDA, evaluated together with the evidence available when the application or abbreviated application was approved, the methods used in, or the facilities and controls used for, the manufacture, processing, and packing of the drug are

inadequate to ensure and preserve its identity, strength, quality, and purity and were not made adequate within a reasonable time after receipt of written notice from the agency.

(3) That on the basis of new information before FDA, evaluated together with the evidence available when the application or abbreviated application was approved, the labeling of the drug, based on a fair evaluation of all material facts, is false or misleading in any particular, and the labeling was not corrected by the applicant within a reasonable time after receipt of written notice from the agency.

(4) That the applicant has failed to comply with the notice requirements of section 510(j)(2) of the act.

(5) That the applicant has failed to submit bioavailability or bioequivalence data required under part 320 of this chapter.

(6) The application or abbreviated application does not contain an explanation of the omission of a report of any investigation of the drug product sponsored by the applicant, or an explanation of the omission of other information about the drug pertinent to an evaluation of the application or abbreviated application that is received or otherwise obtained by the applicant from any source.

(7) That any nonclinical laboratory study that is described in the application or abbreviated application and that is essential to show that the drug is safe for use under the conditions prescribed, recommended, or suggested in its labeling was not conducted in compliance with the good laboratory practice regulations in part 58 of this chapter and no reason for the noncompliance was provided or, if it was, the differences between the practices used in conducting the study and the good laboratory practice regulations do not support the validity of the study.

(8) Any clinical investigation involving human subjects described in the application or abbre-

viated application, subject to the institutional review board regulations in part 56 of this chapter or informed consent regulations in part 50 of this chapter, was not conducted in compliance with those regulations such that the rights or safety of human subjects were not adequately protected.

(9) That the applicant or contract research organization that conducted a bioavailability or bioequivalence study described in § 320.38 or § 320.63 of this chapter that is contained in the application or abbreviated application refuses to permit an inspection of facilities or records relevant to the study by a properly authorized officer or employee of the Department of Health and Human Services or refuses to submit reserve samples of the drug products used in the study when requested by FDA.

(10) That the labeling for the drug product that is the subject of the abbreviated new drug application is no longer consistent with that for the listed drug referred to in the abbreviated new drug application, except for differences approved in the abbreviated new drug application or those differences resulting from:

(i) A patent on the listed drug issued after approval of the abbreviated new drug application; or

(ii) Exclusivity accorded to the listed drug after approval of the abbreviated new drug application that do not render the drug product less safe or effective than the listed drug for any remaining, nonprotected condition(s) of use.

(c) FDA will withdraw approval of an application or abbreviated application if the applicant requests its withdrawal because the drug subject to the application or abbreviated application is no longer being marketed, provided none of the conditions listed in paragraphs (a) and (b) of this section applies to the drug. FDA will consider a written request for a withdrawal under this paragraph to be a waiver of an opportunity for hearing otherwise provided for in this section.

Withdrawal of approval of an application or abbreviated application under this paragraph is without prejudice to refiling.

(d) FDA may notify an applicant that it believes a potential problem associated with a drug is sufficiently serious that the drug should be removed from the market and may ask the applicant to waive the opportunity for hearing otherwise provided for under this section, to permit FDA to withdraw approval of the application or abbreviated application for the product, and to remove voluntarily the product from the market. If the applicant agrees, the agency will not make a finding under paragraph (b) of this section, but will withdraw approval of the application or abbreviated application in a notice published in the Federal Register that contains a brief summary of the agency's and the applicant's views of the reasons for withdrawal.

[57 FR 17993, Apr. 28, 1992, as amended at 58 FR 25927, Apr. 28, 1993; 64 FR 402, Jan. 5, 1999]

§ 314.151   Withdrawal of approval of an abbreviated new drug application under section 505(j)(5) of the act.

(a) Approval of an abbreviated new drug application approved under § 314.105(d) may be withdrawn when the agency withdraws approval, under § 314.150(a) or under this section, of the approved drug referred to in the abbreviated new drug application. If the agency proposed to withdraw approval of a listed drug under § 314.150(a), the holder of an approved application for the listed drug has a right to notice and opportunity for hearing. The published notice of opportunity for hearing will identify all drug products approved under § 314.105(d) whose applications are subject to withdrawal under this section if the listed drug is withdrawn, and will propose to withdraw such drugs. Holders of approved applications for the identified drug products will be provided notice and an opportunity to respond to the proposed withdrawal of their applications as described in paragraphs (b) and (c) of this section.

(b)(1) The published notice of opportunity for hearing on the withdrawal of the listed drug will serve as notice to holders of identified abbreviated new drug applications of the grounds for the proposed withdrawal.

(2) Holders of applications for drug products identified in the notice of opportunity for hearing may submit written comments on the notice of opportunity for hearing issued on the proposed withdrawal of the listed drug. If an abbreviated new drug application holder submits comments on the notice of opportunity for hearing and a hearing is granted, the abbreviated new drug application holder may participate in the hearing as a nonparty participant as provided for in § 12.89 of this chapter.

(3) Except as provided in paragraphs (c) and (d) of this section, the approval of an abbreviated new drug application for a drug product identified in the notice of opportunity for hearing on the withdrawal of a listed drug will be withdrawn when the agency has completed the withdrawal of approval of the listed drug.

(c)(1) If the holder of an application for a drug identified in the notice of opportunity for hearing has submitted timely comments but does not have an opportunity to participate in a hearing because a hearing is not requested or is settled, the submitted comments will be considered by the agency, which will issue an initial decision. The initial decision will respond to the comments, and contain the agency's decision whether there are grounds to withdraw approval of the listed drug and of the abbreviated new drug applications on which timely comments were submitted. The initial decision will be sent to each abbreviated new drug application holder that has submitted comments.

(2) Abbreviated new drug application holders to whom the initial decision was sent may, within 30 days of the issuance of the initial decision, submit written objections.

(3) The agency may, at its discretion, hold a lim-

ited oral hearing to resolve dispositive factual issues that cannot be resolved on the basis of written submissions.

(4) If there are no timely objections to the initial decision, it will become final at the expiration of 30 days.

(5) If timely objections are submitted, they will be reviewed and responded to in a final decision.

(6) The written comments received, the initial decision, the evidence relied on in the comments and in the initial decision, the objections to the initial decision, and, if a limited oral hearing has been held, the transcript of that hearing and any documents submitted therein, shall form the record upon which the agency shall make a final decision.

(7) Except as provided in paragraph (d) of this section, any abbreviated new drug application whose holder submitted comments on the notice of opportunity for hearing shall be withdrawn upon the issuance of a final decision concluding that the listed drug should be withdrawn for grounds as described in § 314.150(a). The final decision shall be in writing and shall constitute final agency action, reviewable in a judicial proceeding.

(8) Documents in the record will be publicly available in accordance with § 10.20(j) of this chapter. Documents available for examination or copying will be placed on public display in the Division of Dockets Management (HFA-305), Food and Drug Administration, room. 1-23, 12420 Parklawn Dr., Rockville, MD 20857, promptly upon receipt in that office.

(d) If the agency determines, based upon information submitted by the holder of an abbreviated new drug application, that the grounds for withdrawal of the listed drug are not applicable to a drug identified in the notice of opportunity for hearing, the final decision will state that the approval of the abbreviated new drug application for such drug is not withdrawn.

[57 FR 17994, Apr. 28, 1992]

§ 314.152   Notice of withdrawal of approval of an application or abbreviated application for a new drug.

If the Food and Drug Administration withdraws approval of an application or abbreviated application for a new drug, FDA will publish a notice in the Federal Register announcing the withdrawal of approval. If the application or abbreviated application was withdrawn for grounds described in § 314.150(a) or § 314.151, the notice will announce the removal of the drug from the list of approved drugs published under section 505(j)(6) of the act and shall satisfy the requirement of § 314.162(b).

[57 FR 17994, Apr. 28, 1992]

§ 314.153   Suspension of approval of an abbreviated new drug application.

(a) Suspension of approval. The approval of an abbreviated new drug application approved under § 314.105(d) shall be suspended for the period stated when:

(1) The Secretary of the Department of Health and Human Services, under the imminent hazard authority of section 505(e) of the act or the authority of this paragraph, suspends approval of a listed drug referred to in the abbreviated new drug application, for the period of the suspension;

(2) The agency, in the notice described in paragraph (b) of this section, or in any subsequent written notice given an abbreviated new drug application holder by the agency, concludes that the risk of continued marketing and use of the drug is inappropriate, pending completion of proceedings to withdraw or suspend approval under § 314.151 or paragraph (b) of this section; or

(3) The agency, under the procedures set forth in paragraph (b) of this section, issues a final decision stating the determination that the abbreviated application is suspended because

371

the listed drug on which the approval of the abbreviated new drug application depends has been withdrawn from sale for reasons of safety or effectiveness or has been suspended under paragraph (b) of this section. The suspension will take effect on the date stated in the decision and will remain in effect until the agency determines that the marketing of the drug has resumed or that the withdrawal is not for safety or effectiveness reasons.

(b) Procedures for suspension of abbreviated new drug applications when a listed drug is voluntarily withdrawn for safety or effectiveness reasons. (1) If a listed drug is voluntarily withdrawn from sale, and the agency determines that the withdrawal from sale was for reasons of safety or effectiveness, the agency will send each holder of an approved abbreviated new drug application that is subject to suspension as a result of this determination a copy of the agency's initial decision setting forth the reasons for the determination. The initial decision will also be placed on file with the Division of Dockets Management (HFA-305), Food and Drug Administration, room 1-23, 12420 Parklawn Dr., Rockville, MD 20857.

(2) Each abbreviated new drug application holder will have 30 days from the issuance of the initial decision to present, in writing, comments and information bearing on the initial decision. If no comments or information is received, the initial decision will become final at the expiration of 30 days.

(3) Comments and information received within 30 days of the issuance of the initial decision will be considered by the agency and responded to in a final decision.

(4) The agency may, in its discretion, hold a limited oral hearing to resolve dispositive factual issues that cannot be resolved on the basis of written submissions.

(5) If the final decision affirms the agency's initial decision that the listed drug was withdrawn

for reasons of safety or effectiveness, the decision will be published in the Federal Register in compliance with § 314.152, and will, except as provided in paragraph (b)(6) of this section, suspend approval of all abbreviated new drug applications identified under paragraph (b)(1) of this section and remove from the list the listed drug and any drug whose approval was suspended under this paragraph. The notice will satisfy the requirement of § 314.162(b). The agency's final decision and copies of materials on which it relies will also be filed with the Division of Dockets Management (address in paragraph (b)(1) of this section).

(6) If the agency determines in its final decision that the listed drug was withdrawn for reasons of safety or effectiveness but, based upon information submitted by the holder of an abbreviated new drug application, also determines that the reasons for the withdrawal of the listed drug are not relevant to the safety and effectiveness of the drug subject to such abbreviated new drug application, the final decision will state that the approval of such abbreviated new drug application is not suspended.

(7) Documents in the record will be publicly available in accordance with § 10.20(j) of this chapter. Documents available for examination or copying will be placed on public display in the Division of Dockets Management (address in paragraph (b)(1) of this section) promptly upon receipt in that office.

[57 FR 17995, Apr. 28, 1992]

§ 314.160 Approval of an application or abbreviated application for which approval was previously refused, suspended, or withdrawn.

Upon the Food and Drug Administration's own initiative or upon request of an applicant, FDA may, on the basis of new data, approve an application or abbreviated application which it had previously refused, suspended, or withdrawn approval. FDA will publish a notice in the Federal Register announcing the approval.

[57 FR 17995, Apr. 28, 1992]

§ 314.161   Determination of reasons for voluntary withdrawal of a listed drug.

(a) A determination whether a listed drug that has been voluntarily withdrawn from sale was withdrawn for safety or effectiveness reasons may be made by the agency at any time after the drug has been voluntarily withdrawn from sale, but must be made:

(1) Prior to approving an abbreviated new drug application that refers to the listed drug;

(2) Whenever a listed drug is voluntarily withdrawn from sale and abbreviated new drug applications that referred to the listed drug have been approved; and

(3) When a person petitions for such a determination under §§ 10.25(a) and 10.30 of this chapter.

(b) Any person may petition under §§ 10.25(a) and 10.30 of this chapter for a determination whether a listed drug has been voluntarily withdrawn for safety or effectiveness reasons. Any such petition must contain all evidence available to the petitioner concerning the reason that the drug is withdrawn from sale.

(c) If the agency determines that a listed drug is withdrawn from sale for safety or effectiveness reasons, the agency will, except as provided in paragraph (d) of this section, publish a notice of the determination in the Federal Register.

(d) If the agency determines under paragraph (a) of this section that a listed drug is withdrawn from sale for safety and effectiveness reasons and there are approved abbreviated new drug applications that are subject to suspension under section 505(j)(5) of the act, FDA will initiate a proceeding in accordance with § 314.153(b).

(e) A drug that the agency determines is withdrawn for safety or effectiveness reasons will be removed from the list, under § 314.162. The

drug may be relisted if the agency has evidence that marketing of the drug has resumed or that the withdrawal is not for safety or effectiveness reasons. A determination that the drug is not withdrawn for safety or effectiveness reasons may be made at any time after its removal from the list, upon the agency's initiative, or upon the submission of a petition under §§ 10.25(a) and 10.30 of this chapter. If the agency determines that the drug is not withdrawn for safety or effectiveness reasons, the agency shall publish a notice of this determination in the Federal Register. The notice will also announce that the drug is relisted, under § 314.162(c). The notice will also serve to reinstate approval of all suspended abbreviated new drug applications that referred to the listed drug.

[57 FR 17995, Apr. 28, 1992]

§ 314.162   Removal of a drug product from the list.

(a) FDA will remove a previously approved new drug product from the list for the period stated when:

(1) The agency withdraws or suspends approval of a new drug application or an abbreviated new drug application under § 314.150(a) or § 314.151 or under the imminent hazard authority of section 505(e) of the act, for the same period as the withdrawal or suspension of the application; or

(2) The agency, in accordance with the procedures in § 314.153(b) or § 314.161, issues a final decision stating that the listed drug was withdrawn from sale for safety or effectiveness reasons, or suspended under § 314.153(b), until the agency determines that the withdrawal from the market has ceased or is not for safety or effectiveness reasons.

(b) FDA will publish in the Federal Register a notice announcing the removal of a drug from the list.

(c) At the end of the period specified in paragraph (a)(1) or (a)(2) of this section, FDA will relist a drug that has been removed from the list. The agency will publish in the Federal Register a notice announcing the relisting of the drug.

[57 FR 17996, Apr. 28, 1992]

§ 314.170 Adulteration and misbranding of an approved drug.

All drugs, including those the Food and Drug Administration approves under section 505 of the act and this part, are subject to the adulteration and misbranding provisions in sections 501, 502, and 503 of the act. FDA is authorized to regulate approved new drugs by regulations issued through informal rulemaking under sections 501, 502, and 503 of the act.

[50 FR 7493, Feb. 22, 1985. Redesignated at 57 FR 17983, Apr. 28, 1992, and amended at 64 FR 402, Jan. 5, 1999]

Subpart E—Hearing Procedures for New Drugs

Source:

50 FR 7493, Feb. 22, 1985, unless otherwise noted. Redesignated at 57 FR 17983, Apr. 28, 1992.

§ 314.200 Notice of opportunity for hearing; notice of participation and request for hearing; grant or denial of hearing.

(a) Notice of opportunity for hearing. The Director of the Center for Drug Evaluation and Research, Food and Drug Administration, will give the applicant, and all other persons who manufacture or distribute identical, related, or similar drug products as defined in § 310.6 of this chapter, notice and an opportunity for a hearing on the Center's proposal to refuse to approve an application or to withdraw the approval of an application or abbreviated application under section 505(e) of the act. The notice will state the reasons for the action and the proposed grounds for the order.

(1) The notice may be general (that is, simply summarizing in a general way the information resulting in the notice) or specific (that is, either referring to specific requirements in the statute and regulations with which there is a lack of compliance, or providing a detailed description and analysis of the specific facts resulting in the notice).

(2) FDA will publish the notice in the Federal Register and will state that the applicant, and other persons subject to the notice under § 310.6, who wishes to participate in a hearing, has 30 days after the date of publication of the notice to file a written notice of participation and request for hearing. The applicant, or other persons subject to the notice under § 310.6, who fails to file a written notice of participation and request for hearing within 30 days, waives the opportunity for a hearing.

(3) It is the responsibility of every manufacturer and distributor of a drug product to review every notice of opportunity for a hearing published in the Federal Register to determine whether it covers any drug product that person manufactures or distributes. Any person may request an opinion of the applicability of a notice to a specific product that may be identical, related, or similar to a product listed in a notice by writing to the Division of New Drugs and Labeling Compliance, Office of Compliance, Center for Drug Evaluation and Research, Food and Drug Administration, 10903 New Hampshire Ave., Silver Spring, MD 20993-0002. A person shall request an opinion within 30 days of the date of publication of the notice to be eligible for an opportunity for a hearing under the notice. If a person requests an opinion, that person's time for filing an appearance and request for a hearing and supporting studies and analyses begins on the date the person receives the opinion from FDA.

(b) FDA will provide the notice of opportunity for a hearing to applicants and to other persons subject to the notice under § 310.6, as follows:

(1) To any person who has submitted an application or abbreviated application, by delivering

the notice in person or by sending it by registered or certified mail to the last address shown in the application or abbreviated application.

(2) To any person who has not submitted an application or abbreviated application but who is subject to the notice under § 310.6 of this chapter, by publication of the notice in the Federal Register.

(c)(1) Notice of participation and request for a hearing, and submission of studies and comments. The applicant, or any other person subject to the notice under § 310.6, who wishes to participate in a hearing, shall file with the Division of Dockets Management (HFA-305), Food and Drug Administration, 5630 Fishers Lane, rm. 1061, Rockville, MD 20852, (i) within 30 days after the date of the publication of the notice (or of the date of receipt of an opinion requested under paragraph (a)(3) of this section) a written notice of participation and request for a hearing and (ii) within 60 days after the date of publication of the notice, unless a different period of time is specified in the notice of opportunity for a hearing, the studies on which the person relies to justify a hearing as specified in paragraph (d) of this section. The applicant, or other person, may incorporate by reference the raw data underlying a study if the data were previously submitted to FDA as part of an application, abbreviated application, or other report.

(2) FDA will not consider data or analyses submitted after 60 days in determining whether a hearing is warranted unless they are derived from well-controlled studies begun before the date of the notice of opportunity for hearing and the results of the studies were not available within 60 days after the date of publication of the notice. Nevertheless, FDA may consider other studies on the basis of a showing by the person requesting a hearing of inadvertent omission and hardship. The person requesting a hearing shall list in the request for hearing all studies in progress, the results of which the person intends later to submit in support of the

request for a hearing. The person shall submit under paragraph (c)(1)(ii) of this section a copy of the complete protocol, a list of the participating investigators, and a brief status report of the studies.

(3) Any other interested person who is not subject to the notice of opportunity for a hearing may also submit comments on the proposal to withdraw approval of the application or abbreviated application. The comments are requested to be submitted within the time and under the conditions specified in this section.

(d) The person requesting a hearing is required to submit under paragraph (c)(1)(ii) of this section the studies (including all protocols and underlying raw data) on which the person relies to justify a hearing with respect to the drug product. Except, a person who requests a hearing on the refusal to approve an application is not required to submit additional studies and analyses if the studies upon which the person relies have been submitted in the application and in the format and containing the summaries required under § 314.50.

(1) If the grounds for FDA's proposed action concern the effectiveness of the drug, each request for hearing is required to be supported only by adequate and well-controlled clinical studies meeting all of the precise requirements of § 314.126 and, for combination drug products, § 300.50, or by other studies not meeting those requirements for which a waiver has been previously granted by FDA under § 314.126. Each person requesting a hearing shall submit all adequate and well-controlled clinical studies on the drug product, including any unfavorable analyses, views, or judgments with respect to the studies. No other data, information, or studies may be submitted.

(2) The submission is required to include a factual analysis of all the studies submitted. If the grounds for FDA's proposed action concern the effectiveness of the drug, the analysis is required to specify how each study accords, on

a point-by-point basis, with each criterion required for an adequate well-controlled clinical investigation established under § 314.126 and, if the product is a combination drug product, with each of the requirements for a combination drug established in § 300.50, or the study is required to be accompanied by an appropriate waiver previously granted by FDA. If a study concerns a drug or dosage form or condition of use or mode of administration other than the one in question, that fact is required to be clearly stated. Any study conducted on the final marketed form of the drug product is required to be clearly identified.

(3) Each person requesting a hearing shall submit an analysis of the data upon which the person relies, except that the required information relating either to safety or to effectiveness may be omitted if the notice of opportunity for hearing does not raise any issue with respect to that aspect of the drug; information on compliance with § 300.50 may be omitted if the drug product is not a combination drug product. A financial certification or disclosure statement or both as required by part 54 of this chapter must accompany all clinical data submitted. FDA can most efficiently consider submissions made in the following format.

I. Safety data.

A. Animal safety data.

1. Individual active components.

a. Controlled studies.

b. Partially controlled or uncontrolled studies.

2. Combinations of the individual active components.

a. Controlled studies.

b. Partially controlled or uncontrolled studies.

B. Human safety data.

1. Individual active components.

a. Controlled studies.

b. Partially controlled or uncontrolled studies.

c. Documented case reports.

d. Pertinent marketing experiences that may influence a determination about the safety of each individual active component.

2. Combinations of the individual active components.

a. Controlled studies.

b. Partially controlled or uncontrolled studies.

c. Documented case reports.

d. Pertinent marketing experiences that may influence a determination about the safety of each individual active component.

II. Effectiveness data.

A. Individual active components: Controlled studies, with an analysis showing clearly how each study satisfies, on a point-by-point basis, each of the criteria required by § 314.126.

B. Combinations of individual active components.

1. Controlled studies with an analysis showing clearly how each study satisfies on a point-by-point basis, each of the criteria required by § 314.126.

2. An analysis showing clearly how each requirement of § 300.50 has been satisfied.

III. A summary of the data and views setting forth the medical rationale and purpose for the drug and its ingredients and the scientific basis for the conclusion that the drug and its ingredients have been proven safe and/or effective for the intended use. If there is an absence of controlled studies in the material submitted or the requirements of any element of § 300.50 or § 314.126 have not been fully met, that fact is required to be stated clearly and a waiver obtained under § 314.126 is required to be submitted.

IV. A statement signed by the person responsible for such submission that it includes in full (or incorporates by reference as permitted in § 314.200(c)(2)) all studies and information specified in § 314.200(d).

(Warning: A willfully false statement is a criminal offense, 18 U.S.C. 1001.)

(e) Contentions that a drug product is not subject to the new drug requirements. A notice of opportunity for a hearing encompasses all issues relating to the legal status of each drug product subject to it, including identical, related, and similar drug products as defined in § 310.6. A notice of appearance and request for a hearing under paragraph (c)(1)(i) of this section is required to contain any contention that the product is not a new drug because it is generally recognized as safe and effective within the meaning of section 201(p) of the act, or because it is exempt from part or all of the new drug provisions of the act under the exemption for products marketed before June 25, 1938, contained in section 201(p) of the act or under section 107(c) of the Drug Amendments of 1962, or for any other reason. Each contention is required to be supported by a submission under paragraph (c)(1)(ii) of this section and the Commissioner of Food and Drugs will make an administrative determination on each contention. The failure of any person subject to a notice of opportunity for a hearing, including any person who manufactures or distributes an identical, related, or similar drug product as defined in § 310.6, to submit a notice of participation and request for hearing or to raise all such contentions constitutes a waiver of any contentions not raised.

(1) A contention that a drug product is generally recognized as safe and effective within the meaning of section 201(p) of the act is required to be supported by submission of the same quantity and quality of scientific evidence that is required to obtain approval of an application for the product, unless FDA has waived a requirement for effectiveness (under § 314.126) or safety, or both. The submission should be in the format and with the analyses required under paragraph (d) of this section. A person who fails to submit the required scientific evidence required under paragraph (d) waives the contention. General recognition of safety and effectiveness shall ordinarily be based upon published studies which may be corroborated by unpublished studies and other data and information.

(2) A contention that a drug product is exempt from part or all of the new drug provisions of the act under the exemption for products marketed before June 25, 1938, contained in section 201(p) of the act, or under section 107(c) of the Drug Amendments of 1962, is required to be supported by evidence of past and present quantitative formulas, labeling, and evidence of marketing. A person who makes such a contention should submit the formulas, labeling, and evidence of marketing in the following format.

I. Formulation.

A. A copy of each pertinent document or record to establish the exact quantitative formulation of the drug (both active and inactive ingredients) on the date of initial marketing of the drug.

B. A statement whether such formulation has at any subsequent time been changed in any manner. If any such change has been made, the exact date, nature, and rationale for each change in formulation, including any deletion or change in the concentration of any active ingredient and/or inactive ingredient, should be stated, together with a copy of each pertinent document or record to establish the date and nature of each such change, including, but not limited to, the formula which resulted from each such change. If no such change has been made, a copy of representative documents or records showing the formula at representative points in time should be submitted to support the statement.

II. Labeling.

A. A copy of each pertinent document or record to establish the identity of each item of written, printed, or graphic matter used as labeling on the date the drug was initially marketed.

B. A statement whether such labeling has at any subsequent time been discontinued or changed in any manner. If such discontinuance or change has been made, the exact date, nature, and rationale for each discontinuance or change and a copy of each pertinent document or record to establish each such discontinuance or change should be submitted, including, but not limited to, the labeling which resulted from each such discontinuance or change. If no such discontinuance or change has been made, a copy of representative documents or records showing labeling at representative points in time should be submitted to support the statement.

III. Marketing.

A. A copy of each pertinent document or record to establish the exact date the drug was initially marketed.

B. A statement whether such marketing has at any subsequent time been discontinued. If such marketing has been discontinued, the exact date of each such discontinuance should be submitted, together with a copy of each pertinent document or record to establish each such date.

IV. Verification.

A statement signed by the person responsible for such submission, that all appropriate records have been searched and to the best of that person's knowledge and belief it includes a true and accurate presentation of the facts.

(Warning: A willfully false statement is a criminal offense, 18 U.S.C. 1001.)

(3) The Food and Drug Administration will not find a drug product, including any active ingredient, which is identical, related, or similar, as described in § 310.6, to a drug product, including any active ingredient for which an application is or at any time has been effective or deemed approved, or approved under section 505 of the act, to be exempt from part or all of the new drug provisions of the act.

(4) A contention that a drug product is not a new drug for any other reason is required to be supported by submission of the factual records, data, and information that are necessary and appropriate to support the contention.

(5) It is the responsibility of every person who manufactures or distributes a drug product in reliance upon a "grandfather" provision of the act to maintain files that contain the data and information necessary fully to document and support that status.

(f) Separation of functions. Separation of functions commences upon receipt of a request for hearing. The Director of the Center for Drug Evaluation and Research, Food and Drug Administration, will prepare an analysis of the request and a proposed order ruling on the matter. The analysis and proposed order, the request for hearing, and any proposed order denying a hearing and response under paragraph (g) (2) or (3) of this section will be submitted to the Office of the Commissioner of Food and Drugs for review and decision. When the Center for Drug Evaluation and Research recommends denial of a hearing on all issues on which a hearing is requested, no representative of the Center will participate or advise in the review and decision by the Commissioner. When the Center for Drug Evaluation and Research recommends that a hearing be granted on one or more issues on which a hearing is requested, separation of functions terminates as to those issues, and representatives of the Center may participate or advise in the review and decision by the Commissioner on those issues. The Commissioner may modify the text of the issues, but may not deny a hearing on those issues. Separation of functions continues with respect to issues on which the Center for Drug Evaluation and Research has recommended denial of a hearing. The Commissioner will neither evaluate nor rule on the Center's recommendation on such issues and such issues will not be included in the notice of hearing. Participants in the hearing may make a motion to the presiding officer for the inclusion of any such issue in the hearing. The ruling on such a motion is subject to review in accordance with § 12.35(b). Failure to so move constitutes a waiver of the right to a hearing on such an issue. Separation of functions on all issues resumes upon issuance of a notice of hearing. The Office of the General Counsel, Department of Health and Human Services, will observe the same separation of functions.

(g) Summary judgment. A person who requests a hearing may not rely upon allegations or denials but is required to set forth specific facts showing that there is a genuine and substantial issue of fact that requires a hearing with respect to a particular drug product specified in the request for hearing.

(1) Where a specific notice of opportunity for hearing (as defined in paragraph (a)(1) of this section) is used, the Commissioner will enter summary judgment against a person who requests a hearing, making findings and conclusions, denying a hearing, if it conclusively appears from the face of the data, information, and factual analyses in the request for the hearing that there is no genuine and substantial issue of fact which precludes the refusal to approve the application or abbreviated application or the withdrawal of approval of the application or abbreviated application; for example, no adequate and well-controlled clinical investigations meeting each of the precise elements of § 314.126 and, for a combination drug product, § 300.50 of this chapter, showing effectiveness have been identified. Any order entering summary judgment is required to set forth the Commissioner's findings and conclusions in detail and is required to specify why each study submitted fails to meet the requirements of the statute and regulations or why the request for hearing does not raise a genuine and substantial issue of fact.

(2) When following a general notice of opportunity for a hearing (as defined in paragraph (a)(1) of this section) the Director of the Center for Drug Evaluation and Research concludes that summary judgment against a person requesting a hearing should be considered, the Director will serve upon the person requesting a hearing by registered mail a proposed order denying a hearing. This person has 60 days after receipt of the proposed order to respond with sufficient data, information, and analyses to demonstrate that there is a genuine and substantial issue of fact which justifies a hearing.

(3) When following a general or specific notice of opportunity for a hearing a person requesting a hearing submits data or information of a type required by the statute and regulations, and the Director of the Center for Drug Evaluation and Research concludes that summary judgment against the person should be considered, the Director will serve upon the person by registered mail a proposed order denying a hearing. The person has 60 days after receipt of the proposed order to respond with sufficient data, information, and analyses to demonstrate that there is a genuine and substantial issue of fact which justifies a hearing.

(4) If review of the data, information, and analyses submitted show that the grounds cited in the notice are not valid, for example, that substantial evidence of effectiveness exists, the Commissioner will enter summary judgment for the person requesting the hearing, and rescind the notice of opportunity for hearing.

(5) If the Commissioner grants a hearing, it will begin within 90 days after the expiration of the time for requesting the hearing unless the parties otherwise agree in the case of denial of approval, and as soon as practicable in the case of withdrawal of approval.

(6) The Commissioner will grant a hearing if there exists a genuine and substantial issue of fact or if the Commissioner concludes that a hearing would otherwise be in the public interest.

(7) If the manufacturer or distributor of an identical, related, or similar drug product requests and is granted a hearing, the hearing may consider whether the product is in fact identical, related, or similar to the drug product named in the notice of opportunity for a hearing.

(8) A request for a hearing, and any subsequent grant or denial of a hearing, applies only to the drug products named in such documents.

(h) FDA will issue a notice withdrawing approval and declaring all products unlawful for drug products subject to a notice of opportunity for a hearing, including any identical, related, or similar drug product under § 310.6, for which an opportunity for a hearing is waived or for which a hearing is denied. The Commissioner may defer or stay the action pending a ruling on any related request for a hearing or pending any related hearing or other administrative or judicial proceeding.

[50 FR 7493, Feb. 22, 1985; 50 FR 14212, Apr. 11, 1985, as amended at 50 FR 21238, May 23, 1985; 55 FR 11580, Mar. 29, 1990; 57 FR 17996, Apr. 28, 1992; 59 FR 14364, Mar. 28, 1994; 63 FR 5252, Feb. 2, 1998; 67 FR 9586, Mar. 4, 2002; 68 FR 24879, May 9, 2003; 69 FR 48775, Aug. 11, 2004; 74 FR 13113, Mar. 26, 2009]

§ 314.201 Procedure for hearings.

Parts 10 through 16 apply to hearings relating to new drugs under section 505 (d) and (e) of the act.

§ 314.235 Judicial review.

(a) The Commissioner of Food and Drugs will certify the transcript and record. In any case in which the Commissioner enters an order without a hearing under § 314.200(g), the record certified by the Commissioner is required to include the requests for hearing together with the data and information submitted and the Commissioner's findings and conclusion.

(b) A manufacturer or distributor of an identical, related, or similar drug product under § 310.6

may seek judicial review of an order withdrawing approval of a new drug application, whether or not a hearing has been held, in a United States court of appeals under section 505(h) of the act.

Subpart F [Reserved]

Subpart G—Miscellaneous Provisions

Source:

50 FR 7493, Feb. 22, 1985, unless otherwise noted. Redesignated at 57 FR 17983, Apr. 28, 1992.

§ 314.410 Imports and exports of new drugs.

(a) Imports. (1) A new drug may be imported into the United States if: (i) It is the subject of an approved application under this part; or (ii) it complies with the regulations pertaining to investigational new drugs under part 312; and it complies with the general regulations pertaining to imports under subpart E of part 1.

(2) A drug substance intended for use in the manufacture, processing, or repacking of a new drug may be imported into the United States if it complies with the labeling exemption in § 201.122 pertaining to shipments of drug substances in domestic commerce.

(b) Exports. (1) A new drug may be exported if it is the subject of an approved application under this part or it complies with the regulations pertaining to investigational new drugs under part 312.

(2) A new drug substance that is covered by an application approved under this part for use in the manufacture of an approved drug product may be exported by the applicant or any person listed as a supplier in the approved application, provided the drug substance intended for export meets the specification of, and is shipped with a copy of the labeling required for, the approved drug product.

(3) Insulin or an antibiotic drug may be exported without regard to the requirements in

section 802 of the act if the insulin or antibiotic drug meets the requirements of section 801(e)(1) of the act.

[50 FR 7493, Feb. 22, 1985, unless otherwise noted. Redesignated at 57 FR 17983, Apr. 28, 1992, and amended at 64 FR 402, Jan. 5, 1999; 69 FR 18766, Apr. 8, 2004]

§ 314.420   Drug master files.

(a) A drug master file is a submission of information to the Food and Drug Administration by a person (the drug master file holder) who intends it to be used for one of the following purposes: To permit the holder to incorporate the information by reference when the holder submits an investigational new drug application under part 312 or submits an application or an abbreviated application or an amendment or supplement to them under this part, or to permit the holder to authorize other persons to rely on the information to support a submission to FDA without the holder having to disclose the information to the person. FDA ordinarily neither independently reviews drug master files nor approves or disapproves submissions to a drug master file. Instead, the agency customarily reviews the information only in the context of an application under part 312 or this part. A drug master file may contain information of the kind required for any submission to the agency, including information about the following:

(1) [Reserved]

(2) Drug substance, drug substance intermediate, and materials used in their preparation, or drug product;

(3) Packaging materials;

(4) Excipient, colorant, flavor, essence, or materials used in their preparation;

(5) FDA-accepted reference information. (A person wishing to submit information and supporting data in a drug master file (DMF) that is not covered by Types II through IV DMF's must first submit a letter of intent to the Drug Master File Staff, Food and Drug Administration, 5901-B Ammendale Rd., Beltsville, MD 20705-1266.) FDA will then contact the person to discuss the proposed submission.

(b) An investigational new drug application or an application, abbreviated application, amendment, or supplement may incorporate by reference all or part of the contents of any drug master file in support of the submission if the holder authorizes the incorporation in writing. Each incorporation by reference is required to describe the incorporated material by name, reference number, volume, and page number of the drug master file.

(c) A drug master file is required to be submitted in two copies. The agency has prepared guidance that provides information about how to prepare a well-organized drug master file. If the drug master file holder adds, changes, or deletes any information in the file, the holder shall notify in writing, each person authorized to reference that information. Any addition, change, or deletion of information in a drug master file (except the list required under paragraph (d) of this section) is required to be submitted in two copies and to describe by name, reference number, volume, and page number the information affected in the drug master file.

(d) The drug master file is required to contain a complete list of each person currently authorized to incorporate by reference any information in the file, identifying by name, reference number, volume, and page number the information that each person is authorized to incorporate. If the holder restricts the authorization to particular drug products, the list is required to include the name of each drug product and the application number, if known, to which the authorization applies.

(e) The public availability of data and information in a drug master file, including the availability of data and information in the file to a person authorized to reference the file, is determined under part 20 and § 314.430.

[50 FR 7493, Feb. 22, 1985, as amended at 50 FR 21238, May 23, 1985; 53 FR 33122, Aug. 30, 1988; 55 FR 28380, July 11, 1990; 65 FR 1780, Jan. 12, 2000; 65 FR 56479, Sept. 19, 2000; 67 FR 9586, Mar. 4, 2002; 69 FR 13473, Mar. 23, 2004]

§ 314.430   Availability for public disclosure of data and information in an application or abbreviated application.

(a) The Food and Drug Administration will determine the public availability of any part of an application or abbreviated application under this section and part 20 of this chapter. For purposes of this section, the application or abbreviated application includes all data and information submitted with or incorporated by reference in the application or abbreviated application, including investigational new drug applications, drug master files under § 314.420, supplements submitted under § 314.70 or § 314.97, reports under § 314.80 or § 314.98, and other submissions. For purposes of this section, safety and effectiveness data include all studies and tests of a drug on animals and humans and all studies and tests of the drug for identity, stability, purity, potency, and bioavailability.

(b) FDA will not publicly disclose the existence of an application or abbreviated application before an approval letter is sent to the applicant under § 314.105 or tentative approval letter is sent to the applicant under § 314.107, unless the existence of the application or abbreviated application has been previously publicly disclosed or acknowledged.

(c) If the existence of an unapproved application or abbreviated application has not been publicly disclosed or acknowledged, no data or information in the application or abbreviated application is available for public disclosure.

(d)(1) If the existence of an application or abbreviated application has been publicly disclosed or acknowledged before the agency sends an approval letter to the applicant, no data or information contained in the application or abbreviated application is available for public disclosure before the agency sends an approval letter, but the Commissioner may, in his or her discretion, disclose a summary of selected portions of the safety and effectiveness data that are appropriate for public consideration of a specific pending issue; for example, for consideration of an open session of an FDA advisory committee.

(2) Notwithstanding paragraph (d)(1) of this section, FDA will make available to the public upon request the information in the investigational new drug application that was required to be filed in Docket Number 95S-0158 in the Division of Dockets Management (HFA-305), Food and Drug Administration, 5630 Fishers Lane, rm. 1061, Rockville, MD 20852, for investigations involving an exception from informed consent under § 50.24 of this chapter. Persons wishing to request this information shall submit a request under the Freedom of Information Act.

(e) After FDA sends an approval letter to the applicant, the following data and information in the application or abbreviated application are immediately available for public disclosure, unless the applicant shows that extraordinary circumstances exist. A list of approved applications and abbreviated applications, entitled "Approved Drug Products with Therapeutic Equivalence Evaluations," is available from the Government Printing Office, Washington, DC 20402. This list is updated monthly.

(1) [Reserved]

(2) If the application applies to a new drug, all safety and effectiveness data previously disclosed to the public as set forth in § 20.81 and a summary or summaries of the safety and effectiveness data and information submitted with or incorporated by reference in the application. The summaries do not constitute the full reports of investigations under section 505(b)(1) of the act (21 U.S.C. 355(b)(1)) on which the safety or effectiveness of the drug may be approved. The summaries consist of the following:

(i) For an application approved before July 1, 1975, internal agency records that describe safety and effectiveness data and information, for example, a summary of the basis for approval or internal reviews of the data and information, after deletion of the following:

(a) Names and any information that would identify patients or test subjects or investigators.

(b) Any inappropriate gratuitous comments unnecessary to an objective analysis of the data and information.

(ii) For an application approved on or after July 1, 1975, a Summary Basis of Approval (SBA) document that contains a summary of the safety and effectiveness data and information evaluated by FDA during the drug approval process. The SBA is prepared in one of the following ways:

(a) Before approval of the application, the applicant may prepare a draft SBA which the Center for Drug Evaluation and Research will review and may revise. The draft may be submitted with the application or as an amendment.

(b) The Center for Drug Evaluation and Research may prepare the SBA.

(3) A protocol for a test or study, unless it is shown to fall within the exemption established for trade secrets and confidential commercial information in § 20.61.

(4) Adverse reaction reports, product experience reports, consumer complaints, and other similar data and information after deletion of the following:

(i) Names and any information that would identify the person using the product.

(ii) Names and any information that would identify any third party involved with the report, such as a physician or hospital or other institution.

(5) A list of all active ingredients and any inactive ingredients previously disclosed to the public as set forth in § 20.81.

(6) An assay procedure or other analytical procedure, unless it serves no regulatory or compliance purpose and is shown to fall within the exemption established for trade secrets and confidential commercial information in § 20.61.

(7) All correspondence and written summaries of oral discussions between FDA and the applicant relating to the application, under the provisions of part 20.

(f) All safety and effectiveness data and information which have been submitted in an application and which have not previously been disclosed to the public are available to the public, upon request, at the time any one of the following events occurs unless extraordinary circumstances are shown:

(1) No work is being or will be undertaken to have the application approved.

(2) A final determination is made that the application is not approvable and all legal appeals have been exhausted.

(3) Approval of the application is withdrawn and all legal appeals have been exhausted.

(4) A final determination has been made that the drug is not a new drug.

(5) For applications submitted under section 505(b) of the act, the effective date of the approval of the first abbreviated application submitted under section 505(j) of the act which refers to such drug, or the date on which the approval of an abbreviated application under section 505(j) of the act which refers to such drug could be made effective if such an abbreviated application had been submitted.

(6) For abbreviated applications submitted under section 505(j) of the act, when FDA sends an approval letter to the applicant.

(g) The following data and information in an application or abbreviated application are not available for public disclosure unless they have been previously disclosed to the public as set forth in § 20.81 of this chapter or they relate to a product or ingredient that has been abandoned and they do not represent a trade secret or confidential commercial or financial information under § 20.61 of this chapter:

(1) Manufacturing methods or processes, including quality control procedures.

(2) Production, sales distribution, and similar data and information, except that any compilation of that data and information aggregated and prepared in a way that does not reveal data or information which is not available for public disclosure under this provision is available for public disclosure.

(3) Quantitative or semiquantitative formulas.

(h) The compilations of information specified in § 20.117 are available for public disclosure.

[50 FR 7493, Feb. 22, 1985, as amended at 50 FR 21238, May 23, 1985; 55 FR 11580, Mar. 29, 1990; 57 FR 17996, Apr. 28, 1992; 61 FR 51530, Oct. 2, 1996; 64 FR 26698, May 13, 1998; 64 FR 402, Jan. 5, 1999; 66 FR 1832, Jan. 10, 2001; 68 FR 24879, May 9, 2003; 69 FR 18766, Apr. 8, 2004; 73 FR 39610, July 10, 2008]

§ 314.440   Addresses for applications and abbreviated applications.

(a) Applicants shall send applications, abbreviated applications, and other correspondence relating to matters covered by this part, except for products listed in paragraph (b) of this section, to the appropriate office identified below:

(1) Except as provided in paragraph (a)(4) of this section, an application under § 314.50 or § 314.54 submitted for filing should be directed to the Central Document Room, 5901-B Ammendale Rd., Beltsville, MD 20705-1266. Applicants may obtain information about folders for binding applications on the Internet at http://www.fda.gov/cder/ddms/binders.htm.   After FDA has filed the application, the agency will inform the applicant which division is responsible for the application. Amendments, supplements,

resubmissions, requests for waivers, and other correspondence about an application that has been filed should be addressed to 5901-B Ammendale Rd., Beltsville, MD 20705-1266, to the attention of the appropriate division.

(2) Except as provided in paragraph (a)(4) of this section, an abbreviated application under § 314.94, and amendments, supplements, and resubmissions should be directed to the Office of Generic Drugs (HFD-600), Center for Drug Evaluation and Research, Food and Drug Administration, Metro Park North II, 7500 Standish Place, rm. 150, Rockville, MD 20855. This includes items sent by parcel post or overnight courier service. Correspondence not associated with an abbreviated application should be addressed specifically to the intended office or division and to the person as follows: Office of Generic Drugs, Center for Drug Evaluation and Research, Food and Drug Administration, Attn: [insert name of person], Metro Park North II, HFD-[insert mail code of office or division], 7500 Standish Place, rm. 150, Rockville, MD 20855. The mail code for the Office of Generic Drugs is HFD-600, the mail codes for the Divisions of Chemistry I, II, and III are HFD-620, HFD-640, and HFD-630, respectively, and the mail code for the Division of Bioequivalence is HFD-650.

(3) A request for an opportunity for a hearing under § 314.110 on the question of whether there are grounds for denying approval of an application, except an application under paragraph (b) of this section, should be directed to the Associate Director for Policy (HFD-5).

(4) The field copy of an application, an abbreviated application, amendments, supplements, resubmissions, requests for waivers, and other correspondence about an application and an abbreviated application shall be sent to the applicant's home FDA district office, except that a foreign applicant shall send the field copy to the appropriate address identified in paragraphs (a) (1) and (a)(2) of this section.

(b) Applicants shall send applications and other

correspondence relating to matters covered by this part for the drug products listed below to the Document Control Center (HFM-99), Center for Biologics Evaluation and Research, 1401 Rockville Pike, suite 200N, Rockville, MD 20852-1448, except applicants shall send a request for an opportunity for a hearing under § 314.110 on the question of whether there are grounds for denying approval of an application to the Director, Center for Biologics Evaluation and Research (HFM-1), at the same address.

(1) Ingredients packaged together with containers intended for the collection, processing, or storage of blood and blood components;

(2) Plasma volume expanders and hydroxyethyl starch for leukapheresis;

(3) Blood component processing solutions and shelf life extenders; and

(4) Oxygen carriers.

[50 FR 7493, Feb. 22, 1985, as amended at 50 FR 21238, May 23, 1985; 55 FR 11581, Mar. 29, 1990; 57 FR 17997, Apr. 28, 1992; 58 FR 47352, Sept. 8, 1993; 62 FR 43639, Aug. 15, 1997; 69 FR 13473, Mar. 23, 2004; 70 FR 14981, Mar. 24, 2005; 73 FR 39610, July 10, 2008; 74 FR 13113, Mar. 26, 2009]

§ 314.445   Guidance documents.

(a) FDA has made available guidance documents under § 10.115 of this chapter to help you to comply with certain requirements of this part.

(b) The Center for Drug Evaluation and Research (CDER) maintains a list of guidance documents that apply to CDER's regulations. The list is maintained on the Internet and is published annually in the Federal Register. A request for a copy of the CDER list should be directed to the Office of Training and Communications, Division of Drug Information, Center for Drug Evaluation and Research, Food and Drug Administration, 10903 New Hampshire Ave., Silver Spring, MD 20993-0002.

[65 FR 56480, Sept. 19, 2000, as amended at 74 FR 13113, Mar. 26, 2009]

Subpart H—Accelerated Approval of New Drugs for Serious or Life-Threatening Illnesses

Source:

57 FR 58958, Dec. 11, 1992, unless otherwise noted.

§ 314.500   Scope.

This subpart applies to certain new drug products that have been studied for their safety and effectiveness in treating serious or life-threatening illnesses and that provide meaningful therapeutic benefit to patients over existing treatments (e.g., ability to treat patients unresponsive to, or intolerant of, available therapy, or improved patient response over available therapy).

[57 FR 58958, Dec. 11, 1992, as amended at 64 FR 402, Jan. 5, 1999]

§ 314.510   Approval based on a surrogate endpoint or on an effect on a clinical endpoint other than survival or irreversible morbidity.

FDA may grant marketing approval for a new drug product on the basis of adequate and well-controlled clinical trials establishing that the drug product has an effect on a surrogate endpoint that is reasonably likely, based on epidemiologic, therapeutic, pathophysiologic, or other evidence, to predict clinical benefit or on the basis of an effect on a clinical endpoint other than survival or irreversible morbidity. Approval under this section will be subject to the requirement that the applicant study the drug further, to verify and describe its clinical benefit, where there is uncertainty as to the relation of the surrogate endpoint to clinical benefit, or of the observed clinical benefit to ultimate outcome. Postmarketing studies would usually be studies already underway. When required to be conducted, such studies must also be adequate and well-controlled. The applicant shall carry out any such studies with due diligence.

§ 314.520   Approval with restrictions to assure safe use.

(a) If FDA concludes that a drug product shown to be effective can be safely used only if distribution or use is restricted, FDA will require such postmarketing restrictions as are needed to assure safe use of the drug product, such as:

(1) Distribution restricted to certain facilities or physicians with special training or experience; or

(2) Distribution conditioned on the performance of specified medical procedures.

(b) The limitations imposed will be commensurate with the specific safety concerns presented by the drug product.

§ 314.530   Withdrawal procedures.

(a) For new drugs approved under §§ 314.510 and 314.520, FDA may withdraw approval, following a hearing as provided in part 15 of this chapter, as modified by this section, if:

(1) A postmarketing clinical study fails to verify clinical benefit;

(2) The applicant fails to perform the required postmarketing study with due diligence;

(3) Use after marketing demonstrates that postmarketing restrictions are inadequate to assure safe use of the drug product;

(4) The applicant fails to adhere to the postmarketing restrictions agreed upon;

(5) The promotional materials are false or misleading; or

(6) Other evidence demonstrates that the drug product is not shown to be safe or effective under its conditions of use.

(b) Notice of opportunity for a hearing. The Director of the Center for Drug Evaluation and Research will give the applicant notice of an opportunity for a hearing on the Center's proposal to withdraw the approval of an application approved under § 314.510 or § 314.520. The notice, which will ordinarily be a letter, will state generally the reasons for the action and the proposed grounds for the order.

(c) Submission of data and information. (1) If the applicant fails to file a written request for a hearing within 15 days of receipt of the notice, the applicant waives the opportunity for a hearing.

(2) If the applicant files a timely request for a hearing, the agency will publish a notice of hearing in the Federal Register in accordance with §§ 12.32(e) and 15.20 of this chapter.

(3) An applicant who requests a hearing under this section must, within 30 days of receipt of the notice of opportunity for a hearing, submit the data and information upon which the applicant intends to rely at the hearing.

(d) Separation of functions. Separation of functions (as specified in § 10.55 of this chapter) will not apply at any point in withdrawal proceedings under this section.

(e) Procedures for hearings. Hearings held under this section will be conducted in accordance with the provisions of part 15 of this chapter, with the following modifications:

(1) An advisory committee duly constituted under part 14 of this chapter will be present at the hearing. The committee will be asked to review the issues involved and to provide advice and recommendations to the Commissioner of Food and Drugs.

(2) The presiding officer, the advisory committee members, up to three representatives of the applicant, and up to three representatives of the Center may question any person during or at the conclusion of the person's presentation. No other person attending the hearing may question a person making a presentation. The presiding officer may, as a matter of discretion, permit questions to be submitted to the presiding officer for response by a person making a

presentation.

(f) Judicial review. The Commissioner's decision constitutes final agency action from which the applicant may petition for judicial review. Before requesting an order from a court for a stay of action pending review, an applicant must first submit a petition for a stay of action under § 10.35 of this chapter.

[57 FR 58958, Dec. 11, 1992, as amended at 64 FR 402, Jan. 5, 1999]

§ 314.540   Postmarketing safety reporting.

Drug products approved under this program are subject to the postmarketing recordkeeping and safety reporting applicable to all approved drug products, as provided in §§ 314.80 and 314.81.

§ 314.550   Promotional materials.

For drug products being considered for approval under this subpart, unless otherwise informed by the agency, applicants must submit to the agency for consideration during the preapproval review period copies of all promotional materials, including promotional labeling as well as advertisements, intended for dissemination or publication within 120 days following marketing approval. After 120 days following marketing approval, unless otherwise informed by the agency, the applicant must submit promotional materials at least 30 days prior to the intended time of initial dissemination of the labeling or initial publication of the advertisement.

§ 314.560   Termination of requirements.

If FDA determines after approval that the requirements established in § 314.520, § 314.530, or § 314.550 are no longer necessary for the safe and effective use of a drug product, it will so notify the applicant. Ordinarily, for drug products approved under § 314.510, these requirements will no longer apply when FDA determines that the required postmarketing study verifies and describes the drug product's

clinical benefit and the drug product would be appropriate for approval under traditional procedures. For drug products approved under § 314.520, the restrictions would no longer apply when FDA determines that safe use of the drug product can be assured through appropriate labeling. FDA also retains the discretion to remove specific postapproval requirements upon review of a petition submitted by the sponsor in accordance with § 10.30.

Subpart I—Approval of New Drugs When Human Efficacy Studies Are Not Ethical or Feasible

Source:

67 FR 37995, May 31, 2002, unless otherwise noted.

§ 314.600   Scope.

This subpart applies to certain new drug products that have been studied for their safety and efficacy in ameliorating or preventing serious or life threatening conditions caused by exposure to lethal or permanently disabling toxic biological, chemical, radiological, or nuclear substances. This subpart applies only to those new drug products for which: Definitive human efficacy studies cannot be conducted because it would be unethical to deliberately expose healthy human volunteers to a lethal or permanently disabling toxic biological, chemical, radiological, or nuclear substance; and field trials to study the product's effectiveness after an accidental or hostile exposure have not been feasible. This subpart does not apply to products that can be approved based on efficacy standards described elsewhere in FDA's regulations (e.g., accelerated approval based on surrogate markers or clinical endpoints other than survival or irreversible morbidity), nor does it address the safety evaluation for the products to which it does apply.

§ 314.610   Approval based on evidence of effectiveness from studies in animals.

(a) FDA may grant marketing approval for a new drug product for which safety has been established and for which the requirements of § 314.600 are met based on adequate and well-controlled animal studies when the results of those animal studies establish that the drug product is reasonably likely to produce clinical benefit in humans. In assessing the sufficiency of animal data, the agency may take into account other data, including human data, available to the agency. FDA will rely on the evidence from studies in animals to provide substantial evidence of the effectiveness of these products only when:

(1) There is a reasonably well-understood pathophysiological mechanism of the toxicity of the substance and its prevention or substantial reduction by the product;

(2) The effect is demonstrated in more than one animal species expected to react with a response predictive for humans, unless the effect is demonstrated in a single animal species that represents a sufficiently well-characterized animal model for predicting the response in humans;

(3) The animal study endpoint is clearly related to the desired benefit in humans, generally the enhancement of survival or prevention of major morbidity; and

(4) The data or information on the kinetics and pharmacodynamics of the product or other relevant data or information, in animals and humans, allows selection of an effective dose in humans.

(b) Approval under this subpart will be subject to three requirements:

(1) Postmarketing studies. The applicant must conduct postmarketing studies, such as field studies, to verify and describe the drug's clinical benefit and to assess its safety when used as indicated when such studies are feasible and ethical. Such postmarketing studies would not be feasible until an exigency arises. When such studies are feasible, the applicant must conduct such studies with due diligence. Applicants must include as part of their application a plan or approach to postmarketing study commitments in the event such studies become ethical and feasible.

(2) Approval with restrictions to ensure safe use. If FDA concludes that a drug product shown to be effective under this subpart can be safely used only if distribution or use is restricted, FDA will require such postmarketing restrictions as are needed to ensure safe use of the drug product, commensurate with the specific safety concerns presented by the drug product, such as:

(i) Distribution restricted to certain facilities or health care practitioners with special training or experience;

(ii) Distribution conditioned on the performance of specified medical procedures, including medical followup; and

(iii) Distribution conditioned on specified recordkeeping requirements.

(3) Information to be provided to patient recipients. For drug products or specific indications approved under this subpart, applicants must prepare, as part of their proposed labeling, labeling to be provided to patient recipients. The patient labeling must explain that, for ethical or feasibility reasons, the drug's approval was based on efficacy studies conducted in animals alone and must give the drug's indication(s), directions for use (dosage and administration), contraindications, a description of any reasonably foreseeable risks, adverse reactions, anticipated benefits, drug interactions, and any other relevant information required by FDA at the time of approval. The patient labeling must be available with the product to be provided to patients prior to administration or dispensing of the drug product for the use approved under this subpart, if possible.

§ 314.620   Withdrawal procedures.

(a) Reasons to withdraw approval. For new drugs approved under this subpart, FDA may withdraw approval, following a hearing as provided in part 15 of this chapter, as modified by this section, if:

(1) A postmarketing clinical study fails to verify clinical benefit;

(2) The applicant fails to perform the postmarketing study with due diligence;

(3) Use after marketing demonstrates that postmarketing restrictions are inadequate to ensure safe use of the drug product;

(4) The applicant fails to adhere to the postmarketing restrictions applied at the time of approval under this subpart;

(5) The promotional materials are false or misleading; or

(6) Other evidence demonstrates that the drug product is not shown to be safe or effective under its conditions of use.

(b) Notice of opportunity for a hearing. The Director of the Center for Drug Evaluation and Research (CDER) will give the applicant notice of an opportunity for a hearing on CDER's proposal to withdraw the approval of an application approved under this subpart. The notice, which will ordinarily be a letter, will state generally the reasons for the action and the proposed grounds for the order.

(c) Submission of data and information. (1) If the applicant fails to file a written request for a hearing within 15 days of receipt of the notice, the applicant waives the opportunity for a hearing.

(2) If the applicant files a timely request for a hearing, the agency will publish a notice of hearing in the Federal Register in accordance with §§ 12.32(e) and 15.20 of this chapter.

(3) An applicant who requests a hearing under this section must, within 30 days of receipt of the notice of opportunity for a hearing, submit the data and information upon which the applicant intends to rely at the hearing.

(d) Separation of functions. Separation of functions (as specified in § 10.55 of this chapter) will not apply at any point in withdrawal proceedings under this section.

(e) Procedures for hearings. Hearings held under this section will be conducted in accordance with the provisions of part 15 of this chapter, with the following modifications:

(1) An advisory committee duly constituted under part 14 of this chapter will be present at the hearing. The committee will be asked to review the issues involved and to provide advice and recommendations to the Commissioner of Food and Drugs.

(2) The presiding officer, the advisory committee members, up to three representatives of the applicant, and up to three representatives of CDER may question any person during or at the conclusion of the person's presentation. No other person attending the hearing may question a person making a presentation. The presiding officer may, as a matter of discretion, permit questions to be submitted to the presiding officer for response by a person making a presentation.

(f) Judicial review. The Commissioner of Food and Drugs' decision constitutes final agency action from which the applicant may petition for judicial review. Before requesting an order from a court for a stay of action pending review, an applicant must first submit a petition for a stay of action under § 10.35 of this chapter.

§ 314.630   Postmarketing safety reporting.

Drug products approved under this subpart are subject to the postmarketing recordkeeping and safety reporting requirements applicable to all approved drug products, as provided in §§ 314.80 and 314.81.

§ 314.640   Promotional materials.

For drug products being considered for approval

under this subpart, unless otherwise informed by the agency, applicants must submit to the agency for consideration during the preapproval review period copies of all promotional materials, including promotional labeling as well as advertisements, intended for dissemination or publication within 120 days following marketing approval. After 120 days following marketing approval, unless otherwise informed by the agency, the applicant must submit promotional materials at least 30 days prior to the intended time of initial dissemination of the labeling or initial publication of the advertisement.

§ 314.650 Termination of requirements.

If FDA determines after approval under this subpart that the requirements established in §§ 314.610(b)(2), 314.620, and 314.630 are no longer necessary for the safe and effective use of a drug product, FDA will so notify the applicant. Ordinarily, for drug products approved under § 314.610, these requirements will no longer apply when FDA determines that the postmarketing study verifies and describes the drug product's clinical benefit. For drug products approved under § 314.610, the restrictions would no longer apply when FDA determines that safe use of the drug product can be ensured through appropriate labeling. FDA also retains the discretion to remove specific postapproval requirements upon review of a petition submitted by the sponsor in accordance with § 10.30 of this chapter.

Subchapter H—Medical Devices

Part 812—Investigational Device Exemptions
Authority:

21 U.S.C. 331, 351, 352, 353, 355, 360, 360c-360f, 360h-360j, 371, 372, 374, 379e, 381, 382, 383; 42 U.S.C. 216, 241, 262, 263b-263n.

Source:

45 FR 3751, Jan. 18, 1980, unless otherwise noted.

Subpart A—General Provisions

§ 812.1 Scope.

(a) The purpose of this part is to encourage, to the extent consistent with the protection of public health and safety and with ethical standards, the discovery and development of useful devices intended for human use, and to that end to maintain optimum freedom for scientific investigators in their pursuit of this purpose. This part provides procedures for the conduct of clinical investigations of devices. An approved investigational device exemption (IDE) permits a device that otherwise would be required to comply with a performance standard or to have premarket approval to be shipped lawfully for the purpose of conducting investigations of that device. An IDE approved under § 812.30 or considered approved under § 812.2(b) exempts a device from the requirements of the following sections of the Federal Food, Drug, and Cosmetic Act (the act) and regulations issued thereunder: Misbranding under section 502 of the act, registration, listing, and premarket notification under section 510, performance standards under section 514, premarket approval under section 515, a banned device regulation under section 516, records and reports under section 519, restricted device requirements under section 520(e), good manufacturing practice requirements under section 520(f) except for the requirements found in § 820.30, if applicable (unless the sponsor states an intention to comply with these requirements under § 812.20(b) (3) or § 812.140(b)(4)(v)) and color additive requirements under section 721.

(b) References in this part to regulatory sections of the Code of Federal Regulations are to chapter I of title 21, unless otherwise noted.

[45 FR 3751, Jan. 18, 1980, as amended at 59 FR 14366, Mar. 28, 1994; 61 FR 52654, Oct. 7, 1996]

§ 812.2 Applicability.

(a) General. This part applies to all clinical investigations of devices to determine safety and effectiveness, except as provided in paragraph (c) of this section.

(b) Abbreviated requirements. The following categories of investigations are considered to have approved applications for IDE's, unless FDA has notified a sponsor under § 812.20(a) that approval of an application is required:

(1) An investigation of a device other than a significant risk device, if the device is not a banned device and the sponsor:

(i) Labels the device in accordance with § 812.5;

(ii) Obtains IRB approval of the investigation after presenting the reviewing IRB with a brief explanation of why the device is not a significant risk device, and maintains such approval;

(iii) Ensures that each investigator participating in an investigation of the device obtains from each subject under the investigator's care, informed consent under part 50 and documents it, unless documentation is waived by an IRB under § 56.109(c).

(iv) Complies with the requirements of § 812.46 with respect to monitoring investigations;

(v) Maintains the records required under § 812.140(b) (4) and (5) and makes the reports required under § 812.150(b) (1) through (3) and (5) through (10);

(vi) Ensures that participating investigators maintain the records required by § 812.140(a) (3)(i) and make the reports required under § 812.150(a) (1), (2), (5), and (7); and

(vii) Complies with the prohibitions in § 812.7 against promotion and other practices.

(2) An investigation of a device other than one subject to paragraph (e) of this section, if the investigation was begun on or before July 16, 1980, and to be completed, and is completed, on or before January 19, 1981.

(c) Exempted investigations. This part, with the exception of § 812.119, does not apply to investigations of the following categories of devices:

(1) A device, other than a transitional device, in commercial distribution immediately before May 28, 1976, when used or investigated in accordance with the indications in labeling in effect at that time.

(2) A device, other than a transitional device, introduced into commercial distribution on or after May 28, 1976, that FDA has determined to be substantially equivalent to a device in commercial distribution immediately before May 28, 1976, and that is used or investigated in accordance with the indications in the labeling FDA reviewed under subpart E of part 807 in determining substantial equivalence.

(3) A diagnostic device, if the sponsor complies with applicable requirements in § 809.10(c) and if the testing:

(i) Is noninvasive,

(ii) Does not require an invasive sampling procedure that presents significant risk,

(iii) Does not by design or intention introduce energy into a subject, and

(iv) Is not used as a diagnostic procedure without confirmation of the diagnosis by another, medically established diagnostic product or procedure.

(4) A device undergoing consumer preference testing, testing of a modification, or testing of a combination of two or more devices in commercial distribution, if the testing is not for the purpose of determining safety or effectiveness and does not put subjects at risk.

(5) A device intended solely for veterinary use.

(6) A device shipped solely for research on or with laboratory animals and labeled in accordance with § 812.5(c).

(7) A custom device as defined in § 812.3(b), un-

less the device is being used to determine safety or effectiveness for commercial distribution.

(d) Limit on certain exemptions. In the case of class II or class III device described in paragraph (c)(1) or (2) of this section, this part applies beginning on the date stipulated in an FDA regulation or order that calls for the submission of premarket approval applications for an unapproved class III device, or establishes a performance standard for a class II device.

(e) Investigations subject to IND's. A sponsor that, on July 16, 1980, has an effective investigational new drug application (IND) for an investigation of a device shall continue to comply with the requirements of part 312 until 90 days after that date. To continue the investigation after that date, a sponsor shall comply with paragraph (b)(1) of this section, if the device is not a significant risk device, or shall have obtained FDA approval under § 812.30 of an IDE application for the investigation of the device.

[45 FR 3751, Jan. 18, 1980, as amended at 46 FR 8956, Jan. 27, 1981; 46 FR 14340, Feb. 27, 1981; 53 FR 11252, Apr. 6, 1988; 62 FR 4165, Jan, 29, 1997; 62 FR 12096, Mar. 14, 1997]

§ 812.3   Definitions.

(a) Act means the Federal Food, Drug, and Cosmetic Act (sections 201-901, 52 Stat. 1040 et seq., as amended (21 U.S.C. 301-392)).

(b) Custom device means a device that:

(1) Necessarily deviates from devices generally available or from an applicable performance standard or premarket approval requirement in order to comply with the order of an individual physician or dentist;

(2) Is not generally available to, or generally used by, other physicians or dentists;

(3) Is not generally available in finished form for purchase or for dispensing upon prescription;

(4) Is not offered for commercial distribution through labeling or advertising; and

(5) Is intended for use by an individual patient named in the order of a physician or dentist, and is to be made in a specific form for that patient, or is intended to meet the special needs of the physician or dentist in the course of professional practice.

(c) FDA means the Food and Drug Administration.

(d) Implant means a device that is placed into a surgically or naturally formed cavity of the human body if it is intended to remain there for a period of 30 days or more. FDA may, in order to protect public health, determine that devices placed in subjects for shorter periods are also "implants" for purposes of this part.

(e) Institution means a person, other than an individual, who engages in the conduct of research on subjects or in the delivery of medical services to individuals as a primary activity or as an adjunct to providing residential or custodial care to humans. The term includes, for example, a hospital, retirement home, confinement facility, academic establishment, and device manufacturer. The term has the same meaning as "facility" in section 520(g) of the act.

(f) Institutional review board (IRB) means any board, committee, or other group formally designated by an institution to review biomedical research involving subjects and established, operated, and functioning in conformance with part 56. The term has the same meaning as "institutional review committee" in section 520(g) of the act.

(g) Investigational device means a device, including a transitional device, that is the object of an investigation.

(h) Investigation means a clinical investigation or research involving one or more subjects to determine the safety or effectiveness of a device.

(i) Investigator means an individual who actually conducts a clinical investigation, i.e., under whose immediate direction the test article is administered or dispensed to, or used involving, a subject, or, in the event of an investigation conducted by a team of individuals, is the responsible leader of that team.

(j) Monitor, when used as a noun, means an individual designated by a sponsor or contract research organization to oversee the progress of an investigation. The monitor may be an employee of a sponsor or a consultant to the sponsor, or an employee of or consultant to a contract research organization. Monitor, when used as a verb, means to oversee an investigation.

(k) Noninvasive, when applied to a diagnostic device or procedure, means one that does not by design or intention: (1) Penetrate or pierce the skin or mucous membranes of the body, the ocular cavity, or the urethra, or (2) enter the ear beyond the external auditory canal, the nose beyond the nares, the mouth beyond the pharynx, the anal canal beyond the rectum, or the vagina beyond the cervical os. For purposes of this part, blood sampling that involves simple venipuncture is considered noninvasive, and the use of surplus samples of body fluids or tissues that are left over from samples taken for noninvestigational purposes is also considered noninvasive.

(l) Person includes any individual, partnership, corporation, association, scientific or academic establishment, Government agency or organizational unit of a Government agency, and any other legal entity.

(m) Significant risk device means an investigational device that:

(1) Is intended as an implant and presents a potential for serious risk to the health, safety, or welfare of a subject;

(2) Is purported or represented to be for a use in supporting or sustaining human life and presents a potential for serious risk to the health, safety, or welfare of a subject;

(3) Is for a use of substantial importance in diag-nosing, curing, mitigating, or treating disease, or otherwise preventing impairment of human health and presents a potential for serious risk to the health, safety, or welfare of a subject; or

(4) Otherwise presents a potential for serious risk to the health, safety, or welfare of a subject.

(n) Sponsor means a person who initiates, but who does not actually conduct, the investigation, that is, the investigational device is administered, dispensed, or used under the immediate direction of another individual. A person other than an individual that uses one or more of its own employees to conduct an investigation that it has initiated is a sponsor, not a sponsor-investigator, and the employees are investigators.

(o) Sponsor-investigator means an individual who both initiates and actually conducts, alone or with others, an investigation, that is, under whose immediate direction the investigational device is administered, dispensed, or used. The term does not include any person other than an individual. The obligations of a sponsor-investigator under this part include those of an investigator and those of a sponsor.

(p) Subject means a human who participates in an investigation, either as an individual on whom or on whose specimen an investigational device is used or as a control. A subject may be in normal health or may have a medical condition or disease.

(q) Termination means a discontinuance, by sponsor or by withdrawal of IRB or FDA approval, of an investigation before completion.

(r) Transitional device means a device subject to section 520(l) of the act, that is, a device that FDA considered to be a new drug or an antibiotic drug before May 28, 1976.

(s) Unanticipated adverse device effect means any serious adverse effect on health or safety or any life-threatening problem or death caused by, or associated with, a device, if that effect, problem, or death was not previously identified in nature, severity, or degree of incidence in the investigational plan or application (including a supplementary plan or application), or any other unanticipated serious problem associated with a device that relates to the rights, safety, or welfare of subjects.

[45 FR 3751, Jan. 18, 1980, as amended at 46 FR 8956, Jan. 27, 1981; 48 FR 15622, Apr. 12, 1983]

§ 812.5   Labeling of investigational devices.

(a) Contents. An investigational device or its immediate package shall bear a label with the following information: the name and place of business of the manufacturer, packer, or distributor (in accordance with § 801.1), the quantity of contents, if appropriate, and the following statement: "CAUTION—Investigational device. Limited by Federal (or United States) law to investigational use." The label or other labeling shall describe all relevant contraindications, hazards, adverse effects, interfering substances or devices, warnings, and precautions.

(b) Prohibitions. The labeling of an investigational device shall not bear any statement that is false or misleading in any particular and shall not represent that the device is safe or effective for the purposes for which it is being investigated.

(c) Animal research. An investigational device shipped solely for research on or with laboratory animals shall bear on its label the following statement: "CAUTION—Device for investigational use in laboratory animals or other tests that do not involve human subjects."

(d) The appropriate FDA Center Director, according to the procedures set forth in § 801.128 or § 809.11 of this chapter, may grant an exception or alternative to the provisions in paragraphs (a) and (c) of this section, to the extent that these provisions are not explicitly required by statute, for specified lots, batches, or other units of a device that are or will be included in the Strategic National Stockpile.

[45 FR 3751, Jan. 18, 1980, as amended at 45 FR 58842, Sept. 5, 1980; 72 FR 73602, Dec. 28, 2007]

§ 812.7   Prohibition of promotion and other practices.

A sponsor, investigator, or any person acting for or on behalf of a sponsor or investigator shall not:

(a) Promote or test market an investigational device, until after FDA has approved the device for commercial distribution.

(b) Commercialize an investigational device by charging the subjects or investigators for a device a price larger than that necessary to recover costs of manufacture, research, development, and handling.

(c) Unduly prolong an investigation. If data developed by the investigation indicate in the case of a class III device that premarket approval cannot be justified or in the case of a class II device that it will not comply with an applicable performance standard or an amendment to that standard, the sponsor shall promptly terminate the investigation.

(d) Represent that an investigational device is safe or effective for the purposes for which it is being investigated.

§ 812.10   Waivers.

(a) Request. A sponsor may request FDA to waive any requirement of this part. A waiver request, with supporting documentation, may be submitted separately or as part of an application to the address in § 812.19.

(b) FDA action. FDA may by letter grant a waiver of any requirement that FDA finds is not required by the act and is unnecessary to protect the rights, safety, or welfare of human subjects.

(c) Effect of request. Any requirement shall continue to apply unless and until FDA waives it.

§ 812.18   Import and export

requirements.

(a) Imports. In addition to complying with other requirements of this part, a person who imports or offers for importation an investigational device subject to this part shall be the agent of the foreign exporter with respect to investigations of the device and shall act as the sponsor of the clinical investigation, or ensure that another person acts as the agent of the foreign exporter and the sponsor of the investigation.

(b) Exports. A person exporting an investigational device subject to this part shall obtain FDA's prior approval, as required by section 801(e) of the act or comply with section 802 of the act.

[45 FR 3751, Jan. 18, 1980, as amended at 62 FR 26229, May 13, 1997]

§ 812.19   Address for IDE correspondence.

(a) If you are sending an application, supplemental application, report, request for waiver, request for import or export approval, or other correspondence relating to matters covered by this part, you must send the submission to the appropriate address as follows:

(1) For devices regulated by the Center for Devices and Radiological Health, send it to the Document Mail Center (HFZ-401), Center for Devices and Radiological Health, Food and Drug Administration, 9200 Corporate Blvd., Rockville, MD 20850.

(2) For devices regulated by the Center for Biologics Evaluation and Research, send it to the Document Control Center (HFM-99), Center for Biologics Evaluation and Research, Food and Drug Administration, 1401 Rockville Pike, suite 200N, Rockville, MD 20852-1448.

(3) For devices regulated by the Center for Drug Evaluation and Research, send it to Central Document Control Room, Center for Drug Evaluation and Research, Food and Drug Administration, 5901-B Ammendale Rd., Beltsville, MD 20705-1266.

(b) You must state on the outside wrapper of each submission what the submission is, for example, an "IDE application," a "supplemental IDE application," or a "correspondence concerning an IDE (or an IDE application)."

[71 FR 42048, July 25, 2006]

Subpart B—Application and Administrative Action

§ 812.20   Application.

(a) Submission. (1) A sponsor shall submit an application to FDA if the sponsor intends to use a significant risk device in an investigation, intends to conduct an investigation that involves an exception from informed consent under § 50.24 of this chapter, or if FDA notifies the sponsor that an application is required for an investigation.

(2) A sponsor shall not begin an investigation for which FDA's approval of an application is required until FDA has approved the application.

(3) A sponsor shall submit three copies of a signed "Application for an Investigational Device Exemption" (IDE application), together with accompanying materials, by registered mail or by hand to the address in § 812.19. Subsequent correspondence concerning an application or a supplemental application shall be submitted by registered mail or by hand.

(4)(i) A sponsor shall submit a separate IDE for any clinical investigation involving an exception from informed consent under § 50.24 of this chapter. Such a clinical investigation is not permitted to proceed without the prior written authorization of FDA. FDA shall provide a written determination 30 days after FDA receives the IDE or earlier.

(ii) If the investigation involves an exception from informed consent under § 50.24 of this chapter, the sponsor shall prominently identify on the cover sheet that the investigation is subject to the requirements in § 50.24 of this chapter.

(b) Contents. An IDE application shall include, in the following order:

(1) The name and address of the sponsor.

(2) A complete report of prior investigations of the device and an accurate summary of those sections of the investigational plan described in § 812.25(a) through (e) or, in lieu of the summary, the complete plan. The sponsor shall submit to FDA a complete investigational plan and a complete report of prior investigations of the device if no IRB has reviewed them, if FDA has found an IRB's review inadequate, or if FDA requests them.

(3) A description of the methods, facilities, and controls used for the manufacture, processing, packing, storage, and, where appropriate, installation of the device, in sufficient detail so that a person generally familiar with good manufacturing practices can make a knowledgeable judgment about the quality control used in the manufacture of the device.

(4) An example of the agreements to be entered into by all investigators to comply with investigator obligations under this part, and a list of the names and addresses of all investigators who have signed the agreement.

(5) A certification that all investigators who will participate in the investigation have signed the agreement, that the list of investigators includes all the investigators participating in the investigation, and that no investigators will be added to the investigation until they have signed the agreement.

(6) A list of the name, address, and chairperson of each IRB that has been or will be asked to review the investigation and a certification of the action concerning the investigation taken by each such IRB.

(7) The name and address of any institution at which a part of the investigation may be conducted that has not been identified in accordance with paragraph (b)(6) of this section.

(8) If the device is to be sold, the amount to be charged and an explanation of why sale does not constitute commercialization of the device.

(9) A claim for categorical exclusion under § 25.30 or § 25.34 or an environmental assessment under § 25.40.

(10) Copies of all labeling for the device.

(11) Copies of all forms and informational materials to be provided to subjects to obtain informed consent.

(12) Any other relevant information FDA requests for review of the application.

(c) Additional information. FDA may request additional information concerning an investigation or revision in the investigational plan. The sponsor may treat such a request as a disapproval of the application for purposes of requesting a hearing under part 16.

(d) Information previously submitted. Information previously submitted to the Center for Devices and Radiological Health, the Center for Biologics Evaluation and Research, or the Center for Drug Evaluation and Research, as applicable, in accordance with this chapter ordinarily need not be resubmitted, but may be incorporated by reference.

[45 FR 3751, Jan. 18, 1980, as amended at 46 FR 8956, Jan. 27, 1981; 50 FR 16669, Apr. 26, 1985; 53 FR 11252, Apr. 6, 1988; 61 FR 51530, Oct. 2, 1996; 62 FR 40600, July 29, 1997; 64 FR 10942, Mar. 8, 1999; 73 FR 49942, Aug. 25, 2008]

§ 812.25 Investigational plan.

The investigational plan shall include, in the following order:

(a) Purpose. The name and intended use of the device and the objectives and duration of the investigation.

(b) Protocol. A written protocol describing the methodology to be used and an analysis of the protocol demonstrating that the investigation is scientifically sound.

(c) Risk analysis. A description and analysis of all increased risks to which subjects will be exposed by the investigation; the manner in which these risks will be minimized; a justification for the investigation; and a description of the patient population, including the number, age, sex, and condition.

(d) Description of device. A description of each important component, ingredient, property, and principle of operation of the device and of each anticipated change in the device during the course of the investigation.

(e) Monitoring procedures. The sponsor's written procedures for monitoring the investigation and the name and address of any monitor.

(f) Labeling. Copies of all labeling for the device.

(g) Consent materials. Copies of all forms and informational materials to be provided to subjects to obtain informed consent.

(h) IRB information. A list of the names, locations, and chairpersons of all IRB's that have been or will be asked to review the investigation, and a certification of any action taken by any of those IRB's with respect to the investigation.

(i) Other institutions. The name and address of each institution at which a part of the investigation may be conducted that has not been identified in paragraph (h) of this section.

(j) Additional records and reports. A description of records and reports that will be maintained on the investigation in addition to those prescribed in subpart G.

§ 812.27   Report of prior investigations.

(a) General. The report of prior investigations shall include reports of all prior clinical, animal, and laboratory testing of the device and shall be comprehensive and adequate to justify the proposed investigation.

(b) Specific contents. The report also shall include:

(1) A bibliography of all publications, whether adverse or supportive, that are relevant to an evaluation of the safety or effectiveness of the device, copies of all published and unpublished adverse information, and, if requested by an IRB or FDA, copies of other significant publications.

(2) A summary of all other unpublished information (whether adverse or supportive) in the possession of, or reasonably obtainable by, the sponsor that is relevant to an evaluation of the safety or effectiveness of the device.

(3) If information on nonclinical laboratory studies is provided, a statement that all such studies have been conducted in compliance with applicable requirements in the good laboratory practice regulations in part 58, or if any such study was not conducted in compliance with such regulations, a brief statement of the reason for the noncompliance. Failure or inability to comply with this requirement does not justify failure to provide information on a relevant nonclinical test study.

[45 FR 3751, Jan. 18, 1980, as amended at 50 FR 7518, Feb. 22, 1985]

§ 812.30   FDA action on applications.

(a) Approval or disapproval. FDA will notify the sponsor in writing of the date it receives an application. FDA may approve an investigation as proposed, approve it with modifications, or disapprove it. An investigation may not begin until:

(1) Thirty days after FDA receives the application at the address in § 812.19 for the investigation of a device other than a banned device, unless FDA notifies the sponsor that the investigation may not begin; or

(2) FDA approves, by order, an IDE for the investigation.

(b) Grounds for disapproval or withdrawal. FDA may disapprove or withdraw approval of an application if FDA finds that:

(1) There has been a failure to comply with any requirement of this part or the act, any other applicable regulation or statute, or any condition of approval imposed by an IRB or FDA.

(2) The application or a report contains an untrue statement of a material fact, or omits material information required by this part.

(3) The sponsor fails to respond to a request for additional information within the time prescribed by FDA.

(4) There is reason to believe that the risks to the subjects are not outweighed by the anticipated benefits to the subjects and the importance of the knowledge to be gained, or informed consent is inadquate, or the investigation is scientifically unsound, or there is reason to believe that the device as used is ineffective.

(5) It is otherwise unreasonable to begin or to continue the investigation owing to the way in which the device is used or the inadequacy of:

(i) The report of prior investigations or the investigational plan;

(ii) The methods, facilities, and controls used for the manufacturing, processing, packaging, storage, and, where appropriate, installation of the device; or

(iii) Monitoring and review of the investigation.

(c) Notice of disapproval or withdrawal. If FDA disapproves an application or proposes to withdraw approval of an application, FDA will notify the sponsor in writing.

(1) A disapproval order will contain a complete statement of the reasons for disapproval and a statement that the sponsor has an opportunity to request a hearing under part 16.

(2) A notice of a proposed withdrawal of approval will contain a complete statement of the reasons for withdrawal and a statement that the sponsor has an opportunity to request a

hearing under part 16. FDA will provide the opportunity for hearing before withdrawal of approval, unless FDA determines in the notice that continuation of testing under the exemption will result in an unreasonble risk to the public health and orders withdrawal of approval before any hearing.

[45 FR 3751, Jan. 18, 1980, as amended at 45 FR 58842, Sept. 5, 1980]

§ 812.35   Supplemental applications.

(a) Changes in investigational plan—(1) Changes requiring prior approval. Except as described in paragraphs (a)(2) through (a)(4) of this section, a sponsor must obtain approval of a supplemental application under § 812.30(a), and IRB approval when appropriate (see §§ 56.110 and 56.111 of this chapter), prior to implementing a change to an investigational plan. If a sponsor intends to conduct an investigation that involves an exception to informed consent under § 50.24 of this chapter, the sponsor shall submit a separate investigational device exemption (IDE) application in accordance with § 812.20(a).

(2) Changes effected for emergency use. The requirements of paragraph (a)(1) of this section regarding FDA approval of a supplement do not apply in the case of a deviation from the investigational plan to protect the life or physical well-being of a subject in an emergency. Such deviation shall be reported to FDA within 5-working days after the sponsor learns of it (see § 812.150(a)(4)).

(3) Changes effected with notice to FDA within 5 days. A sponsor may make certain changes without prior approval of a supplemental application under paragraph (a)(1) of this section if the sponsor determines that these changes meet the criteria described in paragraphs (a)(3)(i) and (a)(3)(ii) of this section, on the basis of credible information defined in paragraph (a)(3)(iii) of this section, and the sponsor provides notice to FDA within 5-working days of making

these changes.

(i) Developmental changes. The requirements in paragraph (a)(1) of this section regarding FDA approval of a supplement do not apply to developmental changes in the device (including manufacturing changes) that do not constitute a significant change in design or basic principles of operation and that are made in response to information gathered during the course of an investigation.

(ii) Changes to clinical protocol. The requirements in paragraph (a)(1) of this section regarding FDA approval of a supplement do not apply to changes to clinical protocols that do not affect:

(A) The validity of the data or information resulting from the completion of the approved protocol, or the relationship of likely patient risk to benefit relied upon to approve the protocol;

(B) The scientific soundness of the investigational plan; or

(C) The rights, safety, or welfare of the human subjects involved in the investigation.

(iii) Definition of credible information. (A) Credible information to support developmental changes in the device (including manufacturing changes) includes data generated under the design control procedures of § 820.30, preclinical/animal testing, peer reviewed published literature, or other reliable information such as clinical information gathered during a trial or marketing.

(B) Credible information to support changes to clinical protocols is defined as the sponsor's documentation supporting the conclusion that a change does not have a significant impact on the study design or planned statistical analysis, and that the change does not affect the rights, safety, or welfare of the subjects. Documentation shall include information such as peer reviewed published literature, the recommendation of the clinical investigator(s), and/or the data gathered

during the clinical trial or marketing.

(iv) Notice of IDE change. Changes meeting the criteria in paragraphs (a)(3)(i) and (a)(3)(ii) of this section that are supported by credible information as defined in paragraph (a)(3)(iii) of this section may be made without prior FDA approval if the sponsor submits a notice of the change to the IDE not later than 5-working days after making the change. Changes to devices are deemed to occur on the date the device, manufactured incorporating the design or manufacturing change, is distributed to the investigator(s). Changes to a clinical protocol are deemed to occur when a clinical investigator is notified by the sponsor that the change should be implemented in the protocol or, for sponsor-investigator studies, when a sponsor-investigator incorporates the change in the protocol. Such notices shall be identified as a "notice of IDE change."

(A) For a developmental or manufacturing change to the device, the notice shall include a summary of the relevant information gathered during the course of the investigation upon which the change was based; a description of the change to the device or manufacturing process (cross-referenced to the appropriate sections of the original device description or manufacturing process); and, if design controls were used to assess the change, a statement that no new risks were identified by appropriate risk analysis and that the verification and validation testing, as appropriate, demonstrated that the design outputs met the design input requirements. If another method of assessment was used, the notice shall include a summary of the information which served as the credible information supporting the change.

(B) For a protocol change, the notice shall include a description of the change (cross-referenced to the appropriate sections of the original protocol); an assessment supporting the conclusion that the change does not have a significant impact on the study design or planned statistical analysis; and a summary of the information that served as the credible information supporting the sponsor's determination that the change does not affect the rights, safety, or welfare of the subjects.

(4) Changes submitted in annual report. The requirements of paragraph (a)(1) of this section do not apply to minor changes to the purpose of the study, risk analysis, monitoring procedures, labeling, informed consent materials, and IRB information that do not affect:

(i) The validity of the data or information resulting from the completion of the approved protocol, or the relationship of likely patient risk to benefit relied upon to approve the protocol;

(ii) The scientific soundness of the investigational plan; or

(iii) The rights, safety, or welfare of the human subjects involved in the investigation. Such changes shall be reported in the annual progress report for the IDE, under § 812.150(b)(5).

(b) IRB approval for new facilities. A sponsor shall submit to FDA a certification of any IRB approval of an investigation or a part of an investigation not included in the IDE application. If the investigation is otherwise unchanged, the supplemental application shall consist of an updating of the information required by § 812.20(b) and (c) and a description of any modifications in the investigational plan required by the IRB as a condition of approval. A certification of IRB approval need not be included in the initial submission of the supplemental application, and such certification is not a precondition for agency consideration of the application. Nevertheless, a sponsor may not begin a part of an investigation at a facility until the IRB has approved the investigation, FDA has received the certification of IRB approval, and FDA, under § 812.30(a), has approved the supplemental application relating to that part of the investigation (see § 56.103(a)).

[50 FR 25909, June 24, 1985; 50 FR 28932, July 17, 1985, as amended at 61 FR 51531, Oct. 2, 1996; 63 FR 64625, Nov. 23, 1998]

§ 812.36 Treatment use of an investigational device.

(a) General. A device that is not approved for marketing may be under clinical investigation for a serious or immediately life-threatening disease or condition in patients for whom no comparable or satisfactory alternative device or other therapy is available. During the clinical trial or prior to final action on the marketing application, it may be appropriate to use the device in the treatment of patients not in the trial under the provisions of a treatment investigational device exemption (IDE). The purpose of this section is to facilitate the availability of promising new devices to desperately ill patients as early in the device development process as possible, before general marketing begins, and to obtain additional data on the device's safety and effectiveness. In the case of a serious disease, a device ordinarily may be made available for treatment use under this section after all clinical trials have been completed. In the case of an immediately life-threatening disease, a device may be made available for treatment use under this section prior to the completion of all clinical trials. For the purpose of this section, an "immediately life-threatening" disease means a stage of a disease in which there is a reasonable likelihood that death will occur within a matter of months or in which premature death is likely without early treatment. For purposes of this section, "treatment use" of a device includes the use of a device for diagnostic purposes.

(b) Criteria. FDA shall consider the use of an investigational device under a treatment IDE if:

(1) The device is intended to treat or diagnose a serious or immediately life-threatening disease or condition;

(2) There is no comparable or satisfactory alternative device or other therapy available to treat or diagnose that stage of the disease or condition in the intended patient population;

(3) The device is under investigation in a controlled clinical trial for the same use under an approved IDE, or such clinical trials have been completed; and

(4) The sponsor of the investigation is actively pursuing marketing approval/clearance of the investigational device with due diligence.

(c) Applications for treatment use. (1) A treatment IDE application shall include, in the following order:

(i) The name, address, and telephone number of the sponsor of the treatment IDE;

(ii) The intended use of the device, the criteria for patient selection, and a written protocol describing the treatment use;

(iii) An explanation of the rationale for use of the device, including, as appropriate, either a list of the available regimens that ordinarily should be tried before using the investigational device or an explanation of why the use of the investigational device is preferable to the use of available marketed treatments;

(iv) A description of clinical procedures, laboratory tests, or other measures that will be used to evaluate the effects of the device and to minimize risk;

(v) Written procedures for monitoring the treatment use and the name and address of the monitor;

(vi) Instructions for use for the device and all other labeling as required under § 812.5(a) and (b);

(vii) Information that is relevant to the safety and effectiveness of the device for the intended treatment use. Information from other IDE's may be incorporated by reference to support the treatment use;

(viii) A statement of the sponsor's commitment to meet all applicable responsibilities under this part and part 56 of this chapter and to ensure compliance of all participating investigators

with the informed consent requirements of part 50 of this chapter;

(ix) An example of the agreement to be signed by all investigators participating in the treatment IDE and certification that no investigator will be added to the treatment IDE before the agreement is signed; and

(x) If the device is to be sold, the price to be charged and a statement indicating that the price is based on manufacturing and handling costs only.

(2) A licensed practitioner who receives an investigational device for treatment use under a treatment IDE is an "investigator" under the IDE and is responsible for meeting all applicable investigator responsibilities under this part and parts 50 and 56 of this chapter.

(d) FDA action on treatment IDE applications—
(1) Approval of treatment IDE's. Treatment use may begin 30 days after FDA receives the treatment IDE submission at the address specified in § 812.19, unless FDA notifies the sponsor in writing earlier than the 30 days that the treatment use may or may not begin. FDA may approve the treatment use as proposed or approve it with modifications.

(2) Disapproval or withdrawal of approval of treatment IDE's. FDA may disapprove or withdraw approval of a treatment IDE if:

(i) The criteria specified in § 812.36(b) are not met or the treatment IDE does not contain the information required in § 812.36(c);

(ii) FDA determines that any of the grounds for disapproval or withdrawal of approval listed in § 812.30(b)(1) through (b)(5) apply;

(iii) The device is intended for a serious disease or condition and there is insufficient evidence of safety and effectiveness to support such use;

(iv) The device is intended for an immediately life-threatening disease or condition and the available scientific evidence, taken as a whole, fails to provide a reasonable basis for concluding that the device:

(A) May be effective for its intended use in its intended population; or

(B) Would not expose the patients to whom the device is to be administered to an unreasonable and significant additional risk of illness or injury;

(v) There is reasonable evidence that the treatment use is impeding enrollment in, or otherwise interfering with the conduct or completion of, a controlled investigation of the same or another investigational device;

(vi) The device has received marketing approval/clearance or a comparable device or therapy becomes available to treat or diagnose the same indication in the same patient population for which the investigational device is being used;

(vii) The sponsor of the controlled clinical trial is not pursuing marketing approval/clearance with due diligence;

(viii) Approval of the IDE for the controlled clinical investigation of the device has been withdrawn; or

(ix) The clinical investigator(s) named in the treatment IDE are not qualified by reason of their scientific training and/or experience to use the investigational device for the intended treatment use.

(3) Notice of disapproval or withdrawal. If FDA disapproves or proposes to withdraw approval of a treatment IDE, FDA will follow the procedures set forth in § 812.30(c).

(e) Safeguards. Treatment use of an investigational device is conditioned upon the sponsor and investigators complying with the safeguards of the IDE process and the regulations governing informed consent (part 50 of this chapter) and institutional review boards (part 56 of this chapter).

(f) Reporting requirements. The sponsor of a treatment IDE shall submit progress reports on a semi-annual basis to all reviewing IRB's and FDA until the filing of a marketing application. These reports shall be based on the period of time since initial approval of the treatment IDE and shall include the number of patients treated with the device under the treatment IDE, the names of the investigators participating in the treatment IDE, and a brief description of the sponsor's efforts to pursue marketing approval/clearance of the device. Upon filing of a marketing application, progress reports shall be submitted annually in accordance with § 812.150(b)(5). The sponsor of a treatment IDE is responsible for submitting all other reports required under § 812.150.

[62 FR 48947, Sept. 18, 1997]

§ 812.38 Confidentiality of data and information.

(a) Existence of IDE. FDA will not disclose the existence of an IDE unless its existence has previously been publicly disclosed or acknowledged, until FDA approves an application for premarket approval of the device subject to the IDE; or a notice of completion of a product development protocol for the device has become effective.

(b) Availability of summaries or data. (1) FDA will make publicly available, upon request, a detailed summary of information concerning the safety and effectiveness of the device that was the basis for an order approving, disapproving, or withdrawing approval of an application for an IDE for a banned device. The summary shall include information on any adverse effect on health caused by the device.

(2) If a device is a banned device or if the existence of an IDE has been publicly disclosed or acknowledged, data or information contained in the file is not available for public disclosure before approval of an application for premarket approval or the effective date of a notice of completion of a product development protocol except as provided in this section. FDA may, in

its discretion, disclose a summary of selected portions of the safety and effectiveness data, that is, clinical, animal, or laboratory studies and tests of the device, for public consideration of a specific pending issue.

(3) If the existence of an IDE file has not been publicly disclosed or acknowledged, no data or information in the file are available for public disclosure except as provided in paragraphs (b) (1) and (c) of this section.

(4) Notwithstanding paragraph (b)(2) of this section, FDA will make available to the public, upon request, the information in the IDE that was required to be filed in Docket Number 95S-0158 in the Division of Dockets Management (HFA-305), Food and Drug Administration, 5630 Fishers Lane, rm. 1061, Rockville, MD 20852, for investigations involving an exception from informed consent under § 50.24 of this chapter. Persons wishing to request this information shall submit a request under the Freedom of Information Act.

(c) Reports of adverse effects. Upon request or on its own initiative, FDA shall disclose to an individual on whom an investigational device has been used a copy of a report of adverse device effects relating to that use.

(d) Other rules. Except as otherwise provided in this section, the availability for public disclosure of data and information in an IDE file shall be handled in accordance with § 814.9.

[45 FR 3751, Jan. 18, 1980, as amended at 53 FR 11253, Apr. 6, 1988; 61 FR 51531, Oct. 2, 1996]

Subpart C—Responsibilities of Sponsors

§ 812.40   General responsibilities of sponsors.

Sponsors are responsible for selecting qualified investigators and providing them with the information they need to conduct the investigation properly, ensuring proper monitoring of the investigation, ensuring that IRB review and approval are obtained, submitting an IDE application to FDA, and ensuring that any reviewing IRB and FDA are promptly informed of significant new information about an investigation. Additional responsibilities of sponsors are described in subparts B and G.

§ 812.42   FDA and IRB approval.

A sponsor shall not begin an investigation or part of an investigation until an IRB and FDA have both approved the application or supplemental application relating to the investigation or part of an investigation.

[46 FR 8957, Jan. 27, 1981]

§ 812.43   Selecting investigators and monitors.

(a) Selecting investigators. A sponsor shall select investigators qualified by training and experience to investigate the device.

(b) Control of device. A sponsor shall ship investigational devices only to qualified investigators participating in the investigation.

(c) Obtaining agreements. A sponsor shall obtain from each participating investigator a signed agreement that includes:

(1) The investigator's curriculum vitae.

(2) Where applicable, a statement of the investigator's relevant experience, including the dates, location, extent, and type of experience.

(3) If the investigator was involved in an investigation or other research that was terminated, an explanation of the circumstances that led to termination.

(4) A statement of the investigator's commitment to:

(i) Conduct the investigation in accordance with the agreement, the investigational plan, this part and other applicable FDA regulations, and conditions of approval imposed by the reviewing IRB or FDA;

(ii) Supervise all testing of the device involving

human subjects; and

(iii) Ensure that the requirements for obtaining informed consent are met.

(5) Sufficient accurate financial disclosure information to allow the sponsor to submit a complete and accurate certification or disclosure statement as required under part 54 of this chapter. The sponsor shall obtain a commitment from the clinical investigator to promptly update this information if any relevant changes occur during the course of the investigation and for 1 year following completion of the study. This information shall not be submitted in an investigational device exemption application, but shall be submitted in any marketing application involving the device.

(d) Selecting monitors. A sponsor shall select monitors qualified by training and experience to monitor the investigational study in accordance with this part and other applicable FDA regulations.

[45 FR 3751, Jan. 18, 1980, as amended at 63 FR 5253, Feb. 2, 1998]

§ 812.45   Informing investigators.

A sponsor shall supply all investigators participating in the investigation with copies of the investigational plan and the report of prior investigations of the device.

§ 812.46   Monitoring investigations.

(a) Securing compliance. A sponsor who discovers that an investigator is not complying with the signed agreement, the investigational plan, the requirements of this part or other applicable FDA regulations, or any conditions of approval imposed by the reviewing IRB or FDA shall promptly either secure compliance, or discontinue shipments of the device to the investigator and terminate the investigator's participation in the investigation. A sponsor shall also require such an investigator to dispose of or return the device, unless this action would jeopardize the rights, safety, or welfare of a subject.

(b) Unanticipated adverse device effects. (1) A sponsor shall immediately conduct an evaluation of any unanticipated adverse device effect.

(2) A sponsor who determines that an unanticipated adverse device effect presents an unreasonable risk to subjects shall terminate all investigations or parts of investigations presenting that risk as soon as possible. Termination shall occur not later than 5 working days after the sponsor makes this determination and not later than 15 working days after the sponsor first received notice of the effect.

(c) Resumption of terminated studies. If the device is a significant risk device, a sponsor may not resume a terminated investigation without IRB and FDA approval. If the device is not a significant risk device, a sponsor may not resume a terminated investigation without IRB approval and, if the investigation was terminated under paragraph (b)(2) of this section, FDA approval.

§ 812.47   Emergency research under § 50.24 of this chapter.

(a) The sponsor shall monitor the progress of all investigations involving an exception from informed consent under § 50.24 of this chapter. When the sponsor receives from the IRB information concerning the public disclosures under § 50.24(a)(7)(ii) and (a)(7)(iii) of this chapter, the sponsor shall promptly submit to the IDE file and to Docket Number 95S-0158 in the Division of Dockets Management (HFA-305), Food and Drug Administration, 5630 Fishers Lane, rm. 1061, Rockville, MD 20852, copies of the information that was disclosed, identified by the IDE number.

(b) The sponsor also shall monitor such investigations to determine when an IRB determines that it cannot approve the research because it does not meet the criteria in the exception in § 50.24(a) of this chapter or because of other relevant ethical concerns. The sponsor promptly shall provide this information in writing to FDA, investigators who are asked to participate in this or a substantially equivalent clinical investigation, and other IRB's that are asked to review this or a substantially equivalent investigation.

[61 FR 51531, Oct. 2, 1996, as amended at 64 FR 10943, Mar. 8, 1999]

Subpart D—IRB Review and Approval

§ 812.60   IRB composition, duties, and functions.

An IRB reviewing and approving investigations under this part shall comply with the requirements of part 56 in all respects, including its composition, duties, and functions.

[46 FR 8957, Jan. 27, 1981]

§ 812.62   IRB approval.

(a) An IRB shall review and have authority to approve, require modifications in (to secure approval), or disapprove all investigations covered by this part.

(b) If no IRB exists or if FDA finds that an IRB's review is inadequate, a sponsor may submit an application to FDA.

[46 FR 8957, Jan. 27, 1981]

§ 812.64   IRB's continuing review.

The IRB shall conduct its continuing review of an investigation in accordance with part 56.

[46 FR 8957, Jan. 27, 1981]

§ 812.65   [Reserved]

§ 812.66   Significant risk device determinations.

If an IRB determines that an investigation, presented for approval under § 812.2(b)(1)(ii), involves a significant risk device, it shall so notify the investigator and, where appropriate, the sponsor. A sponsor may not begin the investigation except as provided in § 812.30(a).

[46 FR 8957, Jan. 27, 1981]

Subpart E—Responsibilities of Investigators

§ 812.100   General responsibilities of investigators.

An investigator is responsible for ensuring that an investigation is conducted according to the signed agreement, the investigational plan and applicable FDA regulations, for protecting the rights, safety, and welfare of subjects under the investigator's care, and for the control of devices under investigation. An investigator also is responsible for ensuring that informed consent is obtained in accordance with part 50 of this chapter. Additional responsibilities of investigators are described in subpart G.

[45 FR 3751, Jan. 18, 1980, as amended at 46 FR 8957, Jan. 27, 1981]

§ 812.110   Specific responsibilities of investigators.

(a) Awaiting approval. An investigator may determine whether potential subjects would be interested in participating in an investigation, but shall not request the written informed consent of any subject to participate, and shall not allow any subject to participate before obtaining IRB and FDA approval.

(b) Compliance. An investigator shall conduct an investigation in accordance with the signed agreement with the sponsor, the investigational plan, this part and other applicable FDA regulations, and any conditions of approval imposed by an IRB or FDA.

(c) Supervising device use. An investigator shall permit an investigational device to be used only with subjects under the investigator's supervision. An investigator shall not supply an investigational device to any person not authorized under this part to receive it.

(d) Financial disclosure. A clinical investigator shall disclose to the sponsor sufficient accurate financial information to allow the applicant to submit complete and accurate certification or disclosure statements required under part 54 of this chapter. The investigator shall promptly update this information if any relevant changes occur during the course of the investigation and for 1 year following completion of the study.

(e) Disposing of device. Upon completion or termination of a clinical investigation or the investigator's part of an investigation, or at the sponsor's request, an investigator shall return to the sponsor any remaining supply of the device or otherwise dispose of the device as the sponsor directs.

[45 FR 3751, Jan. 18, 1980, as amended at 63 FR 5253, Feb. 2, 1998]

§ 812.119 Disqualification of a clinical investigator.

(a) If FDA has information indicating that an investigator has repeatedly or deliberately failed to comply with the requirements of this part, part 50, or part 56 of this chapter, or has repeatedly or deliberately submitted false information either to the sponsor of the investigation or in any required report, the Center for Devices and Radiological Health, the Center for Biologics Evaluation and Research, or the Center for Drug Evaluation and Research will furnish the investigator written notice of the matter under complaint and offer the investigator an opportunity to explain the matter in writing, or, at the option of the investigator, in an informal conference. If an explanation is offered and accepted by the applicable Center, the disqualification process will be terminated. If an explanation is offered but not accepted by the Center, the investigator will be given an opportunity for a regulatory hearing under part 16 of this chapter on the question of whether the investigator is entitled to receive investigational devices.

(b) After evaluating all available information, including any explanation presented by the investigator, if the Commissioner determines that the investigator has repeatedly or deliberately failed to comply with the requirements of this part, part 50, or part 56 of this chapter, or has deliberately or repeatedly submitted false infor-

mation either to the sponsor of the investigation or in any required report, the Commissioner will notify the investigator, the sponsor of any investigation in which the investigator has been named as a participant, and the reviewing IRB that the investigator is not entitled to receive investigational devices. The notification will provide a statement of basis for such determination.

(c) Each investigational device exemption (IDE) and each cleared or approved application submitted under this part, subpart E of part 807 of this chapter, or part 814 of this chapter containing data reported by an investigator who has been determined to be ineligible to receive investigational devices will be examined to determine whether the investigator has submitted unreliable data that are essential to the continuation of the investigation or essential to the approval or clearance of any marketing application.

(d) If the Commissioner determines, after the unreliable data submitted by the investigator are eliminated from consideration, that the data remaining are inadequate to support a conclusion that it is reasonably safe to continue the investigation, the Commissioner will notify the sponsor who shall have an opportunity for a regulatory hearing under part 16 of this chapter. If a danger to the public health exists, however, the Commissioner shall terminate the IDE immediately and notify the sponsor and the reviewing IRB of the determination. In such case, the sponsor shall have an opportunity for a regulatory hearing before FDA under part 16 of this chapter on the question of whether the IDE should be reinstated.

(e) If the Commissioner determines, after the unreliable data submitted by the investigator are eliminated from consideration, that the continued clearance or approval of the marketing application for which the data were submitted cannot be justified, the Commissioner will proceed to withdraw approval or rescind clearance of the medical device in accordance with the applicable provisions of the act.

(f) An investigator who has been determined to be ineligible to receive investigational devices may be reinstated as eligible when the Commissioner determines that the investigator has presented adequate assurances that the investigator will employ investigational devices solely in compliance with the provisions of this part and of parts 50 and 56 of this chapter.

[62 FR 12096, Mar. 14, 1997, as amended at 71 FR 76902, Dec. 22, 2006]

Subpart F [Reserved]

Subpart G—Records and Reports

§ 812.140   Records.

(a) Investigator records. A participating investigator shall maintain the following accurate, complete, and current records relating to the investigator's participation in an investigation:

(1) All correspondence with another investigator, an IRD, the sponsor, a monitor, or FDA, including required reports

(2) Records of receipt, use or disposition of a device that relate to:

(i) The type and quantity of the device, the dates of its receipt, and the batch number or code mark.

(ii) The names of all persons who received, used, or disposed of each device.

(iii) Why and how many units of the device have been returned to the sponsor, repaired, or otherwise disposed of.

(3) Records of each subject's case history and exposure to the device. Case histories include the case report forms and supporting data including, for example, signed and dated consent forms and medical records including, for example, progress notes of the physician, the individual's hospital chart(s), and the nurses' notes. Such records shall include:

(i) Documents evidencing informed consent and, for any use of a device by the investigator without informed consent, any written concurrence of a licensed physician and a brief description of the circumstances justifying the failure to obtain informed consent. The case history for each individual shall document that informed consent was obtained prior to participation in the study.

(ii) All relevant observations, including records concerning adverse device effects (whether anticipated or unanticipated), information and data on the condition of each subject upon entering, and during the course of, the investigation, including information about relevant previous medical history and the results of all diagnostic tests.

(iii) A record of the exposure of each subject to the investigational device, including the date and time of each use, and any other therapy.

(4) The protocol, with documents showing the dates of and reasons for each deviation from the protocol.

(5) Any other records that FDA requires to be maintained by regulation or by specific requirement for a category of investigations or a particular investigation.

(b) Sponsor records. A sponsor shall maintain the following accurate, complete, and current records relating to an investigation:

(1) All correspondence with another sponsor, a monitor, an investigator, an IRB, or FDA, including required reports.

(2) Records of shipment and disposition. Records of shipment shall include the name and address of the consignee, type and quantity of device, date of shipment, and batch number or code mark. Records of disposition shall describe the batch number or code marks of any devices returned to the sponsor, repaired, or disposed of in other ways by the investigator or another person, and the reasons for and method of disposal.

(3) Signed investigator agreements including the financial disclosure information required to

be collected under § 812.43(c)(5) in accordance with part 54 of this chapter.

(4) For each investigation subject to § 812.2(b)(1) of a device other than a significant risk device, the records described in paragraph (b)(5) of this section and the following records, consolidated in one location and available for FDA inspection and copying:

(i) The name and intended use of the device and the objectives of the investigation;

(ii) A brief explanation of why the device is not a significant risk device:

(iii) The name and address of each investigator:

(iv) The name and address of each IRB that has reviewed the investigation:

(v) A statement of the extent to which the good manufacturing practice regulation in part 820 will be followed in manufacturing the device; and

(vi) Any other information required by FDA.

(5) Records concerning adverse device effects (whether anticipated or unanticipated) and complaints and

(6) Any other records that FDA requires to be maintained by regulation or by specific requirement for a category of investigation or a particular investigation.

(c) IRB records. An IRB shall maintain records in accordance with part 56 of this chapter.

(d) Retention period. An investigator or sponsor shall maintain the records required by this subpart during the investigation and for a period of 2 years after the latter of the following two dates: The date on which the investigation is terminated or completed, or the date that the records are no longer required for purposes of supporting a premarket approval application or a notice of completion of a product development protocol.

(e) Records custody. An investigator or sponsor may withdraw from the responsibility to main-

tain records for the period required in paragraph (d) of this section and transfer custody of the records to any other person who will accept responsibility for them under this part, including the requirements of § 812.145. Notice of a transfer shall be given to FDA not later than 10 working days after transfer occurs.

[45 FR 3751, Jan. 18, 1980, as amended at 45 FR 58843, Sept. 5, 1980; 46 FR 8957, Jan. 27, 1981; 61 FR 57280, Nov. 5, 1996; 63 FR 5253, Feb. 2, 1998]

§ 812.145   Inspections.

(a) Entry and inspection. A sponsor or an investigator who has authority to grant access shall permit authorized FDA employees, at reasonable times and in a reasonable manner, to enter and inspect any establishment where devices are held (including any establishment where devices are manufactured, processed, packed, installed, used, or implanted or where records of results from use of devices are kept).

(b) Records inspection. A sponsor, IRB, or investigator, or any other person acting on behalf of such a person with respect to an investigation, shall permit authorized FDA employees, at reasonable times and in a reasonable manner, to inspect and copy all records relating to an investigation.

(c) Records identifying subjects. An investigator shall permit authorized FDA employees to inspect and copy records that identify subjects, upon notice that FDA has reason to suspect that adequate informed consent was not obtained, or that reports required to be submitted by the investigator to the sponsor or IRB have not been submitted or are incomplete, inaccurate, false, or misleading.

§ 812.150   Reports.

(a) Investigator reports. An investigator shall prepare and submit the following complete, accurate, and timely reports:

(1) Unanticipated adverse device effects. An

investigator shall submit to the sponsor and to the reviewing IRB a report of any unanticipated adverse device effect occurring during an investigation as soon as possible, but in no event later than 10 working days after the investigator first learns of the effect.

(2) Withdrawal of IRB approval. An investigator shall report to the sponsor, within 5 working days, a withdrawal of approval by the reviewing IRB of the investigator's part of an investigation.

(3) Progress. An investigator shall submit progress reports on the investigation to the sponsor, the monitor, and the reviewing IRB at regular intervals, but in no event less often than yearly.

(4) Deviations from the investigational plan. An investigator shall notify the sponsor and the reviewing IRB (see § 56.108(a) (3) and (4)) of any deviation from the investigational plan to protect the life or physical well-being of a subject in an emergency. Such notice shall be given as soon as possible, but in no event later than 5 working days after the emergency occurred. Except in such an emergency, prior approval by the sponsor is required for changes in or deviations from a plan, and if these changes or deviations may affect the scientific soundness of the plan or the rights, safety, or welfare of human subjects, FDA and IRB in accordance with § 812.35(a) also is required.

(5) Informed consent. If an investigator uses a device without obtaining informed consent, the investigator shall report such use to the sponsor and the reviewing IRB within 5 working days after the use occurs.

(6) Final report. An investigator shall, within 3 months after termination or completion of the investigation or the investigator's part of the investigation, submit a final report to the sponsor and the reviewing IRB.

(7) Other. An investigator shall, upon request by a reviewing IRB or FDA, provide accurate, complete, and current information about any aspect of the investigation.

(b) Sponsor reports. A sponsor shall prepare and submit the following complete, accurate, and timely reports:

(1) Unanticipated adverse device effects. A sponsor who conducts an evaluation of an unanticipated adverse device effect under § 812.46(b) shall report the results of such evaluation to FDA and to all reviewing IRB's and participating investigators within 10 working days after the sponsor first receives notice of the effect. Thereafter the sponsor shall submit such additional reports concerning the effect as FDA requests.

(2) Withdrawal of IRB approval. A sponsor shall notify FDA and all reviewing IRB's and participating investigators of any withdrawal of approval of an investigation or a part of an investigation by a reviewing IRB within 5 working days after receipt of the withdrawal of approval.

(3) Withdrawal of FDA approval. A sponsor shall notify all reviewing IRB's and participating investigators of any withdrawal of FDA approval of the investigation, and shall do so within 5 working days after receipt of notice of the withdrawal of approval.

(4) Current investigator list. A sponsor shall submit to FDA, at 6-month intervals, a current list of the names and addresses of all investigators participating in the investigation. The sponsor shall submit the first such list 6 months after FDA approval.

(5) Progress reports. At regular intervals, and at least yearly, a sponsor shall submit progress reports to all reviewing IRB's. In the case of a significant risk device, a sponsor shall also submit progress reports to FDA. A sponsor of a treatment IDE shall submit semi-annual progress reports to all reviewing IRB's and FDA in accordance with § 812.36(f) and annual reports in accordance with this section.

(6) Recall and device disposition. A sponsor shall notify FDA and all reviewing IRB's of any request that an investigator return, repair, or otherwise dispose of any units of a device. Such notice

shall occur within 30 working days after the request is made and shall state why the request was made.

(7) Final report. In the case of a significant risk device, the sponsor shall notify FDA within 30 working days of the completion or termination of the investigation and shall submit a final report to FDA and all reviewing the IRB's and participating investigators within 6 months after completion or termination. In the case of a device that is not a significant risk device, the sponsor shall submit a final report to all reviewing IRB's within 6 months after termination or completion.

(8) Informed consent. A sponsor shall submit to FDA a copy of any report by an investigator under paragraph (a)(5) of this section of use of a device without obtaining informed consent, within 5 working days of receipt of notice of such use.

(9) Significant risk device determinations. If an IRB determines that a device is a significant risk device, and the sponsor had proposed that the IRB consider the device not to be a significant risk device, the sponsor shall submit to FDA a report of the IRB's determination within 5 working days after the sponsor first learns of the IRB's determination.

(10) Other. A sponsor shall, upon request by a reviewing IRB or FDA, provide accurate, complete, and current information about any aspect of the investigation.

[45 FR 3751, Jan. 18, 1980, as amended at 45 FR 58843, Sept. 5, 1980; 48 FR 15622, Apr. 12, 1983; 62 FR 48948, Sept. 18, 1997]

Part 814—Pre-market Approval of Medical Devices

Authority:

21 U.S.C. 351, 352, 353, 360, 360c-360j, 371, 372, 373, 374, 375, 379, 379e, 381.

Source:

51 FR 26364, July 22, 1986, unless otherwise noted.

Subpart A—General

§ 814.1   Scope.

Link to an amendment published at 75 FR 16350, Apr. 1, 2010.

(a) This part implements section 515 of the act by providing procedures for the premarket approval of medical devices intended for human use.

(b) References in this part to regulatory sections of the Code of Federal Regulations are to chapter I of title 21, unless otherwise noted.

(c) This part applies to any class III medical device, unless exempt under section 520(g) of the act, that:

(1) Was not on the market (introduced or delivered for introduction into commerce for commercial distribution) before May 28, 1976, and is not substantially equivalent to a device on the market before May 28, 1976, or to a device first marketed on, or after that date, which has been classified into class I or class II; or

(2) Is required to have an approved premarket approval application (PMA) or a declared completed product development protocol under a regulation issued under section 515(b) of the act; or

(3) Was regulated by FDA as a new drug or antibiotic drug before May 28, 1976, and therefore is governed by section 520(1) of the act.

(d) This part amends the conditions to approval for any PMA approved before the effective date of this part. Any condition to approval for an approved PMA that is inconsistent with this part is revoked. Any condition to approval for an approved PMA that is consistent with this part remains in effect.

Effective Date Note:

At 75 FR 16350, Apr. 1, 2010, § 814.1 was amended by revising paragraph (a), effective Aug. 16, 2010. For the convenience of the user, the revised text is set forth as follows:

§ 814.1   Scope.

(a) This section implements sections 515 and 515A of the act by providing procedures for the premarket approval of medical devices intended for human use.

§ 814.2   Purpose.

Link to an amendment published at 75 FR 16350, Apr. 1, 2010.

The purpose of this part is to establish an efficient and thorough device review process—

(a) To facilitate the approval of PMA's for devices that have been shown to be safe and effective and that otherwise meet the statutory criteria for approval; and

(b) To ensure the disapproval of PMA's for devices that have not been shown to be safe and effective or that do not otherwise meet the statutory criteria for approval. This part shall be construed in light of these objectives.

Effective Date Note:

At 75 FR 16350, Apr. 1, 2010, § 814.2 was revised, effective Aug. 16, 2010. For the convenience of the user, the revised text is set forth as follows:

§ 814.2   Purpose.

The purpose of this part is to establish an efficient and thorough device review process—

(a) To facilitate the approval of PMAs for devices that have been shown to be safe and effective and that otherwise meet the statutory criteria for approval;

(b) To ensure the disapproval of PMAs that have not been shown to be safe and effective or that do not otherwise meet the statutory criteria for

approval; and

(c) To ensure PMAs include readily available information concerning actual and potential pediatric uses of medical devices.

§ 814.3   Definitions.

For the purposes of this part:

(a) Act means the Federal Food, Drug, and Cosmetic Act (sections 201-902, 52 Stat. 1040 et seq., as amended (21 U.S.C. 321-392)).

(b) FDA means the Food and Drug Administration.

(c) IDE means an approved or considered approved investigational device exemption under section 520(g) of the act and parts 812 and 813.

(d) Master file means a reference source that a person submits to FDA. A master file may contain detailed information on a specific manufacturing facility, process, methodology, or component used in the manufacture, processing, or packaging of a medical device.

(e) PMA means any premarket approval application for a class III medical device, including all information submitted with or incorporated by reference therein. "PMA" includes a new drug application for a device under section 520(1) of the act.

(f) PMA amendment means information an applicant submits to FDA to modify a pending PMA or a pending PMA supplement.

(g) PMA supplement means a supplemental application to an approved PMA for approval of a change or modification in a class III medical device, including all information submitted with or incorporated by reference therein.

(h) Person includes any individual, partnership, corporation, association, scientific or academic establishment, Government agency, or organizational unit thereof, or any other legal entity.

(i) Statement of material fact means a representation that tends to show that the safety or effectiveness of a device is more probable than it would be in the absence of such a representation. A false affirmation or silence or an omission that would lead a reasonable person to draw a particular conclusion as to the safety or effectiveness of a device also may be a false statement of material fact, even if the statement was not intended by the person making it to be misleading or to have any probative effect.

(j) 30-day PMA supplement means a supplemental application to an approved PMA in accordance with § 814.39(e).

(k) Reasonable probability means that it is more likely than not that an event will occur.

(l) Serious, adverse health consequences means any significant adverse experience, including those which may be either life-threatening or involve permanent or long term injuries, but excluding injuries that are nonlife-threatening and that are temporary and reasonably reversible.

(m) HDE means a premarket approval application submitted pursuant to this subpart seeking a humanitarian device exemption from the effectiveness requirements of sections 514 and 515 of the act as authorized by section 520(m)(2) of the act.

(n) HUD (humanitarian use device) means a medical device intended to benefit patients in the treatment or diagnosis of a disease or condition that affects or is manifested in fewer than 4,000 individuals in the United States per year.

(o) Newly acquired information means data, analyses, or other information not previously submitted to the agency, which may include (but are not limited to) data derived from new clinical studies, reports of adverse events, or new analyses of previously submitted data (e.g., meta-analyses) if the studies, events or analyses reveal risks of a different type or greater severity or frequency than previously included in submissions to FDA.

[51 FR 26364, July 22, 1986, as amended at 61 FR 15190, Apr. 5, 1996; 61 FR 33244, June 26, 1996; 73 FR 49610, Aug. 22, 2008]

§ 814.9 Confidentiality of data and information in a premarket approval application (PMA) file.

(a) A "PMA file" includes all data and information submitted with or incorporated by reference in the PMA, any IDE incorporated into the PMA, any PMA supplement, any report under § 814.82, any master file, or any other related submission. Any record in the PMA file will be available for public disclosure in accordance with the provisions of this section and part 20. The confidentiality of information in a color additive petition submitted as part of a PMA is governed by § 71.15.

(b) The existence of a PMA file may not be disclosed by FDA before an approval order is issued to the applicant unless it previously has been publicly disclosed or acknowledged.

(c) If the existence of a PMA file has not been publicly disclosed or acknowledged, data or information in the PMA file are not available for public disclosure.

(d)(1) If the existence of a PMA file has been publicly disclosed or acknowledged before an order approving, or an order denying approval of the PMA is issued, data or information contained in the file are not available for public disclosure before such order issues. FDA may, however, disclose a summary of portions of the safety and effectiveness data before an approval order or an order denying approval of the PMA issues if disclosure is relevant to public consideration of a specific pending issue.

(2) Notwithstanding paragraph (d)(1) of this section, FDA will make available to the public upon request the information in the IDE that was required to be filed in Docket Number 95S-0158 in the Division of Dockets Management (HFA-305), Food and Drug Administration, 12420 Parklawn Dr., rm. 1-23, Rockville, MD 20857, for investigations involving an ex-

ception from informed consent under § 50.24 of this chapter. Persons wishing to request this information shall submit a request under the Freedom of Information Act.

(e) Upon issuance of an order approving, or an order denying approval of any PMA, FDA will make available to the public the fact of the existence of the PMA and a detailed summary of information submitted to FDA respecting the safety and effectiveness of the device that is the subject of the PMA and that is the basis for the order.

(f) After FDA issues an order approving, or an order denying approval of any PMA, the following data and information in the PMA file are immediately available for public disclosure:

(1) All safety and effectiveness data and information previously disclosed to the public, as such disclosure is defined in § 20.81.

(2) Any protocol for a test or study unless the protocol is shown to constitute trade secret or confidential commercial or financial information under § 20.61.

(3) Any adverse reaction report, product experience report, consumer complaint, and other similar data and information, after deletion of:

(i) Any information that constitutes trade secret or confidential commercial or financial information under § 20.61; and

(ii) Any personnel, medical, and similar information disclosure of which would constitute a clearly unwarranted invasion of personal privacy under § 20.63; provided, however, that except for the information that constitutes trade secret or confidential commercial or financial information under § 20.61, FDA will disclose to a patient who requests a report all the information in the report concerning that patient.

(4) A list of components previously disclosed to the public, as such disclosure is defined in § 20.81.

(5) An assay method or other analytical method, unless it does not serve any regulatory purpose and is shown to fall within the exemption in § 20.61 for trade secret or confidential commercial or financial information.

(6) All correspondence and written summaries of oral discussions relating to the PMA file, in accordance with the provisions of §§ 20.103 and 20.104.

(g) All safety and effectiveness data and other information not previously disclosed to the public are available for public disclosure if any one of the following events occurs and the data and information do not constitute trade secret or confidential commercial or financial information under § 20.61:

(1) The PMA has been abandoned. FDA will consider a PMA abandoned if:

(i)(A) The applicant fails to respond to a request for additional information within 180 days after the date FDA issues the request or

(B) Other circumstances indicate that further work is not being undertaken with respect to it, and

(ii) The applicant fails to communicate with FDA within 7 days after the date on which FDA notifies the applicant that the PMA appears to have been abandoned.

(2) An order denying approval of the PMA has issued, and all legal appeals have been exhausted.

(3) An order withdrawing approval of the PMA has issued, and all legal appeals have been exhausted.

(4) The device has been reclassified.

(5) The device has been found to be substantially equivalent to a class I or class II device.

(6) The PMA is considered voluntarily withdrawn under § 814.44(g).

(h) The following data and information in a PMA file are not available for public disclosure unless they have been previously disclosed to the public, as such disclosure is defined in § 20.81, or they relate to a device for which a PMA has been abandoned and they no longer represent a trade secret or confidential commercial or financial information as defined in § 20.61:

(1) Manufacturing methods or processes, including quality control procedures.

(2) Production, sales, distribution, and similar data and information, except that any compilation of such data and information aggregated and prepared in a way that does not reveal data or information which are not available for public disclosure under this provision is available for public disclosure.

(3) Quantitative or semiquantitative formulas.

[51 FR 26364, July 22, 1986, as amended at 61 FR 51531, Oct. 2, 1996]

§ 814.15 Research conducted outside the United States.

(a) A study conducted outside the United States submitted in support of a PMA and conducted under an IDE shall comply with part 812. A study conducted outside the United States submitted in support of a PMA and not conducted under an IDE shall comply with the provisions in paragraph (b) or (c) of this section, as applicable.

(b) Research begun on or after effective date. FDA will accept studies submitted in support of a PMA which have been conducted outside the United States and begun on or after November 19, 1986, if the data are valid and the investigator has conducted the studies in conformance with the "Declaration of Helsinki" or the laws and regulations of the country in which the research is conducted, whichever accords greater protection to the human subjects. If the standards of the country are used, the applicant shall state in detail any differences between those standards and the "Declaration of Helsinki" and explain why they offer greater protection to the human subjects.

(c) Research begun before effective date. FDA will accept studies submitted in support of a PMA which have been conducted outside the United States and begun before November 19, 1986, if FDA is satisfied that the data are scientifically valid and that the rights, safety, and welfare of human subjects have not been violated.

(d) As sole basis for marketing approval. A PMA based solely on foreign clinical data and otherwise meeting the criteria for approval under this part may be approved if:

(1) The foreign data are applicable to the U.S. population and U.S. medical practice;

(2) The studies have been performed by clinical investigators of recognized competence; and

(3) The data may be considered valid without the need for an on-site inspection by FDA or, if FDA considers such an inspection to be necessary, FDA can validate the data through an on-site inspection or other appropriate means.

(e) Consultation between FDA and applicants. Applicants are encouraged to meet with FDA officials in a "presubmission" meeting when approval based solely on foreign data will be sought.

(Approved by the Office of Management and Budget under control number 0910-0231)

[51 FR 26364, July 22, 1986; 51 FR 40415, Nov. 7, 1986, as amended at 51 FR 43344, Dec. 2, 1986]

§ 814.17 Service of orders.

Orders issued under this part will be served in person by a designated officer or employee of FDA on, or by registered mail to, the applicant or the designated agent at the applicant's or designated agent's last known address in FDA's records.

§ 814.19 Product development protocol (PDP).

A class III device for which a product development protocol has been declared completed by FDA under this chapter will be considered to have an approved PMA.

Subpart B—Premarket Approval Application (PMA)

§ 814.20   Application.

Link to an amendment published at 75 FR 16351, Apr. 1, 2010.

(a) The applicant or an authorized representative shall sign the PMA. If the applicant does not reside or have a place of business within the United States, the PMA shall be countersigned by an authorized representative residing or maintaining a place of business in the United States and shall identify the representative's name and address.

(b) Unless the applicant justifies an omission in accordance with paragraph (d) of this section, a PMA shall include:

(1) The name and address of the applicant.

(2) A table of contents that specifies the volume and page number for each item referred to in the table. A PMA shall include separate sections on nonclinical laboratory studies and on clinical investigations involving human subjects. A PMA shall be submitted in six copies each bound in one or more numbered volumes of reasonable size. The applicant shall include information that it believes to be trade secret or confidential commercial or financial information in all copies of the PMA and identify in at least one copy the information that it believes to be trade secret or confidential commercial or financial information.

(3) A summary in sufficient detail that the reader may gain a general understanding of the data and information in the application. The summary shall contain the following information:

(i) Indications for use. A general description of the disease or condition the device will diagnose, treat, prevent, cure, or mitigate, includ-

ing a description of the patient population for which the device is intended.

(ii) Device description. An explanation of how the device functions, the basic scientific concepts that form the basis for the device, and the significant physical and performance characteristics of the device. A brief description of the manufacturing process should be included if it will significantly enhance the reader's understanding of the device. The generic name of the device as well as any proprietary name or trade name should be included.

(iii) Alternative practices and procedures. A description of existing alternative practices or procedures for diagnosing, treating, preventing, curing, or mitigating the disease or condition for which the device is intended.

(iv) Marketing history. A brief description of the foreign and U.S. marketing history, if any, of the device, including a list of all countries in which the device has been marketed and a list of all countries in which the device has been withdrawn from marketing for any reason related to the safety or effectiveness of the device. The description shall include the history of the marketing of the device by the applicant and, if known, the history of the marketing of the device by any other person.

(v) Summary of studies. An abstract of any information or report described in the PMA under paragraph (b)(8)(ii) of this section and a summary of the results of technical data submitted under paragraph (b)(6) of this section. Such summary shall include a description of the objective of the study, a description of the experimental design of the study, a brief description of how the data were collected and analyzed, and a brief description of the results, whether positive, negative, or inconclusive. This section shall include the following:

(A) A summary of the nonclinical laboratory studies submitted in the application;

(B) A summary of the clinical investigations

involving human subjects submitted in the application including a discussion of subject selection and exclusion criteria, study population, study period, safety and effectiveness data, adverse reactions and complications, patient discontinuation, patient complaints, device failures and replacements, results of statistical analyses of the clinical investigations, contraindications and precautions for use of the device, and other information from the clinical investigations as appropriate (any investigation conducted under an IDE shall be identified as such).

(vi) Conclusions drawn from the studies. A discussion demonstrating that the data and information in the application constitute valid scientific evidence within the meaning of § 860.7 and provide reasonable assurance that the device is safe and effective for its intended use. A concluding discussion shall present benefit and risk considerations related to the device including a discussion of any adverse effects of the device on health and any proposed additional studies or surveillance the applicant intends to conduct following approval of the PMA.

(4) A complete description of:

(i) The device, including pictorial representations;

(ii) Each of the functional components or ingredients of the device if the device consists of more than one physical component or ingredient;

(iii) The properties of the device relevant to the diagnosis, treatment, prevention, cure, or mitigation of a disease or condition;

(iv) The principles of operation of the device; and

(v) The methods used in, and the facilities and controls used for, the manufacture, processing, packing, storage, and, where appropriate, installation of the device, in sufficient detail so that a person generally familiar with current good manufacturing practice can make a knowledgeable judgment about the quality control used in the manufacture of the device.

(5) Reference to any performance standard under section 514 of the act or under section 534 of Subchapter C—Electronic Product Radiation Control of the Federal Food, Drug, and Cosmetic Act (formerly the Radiation Control for Health and Safety Act of 1968) in effect or proposed at the time of the submission and to any voluntary standard that is relevant to any aspect of the safety or effectiveness of the device and that is known to or that should reasonably be known to the applicant. The applicant shall—

(i) Provide adequate information to demonstrate how the device meets, or justify any deviation from, any performance standard established under section 514 of the act or under section 534 of Subchapter C—Electronic Product Radiation Control of the Federal Food, Drug, and Cosmetic Act (formerly the Radiation Control for Health and Safety Act of 1968), and

(ii) Explain any deviation from a voluntary standard.

(6) The following technical sections which shall contain data and information in sufficient detail to permit FDA to determine whether to approve or deny approval of the application:

(i) A section containing results of the nonclinical laboratory studies with the device including microbiological, toxicological, immunological, biocompatibility, stress, wear, shelf life, and other laboratory or animal tests as appropriate. Information on nonclinical laboratory studies shall include a statement that each such study was conducted in compliance with part 58, or, if the study was not conducted in compliance with such regulations, a brief statement of the reason for the noncompliance.

(ii) A section containing results of the clinical investigations involving human subjects with the device including clinical protocols, number of investigators and subjects per investigator, subject selection and exclusion criteria, study population, study period, safety and effectiveness data, adverse reactions and complications, patient discontinuation, patient complaints, device failures and replacements, tabulations of data from all individual subject report forms and copies of such forms for each subject who died during a clinical investigation or who did not complete the investigation, results of statistical analyses of the clinical investigations, device failures and replacements, contraindications and precautions for use of the device, and any other appropriate information from the clinical investigations. Any investigation conducted under an IDE shall be identified as such. Information on clinical investigations involving human subjects shall include the following:

(A) A statement with respect to each study that it either was conducted in compliance with the institutional review board regulations in part 56, or was not subject to the regulations under § 56.104 or § 56.105, and that it was conducted in compliance with the informed consent regulations in part 50; or if the study was not conducted in compliance with those regulations, a brief statement of the reason for the noncompliance.

(B) A statement that each study was conducted in compliance with part 812 or part 813 concerning sponsors of clinical investigations and clinical investigators, or if the study was not conducted in compliance with those regulations, a brief statement of the reason for the noncompliance.

(7) For a PMA supported solely by data from one investigation, a justification showing that data and other information from a single investigator are sufficient to demonstrate the safety and effectiveness of the device and to ensure reproducibility of test results.

(8)(i) A bibliography of all published reports not submitted under paragraph (b)(6) of this section, whether adverse or supportive, known to or that should reasonably be known to the applicant and that concern the safety or effectiveness of the device.

(ii) An identification, discussion, and analysis of any other data, information, or report relevant to an evaluation of the safety and effectiveness of the device known to or that should reasonably be known to the applicant from any source, foreign or domestic, including information derived from investigations other than those proposed in the application and from commercial marketing experience.

(iii) Copies of such published reports or unpublished information in the possession of or reasonably obtainable by the applicant if an FDA advisory committee or FDA requests.

(9) One or more samples of the device and its components, if requested by FDA. If it is impractical to submit a requested sample of the device, the applicant shall name the location at which FDA may examine and test one or more devices.

(10) Copies of all proposed labeling for the device. Such labeling may include, e.g., instructions for installation and any information, literature, or advertising that constitutes labeling under section 201(m) of the act.

(11) An environmental assessment under § 25.20(n) prepared in the applicable format in § 25.40, unless the action qualifies for exclusion under § 25.30 or § 25.34. If the applicant believes that the action qualifies for exclusion, the PMA shall under § 25.15(a) and (d) provide information that establishes to FDA's satisfaction that the action requested is included within the excluded category and meets the criteria for the applicable exclusion.

(12) A financial certification or disclosure statement or both as required by part 54 of this chapter.

(13) Such other information as FDA may request. If necessary, FDA will obtain the concurrence of the appropriate FDA advisory committee before requesting additional information.

(c) Pertinent information in FDA files specifically referred to by an applicant may be incorporated into a PMA by reference. Information in a master file or other information submitted to FDA by a person other than the applicant will not be considered part of a PMA unless such reference is authorized in writing by the person who submitted the information or the master file. If a master file is not referenced within 5 years after the date that it is submitted to FDA, FDA will return the master file to the person who submitted it.

(d) If the applicant believes that certain information required under paragraph (b) of this section to be in a PMA is not applicable to the device that is the subject of the PMA, and omits any such information from its PMA, the applicant shall submit a statement that identifies the omitted information and justifies the omission. The statement shall be submitted as a separate section in the PMA and identified in the table of contents. If the justification for the omission is not accepted by the agency, FDA will so notify the applicant.

(e) The applicant shall periodically update its pending application with new safety and effectiveness information learned about the device from ongoing or completed studies that may reasonably affect an evaluation of the safety or effectiveness of the device or that may reasonably affect the statement of contraindications, warnings, precautions, and adverse reactions in the draft labeling. The update report shall be consistent with the data reporting provisions of the protocol. The applicant shall submit three copies of any update report and shall include in the report the number assigned by FDA to the PMA. These updates are considered to be amendments to the PMA. The time frame for review of a PMA will not be extended due to the submission of an update report unless the update is a major amendment under § 814.37(c) (1). The applicant shall submit these reports—

(1) 3 months after the filing date,

(2) Following receipt of an approvable letter, and

(3) At any other time as requested by FDA.

(f) If a color additive subject to section 721 of the act is used in or on the device and has not previously been listed for such use, then, in lieu of submitting a color additive petition under part 71, at the option of the applicant, the information required to be submitted under part 71 may be submitted as part of the PMA. When submitted as part of the PMA, the information shall be submitted in three copies each bound in one or more numbered volumes of reasonable size. A PMA for a device that contains a color additive that is subject to section 721 of the act will not be approved until the color additive is listed for use in or on the device.

(g) Additional information on FDA policies and procedures, as well as links to PMA guidance documents, is available on the Internet at http://www.fda.gov/cdrh/devadvice/pma/.

(h) If you are sending a PMA, PMA amendment, PMA supplement, or correspondence with respect to a PMA, you must send the submission to the appropriate address as follows:

(1) For devices regulated by the Center for Devices and Radiological Health, send it to: Document Mail Center (HFZ-401), Center for Devices and Radiological Health, Food and Drug Administration, 9200 Corporate Blvd., Rockville, MD 20850.

(2) For devices regulated by the Center for Biologics Evaluation and Research, send it to: Document Control Center (HFM-99), Center for Biologics Evaluation and Research, Food and Drug Administration, 1401 Rockville Pike, suite 200N, Rockville, MD 20852-1448.

(3) For devices regulated by the Center for Drug Evaluation and Research, send it to: Central Document Control Room, Center for Drug Evaluation and Research, Food and Drug Administration, 5901-B Ammendale Rd., Beltsville, MD 20705-1266.

[51 FR 26364, July 22, 1986; 51 FR 40415, Nov. 7,

1986, as amended at 51 FR 43344, Dec. 2, 1986; 55 FR 11169, Mar. 27, 1990; 62 FR 40600, July 29, 1997; 63 FR 5253, Feb. 2, 1998; 65 FR 17137, Mar. 31, 2000; 65 FR 56480, Sept. 19, 2000; 67 FR 9587, Mar. 4, 2002; 71 FR 42048, July 25, 2006; 72 FR 17399, Apr. 9, 2007; 73 FR 34859, June 19, 2008; 74 FR 14478, Mar. 31, 2009]

Effective Date Note:

At 75 FR 16351, Apr. 1, 2010, § 814.20; was amended by revising paragraph (b)(3)(i), effective Aug. 16, 2010. For the convenience of the user, the revised text is set forth as follows:

§ 814.20   Application.

(b) * * *

(3) * * *

(i) Indications for use. (A) A general description of the disease or condition the device will diagnose, treat, prevent, cure, or mitigate, including a description of the patient population for which the device is intended.

(B) Information concerning uses in pediatric patients who are 21 years of age or younger: The application must include the following information, if readily available:

(1) A description of any pediatric subpopulations (neonates, infants, children, adolescents) that suffer from the disease or condition that the device is intended to treat, diagnose, or cure; and

(2) The number of affected pediatric patients.

§ 814.37   PMA amendments and resubmitted PMA's.

Link to an amendment published at 75 FR 16351, Apr. 1, 2010.

(a) An applicant may amend a pending PMA or PMA supplement to revise existing information or provide additional information.

(b) FDA may request the applicant to amend a PMA or PMA supplement with any information regarding the device that is necessary for FDA or the appropriate advisory committee to complete the review of the PMA or PMA supplement.

(c) A PMA amendment submitted to FDA shall include the PMA or PMA supplement number assigned to the original submission and, if submitted on the applicant's own initiative, the reason for submitting the amendment. FDA may extend the time required for its review of the PMA, or PMA supplement, as follows:

(1) If the applicant on its own initiative or at FDA's request submits a major PMA amendment (e.g., an amendment that contains significant new data from a previously unreported study, significant updated data from a previously reported study, detailed new analyses of previously submitted data, or significant required information previously omitted), the review period may be extended up to 180 days.

(2) If an applicant declines to submit a major amendment requested by FDA, the review period may be extended for the number of days that elapse between the date of such request and the date that FDA receives the written response declining to submit the requested amendment.

(d) An applicant may on its own initiative withdraw a PMA or PMA supplement. If FDA requests an applicant to submit a PMA amendment and a written response to FDA's request is not received within 180 days of the date of the request, FDA will consider the pending PMA or PMA supplement to be withdrawn voluntarily by the applicant.

(e) An applicant may resubmit a PMA or PMA supplement after withdrawing it or after it is considered withdrawn under paragraph (d) of this section, or after FDA has refused to accept it for filing, or has denied approval of the PMA or PMA supplement. A resubmitted PMA or PMA supplement shall comply with the requirements of § 814.20 or § 814.39, respectively, and shall include the PMA number assigned to the original submission and the applicant's reasons for resubmission of the PMA or PMA supplement.

Effective Date Note:

At 75 FR 16351, Apr. 1, 2010, § 814.37 was amended by revising the section heading and paragraph (b), effective Aug. 16, 2010. For the convenience of the user, the revised text is set forth as follows:

§ 814.37   PMA amendments and resubmitted PMAs.

(b)(1) FDA may request the applicant to amend a PMA or PMA supplement with any information regarding the device that is necessary for FDA or the appropriate advisory committee to complete the review of the PMA or PMA supplement.

(2) FDA may request the applicant to amend a PMA or PMA supplement with information concerning pediatric uses as required under § 814.20(b)(3)(i).

§ 814.39   PMA supplements.

Link to an amendment published at 75 FR 16351, Apr. 1, 2010.

(a) After FDA's approval of a PMA, an applicant shall submit a PMA supplement for review and approval by FDA before making a change affecting the safety or effectiveness of the device for which the applicant has an approved PMA, unless the change is of a type for which FDA, under paragraph (e) of this section, has advised that an alternate submission is permitted or is of a type which, under section 515(d)(6) (A) of the act and paragraph (f) of this section, does not require a PMA supplement under this paragraph. While the burden for determining whether a supplement is required is primarily on the PMA holder, changes for which an applicant shall submit a PMA supplement include, but are not limited to, the following types of changes if they affect the safety or effectiveness of the device:

(1) New indications for use of the device.

(2) Labeling changes.

(3) The use of a different facility or establishment to manufacture, process, or package the device.

(4) Changes in sterilization procedures.

(5) Changes in packaging.

(6) Changes in the performance or design specifications, circuits, components, ingredients, principle of operation, or physical layout of the device.

(7) Extension of the expiration date of the device based on data obtained under a new or revised stability or sterility testing protocol that has not been approved by FDA. If the protocol has been approved, the change shall be reported to FDA under paragraph (b) of this section.

(b) An applicant may make a change in a device after FDA's approval of a PMA for the device without submitting a PMA supplement if the change does not affect the device's safety or effectiveness and the change is reported to FDA in postapproval periodic reports required as a condition to approval of the device, e.g., an editorial change in labeling which does not affect the safety or effectiveness of the device.

(c) All procedures and actions that apply to an application under § 814.20 also apply to PMA supplements except that the information required in a supplement is limited to that needed to support the change. A summary under § 814.20(b)(3) is required for only a supplement submitted for new indications for use of the device, significant changes in the performance or design specifications, circuits, components, ingredients, principles of operation, or physical layout of the device, or when otherwise required by FDA. The applicant shall submit three copies of a PMA supplement and shall include information relevant to the proposed changes in the device. A PMA supplement shall include a separate section that identifies each change for which approval is being requested and explains the reason for each such change. The applicant shall submit additional copies and additional information if requested by FDA. The time frames for review of, and FDA action on, a PMA supplement are the same as those provided in § 814.40 for a PMA.

(d)(1) After FDA approves a PMA, any change described in paragraph (d)(2) of this section to reflect newly acquired information that enhances the safety of the device or the safety in the use of the device may be placed into effect by the applicant prior to the receipt under § 814.17 of a written FDA order approving the PMA supplement provided that:

(i) The PMA supplement and its mailing cover are plainly marked "Special PMA Supplement—Changes Being Effected";

(ii) The PMA supplement provides a full explanation of the basis for the changes;

(iii) The applicant has received acknowledgement from FDA of receipt of the supplement; and

(iv) The PMA supplement specifically identifies the date that such changes are being effected.

(2) The following changes are permitted by paragraph (d)(1) of this section:

(i) Labeling changes that add or strengthen a contraindication, warning, precaution, or information about an adverse reaction for which there is reasonable evidence of a causal association.

(ii) Labeling changes that add or strengthen an instruction that is intended to enhance the safe use of the device.

(iii) Labeling changes that delete misleading, false, or unsupported indications.

(iv) Changes in quality controls or manufacturing process that add a new specification or test method, or otherwise provide additional assurance of purity, identity, strength, or reliability of the device.

(e)(1) FDA will identify a change to a device for which an applicant has an approved PMA and for which a PMA supplement under paragraph (a) is not required. FDA will identify such a change in an advisory opinion under § 10.85, if the change applies to a generic type of device, or in correspondence to the applicant, if the change applies only to the applicant's device. FDA will require that a change for which a PMA supplement under paragraph (a) is not required be reported to FDA in:

(i) A periodic report under § 814.84 or

(ii) A 30-day PMA supplement under this paragraph.

(2) FDA will identify, in the advisory opinion or correspondence, the type of information that is to be included in the report or 30-day PMA supplement. If the change is required to be reported to FDA in a periodic report, the change may be made before it is reported to FDA. If the change is required to be reported in a 30-day PMA supplement, the change may be made 30 days after FDA files the 30-day PMA supplement unless FDA requires the PMA holder to provide additional information, informs the PMA holder that the supplement is not approvable, or disapproves the supplement. The 30-day PMA supplement shall follow the instructions in the correspondence or advisory opinion. Any 30-day PMA supplement that does not meet the requirements of the correspondence or advisory opinion will not be filed and, therefore, will not be deemed approved 30 days after receipt.

(f) Under section 515(d) of the act, modifications to manufacturing procedures or methods of manufacture that affect the safety and effectiveness of a device subject to an approved PMA do not require submission of a PMA supplement under paragraph (a) of this section and are eligible to be the subject of a 30-day notice. A 30-day notice shall describe in detail the change, summarize the data or information supporting the change, and state that the change has been made in accordance with the requirements of part 820 of this chapter. The manufacturer may distribute the device 30 days after the date on which FDA receives the 30-day notice, unless FDA notifies the applicant within 30 days from receipt of the notice that the notice is not adequate. If the notice is not adequate, FDA shall inform the applicant in writing that a 135-day PMA supplement is needed and shall describe what further information or action is required for acceptance of such change. The number of days under review as a 30-day notice shall be deducted from the 135-day PMA supplement review period if the notice meets appropriate content requirements for a PMA supplement.

(g) The submission and grant of a written request for an exception or alternative under § 801.128 or § 809.11 of this chapter satisfies the requirement in paragraph (a) of this section.

[51 FR 26364, July 22, 1986, as amended at 51 FR 43344, Dec. 2, 1986; 63 FR 54044, Oct. 8, 1998; 67 FR 9587, Mar. 4, 2002; 69 FR 11313, Mar. 10, 2004; 72 FR 73602, Dec. 28, 2007; 73 FR 49610, Aug. 22, 2008]

Effective Date Note:

At 75 FR 16351, Apr. 1 2010, § 814.39 was amended by adding paragraph (h), effective Aug. 16, 2010. For the convenience of the user, the added text is set forth as follows:

§ 814.39   PMA supplements.

(h) The application must include the following information, if readily available:

(1) A description of any pediatric subpopulations (neonates, infants, children, adolescents) that suffer from the disease or condition that the device is intended to treat, diagnose, or cure; and

(2) The number of affected pediatric patients who are 21 years of age or younger.

(3) If information concerning the device that is the subject of the supplement was previously submitted under § 814.20(b)(3)(i), that infor-

mation may be incorporated by reference to the application or submission that contains the information. However, if additional information required under § 814.20(b)(3)(i) has become readily available to the applicant since the previous submission, the applicant must submit that information as part of the supplement.

Subpart C—FDA Action on a PMA

§ 814.40   Time frames for reviewing a PMA.

Within 180 days after receipt of an application that is accepted for filing and to which the applicant does not submit a major amendment, FDA will review the PMA and, after receiving the report and recommendation of the appropriate FDA advisory committee, send the applicant an approval order under § 814.44(d), an approvable letter under § 814.44(e), a not approvable letter under § 814.44(f), or an order denying approval under § 814.45. The approvable letter and the not approvable letter will provide an opportunity for the applicant to amend or withdraw the application, or to consider the letter to be a denial of approval of the PMA under § 814.45 and to request administrative review under section 515 (d)(3) and (g) of the act.

§ 814.42   Filing a PMA.

(a) The filing of an application means that FDA has made a threshold determination that the application is sufficiently complete to permit a substantive review. Within 45 days after a PMA is received by FDA, the agency will notify the applicant whether the application has been filed.

(b) If FDA does not find that any of the reasons in paragraph (e) of this section for refusing to file the PMA applies, the agency will file the PMA and will notify the applicant in writing of the filing. The notice will include the PMA reference number and the date FDA filed the PMA. The date of filing is the date that a PMA accepted for filing was received by the agency. The 180-day period for review of a PMA starts on the date of filing.

(c) If FDA refuses to file a PMA, the agency will notify the applicant of the reasons for the refusal. This notice will identify the deficiencies in the application that prevent filing and will include the PMA reference number.

(d) If FDA refuses to file the PMA, the applicant may:

(1) Resubmit the PMA with additional information necessary to comply with the requirements of section 515(c)(1) (A)-(G) of the act and § 814.20. A resubmitted PMA shall include the PMA reference number of the original submission. If the resubmitted PMA is accepted for filing, the date of filing is the date FDA receives the resubmission;

(2) Request in writing within 10 working days of the date of receipt of the notice refusing to file the PMA, an informal conference with the Director of the Office of Device Evaluation to review FDA's decision not to file the PMA. FDA will hold the informal conference within 10 working days of its receipt of the request and will render its decision on filing within 5 working days after the informal conference. If, after the informal conference, FDA accepts the PMA for filing, the date of filing will be the date of the decision to accept the PMA for filing. If FDA does not reverse its decision not to file the PMA, the applicant may request reconsideration of the decision from the Director of the Center for Devices and Radiological Health, the Director of the Center for Biologics Evaluation and Research, or the Director of the Center for Drug Evaluation and Research, as applicable. The Director's decision will constitute final administrative action for the purpose of judicial review.

(e) FDA may refuse to file a PMA if any of the following applies:

(1) The application is incomplete because it does not on its face contain all the information required under section 515(c)(1) (A)-(G) of the act;

(2) The PMA does not contain each of the items required under § 814.20 and justification for omission of any item is inadequate;

(3) The applicant has a pending premarket notification under section 510(k) of the act with respect to the same device, and FDA has not determined whether the device falls within the scope of § 814.1(c).

(4) The PMA contains a false statement of material fact.

(5) The PMA is not accompanied by a statement of either certification or disclosure as required by part 54 of this chapter.

[51 FR 26364, July 22, 1986, as amended at 63 FR 5254, Feb. 2, 1998; 73 FR 49942, Aug. 25, 2008]

§ 814.44   Procedures for review of a PMA.

Link to an amendment published at 75 FR 16351, Apr. 1, 2010.

(a) FDA will begin substantive review of a PMA after the PMA is accepted for filing under § 814.42. FDA may refer the PMA to a panel on its own initiative, and will do so upon request of an applicant, unless FDA determines that the application substantially duplicates information previously reviewed by a panel. If FDA refers an application to a panel, FDA will forward the PMA, or relevant portions thereof, to each member of the appropriate FDA panel for review. During the review process, FDA may communicate with the applicant as set forth under § 814.37(b), or with a panel to respond to questions that may be posed by panel members or to provide additional information to the panel. FDA will maintain a record of all communications with the applicant and with the panel.

(b) The advisory committee shall submit a report to FDA which includes the committee's recommendation and the basis for such recommendation on the PMA. Before submission of this report, the committee shall hold a public meeting to review the PMA in accordance with part 14. This meeting may be held by a telephone conference under § 14.22(g). The advisory committee report and recommendation may be in the form of a meeting transcript signed by the chairperson of the committee.

(c) FDA will complete its review of the PMA and the advisory committee report and recommendation and, within the later of 180 days from the date of filing of the PMA under § 814.42 or the number of days after the date of filing as determined under § 814.37(c), issue an approval order under paragraph (d) of this section, an approvable letter under paragraph (e) of this section, a not approvable letter under paragraph (f) of this section, or an order denying approval of the application under § 814.45(a).

(d)(1) FDA will issue to the applicant an order approving a PMA if none of the reasons in § 814.45 for denying approval of the application applies. FDA will approve an application on the basis of draft final labeling if the only deficiencies in the application concern editorial or similar minor deficiencies in the draft final labeling. Such approval will be conditioned upon the applicant incorporating the specified labeling changes exactly as directed and upon the applicant submitting to FDA a copy of the final printed labeling before marketing. FDA will also give the public notice of the order, including notice of and opportunity for any interested persons to request review under section 515(d)(3) of the act. The notice of approval will be placed on FDA's home page on the Internet (http://www.fda.gov), and it will state that a detailed summary of information respecting the safety and effectiveness of the device, which was the basis for the order approving the PMA, including information about any adverse effects of the device on health, is available on the Internet and has been placed on public display, and that copies are available upon request. FDA will publish in the Federal Register after each quarter a list of the approvals announced in that quarter. When a notice of approval is published, data and information in the PMA file will be available for public disclosure in accordance with § 814.9.

(2) A request for copies of the current PMA approvals and denials document and for copies of summaries of safety and effectiveness shall be sent in writing to the Division of Dockets Management (HFA-305), Food and Drug Administration, 5630 Fishers Lane, rm. 1061, Rockville, MD 20852.

(e) FDA will send the applicant an approvable letter if the application substantially meets the requirements of this part and the agency believes it can approve the application if specific additional information is submitted or specific conditions are agreed to by the applicant.

(1) The approvable letter will describe the information FDA requires to be provided by the applicant or the conditions the applicant is required to meet to obtain approval. For example, FDA may require, as a condition to approval:

(i) The submission of certain information identified in the approvable letter, e.g., final labeling;

(ii) An FDA inspection that finds the manufacturing facilities, methods, and controls in compliance with part 820 and, if applicable, that verifies records pertinent to the PMA;

(iii) Restrictions imposed on the device under section 515(d)(1)(B)(ii) or 520(e) of the act;

(iv) Postapproval requirements as described in subpart E of this part.

(2) In response to an approvable letter the applicant may:

(i) Amend the PMA as requested in the approvable letter; or

(ii) Consider the approvable letter to be a denial of approval of the PMA under § 814.45 and request administrative review under section 515(d)(3) of the act by filing a petition in the form of a petition for reconsideration under § 10.33; or

(iii) Withdraw the PMA.

(f) FDA will send the applicant a not approvable

letter if the agency believes that the application may not be approved for one or more of the reasons given in § 814.45(a). The not approvable letter will describe the deficiencies in the application, including each applicable ground for denial under section 515(d)(2) (A)-(E) of the act, and, where practical, will identify measures required to place the PMA in approvable form. In response to a not approvable letter, the applicant may:

(1) Amend the PMA as requested in the not approvable letter (such an amendment will be considered a major amendment under § 814.37(c)(1)); or

(2) Consider the not approvable letter to be a denial of approval of the PMA under § 814.45 and request administrative review under section 515(d)(3) of the act by filing a petition in the form of a petition for reconsideration under § 10.33; or

(3) Withdraw the PMA.

(g) FDA will consider a PMA to have been withdrawn voluntarily if:

(1) The applicant fails to respond in writing to a written request for an amendment within 180 days after the date FDA issues such request;

(2) The applicant fails to respond in writing to an approvable or not approvable letter within 180 days after the date FDA issues such letter; or

(3) The applicant submits a written notice to FDA that the PMA has been withdrawn.

[51 FR 26364, July 22, 1986, as amended at 57 FR 58403, Dec. 10, 1992; 63 FR 4572, Jan. 30, 1998]

Effective Date Note:

At 75 FR 16351, Apr. 1, 2010, § 814.44 was amended by redesignating paragraphs(e)(1)(ii) through (e)(1)(iv) as paragraphs (e)(1)(iii) through (e)(1)(v) respectively, and adding a new paragraph (e)(1)(ii), effective Aug. 16, 2010. For the convenience of the user, the added text is set forth as follows:

§ 814.44   Procedures for review of a PMA.

(e) * * *

(1) * * *

(ii) The submission of additional information concerning potential pediatric uses required by § 814.20(b)(3)(i) that is readily available to the applicant;

§ 814.45   Denial of approval of a PMA.

(a) FDA may issue an order denying approval of a PMA if the applicant fails to follow the requirements of this part or if, upon the basis of the information submitted in the PMA or any other information before the agency, FDA determines that any of the grounds for denying approval of a PMA specified in section 515(d)(2) (A)-(E) of the act applies. In addition, FDA may deny approval of a PMA for any of the following reasons:

(1) The PMA contains a false statement of material fact;

(2) The device's proposed labeling does not comply with the requirements in part 801 or part 809;

(3) The applicant does not permit an authorized FDA employee an opportunity to inspect at a reasonable time and in a reasonable manner the facilities, controls, and to have access to and to copy and verify all records pertinent to the application;

(4) A nonclinical laboratory study that is described in the PMA and that is essential to show that the device is safe for use under the conditions prescribed, recommended, or suggested in its proposed labeling, was not conducted in compliance with the good laboratory practice regulations in part 58 and no reason for the noncompliance is provided or, if it is, the differences between the practices used in conducting the study and the good laboratory practice regulations do not support the validity of the study; or

(5) Any clinical investigation involving human subjects described in the PMA, subject to the institutional review board regulations in part 56 or informed consent regulations in part 50, was not conducted in compliance with those regulations such that the rights or safety of human subjects were not adequately protected.

(b) FDA will issue any order denying approval of the PMA in accordance with § 814.17. The order will inform the applicant of the deficiencies in the PMA, including each applicable ground for denial under section 515(d)(2) of the act and the regulations under this part, and, where practical, will identify measures required to place the PMA in approvable form. The order will include a notice of an opportunity to request review under section 515(d)(4) of the act.

(c) FDA will use the criteria specified in § 860.7 to determine the safety and effectiveness of a device in deciding whether to approve or deny approval of a PMA. FDA may use information other than that submitted by the applicant in making such determination.

(d)(1) FDA will give the public notice of an order denying approval of the PMA. The notice will be placed on the FDA's home page on the Internet (http://www.fda.gov), and it will state that a detailed summary of information respecting the safety and effectiveness of the device, including information about any adverse effects of the device on health, is available on the Internet and has been placed on public display and that copies are available upon request. FDA will publish in the Federal Register after each quarter a list of the denials announced in that quarter. When a notice of denial of approval is made publicly available, data and information in the PMA file will be available for public disclosure in accordance with § 814.9.

(2) A request for copies of the current PMA approvals and denials document and copies of summaries of safety and effectiveness shall be sent in writing to the Freedom of Information Staff (HFI-35), Food and Drug Administration,

5600 Fishers Lane, Rockville, MD 20857.

(e) FDA will issue an order denying approval of a PMA after an approvable or not approvable letter has been sent and the applicant:

(1) Submits a requested amendment but any ground for denying approval of the application under section 515(d)(2) of the act still applies; or

(2) Notifies FDA in writing that the requested amendment will not be submitted; or

(3) Petitions for review under section 515(d)(3) of the act by filing a petition in the form of a petition for reconsideration under § 10.33.

[51 FR 26364, July 22, 1986, as amended at 63 FR 4572, Jan. 30, 1998; 73 FR 34859, June 19, 2008]

§ 814.46 Withdrawal of approval of a PMA.

(a) FDA may issue an order withdrawing approval of a PMA if, from any information available to the agency, FDA determines that:

(1) Any of the grounds under section 515(e)(1) (A)-(G) of the act applies.

(2) Any postapproval requirement imposed by the PMA approval order or by regulation has not been met.

(3) A nonclinical laboratory study that is described in the PMA and that is essential to show that the device is safe for use under the conditions prescribed, recommended, or suggested in its proposed labeling, was not conducted in compliance with the good laboratory practice regulations in part 58 and no reason for the noncompliance is provided or, if it is, the differences between the practices used in conducting the study and the good laboratory practice regulations do not support the validity of the study.

(4) Any clinical investigation involving human subjects described in the PMA, subject to the institutional review board regulations in part 56 or informed consent regulations in part 50, was

not conducted in compliance with those regulations such that the rights or safety of human subjects were not adequately protected.

(b)(1) FDA may seek advice on scientific matters from any appropriate FDA advisory committee in deciding whether to withdraw approval of a PMA.

(2) FDA may use information other than that submitted by the applicant in deciding whether to withdraw approval of a PMA.

(c) Before issuing an order withdrawing approval of a PMA, FDA will issue the holder of the approved application a notice of opportunity for an informal hearing under part 16.

(d) If the applicant does not request a hearing or if after the part 16 hearing is held the agency decides to proceed with the withdrawal, FDA will issue to the holder of the approved application an order withdrawing approval of the application. The order will be issued under § 814.17, will state each ground for withdrawing approval, and will include a notice of an opportunity for administrative review under section 515(e)(2) of the act.

(e) FDA will give the public notice of an order withdrawing approval of a PMA. The notice will be published in the Federal Register and will state that a detailed summary of information respecting the safety and effectiveness of the device, including information about any adverse effects of the device on health, has been placed on public display and that copies are available upon request. When a notice of withdrawal of approval is published, data and information in the PMA file will be available for public disclosure in accordance with § 814.9.

§ 814.47   Temporary suspension of approval of a PMA.

(a) Scope. (1) This section describes the procedures that FDA will follow in exercising its authority under section 515(e)(3) of the act (21 U.S.C. 360e(e)(3)). This authority applies to the original PMA, as well as any PMA supplement(s), for a medical device.

(2) FDA will issue an order temporarily suspending approval of a PMA if FDA determines that there is a reasonable probability that continued distribution of the device would cause serious, adverse health consequences or death.

(b) Regulatory hearing. (1) If FDA believes that there is a reasonable probability that the continued distribution of a device subject to an approved PMA would cause serious, adverse health consequences or death, FDA may initiate and conduct a regulatory hearing to determine whether to issue an order temporarily suspending approval of the PMA.

(2) Any regulatory hearing to determine whether to issue an order temporarily suspending approval of a PMA shall be initiated and conducted by FDA pursuant to part 16 of this chapter. If FDA believes that immediate action to remove a dangerous device from the market is necessary to protect the public health, the agency may, in accordance with § 16.60(h) of this chapter, waive, suspend, or modify any part 16 procedure pursuant to § 10.19 of this chapter.

(3) FDA shall deem the PMA holder's failure to request a hearing within the timeframe specified by FDA in the notice of opportunity for hearing to be a waiver.

(c) Temporary suspension order. If the PMA holder does not request a regulatory hearing or if, after the hearing, and after consideration of the administrative record of the hearing, FDA determines that there is a reasonable probability that the continued distribution of a device under an approved PMA would cause serious, adverse health consequences or death, the agency shall, under the authority of section 515(e)(3) of the act, issue an order to the PMA holder temporarily suspending approval of the PMA.

(d) Permanent withdrawal of approval of the PMA. If FDA issues an order temporarily suspending approval of a PMA, the agency shall proceed expeditiously, but within 60 days, to hold a hearing on whether to permanently withdraw approval of the PMA in accordance with section 515(e)(1) of the act and the procedures set out in § 814.46.

[61 FR 15190, Apr. 5, 1996]

Subpart D—Administrative Review [Reserved]

Subpart E—Postapproval Requirements

§ 814.80   General.

A device may not be manufactured, packaged, stored, labeled, distributed, or advertised in a manner that is inconsistent with any conditions to approval specified in the PMA approval order for the device.

§ 814.82   Postapproval requirements.

(a) FDA may impose postapproval requirements in a PMA approval order or by regulation at the time of approval of the PMA or by regulation subsequent to approval. Postapproval requirements may include as a condition to approval of the device:

(1) Restriction of the sale, distribution, or use of the device as provided by section 515(d)(1)(B) (ii) or 520(e) of the act.

(2) Continuing evaluation and periodic reporting on the safety, effectiveness, and reliability of the device for its intended use. FDA will state in the PMA approval order the reason or purpose for such requirement and the number of patients to be evaluated and the reports required to be submitted.

(3) Prominent display in the labeling of a device and in the advertising of any restricted device of warnings, hazards, or precautions important for the device's safe and effective use, including patient information, e.g., information provided to the patient on alternative modes of therapy and on risks and benefits associated with the use of the device.

(4) Inclusion of identification codes on the device or its labeling, or in the case of an implant, on cards given to patients if necessary to protect the public health.

(5) Maintenance of records that will enable the applicant to submit to FDA information needed to trace patients if such information is necessary to protect the public health. Under section 519(a)(4) of the act, FDA will require that the identity of any patient be disclosed in records maintained under this paragraph only to the extent required for the medical welfare of the individual, to determine the safety or effectiveness of the device, or to verify a record, report, or information submitted to the agency.

(6) Maintenance of records for specified periods of time and organization and indexing of records into identifiable files to enable FDA to determine whether there is reasonable assurance of the continued safety and effectiveness of the device.

(7) Submission to FDA at intervals specified in the approval order of periodic reports containing the information required by § 814.84(b).

(8) Batch testing of the device.

(9) Such other requirements as FDA determines are necessary to provide reasonable assurance, or continued reasonable assurance, of the safety and effectiveness of the device.

(b) An applicant shall grant to FDA access to any records and reports required under the provisions of this part, and shall permit authorized FDA employees to copy and verify such records and reports and to inspect at a reasonable time and in a reasonable manner all manufacturing facilities to verify that the device is being manufactured, stored, labeled, and shipped under approved conditions.

(c) Failure to comply with any postapproval requirement constitutes a ground for withdrawal of approval of a PMA.

(Approved by the Office of Management and Budget under control number 0910-0231)

[51 FR 26364, July 22, 1986, as amended at 51 FR 43344, Dec. 2, 1986]

§ 814.84   Reports.

(a) The holder of an approved PMA shall comply with the requirements of part 803 and with any other requirements applicable to the device by other regulations in this subchapter or by order approving the device.

(b) Unless FDA specifies otherwise, any periodic report shall:

(1) Identify changes described in § 814.39(a) and changes required to be reported to FDA under § 814.39(b).

(2) Contain a summary and bibliography of the following information not previously submitted as part of the PMA:

(i) Unpublished reports of data from any clinical investigations or nonclinical laboratory studies involving the device or related devices and known to or that reasonably should be known to the applicant.

(ii) Reports in the scientific literature concerning the device and known to or that reasonably should be known to the applicant. If, after reviewing the summary and bibliography, FDA concludes that the agency needs a copy of the unpublished or published reports, FDA will notify the applicant that copies of such reports shall be submitted.

(3) Identify changes made pursuant to an exception or alternative granted under § 801.128 or § 809.11 of this chapter.

[51 FR 26364, July 22, 1986, as amended at 51 FR 43344, Dec. 2, 1986; 67 FR 9587, Mar. 4, 2002; 72 FR 73602, Dec. 28, 2007]

Subparts F-G [Reserved]

Subpart H—Humanitarian Use Devices

Source:

61 FR 33244, June 26, 1996, unless otherwise noted.

§ 814.100   Purpose and scope.

Link to an amendment published at 75 FR 16351, Apr. 1, 2010.

(a) This subpart H implements section 520(m) of the act. The purpose of section 520(m) is, to the extent consistent with the protection of the public health and safety and with ethical standards, to encourage the discovery and use of devices intended to benefit patients in the treatment or diagnosis of diseases or conditions that affect or are manifested in fewer than 4,000 individuals in the United States per year. This subpart provides procedures for obtaining:

(1) HUD designation of a medical device; and

(2) Marketing approval for the HUD notwithstanding the absence of reasonable assurance of effectiveness that would otherwise be required under sections 514 and 515 of the act.

(b) Although a HUD may also have uses that differ from the humanitarian use, applicants seeking approval of any non-HUD use shall submit a PMA as required under § 814.20, or a premarket notification as required under part 807 of this chapter.

(c) Obtaining marketing approval for a HUD involves two steps:

(1) Obtaining designation of the device as a HUD from FDA's Office of Orphan Products Development, and

(2) Submitting an HDE to the Office of Device Evaluation (ODE), Center for Devices and Radiological Health (CDRH), the Center for Biologics Evaluation and Research (CBER), or the Center for Drug Evaluation and Research (CDER), as applicable.

(d) A person granted an exemption under section 520(m) of the act shall submit periodic reports as described in § 814.126(b).

(e) FDA may suspend or withdraw approval of an HDE after providing notice and an opportunity for an informal hearing.

[61 FR 33244, June 26, 1996, as amended at 63 FR 59220, Nov. 3, 1998; 73 FR 49942, Aug. 25, 2008]

Effective Date Note:

At 75 FR 16351, Apr. 1, 2010, § 814.100 was amended by redesignating paragraphs (b) through (e) as paragraphs (d) through (g) respectively; redesignating paragraph (a) as paragraph (b), removing the first sentence of the newly redesignated paragraph (b); and adding new paragraphs (a) and (c), effective Aug. 16, 2010. For the convenience of the user, the added text is set forth as follows:

§ 814.100 Purpose and scope.

(a) This subpart H implements sections 515A and 520(m) of the act.

(c) Section 515A of the act is intended to ensure the submission of readily available information concerning actual and potential pediatric uses of medical devices.

§ 814.102 Designation of HUD status.

(a) Request for designation. Prior to submitting an HDE application, the applicant shall submit a request for HUD designation to FDA's Office of Orphan Products Development. The request shall contain the following:

(1) A statement that the applicant requests HUD designation for a rare disease or condition or a valid subset of a disease or condition which shall be identified with specificity;

(2) The name and address of the applicant, the name of the applicant's primary contact person and/or resident agent, including title, address, and telephone number;

(3) A description of the rare disease or condition for which the device is to be used, the proposed indication or indications for use of the device, and the reasons why such therapy is needed. If the device is proposed for an indication that represents a subset of a common disease or condition, a demonstration that the subset is medically plausible should be included;

(4) A description of the device and a discussion of the scientific rationale for the use of the device for the rare disease or condition; and

(5) Documentation, with appended authoritative references, to demonstrate that the device is designed to treat or diagnose a disease or condition that affects or is manifested in fewer than 4,000 people in the United States per year. If the device is for diagnostic purposes, the documentation must demonstrate that fewer than 4,000 patients per year would be subjected to diagnosis by the device in the United States. Authoritative references include literature citations in specialized medical journals, textbooks, specialized medical society proceedings, or governmental statistics publications. When no such studies or literature citations exist, the applicant may be able to demonstrate the prevalence of the disease or condition in the United States by providing credible conclusions from appropriate research or surveys.

(b) FDA action. Within 45 days of receipt of a request for HUD designation, FDA will take one of the following actions:

(1) Approve the request and notify the applicant that the device has been designated as a HUD based on the information submitted;

(2) Return the request to the applicant pending further review upon submission of additional information. This action will ensue if the request is incomplete because it does not on its face contain all of the information required under § 814.102(a). Upon receipt of this additional information, the review period may be extended up to 45 days; or

(3) Disapprove the request for HUD designation based on a substantive review of the information submitted. FDA may disapprove a request for HUD designation if:

(i) There is insufficient evidence to support the estimate that the disease or condition for which the device is designed to treat or diagnose affects or is manifested in fewer than 4,000 people in the United States per year;

(ii) FDA determines that, for a diagnostic device, 4,000 or more patients in the United States would be subjected to diagnosis using the device per year; or

(iii) FDA determines that the patient population defined in the request is not a medically plausible subset of a larger population.

(c) Revocation of designation. FDA may revoke a HUD designation if the agency finds that:

(1) The request for designation contained an untrue statement of material fact or omitted material information; or

(2) Based on the evidence available, the device is not eligible for HUD designation.

(d) Submission. The applicant shall submit two copies of a completed, dated, and signed request for HUD designation to: Office of Orphan Products Development (HF-35), Food and Drug Administration, 5600 Fishers Lane, Rockville, MD 20857.

§ 814.104   Original applications.

Link to an amendment published at 75 FR 16351, Apr. 1, 2010.

(a) United States applicant or representative. The applicant or an authorized representative shall sign the HDE. If the applicant does not reside or have a place of business within the United States, the HDE shall be countersigned by an authorized representative residing or maintaining a place of business in the United States and shall identify the representative's name and address.

(b) Contents. Unless the applicant justifies an omission in accordance with paragraph (d) of this section, an HDE shall include:

(1) A copy of or reference to the determination made by FDA's Office of Orphan Products Development (in accordance with § 814.102) that the device qualifies as a HUD;

(2) An explanation of why the device would not be available unless an HDE were granted and a statement that no comparable device (other than another HUD approved under this subpart or a device under an approved IDE) is available to treat or diagnose the disease or condition. The application also shall contain a discussion of the risks and benefits of currently available devices or alternative forms of treatment in the United States;

(3) An explanation of why the probable benefit to health from the use of the device outweighs the risk of injury or illness from its use, taking into account the probable risks and benefits of currently available devices or alternative forms of treatment. Such explanation shall include a description, explanation, or theory of the underlying disease process or condition, and known or postulated mechanism(s) of action of the device in relation to the disease process or condition;

(4) All of the information required to be submitted under § 814.20(b), except that:

(i) In lieu of the summaries, conclusions, and results from clinical investigations required under §§ 814.20(b)(3)(v)(B), (b)(3)(vi), and (b)(6)(ii), the applicant shall include the summaries, conclusions, and results of all clinical experience or investigations (whether adverse or supportive) reasonably obtainable by the applicant that are relevant to an assessment of the risks and probable benefits of the device; and

(ii) In addition to the proposed labeling requirement set forth in § 814.20(b)(10), the labeling shall bear the following statement: Humanitarian Device. Authorized by Federal law for use in the [treatment or diagnosis] of [specify disease or condition]. The effectiveness of this device for this use has not been demonstrated; and

(5) The amount to be charged for the device and, if the amount is more than $250, a report by an independent certified public accountant, made in accordance with the Statement on Standards for Attestation established by the American Institute of Certified Public Accountants, or in lieu of such a report, an attestation by a responsible individual of the organization, verifying that the amount charged does not exceed the costs of the device's research, development, fabrication, and distribution. If the amount charged is $250 or less, the requirement for a report by an independent certified public accountant or an attestation by a responsible individual of the organization is waived.

(c) Omission of information. If the applicant believes that certain information required under paragraph (b) of this section is not applicable to the device that is the subject of the HDE, and omits any such information from its HDE, the applicant shall submit a statement that identifies and justifies the omission. The statement shall be submitted as a separate section in the HDE and identified in the table of contents. If the justification for the omission is not accepted by the agency, FDA will so notify the applicant.

(d) Address for submissions and correspondence. Copies of all original HDEs amendments and supplements, as well as any correspondence relating to an HDE, must be sent or delivered to the following:

(1) For devices regulated by the Center for Devices and Radiological Health, send this information to the Document Mail Center (HFZ-401), Office of Device Evaluation, Center for Devices and Radiological Health, Food and Drug Administration, 9200 Corporate Blvd., Rockville, MD 20850.

(2) For devices regulated by the Center for Biologics Evaluation and Research, send this information to the Document Control Center (HFM-99), Center for Biologics Evaluation and Research, Food and Drug Administration, 1401 Rockville Pike, suite 200N, Rockville, MD 20852-1448.

(3) For devices regulated by the Center for Drug Evaluation and Research, send this information to the Central Document Control Room, Center for Drug Evaluation and Research, Food and Drug Administration, 5901-B Ammendale Rd., Beltsville, MD 20705-1266.

[61 FR 33244, June 26, 1996, as amended at 63 FR 59220, Nov. 3, 1998; 73 FR 49942, Aug. 25, 2008]

Effective Date Note:

At 75 FR 16351, Apr. 1, 2010, § 814.104 was amended by revising the last sentence of paragraph (b)(4)(ii); revising the last sentence of paragraph (b)(5); and adding paragraph (b)(6), effective Aug. 16, 2010. For the convenience of the user, the added and revised text is set forth as follows:

§ 814.104   Original applications.

(b) * * *

(4) * * *

(ii) * * * The effectiveness of this device for this use has not been demonstrated.

(5) * * * If the amount charged is $250 or less, the requirement for a report by an independent certified public accountant or an attestation by a responsible individual of the organization is waived; and

(6) Readily available information concerning actual and potential pediatric uses of the device, as required by § 814.20(b)(3)(i).

§ 814.106   HDE amendments and resubmitted HDE's.

An HDE or HDE supplement may be amended

ubmitted upon an applicant's own initia-
r at the request of FDA, for the same rea-
nd in the same manner as prescribed for
in § 814.37, except that the timeframes
th in § 814.37(c)(1) and (d) do not apply.
requests an HDE applicant to submit an
amendment, and a written response to
request is not received within 75 days of
ite of the request, FDA will consider the
ng HDE or HDE supplement to be with-
voluntarily by the applicant. Further-
if the HDE applicant, on its own initiative
FDA's request, submits a major amend-
as described in § 814.37(c)(1), the review
l may be extended up to 75 days.

[59220, Nov. 3, 1998]

.108   Supplemental applications.

FDA approval of an original HDE, an ap
t shall submit supplements in accordance
he requirements for PMA's under § 814.39,
t that a request for a new indication for use
HUD shall comply with requirements set
in § 814.110. The timeframes for review of,
DA action on, an HDE supplement are the
as those provided in § 814.114 for an HDE.

[59220, Nov. 3, 1998]

.110   New indications for use.

n applicant seeking a new indication for
f a HUD approved under this subpart H
obtain a new designation of HUD status in
dance with § 814.102 and shall submit an
al HDE in accordance with § 814.104.

n application for a new indication for use
under § 814.104 may incorporate by ref-
e any information or data previously sub-
d to the agency under an HDE.

.112   Filing an HDE.

e filing of an HDE means that FDA has
a threshold determination that the ap-
ion is sufficiently complete to permit sub-
ve review. Within 30 days from the date an

HDE is received by FDA, the agency will notify
the applicant whether the application has been
filed. FDA may refuse to file an HDE if any of the
following applies:

(1) The application is incomplete because it
does not on its face contain all the information
required under § 814.104(b);

(2) FDA determines that there is a comparable
device available (other than another HUD approved under this subpart or a device under an
approved IDE) to treat or diagnose the disease
or condition for which approval of the HUD is
being sought; or

(3) The application contains an untrue statement
of material fact or omits material information.

(4) The HDE is not accompanied by a statement
of either certification or disclosure, or both, as
required by part 54 of this chapter.

(b) The provisions contained in § 814.42(b), (c),
and (d) regarding notification of filing decisions,
filing dates, the start of the 75-day review period, and applicant's options in response to FDA
refuse to file decisions shall apply to HDE's.

[61 FR 33244, June 26, 1996, as amended at 63
FR 5254, Feb. 2, 1998; 63 FR 59221, Nov. 3, 1998]

**§ 814.114   Timeframes for reviewing an
HDE.**

Within 75 days after receipt of an HDE that is
accepted for filing and to which the applicant
does not submit a major amendment, FDA shall
send the applicant an approval order, an approvable letter, a not approvable letter (under §
814.116), or an order denying approval (under
§ 814.118).

[63 FR 59221, Nov. 3, 1998]

**§ 814.116   Procedures for review of an
HDE.**

**Link to an amendment published at 75 FR
16351, Apr. 1, 2010.**

(a) Substantive review. FDA will begin substantive review of an HDE after the HDE is accepted for filing under § 814.112. FDA may refer an original HDE application to a panel on its own initiative, and shall do so upon the request of an applicant, unless FDA determines that the application substantially duplicates information previously reviewed by a panel. If the HDE is referred to a panel, the agency shall follow the procedures set forth under § 814.44, with the exception that FDA will complete its review of the HDE and the advisory committee report and recommendations within 75 days from receipt of an HDE that is accepted for filing under § 814.112 or the date of filing as determined under § 814.106, whichever is later. Within the later of these two timeframes, FDA will issue an approval order under paragraph (b) of this section, an approvable letter under paragraph (c) of this section, a not approvable letter under paragraph (d) of this section, or an order denying approval of the application under § 814.118(a).

(b) Approval order. FDA will issue to the applicant an order approving an HDE if none of the reasons in § 814.118 for denying approval of the application applies. FDA will approve an application on the basis of draft final labeling if the only deficiencies in the application concern editorial or similar minor deficiencies in the draft final labeling. Such approval will be conditioned upon the applicant incorporating the specified labeling changes exactly as directed and upon the applicant submitting to FDA a copy of the final printed labeling before marketing. The notice of approval of an HDE will be published in the Federal Register in accordance with the rules and policies applicable to PMA's submitted under § 814.20. Following the issuance of an approval order, data and information in the HDE file will be available for public disclosure in accordance with § 814.9(b) through (h), as applicable.

(c) Approvable letter. FDA will send the applicant an approvable letter if the application substantially meets the requirements of this subpart and the agency believes it can approve the application if specific additional information is submitted or specific conditions are agreed to by the applicant. The approvable letter will describe the information FDA requires to be provided by the applicant or the conditions the applicant is required to meet to obtain approval. For example, FDA may require as a condition to approval:

(1) The submission of certain information identified in the approvable letter, e.g., final labeling;

(2) Restrictions imposed on the device under section 520(e) of the act;

(3) Postapproval requirements as described in subpart E of this part; and

(4) An FDA inspection that finds the manufacturing facilities, methods, and controls in compliance with part 820 of this chapter and, if applicable, that verifies records pertinent to the HDE.

(d) Not approvable letter. FDA will send the applicant a not approvable letter if the agency believes that the application may not be approved for one or more of the reasons given in § 814.118. The not approvable letter will describe the deficiencies in the application and, where practical, will identify measures required to place the HDE in approvable form. The applicant may respond to the not approvable letter in the same manner as permitted for not approvable letters for PMA's under § 814.44(f), with the exception that if a major HDE amendment is submitted, the review period may be extended up to 75 days.

(e) FDA will consider an HDE to have been withdrawn voluntarily if:

(1) The applicant fails to respond in writing to a written request for an amendment within 75 days after the date FDA issues such request;

(2) The applicant fails to respond in writing to an approvable or not approvable letter within

75 days after the date FDA issues such letter; or

(3) The applicant submits a written notice to FDA that the HDE has been withdrawn.

[61 FR 33244, June 26, 1996, as amended at 63 FR 59221, Nov. 3, 1998]

Effective Date Note:

At 75 FR 16351, Apr. 1 2010, § 814.116 was amended by redesignating paragraphs (c)(2) through (c)(4) as paragraphs (c)(3) through (c) (5) respectively, and adding a new paragraph (c) (2), effective Aug. 16, 2010. For the convenience of the user, the added text is set forth as follows:

§ 814.116   Procedures for review of an HDE.

(c) * * *

(2) The submission of additional information concerning potential pediatric uses required by § 814.20(b)(3)(i) that is readily available to the applicant;

§ 814.118   Denial of approval or withdrawal of approval of an HDE.

(a) FDA may deny approval or withdraw approval of an application if the applicant fails to meet the requirements of section 520(m) of the act or of this part, or of any condition of approval imposed by an IRB or by FDA, or any postapproval requirements imposed under § 814.126. In addition, FDA may deny approval or withdraw approval of an application if, upon the basis of the information submitted in the HDE or any other information before the agency, FDA determines that:

(1) There is a lack of a showing of reasonable assurance that the device is safe under the conditions of use prescribed, recommended, or suggested in the labeling thereof;

(2) The device is ineffective under the conditions of use prescribed, recommended, or suggested in the labeling thereof;

(3) The applicant has not demonstrated that

there is a reasonable basis from which to conclude that the probable benefit to health from the use of the device outweighs the risk of injury or illness, taking into account the probable risks and benefits of currently available devices or alternative forms of treatment;

(4) The application or a report submitted by or on behalf of the applicant contains an untrue statement of material fact, or omits material information;

(5) The device's labeling does not comply with the requirements in part 801 or part 809 of this chapter;

(6) A nonclinical laboratory study that is described in the HDE and that is essential to show that the device is safe for use under the conditions prescribed, recommended, or suggested in its proposed labeling, was not conducted in compliance with the good laboratory practice regulations in part 58 of this chapter and no reason for the noncompliance is provided or, if it is, the differences between the practices used in conducting the study and the good laboratory practice regulations do not support the validity of the study;

(7) Any clinical investigation involving human subjects described in the HDE, subject to the institutional review board regulations in part 56 of this chapter or the informed consent regulations in part 50 of this chapter, was not conducted in compliance with those regulations such that the rights or safety of human subjects were not adequately protected;

(8) The applicant does not permit an authorized FDA employee an opportunity to inspect at a reasonable time and in a reasonable manner the facilities and controls, and to have access to and to copy and verify all records pertinent to the application; or

(9) The device's HUD designation should be revoked in accordance with § 814.102(c).

(b) If FDA issues an order denying approval of

an application, the agency will comply with the same notice and disclosure provisions required for PMA's under § 814.45(b) and (d), as applicable.

(c) FDA will issue an order denying approval of an HDE after an approvable or not approvable letter has been sent and the applicant:

(1) Submits a requested amendment but any ground for denying approval of the application under § 814.118(a) still applies;

(2) Notifies FDA in writing that the requested amendment will not be submitted; or

(3) Petitions for review under section 515(d)(3) of the act by filing a petition in the form of a petition for reconsideration under § 10.33 of this chapter.

(d) Before issuing an order withdrawing approval of an HDE, FDA will provide the applicant with notice and an opportunity for a hearing as required for PMA's under § 814.46(c) and (d), and will provide the public with notice in accordance with § 814.46(e), as applicable.

[61 FR 33244, June 26, 1996, as amended at 63 FR 59221, Nov. 3, 1998]

§ 814.120   Temporary suspension of approval of an HDE.

An HDE or HDE supplement may be temporarily suspended for the same reasons and in the same manner as prescribed for PMA's in § 814.47.

[63 FR 59221, Nov. 3, 1998]

§ 814.122   Confidentiality of data and information.

(a) Requirement for disclosure. The "HDE file" includes all data and information submitted with or referenced in the HDE, any IDE incorporated into the HDE, any HDE amendment or supplement, any report submitted under § 814.126, any master file, or any other related submission. Any record in the HDE file will be available for public disclosure in accordance with the provisions of this section and part 20 of this chapter.

(b) Extent of disclosure. Disclosure by FDA of the existence and contents of an HDE file shall be subject to the same rules that pertain to PMA's under § 814.9(b) through (h), as applicable.

§ 814.124   Institutional Review Board requirements.

(a) IRB approval. The HDE holder is responsible for ensuring that a HUD approved under this subpart is administered only in facilities having an Institutional Review Board (IRB) constituted and acting pursuant to part 56 of this chapter, including continuing review of use of the device. In addition, a HUD may be administered only if such use has been approved by the IRB located at the facility or by a similarly constituted IRB that has agreed to oversee such use and to which the local IRB has deferred in a letter to the HDE holder, signed by the IRB chair or an authorized designee. If, however, a physician in an emergency situation determines that approval from an IRB cannot be obtained in time to prevent serious harm or death to a patient, a HUD may be administered without prior approval by the IRB located at the facility or by a similarly constituted IRB that has agreed to oversee such use. In such an emergency situation, the physician shall, within 5 days after the use of the device, provide written notification to the chairman of the IRB of such use. Such written notification shall include the identification of the patient involved, the date on which the device was used, and the reason for the use.

(b) Withdrawal of IRB approval. A holder of an approved HDE shall notify FDA of any withdrawal of approval for the use of a HUD by a reviewing IRB within 5 working days after being notified of the withdrawal of approval.

[61 FR 33244, June 26, 1996, as amended at 63 FR 59221, Nov. 3, 1998]

§ 814.126   Postapproval requirements and reports.

(a) An HDE approved under this subpart H shall be subject to the postapproval requirements and reports set forth under subpart E of this part, as applicable, with the exception of § 814.82(a)(7). In addition, medical device reports submitted to FDA in compliance with the requirements of part 803 of this chapter shall also be submitted to the IRB of record.

(b) In addition to the reports identified in paragraph (a) of this section, the holder of an approved HDE shall prepare and submit the following complete, accurate, and timely reports:

(1) Periodic reports. An HDE applicant is required to submit reports in accordance with the approval order. Unless FDA specifies otherwise, any periodic report shall include:

(i) An update of the information required under § 814.102(a) in a separately bound volume;

(ii) An update of the information required under § 814.104(b)(2), (b)(3), and (b)(5);

(iii) The number of devices that have been shipped or sold since initial marketing approval under this subpart H and, if the number shipped or sold exceeds 4,000, an explanation and estimate of the number of devices used per patient. If a single device is used on multiple patients, the applicant shall submit an estimate of the number of patients treated or diagnosed using the device together with an explanation of the basis for the estimate;

(iv) Information describing the applicant's clinical experience with the device since the HDE was initially approved. This information shall include safety information that is known or reasonably should be known to the applicant, medical device reports made under part 803 of this chapter, any data generated from the post-marketing studies, and information (whether published or unpublished) that is known or reasonably expected to be known by the applicant that may affect an evaluation of the safety of the device or that may affect the statement of contraindications, warnings, precautions, and adverse reactions in the device's labeling; and

(v) A summary of any changes made to the device in accordance with supplements submitted under § 814.108. If information provided in the periodic reports, or any other information in the possession of FDA, gives the agency reason to believe that a device raises public health concerns or that the criteria for exemption are no longer met, the agency may require the HDE holder to submit additional information to demonstrate continued compliance with the HDE requirements.

(2) Other. An HDE holder shall maintain records of the names and addresses of the facilities to which the HUD has been shipped, correspondence with reviewing IRB's, as well as any other information requested by a reviewing IRB or FDA. Such records shall be maintained in accordance with the HDE approval order.

[61 FR 33244, June 26, 1996, as amended at 63 FR 59221, Nov. 3, 1998, 71 FR 16228, Mar. 31, 2006]

Title 45—Public Welfare

Department of Health and Human Services

Part 46—Protection of Human Subjects

Revised January 15, 2009
Effective July 14, 2009

Subpart A—Basic HHS Policy for Protection of Human Research Subjects

Authority:
5 U.S.C. 301; 42 U.S.C. 289;
42 U.S.C. 300v-1(b).

Source:
56 FR 28012, 28022, June 18, 1991, unless otherwise noted.

§46.101 To what does this policy apply?

(a) Except as provided in paragraph (b) of this section, this policy applies to all research involving human subjects conducted, supported or otherwise subject to regulation by any federal department or agency which takes appropriate administrative action to make the policy applicable to such research. This includes research conducted by federal civilian employees or military personnel, except that each department or agency head may adopt such procedural modifications as may be appropriate from an administrative standpoint. It also includes research conducted, supported, or otherwise subject to regulation by the federal government outside the United States.

(1) Research that is conducted or supported by a federal department or agency, whether or not it is regulated as defined in §46.102(e), must comply with all sections of this policy.

(2) Research that is neither conducted nor supported by a federal department or agency but is subject to regulation as defined in §46.102(e) must be reviewed and approved, in compliance with §46.101, §46.102, and §46.107 through §46.117 of this policy, by an institutional review board (IRB) that operates in accordance with the pertinent requirements of this policy.

(b) Unless otherwise required by department or agency heads, research activities in which the only involvement of human subjects will be in one or more of the following categories are exempt from this policy:

(1) Research conducted in established or commonly accepted educational settings, involving normal educational practices, such as (i) research on regular and special education instructional strategies, or (ii) research on the effectiveness of or the comparison among instructional techniques, curricula, or classroom management methods.

(2) Research involving the use of educational tests (cognitive, diagnostic, aptitude, achievement), survey procedures, interview procedures or observation of public behavior, unless: (i) information obtained is recorded in such manner that human subjects can be identified, directly or through identifiers linked to the subjects; and (ii) any disclosure of the human subjects' responses outside the research could reasonably place the subjects at risk of criminal or civil liability or be damaging to the subjects' financial standing, employability, or reputation.

(3) Research involving the use of educational tests (cognitive, diagnostic, aptitude, achievement), survey procedures, interview procedures, or observation of public behavior that is not exempt under paragraph (b)(2) of this section, if:

(i) the human subjects are elected or appointed public officials or candidates for public office; or (ii) federal statute(s) require(s) without exception that the confidentiality of the personally identifiable information will be maintained throughout the research and thereafter.

(4) Research involving the collection or study of existing data, documents, records, pathological specimens, or diagnostic specimens, if these sources are publicly available or if the information is recorded by the investigator in such a manner that subjects cannot be identified, directly or through identifiers linked to the subjects.

(5) Research and demonstration projects which are conducted by or subject to the approval of department or agency heads, and which are designed to study, evaluate, or otherwise examine: (i) Public benefit or service programs; (ii) procedures for obtaining benefits or services under those programs; (iii) possible changes in or alternatives to those programs or procedures; or (iv) possible changes in methods or levels of payment for benefits or services under those programs.

(6) Taste and food quality evaluation and consumer acceptance studies, (i) if wholesome foods without additives are consumed or (ii) if a food is consumed that contains a food ingredient at or below the level and for a use found to be safe, or agricultural chemical or environmental contaminant at or below the level found to be safe, by the Food and Drug Administration or approved by the Environmental Protection Agency or the Food Safety and Inspection Service of the U.S. Department of Agriculture.

(c) Department or agency heads retain final judgment as to whether a particular activity is covered by this policy.

(d) Department or agency heads may require that specific research activities or classes of research activities conducted, supported, or otherwise subject to regulation by the department or agency but not otherwise covered by this policy, comply with some or all of the requirements of this policy.

(e) Compliance with this policy requires compliance with pertinent federal laws or regulations which provide additional protections for human subjects.

(f) This policy does not affect any state or local laws or regulations which may otherwise be applicable and which provide additional protections for human subjects.

(g) This policy does not affect any foreign laws or regulations which may otherwise be applicable and which provide additional protections to human subjects of research. h) When research covered by this policy takes place in foreign countries, procedures normally followed in the foreign countries to protect human subjects may differ from those set forth in this policy. [An example is a foreign institution which complies with guidelines consistent with the World Medical Assembly Declaration (Declaration of Helsinki amended 1989) issued either by sovereign states or by an organization whose function for the protection of human research subjects is internationally recognized.] In these circumstances, if a department or agency head determines that the procedures prescribed by the institution afford protections that are at least equivalent to those provided in this policy, the department or agency head may approve the substitution of the foreign procedures in lieu of the procedural requirements provided in this policy. Except when otherwise required by statute, Executive Order, or the department or agency head, notices of these actions as they occur will be published in the FEDERAL REGISTER or will be otherwise published as provided in department or agency procedures. (i) Unless otherwise required by law, department or agency heads may waive the applicability of some or all of the provisions of this policy to specific research activities or classes of research activities otherwise covered by this policy. Except when otherwise required by statute or Executive Order, the department or agency head shall forward advance notices of these actions to the Office for Human Research Protections,

Department of Health and Human Services (HHS), or any successor office, and shall also publish them in the FEDERAL REGISTER or in such other manner as provided in department or agency procedures.[1]

[56 FR 28012, 28022, June 18, 1991; 56 FR 29756, June 28, 1991, as amended at 70 FR 36328, June 23, 2005]

§46.102 Definitions.

(a) *Department or agency head* means the head of any federal department or agency and any other officer or employee of any department or agency to whom authority has been delegated.

(b) *Institution* means any public or private entity or agency (including federal, state, and other agencies).

(c) *Legally authorized representative* means an individual or judicial or other body authorized under applicable law to consent on behalf of a prospective subject to the subject's participation in the procedure(s) involved in the research.

(d) *Research* means a systematic investigation, including research development, testing and evaluation, designed to develop or contribute to generalizable knowledge. Activities which meet this definition constitute research for purposes of this policy, whether or not they are conducted or supported under a program which is considered research for other purposes. For example, some demonstration and service programs may include research activities.

(e) *Research subject to regulation*, and similar terms are intended to encompass those research activities for which a federal department or agency has specific responsibility for regulating as a research activity (for example, Investigational New Drug requirements administered by the Food and Drug Administration). It does not include research activities which are incidentally regulated by a federal department or agency solely as part of the department's or agency's broader responsibility to regulate certain types of activities whether research or non-research in nature (for example, Wage and Hour requirements administered by the Department of Labor).

(f) *Human subject* means a living individual about whom an investigator (whether professional or student) conducting research obtains

(1) Data through intervention or interaction with the individual, or

(2) Identifiable private information.

Intervention includes both physical procedures by which data are gathered (for example, venipuncture) and manipulations of the subject or the subject's environment that are performed for research purposes. Interaction includes communication or interpersonal contact between investigator and subject. Private information includes information about behavior that occurs in a context in which an individual can reasonably expect that no observation or recording is taking place, and information which has been provided for specific purposes by an individual and which the individual can reasonably expect will not be made public (for example, a medical record).

Private information must be individually identifiable (i.e., the identity of the subject is or may readily be ascertained by the investigator or associated with the information) in order for ob-

---

[1]Institutions with HHS-approved assurances on file will abide by provisions of Title 45 CFR part 46 subparts A-D. Some of the other departments and agencies have incorporated all provisions of Title 45 CFR part 46 into their policies and procedures as well. However, the exemptions at 45 CFR 46.101(b) do not apply to research involving prisoners, subpart C. The exemption at 45 CFR 46.101(b)(2), for research involving survey or interview procedures or observation of public behavior, does not apply to research with children, subpart D, except for research involving observations of public behavior when the investigator(s) do not participate in the activities being observed.

taining the information to constitute research involving human subjects.

(g) *IRB* means an institutional review board established in accord with and for the purposes expressed in this policy.

(h) *IRB approval* means the determination of the IRB that the research has been reviewed and may be conducted at an institution within the constraints set forth by the IRB and by other institutional and federal requirements.

(i) *Minimal risk* means that the probability and magnitude of harm or discomfort anticipated in the research are not greater in and of themselves than those ordinarily encountered in daily life or during the performance of routine physical or psychological examinations or tests.

h) When research covered by this policy takes place in foreign countries, procedures normally followed in the foreign countries to protect human subjects may differ from those set forth in this policy. [An example is a foreign institution which complies with guidelines consistent with the World Medical Assembly Declaration (Declaration of Helsinki amended 1989) issued either by sovereign states or by an organization whose function for the protection of human research subjects is internationally recognized.] In these circumstances, if a department or agency head determines that the procedures prescribed by the institution afford protections that are at least equivalent to those provided in this policy, the department or agency head may approve the substitution of the foreign procedures in lieu of the procedural requirements provided in this policy. Except when otherwise required by statute, Executive Order, or the department or agency head, notices of these actions as they occur will be published in the FEDERAL REGISTER or will be otherwise published as provided in department or agency procedures.

§46.103 Assuring compliance with this policy—research conducted or supported by any Federal Department or Agency.

(a) Each institution engaged in research which is covered by this policy and which is conducted or supported by a federal department or agency shall provide written assurance satisfactory to the department or agency head that it will comply with the requirements set forth in this policy. In lieu of requiring submission of an assurance, individual department or agency heads shall accept the existence of a current assurance, appropriate for the research in question, on file with the Office for Human Research Protections, HHS, or any successor office, and approved for federalwide use by that office. When the existence of an HHSapproved assurance is accepted in lieu of requiring submission of an assurance, reports (except certification) required by this policy to be made to department and agency heads shall also be made to the Office for Human Research Protections, HHS, or any successor office.

(b) Departments and agencies will conduct or support research covered by this policy only if the institution has an assurance approved as provided in this section, and only if the institution has certified to the department or agency head that the research has been reviewed and approved by an IRB provided for in the assurance, and will be subject to continuing review by the IRB. Assurances applicable to federally supported or conducted research shall at a minimum include:

(1)A statement of principles governing the institution in the discharge of its responsibilities for protecting the rights and welfare of human subjects of research conducted at or sponsored by the institution, regardless of whether the research is subject to Federal regulation. This may include an appropriate existing code, declaration, or statement of ethical principles, or a statement formulated by the institution itself. This requirement does not preempt provisions of this policy applicable to department- or agency-supported or regulated research and need not be applicable to any research exempted or waived under §46.101(b) or (i).

(2)Designation of one or more IRBs established in accordance with the requirements of this policy, and for which provisions are made for meeting space and sufficient staff to support the IRB's review and recordkeeping duties.

(3)A list of IRB members identified by name; earned degrees; representative capacity; indications of experience such as board certifications, licenses, etc., sufficient to describe each member's chief anticipated contributions to IRB deliberations; and any employment or other relationship between each member and the institution; for example: full-time employee, part-time employee, member of governing panel or board, stockholder, paid or unpaid consultant. Changes in IRB membership shall be reported to the department or agency head, unless in accord with §46.103(a) of this policy, the existence of an HHS-approved assurance is accepted. In this case, change in IRB membership shall be reported to the Office for Human Research Protections, HHS, or any successor office.

(4)Written procedures which the IRB will follow (i) for conducting its initial and continuing review of research and for reporting its findings and actions to the investigator and the institution; (ii) for determining which projects require review more often than annually and which projects need verification from sources other than the investigators that no material changes have occurred since previous IRB review; and (iii) for ensuring prompt reporting to the IRB of proposed changes in a research activity, and for ensuring that such changes in approved research, during the period for which IRB approval has already been given, may not be initiated without IRB review and approval except when necessary to eliminate apparent immediate hazards to the subject.

(5)Written procedures for ensuring prompt reporting to the IRB, appropriate institutional

officials, and the department or agency head of (i) any unanticipated problems involving risks to subjects or others or any serious or continuing noncompliance with this policy or the requirements or determinations of the IRB; and (ii) any suspension or termination of IRB approval.

(c) The assurance shall be executed by an individual authorized to act for the institution and to assume on behalf of the institution the obligations imposed by this policy and shall be filed in such form and manner as the department or agency head prescribes.

(d) The department or agency head will evaluate all assurances submitted in accordance with this policy through such officers and employees of the department or agency and such experts or consultants engaged for this purpose as the department or agency head determines to be appropriate. The department or agency head's evaluation will take into consideration the adequacy of the proposed IRB in light of the anticipated scope of the institution's research activities and the types of subject populations likely to be involved, the appropriateness of the proposed initial and continuing review procedures in light of the probable risks, and the size and complexity of the institution.

(e) On the basis of this evaluation, the department or agency head may approve or disapprove the assurance, or enter into negotiations to develop an approvable one. The department or agency head may limit the period during which any particular approved assurance or class of approved assurances shall remain effective or otherwise condition or restrict approval.

(f) Certification is required when the research is supported by a federal department or agency and not otherwise exempted or waived under §46.101(b) or (i). An institution with an approved assurance shall certify that each application or proposal for research covered by the assurance and by §46.103 of this Policy has been reviewed and approved by the IRB. Such certification must be submitted with the application or proposal or by such later date as may be prescribed by the department or agency to which the application or proposal is submitted. Under no condition shall research covered by §46.103 of the Policy be supported prior to receipt of the certification that the research has been reviewed and approved by the IRB. Institutions without an approved assurance covering the research shall certify within 30 days after receipt of a request for such a certification from the department or agency, that the application or proposal has been approved by the IRB. If the certification is not submitted within these time limits, the application or proposal may be returned to the institution.

(Approved by the Office of Management and Budget under Control Number 0990-0260.)

[56 FR 28012, 28022, June 18, 1991; 56 FR 29756, June 28, 1991, as amended at 70 FR 36328, June 23, 2005]

§§46.104--46.106 [Reserved]

§46.107 IRB membership.

(a) Each IRB shall have at least five members, with varying backgrounds to promote complete and adequate review of research activities commonly conducted by the institution. The IRB shall be sufficiently qualified through the experience and expertise of its members, and the diversity of the members, including consideration of race, gender, and cultural backgrounds and sensitivity to such issues as community attitudes, to promote respect for its advice and counsel in safeguarding the rights and welfare of human subjects. In addition to possessing the professional competence necessary to review specific research activities, the IRB shall be able to ascertain the acceptability of proposed research in terms of institutional commitments and regulations, applicable law, and standards of professional conduct and practice. The IRB shall therefore include persons knowledgeable in these areas. If an IRB regu-

larly reviews research that involves a vulnerable category of subjects, such as children, prisoners, pregnant women, or handicapped or mentally disabled persons, consideration shall be given to the inclusion of one or more individuals who are knowledgeable about and experienced in working with these subjects.

(b) Every nondiscriminatory effort will be made to ensure that no IRB consists entirely of men or entirely of women, including the institution's consideration of qualified persons of both sexes, so long as no selection is made to the IRB on the basis of gender. No IRB may consist entirely of members of one profession.

(c) Each IRB shall include at least one member whose primary concerns are in scientific areas and at least one member whose primary concerns are in nonscientific areas.

(d) Each IRB shall include at least one member who is not otherwise affiliated with the institution and who is not part of the immediate family of a person who is affiliated with the institution.

(e) No IRB may have a member participate in the IRB's initial or continuing review of any project in which the member has a conflicting interest, except to provide information requested by the IRB.

(f) An IRB may, in its discretion, invite individuals with competence in special areas to assist in the review of issues which require expertise beyond or in addition to that available on the IRB. These individuals may not vote with the IRB

§46.108 IRB functions and operations.

In order to fulfill the requirements of this policy each IRB shall:

(a) Follow written procedures in the same detail as described in §46.103(b)(4) and, to the extent required by, §46.103(b)(5).

(b) Except when an expedited review procedure is used (see §46.110), review proposed research at convened meetings at which a majority of the members of the IRB are present, including at least one member whose primary concerns are in nonscientific areas. In order for the research to be approved, it shall receive the approval of a majority of those members present at the meeting.

§46.109 IRB review of research.

(a) An IRB shall review and have authority to approve, require modifications in (to secure approval), or disapprove all research activities covered by this policy.

(b) An IRB shall require that information given to subjects as part of informed consent is in accordance with §46.116. The IRB may require that information, in addition to that specifically mentioned in §46.116, be given to the subjects when in the IRB's judgment the information would meaningfully add to the protection of the rights and welfare of subjects.

(c) An IRB shall require documentation of informed consent or may waive documentation in accordance with §46.117.

(d) An IRB shall notify investigators and the institution in writing of its decision to approve or disapprove the proposed research activity, or of modifications required to secure IRB approval of the research activity. If the IRB decides to disapprove a research activity, it shall include in its written notification a statement of the reasons for its decision and give the investigator an opportunity to respond in person or in writing.

(e) An IRB shall conduct continuing review of research covered by this policy at intervals appropriate to the degree of risk, but not less than once per year, and shall have authority to observe or have a third party observe the consent process and the research.

(Approved by the Office of Management and Budget under Control Number 0990-0260.)

[56 FR 28012, 28022, June 18, 1991, as amended at 70 FR 36328, June 23, 2005]

§46.110 Expedited review procedures for certain kinds of research involving no more than minimal risk, and for minor changes in approved research.

(a) The Secretary, HHS, has established, and published as a Notice in the FEDERAL REGISTER, a list of categories of research that may be reviewed by the IRB through an expedited review procedure. The list will be amended, as appropriate, after consultation with other departments and agencies, through periodic republication by the Secretary, HHS, in the FEDERAL REGISTER. A copy of the list is available from the Office for Human Research Protections, HHS, or any successor office.

(b) An IRB may use the expedited review procedure to review either or both of the following:

(1) some or all of the research appearing on the list and found by the reviewer(s) to involve no more than minimal risk,

(2) minor changes in previously approved research during the period (of one year or less) for which approval is authorized. Under an expedited review procedure, the review may be carried out by the IRB chairperson or by one or more experienced reviewers designated by the chairperson from among members of the IRB. In reviewing the research, the reviewers may exercise all of the authorities of the IRB except that the reviewers may not disapprove the research. A research activity may be disapproved only after review in accordance with the nonexpedited procedure set forth in §46.108(b).

(c) Each IRB which uses an expedited review procedure shall adopt a method for keeping all members advised of research proposals which have been approved under the procedure.

(d) The department or agency head may restrict, suspend, terminate, or choose not to authorize an institution's or IRB's use of the expedited review procedure.

[56 FR 28012, 28022, June 18, 1991, as amended at 70 FR 36328, June 23, 2005]

§46.111 Criteria for IRB approval of research.

(a) In order to approve research covered by this policy the IRB shall determine that all of the following requirements are satisfied:

(1) Risks to subjects are minimized: (i) By using procedures which are consistent with sound research design and which do not unnecessarily expose subjects to risk, and (ii) whenever appropriate, by using procedures already being performed on the subjects for diagnostic or treatment purposes.

(2) Risks to subjects are reasonable in relation to anticipated benefits, if any, to subjects, and the importance of the knowledge that may reasonably be expected to result. In evaluating risks and benefits, the IRB should consider only those risks and benefits that may result from the research (as distinguished from risks and benefits of therapies subjects would receive even if not participating in the research). The IRB should not consider possible long-range effects of applying knowledge gained in the research (for example, the possible effects of the research on public policy) as among those research risks that fall within the purview of its responsibility.

(3) Selection of subjects is equitable. In making this assessment the IRB should take into account the purposes of the research and the setting in which the research will be conducted and should be particularly cognizant of the special problems of research involving vulnerable populations, such as children, prisoners, pregnant women, mentally disabled persons, or economically or educationally disadvantaged persons.

(4) Informed consent will be sought from each prospective subject or the subject's legally authorized representative, in accordance with, and to the extent required by §46.116.

(5) Informed consent will be appropriately documented, in accordance with, and to the extent required by §46.117.

(6) When appropriate, the research plan makes adequate provision for monitoring the data collected to ensure the safety of subjects.

(7) When appropriate, there are adequate provisions to protect the privacy of subjects and to maintain the confidentiality of data.

(b) When some or all of the subjects are likely to be vulnerable to coercion or undue influence, such as children, prisoners, pregnant women, mentally disabled persons, or economically or educationally disadvantaged persons, additional safeguards have been included in the study to protect the rights and welfare of these subjects.

§46.112 Review by institution.

Research covered by this policy that has been approved by an IRB may be subject to further appropriate review and approval or disapproval by officials of the institution. However, those officials may not approve the research if it has not been approved by an IRB.

§46.113 Suspension or termination of IRB approval of research.

An IRB shall have authority to suspend or terminate approval of research that is not being conducted in accordance with the IRB's requirements or that has been associated with unexpected serious harm to subjects. Any suspension or termination of approval shall include a statement of the reasons for the IRB's action and shall be reported promptly to the investigator, appropriate institutional officials, and the department or agency head.

(Approved by the Office of Management and Budget under Control Number 0990-0260.)

[56 FR 28012, 28022, June 18, 1991, as amended at 70 FR 36328, June 23, 2005]

§46.114 Cooperative research.

Cooperative research projects are those projects covered by this policy which involve more than one institution. In the conduct of cooperative research projects, each institution is responsible for safeguarding the rights and welfare of human subjects and for complying with this policy. With the approval of the department or agency head, an institution participating in a cooperative project may enter into a joint review arrangement, rely upon the review of another qualified IRB, or make similar arrangements for avoiding duplication of effort.

§46.115 IRB records.

(a) An institution, or when appropriate an IRB, shall prepare and maintain adequate documentation of IRB activities, including the following:

(1) Copies of all research proposals reviewed, scientific evaluations, if any, that accompany the proposals, approved sample consent documents, progress reports submitted by investigators, and reports of injuries to subjects.

(2) Minutes of IRB meetings which shall be in sufficient detail to show attendance at the meetings; actions taken by the IRB; the vote on these actions including the number of members voting for, against, and abstaining; the basis for requiring changes in or disapproving research; and a written summary of the discussion of controverted issues and their resolution.

(3) Records of continuing review activities.

(4) Copies of all correspondence between the IRB and the investigators.

(5) A list of IRB members in the same detail as described in §46.103(b)(3).

(6) Written procedures for the IRB in the same detail as described in §46.103(b)(4) and §46.103(b)(5).

(7) Statements of significant new findings provided to subjects, as required by §46.116(b)(5).

(b) The records required by this policy shall be retained for at least 3 years, and records relating to research which is conducted shall be retained for at least 3 years after completion of the research. All records shall be accessible for inspection and copying by authorized representatives of the department or agency at reasonable times and in a reasonable manner.

(Approved by the Office of Management and Budget under Control Number 0990-0260.)

[56 FR 28012, 28022, June 18, 1991, as amended at 70 FR 36328, June 23, 2005]

§46.116 General requirements for informed consent.

Except as provided elsewhere in this policy, no investigator may involve a human being as a subject in research covered by this policy unless the investigator has obtained the legally effective informed consent of the subject or the subject's legally authorized representative. An investigator shall seek such consent only under circumstances that provide the prospective subject or the representative sufficient opportunity to consider whether or not to participate and that minimize the possibility of coercion or undue influence. The information that is given to the subject or the representative shall be in language understandable to the subject or the representative. No informed consent, whether oral or written, may include any exculpatory language through which the subject or the representative is made to waive or appear to waive any of the subject's legal rights, or releases or appears to release the investigator, the sponsor, the institution or its agents from liability for negligence.

(a) Basic elements of informed consent. Except as provided in paragraph (c) or (d) of this section, in seeking informed consent the following information shall be provided to each subject:

(1) A statement that the study involves research, an explanation of the purposes of the research and the expected duration of the

subject's participation, a description of the procedures to be followed, and identification of any procedures which are experimental;

(2) A description of any reasonably foreseeable risks or discomforts to the subject;

(3) A description of any benefits to the subject or to others which may reasonably be expected from the research;

(4) A disclosure of appropriate alternative procedures or courses of treatment, if any, that might be advantageous to the subject;

(5) A statement describing the extent, if any, to which confidentiality of records identifying the subject will be maintained;

(6) For research involving more than minimal risk, an explanation as to whether any compensation and an explanation as to whether any medical treatments are available if injury occurs and, if so, what they consist of, or where further information may be obtained;

(7) An explanation of whom to contact for answers to pertinent questions about the research and research subjects' rights, and whom to contact in the event of a research-related injury to the subject; and

(8) A statement that participation is voluntary, refusal to participate will involve no penalty or loss of benefits to which the subject is otherwise entitled, and the subject may discontinue participation at any time without penalty or loss of benefits to which the subject is otherwise entitled.

(b) Additional elements of informed consent. When appropriate, one or more of the following elements of information shall also be provided to each subject:

(1) A statement that the particular treatment or procedure may involve risks to the subject (or to the embryo or fetus, if the subject is or may become pregnant) which are currently unforeseeable;

(2) Anticipated circumstances under which the subject's participation may be terminated by the investigator without regard to the subject's consent;

(3) Any additional costs to the subject that may result from participation in the research;

(4) The consequences of a subject's decision to withdraw from the research and procedures for orderly termination of participation by the subject;

(5) A statement that significant new findings developed during the course of the research which may relate to the subject's willingness to continue participation will be provided to the subject; and

(6) The approximate number of subjects involved in the study.

(c) An IRB may approve a consent procedure which does not include, or which alters, some or all of the elements of informed consent set forth above, or waive the requirement to obtain informed consent provided the IRB finds and documents that:

(1) The research or demonstration project is to be conducted by or subject to the approval of state or local government officials and is designed to study, evaluate, or otherwise examine: (i) public benefit or service programs; (ii) procedures for obtaining benefits or services under those programs; (iii) possible changes in or alternatives to those programs or procedures; or (iv) possible changes in methods or levels of payment for benefits or services under those programs; and

(2) The research could not practicably be carried out without the waiver or alteration.

(d) An IRB may approve a consent procedure which does not include, or which alters, some or all of the elements of informed consent set forth in this section, or waive the requirements to obtain informed consent provided the IRB finds and documents that:

1) The research involves no more than minimal risk to the subjects;

(2) The waiver or alteration will not adversely affect the rights and welfare of the subjects;

(3) The research could not practicably be carried out without the waiver or alteration; and

(4) Whenever appropriate, the subjects will be provided with additional pertinent information after participation.

(e) The informed consent requirements in this policy are not intended to preempt any applicable federal, state, or local laws which require additional information to be disclosed in order for informed consent to be legally effective.

(f) Nothing in this policy is intended to limit the authority of a physician to provide emergency medical care, to the extent the physician is permitted to do so under applicable federal, state, or local law.

(Approved by the Office of Management and Budget under Control Number 0990-0260.)

[56 FR 28012, 28022, June 18, 1991, as amended at 70 FR 36328, June 23, 2005]

§46.117 Documentation of informed consent.

(a) Except as provided in paragraph (c) of this section, informed consent shall be documented by the use of a written consent form approved by the IRB and signed by the subject or the subject's legally authorized representative. A copy shall be given to the person signing the form.

(b) Except as provided in paragraph (c) of this section, the consent form may be either of the following:

(1) A written consent document that embodies the elements of informed consent required by §46.116. This form may be read to the subject or the subject's legally authorized representative, but in any event, the investigator shall give either the subject or the representative adequate opportunity to read it before it is signed; or

(2) A short form written consent document stating that the elements of informed consent required by §46.116 have been presented orally to the subject or the subject's legally authorized representative. When this method is used, there shall be a witness to the oral presentation. Also, the IRB shall approve a written summary of what is to be said to the subject or the representative. Only the short form itself is to be signed by the subject or the representative. However, the witness shall sign both the short form and a copy of the summary, and the person actually obtaining consent shall sign a copy of the summary. A copy of the summary shall be given to the subject or the representative, in addition to a copy of the short form.

(c) An IRB may waive the requirement for the investigator to obtain a signed consent form for some or all subjects if it finds either:

(1) That the only record linking the subject and the research would be the consent document and the principal risk would be potential harm resulting from a breach of confidentiality. Each subject will be asked whether the subject wants documentation linking the subject with the research, and the subject's wishes will govern; or

(2) That the research presents no more than minimal risk of harm to subjects and involves no procedures for which written consent is normally required outside of the research context.

In cases in which the documentation requirement is waived, the IRB may require the investigator to provide subjects with a written statement regarding the research.

(Approved by the Office of Management and Budget under Control Number 0990-0260.)

[56 FR 28012, 28022, June 18, 1991, as amended at 70 FR 36328, June 23, 2005]

§46.118 Applications and proposals lacking definite plans for involvement of human subjects.

Certain types of applications for grants, cooperative agreements, or contracts are submitted to departments or agencies with the knowledge that subjects may be involved within the period of support, but definite plans would not normally be set forth in the application or proposal. These include activities such as institutional type grants when selection of specific projects is the institution's responsibility; research training grants in which the activities involving subjects remain to be selected; and projects in which human subjects' involvement will depend upon completion of instruments, prior animal studies, or purification of compounds. These applications need not be reviewed by an IRB before an award may be made. However, except for research exempted or waived under §46.101(b) or (i), no human subjects may be involved in any project supported by these awards until the project has been reviewed and approved by the IRB, as provided in this policy, and certification submitted, by the institution, to the department or agency.

§46.119 Research undertaken without the intention of involving human subjects.

In the event research is undertaken without the intention of involving human subjects, but it is later proposed to involve human subjects in the research, the research shall first be reviewed and approved by an IRB, as provided in this policy, a certification submitted, by the institution, to the department or agency, and final approval given to the proposed change by the department or agency.

§46.120 Evaluation and disposition of applications and proposals for research to be conducted or supported by a Federal Department or Agency.

(a) The department or agency head will evaluate all applications and proposals involving human subjects submitted to the department or agency through such officers and employees of the department or agency and such experts and consultants as the department or agency head determines to be appropriate. This evaluation will take into consideration the risks to the subjects, the adequacy of protection against these risks, the potential benefits of the research to the subjects and others, and the importance of the knowledge gained or to be gained.

(b) On the basis of this evaluation, the department or agency head may approve or disapprove the application or proposal, or enter into negotiations to develop an approvable one.

§46.121 [Reserved]

§46.122 Use of Federal funds.

Federal funds administered by a department or agency may not be expended for research involving human subjects unless the requirements of this policy have been satisfied.

§46.123 Early termination of research support: Evaluation of applications and proposals.

(a) The department or agency head may require that department or agency support for any project be terminated or suspended in the manner prescribed in applicable program requirements, when the department or agency head finds an institution has materially failed to comply with the terms of this policy.

(b) In making decisions about supporting or approving applications or proposals covered by this policy the department or agency head may take into account, in addition to all other eligibility requirements and program criteria, factors such as whether the applicant has been subject to a termination or suspension under paragraph (a) of this section and whether the applicant or the person or persons who would direct or has/have directed the scientific and technical aspects of an activity has/have, in the judgment of the department or agency head, materially failed to discharge responsibility for the protection of the rights and welfare of human subjects (whether or not the research was subject to federal regulation).

§46.124 Conditions.

With respect to any research project or any class of research projects the department or agency head may impose additional conditions prior to or at the time of approval when in the judgment of the department or agency head additional conditions are necessary for the protection of human subjects.

Subpart B—Additional Protections for Pregnant Women, Human Fetuses and Neonates Involved in Research

Source:
66 FR 56778, Nov. 13, 2001, unless otherwise noted.

§46.201 To what do these regulations apply?

(a) Except as provided in paragraph (b) of this section, this subpart applies to all research involving pregnant women, human fetuses, neonates of uncertain viability, or nonviable neonates conducted or supported by the Department of Health and Human Services (DHHS). This includes all research conducted in DHHS facilities by any person and all research conducted in any facility by DHHS employees.

(b) The exemptions at §46.101(b)(1) through (6) are applicable to this subpart.

(c) The provisions of §46.101(c) through (i) are applicable to this subpart. Reference to State or local laws in this subpart and in §46.101(f) is intended to include the laws of federally recognized American Indian and Alaska Native Tribal Governments.

(d) The requirements of this subpart are in addition to those imposed under the other subparts of this part.

§46.202 Definitions.

The definitions in §46.102 shall be applicable to this subpart as well. In addition, as used in this subpart:

(a) Dead fetus means a fetus that exhibits neither heartbeat, spontaneous respiratory activity, spontaneous movement of voluntary muscles, nor pulsation of the umbilical cord.

(b) Delivery means complete separation of the fetus from the woman by expulsion or extraction or any other means.

(c) Fetus means the product of conception from implantation until delivery.

(d) Neonate means a newborn.

(e) Nonviable neonate means a neonate after delivery that, although living, is not viable.

(f) Pregnancy encompasses the period of time from implantation until delivery. A woman shall be assumed to be pregnant if she exhibits any of the pertinent presumptive signs of pregnancy, such as missed menses, until the results of a pregnancy test are negative or until delivery.

(g) Secretary means the Secretary of Health and Human Services and any other officer or employee of the Department of Health and Human Services to whom authority has been delegated.

(h) Viable, as it pertains to the neonate, means being able, after delivery, to survive (given the benefit of available medical therapy) to the point of independently maintaining heartbeat and respiration. The Secretary may from time to time, taking into account medical advances, publish in the FEDERAL REGISTER guidelines to assist in determining whether a neonate is viable for purposes of this subpart. If a neonate is viable then it may be included in research only to the extent permitted and in accordance with the requirements of subparts A and D of this part.

§46.203 Duties of IRBs in connection with

research involving pregnant women, fetuses, and neonates.

In addition to other responsibilities assigned to IRBs under this part, each IRB shall review research covered by this subpart and approve only research which satisfies the conditions of all applicable sections of this subpart and the other subparts of this part.

§46.204 Research involving pregnant women or fetuses.

Pregnant women or fetuses may be involved in research if all of the following conditions are met:

(a) Where scientifically appropriate, preclinical studies, including studies on pregnant animals, and clinical studies, including studies on nonpregnant women, have been conducted and provide data for assessing potential risks to pregnant women and fetuses;

(b) The risk to the fetus is caused solely by interventions or procedures that hold out the prospect of direct benefit for the woman or the fetus; or, if there is no such prospect of benefit, the risk to the fetus is not greater than minimal and the purpose of the research is the development of important biomedical knowledge which cannot be obtained by any other means;

(c) Any risk is the least possible for achieving the objectives of the research;

(d) If the research holds out the prospect of direct benefit to the pregnant woman, the prospect of a direct benefit both to the pregnant woman and the fetus, or no prospect of benefit for the woman nor the fetus when risk to the fetus is not greater than minimal and the purpose of the research is the development of important biomedical knowledge that cannot be obtained by any other means, her consent is obtained in accord with the informed consent provisions of subpart A of this part;

(e) If the research holds out the prospect of direct benefit solely to the fetus then the con-sent of the pregnant woman and the father is obtained in accord with the informed consent provisions of subpart A of this part, except that the father's consent need not be obtained if he is unable to consent because of unavailability, incompetence, or temporary incapacity or the pregnancy resulted from rape or incest.

(f) Each individual providing consent under paragraph (d) or (e) of this section is fully informed regarding the reasonably foreseeable impact of the research on the fetus or neonate;

(g) For children as defined in §46.402(a) who are pregnant, assent and permission are obtained in accord with the provisions of subpart D of this part;

(h) No inducements, monetary or otherwise, will be offered to terminate a pregnancy;

(i) Individuals engaged in the research will have no part in any decisions as to the timing, method, or procedures used to terminate a pregnancy; and

(j) Individuals engaged in the research will have no part in determining the viability of a neonate.

§46.205 Research involving neonates.

(a) Neonates of uncertain viability and nonviable neonates may be involved in research if all of the following conditions are met:

(1) Where scientifically appropriate, preclinical and clinical studies have been conducted and provide data for assessing potential risks to neonates.

(2) Each individual providing consent under paragraph (b)(2) or (c)(5) of this section is fully informed regarding the reasonably foreseeable impact of the research on the neonate.

(3) Individuals engaged in the research will have no part in determining the viability of a neonate.

(4) The requirements of paragraph (b) or (c) of

this section have been met as applicable.

(b) Neonates of uncertain viability. Until it has been ascertained whether or not a neonate is viable, a neonate may not be involved in research covered by this subpart unless the following additional conditions have been met:

(1) The IRB determines that:

(i) The research holds out the prospect of enhancing the probability of survival of the neonate to the point of viability, and any risk is the least possible for achieving that objective, or

(ii) The purpose of the research is the development of important biomedical knowledge which cannot be obtained by other means and there will be no added risk to the neonate resulting from the research; and

(2) The legally effective informed consent of either parent of the neonate or, if neither parent is able to consent because of unavailability, incompetence, or temporary incapacity, the legally effective informed consent of either parent's legally authorized representative is obtained in accord with subpart A of this part, except that the consent of the father or his legally authorized representative need not be obtained if the pregnancy resulted from rape or incest.

(c) Nonviable neonates. After delivery nonviable neonate may not be involved in research covered by this subpart unless all of the following additional conditions are met:

(1) Vital functions of the neonate will not be artificially maintained;

(2) The research will not terminate the heartbeat or respiration of the neonate;

(3) There will be no added risk to the neonate resulting from the research;

(4) The purpose of the research is the development of important biomedical knowledge that cannot be obtained by other means; and

(5) The legally effective informed consent of both parents of the neonate is obtained in accord with subpart A of this part, except that the waiver and alteration provisions of §46.116(c) and (d) do not apply. However, if either parent is unable to consent because of unavailability, incompetence, or temporary incapacity, the informed consent of one parent of a nonviable neonate will suffice to meet the requirements of this paragraph (c) (5), except that the consent of the father need not be obtained if the pregnancy resulted from rape or incest. The consent of a legally authorized representative of either or both of the parents of a nonviable neonate will not suffice to meet the requirements of this paragraph (c)(5).

(d) Viable neonates. A neonate, after delivery, that has been determined to be viable may be included in research only to the extent permitted by and in accord with the requirements of subparts A and D of this part.

§46.206 Research involving, after delivery, the placenta, the dead fetus or fetal material.

(a) Research involving, after delivery, the placenta; the dead fetus; macerated fetal material; or cells, tissue, or organs excised from a dead fetus, shall be conducted only in accord with any applicable federal, state, or local laws and regulations regarding such activities.

(b) If information associated with material described in paragraph (a) of this section is recorded for research purposes in a manner that living individuals can be identified, directly or through identifiers linked to those individuals, those individuals are research subjects and all pertinent subparts of this part are applicable.

§46.207 Research not otherwise approvable which presents an opportunity to understand, prevent, or alleviate a serious problem affecting the health or welfare of pregnant women, fetuses, or neonates.

The Secretary will conduct or fund research that the IRB does not believe meets the requirements of §46.204 or §46.205 only if:

(a) The IRB finds that the research presents a reasonable opportunity to further the understanding, prevention, or alleviation of a serious problem affecting the health or welfare of pregnant women, fetuses or neonates; and

(b) The Secretary, after consultation with a panel of experts in pertinent disciplines (for example: science, medicine, ethics, law) and following opportunity for public review and comment, including a public meeting announced in the FEDERAL REGISTER, has determined either:

(1) That the research in fact satisfies the conditions of §46.204, as applicable; or

(2) The following:

(i) The research presents a reasonable opportunity to further the understanding, prevention, or alleviation of a serious problem affecting the health or welfare of pregnant women, fetuses or neonates;

(II) The research will be conducted in accord with sound ethical principles; and

(iii) Informed consent will be obtained in accord with the informed consent provisions of subpart A and other applicable subparts of this part.

Subpart C—Additional Protections Pertaining to Biomedical and Behavioral Research Involving Prisoners as Subjects

Source:
43 FR 53655, Nov. 16, 1978, unless otherwise noted.

§46.301 Applicability.

(a) The regulations in this subpart are applicable to all biomedical and behavioral research conducted or supported by the Department of Health and Human Services involving prisoners as subjects.

(b) Nothing in this subpart shall be construed as indicating that compliance with the procedures set forth herein will authorize research involving prisoners as subjects, to the extent such research is limited or barred by applicable State or local law.

(c) The requirements of this subpart are in addition to those imposed under the other subparts of this part.

§46.302 Purpose.

Inasmuch as prisoners may be under constraints because of their incarceration which could affect their ability to make a truly voluntary and uncoerced decision whether or not to participate as subjects in research, it is the purpose of this subpart to provide additional safeguards for the protection of prisoners involved in activities to which this subpart is applicable.

§46.303 Definitions.

As used in this subpart:

(a) *Secretary* means the Secretary of Health and Human Services and any other officer or employee of the Department of Health and Human Services to whom authority has been delegated.

(b) *DHHS* means the Department of Health and Human Services.

(c) *Prisoner* means any individual involuntarily confined or detained in a penal institution. The term is intended to encompass individuals sentenced to such an institution under a criminal or civil statute, individuals detained in other facilities by virtue of statutes or commitment procedures which provide alternatives to criminal prosecution or incarceration in a penal institution, and individuals detained pending arraignment, trial, or sentencing.

(d) *Minimal risk* is the probability and magnitude of physical or psychological harm that is normally encountered in the daily lives, or in the routine medical, dental, or psychological examination of healthy persons.

§46.304 Composition of Institutional Review Boards where prisoners are involved.

In addition to satisfying the requirements in §46.107 of this part, an Institutional Review Board, carrying out responsibilities under this part with respect to research covered by this subpart, shall also meet the following specific requirements:

(a) A majority of the Board (exclusive of prisoner members) shall have no association with the prison(s) involved, apart from their membership on the Board.

(b) At least one member of the Board shall be a prisoner, or a prisoner representative with appropriate background and experience to serve in that capacity, except that where a particular research project is reviewed by more than one Board only one Board need satisfy this requirement.

[43 FR 53655, Nov. 16, 1978, as amended at 46 FR 8366, Jan. 26, 1981]

§46.305 Additional duties of the Institutional Review Boards where prisoners are involved.

(a) In addition to all other responsibilities prescribed for Institutional Review Boards under this part, the Board shall review research covered by this subpart and approve such research only if it finds that:

(1) The research under review represents one of the categories of research permissible under §46.306(a)(2);

(2) Any possible advantages accruing to the prisoner through his or her participation in the research, when compared to the general living conditions, medical care, quality of food, amenities and opportunity for earnings in the prison, are not of such a magnitude that his or her ability to weigh the risks of the research against the value of such advantages in the limited choice environment of the prison is impaired;

(3) The risks involved in the research are commensurate with risks that would be accepted by nonprisoner volunteers;

(4) Procedures for the selection of subjects within the prison are fair to all prisoners and immune from arbitrary intervention by prison authorities or prisoners. Unless the principal investigator provides to the Board justification in writing for following some other procedures, control subjects must be selected randomly from the group of available prisoners who meet the characteristics needed for that particular research project;

(5) The information is presented in language which is understandable to the subject population;

(6) Adequate assurance exists that parole boards will not take into account a prisoner's participation in the research in making decisions regarding parole, and each prisoner is clearly informed in advance that participation in the research will have no effect on his or her parole; and

(7) Where the Board finds there may be a need for follow-up examination or care of participants after the end of their participation, adequate provision has been made for such examination or care, taking into account the varying lengths of individual prisoners' sentences, and for informing participants of this fact.

(b) The Board shall carry out such other duties as may be assigned by the Secretary.

(c) The institution shall certify to the Secretary, in such form and manner as the Secretary may require, that the duties of the Board under this section have been fulfilled.

§46.306 Permitted research involving prisoners.

(a) Biomedical or behavioral research conducted or supported by DHHS may involve prisoners as subjects only if:

(1) The institution responsible for the conduct of the research has certified to the Secretary that the Institutional Review Board has approved the research under §46.305 of this subpart; and

(2) In the judgment of the Secretary the proposed research involves solely the following:

(i) Study of the possible causes, effects, and processes of incarceration, and of criminal behavior, provided that the study presents no more than minimal risk and no more than inconvenience to the subjects;

(ii) Study of prisons as institutional structures or of prisoners as incarcerated persons, provided that the study presents no more than minimal risk and no more than inconvenience to the subjects;

(iii) Research on conditions particularly affecting prisoners as a class (for example, vaccine trials and other research on hepatitis which is much more prevalent in prisons than elsewhere; and research on social and psychological problems such as alcoholism, drug addiction, and sexual assaults) provided that the study may proceed only after the Secretary has consulted with appropriate experts including experts in penology, medicine, and ethics, and published notice, in the FEDERAL REGISTER, of his intent to approve such research; or

(iv) Research on practices, both innovative and accepted, which have the intent and reasonable probability of improving the health or well-being of the subject. In cases in which those studies require the assignment of prisoners in a manner consistent with protocols approved by the IRB to control groups which may not benefit from the research, the study may proceed only after the Secretary has consulted with appropriate experts, including experts in penology, medicine, and ethics, and published notice, in the FEDERAL REGISTER, of the intent to approve such research.

(b) Except as provided in paragraph (a) of this section, biomedical or behavioral research conducted or supported by DHHS shall not involve prisoners as subjects.

Subpart D—Additional Protections for Children Involved as Subjects in Research

Source:

48 FR 9818, March 8, 1983, unless otherwise noted.

§46.401 To what do these regulations apply?

(a) This subpart applies to all research involving children as subjects, conducted or supported by the Department of Health and Human Services.

(1) This includes research conducted by Department employees, except that each head of an Operating Division of the Department may adopt such nonsubstantive, procedural modifications as may be appropriate from an administrative standpoint.

(2) It also includes research conducted or supported by the Department of Health and Human Services outside the United States, but in appropriate circumstances, the Secretary may, under paragraph (i) of §46.101 of subpart A, waive the applicability of some or all of the requirements of these regulations for research of this type.

(b) Exemptions at §46.101(b)(1) and (b)(3) through (b)(6) are applicable to this subpart. The exemption at §46.101(b)(2) regarding educational tests is also applicable to this subpart. However, the exemption at §46.101 (b)(2) for research involving survey or interview procedures or observations of public behavior does not apply to research covered by this subpart, except for research involving observation of public behavior when the investigator(s) do not participate in the activities being observed.

(c) The exceptions, additions, and provisions for waiver as they appear in paragraphs (c) through (i) of §46.101 of subpart A are applicable to this subpart.

[48 FR 9818, Mar.8, 1983; 56 FR 28032, June 18, 1991; 56 FR 29757, June 28, 1991.]

§46.402 Definitions.

The definitions in §46.102 of subpart A shall be applicable to this subpart as well. In addition, as used in this subpart:

(a) *Children* are persons who have not attained the legal age for consent to treatments or procedures involved in the research, under the applicable law of the jurisdiction in which the research will be conducted.

(b) *Assent* means a child's affirmative agreement to participate in research. Mere failure to object should not, absent affirmative agreement, be construed as assent.

(c) *Permission* means the agreement of parent (s) or guardian to the participation of their child or ward in research.

(d) *Parent* means a child's biological or adoptive parent.

(e) *Guardian* means an individual who is authorized under applicable State or local law to consent on behalf of a child to general medical care.

§46.403 IRB duties.

In addition to other responsibilities assigned to IRBs under this part, each IRB shall review research covered by this subpart and approve only research which satisfies the conditions of all applicable sections of this subpart.

§46.404 Research not involving greater than minimal risk.

HHS will conduct or fund research in which the IRB finds that no greater than minimal risk to children is presented, only if the IRB finds that

adequate provisions are made for soliciting the assent of the children and the permission of their parents or guardians, as set forth in §46.408.

§46.405 Research involving greater than minimal risk but presenting the prospect of direct benefit to the individual subjects.

HHS will conduct or fund research in which the IRB finds that more than minimal risk to children is presented by an intervention or procedure that holds out the prospect of direct benefit for the individual subject, or by a monitoring procedure that is likely to contribute to the subject's well-being, only if the IRB finds that:

(a) The risk is justified by the anticipated benefit to the subjects;

(b) The relation of the anticipated benefit to the risk is at least as favorable to the subjects as that presented by available alternative approaches; and

(c) Adequate provisions are made for soliciting the assent of the children and permission of their parents or guardians, as set forth in §46.408.

§46.406 Research involving greater than minimal risk and no prospect of direct benefit to individual subjects, but likely to yield generalizable knowledge about the subject's disorder or condition.

HHS will conduct or fund research in which the IRB finds that more than minimal risk to children is presented by an intervention or procedure that does not hold out the prospect of direct benefit for the individual subject, or by a monitoring procedure which is not likely to contribute to the well-being of the subject, only if the IRB finds that:

(a) The risk represents a minor increase over minimal risk;

(b) The intervention or procedure presents experiences to subjects that are reasonably commensurate with those inherent in their actual or expected medical, dental, psychological, social, or educational situations;

(c) The intervention or procedure is likely to yield generalizable knowledge about the subjects' disorder or condition which is of vital importance for the understanding or amelioration of the subjects' disorder or condition; and

(d) Adequate provisions are made for soliciting assent of the children and permission of their parents or guardians, as set forth in §46.408.

§46.407 Research not otherwise approvable which presents an opportunity to understand, prevent, or alleviate a serious problem affecting the health or welfare of children.

HHS will conduct or fund research that the IRB does not believe meets the requirements of §46.101, §46.105, or §46.406 only if:

(a) the IRB finds that the research presents a reasonable opportunity to further the understanding, prevention, or alleviation of a serious problem affecting the health or welfare of children; and

(b) the Secretary, after consultation with a panel of experts in pertinent disciplines (for example: science, medicine, education, ethics, law) and following opportunity for public review and comment, has determined either:

(1) that the research in fact satisfies the conditions of §46.404, §46.405, or §46.406, as applicable, or (2) the following:

(i) the research presents a reasonable opportunity to further the understanding, prevention, or alleviation of a serious problem affecting the health or welfare of children;

(ii) the research will be conducted in accordance with sound ethical principles;

(iii) adequate provisions are made for soliciting the assent of children and the permission of their parents or guardians, as set forth in §46.408.

§46.408 Requirements for permission by parents or guardians and for assent by children.

(a) In addition to the determinations required under other applicable sections of this subpart, the IRB shall determine that adequate provisions are made for soliciting the assent of the children, when in the judgment of the IRB the children are capable of providing assent. In determining whether children are capable of assenting, the IRB shall take into account the ages, maturity, and psychological state of the children involved. This judgment may be made for all children to be involved in research under a particular protocol, or for each child, as the IRB deems appropriate. If the IRB determines that the capability of some or all of the children is so limited that they cannot reasonably be consulted or that the intervention or procedure involved in the research holds out a prospect of direct benefit that is important to the health or well-being of the children and is available only in the context of the research, the assent of the children is not a necessary condition for proceeding with the research. Even where the IRB determines that the subjects are capable of assenting, the IRB may still waive the assent requirement under circumstances in which consent may be waived in accord with §46.116 of Subpart A.

(b) In addition to the determinations required under other applicable sections of this subpart, the IRB shall determine, in accordance with and to the extent that consent is required by §46.116 of Subpart A, that adequate provisions are made for soliciting the permission of each child's parents or guardian. Where parental permission is to be obtained, the IRB may find that the permission of one parent is sufficient for research to be conducted under §46.404 or §46.405. Where research is covered by §§46.406 and 46.407 and permission is to be obtained from parents, both parents must give their permission unless one parent is deceased, unknown, incompetent, or not reasonably available, or when only one parent has legal responsibility for the care and custody of the child.

(c) In addition to the provisions for waiver contained in §46.116 of subpart A, if the IRB determines that a research protocol is designed for conditions or for a subject population for which parental or guardian permission is not a reasonable requirement to protect the subjects (for example, neglected or abused children), it may waive the consent requirements in Subpart A of this part and paragraph (b) of this section, provided an appropriate mechanism for protecting the children who will participate as subjects in the research is substituted, and provided further that the waiver is not inconsistent with federal, state, or local law. The choice of an appropriate mechanism would depend upon the nature and purpose of the activities described in the protocol, the risk and anticipated benefit to the research subjects, and their age, maturity, status, and condition.

(d) Permission by parents or guardians shall be documented in accordance with and to the extent required by §46.117 of subpart A. (e) When the IRB determines that assent is required, it shall also determine whether and how assent must be documented.

§46.409 Wards.

(a) Children who are wards of the state or any other agency, institution, or entity can be included in research approved under §46.406 or §46.407 only if such research is:

(1) Related to their status as wards; or

(2) Conducted in schools, camps, hospitals, institutions, or similar settings in which the majority of children involved as subjects are not wards.

(b) If the research is approved under paragraph (a) of this section, the IRB shall require appointment of an advocate for each child who is a ward, in addition to any other individual acting on behalf of the child as guardian or in loco parentis. One individual may serve as advocate for more than one child. The advocate shall be an individual who has the background and experience to act in, and agrees to act in, the best interests of the child for the duration of the child's participation in the research and who is not associated in any way (except in the role as advocate or member of the IRB) with the research, the investigator(s), or the guardian organization.

Subpart E—Registration of Institutional Review Boards

Source:

74 FR 2399, January 15, 2009, unless otherwise noted.

§46.501 What IRBs must be registered?

Each IRB that is designated by an institution under an assurance of compliance approved for federalwide use by the Office for Human Research Protections (OHRP) under §46.103(a) and that reviews research involving human subjects conducted or supported by the Department of Health and Human Services (HHS) must be registered with HHS. An individual authorized to act on behalf of the institution or organization operating the IRB must submit the registration information.

§46.502 What information must be provided when registering an IRB?

The following information must be provided to HHS when registering an IRB:

(a) The name, mailing address, and street address (if different from the mailing address) of the institution or organization operating the IRB(s); and the name, mailing address, phone number, facsimile number, and electronic mail address of the senior officer or head official of that institution or organization who is responsible for overseeing activities performed by the IRB.

(b) The name, mailing address, phone number, facsimile number, and electronic mail address of the contact person providing the registration information.

(c) The name, if any, assigned to the IRB by the institution or organization, and the IRB's mailing address, street address (if different from the mailing address), phone number, facsimile number, and electronic mail address.

(d) The name, phone number, and electronic mail address of the IRB chairperson.

(e)(1) The approximate numbers of:

(i) All active protocols; and

(ii) Active protocols conducted or supported by HHS.

(2) For purpose of this regulation, an "active protocol" is any protocol for which the IRB conducted an initial review or a continuing review at a convened meeting or under an expedited review procedure during the preceding twelve months.

(f) The approximate number of full-time equivalent positions devoted to the IRB's administrative activities.

§46.503 When must an IRB be registered?

An IRB must be registered before it can be designated under an assurance approved for federalwide use by OHRP under §46.103(a). IRB registration becomes effective when reviewed and accepted by OHRP. The registration will be effective for 3 years.

§46.504 How must an IRB be registered?

Each IRB must be registered electronically through http://ohrp.cit.nih.gov/efile unless an institution or organization lacks the ability to register its IRB(s) electronically. If an institution or organization lacks the ability to register an IRB electronically, it must send its IRB registration information in writing to OHRP.

§46.505 When must IRB registration infor-

mation be renewed or updated?

(a) Each IRB must renew its registration every 3 years.

(b) The registration information for an IRB must be updated within 90 days after changes occur regarding the contact person who provided the IRB registration information or the IRB chairperson. The updated registration information must be submitted in accordance with §46.504.

(c) Any renewal or update that is submitted to, and accepted by, OHRP begins a new 3- year effective period.

(d) An institution's or organization's decision to disband a registered IRB which it is operating also must be reported to OHRP in writing within 30 days after permanent cessation of the IRB's review of HHSconducted or -supported research.

Glossary

Adverse Event
(AE) Any unfavorable or unintended event associated with a research study.

Association for the Accreditation of Human Research Protection Programs (AAHRPP)
An organization that accredits IRBs, with the goal of helping to ensure that all human research participants are respected and protected from harm.

Accountability Records
Forms that are used to provide evidence that, at the conclusion of a drug or device investigation, all materials are accounted for and that their final disposition is controlled.

Adverse Event (AE)
Any unfavorable or unintended event associated with a research study.

Adverse Event Reports
Investigator reports of all serious and adverse events, injury and deaths given to the sponsor, the IRB and the FDA.

Assent
A child's affirmative agreement to participate in a clinical investigation.

Assurance
Renewable permit granted by a federal department to an institution to conduct research, can be given for individual or multiple projects.

Belmont Report
Ethical Principles and Guidelines for the Protection of Human Subjects of Research. Cornerstone document of ethical principles. Federal regulation of subject protection based on respect for persons, beneficence and justice.

Beneficence
Doing no harm, maximizing benefits while minimizing risks.

Bioresearch Monitoring Program (BIMO)
The FDA's inspection program that conducts routine and "for cause" audits of FDA-regulated research.

Case Report Forms
Study document of all data required by protocol on each subject.

Certificates of Confidentiality
Issued by the National Institutes of Health (NIH) and other DHHS agencies to protect the privacy of research subjects by protecting investigators and institutions from being compelled to release information (i.e., forced disclosure) that could be used to identify subjects in a research project.

Certified Clinical Research Coordinator (CCRC)
CRC with more than two years experience and with certification earned by passing required program and exam.

Certified IRB Professional (CIP)
IRB administrative personnel with more than two years experience and with certification earned by passing required exam.

Clinical Research
Study of drug, biologic or device in human subjects with the intent to discover potential beneficial effects and/or determine its safety and efficacy. Also called clinical study and clinical investigation. Note that in this manual, this term is used in its narrow sense as used by the FDA. Thus, it does not encompass all the research that is carried out in the clinical setting (e.g., health services research). See also, patient-oriented research.

Clinical Research Associate (CRA)
Person employed by the study sponsor or CRO to monitor a clinical study at all participating sites. See also, monitor.

Clinical Research Coordinator (CRC)
Site administer for the clinical study. Duties are delegated by the investigator. Also called research, study or healthcare coordinator, and data manager, research nurse or protocol nurse.

Clinical Study Materials
Study supplies (i.e., study test article, laboratory supplies case report forms) provided by the study sponsor to the investigator.

Clinical Trial Steering Committee
A committee appointed by a sponsor to design a study, ensure the quality of the study conduct and write the final study report. The committee is usually comprised of investigators, sponsor representatives and experts not directly involved in the study.

Common Rule
1991 agreement to cover all federally-sponsored and federally-conducted research by a common set of regulations.

Consent Form
Contains all relevant study information explained in lay terms and documents voluntary participation of subject. Presented to and signed by subject.

Contract Research Organization (CRO)
A person or an organization (commercial, academic or other) contracted by the sponsor to perform one or more of a sponsor's study-related duties and functions.

Data
Legally defined according to institution. Generally refers to recorded information regardless of form. Most institutions hold title to data while researchers have rights to access data.

Data Monitoring Committee
An independent review/advisory board whose primary mission is to measure and report on the continuing safety of current research subjects as well as subjects who have not yet enrolled in a clinical trial. (Sometimes called Data Safety Monitoring Boards (DSMB).)

Deception
Intentionally misleading or withholding information about nature of experiment.

Declaration of Helsinki
Statement of ethical principles first published by World Medical Association in 1964 to define rules for therapeutic and nontherapeutic research.

Delegation of Authority Log
A written document listing the responsibilities delegated to all members of the research team and the time period that each team member participated.

Documentation
All forms of records that describe or document study methods, conduct and results, including any adverse events and actions taken.

Drug or Device Accountability Records (DAR)
Required documentation for material accountability, quantity used and left over, and date of disposal.

Ethical Principles and Guidelines for the Protection of Human Subjects of Research
See Belmont Report.

Family Educational Rights and Privacy Act (FERPA)
Covers rights of parents of school children regarding reviewing, amending and disclosing educational records.

Federalwide Assurance (FWA)
Permit given to institution for multiple federally funded research grants for a specified period of time. States institution retains responsibility for all research involving humans and that the institution must have an established IRB.

Food and Drug Administration (FDA)
Within DHHS. Enforces Food, Drug and Cosmetics Act and related federal public health laws. Grants IND, IDE, PMA and NDA approvals.

Food and Drug Administration Amendments Act (FDAAA)
This act, passed in 2007, mandates the submission (to the FDA) of summary clinical trial results data for phase IIb – IV studies whether the results are conclusive, inconclusive, published or not.

Food and Drug Administration Modernization Act (FDAMA)
Legislation passed in 1997 that contains a provision requiring that information about clinical trials for serious or life-threatening diseases be accessible to potential subjects.

Food Drug and Cosmetic Act (FD&C Act)
States only drugs, biologics and devices proven safe and effective can be marketed.

FDA Form 1572
List of commitments and conduct required by FDA for each investigator performing drug/biologics study. Also referred to as statement of investigator.

Gene Transfer
A technique to substitute absent or faulty genes causing diseases with working genes so that cells make the correct enzyme or protein.

Good Clinical Practice (GCP)
International ethical and scientific quality standard for designing, conducting, monitoring, recording, auditing, analyzing and reporting studies. In-

sures that the data reported is credible and accurate and that subject's rights and confidentiality are protected.

Health Information
Information in any form or medium that relates to a living or deceased individual's past, present or future physical or mental health or condition.

Health Information Technology for Economic and Clinical Health Act (HITECH Act)
Enacted by Congress in 2009, this act includes incentives for health care providers who adopt electronic health records (EHR) and expands the scope of HIPAA.

Health Insurance Portability and Accountability Act of 1996 (HIPAA)
Law that requires parties who participate in certain healthcare transactions to conduct the transactions electronically using standardized formats and code sets.

Human Subject
A patient or healthy individual participating in a research study. A living individual about whom an investigator obtains private information or data through intervention or interaction.

Inclusion Criteria
A list of criteria that must be met by all study subjects.

IND Safety Report
A formal written report of an adverse experience that is associated with the drug, serious, and unexpected. The sponsor must send this report to the FDA and all investigators working with the drug.

Informed Consent
Information exchange including subject recruitment materials, verbal instructions, written materials, question and answer sessions and signature documenting consent with date. Subjects are given opportunity to choose involvement based on information, comprehension and voluntariness.

International Conference on Harmonization (ICH)
An organization composed of expert working groups from industry and regulatory bodies in the European Union, Japan and the United States. ICH publishes guidelines for worldwide GCP with the goal of standardization for clinical trials of drugs.

International Ethics Guidelines for Biomedical Research Involving Human Subjects
(CIOMS guidelines) Developed by the Council for International Organizations of Medical Sciences in 1982 to guide cross-cultural research.

Institution
Location of research. Retains ultimate responsibility for human subject regulation compliance.

Institutional Review Board (IRB)
Reviews research and consent forms to determine if rights and welfare of subjects are protected.

Investigational Device Exemption (IDE)
Exemption from FD&C Act to study investigational medical devices.

Investigational Materials
Test articles under clinical investigation.

Investigational New Drug Application (IND)
Exemption from FD&C Act to study investigational drug or biologic.

Investigator
Conducts and directs study. Carries ultimate responsibility for research. Is referred to as the principle investigator when acts as a leader for an investigational team. Also referred to as Clinical Investigator by the FDA.

Investigator Brochure (IB)
A document containing the results of animal studies, pharmacokinetic and pharmacodynamic information, any previous clinical studies and other pertinent information about a drug under development.

Investigator-Sponsor
Individual with both responsibilities of initiating and conducting a clinical study.

Investigator's Brochure
Relevant clinical and nonclinical data compiled on the investigational drug, biologic or device being studied.

Kefauver-Harris Amendments
Amendment to FD&C Act that requires informed consent for experimental drugs.

Legally Authorized Representative

An individual or judicial or other body authorized under applicable law to consent on behalf of a prospective subject to the subject's participation in a research trial.

Life-threatening Adverse Event or Life-threatening Suspected Adverse Reaction

An adverse event or suspected adverse reaction is considered "life-threatening" if, in the view of either the investigator or sponsor, its occurrence places the patient or subject at immediate risk of death.

Misconduct

Fabrication, falsification, plagiarism or other practices that seriously deviate from those accepted within scientific community for conducting and reporting research.

Monitor

Person employed by the sponsor or CRO who reviews study records to determine that a study is being conducted in accordance with the protocol. A monitor's duties may include, but are not limited to, helping to plan and initiate a study, and assessing the conduct of studies. Monitors work with the clinical research coordinator to check all data and documentation from the study. See also CRA.

Monitoring

Reviewing a clinical study, ensuring conduct, proper records and reports are performed as stated in the clinical protocol, standard operating procedures, GCP and by regulatory requirements.

National Research Act

Act created the National Commission for Protection of Human Subjects of Biomedical and Behavioral research in 1974 and mandated review of studies by institutional review boards and subject protection by informed consent.

New Drug Application (NDA)

An FDA application to market a new drug in the United States.

National Institutes of Health (NIH)

Agency within DHHS that provides funding for research, conducts studies and funds multi-site national studies.

Nuremberg Code

Set of standards proclaimed following trial of Nazi doctors in 1947.

Non-significant Risk Device (NSR)

A device that has not been classified as a significant risk (SR) device.

Office for Human Research Protection (OHRP)
Federal government office that issues Assurances and overseas compliance.

Office of Research Integrity (ORI)
ORI is the division of the PHS which oversees investigations of allegations of scientific misconduct.

Patient
Individual seeking medical care.

Patient Oriented Research
Research conducted with human subjects (or on material of human origin) in which an investigator or colleague directly interacts with human subjects. (NIH definition of clinical research)

Physician Payment Sunshine Act
A law enacted in 2010 that requires pharmaceutical, medical device, biological, and medical supply manufacturers to report to Health and Human Services (HHS) any "payment or other transfer of value" to physicians and teaching hospitals.

Placebo
An inert substance used as a comparison to an active ingredient in clinical trials.

Privacy Certificate
Investigators receiving NIJ funding must apply for a Privacy Certificate per the Department of Justice Confidentiality statute (42 USC 3789g). This makes identifiable data collected during the course of the research immune from legal action.

Privacy Rule
A standard issued by HHS in 2003 that restricts the use and disclosure of identifiable health information maintained by individuals or organizations covered by the HIPAA regulation.

Protected Health Information
Information about a person that is individually identifiable.

Protection of Pupil Rights Amendment (PPRA)
Department of Education regulation that states that surveys, questionnaires and instructional materials for school children must be inspected by parents/guardians.

Protocol

Documentation of study objective, design, methods, statistical methods and organization. The term also includes amendments made to the original document.

Protocol Amendment

Changes or clarifications made in writing to the original protocol.

Recruitment

Act of enrolling subjects with the proper inclusion criteria into a study.

Recruitment Period

Time allowed to recruit all subjects for a study.

Representative Population

Generally means that a study should include men, women, minorities and age-appropriate participants, in keeping with the proportion of individuals afflicted with the disease or condition being studied.

Research

Systematic investigation designed to develop or contribute to generalizable knowledge. Includes Clinical Research.

Research Team

Investigator, subinvestigator and clinical research coordinator involved with study.

Risk-Benefit Ratio

Risk to individual subject vs. potential benefits. Also called Risk-Benefit Analysis.

Safety Reports

FDA report required by investigator for any serious and unexpected adverse experience.

Secondary Subjects Research

Research that involves the collection of information about individuals from sources other than through direct intervention.

Security Rule

A standard issued by HHS in 2003 that requires appropriate administrative, physical and technical safeguards to ensure the confidentiality, integrity, and security of identifiable health information that is maintained in an electronic format.

Serious Adverse Event or Serious Suspected Adverse Reaction

Any event that results in death, a life threatening situation, hospitalization or prolonged hospitalization, disability, incapacity or a congenital anomaly/ birth defect.

Significant Risk Device

An investigational device that: (1) is intended as an implant and presents a potential for serious risk to the health, safety, or welfare of a subject; (2) is for use in supporting or sustaining human life and represents a potential for serious risk to the health, safety, or welfare of a subject; (3) is for a use of substantial importance in diagnosing, curing, mitigating, or treating disease or otherwise preventing impairment of human health and presents a potential for serious risk to the health, safety, or welfare of a subject; or (4) otherwise presents a potential for serious risk to a subject.

Source Data

All information contained in original records and certified copies of results, observations or other facets required for the reconstruction and evaluation of the study that is contained in source documents.

Source Documentation

Location that information is first recorded including original documents, data and records.

Sponsor

Individual, company, institution or organization taking responsibility for initiation, management and financing of study.

Standard Operating Procedures (SOP)

Detailed, written procedures for the uniform performance of a function.

Subinvestigator

Helps design and conduct investigation at a study site.

Subject/Study Subject

Participant in a study. See Human Subject.

Suspected Adverse Reaction

Any adverse event for which there is a reasonable possibility that the drug caused the adverse event.

Telephone Report

Notification via telephone to the FDA of unexpected fatal or life threatening advent associated with clinical study.

Unanticipated Adverse Device Effect (UADE)
An adverse effect occurring in a device trial that presents an unreasonable risk to study participants.

Unexpected Adverse Event or Unexpected Suspected Adverse Reaction
An adverse event or suspected adverse reaction is considered "unexpected" if it is not listed in the investigator brochure or is not listed at the specificity or severity that has been observed.

Unexpected Event
Any incident or reaction that puts subjects or others at risk and is not described in the study plan and/or study application.

Vulnerable Subjects
Group/individual that cannot give informed consent because of limited autonomy (e.g., children, mentally ill and prisoners). Also refers to subjects who may be unduly influenced to participate (e.g., students, subordinates and patients).

Well-being
Subject's physical and mental soundness.

Whistle-blower
An individuals who has, in good faith, made an allegation of misconduct against an organization or individual.

Withdrawal Application
Investigator/sponsor letter to FDA requesting application withdrawal when no additional work is envisioned.

Abbreviations and Acronyms

Abbreviation	Term
AAHRPP	Association for the Accreditation of Human Research Protection Programs
AAMC	American Association of Medical Colleges
AAU	Association of American Universities
ACE	Affiliated Covered Entity
ACHRE	Advisory Committee on Human Radiation Experiments
AE	Adverse Event
AEC	Atomic Energy Commission
AHA	American Historical Association
AHRQ	Agency for Healthcare Research and Quality
AMA	American Medical Association
ARRA	American Recovery and Reinvestment Act of 2009
ATS	American Thoracic Society
BIMO	Bioresearch Monitoring Program
BMJ	British Medical Journal
CBQR	Community-Based Qualitative Research
CCRC	Certified Clinical Research Coordinator
CDC	Centers for Disease Control and Prevention
CFR	Code of Federal Regulations
CI	Clinical Investigator
CIOMS	Council for International Organizations of Medical Sciences
COI	Conflict of Interest
COIC	Conflict of Interest Committee
CRA	Clinical Research Associate
CRC	Clinical Research Coordinator
CRF	Case Report Form
CRO	Contract Research Organization
DAR	Drug or Device Accountability Record
DHHS	Department of Health and Human Services
DMC	Data Monitoring Committee
DOD	Department of Defense

Abbreviation	Term
DOE	U.S. Department of Education
DSMB	Data Safety Monitoring Board
EHR	Electronic Health Records
EMA	European Medicines Agency
FAQ	Frequently Asked Questions
FDA	Food and Drug Administration
FDAAA	Food and Drug Administration Amendments Act
FDAMA	Food and Drug Administration Modernization Act
FERPA	Family Educational Rights and Privacy Act
FWA	Federal-Wide Assurance
GAO	General Accounting Office
GCP	Good Clinical Practice
HGT	Human Gene Transfer
HHS	Health and Human Services (Department of)
HIPAA	Health Insurance Portability and Accountability Act
HITECH	Health Information Technology for Economic and Clinical Health Act
IBC	Institutional Biosafety Committee
ICH	International Conference on Harmonization
ICMJE	International Committee of Medical Journal Editors
IDE	Investigational Device Exemption
IIHI	Individually Identifiable Health Information
ILD	Interstitial Lung Disease
IND	Investigational New Drug Application
IOM	Institute of Medicine
IRB	Institutional Review Board
JAMA	Journal of the American Medical Association
LAR	Legally Authorized Representative
MPA	Multiple Project Assurance
NBAC	National Bioethics Advisory Commission
NCI	National Cancer Institute
NDA	New Drug Application
NEJM	New England Journal of Medicine
NFS	National Science Foundation
NIH	National Institutes of Health
NIJ	National Institute of Justice
NIOSH	National Institute for Occupational Safety & Health
MHRA	Medical and Healthcare Products Regulatory Agency (England)
NPP	Notice of Privacy Practices
NYS-DH	New York State Department of Health
OCR	Office of Civil Rights
OHA	Oral History Association
OHCA	Organized Health Care Arrangement
OHRP	Office for Human Research Protection

Abbreviation	Term
ORI	Office of Research Integrity
PAR	Participatory Action Research
PCB	President's Commission on Bioethics
PHI	Protected Health Information
PHS	Public Health Service
PI	Principal Investigator
PMA	Premarket Approval Application
PPRA	Protection of Pupil Rights Amendment
QA	Quality Assurance
RAC	Recombinant DNA Advisory Committee
SADR	Suspected Adverse Drug Reaction
SAE	Serious Adverse Event
SAR	Suspected Adverse Reaction
SMO	Site Management Organization
SOP	Standard Operating Procedure
TBI	Total Body Irradiation
TPO	Treatment, Payment for Healthcare or Healthcare Operations
UADE	Unanticipated Adverse Device Effect
WMA	World Medical Association

R

S

T

U

V

W

Protecting Study Volunteers in Research Examination

In an effort to make this manual as useful to as many investigators as possible, it focuses on topics, regulations, and guidelines that are most pertinent to both biomedical and behavioral researchers. The manual does include some information and chapters that are specific to biomedical research and clinical trials in particular. Recognizing that those individuals engaged in behavioral research may not need to be tested on biomedical topics, the following examination was designed to allow individuals and institutions to easily adapt the examination process to meet specific needs.

The examination is presented in two parts. Part 1 is 32 multiple choice questions that cover the general topics that all researchers should be familiar with and should be applied when conducting any research with human subjects. Part 2 consists of 20 true/false case-oriented questions that cover topics in biomedical research. To obtain CME or CE credit, both sections must be completed. Those institutions and individuals who focus exclusively on research in the social and behavioral sciences, however, would be able to complete part 1 without the focus on biomedical research. Institutions may wish to develop their own part 2 examination to cover topics specific to the types of research conducted at the institution.

Part 1: Multiple Choice

Please read the following questions and choose the answer that is the most accurate or best answers the question.

1. The Syphilis Study, the Willowbrook Study and others are frequently cited as examples of research with ethical problems. An important lesson from these studies is that:

   a. Researchers may violate ethical norms even though they have good intentions

   b. Only biomedical research has been associated with ethical problems

    c. Research scandals never result in national legislation or regulations

    d. Mistakes of the past can never be repeated

2. In 1981, the FDA and DHHS published federal regulations for the protection of human subjects in biomedical and behavioral research. These regulations were also adopted by other federal agencies in 1991. What two protections do these "Common Rule" regulations mandate?

    a. Payment to subjects and compensation for injury

    b. Informed consent of subjects and IRB review

    c. Confidentiality of research records and privacy guarantees

    d. Direct benefit to subjects and elimination of all risks

3. As defined in the Belmont Report, the ethical principle of respect for persons relates to the general rule:

    a. Obtain consent from subjects

    b. Maximize possible benefits and minimize potential risks

    c. The burdens of research should be shared equally

    d. Children should not be enrolled in research

4. As defined in the Belmont Report, the ethical principle of beneficence relates to the general rule:

    a. Obtain consent from subjects

    b. Maximize possible benefits and minimize potential risks

    c. The burdens of research should be shared equally

    d. The benefits from research should be applied first to those who cannot afford them

5. As defined in the Belmont Report, the ethical principle of justice relates to the general rule:

    a. Obtain consent from subjects

    b. Maximize possible benefits and minimize potential risks

    c. The burdens of research should be shared equally

    d. Local courts have ultimate jurisdiction over research

6. What is included in the official definition of scientific misconduct?

    a. Negligence, errors and omissions

    b. Fabrication, falsification and plagiarism

    c. Incompetence, misbehavior and deviations

d. Differences in interpretations of data

7. Under federal regulations and guidelines, institutions conducting federally funded research are required to:

   a. Report all honest errors to the Office of Research Integrity (ORI)

   b. Be registered with the OHRP, ORI and FDA

   c. Establish a sponsored-programs office that provides peer review of research protocols

   d. Provide training in research ethics to investigators and investigate reports of scientific misconduct

8. To conduct federally funded research, the regulations require institutions to have which of the following?

   a. A Certificate of Confidentiality

   b. A contract for goods and services

   c. An assurance of compliance with the human subject protection regulations (e.g., Federal-Wide Assurance)

   d. A Business Associate agreement

9. When reviewing research, the IRB has the authority to:

   a. Require modifications in consent forms, but not to protocols

   b. Disapprove any research with human subject concerns

   c. Modify research before it starts, but not afterwards

   d. Override an institutional official's disapproval of research

10. What actions must an investigator take to amend/modify the way a study is being conducted?

    a. Obtain IRB approval of the change before implementing it

    b. Only notify the IRB at the time of study renewal/review

    c. Obtain prior IRB approval only if the consent form is to be changed

    d. No action is necessary for already approved studies

11. Investigators must follow the IRB approved protocol. This is:

    a. Required even if immediate danger to subjects may result.

    b. Only required for federally sponsored research.

    c. A specific requirement for compliance with the regulations.

    d. Primarily to prevent sponsors from defaulting on payments for protocol violations.

12. The investigator's professional judgment is essential to maintain the integrity of the research process. Investigators should always:

    a. Value human rights and subject welfare more highly than scientific knowledge

    b. Value scientific knowledge more highly than human rights and subject welfare

    c. Value commercial success over scientific knowledge

    d. Value commercial success over human rights and subject welfare

13. The greatest concern for most volunteers in behavioral and social science research is usually:

    a. Deception

    b. Risk of physical harm

    c. Payment for time

    d. Privacy and confidentiality

14. In designing and conducting behavioral and social science research, the following is true:

    a. Intrusions on privacy are justified by the requirement for absolute confidentiality

    b. Deception should never be used

    c. No additional safeguards are needed when studying vulnerable populations

    d. Stress, discomfort and other harms should be minimized

15. Certificates of Confidentiality from the Department of Health and Human Services

    a. Guarantee absolute confidentiality of research data.

    b. Are issued for all research studies.

    c. Do not prevent voluntary disclosures.

    d. Prohibit subjects from disclosing research data or involvement.

16. When research is sponsored by a company or agency, a contract should be negotiated that protects the researcher's publication rights. These research contracts are:

    a. Not legally enforceable, but provide guidance on study conduct

    b. Usually are required to be negotiated and signed by an authorized institutional representative

    c. Always signed solely by the investigator as part of the responsibility for conducting the study

    d. Illegal if they place limitations on publication rights

17. An example of scientific misconduct in publication is:

    a. Changing the results to be reported in a publication for personal gain

    b. Accepting financial support to present data or to publish a manuscript

    c. Delaying publication of results for two weeks to allow a sponsor to file patent applications

    d. Publication of negative results

18. Regarding genetic research,

    a. It is only regulated by federal law, not State law.

    b. It always involves sampling and testing DNA or RNA.

    c. Knowledge about the implications for specific genetic mutations is constantly evolving.

    d. The risk associated with genetic testing studies is small.

19. Regarding human gene transfer (HGT) studies carried out at an institution that receives federal support for recombinant DNA research:

    a. By federal regulation, only germline cells can be modified by HGT

    b. Investigatorsmust comply with"Appendix M"of the NIH Guidelines on HGT

    c. Privately funded HGT is not regulated by either NIH or FDA

    d. IBC review is required but it substitutes for IRB review

20. Regarding conflicts of interest in research,

    a. There is only one type of conflict that matters, i.e., financial conflicts.

    b. They indicate a character flaw in the person who has the conflict.

    c. Disclosure in consent forms is always required by federal regulation.

    d. Public concern may lead to additional regulations for investigators to follow.

21. It is important to address conflicts of interest on the part of investigators and institutions because subject safety may be compromised and/or:

    a. Journals will not publish research with conflicts, hidden or apparent.

    b. The knowledge produced from the research may be biased.

    c. Proper management requires elimination of all conflicts.

    d. They cause obvious bias, and damage the institution's reputation

22. Research with tissues may require informed consent from subjects. When consent will be obtained,

    a. Risks of disclosure of the information need not be part of the consent process because they do not cause physical harm

    b. Federal regulations for consent always take precedence over State laws

    c. The type of research to be conducted, including whether genetic analysis will be performed should be stated in the consent form.

    d. The consent form should contain a waiver of profits from any commercial products

23. Recruitment advertisements for subjects are considered to be part of the informed consent process. Therefore, ads must

    a. Contain all the federal elements of consent

    b. Be reviewed and approved by the IRB

    c. Only be in written formats

    d. Be in both English and expected non-English languages

24. Including representative populations (men, women, minorities and age appropriate participants) in research helps ensure applicability/generalizability of results. Including a representative population is

    a. Generally mandatory for NIH-funded and FDA-regulated studies

    b. Never to be reviewed by the IRB

    c. Only important for adult populations, not for children

    d. Only important for human gene transfer studies

25. An example of addressing barriers to minority participation is:

    a. Avoiding participation by minority researchers and research staff

    b. Providing study materials in languages other than English

    c. Being available only during normal business hours

    d. Charging for transportation services

26. Community-based qualitative research (CBQR) assumes that:

    a. The community is the authority on its own situation and potential solutions

    b. Consent of individual subjects is not necessary

c. The research team's own cultural values do not differ from those of the study community

d. Unbiased research can only be conducted at sites near the research institution

27. Responsibility for maintaining confidentiality in community-based qualitative research (CBQR) rests with the researcher, however:

a. Masking identities is only permissible for Participatory Action Research (PAR)

b. Gathering and reporting identifying information is required for Participatory Action Research (PAR)

c. Written informed consent may threaten a participant's desire to remain anonymous

d. Certificates of Confidentiality are required to use this technique

28. According to the Belmont Report, the process of informed consent requires three key components to be adequately addressed to be considered ethically valid. These are:

a. Confidentiality, compassion and comprehension

b. Information, understanding and voluntary agreement

c. Signatures of subject, person obtaining consent and a witness

d. Subject's signature and date plus receipt of a copy of the form

29. When designing the consent process for a study, investigators should consider:

a. Inclusion of required elements of consent

b. Timing of the consent process

c. Who will discuss consent with the potential subject

d. All of the above

30. When obtaining informed consent, coercion and undue influence should be avoided. Undue influences are harder to control because:

a. Subjects are always in dependent relationships with investigators

b. Research always includes some benefit for subjects

c. They may be situational/environmental, and are dependent on each subject's personal circumstances

d. They are known to the investigator but not to the subject

31. Failure to comply with the HIPAA Privacy Rule can result in:

    a. Civil penalties and criminal sanctions against both organizations and investigators

    b. Administrative sanctions against the organization only

    c. Civil penalties and criminal sanctions, but only against investigators

    d. Civil penalties and criminal sanctions, but only against the actual violator, not the investigator

32. According to the HIPAA Privacy Rule, "protected health information" (PHI) includes:

    a. All individually identifiable health information in medical records only

    b. Health information that is individually identifiable and created or received by a covered entity

    c. Only electronically stored information

    d. De-identified health information held by a covered entity

Part 2: Biomedical Case Studies (True /False)

Please read the following case studies and answer the corresponding questions.

Case Study 1: The drug, "Seizure-stop" is an FDA-approved product marketed in tablet form for treatment of epileptic seizures in patients over 12 years old. Based upon a report in the literature, an investigator wants to conduct an open-label study (i.e., no placebo, no blinding) with this drug for treatment of life-threatening refractory seizures. The study will be conducted with pediatric patients aged 5 to 15.

33. Approved drugs that are used in a research context are governed by the FDA human subject protection regulations.

    a. True

    b. False

34. This study may require an IND because of the change in population from the approved labeling.

    a. True

    b. False

35. If the IRB finds that it is not appropriate to get assent from the children, it may waive the requirement for assent and just require parental permission.

    a. True

    b. False

Case Study 2: A surgeon designs an investigational medical device that is to be used in a study to place sutures in heart valve repairs. The subject population will be adults scheduled for non-emergent surgical repair. Because the "investigator" will also be the patients' surgeon, the protocol calls for an independent physician to obtain consent. Tissue removed from the valves will be provided to another researcher at the institution who is studying why the valves fail. The "tissue" study also involves reviewing the patient records and comparing prior medical histories to the types of defects seen in the valves.

36. If the IRB makes a determination that this is a "significant risk" device, then an IDE is required before the study may start.

    a. True

    b. False

37. The use of another physician to obtain consent will always confuse subjects and will never avoid undue influence.

    a. True

    b. False

38. Because it is "practicable" to obtain consent, a waiver of consent for the specimen study could not be approved by the IRB.

    a. True

    b. False

Case Study 3: The drug, "Snooze-away" is an investigational drug, currently in phase 3 trials as a sedative. The study protocol is a multi-center randomized placebo controlled, double blind design in persons age 21 or over with mild insomnia. The "placebo effect" is expected to be high. Each subject will participate for 2 weeks in this study.

39. The assessment of the risks and benefits of the use of placebo versus the use of available standard sedatives is a required step for investigators and IRBs.

    a. True

    b. False

40. Part of the ethical justification for the acceptable use of placebo in this research study is the IRB's assessment that the use of the placebo will not expose the subject to excessive or unnecessary risks.

    a. True

    b. False

41. A central question that must be answered in this clinical trial is whether the subjects in the placebo control group are being unfairly denied a medical benefit.

    a. True

    b. False

42. The fact that there are standard treatments for insomnia that are available without enrolling in this study must be clearly stated in the consent form.

    a. True

    b. False

43. If a large percentage of potential subjects are known to be non-English speaking, the regulations allow an investigator to enroll them with the English consent form, but require using a translator.

    a. True

    b. False

44. Each principal investigator in this study must have a Form-1572 on file with the FDA.

    a. True

    b. False

45. During a routine site visit, the sponsor's study monitor is permitted to review the accuracy of the case report forms, but cannot review source documents.

    a. True

    b. False

46. After the study has been enrolling for a few weeks, one investigator wants to change the procedure for the initial work-up of subjects. Both the sponsor and the IRB must approve this change.

    a. True

    b. False

Case Study 4: An industry-sponsored clinical trial of an unapproved optical laser system to correct corneal malformations will compare eyes treated with the investigational system to those treated using normal standard of care techniques. A data monitoring Committee (DMC) is established to monitor the study. A protocol, a sample consent form and a confidential document listing known risks and background on prior studies are provided to the investigator by the sponsor.

47. The sponsor is permitted to ship the laser device to investigational sites for training before the IDE is filed with FDA.

   a. True

   b. False

48. If the study is put on hold by the sponsor because of "unreasonable risk" to subjects, the sponsor may correct the device and/or protocol procedures and resume the study without further review by the IRB or FDA.

   a. True

   b. False

49. An important role for the DMC in this study is making judgments about early termination of the trial based on the type and extent of reported adverse events, or the efficacy of the laser system.

   a. True

   b. False

50. The investigator should present the consent form and obtain consent from subjects at a pre-operative visit, rather than waiting until the day of the procedure.

   a. True

   b. False

51. Because this is a study conducted under an IDE, the principal investigator can not delegate obtaining informed consent process to any other study personnel.

   a. True

   b. False

52. If the investigator violates the FDA regulations, fines, debarment, and criminal charges may result.

   a. True

   b. False

Founded in 1994, CenterWatch is a trusted source and global destination of clinical trials information for both professionals and patients. CenterWatch provides a wide variety of information services including grant leads for investigative sites; business development leads for contract service providers; postings of career opportunities; listings of clinical trials actively seeking patients; advertising and promotional opportunities; and proprietary business analysis and data about the global clinical trials industry.

As a pioneer in publishing clinical trials information, CenterWatch was the first web site to publish detailed information about clinical trials that could be freely accessed by patients and their advocates. Today, we have the largest online database of actively recruiting, industry-sponsored clinical trials.

Visit centerwatch.com, call (617) 948-5100 or email customerservice@ centerwatch.com for more in-depth information on the wide variety of products and services CenterWatch offers.

CenterWatch Products and Service Offerings

- Periodicals and Business News
- Grant Notification and Site Identification Services
- Market Intelligence Services
- Patient Enrollment Services
- Patient Education
- Career Services
- Clinical Research Training Guides
- Regulatory Compliance
- Medical Writing Services
- Information Solutions and Content Licensing
- Business Development and Partnership Opportunities

Periodicals and Business News

The CenterWatch Monthly

The CenterWatch Monthly, our flagship publication, is a premier industry resource providing in-depth, authoritative business coverage for the clinical trials community, including unparalleled competitive market intelligence and clinical study leads and the most detailed drug pipeline analysis in the industry—all in one comprehensive publication featuring original CenterWatch data.

CWWeekly

CWWeekly is a leading news source providing expanded analysis on the week's top business and financial headlines and trends. Other features include: market intelligence, patient recruitment tips, drug intelligence and clinical study leads.

Research Practitioner

This bi-monthly journal is a valuable, educational and career advancement resource that provides in-depth and practical "how-to" articles about clinical research management trends, ethical and legal principles, regulatory issues and more. Subscribers can earn up to 18 CNE credits per year.

CenterWatch News Online

CenterWatch News Online (centerwatch.com/news-online) is a dynamic and easy-to-navigate online service featuring real-time objective news reports covering timely stories and emerging trends in the global clinical research industry. Features include: breaking news and top headlines as selected by the CenterWatch editorial staff, news beats featuring relevant content on various industry segments and proprietary CenterWatch data.

Grant Notification and Site Identification Services

TrialWatch for Sites

A complimentary grant notification service designed to help research centers easily connect with sponsors and CROs seeking qualified investigators for upcoming or ongoing active trials. Sites complete a brief online profile that is stored in a database and then matched against grant requests from sponsors and CROs. When a match is found, the site information is forwarded to the requesting company for consideration. Site profiles can be completed at centerwatch.com/trialwatch_signup.

TrialWatch for Sponsors and CROs

A complimentary site identification service that helps companies quickly and effectively identify active and qualified investigative sites worldwide to conduct upcoming and active phase I through phase IV clinical trials. Confidential requests can be submitted online at centerwatch.com/clinical-trials/trialwatch.

Research Center Profile Pages

Research Center Profile Pages, located on centerwatch.com, are an easy and cost-effective way for sites to showcase detailed information online about their site offerings and expertise to secure clinical research grants and contracts, increase their site's exposure and reach a captive and targeted audience. Profile Pages are completely customizable and can include images, video presentations, links to company documents, trial listings and more.

Market Intelligence Services

Custom Market Intelligence Services

Unprecedented business knowledge of the clinical research enterprise, combined with proprietary data and global contacts, gives CenterWatch a unique and objective position to perform rich and insightful quantitative and qualitative market intelligence services.

Our comprehensive offerings focus on all aspects of the life sciences and clinical trials industry and include secondary data analysis, interviews, focus group research and a broad range of customer surveys such as outsourcing and vendor evaluations, research and examination of new industry technologies, company performance and relationships, post-trial analysis to gauge site success, volatility of global investigative site infrastructure and more.

Our experienced market research team works directly with companies to provide mission-critical information and detailed market analysis their organizations need to make more effective business decisions. We provide final reports for all commissioned studies and also offer presentations and facilitated discussions.

Clinical Trials Data Library

The *CenterWatch Clinical Trials Data Library* is a valuable online and searchable resource providing access to comprehensive data on the life sciences and clinical research industry. Derived from several industry sources, including proprietary, CenterWatch-conducted surveys, data charts range from analysis of global economic trends and clinical research practices to examinations of partnerships and drug development pipelines and performance. Charts can be conveniently downloaded, copied and pasted into PowerPoint or Word documents to create dynamic, data-driven business reports and conference presentations, prepare strategic marketing, financial and business development plans and study current and historical activity for training and roundtable discussions.

Patient Enrollment Services

Clinical Trials Listing Service™

As one of the first web sites to publish clinical trials actively seeking study volunteers, CenterWatch continues to be a leading resource for patients interested in clinical trial participation receiving more than one million visitors annually to our listings. When companies post a trial on our *Clinical Trials Listing Service™*, now the largest online database of industry-funded global clinical trials, this targeted population has direct access to these listings via a range of distribution channels including: email messaging programs, email alerts for new trial postings, social media efforts, top search engine rankings including Search Clinical Trials, RSS clinical news feeds and collaborative relationships with health associations and other non-profit organizations.

Patient Education

Volunteering for a Clinical Trial

An easy-to-read, IRB-approved pamphlet designed as a quick reference guide for potential volunteers interested in participating in a research study. It includes an overview of the clinical trials process and answers some of the most commonly asked questions about volunteering for a clinical trial. Translations available in Spanish, French, Italian, Portuguese, Dutch and German.

Understanding the Informed Consent Process

A comprehensive, IRB-approved brochure providing study volunteers with important information regarding the informed consent process, including facts and information about the volunteer's "Bill of Rights." Translation available in Spanish.

Career Services

JobWatch

JobWatch (centerwatch.com/jobwatch) is a key clinical research recruitment and career resource for professionals currently involved in the industry or professionals interested in obtaining a career in the life sciences or clinical research field.

JobWatch provides job listings, upcoming industry events, educational programs, company profiles and more. Registered job seekers can also manage resumes, set up email alerts and apply directly for positions online. Employers can review resumes, post and manage current openings and maximize exposure with a variety of recruitment and advertising opportunities online along with utilizing the various distribution channels *JobWatch* offers to reach professionals.

Clinical Research Training Guides

CenterWatch's training guide series offers effective and practical tools for those interested in clinical research as well as seasoned professionals seeking to better understand their roles and improve the management of their clinical trials operations in a safe and ethical manner.

- *Becoming a Successful Clinical Research Investigator*
- *The CRA's Guide to Monitoring Clinical Research*
- *The CRC's Guide to Coordinating Clinical Research*
- *Global Issues in Patient Recruitment and Retention*
- *Global Regulatory Systems: A Strategic Primer for Biopharmaceutical Product Development and Registration*

Regulatory Compliance

Standard Operating Procedures for the Conduct of Clinical Research

Developed to help clinical research sites meet the challenge of maintaining rigorous standards in a world of diminishing resources. The template has been expanded to include more procedures to assess study feasibility, recruit subjects and ensure regulatory compliance and is based on the Code of Federal Regulations and GCP Consolidated Guidelines.

Policies and Standard Operating Procedures for the Institutional Review Board

An efficient way for IRBs to document policies and procedures that reflect their organization's philosophies, standards and innovations while continuing to comply with federal regulations. The SOP template is based on the Code of Federal Regulations, guidance and ICH/GCP Consolidated Guideline and the Association for the Accreditation of Human Research Protection Program's (AAHRPP) standards for human subject protection.

Standard Operating Procedures for Good Clinical Practice by Sponsors of Clinical Trials

Developed to assist pharmaceutical and biotechnology companies maintain the quality performance and ethical conduct of clinical trials while adhering to U.S. federal regulations. The template contains 30 procedures addressing all Good Clinical Practice requirements and is based on FDA regulations and ICH guidelines.

Standard Operating Procedures for Good Clinical Practice by Sponsors of Medical Device Clinical Trials

Provides detailed SOPs to address specific requirements for medical device research practices to adhere to a discrete set of FDA regulations and guidance. Organizations that sponsor clinical research on new medical devices must implement procedures that comply with both Good Clinical Practice guidelines and federal regulations.

Medical Writing Services

Medical Writing Services

CenterWatch provides comprehensive medical writing and custom publishing services for pharmaceutical, biotech and contract research organizations to support their clinical development initiatives through post-approval marketing.

Medical Writing Services also has expanded offerings and expertise in the healthcare, academia and medical communications sectors.

Information Solutions and Content Licensing

Drugs in Clinical Trials Database

With more than 4,000 new investigational treatments in clinical trials worldwide, this database is updated weekly and is an effective resource for sponsors, CROs, research centers, service providers and analysts seeking to monitor drug performance, track competitors' development activity, identify development partners and clinical grant opportunities and analyze drug information for potential investments. Detailed drug profiles are completely searchable and include indications for use, current trial results, study phase status and manufacturer contact information.

Content Licensing

CenterWatch offers licensing of our database-driven and static-text content to provide companies with the latest in scientific clinical trial activity and drug development information using market intelligence and knowledge resources. Content can be offered as data feeds and co-branded to seamlessly integrate with a company's web site or Intranet. Our offerings include:

- Clinical Trials Listing Service™
- Drugs in Clinical Trials Database
- Recently Approved Drugs by the FDA
- New Medical Therapies™
- Patient Education
- Publication Content Portal

Business Development and Partnership Opportunities

Industry Provider Profile Pages

Industry Provider Profile Pages, located on centerwatch.com, create visibility for contract service providers to showcase their products and services online to the clinical trials community making it a useful and cost-effective way for providers to generate new business leads, increase exposure and reach a captive and targeted audience. Profile Pages are completely customizable and can include images and links to video presentations, demos and company documents.

Partnership Opportunities

CenterWatch has developed numerous partnerships and professional relationships with sponsors, CROs, health associations, niche providers and other organizations in order to better provide the clinical research community and patients with access to the most current and relevant industry, educational and patient-related information possible.

As market research experts, we also collaborate with organizations on various custom projects to conduct both broad and targeted industry-related surveys and to provide detailed data analysis about the clinical research industry.